Destination Baja & Los Cabos

Think of Baja like this: Escape. Once you're on the peninsula, margarita in hand – or your hand on the steering wheel – it's *adios* world. Unroll the car windows, slap a bag of flour tortillas on the dash and get ready for the ride: wild, boulder-strewn plateaus, towering *cardón* cacti, those pointy Dr Seussian *cirios*, elephant trees. As you head south, nothingness morphs into jagged badlands that finally give way to the crystalline, island-studded bays of the Sea of Cortez. Can't pick up Radio Frontera down here.

Meanwhile, on the Pacific side, folks have their eyes on something different: the majestic gray whales calving in the lagoons along the coast. The mothers literally nudge their calves up to the outstretched arms of whale-watchers in their skiffs. Farther south, fly-ins are lounging on Los Cabos' beaches getting ready for another show: sunset over Land's End, a gourmet seafood dinner and a night on the town.

You can sleep beneath the stars on a sandy beach on Bahía Concepción, with your crackling campfire throwing shadows over your kayak, or party till dawn beneath the nightclub lights of Tijuana or Cabo San Lucas. You can stroll down a lush green fairway overlooking the Sea of Cortez, or hike canyons to the pre-Columbian cave paintings in the Sierra de San Francisco.

Spanish explorers used to think this place was an island. Time and exploration certainly settled that one, but Baja remains – in both geography and in mindset – an island. A frontier spirit pervades, even in developed areas like Los Cabos. *Bajacalifornianos* (people from Baja) are a breed of their own – friendly, independent and proud of their intrepid past. They're the icing on the cake, really, making Baja one fun place for an escape.

ROSS BARNETT

Dividing the tranquil Sea of Cortez from the mighty Pacific, Baja is a sliver of surreal desert landscapes surrounded by an endless liquid paradise. Drive along the **Los Cabos Corridor** (p199), a visual feast of coves, jutting points, sandy beaches and stunning ocean views. Admire the old buildings, verdant river and palm trees of subtropical **Mulegé** (p143). Gaze at the boulder-strewn landscape and giant granite rock pile of El Pedregoso, near **Cataviña** (p126). Visit the fascinating indigenous rock art sites in the **Sierra de San Francisco** (p138). Mellow out and watch fabulous sunsets over the waterfront promenade in **La Paz** (p161). Wonder if you've ever seen a bay as beautiful as **Bahía de Los Angeles** (p128).

KRAIG LIEB

Survey miles of coastline and camp on the beach at **Bahía Concepción** (p147)

DAVID PEEVERS

View hills of grapes in **Valle de Guadalupe** (p90), Baja's wine country

Gaze up at giant cacti and **cirios** ('boojum trees') in central Baja (p124)

WOODS WHEATCR

JIM WARK

Escape the crowds at desolate **Bahía San Luis Gonzaga** (p126)

DAVID PEEVERS

Watch for crazy **sculptures** along the Transpeninsular in northern Baja (p50)

Visit the restored **Misión Santa Rosalía de Mulegé** (p143) and admire the palm-filled view below

BRENT WINEBRENNER

From water and wind sports to fairways and fishing, Baja abounds with op-portunities to get active outside – even if it means tipping margaritas in the sun. **Snorkel** or **scuba dive** with giant manta rays at Cabo Pulmo (p180), home of the only living reef on North America's west coast. Dirty your knobbies **mountain biking** the spectacular dirt road from Los Barriles to Bahía de los Muertos (p178). Brave the high winds **kite surfing** or **windsurfing** at Los Barriles (p177). **Surf** the waves at Scorpion Bay, San Juanico (p149). **Hike** through a landscape of cacti, palms, canyons and thermal springs in the mountainous Sierra de la Laguna (p175).

LEE FOSTER

Stroll along the river path and spot birds at **Estero San José** (p192)

Kayak (p38) in the calm, crystalline Sea of Cortez

RALPH LEE HOPKINS

RALPH LEE HOPKINS

Get friendly with California gray whales on a **whale-watching** trip (p35)

LEE FOSTER

Try your angler's luck on a chartered **fishing** excursion in the waters off Los Cabos, Baja's billfish capital (p208)

STUART WASSERMAN

Watch for the enormous sand traps at **Cabo Real Golf Course** (p202)

Stop for a quick dip in one of the **swimming** holes on the way to Misión San Javier (p154)

WOODS WHEATLKUFT

Paradise for the Palate

Combine Baja's penchant for seafood with Mexico's rich culinary tradition and you have an epicure's dream. Stuff yourself on **lobster** at a seaside restaurant in Puerto Nuevo (p75). Suck up a plate of San Quintín's famous **clams** (p96). Douse your taste buds in **wine** at Valle de Guadalupe (p90) or Mexican beer in **Tecate** (p102). Experience the heights of *alta cocina* (haute cuisine) in San José del Cabo (p195). Join the locals for *carnitas* (slow-roasted or fried pork) on a Sunday afternoon.

RICHARD I'ANSON

Tequila, wine, beer, margaritas – choose your Baja beverage (p45)

Feast on tasty **fish tacos** in Ensenada (p85) and throughout Baja

DAVID PEEVERS

Snack on *ceviche,* chips and salsa with your feet in the sand at a **Playa Médano** restaurant (p216), Cabo San Lucas

MARK & AUDREY GIBSON

Getting Started

Planning a trip is half the fun. Even though you can jump a plane to Los Cabos on a day's notice and be sucking down margaritas beachside the next, you might as well milk your vacation for all the pre-trip daydreaming you can. Dissect maps, read books, pack, repack, gear-check... This section will help you decide where and when to get Peninsular as well as steer you to the literary and practical resources that will pump you up for the trip and make it smoother and more fulfilling once you're there.

WHEN TO GO

Baja is a year-round destination, but the best time to visit depends on where you're going and what you want to do.

The northwestern Pacific coast is busiest from May to October, when the weather is reliably dry and warm. Winter here brings cooler temperatures and occasional rain but also smaller crowds and lower prices. During spring break, American students jam all the resort areas down to San Felipe and even trickle down to Cabo San Lucas.

On the Sea of Cortez and in the Cape Region, tourist season peaks from November through March. The nicest time to visit here may be spring, when temperatures are moderate and tourists few. Summer is *chubasco* (tropical storm) season and can be hot, humid and unpleasant, unless fishing is your bailiwick: the biggest catches are usually brought in between July and September.

Visitors with special interests should tailor their itineraries accordingly. Whale-watching season generally runs from January to the end of March, while bird-watchers may find the colonies in the Bahía de los Angeles area most active in May. Desert bighorn sheep are easiest to spot in summer in the eastern escarpment of the Sierra de Juárez and Sierra San Pedro Mártir. In general, it's best to skirt the desert areas between May and October.

DON'T LEAVE HOME WITHOUT...

- Hat, sunglasses and sunscreen
- Water bottles (pilfer that free hotel water when you can!)
- At least one good book
- Universal sink plug (for washing clothes)
- A sweater (wool or fleece) for chilly desert nights and mornings on the water
- Snorkel gear (it's always best to have your own)
- Camera
- Swiss Army knife
- Cigar cutter
- Sense of humor (essential)

Drivers:

- Auto insurance (a must)
- Duct tape – and lots of it
- Electrical tape
- Bailing (mechanic's) wire
- Spare fuses
- Motor oil and a spare oil filter
- Radiator water and/or engine coolant
- Basic tool set
- Rags and paper towels
- Spare car key
- 26 cans of Red Bull

See Climate Charts (p225)
for more information

Hiking in the mountains is best in summer, when temperatures are mild; in winter be prepared for snow and icy conditions. Spring-flower season peaks in April and May in the northern ranges, and September and October in the Cape Region mountains.

COSTS

The cost of travel in Baja depends a great deal on the degree of comfort you require. Food and lodgings cost more in Baja than in the rest of Mexico, often only slightly less than in the USA. Prices are highest near the border and in tourist centers like La Paz and Los Cabos.

Unless you're camping or traveling with an RV, lodging will probably take the biggest chunk out of your travel budget. It's hard to find a decent double for less than US$30 per night. Prices are lower in RV parks or campgrounds, and beach camping is free and legal. Most luxury resort hotels are in Los Cabos, where doubles *start* around US$180 per night.

You can save money by buying food from supermarkets, bakeries, and fruit and vegetable stands (wash the fruits and veggies first), or by eating at

TOP FIVES

NATURAL WONDERS

The Baja magic is all about the outdoors, so daydream of the following before heading out. See p4 for more natural highlights.

- The coral reef of Cabo Pulmo (p180)
- Islas Espíritu Santo (p167)
- Cañón de Guadalupe hot springs (p117)
- The California gray whales of Laguna San Ignacio (p140)
- Cardón cacti of Cataviña (p126)

DRIVES

As you're staring at that road map wondering where to go, ponder these top drives. See p236 for more on driving.

- Mulegé to Loreto (p147) – spectacular views of island-studded bays
- México 1 to Misión San Javier (p154) – cliffside drive into dramatic mountains
- Eastern Cape Road (p176) – a Baja classic along the rocky southern coast
- San Felipe to Rancho Grande/Bahía San Luis Gonzaga (p122) – endless ocean views and empty road
- El Rosario through Cataviña (p126) – massive boulders and giant cardón cacti

FESTIVALS & EVENTS

Mexicans love a good party, and timing your trip around a fiesta is the best way to be certain you'll rub shoulders with the locals. See p227 for more festivals and events.

- Fiesta de la Vendimia (Valle de Guadalupe) August (p83)
- Carnaval (La Paz) February/March (p168)
- Dia de Nuestra Señora de Guadalupe (Tecate) December 12 (p104)
- Fiesta de San Javier (Misión San Javier) December 3 (p154)
- Festival de Artes (Todos Santos) February (p184)

roadside *taquerías* (taco stands) or casual restaurants, where filling meals can cost less than US$4. Prices at better restaurants equal or even exceed those in the USA. Buying warm fresh tortillas, avocados and *carnitas* (slow-roasted pork) is a great way pick up cheap lunches for the road.

Gasoline is not cheap, so using the bus and public transportation can be a money-saver. However, it will also limit your mobility and prevent you from accessing the most fascinating and remote parts of the peninsula.

PREDEPARTURE READING

To really fire yourself up about Baja, pick up a copy of Bruce Berger's *Almost an Island*, an eloquent travelogue with the perfect combination of adventure, history, culture and humor. Berger's love and knowledge of the peninsula brings to life one of the best books on Baja to date.

Cartwheels in the Sand: Baja California, Four Women and a Motor Home, by Ann Hazard, is an amusing account of a journey down México 1 by four women in a 1978 RV. Her newest book, *Agave Sunsets*, weaves 50 tales of Baja, from the 1890s (when her grandfather wandered south of the border) to the present.

No Baja reading list is complete without John Steinbeck's classic *The Log from the Sea of Cortez*. The combination travelogue and natural history essay was one of the earliest studies of marine life in the Sea of Cortez. Steinbeck's biologist companion, Ed Ricketts, was the model for Doc in the novelist's famous *Cannery Row*.

Another excellent escape into Baja of old – before the Transpeninsular was carved into the scenery – is *The Forgotten Peninsula: A Naturalist in Baja California*, by literary naturalist Joseph Wood Krutch.

Even with the Transpeninsular now paved to Cabo, some still take things slowly: witness *Into a Desert Place*, Graham Mackintosh's narrative of his two-year, 3000-mile walk (walk?!) around the Baja coast, deemed 'one of the most grueling and challenging solo bipedal treks ever taken.'

Baja has many sides. Luis Alberto Urrea's grim but fascinating *Across the Wire: Life and Hard Times on the Mexican Border* focuses on the problems of immigrants and shantytowns in a Tijuana that very few tourists see.

Harry Crosby's detailed and readable *Cave Paintings of Baja California*, both history and eye-candy (it's loaded with juicy glossy photos), will inspire you to see Baja's famous cave paintings.

INTERNET RESOURCES

The following sites are great places to start your research. More websites are listed throughout the book.

Baja Information Pages (http://math.ucr.edu/~ftm/bajainfoPage.html) Tough to navigate but packed with travelers' experiences and information about many subjects, from pets to tides to ATMs to weather; mostly focused on Baja Sur. Some areas need updating.

Baja Links (www.bajalinks.com) The most extensive compilation of links to Baja-related websites.

Baja.com (www.baja.com) Loaded with information and history on destinations throughout Baja. Hourly updates on border traffic, message boards, articles, city highlights and more.

Baja Nomad (www.bajanomad.com) Online travelers' guide to all major Baja destinations, plus forums and newsletter. It has what's likely the best archive of Baja articles on the Internet.

Baja Web (www.baja-web.com) Tome of destination-specific information from Tijuana to Los Cabos, plus general information about ferries, immigration and activities; lots of links.

Lonely Planet (www.lonelyplanet.com) Succinct summaries on traveling to most places on earth, and the invaluable Thorn Tree bulletin board, where you can ask questions before you go or dispense advice when you get back.

MexOnline Baja (www.mexonline.com/baja) A comprehensive travelers' guide to Baja, plus invaluable information on travel to Mexico in general.

HOW MUCH?

Gasoline US$0.62/2.35 per liter/US gallon

One dozen freshly made tortillas US$0.35

Standard car rental US$50-60 per day

Cybercafé in Los Cabos/ elsewhere US$5/1.50 per hour

Admission to archaeological site US$3

Small bottled water US$0.70

Tecate beer US$1.50

Souvenir T-shirt US$5

Street taco US$1

Itineraries

CLASSIC ROUTE

BORDER TO CAPE   Four Days to Three Weeks

Tijuana to Los Cabos is Baja's classic road trip, driven by thousands of North Americans in their RVs, SUVs, trailer rigs, pickups, cars and, occasionally, old Volkswagen campers (someone has to keep the faith!). You can make it to Los Cabos in two days of hard driving: **Tijuana** (p53) to Guerrero Negro, Guerrero Negro to Land's End (Cabo San Lucas), 12 hours a leg. If you're a masochist, turn around and drive back. You'll have seen a lot.

With more time under your tires, you'll see a lot more. Stop in **San Quintín** (p96) for clams (it's an unwritten rule) or a day of sportfishing and a night's rest. South of the blink-and-you'll-miss-it town of **El Rosario** (p101), the real Baja begins; the boulder-scapes and cacti of **Cataviña** (p126) warrant at least a day's exploration. Catch some Zs here and gas up for a side trip to spectacular **Bahía de Los Angeles** (p128) for fishing or kayaking. Back on the road, continue south to **Guerrero Negro** and nearby **Laguna Ojo de Liebre** (p133), Baja's northernmost whale-watching site.

From here it's a long haul over the Vizcaíno Desert. (If you have time, take a detour to **Laguna San Ignacio** (p140) for whale-watching, check out the beautifully preserved mission at **San Ignacio** (p136), or take a multi-day trek into the **Sierra de San Francisco** (p138) to marvel at Baja's world-famous indigenous rock art.) Stop at the old French mining town of **Santa Rosalía** (p140) on the Sea of Cortez, where old French clapboard houses make it one of the strangest towns in Baja. From here, it's a short hop south to the tropical oasis town of **Mulegé** (p143), where faded adobe-style buildings and narrow streets resemble those of small towns in mainland Mexico. Shack up here for a night or two, or sleep under the stars at one of several beautifully set beachside campgrounds along nearby **Bahía Concepción** (p147).

About two hours south of Mulegé, colonial-style **Loreto** (p149) was the first capital of the Californias, and is a must-see. It boasts one of the peninsula's best-preserved missions, plenty of hotels and a long waterfront for peaceful evening walks. South of Loreto, the Transpeninsular doglegs west, over the Sierra de la Giganta, passing the roads to premier whale-watching destinations **Puerto López Mateos** (p157) and **Puerto San Carlos** (p157).

Back on the east coast, **La Paz** (p161) is arguably the best city in Baja California. You could spend *at least* a day exploring its curious shops and excellent restaurants, or kayaking the spectacular islands of Isla Espíritu Santo. Then wind down the evening wandering along the *malecón* (waterfront promenade) at sunset. After La Paz, head south to **San José del Cabo** (p189) and **Cabo San Lucas** (p204) for excellent seafood, all-night dancing, sportfishing and beaches, beaches, beaches. Hit the brakes at Land's End.

Tijuana

Baja
California

San Quintín

El Rosario

Cataviña

Bahía de Los Angeles

Sea of Cortez

Guerrero
Negro

*Sierra de
San Francisco*

*Laguna Ojo
de Liebre*

*Laguna San
Ignacio*

San
Ignacio

Santa Rosalía

Baja
California
Sur

Mulegé

Bahía Concepción

*PACIFIC
OCEAN*

Loreto

Puerto López Mateos

Puerto San Carlos

La Paz

San José
del Cabo

Cabo San Lucas

**Tune up the car
and roll down the
windows for the
legendary 1061-
mile (1711km)
drive from the
USA/Mexico border
to Cabo San Lucas,
the peninsula's
southernmost
point. By bus it's 24
to 27 hours, and by
car about 24. While
two to three weeks
is ideal, you could
spend months
exploring – or, if
you're insane, pull
a four-day whirl-
wind dash.**

TAILORED TRIPS

SOUTHERN BEACHES & BAYS

The Southern Beaches & Bays route covers more than 60 miles (96km)of spectacular coastline, allowing those with about a week in Los Cabos to take in the area's finest beaches, from Playa del Amor in Cabo San Lucas to the coral reefs of Cabo Pulmo.

Spend your first days in Cabo San Lucas, being certain to hit **Playa del Amor** (Lover's Beach; p208), near the famous arches of Land's End. Just around the point lies the Pacific beach of **Playa Solmar** (Divorce Beach; p208). Eating, drinking and lounging in one of **Playa Médano's** beachside restaurants (p216) is a must.

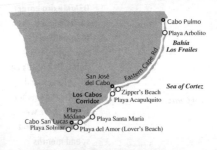

When you've had your fill of Cabo's busy beaches, explore the sandy coves along **Los Cabos Corridor** (p199), especially **Playa Santa María** (p200). **Zipper's Beach** and **Playa Acapulquito** (p200) spell s-u-r-f. Spend a night in San José del Cabo (p189) before heading northeast to the spectacular beach-hugging **Eastern Cape Road** (p176). Spend the night at **Bahía Los Frailes** (p181) or **Cabo Pulmo** (p180) to maximize your time in the sand. And be sure to stop at exquisite **Playa Arbolito** (p180), with its glassy turquoise water and excellent snorkeling.

NORTHERN ELIXIR TRAIL

By car or bus and with an interest in swill, you're set to explore northern Baja's finest treasures, both natural and humanmade. On this quest to see what Baja brews best – margaritas, wine and Tecate beer – this 175-mile (282km) loop will also give you a dose of everything from beaches to scenic valleys to northern Baja's most exciting towns.

First step: spend a night knocking back icy margaritas on Tijuana's infamous **Av Revolución** (p56). The following day, hit **Ensenada** (p77) and **Hussong's Cantina** (p86), the oldest bar in the Americas. While no one has proven the origin of the margarita, Ensenada's historic **Bar Andaluz**

(p87) claims to have invented it. After a day or two in Ensenada, head northeast to the **Valle de Guadalupe** (p90) to visit Mexico's best wineries. After your day in wine country, spend the night in Tecate, home of the **Tecate Brewery** (p104), which brews Carta Blanca, XX, Bohemia and, of course, the town's namesake. After exploring Tecate, cut back to Tijuana and have a pilsner at the city's very own **Tijuana Brewery** (Cervecería Tijuana; p57) before heading home.

The Author

DANNY PALMERLEE

The city of La Paz gave Danny his first taste of Mexico in 1991, and he's been no less than obsessed with the country ever since (it was the blue walls and dusty bric-a-brac of Pensión California). He has traveled extensively throughout Mexico and Central and South America, and works as a freelance writer in San Francisco, California. Danny has written about Mexico for the *San Francisco Chronicle, The Dallas Morning News* and *The Miami Herald,* and his travel writing has appeared in *The Oregonian* and the *San Francisco Bay Guardian.* He was the coordinating author of Lonely Planet's *Mexico's Pacific Coast* and several South America titles.

My Baja

For this research trip, I drove a 1985 Subaru around the peninsula, and it couldn't have been a better way to meet people – engine trouble has a way of introducing you to strangers. San Ignacio's historic plaza (p135) is one of my favorite places, I think because I spent hours beneath its laurel trees, discussing with a group of men the mechanics of my overheating motor. The car also allowed me to spend more time than anticipated in Mulegé (p143), confirming my feeling that it's one of Baja's loveliest towns. If you're flying into Los Cabos, La Paz or Loreto and visiting Baja for the first time, by all means rent a car and beat the hell out of it, exploring the region's back roads. Drive the road north of La Paz to San Evaristo (p173), the hair-raising road from Loreto to Misión San Javier (p154) and, needless to say, the Eastern Cape Road (p176 & p199) from San José del Cabo.

CONTRIBUTING AUTHORS

Jim Peyton wrote the Food & Drink chapter (p43). Jim has written three books on Mexican cooking as well as articles for magazines such as *Fine Cooking, Texas Highways* and *Food & Wine.* He appears on television, conducts cooking classes and lectures on Mexican cuisine. In addition Jim maintains a website, *Jim Peyton's Lo Mexicano* at www.lomexicano.com, providing information about Mexico and Mexican cooking. Jim also consults on recipe development and menu design for the Mexican food industry. Jim's recipes were selected to appear in the 2000 and 2001 issues of Houghton Mifflin's *The Best American Recipes.* His latest book is *Jim Peyton's New Cooking from Old Mexico.*

David Goldberg MD wrote the Health chapter (p244). Dr Goldberg completed his training in internal medicine and infectious diseases at Columbia-Presbyterian Medical Center in New York City, where he has also served as voluntary faculty. At present, he is an infectious diseases specialist in Scarsdale NY and the editor-in-chief of the website MDTravelHealth.com.

Keith Jones wrote the 'Gray Whales of Baja' boxed text (p36). He studied oceanography and biology before starting Baja Jones Adventures, a tour company offering whale-watching expeditions in Baja (www.greywhale.com). Keith has logged more than 2000 hours observing whales in Baja, and has also contributed photos and articles for numerous magazines, newspapers and websites. He's always searching the world for new marine animal encounters.

Snapshot

Baja California has long been called 'the forgotten peninsula,' both for its geographical detachment from mainland Mexico and its geopolitical detachment from the USA. But when President Vicente Fox announced in 2001 his grand plan to turn Baja into the Cancún of the 21st century, the peninsula was surely 'forgotten' no longer – at least for a while anyway. Fox, former president of Coca Cola Mexico, was thinking *big*.

With the backing of Fonatur (the Mexican tourist development agency), Fox unveiled the Escalera Nautical (Nautical Stairway), a land bridge that would bisect the peninsula east-to-west and allow yachters to sail down the Pacific Coast to Santa Rosalillita (p130), haul their US$900,000 yachts ashore and trailer them across Baja to the Sea of Cortez.

Construction began with a new marina at Santa Rosalillita and a road twice the width of the Transpeninsular from the marina to México 1. But little has happened since, and the whole plan (which was to be finished by 2014) may go overboard. Time will tell. Meanwhile, North American boaters continue to haul their fishing boats south – to fish rather than resort-hop.

As vacationing North Americans move south, thousands of underemployed Mexicans move north, hoping to cross illegally into California, where the economy depends on an immigrant Mexican labor force. Despite this dependence, the USA has cinched up the border in recent years, contributing to the most pressing dilemma faced today by the Mexican border states. Each year hundreds of 'walkers' die trying to cross the desert as the USA, through campaigns such as Operation Gatekeeper, effectively seals off the safer urban crossings in and around Tijuana and Mexicali. Mexican migrants now pay big bucks (up to US$1600) for *coyotes* or *polleros* (guides) to smuggle them across the border.

Despite the fact that coyotes regularly abandon their clients to die in the desert, countless *narcocorridos* (ballads about drugs and Mexican mafiosos) pour from car stereos in Baja romanticizing them as anti-establishment outlaw heroes. You'll surely hear them while you're here (and many narcocorridos are fabulous stories from the underworld), but you won't hear them on the airwaves. In 2002 all Tijuana radio stations voluntarily banned narcocorridos from being played – which, of course, has made them all the more popular.

Tijuana itself has been spiffing up its image in recent years, swapping its Sin City rap for a suit of art, culture and haute cuisine. In fact, Tijuana now has more fine-dining establishments than Cabo San Lucas, and its rebirth as a vibrant, cultured city continues to make international press. Tijuana's Nortec music collective gained international fame with its techno beats by fusing the trumpets, drums and bass of Mexican *banda* and *norteño* music with electronica.

At the bottom of the peninsula – and worlds away – the big issue is development. From Cabo San Lucas to Los Barriles, the Eastern Cape is poised for a building boom that will have no small effect on the fragile coastal environment (for details, see p34). For the time being, however, this playground in paradise has vast coastal stretches that still feel forgotten.

History

Traipsing around Baja you'll encounter an odd collage of historical sites alluding to the peninsula's peculiar past: English flour mills near San Quintín; pre-Columbian cave paintings in the Sierra de San Francisco; a French mining town on the Sea of Cortez; splendid stone missions plunked into the middle of nowhere; businesses everywhere named after Dutch and English pirates.

It's fitting that for years the Spanish explorers on mainland Mexico thought the mysterious California they kept hearing about was an island. Except for the minor disqualifier that the peninsula *is* attached to the North American landmass at one end, Baja California remains, in many other respects, an island. From the beginning of human settlement here, the peninsula's disconnection from mainland Mexico has defined its history, which is indeed peculiar.

HOMO MIGRATORIUS (YO, IS THAT A BRIDGE?)

It's generally accepted that human settlement of North America began at least 12,000 years ago with one of the most significant human migrations ever. The ancestors of Amerindians, taking advantage of lowered sea levels during the Pleistocene Epoch, walked from Siberia to Alaska via a land bridge across the Bering Strait. They weren't exactly speedy about moving south, and, according to radiocarbon dating of artifacts like shell middens, stone tools and arrowheads, it took descendants of these migrants a good 2000 years to reach the Baja Peninsula. As middens at Punta Minitas in northwestern Baja indicate, shellfish was a main food source for these peoples, who also engaged in hunting, gathering and, later, rudimentary farming.

BAJA CALIFORNIA INDIANS

Until Europeans reached the peninsula in the 16th century, upwards of 48,000 mobile hunter-gatherers lived on the Baja Peninsula, belonging to three major linguistic groups, subdivided into several tribal entities. They lived in groups that became known as *rancherías*, ranging in size from a few families to upwards of 200 people.

While the Maya and Aztecs of mainland Mexico were building their pyramids and living the complex society life, the isolated peninsular Indians hardly advanced beyond the early Stone Age. They usually slept in the open, in caves or in simple dwellings near a dependable water source, and spent their waking hours finding enough sustenance for survival. The men hunted and fished while the women gathered wild plant foods such as pine nuts and the fruit of the pitahaya cactus. They had no written language, formal religious beliefs or agriculture, and they practiced polygamy, apparently because tribal warfare had led to a surplus of women. However, they created the most spectacular petroglyphs and cave paintings in the western hemisphere, still visible at sites throughout the peninsula, including the most impressive of all in the Sierra de San Francisco (p138).

While the Yumano in the north and the Guaycura in the south enjoyed a fairly dependable subsistence, by most accounts the Cochimí of central Baja, the peninsula's harshest desert, were often destitute. In times of stress they even collected pitahaya seeds from their own excrement and toasted them in what Spaniards jokingly called their 'second harvest.'

Few survived European colonization, and the only remaining Indians live in the northernmost part of the peninsula. Collecting pine nuts for food is an important seasonal activity, and women still produce attractive basketry and pottery.

ADIOS CORTÉS

After the conquest of Mexico in the early 16th century, there was much fanciful speculation about a golden island beyond Mexico's western coast. It was California, named even before it was explored after a mythical island queen in a Spanish novel. The precise etymology and meaning of the name 'California' have never been convincingly established, but there is wide consensus that it is a derivation of 'Calafia,' the book's heroine queen, who ruled a race of gold-rich black Amazons.

Of course, rumors of gold and women have a way of making conquistadors fidgety. Not content with his spoils on mainland Mexico, Spanish conquistador Hernán Cortés dispatched a series of expeditions to find the island beginning in 1532. Rather than babes in bracelets, however, the explorers found men with sharp objects who killed many of the intruders and forced the survivors back to the mainland.

Determined to get his hands on more gold, Cortés finally joined a third expedition in 1535 and went ashore at present-day Bahía Pichilingue (p173), where he founded the colony of Santa Cruz. He also found pearls, but harsh desert, disease, hostile Indians, and several food and water shortages forced the colonists, once again, to beat it back to Mexico.

Still, Cortés wouldn't give up. In 1539 he sent out a fourth expedition under Francisco de Ulloa, who would be the first to discover that Baja was a peninsula, not an island. After Ulloa's ship disappeared near Bahía Magdalena, Cortés finally threw in the towel. He'd had enough. He returned to Spain in 1541, leaving the 'golden land' to other adventurers.

For a peek into piracy and the Manila galleons, peruse Peter Gerhard's succinct and readable *Pirates of the Pacific, 1575-1742*.

BOATS & BUCCANEERS

Meanwhile, the peninsula became important in other ways – in particular, as a stopping point for trade ships between Mexico and the Philippines. For 250 years, starting in 1565, these 'Manila galleons' traveled west from Acapulco across the Pacific to Manila, where they loaded up on Asian luxuries. The bloated vessels then embarked on their arduous six- to

---

CALIFORNIA: WHAT'S IN A WORD?

In late Spanish colonial times, the general term 'California' meant Baja California (Lower California), and the present US state of California – then a backwater – became known as Alta California (Upper California). Rather than use the latter term, an anachronism except in its historical context, this book uses the more appropriate (if not precisely accurate) term 'mainland California' to refer to areas north of the Mexican border.

Use of the abbreviated 'Baja' – rather than 'Baja California' – to describe the peninsula became popular among folks north of the border, largely as a result of the Baja 1000 (the peninsula's world famous offroad race from Ensenada to La Paz). Many native *bajacaliforianos* wince at the term 'Baja' (which means low or under) when used alone to describe the original California. You're asking for flack from an immigration official if you write 'Baja' in the destination section of your tourist card. Use the more appropriate Baja California (the name of the peninsula's northern state) or Baja California Sur (the name of the southern state).

When necessary for clarity, this book refers to the individual states as Baja California (Norte) and Baja California Sur.

eight-month return to Mexico. After crossing the Pacific, the crew was usually out of water and starved of food. The Baja Peninsula was the first land and made for an obvious supply stop.

For the Spanish, creating a settlement on the peninsula to reequip the crew became even more crucial after bounty-hungry buccaneers caught wind of the seaborne riches and started to attack the overloaded vessels. Sir Francis Drake was among the first to stage these raids. Many other pirates, mostly from England and the Netherlands, followed suit. The Spaniards tried to hide from the marauders by seeking shelter in the bays of the Cape Region, but they were still outfoxed. In the biggest attack ever, in November 1587, Englishman Thomas Cavendish lay in wait at Cabo San Lucas, then sacked the prize galleon *Santa Ana* in a surprise attack.

Meanwhile, a desperate Spanish crown dispatched a skilled admiral, Sebastián Vizcaíno (after whom a major bay and a large desert in Central Baja were later named), to look for alternative sites to stop the riches from falling into enemy hands. Although he never found a site that would safely harbor the Spanish galleons, he did finally land in a sheltered bay on the Sea of Cortez that would serve as an excellent port; he named the place La Paz.

MISSION IMPROBABLE

Having been thoroughly humiliated by repeated failures to colonize Baja, the Spanish crown felt it was time to bring in the army – of God, that is. The first Jesuit foray into the peninsula came in 1683 when Isidro de Atondo y Antillón crossed the Sea of Cortez with Jesuit priest Eusebio Kino. Together they established a settlement at La Paz, which was soon abandoned because of hostile Indians.

It would take another 14 years before a Jesuit priest named Juan María Salvatierra and six soldiers finally managed to do what had eluded countless explorers for a century and a half: establish the first *permanent* Spanish settlement in Baja California. Loreto, where they set up the first mission (p149), soon became the peninsula's religious and administrative capital. From here, other Jesuits swarmed out to establish a total of 23 missions over the next 70 years.

The Jesuits may have meant well in converting the Indians to Christianity and in instructing them in farming techniques and various crafts, but their altruistic intentions backfired. Along with God, grapes and greener pastures, the missionaries also brought an invisible evil – European microbes to which native peoples had no natural defenses. Epidemics decimated the Indian population, and several revolts against missionization caused further loss of life. By the end of the Jesuit period (1767), the Indian population had dwindled to only about 8000.

Then a decision was made halfway around the world that doomed the Jesuits for good. As word spread that the Jesuit Order had accumulated inordinate power and wealth, King Carlos III of Spain had all Jesuits arrested and expelled from their missionary postings around the world, and the Baja Jesuits were subsequently deported back to Spain.

In their stead came another order – the Franciscans, under the authority of Padre Junípero Serra, who closed or consolidated several of the Jesuit missions before turning his energies toward mainland California.

In 1773 another order, the Dominicans, got into the mission game, setting up nine new missions north of El Rosario (p101). They also continued to operate the former Jesuit missions until after Mexico won independence from Spain in 1821. Three years later, Baja became a federal territory, headed by a governor. In 1832 a newly appointed

DID YOU KNOW?

The infamous pirates Thomas Cavendish and Sir Francis Drake both plied the waters off Cabo San Lucas in their search for the Manila galleons' booty.

Harry Crosby's robust *Antigua California* is a well-written, engaging and comprehensive history of early colonial times (1697-1768), with considerable focus on the Jesuits.

DID YOU KNOW?

Loreto, in Baja California Sur, was the first capital of the Californias.

governor put an end to the mission system by converting nearly all of them into parish churches.

THE MEXICAN-AMERICAN WAR

Meanwhile, on the Mexican mainland, momentous events were taking place that would bring war as far west as the peninsula and forever alter the map of Mexico. Before 1848 most of what is today the southwestern USA belonged to Mexico. North American settlers, initially welcomed by the Mexican authorities, declared Texas independent in 1836 in a surprise move. In 1845, when the US Congress voted to annex Texas and US President Polk (1845–49) demanded further Mexican territory, Mexico resisted. And so it came to the Mexican-American War (1846–48).

The main battles occurred on the Mexican mainland, but Baja was drawn into the conflict as well. American ships arrived in La Paz in 1846 and in San José del Cabo the following spring, where they brought local authorities under their control. In response, the Mexican government swiftly sent in troops under Captain Manuel Piñada. Fighting took place in Mulegé, La Paz and San José del Cabo, with Mexicans putting up such fierce resistance that the US troops had to repeatedly call for reinforcements. It wasn't until March 1848 that they finally captured Piñada and his cohorts. Both sides were oblivious to the fact that war had ended one month earlier.

With the signing of the Treaty of Guadalupe Hidalgo, a destabilized Mexico was forced to sell most of New Mexico and mainland California to the USA. Mexico did, however, retain sovereignty over Baja California.

FOREIGN INTERESTS & INVESTMENT

Since war didn't land the peninsula in US hands, the country attempted to acquire it in other ways – namely through private investment (encouraged by the Mexican government) and agricultural colonization schemes. In 1866 the Lower California Colonization & Mining Company gained title to all Baja lands roughly between San Quintín and La Paz. It embarked on a transparently fraudulent colonization attempt – even issuing bogus paper money – but failed scandalously in the end.

In the 1880s Mexico, under autocratic President Porfirio Díaz (1876–80 and 1884–1911), began encouraging US and European capital investment throughout the country. Eager to raise much-needed funds to grow the Mexican economy, Díaz granted major mining, railroad, manufacturing and other concessions to foreign investors. As a result, northern Baja in particular, which until then had been a complete outback without infrastructure, was transformed.

The main investor was the US-based International Company of Mexico (ICM), which constructed port facilities and flour mills at Ensenada and San Quintín (p96) but failed miserably in its deceptive propaganda campaign to attract many colonists. After too many rainless years, ICM cut its losses and surrendered its 'perfect title' to a gullible English syndicate for US$7 million. Again the rains failed and harvests were nil, and those colonists who didn't end up in San Quintín's first cemetery returned to England or moved to other parts of Baja, where British surnames like Jones and Smith are not unusual.

If agriculture proved to be a futile endeavor, mining did not. Several important mineral discoveries occurred around the peninsula, including gold and silver strikes. One of the largest projects, operated by the French syndicate Compañía del Boleo at Santa Rosalía (p140), produced copper until the 1950s and left a fascinating architectural mark on central Baja.

With history, links, a timeline and forums, PBS's outstanding US-Mexican War Website (www.pbs.org/kera/usmexicanwar) offers an in-depth look into the war that permanently transformed the US-Mexico border.

Norris Hundley's The Great Thirst: Californians and Water, 1770s-1990s details the controversy between the USA and Mexico over the Colorado River delta.

REVOLUTION & REFORM

The Mexican Revolution of 1910 lasted a decade and temporarily interrupted growth on the peninsula. Warfare had very little impact on most of the peninsula, but in 1911 a ragtag army of the Liberal Party, an anarchist force under the influence of exiled Mexican intellectual Ricardo Flores Magón, swept through northern Baja's lightly defended border towns from Mexicali to Tijuana in an attempt to establish a regional power base.

The Magonistas, as Flores Magón's forces were also known, took Tijuana in a single morning but failed to establish any form of government. When the Mexican army finally hit the scene, the rebels quickly crumbled.

After the war, Baja continued in isolation, excluded from most of the grandiose political and economic development plans underway in Mexico City. Ironically, it was the passage of legislation in the USA that pump-primed the Baja economy. The Eighteenth Amendment to the US Constitution – better known as Prohibition – outlawed alcoholic beverages north of the border, and mainland Californians flocked to Tijuana, Ensenada and Mexicali for drinking, gambling and sex.

Border towns both prospered and suffered from this US invasion. Along with the money came an assortment of corrupt characters, and both Tijuana and Mexicali soon had a reputation for tawdriness and sleaze.

A major turning point in the history of Baja came in 1938 with the election of reformist President Lázaro Cárdenas (1934–40), who instituted sweeping reforms throughout Mexico. He banned casino gambling, cracked down on crime and built the Sonora-Mexicali railroad to reduce the territory's economic dependence on the USA and its isolation from mainland Mexico. Reforms later continued with President Miguel Alemán (1946–52), who built hydroelectric stations, irrigation projects and an expanded road system. In 1952, still under Alemán, Baja's political status improved as its northern half became the Mexican state of Baja California.

Michael C Meyer's and William L Sherman's *The Course of Mexican History* is one of the best general accounts of Mexican history and society.

James Blaisdell's *The Desert Revolution* tells of Ricardo Flores Magón's quixotic attempt to influence the Mexican Revolution from the Baja periphery.

FISH TALES & TOURISM

After World War II, tales of fish, perpetual sunshine and beautiful bays filtered north to mainland California, spurring the wealthy and the famous to explore the frontier south of the border. With no access road, private planes and yachts were the only means of access. In 1948 Hollywood bigwigs including Bing Crosby, John Wayne and Desi Arnaz put money toward Baja's first private resort at Las Cruces, just south of La Paz. In 1956 Rod Rodríguez (son of Abelardo L Rodríguez, the Mexican president from 1932 to '34) built the Hotel Palmilla in Los Cabos Corridor. W Matt (Bud) Parr's Hotel Cabo San Lucas, nearby, and Herb Tanzi's Rancho Buena Vista, on the Eastern Cape, followed in 1962. Development came to Cabo San Lucas in 1967, when Rodríguez built the Hotel Hacienda, Luís Coppola put up Hotel Finisterra and Luís Bulnes erected the Hotel Solmar. These five families are commonly considered the founders of Los Cabos.

Despite these developments, tourism stagnated, largely because of inaccessibility. This changed in 1973, when paved México 1 – the Transpeninsular from Tijuana to Cabo San Lucas – opened. The population grew so quickly that less than a year later, south of the 28th parallel, Baja California Sur became Mexico's 30th state.

The highway functioned very much as a bridge to the 20th century, allowing farmers and craftsmen to transport their goods to other parts of Baja while opening up one of the hemisphere's last frontiers to tourism.

The influx of these foreigners further contributed to an improved standard of living for the local population. Southern Baja's fate as a 'destination' was sealed when the international airport near San José del Cabo opened in 1986.

1980s TO THE PRESENT

Following the oil booms of the 1970s, the Mexican economy went into a tailspin in the '80s from which it did not recover until drastic measures to introduce private enterprise and free trade were taken under President Carlos Salinas de Gortari (1988–94). By the time the North American Free Trade Agreement (NAFTA) took effect on January 1, 1994, things seemed to have stabilized and started to move forward. Then all hell broke loose.

The same day, about 2000 indigenous-peasant rebels calling themselves the Ejército Zapatista de Liberación Nacional (EZLN, Zapatista National Liberation Army) surprised Mexico by taking over several towns in the southern Mexican state of Chiapas. Two months later, Luis Donaldo Colosio, Salinas' chosen successor as Partido Revolucionario Institucional (PRI) presidential candidate, was assassinated in Tijuana. Conspiracy theories abound about the killing – relations between Salinas and Colosio had deteriorated markedly – but the only person convicted was the one who pulled the trigger and was captured on the spot.

After ruling Mexico for 71 consecutive years (primarily through rigged elections), the PRI finally lost its hold on the presidency in 2000. In that year's historical elections, with the world watching as Mexicans went to the polls, National Action Party (PAN) candidate Vicente Fox, a former Coca Cola executive, broke the PRI reign by winning 42% of the vote. The PAN victory clearly signified the country's desire for reform and dissatisfaction with PRI corruption and the power of drug cartels, but deep-rooted change has been slow to come.

Baja California has also become a major gateway into the US for the drug trade. Mexican cartels, especially the Tijuana-based Arellano Félix cartel, dominate the drug trade. In 2002 the gang's leader, Benjamin Arellano Felix, was captured, and his brother gunned down by police. Two years later Mexican police nabbed Efrain Perez and Jorge Aureliano Felix, two of the cartel's kingpins, and continued their search for the cartel's main man, Francisco Javier Arellano Felix. Despite increased cooperation between US and Mexican authorities, officials estimate that 90% of production still makes it to market.

Despite such problems, Baja California continues its growth in economic power, population and popularity as a tourist destination. In the 1990s Los Cabos' population tripled, and countless new hotels, condominium complexes and golf courses opened. Currently a colossal 2000-acre (800-hectare) resort development called Puerto Los Cabos (p199) is transforming the coastline north of San José del Cabo. Near Santa Rosalillita, the outrageous Escolera Nautical project (see p16) is billed to turn Baja's Sea of Cortez into the next Cancún.

As Baja develops, growing pains will be inevitable, and sizable tourist projects will potentially wreak havoc upon Baja's natural environment. Awareness and participation by tourists in both ecologically sound travel activities and in programs that seek to minimize the affects of tourism will help the peninsula remain the astounding natural playground it has long been.

For a quick look at the Escolera Nautica project, check out Sean Wagstaff's site (http://laescaleranautica.com) or the official Escolera Nautica site (www.escaleranautica.com/indexenglish.html).

The Culture

REGIONAL IDENTITY

Mexicans are not easily pinned down. They love fun, music and a fiesta, yet in many ways are deeply serious. They work hard but relax to the max in their time off. They're hospitable and warm to guests, yet are most truly themselves only within their family group. They will laugh at death, but have a profound vein of spirituality. You may read about anti-*gringo* sentiment in the media, but as a visitor to their country, Mexicans will treat you as an individual and with refreshing warmth and courtesy. Ask for help or information, and people will go out of their way to give it. (The word *gringo*, incidentally, isn't exactly a compliment, but nor is it necessarily an insult; the term can simply be, and often is, a neutral synonym for 'American' or 'citizen of the USA.')

Mexico is, of course, the home of machismo, that exaggeration of masculinity whose manifestations may range from a certain way of trimming a moustache to aggressive driving, heavy drinking, the carrying of weapons or abuse of women. The other side of the machismo coin is the exaggeratedly feminine, subjugated female. But gender equalization has come a long way in the past few decades: you'll find most Mexican women and men, especially among the increasingly educated and worldly younger generations, ready to relate simply as one person to another – even if the cliché Mexican family dynamic (son adores mother and must protect virtue of sisters and daughters, but all other women are fair game) still contains a dose of truth.

Mexico's 'patron saint' – not actually a saint but a manifestation of the Virgin Mary – is the dark-skinned Virgin of Guadalupe, who made her appearance before an indigenous Mexican in 1531 on a hill near Mexico City. Universally revered, she's both the archetypal mother and the preeminent focus of Mexicans' inborn spirituality, which has its roots both in Spanish Catholicism and in the complex belief systems of Mexico's pre-Hispanic civilizations. Elements of these ancient nature-based beliefs survive alongside Catholicism among the country's many indigenous people. Many Mexicans, when sick, prefer to visit a traditional *curandero* – a kind of cross between a naturopath and a witch doctor – rather than a modern *médico* (doctor). Nor have Mexicans left behind that awareness of death and afterlife that was so central to the pre-Hispanic cultures. The famous Día de Muertos festival (Day of the Dead, November 2; p227), when the departed are believed to revisit the living, is perhaps a way of building a bridge between this life and whatever follows it.

On a more mundane level, you'll find most Mexicans are chiefly concerned with earning a crust for themselves and their tightly knit families – and with enjoying the leisure side of life to the fullest, whether it be raging at clubs, parties, bars or fiestas or relaxing over a long, extended-family Sunday lunch at a beachside restaurant. Nobel Prize–winning Mexican writer Octavio Paz argued in *The Labyrinth of Solitude* that Mexicans' love of noise, music and crowds is no more than a temporary escape from a deeper personal isolation and gloom – but make your own judgment!

On a political level, the country is (slowly) democratizing, but most Mexicans still despair of it ever being governed well. Mexicans mock themselves for their country's failings. At the same time they are proud

– proud of their families, proud of their villages and towns, proud of Mexico. They don't like perceived slurs or any hint of foreign interference. So close to the USA, where millions of Mexicans have spent years of their lives, they accept a certain amount of US technology, fashion and products, but they also strongly value the positives they see in Mexican life – a more human pace, a stronger sense of community and family, their own very distinctive cuisine, their unique heritage and their thriving national culture.

While *bajacalifornianos* (people from Baja California) are Mexican in every sense of the word, they do share their own peninsular identity. The ancestors of today's bajacalifornianos, who settled the peninsula beginning over three hundred years ago (and as recently as 100 years ago), faced a harsh life in an unwelcoming desert. Baja's geographical distance from mainland Mexico and the Mexican government's lack of interest in the peninsula (until recently it invested very little here) meant bajacalifornianos faced life, in a land replete of infrastructure, on their own. Real bajacalifornianos were – and are – a grittier breed of folk. More recent immigrants – those who have come here in search of work over the last 50 years or so – may identify more with mainland Mexico, but still carry with them a sort of frontier spirit.

LIFESTYLE

Daily life for bajacalifornianos depends first and foremost upon place. For those who live in Tijuana or Mexicali (Baja's two largest cities), life is vastly different than it is in the small towns and empty spaces that make up the rest of the region.

Most residents of Tijuana inhabit tightly knit, multigenerational family homes or multistory apartment buildings. Streets are bustling and noisy with traffic, and there are few parks or open areas. On the outskirts of the city, the poorest people live in shacks without electricity or steady water supply. Some neighborhoods are literally jammed up against the corrugated metal fence that separates the city from the US on the other side.

In affluent neighborhoods, houses are closed to the outside by fences and electric gates to protect the building and flashy SUVs from the world outside, while the owners work in air-conditioned buildings here or in San Diego, California. Satellite dishes stand atop roofs, and housekeepers and tradespeople come and go.

The contrasts between poor and rich couldn't be greater: while kids from rich families go out nightclubbing in *carros del ano* (new cars) and attend private universities or schools in the USA, poor kids are lucky to complete primary education and often begin working before they're 15 years old. In other towns, families crowd into ramshackle dwellings and work in the fields or in *maquiladoras* (factories producing goods primarily for export) – in the case of the latter, for an average of between US$2 and US$2.50 per hour.

Elsewhere in Baja, things are strikingly different. In the smallest towns, people regularly take siestas and life maintains a slower pace, especially farther south where the midday summer heat is oppressive. In Baja California Sur (Baja's southern state), some people still live on *ranchos* (rural settlements), both in the mountains and on isolated stretches of the coast, where life is much the same as it was 300 years ago. Take a drive up to La Candelaria (p221) from Cabo San Lucas and you'll find a village, similar to many others in the region, where families still slaughter pigs and goats, grow some of their own food and live a unique semisubsistent lifestyle.

Debbie Nathan's *Women and Other Aliens: Essays from the US-Mexico Border* is an intriguing collection of articles exploring sexual politics on the border and the lives of illegal immigrants.

Oscar Martinez's *Troublesome Border* deals with current borderland issues like population growth, economic development, ecology and international migration.

Throughout Baja, as in the rest of Mexico, family and hometown ties remain strong despite influences that might be expected to drive generations apart, such as youth culture, computers, study and work away from home, and emigration to the USA.

Gender roles are relaxing among the middle class: education and jobs are more accessible for young women, and women now hold 23% of seats in Mexico's Congress and 41% of the country's professional and technical jobs. A Mexican woman today will have 2.8 children on average; in the early 1970s the average was 6.5. Among the poor, women still tend to play out traditional domestic and mothering roles, though they may also have part-time jobs or sell produce at the market.

Mexico is more broad-minded about sexuality than you might expect. Gays and lesbians tend to keep a low profile but rarely attract open discrimination or violence. Relatively open gay scenes exist in Tijuana and, to a lesser extent, Mexicali.

Tradition remains powerful. The calendar (see p227) is filled with saints' days and festivals such as Semana Santa (Holy Week), Día de Muertos (Day of the Dead, November 2), Día de la Virgen de Guadalupe (December 12) and Christmas. These events bring people together for the same processions and rituals year after year.

POPULATION

Anyone who's happiest barreling down an empty road whistling the old Cole Porter tune *Don't Fence Me In* will appreciate this: 85% of the peninsula's population lives in the northern state of Baja California, and 94% of those folks live in Tijuana, Mexicali or Ensenada. That leaves a *lot* of sparsely inhabited country. The biggest towns in Baja California Sur are La Paz (196,900), Los Cabos (San José and Cabo San Lucas combined; 150,000) and Loreto (11,800). The Cape Region's burgeoning tourism and housing developments (principally in and around Los Cabos) have generated a great need for service-industry personnel and construction workers, who migrate from mainland Mexico and continue to swell the region's population. The number of people in the border cities and the Cape Region is probably higher than official statistics suggest.

MULTICULTURALISM

Baja's population consists largely of *mestizos*, individuals of mixed Indian and European heritage, mostly immigrants or descendants of immigrants from mainland Mexico. But you'll also notice the peninsula has its share of fair-skinned, light-haired Mexicans. This is due partially to Baja's proximity to the USA, but also to the number of English and other European immigrants who came to the region in the late 1800s (see p20).

Baja's 1500 or so remaining Indians, often known by the generic term *Cochimí* (after the now extinct peoples of the Desierto Central), live mainly in the Sierra San Pedro Mártir, the Sierra de Juárez and the lowlands near the Río Hardy. They belong to tribal groups like the Diegueño (Tipai), Paipai, Kiliwa, Cucupah and Kamia, but few follow the traditional subsistence economy of hunting and gathering. Nearly all speak Spanish, but indigenous languages are still common among the Tipai, Paipai and Cucupah.

In the 19th century Baja's first fishing villages, ranchos and secular towns appeared along with mining operations that attracted fortune-seekers from around the world. Many established bajacalifornianos are descendants of settlers whose roots were in mainland Mexico or in other parts of the world – some trace their ancestry to the USA, southern and

DID YOU KNOW?

The state of Baja California Sur has the lowest population of any Mexican state: 424,000 people.

For a frightening look at the state of the Mexican-US border, read his Alberto Urrea's *The Devil's Highway*, the brutal story of 26 men who tried to cross the desert into the US in 2001.

Tune into the art, culture and history of the US-Mexico border with *Puro Border* (Luis Humberto Crosthwaite et al), an eclectic collection of essays and stories by journalists, artists and poets.

northern Europe, and even China. Thanks to these enclaves, unexpected surnames like Smith, Jones and even Crosthwaite and McLish are not unusual on the peninsula.

Chinese workers and wealthy Chinese labor contractors from California migrated to the Valle de Mexicali during World War I, and some 2000 Chinese-Mexicans still live in Mexicali (p110). In the early 20th century a group of Russian pacifist refugees settled the Valle de Guadalupe (p90) near Ensenada, and although they later moved to Los Angeles, they left an indelible mark on the cultural landscape. The French had their stay in and around the central Baja town of Santa Rosalía (p140), where the entire town looks like it was dropped out of the French countryside.

The past decade has seen the influx of large numbers of Indians from central Mexico to the city of Tijuana in particular, often as a staging point for crossing the US border. Several thousand Mixtecs from rural Oaxaca have settled in the San Quintín area, driven by poverty in the south and attracted by farming jobs in Baja, despite relatively low wages. For this reason, mainland indigenous languages are more common than in the past; bilingual schools have even been established in Tijuana, San Quintín and elsewhere.

California's Latino population suddenly disappears and chaos ensues in Sergio Arau's mockumentary film *A Day Without a Mexican* (Telvisa Cine; 2004). Though the humor is far from subtle, it's worth a peek for the pondering (and Mexicans love the film!).

Tossed into this continually changing cultural landscape are the Americans and Canadians (and a few Europeans) who have been steadily buying property along the coast, primarily in the Cape Region. They make up about 2% of Baja's population, a number that's growing as real estate moguls and small-time investors do everything they can to attract foreign homebuyers.

Recent large-scale developments such as Puerto Los Cabos (p199) near San José del Cabo, have forced local populations from their land and homes. Not surprisingly, it foments deep resentment both toward foreigners buying land and toward the Mexican developers selling it off to the *yanquis*. On the flip side, tourism in Baja California has given the peninsula one of the country's highest standards of living, and most locals are wonderfully welcoming toward foreigners. Gringos have been a part of the cultural landscape for years now, and intercultural relations are generally warm, albeit tinted with a usually humorous disdain for those wealthy folks from north of the border.

ARTS
Music

In Baja, as in the rest of Mexico, music may start up spontaneously on streets, plazas or even buses. These musicians play for a living and range from *marimba* (wooden xylophone) teams and mariachi bands (trumpeters, violinists, guitarists and a singer, all dressed in smart cowboy-like costumes) to ragged lone buskers with out-of-tune guitars and sandpaper voices. Mariachi music – perhaps the most 'typical' Mexican music of all – originated in the Guadalajara area but is played everywhere in Baja, primarily to tourists (both Mexican and foreign) who request and pay for songs.

Listen to everything from *rock en español* and *norteño* to *banda* and *mariachi* music at Batanga (www.batanga.com).

On a more organized level, Mexico has a thriving popular music business. Its outpourings can be heard live at fiestas, nightspots and concerts or bought from music shops or cheap bootleg vendors – though the latter are becoming harder to find due to crackdowns by local and international authorities.

REGIONAL STYLES
The most common sounds blaring from boom boxes and car stereos

Baja are those of **norteño** music. Its roots are in *corridos,* folk ballads dealing with Latino/Anglo strife in the borderlands in the 19th century, and themes from the Mexican Revolution. The genre today is dominated largely by *narcocorridos,* ballads whose themes are the trials of small-time smugglers and drug-runners trying to survive amid big-time corruption and crime. The Mexican government has officially banned some songs, and Tijuana's radio stations voluntarily banned narcocorridos in general from the air. It's now common practice for a wealthy tough or gang leader to pay a band to write a corrido in his honor, memorializing his valorous deeds (fictitiously or not).

First popularized by Los Tigres del Norte in the early 1970s, norteño's most characteristic sound is the accordion, although backing for the singer is also guitar-based, with bass and drums. Los Tigres del Norte, who got their start in San Jose, California, are by far the superstars of norteño, and their lyrics are more socially conscious than any other norteño band out there. Other chart-topping bands who lean more toward narcocorridos are Los Tucanes de Tijuana, El As de la Sierra, Los Huaracanes del Norte, Grupo Exterminador (if you really like it nasty) and Los Originales de San Juan.

Banda is a 1990s development of norteño, substituting large brass sections for guitars and accordion and playing a combination of Latin and more traditional Mexican rhythms. If you're not used to it, it's almost painful to listen to, as the trumpets and tuba mercilessly pound out the rhythm behind often raspy vocals. Banda Recodo, Banda Machos, Banda Cuisillos and Banda Aguacaliente are big names.

Ranchera is Mexico's urban 'country music.' Developed in the expanding towns and cities of the 20th century, it's mostly melodramatic, sentimental stuff with a nostalgia for rural roots – vocalist-and-combo music, maybe with a mariachi backing. Eugenia León, Juan Gabriel and Alejandro Fernández are among the leading ranchera artists.

ROCK

Baja California has a particularly vibrant *rock en español* (Spanish-language rock) scene, most evident in Tijuana. Bands that have made it big include Staura (a sort of Sonic Youth clone), Solución Mortal (hard-core punk), Tijuana No (The Clash–inspired salsa-punk), Paradoxa (thrash), Mercado Negro (UK-style punk), Beam (California punk), Crime of the Century (a Kiss clone with members from both sides of the border) and Giovanna (pop). Julieta Venegas – who got her start with Tijuana No, has received MTV awards and several nominations for Latin Grammys – is proving to be one of rock en español's powerhouses. Ensenada's claim to fame is heavy-metal act Yeo.

Popular bands from other parts of Mexico include Los Jaguares, Gran Silencio, Elefante and King Crimson–inspired La Barranca. Talented and versatile Mexico City bands such as Café Tacuba and Maldita Vecindad often roar from the jukebox at hip bars. These two bands took rock en español to new heights and new audiences (well beyond Mexico) in the '90s, mixing a huge range of influences – rock 'n' roll, ska, punk, bolero and mariachi.

ELECTRONICA

In 2000 Tijuana's Nortec Collective officially released its album *The Tijuana Sessions Vol 1,* after it became an internationally downloaded hit on the Internet. Fusing the sounds of norteño music with techno beats – hence the name Nortec – the recordings made their way into clubs

DID YOU KNOW?

Los Tigres del Norte have recorded 55 albums in their 33-year career; seven went gold, and the group has been nominated for 11 Latin Grammys.

DID YOU KNOW?

Mexican regional music (norteño, banda etc) accounts for over half of all Latin music sales in the USA. Ricky Martin, ha ha ha.

Elijah Wald's superbly narrated *Narcocorridos: A Journey Into the Music of Guns, Drugs & Guerillas* makes an excellent introduction into norteño music (which you'll surely hear in Baja).

DID YOU KNOW?

Guitar legend Carlos Santana began his musical career in Tijuana, where he played with bands like the TJs in the late 1950s.

around the world. At press time the group was getting ready to rele~
its second disc, which would use live – rather than recorded – norteñ
sounds, with drums, trumpet and accordion all folded into the heavy
bass mix. The group has spawned offshoots in Tijuana, making the city
a great place to groove to some unique techno sounds.

CLASSICAL

Baja's larger cities, most notably Tijuana and La Paz, support classical
music at venues like Tijuana's Centro Cultural. Ensembles also tour
smaller towns and cities. One of the most renowned groupings is Tijuana's Orquesta de Baja California, with musicians from Russia, the USA
and Mexico. Founded by Eduardo García Barrios, a Mexican who studied
at Moscow's Tchaikovsky Conservatory prior to the breakup of the Soviet
Union, the orchestra is led by conductor Eduardo Diazmuños. Barrios
also instigated the formation of Mexico's first orchestra-led music acad-
emy, which has since evolved into the Conservatorio Estatal de Música
(State Music Conservatory).

Film

Early Hollywood directors gave such insulting treatment to the Mexican
borderlands through depictions of casinos and prostitution that Baja
California's first cinematic production in 1927, Raza de Bronce (Race of
Bronze), was a nationalistic response to what director Guillermo Calles
perceived as racist stereotyping. In the 1970s Tecate built a cinema village
to attract US directors of westerns, but local talent did not flourish until
the video format became an inexpensive alternative.

With support from the Universidad Autónoma de Baja California,
bajacalifornianos have produced documentaries on such topics as the
Jesuit colonization and the Chinese community of Mexicali.

In the mid-1990s Hollywood went south again when 20th Century Fox
custom-built a studio just south of Playas de Rosarito for the filming of
James Cameron's epic, *Titanic*. Originally intended as a one-time facility,
it has been turned into the permanent Fox Baja Studios and was used for
other major movies, including *Tomorrow Never Dies* and *Deep Blue Sea*.
See p75 for more details.

Theater

Tijuana, Mexicali and La Paz – all of which have outstanding stage
facilities – are Baja California's dramatic centers. Like film, dance and
painting, peninsular theater grew with the universities and the Casa de
la Cultura. Numerous theater companies have offered aspiring actors
the opportunity to develop their talents. Groups like the well-established
Thalía Company of Mexicali and the more experimental Los Desarraiga-
dos of Tijuana have performed in Mexico City, the USA and overseas.

Visual Arts

Few visitors appreciate what a fertile environment Baja California has
provided for the visual arts. Throughout the peninsula, from Tijuana
to Los Cabos, evidence of cultural links with mainland Mexican move-
ments like the muralist tradition are apparent, but sculpture and painting
flourished even before the creation of the Instituto de Ciencias y Artes
del Estado (ICAE, now part of the Instituto de Bellas Artes) and the
Universidad Autónoma in the 1950s. Both institutions supported local
artists and others who had relocated from mainland Mexico.

DID YOU KNOW?

Troy (2003), starring
Brad Pitt, was filmed in
Los Cabos.

Rubén Martínez describes
Tijuana's thriving inde-
pendent arts community
in great detail in the
essay 'Tijuana Burning,' in
The Other Side, a collection of essays on Mexican
and Mexican-American
culture.

After the Universidad Autónoma abandoned the arts community, individual artists combined to form groups like the Círculo de Escultores y Pintores (Circle of Sculptors and Painters) and the Profesionales de Artes Visuales (Visual Arts Professionals). Since 1977 the Bienal de Artes Plásticas del Noroeste (Northwest Sculpture Festival) has been an important competition for artists from the region.

One informal movement in the local scene is *cholismo*, the equivalent of European or North American punk, often expressed in street murals featuring traditional Mexican figures like the Virgin of Guadalupe in unconventional contexts. Artists from both sides of the border are active in groups like the Taller de Arte Fronterizo (Border Art Workshop) and in the women-only Las Comadres. Both have direct ties to the Centro Cultural de la Raza in San Diego and the Centro Cultural in Tijuana, and often stage performance-art shows and events with borderlands themes.

Baja California Sur also has a lively arts community that revolves around the village of Todos Santos, which partly but by no means exclusively derives from North Americans who have relocated to the area. Their work, however, lacks the urgency of borderland artists' work; it more closely resembles styles and themes of artists from Taos and Santa Fe in the US state of New Mexico.

Luis Alberto Urrea's *By the Lake of the Sleeping Children: The Secret Life of the Mexican Border*, a combined effort with photographer John Lueders-Booth, deals with garbage pickers (the ultimate recyclers) in Tijuana.

Environment

THE LAND

Baja California is a desolate but scenic peninsula of mountains, deserts, headlands and beaches flanked by the Pacific Ocean to the west and the Sea of Cortez (also known as the Gulf of California) to the east. Its irregular, snakelike outline stretches 775 miles (1250km) from mainland California to Los Cabos, though its width ranges only from 30 to 145 miles (50 to 230km). On its northeastern edge, Baja also shares short borders with the US state of Arizona and the Mexican state of Sonora, both across the Río Colorado delta. (The southern part of the cape, loosely from La Paz south, is known as the Cape Region.) With a total landmass of about 55,000 sq miles (143,000 sq km), it is about the size of the US state of Illinois, or of England and Wales combined.

And here's the best part: more than 3000 miles (4800km) of spectacular and varied coastline wrap the peninsula.

Baja's unique topography is partly the result of tectonic uplift, during which the peninsula tilted westward over millions of years to form three of the peninsula's four main mountain ranges: the granitic **Sierra de Juárez** near the US border, home to the **Parque Nacional Constitución de 1857** (p33 & p91); the **Sierra San Pedro Mártir** (p33 & p94), crowned by the 10,154-foot (3046m) Picacho del Diablo; and the **Sierra de la Giganta**, which stretches from Mulegé nearly to La Paz. The fourth range, **Sierra de la Laguna** (p174), is volcanic in origin. With peaks up to 7000 feet (2100m), it divides the southern cape in half.

Similar to mainland California's Sierra Nevada, the western slopes of Baja's ranges feature low foothills gradually giving way to pine forests and granitic mountain peaks. On the eastern side, the mountains rise up rather abruptly, and the landscape is more arid and rugged.

Dotting Baja's Gulf waters are numerous islands, which are undersea extensions of peninsular mountain ranges. The largest island, **Isla Angel de la Guarda** (p129), is 42 miles (68km) long and 10 miles (16km) wide.

The **Tropic of Cancer** runs almost precisely through the towns of Todos Santos and Santiago, about midway between La Paz and Cabo San Lucas.

WILDLIFE

Baja California's desolate desert terrain doesn't mean it lacks wildlife – on the contrary. The peninsula is home to some of the most surreal landscapes you'll find, made all the more spectacular by such bizarre flora as the cardón cactus, the cirio tree, and the stunted, baobab-like elephant tree. As for animals, Baja has some of the best whale-watching in the world, not to mention the other rich sea life and land critters.

Animals

BIRDS

Baja California's bird habitats strongly correlate with the peninsula's plant communities, varying with climate, elevation and latitude. The mountainous Sierra San Pedro Mártir, the deserts of central Baja and the Cape each have characteristic groups of bird species. Ospreys are a common sight on the road to Puerto San Carlos (p157), where they nest atop nearly every available electrical pole.

Large colonies of nesting seabirds populate the many islands in the Sea of Cortez. Among the most noteworthy species are black storm-

DID YOU KNOW?

At 775 miles (1250km), Baja is the third longest peninsula in the world, after the Antarctic Peninsula and Russia's Kamchatka.

For an in-depth look at Baja's birds, pick up a copy of the excellent *Field Guide to the Birds of Mexico and Adjacent Areas*, by Ernest Preston Edwards.

petrels and least storm-petrels, brown pelicans, cormorants, frigate birds, boobies, Craveri's murrelets, Heerman's gulls, yellow-footed gulls, elegant terns and brown noddys.

LAND MAMMALS
Baja is home to a variety of unique mammals, including the black jackrabbit of Isla Espíritu Santo (p167) and the fish-eating bat of the Sea of Cortez. More characteristic, however, are animals like the mule deer, peninsular pronghorn antelope and endangered desert bighorn sheep. The Cedros mule deer is an endangered subspecies on its namesake Pacific island (p134). Smaller and more common land mammals include the coyote, rabbit, fox, squirrel, chipmunk and gopher.

MARINE MAMMALS
From January to April, visitors flock to the lagoons of central Baja to view the migration and mating of the California gray whale (p35). Other whale species (including finback, blue, orca and humpack) and dolphins also frequent the waters of the Pacific and the Gulf.

Other marine mammals include the endangered Gulf of California harbor porpoise, the recovering but still threatened southern sea otter, the threatened Guadalupe fur seal, and the more common sea lion, northern elephant seal and harbor seal. The most easily accessible sea lion colonies (where you can even snorkel with the friendly creatures) are at Bahía Los Frailes (p181), Cabo San Lucas (p212) and Isla Espíritu Santo (p167).

DID YOU KNOW?
Pacific manta rays, common in the Sea of Cortez, can have a wingspan up to 25ft (7.5m) across and weigh up to 4000lb (1800kg). Good thing they're friendly!

FISH & MARINE LIFE
The waters of the Pacific support a cool temperate flora and fauna resembling that off the coast of mainland California, with kelp and mollusks, sea urchins and barnacles. Shallow areas, like Laguna San Ignacio (p140) and Bahía Magdalena (p157), support more tropical life forms.

Because of the range of temperatures in the Sea of Cortez, its flora and fauna are relatively limited in numbers of species, especially in the northern half. Mangrove swamps in some shallow lagoons, especially toward the middle of the peninsula, are incubators for oysters. Crustaceans such as spiny lobsters and rock crabs were already popular fare in aboriginal Baja. The venomous yellow-bellied sea snake frequents the inshore waters of southern Baja.

Most of today's important marine life, especially that of interest to tourists, is pelagic (native to open seas). More than 800 species of fish inhabit the Sea of Cortez. The totuava, known commonly as sea trout or weakfish, is an endangered species in the Sea of Cortez. Parque Nacional Cabo Pulmo (p180), northeast of San José del Cabo, is home to the only living coral reef on North America's west coast.

Daniel Gotshall's *Marine Animals of Baja California: A Guide to the Common Fish & Invertebrates* has lavish color photographs of Baja's sea life.

REPTILES
Desert environments support many reptiles, including snakes, lizards and turtles. Baja has an abundant and varied snake population, including king, gopher, whiptail and, of course, rattlesnakes, which are a serious concern throughout the peninsula. Isla Santa Catalina, southeast of Loreto, is home to the endemic rattleless rattlesnake, so called because it has only a single rattle segment, which by itself is incapable of making any sound. It is also poisonous.

Sea turtles, all of which are endangered species, inhabit the coastal areas, mostly on the Sea of Cortez side. The Pacific green turtle, colloquially known as the *caguama negra* or *tortuga prieta,* is the most important,

Familiarize yourself with the plight of pacific sea turtles through the excellent news archive at Wild Coast (www.wildcoast.net). Through the website you can also learn how to help save these majestic creatures from extinction.

but other species include the leatherback, black, olive ridley, loggerhead and hawksbill.

Plants

Most people think of Baja as a desert largely devoid of vegetation. Fact is, the desert is alive with more than 3000 native and introduced plants, some of which grow nowhere else on earth.

In botanical terms, much of semi-arid northern Baja is very much a continuation of Southern California. At sea level and in the lower elevations, plants like agave, buckeye, buckwheat, and bladderpod dominate. Away from the coast, these give way to chaparral vegetation including manzanita, California lilac, chamise and other plants. Above the chaparral belt, the upper slopes of the Sierra de Juárez and San Pedro

---

THE SAD TALE OF THE TURTLE

The great whales get all the press. Few travelers know as much about the sea turtles that, historically, have been as important to the peoples of the tropics as whales have been to the peoples of the Arctic. Called 'the world's most valuable reptile' by the late geographer James Parsons, the Pacific green turtle *(Chelonia mydas)* is endangered throughout the world, and its conservation should be a major priority in Baja California and the rest of Mexico.

The Pacific green turtle (*caguama negra*, or *tortuga prieta* in Baja) is a grazing reptile that feeds on marine grasses in tropical and subtropical seas. They can weigh up to 800lb (360kg), though most weigh 300lb (135kg) or less. Males rarely leave the sea, but females migrate long distances and haul themselves onto sandy beaches of isolated tropical islands to lay their eggs.

For millennia the green turtle has provided protein to people in the tropics with its meat and eggs, but the Europeans' exploration of the globe marked the beginning of the species' decline. Northern European sailors netted the abundant turtles of the Caribbean, for example, and kept them aboard ships as sources of fresh meat on their trips around Cape Horn. Outside the tropics, turtle has long been a delicacy, and commercial pressures resulted in overhunting in such important areas as the Caribbean coasts of Nicaragua and Costa Rica.

Baja California's turtles shared this unfortunate history. At Bahía Tortugas (p136) on Península Vizcaíno, one 19th-century ship netted almost 200 turtles in a single pass. As recently as the 1960s the Empacadora Baja California in Ensenada was canning as much as 100 tons of turtle soup in a single season.

In the 1970s increasing concern over the green turtle's declining numbers resulted in its placement (and that of all other sea turtles) on Appendix I of the Convention on International Trade in Endangered Species of Wild Fauna and Flora (CITES). Mexico officially outlawed sea-turtle hunting in 1990. Despite this, the turtle populations continue to decline. Pollution, illegal hunting, egg collecting, ATV use on nesting-site beaches, boat traffic and other factors contribute to the turtles' demise.

Several Baja-based nonprofit agencies focus their energies on turtle preservation, including the **Sea Turtle Conservation Network of the Californias** (www.baja.seaturtle.org) and **Asupmatoma** (☎ 624-143-0458; www.mexonline.com/tortuga.htm), which operates a turtle nursery at Rancho Punta San Cristobal, about 15 minutes north of Cabo San Lucas. In the 1999-2000 season, more than 15,000 hatchlings were released into the Pacific Ocean. At Bahía de Los Angeles, **Semarnap** (the Mexican ministry of the environment) operates a modest turtle conservation project, where it's possible to see leatherbacks, hawksbills and greens (see p129).

Baja visitors are unlikely to come across nesting sites, which are usually in remote spots. Nevertheless, greens and other turtle species are not unusual in Baja waters. There are nesting sites on the Eastern Cape north of Cabo Pulmo, and the green has been spotted at numerous sites within the Gulf and on the Pacific as far north as Ensenada. The warmer waters of Baja California Sur are better turtle habitat, and turtles appear in many of the same areas frequented by calving gray whales: Laguna Ojo de Liebre, Laguna San Ignacio and Bahía Magdalena.

Mártir support a lush forest studded with pines, spruce, cedar, fir, aspen and oak.

East of the sierras, the Sonoran Desert botanical region comprises several distinct subregions. From the US border as far as Bahía de los Angeles, there are small-leaved shrubs like ocotillo, the closely related *palo adán*, the cactuslike *nopal* (prickly pear), and the cholla and saguaro cacti.

South of Bahía de los Angeles almost to La Paz, a narrow coastal strip on the Sea of Cortez features imposing cacti like the *cardón,* which reaches heights over 60 feet (18m), and many species of *biznaga* (barrel cactus).

The giant cardón cactus is one of the species endemic to Baja California. Others with this distinction are the *datilillo,* a yucca variety related to the Joshua tree in Southern California, and the curious *cirio* tree. Often likened in appearance to an inverted carrot, this bizarre, slow-growing species stands up to 60 feet (18m) tall. It's also called 'boojum,' in reference to the tall, twisted creature in Lewis Carroll's poem *The Hunting of the Snark.*

Farther south, on the Pacific slope, the Desierto de Vizcaíno and the Llano de Magdalena support different species of agave, plus cacti like the cardón and the galloping cactus.

The Sierra de la Giganta, running from Loreto nearly to La Paz, is home to many common trees and shrubs like acacia and mesquite, a handful of native palms and many cacti, including nopal, the organ pipe cactus and the *pitahaya dulce,* which yields a sweet fruit that was the Cochimí equivalent of candy.

South of the Sierra de la Giganta, most of the Cape Region is an arid tropical zone of acacia and other leguminous trees and shrubs, sumac and fan palm. Pines and oaks, however, appear side by side with palms and cacti at higher elevations in the well-watered Sierra de la Laguna.

In addition to these major zones, more localized plant associations exist that are botanically significant and constitute critical wildlife habitat, especially for birds. These areas include coastal dunes, coastal salt marshes, freshwater marshes, mangrove swamps and vernal pools.

PARKS & RESERVES
National Parks

Mexico has established four major *parques nacionales* (national parks) on the Baja Peninsula. On the plateau and eastern slope of the Sierra de Juárez, the 19-sq-mile (49-sq-km) **Parque Nacional Constitución de 1857** (p91) is barely an hour's drive from Ensenada and a good place for camping and rock climbing. Its shallow Laguna Hanson, surrounded by shady pine forests, is a major stopover for migratory birds on the Pacific flyway.

Reaching altitudes above 10,000 feet (3000m) in its namesake mountain range, **Parque Nacional Sierra San Pedro Mártir** (p94) is roughly 236 sq miles (614 sq km) and contains Baja's highest point, the Picacho del Diablo (Devil's Peak), which tops out at 10,154 feet (3046m). Thanks to the park's remoteness and difficult access, it does not receive many visitors and has little infrastructure. Its varied terrain and vegetation, however, make it a good destination for backcountry camping and backpacking, especially in the spring.

The 799-sq-mile (2077-sq-km) **Parque Marino Nacional Bahía de Loreto** (p149) protects the fish, sealife, islands and water around Loreto. The 27-sq-mile (70-sq-km) **Parque Marino Nacional Cabo Pulmo** (p180) protects the only living coral reef on the west coast of North America.

Norman C Roberts' excellent *Baja California Plant Field Guide* has 285 color photographs to accompany descriptions of more than 400 of Baja's plants.

DID YOU KNOW?

The tallest cactus in the world is in northern Baja – a cardón topping out at 63 feet (19m).

UNESCO WORLD HERITAGE SITES

In 1993 the United Nations Educational, Scientific and Cultural Organization (Unesco) designated three World Heritage Sites within the Vizcaíno Biosphere Reserve: the rock art of Sierra de San Francisco (p138) and the important gray-whale calving sites of Laguna Ojo de Liebre (p133) and Laguna San Ignacio (p140). The sites, three of the most fascinating destinations in Baja, are now protected areas and are managed locally with some assistance and technical support from Unesco.

Biosphere Reserves

Baja also has three Unesco Biosphere Reserves. **Islas del Golfo Biosphere Reserve** includes all the islands in the Sea of Cortez; the reserve overlaps the borders of the marine national parks at Loreto and Cabo Pulmo, mentioned earlier.

The 9833-sq-mile (25,566-sq-km) **Vizcaíno Biosphere Reserve** stretches across the central peninsula just south of the Baja California Sur state border. It is Latin America's largest single protected area.

In the high mountains of the Cape Region, **Sierra de la Laguna Biosphere Reserve** (p175) protects a truly unique mixture of coniferous, deciduous and palm forests.

ENVIRONMENTAL ISSUES

From the international border to Cabo San Lucas, Baja California's fragile desert and maritime environments are facing a variety of challenges. Urban population growth has caused various problems. In Tijuana, for instance, the inability to build adequate housing and sewage facilities has meant serious pollution of the Río Tijuana; about 13 million gallons (58.5 million liters) of raw sewage enter the river daily and flow into the Pacific Ocean off San Diego. The New River, entering California from Mexicali, carries about 100 toxic substances and more than one billion liters of sewage and industrial waste daily.

Other environmental issues include deforestation and erosion in the Sierra de Juárez of northern Baja, potentially deleterious effects of increased salt production on the gray-whale nursery at Laguna San Ignacio and toxic mining residues at sites like Santa Rosalía. San Ignacio won a major environmental victory in 2000 when Mitsubishi and the Mexican government announced they were abandoning plans to build a massive salt-evaporation facility near Laguna San Ignacio.

The proliferation of off-road races throughout the peninsula has done inestimable damage to its flora and fauna. Other recent impacts from the tourist sector include the massive Escolera Nautica land-bridge project (see p16) and resort development around San José del Cabo (p199).

Overfishing is another major problem, especially because of commercial fishing. The Mexican government allows Japanese fishing boats to fish for tuna with longlines within 15 miles off the shores of Baja, with billfish considered incidental catches. This poses a serious threat not just to the fish population but ultimately also to the sportfishing industry. Locals are becoming gradually educated, and most sportfishing operators promote catch and release.

Ron Mader's Planeta: Ecotravels in Latin America (www. planeta.com) is one of the best resources for environmentally conscious travel in Latin America, and his Baja pages (www.planeta. com/baja.html) are no exception.

Baja Outdoors

For nature lovers, Baja is a dream. Outdoor adventure has always been the peninsula's highlight, with endless opportunities to frolic in nature, from sea kayaking and diving in the Sea of Cortez, to whale-watching in the Pacific, to sportfishing just about everywhere.

WHALE-WATCHING

From mid-December to mid-April, the coastal lagoons of Baja California Sur are calving grounds for the California gray whale, and thousands of visitors, both Mexicans and foreigners, gather to observe mothers and their calves cavorting in the lagoons' shallow waters. Witnessing a mother nudge her calf right up to the boat – and people literally reach out and touch them – is truly a spectacle to behold.

In winter you can spot whales from shore from Ensenada all the way to Cabo San Lucas and into the Sea of Cortez. But the whales' primary calving grounds – and the best places to see them – are within three sheltered bays on the Pacific. North to south, they are **Laguna Ojo de Liebre** (p133), **Laguna San Ignacio** (p140) and **Bahía Magdalena** (p157).

For your coffee table, it's hard to beat Stanley Minasian's *The World's Whales*. Incorporate people and politics into your research with Serge Dedina's *Saving the Gray Whale: People, Politics and Conservation in Baja California*.

Whale-Watching Sites

The closest town to Laguna Ojo de Liebre is **Guerrero Negro** (p131), about 20 miles (32km) inland. While definitely not the most attractive town, it has a good choice of mid-range hotels, or you can camp near the lagoon. The bay itself gets more whales than the other two bays.

San Ignacio (p135) is the closest population center to Laguna San Ignacio. It has better accommodations than Guerrero Negro and, because it's a delightful, historic town, it makes a great place to stay. There's also a sprinkling of cabañas and camping areas at the lagoon, nearly two hours – but only 40 miles (64km) – from San Ignacio proper. The lagoon is known for having the 'friendliest' whales.

Bahía Magdalena has two main centers: **Puerto López Mateos** and **Puerto San Carlos** (p157). The latter is the bigger of the two and has better, more comfortable, accommodations. Both are right on the bay, meaning you can get out on the water as soon as you can drag your butt out of bed and to the piers. Boca de Soledad, an inlet near Puerto López Mateos, boasts the highest *density* of whales of all these sites.

Tours

Although it's possible to see the whales from land (especially near Puerto López Mateos), the best way to really see them is by *panga* (skiff). You can set up panga tours in three ways. The cheapest option is to negotiate directly with the *pangueros* (panga owners) down at the piers. They usually charge US$30 to US$50 per hour per boat for up to six people, and you'll want *at least* two hours in the water. The downside to this is that the pangueros generally don't speak English and won't be able to explain – from a 'naturalist's' perspective – what's going on.

The next step up is to arrange a trip through one of the hotels or operators in the towns closest to the lagoons. There will often be a bilingual guide in the boat. These trips generally cost US$50 to US$60 per hour per boat. Similarly tour operators in La Paz (p167) and Loreto (p152) offer full-day trips to Bahía Magdalena and Laguna San Ignacio.

GRAY WHALES OF BAJA *Keith Jones*

There is nowhere else in the world where you can get as close to a wild whale as you will get at any of the lagoons of Baja. Friendly whale activity, where the whales come very close to your boat and sometimes allow you to touch them, is common in these lagoons. If you are visiting Baja in January, February or March, you should take at least one trip on a whale-watching panga.

The Migration

Each year, gray whales make one of the longest migrations of any animal on Earth. Triggered by a drop in water temperature, these 35-to-45-foot-long mammals migrate south from their winter feeding grounds in the Alaskan and Siberian waters beginning in October or November. The first to migrate are usually pregnant females, followed closely by the breeding-age adults. Juvenile whales also make the migration, but their drive to arrive isn't as intense. They are known to linger along the way, frequently stopping well short of the Mexican lagoons.

Swimming day and night, gray whales travel between 5000 and 6000 miles, pausing only for brief 10- or 15-minute catnaps. Although some whales have been observed feeding along the way (they have a set of bristly filters that hang down from their upper jaws called a baleen), it's uncommon. The Vizcaino Biosphere Reserve biologists estimate that an adult migrating whale may lose up to 15,000 pounds of body weight during the migration. (They weigh up to 75,000 pounds.)

Arrival in Baja

Baja's Laguna Ojo de Liebre and the two more southerly bays of Laguna San Ignacio and Bahía Magdalena are the three protected waterways where the gray whales spend three months each year to give birth and mate. The first whales normally enter Laguna Ojo de Liebre between December 15 and 20 and arrive a few weeks later at the other lagoons.

The whale-watching season doesn't officially open until January 1. By then hundreds of whales have arrived inside Laguna Ojo de Liebre. The whale count peaks around February 15, when the average number of whales in Laguna Ojo de Liebre is 1500. (In 2004, the official Vizcaino Biosphere Reserve census was 2000 whales.) In Laguna San Ignacio and Bahía Magdalena, the whale count usually peaks at around 200 to 350 whales. Although the eastern North Pacific gray whale population has been estimated at between 16,000 and 26,000, the population has declined the last few years, likely due to a food shortage.

Mothers and Babies

Female gray whales normally give birth to one baby, weighing in at 1500 to 2000 pounds. The lagoons of Baja provide a unique environment ideally suited for bringing baby whales into the

Finally, you can set up a trip from the USA or elsewhere. These multiday tours are the most expensive way to do it, but are also the most extensive and informative. An English-speaking naturalist guide will always be in the boat, so you'll learn and see a lot. Tours are usually in February and March, and include lodging, ground transport, optional charter flights, food, excursions and guides. If you need specific dates, make reservations one to three months in advance. A five-day trip usually gets you three days of whale-watching.

There are also 12-day cruises aboard 30-person yachts. Sailing from San Diego and ending in Cabo San Lucas, these take you to the Pacific lagoons (usually San Ignacio) as well as to the Sea of Cortez where you can see blue, sperm and humpback whales. You'll have chances to snorkel and hike on islands as well.

Following is a list of recommended USA-based tour operators. Rates here are per person, double occupancy. Cruises do not include return flights from Cabo San Lucas.

world. The shallow water (20 or 30 feet deep) is warmer than in the open ocean, providing needed warmth for the babies, which are born without an insulating layer of blubber. There are virtually no waves inside the lagoons. Orcas, the number-one threat to baby gray whales, never enter Laguna Ojo de Liebre or Laguna San Ignacio because of this shallow water. As baby whales don't know how to swim, the mother whale must assist the newborn to the surface for his first breath of air, then teach him essential survival skills.

The mother whales are tremendously protective of their newborn babies. The mother and baby constantly touch one another. The baby uses his mother as a platform to rest upon, to sleep on and play on and under. Frequently, we see a mother whale swimming with her pectoral fin extended to the side so her baby can swim and rest almost simultaneously.

If you're lucky, you may be able to catch mother whales teaching the youngsters how to breach (leaping out of the water and crashing back down). By early February the youngsters are commonly seen attempting to breach, but they usually aren't strong enough until mid-February, when for just one or two days the mother whales will breach (an unusual sight). Some days you'll see dozens of mothers jumping at the same time, or just before, their baby jumps. It's an exciting time to be on the water.

By late February, the babies have grown large enough to swim away from their mother's side, and groups of whales will play together. The mothers hover around the fringes of this playtime activity.

One Memorable Experience

In 1997 I helped a stranded baby gray whale swim off a muddy-bottomed beach (he became stuck after his mother died). We discovered him after dark. As the tide raised the water level, a small group of people pushed and rolled him out toward deeper water. We waded out to our waists and helped him swim free. Later we stood huddled together on the shore, wet and cold from the onshore wind. There were tears in all of our eyes as we slowly walked the half mile back to our camp.

That night I sat staring out at the black lagoon. I couldn't sleep. I kept thinking about that baby whale who was probably even colder than I was. Certainly he was frightened and very tired out there all alone in the dark lagoon water. Each time I dozed off an image of his glistening black eyes, staring helplessly at our tiny band of rescuers, crept into my dreams. Although I knew we had done a good thing, I was troubled.

The next day while out on a whale-watching boat, we came across a mother whale with two babies feeding and playing. We realized quickly that the mother had adopted the young baby we helped off the mud flat. I've experienced many uplifting moments in the time I've spent with the gray whales, but this was one of the best.

Baja Discovery (☎ 619-262-0700, 800-829-2252; www.bajadiscovery.com) Land-based. Boat-in base camp at Laguna San Ignacio, right on a deepwater channel. Superb location, great outfitter. Five-day trips cost US$1995.

Baja Expeditions (☎ 858-581-3311, 800-843-6967; www.bajaex.com) Land based. Highly reqarded outfitter, long in the business. Base camps at Laguna San Ignacio and Bahía Magdalena. Five-day trips, including charter flights from San Diego, cost US$1950

Baja Jones Adventures (☎ 909-923-8933; www.greywhale.com) Five- and six-day land or air-charter trips to Ojo de Liebre cost US$1695 to US$1995.

Natural Habitat Adventures (☎ 800-543-8917; www.nathab.com) Six-day land-based trips from Loreto to San Ignacio cost US$1995. Two departures in mid-February.

Pacific Sea Fari/H&M Landing (☎ 619-226-8224; www.hmlanding.com/newseafari.htm) Eleven-day cruises cost US$2790. Five departures in February and March.

Oceanic Society (☎ 800-326-7491; www.oceanic-society.org) Twelve-day cruises cost US$2760. One departure in mid-March.

Searcher Natural History Tours (☎ 619-226-2403; www.bajawhale.com) Twelve-day cruises cost US$2975. Three departures in February and March.

SEA KAYAKING

Baja California is a top-rated destination for sea kayaking, which is often the only way to access some of the most pristine and beautiful coves and inlets along the coast and the offshore islands.

The Sea of Cortez offers calmer waters than the Pacific and is a great place to learn or hone your kayaking skills. The most interesting areas are the Gulf islands of the Midriff from Bahía de Los Angeles (p128) south to the Islas Espíritu Santo (p167) near La Paz. These feature abundant wildlife and countless anchorages for well-equipped campers. Sheltered Bahía Concepción (p147), south of Mulegé, is another major hot spot for recreational kayakers and is especially suited for novices. Kayaking can be excellent along the Eastern Cape (p176) as well.

Rougher seas on the Pacific side attract more advanced and adventurous kayakers, although most beginners should also be able to cope with the waters in sheltered Punta Banda (p89), south of Ensenada.

Hazards to sea kayakers include the large swells of the open Pacific and high winds on the Gulf, both of which can swamp unsuspecting novices. But even experts should respect these natural phenomena and inquire about local conditions. Note also that Mexican government regulations prohibit sea kayaking when whales are present in the Pacific coastal lagoons of Baja California Sur.

Many aficionados bring their own equipment, but kayaks are also for rent at hotels, resorts and sports outfitters, many of whom also offer guided tours. Loreto and especially La Paz are two of the best places to arrange kayaking tours. Several outfitters operate in La Paz, offering everything from half- and full-day trips to Espíritu Santo (about US$80 per person) to multiday camping trips (about US$850 to US$1050 per week). You can also rent equipment from several operators in La Paz and arrange shuttle service to/from the islands, allowing you to kayak and camp alone and get picked up when you want. You can even set up meeting points to have your food carried and cooked for you. Outfitters that provide such services (such as Mar y Aventuras and Baja Expeditions in La Paz; see p166) also offer radios, maps, information and assistance if you get into trouble.

To arrange a trip from home, contact one of the following operators, most based in the USA:

Sea Trek (☎ 415-488-1100; www.seatrekkayak.com) Based in San Francisco
Baja Outdoor Activities (www.kayactivities.com) Based in La Paz
Baja Expeditions (☎ 858-581-3311, 800-843-6967; www.bajaex.com) Based in San Diego
Kayak Port Townsend (☎ 360-531-1670, 800-853-2252; www.kayakpt.com) Based in Port Townsend, Washington
Sea Kayak Adventures (☎ 208-765-3116, 800-616-1943; www.seakayakadventures.com) Based in Coeur D'Alene, Idaho

DIVING & SNORKELING

Both the Pacific Ocean and the Sea of Cortez are water wonderlands for divers and snorkelers. Rock and coral reefs, shipwrecks and kelp beds all invite exploration and attract a great variety of ocean dwellers and tropical fish.

Dive sites on the Pacific side, in general, are better suited for advanced divers; thanks to chilly water temperatures, wetsuits are advisable year-round. Both Islas de Todos Santos (near Ensenada; p88) and Islas de los Coronados (p68) are popular playgrounds for Southern Californians. Species you're likely to encounter include rockfish, the luminescent garibaldi, moray eels and bat rays.

The central and southern Sea of Cortez beckons with calmer and warmer waters and an even greater diversity of species: You'll feel as if you're diving in a giant tropical aquarium. There are sites for snorkelers as well as divers of all skill and experience levels. Hubs for underwater explorations are (north to south): Bahiá de Los Angeles (p128) and the Midriff Islands to the south; Isla Santa Inéz near Mulegé (p144) and Bahía Concepción (p147); La Paz (p166) with Isla Espiritú Santo, Isla Partida, Los Islotes and El Bajo Seamount (famous for schooling hammerhead sharks, mantas and whale sharks); the Eastern Cape's Cabo Pulmo (the only coral reef on the North American west coast; p180); and Land's End sandfalls, Playa Santa María and Playa Chileño, near Cabo (p212).

Dive shops at or near all of these areas lead tours and rent equipment, though you may prefer to bring your own.

San Diego–based **Baja Expeditions** (p37) and **Horizon Charters Diving** (☎ 858-277-7823; www.horizoncharters.com) both organize multiday diving excursions. Another outfitter with an outstanding reputation is **Baja Diving & Service** (☎ 612-122-1826; Paseo Obregón 1665, Local 2; www.clubcantamar.com), based in La Paz. It owns the only recompression chamber in La Paz.

Most outfitters charge about US$20 to US$25 per day for full diving-gear rental, provided you're diving with them. It's slightly more if you go on your own. A two-day/three-night dive package, including hotel room in La Paz, costs US$300 to US$400, not including transport to La Paz. Baja Diving & Service offers two- to five-night camp-and-dive packages for US$550 to US$1100 per person. Rates at other outfitters throughout the peninsula are similar.

Snorkel tours cost about US$45 to US$80 per day and include transport to islands or bays accessible only by boat. You can rent snorkeling gear and go on your own in La Paz and Cabo San Lucas, but you don't see nearly as much as you do by boat. Bring your own gear if you can; it will allow you to snorkel whenever and wherever you want, which is especially handy if you're exploring waters of the Eastern Cape Road (p176).

FISHING

Sportfishing, for good reason, is one of the most popular activities off the Pacific coast and in the Sea of Cortez. The waters of Baja are among the most fecund anywhere, and few places offer a greater variety of fish. The southern peninsula enjoys a legendary reputation for big game fish like marlin and dorado.

The most detailed and respected source on Baja fishing is *The Baja Catch*, by Neil Kelly and Gene Kira.

Also see the fish calendars (indicating at what time certain species are most prevalent in a particular area) and additional information that appear in the San Quintín (p99), San Felipe (p119), Puertecitos (p123), Bahía San Luis Gonzaga (p128), Bahía de Los Angeles (p129), Mulegé (p145), Loreto (p151), La Paz (p167), Buena Vista (p179), San José del Cabo (p193) and Cabo San Lucas (p208) sections.

When to Fish

You can catch fish in Baja waters year-round, but what's biting, how many, where and when depends on variables like water temperature, currents, bait supply and fish migrations. In general the biggest catches occur April to July and October to December. Keep in mind that summer through late fall is also prime tropical-storm and hurricane season.

Where to Fish

The waters around Ensenada and San Quintín Bay are known to be rich in yellowtail, halibut, sea bass, bonito and albacore tuna. On the Sea of

HERE, FISHY FISHY FISH...

Who's gonna believe you if you can't even tell them what kind of fish you caught? This little angler's glossary should help. It will also help you communicate with Mexican guides and captains, who can usually tell you what you're most likely to catch.

barracuda	*picuda*	sea bass	*corvina*
black marlin	*marlín negro*	shark	*tiburón*
blue marlin	*marlín azul*	sierra	*Spanish mackerel*
bonito	*bonito*	striped marlin	*marlín rayado*
dolphin fish (mahimahi)	*dorado*	swordfish	*pez espada*
halibut	*lenguado*	tuna	*atún*
mullet	*lisa*	wahoo	*peto, guahu*
red snapper	*huachinango, pargo*	yellowtail	*jurel*
roosterfish	*pez gallo*	yellowfin tuna	*atún de aleta*
sailfish	*pez vela*		

The phrase that will serve you most, however, may turn out to be *se me fue* (it got away). Then throw your hands up and say *te lo juro* (I swear it)!

Cortez side, grouper, sierra and corvina are common off San Felipe. Mulegé and Bahía Concepción have many of the same species as well as yellowtail, dorado and even the occasional marlin. Loreto is famous for roosterfish.

The most abundant fishing grounds are in the Cape Region. Both Los Cabos and the East Cape are rich in migratory species such as dorado, tuna and wahoo, but Cabo San Lucas especially is the epicenter for year-round billfish such as marlin, sailfish and swordfish. Roosterfish swarm around the East Cape.

Charters

Fishing charters are available at all of Baja's fishing hubs, and you'll find reputable local companies listed throughout this book. Always ask what's included in the rates. Fishing licenses, tackle, crew and ice are standard, but sometimes charters may also include bait, cleaning and freezing, meals, drinks and tax. Tips for the crew are at your discretion, but US$20 (per angler) for a successful eight hours is considered adequate. Bring along a hat, sunscreen, polarized sunglasses and Dramamine (or equivalent) if you suffer from seasickness.

Prices depend on boat type and size. The most common is the fly-bridge cruiser, usually 26 to 42 feet (8.6 to 14m) in length. It usually has two fighting chairs in the stern to reel in the big fish. Prices range from US$300 for a 26-footer to US$900-plus for a 42-footer.

The cheapest boats are pangas, the vessel of choice of Mexican commercial fishermen, as they put you right up close with the sea. About 18 to 24 feet (6 to 8m) long, these sturdy skiffs are made from heavy-duty fiberglass and wood and are powered by an outboard motor. They cruise up to 25mph (40km/h) and are capable of beach landings. Superpangas are larger and more comfortable, and they often feature toilets and a canvas shade top. Panga rates start around US$30 per hour for two to three people, with a six-hour minimum.

On the northwest Pacific coast, operators based at San Diego or Ensenada go out on larger powerboats (40 to 60 feet/13 to 20m) that can accommodate up to 30 anglers.

Licenses & Bag Limits

Anyone 16 years or older aboard a private vessel carrying fishing gear must have a Mexican fishing license, whether they're fishing or not. Licenses are usually included in any charters but can also be obtained in the USA from the **Mexican Fisheries Department** (Conapesca; ☎ 619-233-6956; 2550 5th Ave, Suite 101, San Diego, CA 92103). In Mexico licenses are issued by the Oficina de Pesca in the respective towns. The cost of the license is US$10 per day, US$21 per week, US$31 per month and US$40 per year.

The daily bag limit is 10 fish per person with no more than five of any one species. Billfish like marlin, sailfish and swordfish are restricted to one per day per boat; tarpon, roosterfish and halibut to two. Please take the catch and release of billfish seriously, as these majestic lords of the deep are being disastrously overfished, both by sportsmen and Japanese commercial fleets (also see p209). Protected species like *totuava* (a relative of white sea bass) and sea turtles, as well as mollusks and crustaceans, may not be taken at all.

US Customs allows fish caught in Mexico to enter the USA as long as it conforms with Mexican bag limits, the species is somehow identifiable (an ice chest filled with fillets is a no-no; the head, tail or part of the skin should be left on) and you can produce a Mexican fishing license. Contact the **California Department of Fish & Game** (☎ 858 467 4201; in Sacramento ☎ 916-653-6281; www.dfg.ca.gov; 4949 Viewridge Ave, San Diego, CA 92123) for information about declaration forms, permits and limits.

GOLF

With spectacular championship courses flanking the Sea of Cortez, the Los Cabos Corridor reigns supreme when it comes to golf. The region's six signature courses include three by Jack Nicklaus – the 27-hole Palmilla, the 18-hole El Dorado (p202) and the 18-hole Cabo del Sol Ocean Course – a Tom Weiskopf course and a Robert Trent Jones course. With fairways set against the Sea of Cortez and a rolling desert landscape, the courses are some of the most spectacular in the world. The Corridor has hosted the PGA Senior Slam tournament since 1995. However, don't expect to play for cheap. A round of 18 holes, including cart and bottled water, costs US$121 to US$190 during the ball-melting heat of summer and US$176 to US$276 in winter. You can play for less if you wait for the 'twilight fees' to kick in after 11am or noon. Club rentals go for about US$50. For a complete rundown of golf options in the Corridor, see p202.

The flip side to this golf Mecca is that the development has irrevocably transformed the pristine coastline into a 'Palm Springs by the Sea.'

There are also two 18-hole courses near Ensenada (p82) and another at Nopoló (p154), immediately south of Loreto. At US$44, the green fees at the Nopoló course make it the cheapest oceanside course in North America, and it's a surprisingly pretty place to play.

Airline passengers are allowed to check one set of clubs (usually no more than 14 clubs) along with one piece of luggage at no additional cost.

For in-depth information on the types of commercial fishing practices threatening the Sea of Cortez, or to get involved yourself, check out Sea Watch (www.seawatch.org).

HIKING

Hiking and backpacking are less common in Baja than they are north of the border, but there are many areas suitable for these activities – for example, Parque Nacional Constitución de 1857 (p91), Parque Nacional Sierra San Pedro Mártir (p94), the Sierra de San Francisco (p138), the Sierra de la Giganta west of Loreto and Mulegé, and the Sierra de la Laguna (p175) north of Los Cabos. Services anywhere are basically nil.

The two national parks have the best trail infrastructure, often following the routes walked by Indians hundreds of years ago, although trails are not always well maintained. In the central and southern areas, trails are less worn and it's fairly easy to get lost. Even locals rarely venture on multiday trips, and many recommend taking a guide.

Part of the problem is that reliable maps are nonexistent. The **Instituto Nacional de Estadística, Geografía e Informática** (INEGI; www.inegi.gob.mx) publishes large-scale topographical maps covering the entire country, but these are rather outdated. Both Map World and Maplink (p229) are good sources for maps.

Always bring plenty of water and food supplies with you, and be aware of hazards like rattlesnakes (p249), flash floods in *arroyos* (riverbeds) and unanticipated heat (even in winter).

If you prefer not to go at it alone, check out the hiking calendar of Baja Discovery (p37).

MORE TO DO? YEP!

The activities described in this chapter are Baja's biggest draw cards, but there are plenty of other outdoor pursuits to keep you busy in the Baja sun.

Windsurfing & Kite Surfing

Baja's windsurfing capital is Los Barriles (p177), a fast-growing settlement on the East Cape, but Bahía de la Ventana (p173) – southeast of La Paz via a good paved highway – has more consistent wind and is rapidly gaining popularity. The season runs from mid-November to early March. In these areas, equipment is easy to come by, but elsewhere windsurfers have to bring their own.

On the Pacific side, popular spots include Punta Baja (p102), Punta Abreojos (near Laguna San Ignacio) and Punta San Carlos (p102), named 'best wave sailing spot in the world' by *Windsurfing* magazine. Another insider spot is Bahía de Los Angeles (p128). The season here runs from February to October, peaking in the summer.

Vela Windsurf Resorts (p177) and **Baja Expeditions** (p39) both organize windsurfing trips.

Surfing

Virtually the entire Pacific coast of Baja and areas along the East Cape as far north as Punta Arenas contain a multitude of surf sites. To reach the best spots, surfers need sturdy vehicles and should carry extra parts, gasoline, plenty of water and all supplies.

The best book on surfing in Baja is Mike Parise's *The Surfer's Guide to Baja*. The useful *Baja/Mexico Surf Map* is available at surf shops and online.

For organized tours, contact **Baja Surf Adventures** (☎ 760-744-5642, 800-428-7873; www.bajasurfadventures.com).

Bicycling & Mountain Biking

Cycling the Transpeninsular is increasingly popular as both bicycles and roads improve. However, the distance between settlements and lack of water in some areas can be serious drawbacks. Narrow shoulders on most highways can be hazardous, although most drivers are courteous.

Even better than biking along the highway is getting off-road into the backcountry. Tracks take you along ridges, past remote ranches and through cactus forests. 'Slime tubes' (self-sealing puncture tubes) are essential on these thorn-paved trails.

The Baja border areas – particularly the cities of Tecate, Playas de Rosarito and Ensenada – host a variety of bicycling events annually. For additional information about bicycling in Baja, see p239.

Rental bikes are readily available in resort areas like Loreto, La Paz and Los Cabos. Outfitters of organized multiday trips include two Northern California companies: **Backroads Bicycle Touring** (☎ 510-527-1555, 800-462-2848; www.backroads.com) and **Pedaling South** (☎ 707-942-4550, 800-398-6200; www.tourbaja.com/pedlsth.html).

Food & Drink Jim Peyton

What Baja California is not is an extension of Southern California. It is *puro Mexicano* with its own distinctive ambiance and food. Much of its uniqueness comes from its two oceans, the Pacific and the Sea of Cortez – the latter of which has been described as 'a perfect fish trap.' Together these bodies of water provide a quantity and variety of seafood found almost nowhere else. In addition, Baja's inland *ranchos* and farms produce a surprising amount and quality of beef and produce, not to mention some truly fine wines.

If regions rather than restaurants received stars for culinary excellence, the two Mexican states of Baja would recently have vaulted to five big ones. For years the area stretching from Tijuana in the north to Los Cabos at the southern tip was known primarily for its simple but delicious renditions of seafood and charbroiled beef. Although they were prepared with traditional simplicity, the main ingredients were of such pristine quality and so lovingly rendered that the cuisine was still worthy of four stars.

In recent years the development of deluxe resorts, especially in the Los Cabos area, has attracted acclaimed chefs from Mexico and other parts of the world. To provide for their needs, boutique growers have sprouted from traditional farm land. The result is that the area now offers world-class cuisine at all levels, from the Mexican equivalent of Chicago's old-time steak houses to the fish emporiums of Boston to the haute cuisine of New York's upscale restaurants to street food everywhere. In addition, you will find a surprising number of Chinese restaurants, particularly in the north. All this with the special flavor and relaxed atmosphere of Baja!

STAPLES & SPECIALTIES

Although Baja honors many of the traditions of other parts of Mexico, in most places the meal schedule has been adapted to that of its visitors, many of who come from the USA. This means you can usually find lunch at 11:30am or noon instead of considerably later and a main-meal dinner rather than a light supper. You will also find few items, even in non-tourist establishments, that do not appeal to the Western palate.

Meals

Breakfast in Baja consists of everything from a light continental-style affair – crispy French-style rolls (called *bolillos*), *pan dulce* (Mexican-style sweet breads) and toast served with butter and, if you are lucky, a local jam, jelly or honey – to more elaborate dishes. A regional favorite is *chilaquiles*, crispy tortilla chips topped with either a red or green chile sauce, often including meat or chicken and a fried or poached egg. They are often garnished with cheese and a thick dollop of cream.

You will also find the Mexican standby, *huevos rancheros* (lightly fried corn tortillas covered with fried eggs and a mild tomato and chile sauce) served with refried beans garnished with crumbly white cheese, called *queso añejo* or *queso cotija*. Omelets are popular and often filled with *chorizo* (a chile and vinegar-flavored Mexican sausage), mushrooms, *rajas* (mild green chiles fried with onion) and/or a delicious Mexican cheese such as *asadero, ranchero* or Chihuahua. Eggs are often scrambled with the area's delicious shredded dried beef, *machacado*.

Jim Peyton has written three books related to Mexican cooking, including *El Norte: The Cuisine of Northern Mexico* and *Jim Peyton's New Cooking from Old Mexico*. In addition, he has written articles for *Fine Cooking*, *Texas Highways* and *Food & Wine*, appears on TV, conducts cooking classes and lectures on Mexican cuisine.

DID YOU KNOW?

The Caesar salad was invented in Tijuana by Caesar Cardini in 1924. The dish is still served at the original digs and almost everywhere else in Baja – and the world (also see p62).

Cooking with Baja Magic, by Ann Hazard (1997), presents the favorite regional recipes of an experienced Baja traveler.

One site that does a comprehensive job of covering both Mexico and its foods is www. mexconnect.com.

Baja has an abundance of fresh, tropical fruits and berries that are served at breakfast, often with yogurt and granola. Pancakes (or hot cakes) are also common and often are accompanied by homemade syrups and jams.

For lunch and dinner you will find a truly amazing variety of choices, from *antojitos mexicanos* (Mexican-style corn and tortilla specialties such as tacos, enchiladas and quesadillas often made with fish or shellfish) to delicious seafood and steak entrées. And those same luscious fruits that were served at breakfast with yogurt and granola come to the lunch table as salads, tossed with creative dressings and sometimes seafood and sliced avocado.

Seafood lovers interested in light meals will take particular delight in the abundance of seafood cocktails and *ceviches* (seafood 'cooked' in lime juice, chopped and mixed with onion, tomato, green chile, cilantro or more exotic spices). Most are far more interesting than the usual North American shrimp cocktail and standard ceviche.

Dessert brings sweet pastries called *coyotas*. These thin, round pastries sandwiching sweet fillings are originally from the Mexican state of Sonora, and are often made with local dates. Flan flavored with tropical fruits is also popular.

Fish & Seafood

Diana Kennedy's latest book, *From My Mexican Kitchen* (2003), captures the essence of Mexico's complex cuisine.

Tacos, enchiladas, quesadillas and tamales are often rendered with local seafood. The most famous example is the fish taco that originated in Ensenada, a short drive south of Tijuana. Made with an intriguing combination of fish filets fried in beer batter and garnished with shredded cabbage and a special tartar-sauce-like salsa, its popularity has recently spread throughout the USA and to other parts of the world. Other examples of the genre include *burritas de langosta* (lobster burritos, often made with guacamole and garlic butter), steaming shrimp and seafood tamales, tacos made with charbroiled fish and either fresh corn or paper-thin flour tortillas, and elegant enchiladas made with crab in both tomato and cream sauces.

One lobster specialty, *langosta estilo Puerto Nuevo,* originated in this northern Baja fishing village, turning the tiny community into a bustling restaurant metropolis. Although the lobster seems to be broiled, it is actually deep-fried *without* a coating of batter or bread crumbs. It's served with rice pilaf, black beans, lemon-garlic butter, special salsas and *tortillas de agua* – huge, thin, Sonora-style flour tortillas.

In Baja, shrimp, scallops, clams, abalone, octopus and squid are prepared in myriad ways. Perhaps the most popular is *al mojo de ajo* – with garlic sauce. Two of the most unique seafood dishes are an enchanting chorizo made with abalone and shrimp served with a tangy tamarind sauce. Fish and shellfish shiskabobs *(alambres)* are also popular, and not to be missed.

Jim Peyton's website, www.lomexicano.com, is updated quarterly and offers regional Mexican recipes, food-related travel articles and a large glossary of Mexican food terms.

Baja is famous for its seafood soups, which come in all forms and showcase Baja's fresh *fruit de mer:* light, brothy concoctions; thicker tomato-based versions; and those made with *albóndigas de pescado* (fish meatballs). *Caldo Siete Mares* (Soup of the Seven Seas) is a good choice – mixed seafood in a broth flavored with tomato and green chiles.

You will discover a large number of dishes referred to as *en escabeche*, or pickled. Although foods such as quail are sometimes featured, the most common selections are of seafood. They are prepared by lightly sautéing fish or shellfish and adding vegetables, herbs and spices in a mild solution of vinegar and sometimes wine. The liquid is then reduced to an essence, allowed to marinate and cool; the dish is served at room temperature. The result is a light, flavorful meal that can reach epic levels of delectation due to the quality and balance of the ingredients.

Beef & Pork

Baja takes full advantage of the fine beef – much of it grass-fed – that is raised on its numerous inland ranches. Throughout the region you will find beef in everything from tacos to burritos to huge entrée steaks, usually broiled to perfection over mesquite charcoal. Tijuana is famous for its *tacos al carbón* (charbroiled tacos, often made with the New York cut). *Machaca* (sun-dried beef jerky), usually called *machacado* when it is finely shredded, is used in everything from egg dishes to tacos and burritos. Also made with fish, it is often part of upscale culinary creations in the area's best restaurants.

Carnitas, which means 'little meats,' is a specialty of the Mexican state of Michoacán but is also very popular in Baja. Chunks of pork are slowly simmered in pure lard until golden and crispy, then they're shredded and wrapped in corn tortillas with guacamole. Carnitas are surprisingly light and are often found in restaurants that serve virtually nothing else.

DRINKS
Alcoholic

For wine lovers, one of the joys of travel is to sample local vintages, and Baja California is one of a handful of places in Mexico where you can do this.

After Spain banned vineyards, Mexicans grew accustomed to other alcoholic beverages, and wine never became a tradition. Even though vineyards were permitted after Mexican independence, the nation's turmoil and tastes retarded the development of wine to nearly zero. Recently growers found the hot days, cool nights and water necessary to yield premium grapes just inland from Ensenada. Now the region produces nearly 90% of Mexican wines. Study abroad, experimentation and cooperation with foreign producers has vaulted the quality of Mexican wines to international standards. Some of the best brands are Domecq, Monte Xanic and Chateau Camou, all with wineries and tasting rooms in Valle de Guadalupe (p90). Major wineries welcome visitors and have tasting centers in Ensenada.

Visitors to Baja are often in a partying mood, and tequila has become the favorite catalyst. Bars and liquor stores, especially in Tijuana and the Los Cabos area, provide admirable selections of the national liquor, as well as a profusion of mixed drinks. Baja is one of the few places in Mexico where bartenders know how to make margaritas that both meet and surpass the expectations of their *norte americano* visitors. Some of the finest margaritas include the native Baja liqueur *damiana.*

In addition to tequila, Mexico produces some of the world's finest beers, and Baja brews two of the best: Tecate and Pacifico.

Nonalcoholic

Mexico has a long tradition of nonalcoholic drinks, and many of them are common in Baja. The most popular are *tamarindo,* made with tamarind pods; *jamaica,* made with dried hibiscus leaves; *horchata,* a combination of fruit and seeds and/or rice; and lime-aid. These delicious fruity drinks are sold from large, keg-shaped glass containers, often garnished with mint leaves. Note that although these are prepared with boiled water, sometimes the ice is untreated.

DID YOU KNOW?

Fearing competition to its domestic wines, the Spanish once forbade the cultivation of grapes in Mexico. The ban was lifted after Mexican Independence in 1821, but it was not until the 1970s that Mexican wineries bloomed, most of them around the Valle de Guadalupe (p90)

DID YOU KNOW?

The Baja liqueur *damiana* is made from a native plant (of the same name) reputed to have aphrodisiacal qualities. Similar to Triple Sec, Cointreau and Grand Marnier, it gives margaritas that 'something extra.'

You will also discover a variety of smoothies and milkshakes called *licuados*, made with milk, fruits, yogurt and honey. Orange juice, nearly always fresh-squeezed, is available everywhere, as are juices of other fruits and vegetables. Many of these are found in street *puestos* (stalls) and in larger, bar-like establishments.

Some of the best coffee in the world is grown in Mexico, and the uniquely Mexican way of making it is called *café de olla*. This 'coffee from the pot' is brewed in a special clay vessel with a raw sugar called *piloncillo*. *Café con leche* (coffee with milk) is also very popular. Waiters will often pour both coffee and cream at the table according to your instructions. For ordinary coffee, with cream on the side, simply ask for *café con crema*.

Chocolate originated in Mexico and it often includes cinnamon and some crushed almonds, giving it a unique flavor and texture. As a drink, it is mixed with milk or water and sugar, then whipped to a cappuccino-like froth with a decorative wooden implement called a *molinillo*.

CELEBRATIONS

Besides being great entertainment, *Like Water for Chocolate* conveys the importance of food in Mexico, and the magic-realism used in the book/film showcases the way so many Mexicans view life.

Baja Californians celebrate the same feast days as other parts of Mexico, but they are more casual in their observations. For the most part they do not allow their traditions to interfere with the enjoyment of their visitors. However, be aware that on Christmas, New Years, Holy Week and the Day of the Dead (first two days of November), nontourist establishments may be closed. During these times special items are often available, including *pan de muertos* (bread of the dead). Vegetarian specialties are popular during Holy Week, and at Christmas and New Years *bacalao* (dried cod) is often served in a mild chile sauce.

WHERE TO EAT & DRINK

The number of places to eat will thrill you, and where you end up will depend on your mood and budget. Perhaps the most typical places are oceanside *palapas*. These casual thatched-roof structures are found nearly everywhere there is an easily accessible beach. You will discover delicious traditional seafood cocktails and entrees at moderate to low prices. While you are ordering, it's not uncommon to see a boat pull up and deliver the fresh catch you will be served!

Bajas's urban areas are filled with puestos that usually specialize in a single item – tacos, burritos, etc. Many of them serve dishes passed down through generations. As always, take precautions when eating at such informal places. Check overall cleanliness, and especially the availability of bathroom and handwashing facilities. Slightly more formal are *loncherías, comedores* and *taquerías*, small sit-down establishments often found in private homes in villages, and at markets in towns and cities. A step up are cafés that serve Mexican specialties such as antojitos and simple but delicious meat and seafood entrées, usually accompanied by homemade soups, steaming rice pilafs, beans and fresh vegetables.

Resorts and large cities offer upscale dining with local atmosphere – indoor-outdoor dining areas with tropical landscaping and birds – and a combination of international foods and elegant Mexican creations. Many of their chefs practice Mexico's upscale version of fusion cooking, called *nueva cocina mexicana* or *alta cocina* (new Mexican cooking), where regional Mexican ingredients, techniques and recipes are combined in delicious, aesthetically pleasing new ways.

VEGETARIANS & VEGANS

Tourist establishments have learned to cater to their patrons, including vegetarians. However, being in the arid north, Baja's produce is not nearly as prolific as in other parts of Mexico. Most cities have a smattering of vegetarian restaurants, and suitable offerings are usually easy to arrange at other places. One item of special interest to vegetarians is *nopalitos:* a Baja favorite, made by boiling, grilling or frying sliced cactus paddles, and sometimes combining them with other ingredients, such as onions and cheese. *Chiles rellenos,* stuffed mild chiles, are another good option, but be sure to specify the ones filled with cheese rather than meat.

Most waiters in the larger establishments are knowledgeable about what they serve and are anxious to please. However they are often not aware of the specific requirements of vegetarians, and especially vegans, and may find the concept difficult to understand – most Mexicans do without meat only because they cannot afford it, and many Mexican vegetarians eat what they do purely because they believe vegetables are healthy, rather than for ethical or philosophical reasons – so you must make your requirements very plain. One specific problem is that your server may believe he is bringing you a vegetarian meal when the items have been flavored with beef or chicken broth, or cooked in lard. Just to be safe, you can ask *¿Tiene productos de carne, como caldo o manteca?* The more upscale the restaurant, the better your chances of being understood and accommodated.

WHINING & DINING

Mexicans adore children, and Baja is a child-friendly place. Most waiters will cheerfully do anything within reason to please your child, and virtually all restaurants have highchairs; just ask for a *silla para niños.* Supermarkets carry a full range of American and international brands of baby food.

HABITS & CUSTOMS

Bajas's eating customs are less formal than in other parts of Mexico, and those of their visitors are accommodated whenever possible. Baja's attitude toward liquor is quite liberal, but be aware that in many communities liquor cannot be sold on election days or when the president is visiting. Also, while alcoholic beverages are usually considered a normal part of life, drinking while driving is a serious no-no!

In establishments with table service, tipping is expected. Ten percent is considered on the low side with 15% the norm, and 20% and above for an exceptional experience. Most restaurants add on Mexico's value-added tax of 15%, which is noted as IVA.

EAT YOUR WORDS

For non-Spanish speakers, travel and dining in Mexico is no problem; English is understood almost everywhere. However a few words in Spanish will indicate a respect for Mexicans and their culture, not to mention a willingness to risk embarrassment, and that can make a huge difference.

For pronunciation help, please see the Language chapter (p251).

Useful Phrases

Are you open?   *¿Está abierto?*
   e·sta a·be·er·tow

When are you open?	*¿Cuando está abierto?*
kwan-do e-*sta* a-*be*-er-tow	
Are you serving breakfast/lunch/ dinner now?	*¿Ahora, está sirviendo desayuno/la comida/ la cena?*
a-*o*-ra e-*sta* ser-*vyen*-do de-sa-*yoo*-no/la ko-*mee*-da/la *se*-na	
I'd like to see a menu.	*Quisiera ver la carta/el menú.*
kee-*sye*-ra ver la *kar*-ta/el me-*noo*	
Do you have a menu in English?	*¿Tienen un menú en inglés?*
te-en-nen oon me-*noo* en een-*gles*	
Can you recommend something?	*¿Puede recomendar algo?*
pwe-de re-ko-men-*dar* al-*go*	
I'm a vegetarian.	*Soy vegetariano/a.* (m/f)
soy ve-khe-te-*ree*-a-no/a	
I can't eat anything with meat or poultry products, including broth.	*No puedo comer algo de carne o aves, incluyendo caldo.*
no *pwe*-do ko-*mer* al-*go* de *kar*-ne o *a*-ves een-kloo-*yen*-do *kal*-do	
I'd like mineral water/natural bottled water.	*Quiero agua mineral/agua purificada.*
kee-*ye*-ro *a*-gwa mee-ne-*ral*/*a*-gwa poo-ree-fee-*ka*-da	
Is it (spicy) hot?	*¿Es picoso?*
es pee-*ko*-so	
The check, please.	*La cuenta, por favor.*
la *kwen*-ta por fa-*vor*	

Food Glossary

a la parilla – grilled
a la plancha – pan-broiled
adobada – marinated with *adobo* (chile sauce)
agua mineral – mineral water or club soda
agua purificado – bottled uncarbonated water
al carbón – char-broiled
al mojo de ajo – with garlic sauce
alambre – shishkabob
albóndigas – meatballs
antojitos – 'little Mexican whims,' corn- and tortilla-based snacks like tacos and gorditas
arroz – rice
arroz mexicana – pilaf-style rice with a tomato base
aves – poultry
azucar – sugar
biftec – steak
brochete – shishkabob
cajeta – goat's milk and sugar boiled to a paste
calabacita – squash
calamar – squid
caldo – broth or soup
camarones – shrimp
cangrejo – crab
carne – meat
carne de puerco – pork
carne de res – beef
carnitas – pork simmered in lard
cebolla – onion
cerdo – pork
chilaquiles – fried tortilla strips cooked with a red or green chile sauce, and sometimes meat and eggs

chile relleno – chile stuffed with meat or cheese, usually fried with an egg batter
chorizo – Mexican-style bulk sausage made with chile and vinegar
chuleta de puerco – pork chop
coco – coconut
coctel de frutas – fruit cocktail
costillas de res – beef ribs
empanada – pastry turnover filled with meat, cheese or fruits
empanizado – sautéed
enchiladas – corn tortillas dipped in chile sauce, wrapped around meat or poultry and garnished with cheese
ensalada – salad
filete – filet
filete al la tampiqueña – Tampico-style steak: a thin grilled tenderloin served with chile strips, onion, a quesadilla and an enchilada.
fresa – strawberry
frito – fried
helado – ice cream
huevos fritos – fried eggs
huevos rancheros – fried eggs served on a corn tortilla, topped with a sauce of tomato, chiles and onions
huevos revueltos – scrambled eggs
jaiba – crab
jamón – ham
jugo de piña – pineapple juice
jugo de manzano – apple juice
jugo de naranja – orange juice
langosta – lobster
leche – milk
lomo de cerdo – pork loin
mantequilla – butter
mariscos – seafood
nieve – sorbet
nopalitos – sautéed or grilled sliced cactus paddles
ostiones – oysters
pan – bread
papas – potatoes
papas fritas – french fries
pastel – cake
pechuga de pollo – breast of chicken
picadillo – a ground beef filling that often includes fruit and nuts
piña – pineapple
platano – banana or plantain
pollo – chicken
postre – dessert
pulpos – octopus
pozole – a soup or thin stew of hominy, meat, vegetables and chiles
quesadilla – cheese and other items folded inside a tortilla and fried or grilled
queso – cheese
sopa – soup, either 'wet' or 'dry' as in rice and pasta
té de manzanillo – chamomile tea
té negro – black tea
tocino – bacon
verduras – vegetables

Northern Baja

CONTENTS

For weekenders from mainland California, northern Baja is an immediate escape from home. It's a quick jump into Mexico, where towns such as Playas de Rosarito, Ensenada and San Felipe offer beaches, sun and rip-roaring, hedonistic nightlife. Border hoppers drive down to Puerto Nuevo for lobster, to San Quintín for sportfishing and clams, to Cañón de Guadalupe for hot springs and hiking and into the deserts for off-road rampages in every type of souped-up vehicle imaginable. They take meandering afternoon drives from Ensenada to Mexico's blossoming wine country in the Valle de Guadalupe, or they simply walk across the border into Tijuana.

Slowly but surely discarding its image as a bawdy border town, Tijuana has become an important center of art, music, world-class cuisine and nightlife far more sophisticated – and far more 21st century Mexican – than the debauchery still gracing its infamous Av Revolución. Tecate also sits at the US border, yet it is one of the most typically Mexican towns in all of Baja, where an afternoon on its sleepy central plaza is worlds away from the good ol' US of A. Most foreigners blow through Mexicali on their way south to San Felipe, but like Tijuana, it offers fabulous restaurants and exciting nightlife for anyone taking the time to explore.

Northern Baja has many faces and countless opportunities to wine, dine, swim, surf, walk empty beaches, hike spectacular national parks or just slip into a side of Mexico that is distinct from both mainland Mexico and its US neighbor – but is still, in every way, Mexico.

TOP FIVE

- Put your taste buds to the test sampling the fine wines of **Valle de Guadalupe** (p90), Mexico's premier wine region.
- Tear up the night in Tijuana, from crazy Av Revolución to the clubs of **Zona Río** (p63).
- Soak beneath the desert stars in the thermal baths of **Cañón de Guadalupe** (p117).
- Stroll **Tecate's central plaza** (p104), where cowboy-hatted locals and mariachi bands make it Baja's most traditional square.
- Sail through beautiful **Bahía San Quintín** (p96) and into port with your fat catch of the day.

- TIJUANA JANUARY AVERAGE HIGH: 66°F/19°C
- WATER TEMP OFF ENSENADA: 55-64°F/13-18°C

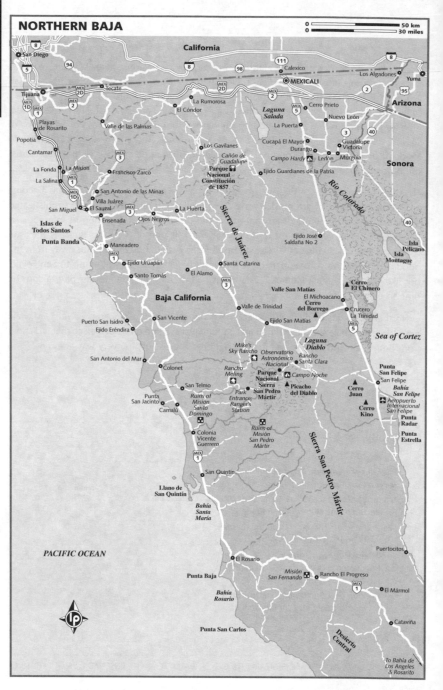

NORTHERN BAJA

0 ————— 50 km
0 ————— 30 miles

California

San Diego

8

5

94

98

111 Calexico

8

Los Algadones

Yuma

8

MEXICALI

95

Tijuana

MEX 1D

MEX 2D

Tecate

MEX 2

La Rumorosa

MEX 2D

MEX 2

Cerro Prieto

Arizona

MEX 1

Playas de Rosarito

El Cóndor

Nuevo León

2

Popotla

Valle de las Palmas

MEX 3

Los Gavilanes

Cañón de Guadalupe

Laguna Salada

La Puerta

Cucapá El Mayor

Durango

Campo Hardy

León

Guadalupe Victoria

Múrguia

40

Sonora

Cantamar

La Fonda

La Misión

La Salina

MEX 1

Francisco Zarco

Parque Nacional Constitución de 1857

Ejido Guadianes de la Patria

Río Colorado

MEX 1D

San Antonio de las Minas

Villa Juárez

El Sauzal

MEX 3

La Huerta

San Miguel

Ensenada

Ojos Negros

Ejido José Saldaña No 2

40

Islas de Todos Santos

Punta Banda

Maneadero

MEX 1

Ejido Uruápan

Santa Catarina

Sierra de Juárez

Isla Pelícano

Isla Montague

Santo Tomás

El Alamo

MEX 3

Baja California

Valle de Trinidad

Valle San Matías

El Michoacano

Cerro del Borrego

Cerro El Chimero

Puerto San Isidro

Ejido Eréndira

San Vicente

Ejido San Matías

Crucero La Trinidad

MEX 5

Sea of Cortez

San Antonio del Mar

Mike's Sky Rancho

Laguna Diablo

Colonet

Observatorio Astronómico Nacional

Rancho Santa Clara

Punta San Felipe

San Telmo

Rancho Meling

Parque Nacional Sierra San Pedro Mártir

Campo Noche

San Felipe

Bahía San Felipe

Punta San Jacinto

Ruins of Misión Santo Domingo

Park Entrance; Ranger's Station

Picacho del Diablo

Cerro Juan

Aeropuerto Internacional San Felipe

Camalú

Cerro Kino

Punta Radar

Colonia Vicente Guerrero

Ruins of Misión San Pedro Mártir

Punta Estrella

MEX 1

San Quintín

Llano de San Quintín

Bahía Santa María

Puertocitos

PACIFIC OCEAN

El Rosario

Misión San Fernando

Rancho El Progreso

Punta Baja

Bahía Rosario

MEX 1

El Mármol

Punta San Carlos

Cataviña

Desierto Central

To Bahía de Los Angeles & Rosarito

TIJUANA

☎ 664 / pop 1,210,820

'Jesus is in Tijuana.'

– Javier (from the film **Born in East LA)**

TJ, as the gringos call it: love it or hate it, there's nowhere like it. Sea Biscuit won the Caliente Handicap here in 1938, and the greatest matadors in the world have fought in the city's bullring-by-the-sea. Jazz great Charles Mingus named an album after the place – *Tijuana Moods* – and Herb Albert, god forbid, named his band after it. Carlos Santana got his start here, and famous US rock-and-rollers have played the city's bars. Tijuana definitely has a history.

The city has long shouldered a reputation as the city of sin, and Southern California college kids, like their thirsty predecessors during Prohibition, still pour across the border for booze, boobs and debauchery. The days of the donkey shows are gone, but notorious Av Revolución – aka La Revo – is still one of the wildest streets in North America. Its curio stores overflowing with kitschy souvenirs while strip club touts bark at every passerby. Everyone should experience it at least once.

But there's so much more. The city's cultural attractions, from art and music to cinema and food, are more vibrant than ever. Escaping La Revo and hitting an upscale restaurant, a café like El Lugar del Nopal (p64) or a Zona Río nightclub offers a side of the city more deeply Tijuana than anything on La Revo.

For all its modern stresses, burgeoning population and seeming inability to deal effectively with drug and infrastructure problems, Tijuana is a dynamic place, where you'll experience a city of hope and a city sandwiched between two cultures at once. If you're at all enamored of cities, you'll find Tijuana one exciting town.

Orientation

Tijuana parallels the US border for about 12 miles (19km). Downtown Tijuana is a 15-minute walk southwest of the San Ysidro border crossing and features a regular grid pattern of north-south *Avs* (avenues) and east-west *calles* (streets). Av Revolución, five blocks to the east, is the city's main tourist-oriented artery; the parallel Av Constitución features shops and other businesses catering more to locals.

Most streets in central Tijuana have numbers (for example, Calle 2a or Calle 7a) that are used more frequently than their

---

THE POROUS BORDER

In recent years, the exploding job market in the border towns has brought hundreds of thousands of migrants from Mexico City and poorer states like Jalisco, Michoacán, Sinaloa, Sonora and Oaxaca to the country's northern edge. Most find work in a *maquiladora* (assembly plant) or elsewhere and settle down, but many use the region as a jumping-off point to the USA.

In 1994 the Clinton administration initiated Operation Gatekeeper, a costly effort to curb illegal immigration. Stepped-up measures included a metal fence, a huge contingent of border patrol agents, and sophisticated equipment such as floodlights, infrared scopes and movement-detecting ground sensors.

While these measures have certainly made life harder for potential border crossers, they have done little to seal off the flow of illegal immigrants, most of whom are now forced to cross the deserts to the east, where vast expanses and temperatures soaring to 110°F cause hundreds of crossers to die each year from heat exposure and dehydration. It is estimated that for every undocumented worker arrested, at least two manage to get through to the USA. In San Diego alone, almost half a million people are caught each year.

Illegal immigration is big business. Many would-be illegal immigrants (derogatively called *pollos*, or chickens) engage the services of a *coyote* or *pollero* (smuggler). These smugglers charge as much as US$1600 for merely crossing the border, then more for transportation to Los Angeles or elsewhere in California. Most coyotes operate as individuals, but others are part of highly organized gangs with members on both sides of the border.

To explore this subject further, read reporter Ken Ellington's *Hard Line: Life & Death on the US-Mexico Border*. Also see The Culture chapter (p23) for more on immigration and additional book recommendations.

names (in this case, Juárez or Galeana). This section uses the numbering system but includes the street name if there is any ambiguity. The map includes both the numbers and the names because people and businesses still use one or the other, or both. Another source of confusion is that some streets have more than one name, such as Paseo de Tijuana, also known as Av del Centenario.

East of downtown, the Zona Río, Tijuana's new commercial center, flanks the Río Tijuana. Paseo de los Héroes, Via Poniente and Blvd Sánchez Taboada, the principal streets in this part of town, all parallel the river. Northeast of here, on a broad hilltop, is the new sector of Mesa de Otay, home to another border crossing, the airport, maquiladoras, residential neighborhoods and shopping areas.

Traffic along Paseo de los Héroes is regulated by several *glorietas* (traffic circles), each anchored by huge monuments. Going west to east, they are the Monument de la Raza, nicknamed 'Scissors' for its spiky shape; the monument to Aztec emperor Cuauhtémoc; the monument to Abraham Lincoln; and the monument to General Ignacio Zaragoza, a war hero during the French invasion of 1862.

Other important glorietas are located north of here along Av Independencia; one is dedicated to Mexican independence martyr Padre Miguel Hidalgo, while another features Diana, the goddess of hunting in Roman mythology.

West of downtown lie both spiffy suburbs and hillside shantytowns, the latter known as *asentamientos irregulares* (literally, irregular settlements). Formally all Tijuana boroughs or neighborhoods are known as *colonias* (or sometimes as *fraccionamientos)*, and addresses are much easier to locate if one knows the name of the colonia.

MAPS

The maps in this book should suffice in most cases, but the tourist offices also hand out an adequate free map. If you're planning an extensive stay or want to look up

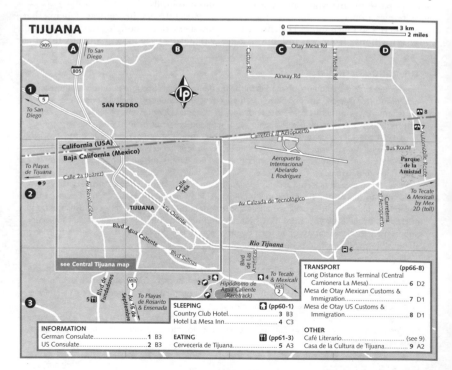

TIJUANA

0 — 3 km
0 — 2 miles

To San Diego
SAN YSIDRO
To San Diego
To Playas de Tijuana
California (USA)
Baja California (Mexico)
Calle 2a (Juárez)
Av Revolución
TIJUANA
Via Oriente
Blvd Agua Caliente
Blvd Salinas
see Central Tijuana map
Blvd de Fundadores
To Playas de Rosarito & Ensenada
Av 16 de Septiembre

Otay Mesa Rd
Airway Rd
Carretera al Aeropuerto
Aeropuerto Internacional Abelardo L. Rodríguez
Av Calzada de Tecnológico
Río Tijuana
Blvd de Las Américas
Hipódromo de Agua Caliente (Racetrack)
To Tecate & Mexicali
Bus Route
Parque de la Amistad
To Tecate & Mexicali by Mex 2D (toll)
Carretera al Aeropuerto
Cactus Rd
La Media Rd
Automobile Route

INFORMATION
German Consulate.................................1 B3
US Consulate.....................................2 B3

SLEEPING (pp60-1)
Country Club Hotel...............................3 B3
Hotel La Mesa Inn...............................4 C3

EATING (pp61-3)
Cervecería de Tijuana............................5 A3

TRANSPORT (pp66-8)
Long Distance Bus Terminal (Central Camionera La Mesa)..................6 D2
Mesa de Otay Mexican Customs & Immigration...................................7 D1
Mesa de Otay US Customs & Immigration...................................8 D1

OTHER
Café Literario.................................(see 9)
Casa de la Cultura de Tijuana............9 A2

specific streets, you will need to buy a more detailed map. These are available in bookstores and also at Sanborn's (below).

Information
BOOKSTORES
Librería El Día (Map pp58-9; ☎ 684-0908; Blvd Sánchez Taboada 10050, Zona Río) Loads of books on Mexican history and culture, all in Spanish. Local publications.

Libros y Arte (Map pp58-9; www.librosyarte.com.mx; Paseo de los Héroes at Av Independencia) Lots of arts and literature books. Inside Cecut (p56).

Sanborn's Department Store (Map pp58-9; ☎ 688-1462; cnr Av Revolución & Calle 8a/Hidalgo) Good book department and the city's best selection of international magazines.

CULTURAL CENTERS
An imposing neoclassical brick building (in the former Escuela Alvaro Obregón, from 1929) houses the **Casa de la Cultura de Tijuana** (Map p54; ☎ 687-2604; Calle Lisboa 5), on pleasant grounds about 1 mile (1.6km) west of Av Revolución. It presents lectures, art exhibitions, film festivals and concerts, and its small **Café Literario** (🕐 1-8pm Mon-Sat and during events) is a quiet place to hang out. Take any blue-and-white taxi (marked 'Colonia Altamira') westbound from Calle 3a (Carrillo Puerto) or walk up Calle 4a (Díaz Mirón); instead of the busy street, go up the hillside staircase for fine city views.

Tijuana's most important cultural center is the **Centro Cultural Tijuana (Cecut)** (p56). The delightful **El Lugar de Nopal** (p64) is a great place for checking out the local cultural scene.

EMERGENCY & MEDICAL SERVICES
Central police station (Map pp58-9; ☎ 060; Av Constitución 1616)

Cruz Roja (Red Cross; ☎ 066) Call for ambulance.

Fire station (Map pp58-9; ☎ 068; Av Constitución at Calle 8a/Hidalgo)

Hospital General (Map pp58-9; ☎ 684-0922; Av Padre Kino)

INTERNET ACCESS
Worldnet (Map pp58-9; Calle 2a 8174; US$1/hr; 🕐 24hrs)

Vacanett (Map pp58-9; Calle 7a 8150; US$1 per hr; 🕐 9am-10pm)

INTERNET RESOURCES
The following are a few websites – all in English – with up-to-date information about Tijuana:

Baja Life Online (www.bajalife.com/tijuana) Commercial site with nightlife, restaurant and hotel listings as well as information about car insurance and business services.

Tijuana.com (www.tijuana.com) Commercial site that's fairly up to date if not too comprehensive.

Tijuana Tourism Board (www.seetijuana.com) Official tourism site with comprehensive information about hotels, restaurants, sightseeing, events and services.

Cotuco Official Tourist Guide (www.tijuanaonline.org) Official site of the Tijuana Convention and Visitors Bureau.

MEDIA
Tune into Tijuana's cultural side by picking up one of these independent newspapers, all of which are available at the bookstores listed earlier:

Arte de Vivir – Monthly gay, lesbian, bi and transgendered focused newspaper with cultural information for all open-minded folks.

Bitácora (www.bitacora-tj.com) – Highly regarded cultural paper with literature, music and entertainment listings. Free every Wednesday.

Bulbo Press – Colorful monthly indie paper (US$0.50) tuned into the local music scene.

Cicuta – Highly respected left-leaning paper (US$1) covering local and national issues.

Tijuana Metro – Monthly paper focused on arts, culture and entertainment

MONEY
Everyone accepts (even prefers) US dollars. Numerous *casas de cambio* (money exchange houses) will change money and traveler's checks at almost any hour. Banks, though slower and more bureaucratic, offer slightly better rates; most also have ATMs. Beware of cambios on the US side, some of which advertise 'no commission' on exchanges of pesos for US dollars but charge up to 8% for converting US-dollar cash or traveler's checks into pesos. Change money on the Mexican side instead. There's also a cambio at the La Mesa long-distance bus terminal (p66).

POST
Post office (Map pp58-9; cnr Av Negrete & Calle 11a/Calles; 🕐 8am-7pm Mon-Fri, 9am-3pm Sat & Sun)

TELEPHONE
Tijuana has many Telnor public telephones and long-distance offices both downtown and in the outskirts. **Vacanett** has several long-distance telephone booths with good rates.

TOURIST INFORMATION

Tijuana has several tourist offices at the border, downtown and in the Zona Río. If you need information prior to arrival, call the number for **Cotuco** (Comité de Turismo y Convenciones or Tijuana Conventions and Visitors Bureau; in the USA ☎ 888-775-2417).

Cotuco tourist information (Map pp58-9; ☎ 683-1405; ☼ 9am-7pm Mon-Sat, 10am-2pm Sun) Just south of the border, next to the yellow cabs (look for the totem pole).

Cotuco tourist information kiosk (Map pp58-9; ☎ 685-2210; Av Revolución btwn Calles 3a & 4a; ☼ 9am-5pm Mon-Thu, 9am-7pm Fri-Sun) Lots of brochures, maps and good advice. English spoken.

Cotuco head office (Map pp58-9; ☎ 684-0537; www.tijuanaonline.org; Paseo de los Héroes 9365, Ste 201, Zona Río; ☼ 9am-6pm Mon-Fri) Some brochures, fewer answers. The Cotuco kiosk is better for tourist questions.

Secture (Map pp58-9; Secretaría de Turismo del Estado; ☎ 973-0424/30; Calle de la Juventud 8800-2523, 2nd Fl; ☼ 8am-8pm Mon-Fri, 9am-2pm Sat & Sun) State tourist office; in Plaza Viva Tijuana, on left as entering from USA. English-speaking staff, brochures, helpful.

TRAVEL AGENCIES

One of Tijuana's most respected travel agencies is **Viajes Honold's** (Map pp58-9; ☎ 688-1111; Av Revolución 828 at Calle 2a). Many others are downtown and in the Zona Río.

Dangers & Annoyances

Ain't no lie: the air quality in Tijuana on any given day will knock a buzzard off a shit wagon. Sleep well away from main traffic thoroughfares, and be aware that your migraine isn't solely due to last night's extra margarita.

Coyotes and *polleros* (smugglers) and *pollos* (their clients, undocumented border-crossers) congregate along the Río Tijuana west of the San Ysidro border crossing. After dark, avoid this area and also Colonia Libertad, east of the crossing.

The Zona Norte, Tijuana's seedy red-light district west of Av Revolución and north of Calle 1a (Artículo 123), is not recommended for foreigners lacking street savvy, at least after dark. City officials prefer not to dwell on its continued existence, but the area is still of sufficient economic importance such that authorities cannot, or will not, eradicate it. Neon-lit Calle Coahuila is especially notorious for its street prostitution and hardcore clubs.

If you are the victim of a crime, you can call the state government's **tourist assistance number** (☎ 078; 688-0555).

Sights

LA REVO

Virtually every visitor to Tijuana has to experience at least a brief stroll up raucous **Av Revolución**, also known as 'La Revo,' between Calle 1a (Artículo 123) and Calle 8a (Hidalgo). It's a mishmash of nightclubs, bellowing hawkers outside seedy strip bars, brash taxi drivers, tacky souvenir stores, street photographers with zebra-striped burros, discount liquor stores and restaurants. If you're walking north to south but find the sensory assault from high-tech sound systems too overwhelming to return the same way, try the more conventional shopping street of Av Constitución, paralleling La Revo one block west.

Oddly baroque in style, **Frontón Palacio Jai Alai** (Map pp58-9) was begun in 1926 but not completed until 1947. This striking Tijuana landmark fronts almost the entire block of Av Revolución between Calle 7a (Galeana) and Calle 8a (Hidalgo). For decades it hosted the fast-moving ball game of jai alai – kind of a hybrid between squash and tennis, originating from Basque Counbtry (in northern Spain). But alas, the game's obscurity and lack of attendance forced the owner to close down the operation. The building now hosts cultural events including music and theater performances.

CENTRO CULTURAL TIJUANA (CECUT)

This modern **cultural center** (Map pp58-9; ☎ 687-4973, 687-9693; www.cecut.gob.mx; Paseo de los Héroes at Av Independencia) goes a long way toward undermining Tijuana's reputation as a cultural wasteland and is a facility that would be the pride of any comparably sized city in the world. It's the city's premier showcase for highbrow events – concerts, theater, readings, conferences, dance recitals and more. Ticket prices vary but tend to be lower than those north of the border; student discounts are usually available.

The distinctive complex is fronted by a humongous cream-colored sphere – sort of a giant golf ball – locally known as La Bola (the ball) and was designed by noted architects Pedro Ramirez Vasquez and Manuel Rosen Morrison. It also houses a fascinating new museum, an Omnimax theater, several art galleries, conference rooms and a well-stocked bookstore.

The state-of-the-art **Museo de las Californias** (☎ 687-9641/42; US$2; ☻ 10am-6pm Tue-Fri, 10am-7pm Sat & Sun) chronicles the history of Baja California from prehistoric times to the present. It's an excellent introduction to the peninsula for any visitor and should not be missed. The exhibit kicks off with replica cave paintings, then covers important historical milestones, including the earliest Spanish expeditions under Hernán Cortés, the mission period, the Treaty of Hidalgo, the Chinese immigration, the irrigation of the Colorado River delta and the advent of the railroad. Displays in glass cases mix with scale replicas of ships, missions, other objects and fairly realistic dioramas. All explanatory paneling is in English and Spanish, and touch-screen terminals provide additional information. It's all presented along gentle ramps in an airy space without encumbering walls.

Housed within Cecut's 'golf ball,' **Cine Planetario** (adult/student US$4/20, 2-for-1 Tue & Wed) is a popular Omnimax-style theater showing a changing roster of films – usually in Spanish – on a 180-degree screen.

The **Jardín Caracol** (☻ 10am-6pm) is a charming garden whose layout is intended to resemble a snail (hence the name) and often hosts free events and exhibits, many of them geared toward children. In summer the Voladores de Papántla (Totonac Indian performers) can be seen here.

MUSEO DE CERA

Elvis is in da house! Leave any expectations at the door and you might actually enjoy a visit to Tijuana's **wax museum** (Map pp58-9; ☎ 688-2478; Calle 1a 8281; US$1.25, ☻ 10am-6pm), strategically placed right along the walking route to downtown from the border. On view are about 90 waxen figures from Mexican history, world politics and entertainment, plus the obligatory House of Horrors. Speaking of horror, things start off rather gruesomely with an Aztec warrior posing triumphantly with the heart of his poor victim. Controversial displays include Iran's Ayatollah Khomeini and Cuba's Fidel Castro, complemented by crowd pleasers like former Tijuana resident Rita Hayworth, an uncanny Frida Kahlo and a really bad Elvis.

GALERÍA DE ARTE DE LA CIUDAD

At press time, the **municipal art gallery** (Map pp58-9; ☎ 685-0104; cnr Av Constitución & Calle 2a) was closed for renovation, with aims to reopen in 2006. It's housed on the ground floor of the former Palacio Municipal (City Hall), and the entire building is getting a facelift. The Palacio Municipal was home to the city government from 1921 until its move to a new, modern **building** (Map pp58-9) on Paseo de Tijuana in the Zona Río in 1986.

VINÍCOLA LA CETTO

Mexico's largest **winery** (Map pp58-9; ☎ 685-3031; Cañón Johnson 8151), just southwest of Av Constitución, has opened its Tijuana branch for tours and tastings. Still operated by descendants of Italian immigrants who arrived in Baja in 1926, it produces some 50 million liters annually, about 30% of which is exported. With vineyards in the fertile Valle de Guadalupe (p90) between Tecate and Ensenada, LA Cetto produces a range of tasty red and white varietals, as well as sparkling wines, decent brandy and quality tequila. You can visit the **tasting room** (☻ 10am-2pm & 3:30-5pm Mon-Fri, 10am-4pm Sat) and sample four wines all for US$2. Bottle prices at the tasting room are about 25% cheaper than around town.

CERVECERÍA DE TIJUANA

If you're a beer-drinker, make a pilgrimage to this **microbrewery** (Tijuana Brewery; Map p54; ☎ 638-8662; Blvd de Fundadores 2951), which opened in early 2000. Owner José González Ibarra's vision was to make a potent brew in the tradition of pilsner beer, which originated in the Czech Republic. He imported not only all the technology from that country but also a young Czech brewmaster whose efforts have clearly paid off. Sold under the brand name Tijuana, this is a superior and full-bodied beer that easily measures up to some of Europe's finest. It is best enjoyed in the atmospheric, timbered brewery pub. The brewery is about 1½ miles (3.2km) south of downtown.

MERCADO HIDALGO

This **market** (Map pp58-9; ☻ 7am-7pm) is where locals come to buy spices, dried chiles, exotic produce, fresh tortillas and seasonal specialties made from Aztec grains. The partially covered stalls open onto a central

CENTRAL TIJUANA

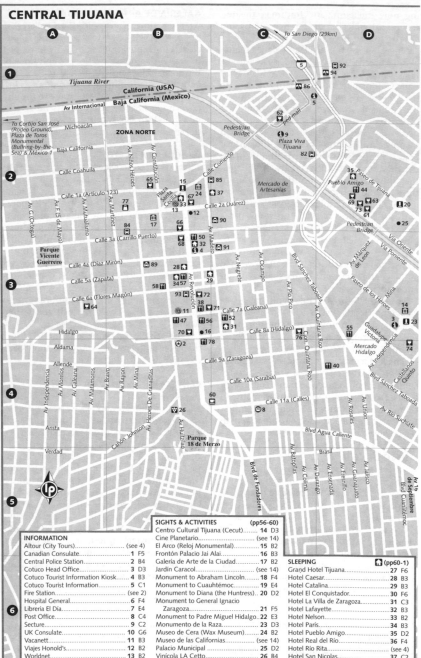

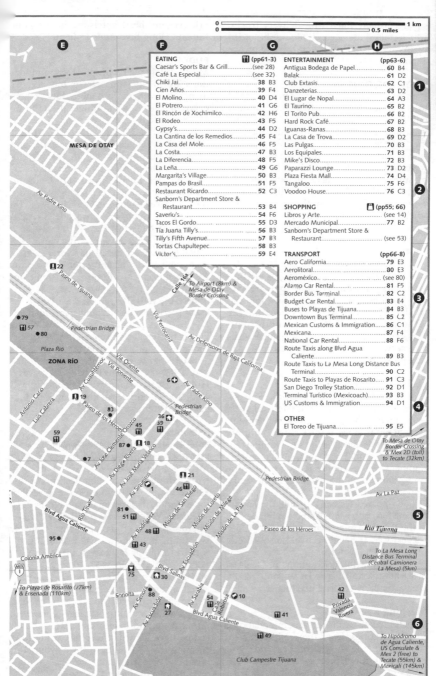

EATING (pp61-3)
Caesar's Sports Bar & Grill.............(see 28)
Café La Especial............................(see 32)
Chiki Jai.....................................**38** B3
Cien Años...................................**39** F4
El Molino....................................**40** D4
El Potrero...................................**41** G6
El Rincón de Xochimilco................**42** H6
El Rodeo....................................**43** F5
Gypsy's......................................**44** D2
La Cantina de los Remedios...........**45** F4
La Casa del Mole.........................**46** F5
La Costa.....................................**47** B3
La Diferencia...............................**48** F5
La Leña......................................**49** G6
Margarita's Village.......................**50** B3
Pampas do Brasil.........................**51** F5
Restaurant Ricardo.......................**52** C3
Sanborn's Department Store &
    Restaurant.............................**53** B4
Saverio's....................................**54** F6
Tacos El Gordo.............................**55** D3
Tía Juana Tilly's...........................**56** B3
Tilly's Fifth Avenue.......................**57** B3
Tortas Chapultepec......................**58** B3
Victor's......................................**59** E4

ENTERTAINMENT (pp63-6)
Antigua Bodega de Papel...............**60** B4
Balak...**61** D2
Club Extasis...............................**62** C1
Danzeterias................................**63** D2
El Lugar de Nopal........................**64** A3
El Taurino..................................**65** B2
El Torito Pub...............................**66** B2
Hard Rock Café...........................**67** B2
Iguanas-Ranas.............................**68** B3
La Casa de Trova..........................**69** D2
Las Pulgas..................................**70** B3
Los Equipales..............................**71** B3
Mike's Disco...............................**72** B3
Paparazzi Lounge.........................**73** D2
Plaza Fiesta Mall..........................**74** D4
Tangaloo....................................**75** F6
Voodoo House.............................**76** C3

SHOPPING (pp55; 66)
Libros y Arte...............................(see 14)
Mercado Municipal.......................**77** B2
Sanborn's Department Store &
    Restaurant.............................(see 53)

TRANSPORT (pp66-8)
Aero California............................**79** E3
Aerolitoral.................................**80** E3
Aeroméxico................................(see 80)
Alamo Car Rental.........................**81** F5
Border Bus Terminal.....................**82** C2
Budget Car Rental........................**83** E4
Buses to Playas de Tijuana.............**84** B3
Downtown Bus Terminal.................**85** C2
Mexican Customs & Immigration......**86** C1
Mexicana...................................**87** F4
National Car Rental.......................**88** F6
Route Taxis along Blvd Agua
    Caliente................................**89** B3
Route Taxis to La Mesa Long Distance Bus
    Terminal................................**90** C2
Route Taxis to Playas de Rosarito....**91** C3
San Diego Trolley Station...............**92** D1
Terminal Turístico (Mexicoach)........**93** B3
US Customs & Immigration.............**94** D1

OTHER
El Toreo de Tijuana......................**95** E5

square, usually filled with delivery trucks, which takes up several blocks bounded by Av Independencia and Blvd Sánchez Taboada.

PLAYAS DE TIJUANA
Popular with locals, Tijuana's beaches tend to get crowded, especially during summer bullfights (the Plaza de Toros Monumental is located here; p65). A blue-and-white bus marked 'Playas' runs along Calle 3a (Carrillo Puerto) from downtown and goes westward to the beaches. If you're driving, be sure to stop for tacos at **Tacos Aaron** (Av Pedegral; 🕑 7:30-2pm), across from the Calimax as you enter Playas from the toll road. The truck whips out some of the best, most imaginative tacos on the entire peninsula.

Tours
In conjunction with Cotuco, **Altour** (Map pp58-9; ☎ 634-6173/74; adult/child under 11 US$25/20) offers city tours on Friday at 1pm and Saturday at noon. The 3½-hour tour hits the jai alai, Tijuana Brewery, wax museum, LA Cetto tasting room and several other city sites. Tours are in English or Spanish. Call to reserve or stop by the Cotuco information kiosk (p56).

Festivals & Events
From late March to early April, Tijuana hosts an international dance festival with performances by regional, national and international troupes at the Centro Cultural.

The **Feria de Tijuana** is the city's annual fair with rides, food, big-name Mexican entertainment and cockfights. It takes place from mid-August to mid-September at the Agua Caliente racetrack.

Food-related festivals include the **Annual Mexican Food Fair**, held around September 10 at the Pueblo Amigo mall, and the 'World's Biggest Caesar Salad Festival,' on Av Revolución in late October.

The nationwide celebrations of **Día de la Independencia** and **Día de los Muertos** (p227) are particularly colorful in Tijuana.

Sleeping
Tijuana has a wealth of accommodations in all categories, from the really seedy to the truly luxurious. The cheapest and most convenient for exploring downtown Tijuana are near Av Revolución, while the priciest (and best) hotels are in the Zon Río and along Blvd Agua Caliente.

BUDGET
Most of Tijuana's cheapest accommodations are in the Zona Norte, but because many places there do double duty as bordellos or safe houses for migrants, none are recommended.

Hotel Catalina (Map pp58-9; ☎ 685-9748; Calle 5a 2039; r with/without TV US$18/27) One of the best budget options downtown, this family-run hotel tolerates zero riffraff, stressing security and cleanliness. Rooms are tiled and tidy, and some have TV. You can even order room service from the cafeteria below. Extra persons (after two) are charged US$5 each.

Hotel San Nicolas (Map pp58-9; ☎ 688-0418; Av Madero 768; s/d US$25/30) This is the closest acceptable place to the Zona Norte, with a surprising artsy vibe and Frida Kahlo posters for decoration. Rooms are small but clean.

Hotel Lafayette (Map pp58-9; ☎ 685-3940; Av Revolución 325; r US$20-26) Spick and span Hotel Lafayette offers plain rooms with TV, phone and bath. It's a safe, reliable budget place, though the staff is far from friendly.

Hotel París (Map pp58-9; ☎ 685-3023; Calle 5a 8181; s/d US$27/30; 🔀) Friendly if a tad tawdry, Hotel París has rooms with telephones and color TV. The pricier double rooms are bigger and better than the singles.

MID-RANGE
Hotel La Mesa Inn (Map p54; ☎ 681-6522, in the USA ☎ 888-226-1033; Blvd Díaz Ordaz 50; r US$70-75; 🅿 🔀 🖳) Tropical gardens and friendly faces behind the reception desk make this 120-room property one of the nicest in town. Modern and immaculate rooms have satellite TV, telephones and bottled water. There's plenty of free parking, a lovely swimming pool and a small restaurant.

Hotel La Villa de Zaragoza (Map pp58-9; ☎ 685-1832; Av Madero 1120; r US$34-55; 🅿 🔀 🔀) Easily one of the best downtown hotels, this is an excellent deal, especially if you're driving: its parking lot is guarded constantly. Staff is very helpful, and the rooms are modern, immaculate and comfortable. The priciest rooms have giant baths, plush white towels and plenty of room to throw your stuff around. There are fully accessible ground-level rooms for disabled persons.

Hotel Caesar (Map pp58-9; ☎ 685-1606; Av Revolución 1079; r US$36) Historic bullfighting posters and knight armor adorn the lobby and hallways of this famous hotel. Famous? Its original restaurant supposedly created the Caesar salad (p62).

Hotel Nelson (Map pp58-9; ☎ 685-4303; Av Revolución 721; r 1st/2nd/3rd fl US$40/50/54) Long a travelers' favorite for its central location and 92 clean, basic and carpeted rooms, Hotel Nelson boasts a bar, an inexpensive coffee shop and a barber shop. Rooms on the upper floors have telephones and satellite TV.

Hotel Río Rita (Map pp58-9; ☎ 685-7777, 685-8810; riorita@bc.cablemas.com; Av Revolución 968; r US$59) This excellent hotel, smack in the middle of La Revo, has spotless rooms with cable TV, fans and carpet. Rooms over the strip have balconies but get noisy from the weekend revelry outside.

Hotel El Conquistador (Map pp58-9; ☎ 681-7955; Blvd Agua Caliente 10750; r from US$50; ❄) All 105 rooms in this comfortable colonial-style hotel have air-con, cable TV and phones.

TOP END

Hotel Pueblo Amigo (Map pp58-9; ☎ 683-5030, in the USA ☎ 800-386-6985; www.hotelpuebloamigo.com; Via Oriente 9211; r/ste US$152/392; P ⊠ ❄) Located in the Pueblo Amigo outdoor mall, this attractive, well-landscaped hotel offers state-of-the-art rooms with all the usual amenities. The mall has several excellent restaurants and hip bars that make the hotel especially inviting.

Hotel Real del Río (Map pp58-9; ☎ 634-3100, in Mexico ☎ 800-025-7325, in the USA ☎ 877-517-6479; www.realdelrio.com; José María Velasco 1409-A; r weekday/weekend US$81/90, ste weekday/weekend US$196/207; P ⊠ ❄) This elegant, modern hotel is especially convenient for exploring the Zona Río. Service is outstanding, and the rooms are excellent. Bonuses include a Jacuzzi, restaurant and bar.

Grand Hotel Tijuana (Map pp58-9; ☎ 681-7000, in the USA 866-472-6385; www.grandhoteltij.com.mx; Blvd Agua Caliente 4500; r US$135, ste US$231-270; P ⊠ ❄ ▣) The city's most prominent hotel occupies the landmark 23-floor twin towers of Agua Caliente. Amenities include cable TV, minibars, a heated pool, Jacuzzi, tennis court, two restaurants and a cocktail bar.

Country Club Hotel (Map p54; ☎ 681-7733, in the USA ☎ 888-226-1033; www.bajainn.com; Tapachula 1; r US$77-107; P ⊠ ❄ ▣) Next to the Agua Caliente racetrack, the Country Club Hotel offers spacious suites and rooms overlooking the golf course and the city. All have air-con, cable TV, telephones, private bath and bottled water. Includes a coffee shop/restaurant.

Eating   Map pp58-9

Tijuana's cuisine scene is one of the city's big surprises. You'll find everything from traditional *antojitos* (Mexican snacks or light meals) to gourmet Chinese, Italian, Spanish and French cuisine.

Most places on Av Revolución cater to tourists, serving the usual Mexican dishes like tacos and enchiladas, while the city's best restaurants are in the Zona Río and along Blvd Agua Caliente.

LA REVO & DOWNTOWN

People coming to Av Revolución for booze, music and raucous partying have plenty of places to pick from. Many places also serve fairly decent Mexican food, albeit calibrated to gringo tastes. The following have stood the test of time.

Chiki Jai (☎ 685-4955; Av Revolución 1388; mains US$6-9) Thanks to its consistently good Spanish/Basque seafood, the small, friendly Chiki Jai has been packed with patrons since 1947. It's a perfect escape from the street outside.

Caesar's Sports Bar & Grill (Av Revolución 1079; mains US$5-9) We may never know for sure whether the Caesar salad really was invented in 1929 at what is now called the Hotel Caesar, but it's definitely fun watching your waiter go through the ritual of preparing one tableside.

Café La Especial (☎ 685-6654; Av Revolución btwn Calles 3 & 4) Hidden away in a small basement shopping arcade on La Revo (next to the Hotel Lafayette), this old-time favorite serves solid Mexican food at reasonable prices.

Sanborn's (☎ 688-1462; cnr Av Revolución & Calle 8a/Hidalgo; mains US$4-12; ☺ 7am-1am Mon-Sat, 7am-11pm Sun) Sanborn's department stores are known for their cafeterias, and this one is a popular meeting place at night.

Tía Juana Tilly's (☎ 685-6024; Av Revolución at Calle 7a; mains US$5-10) Can't go wrong here; the cantina-like atmosphere is great.

La Costa (☎ 685-8494; Calle 7a/Galeana 8131; mains US$7-11) Locals and tourists alike give top marks to this classy, warmly lit seafood restaurant.

Step one block east or west off Av Revolución and you'll find plenty more culinary candidates worth your attention.

Restaurant Ricardo (☎ 681-8655; cnr Av Madero & Calle 7a/Galeana; mains US$4-8; ☻ 24hrs) This former sandwich shop is now a full-fledged diner. It's bright and cheerful, the breakfasts are excellent and the *tortas* (sandwiches) are among the best in town.

Tortas Chapultepec (☎ 685-1412; cnr Av Constitución & Calle 6a/Flores Magón; mains US$3-5) You can't beat the friendly service, good prices, and delicious tortas, burgers and fries at this family-style diner. There are several Mexican dishes on the menu too.

El Molino (☎ 684-9040; Av Quintana Roo at Calle 10a/Sarabia) Pop in for outstanding bakery items. In business since 1928, it makes everything from ordinary *bolillos* (typical Mexican breads) to fanciful wedding cakes.

These places are also recommended:

Margarita's Village (☎ 685-3862; mains US$7-12; Calle 3a at Av Revolución) Longtime favorite, big margaritas, decent food.

Tilly's Fifth Avenue (☎ 685-9015; Av Revolución at Calle 5a; US$5-10) Popular with locals and tourists alike.

ZONA RÍO

The Zona Río has many of the best restaurants in town. A cab ride from La Revo area – about US$2.50 in a Taxi Libre – beats driving.

La Casa del Mole (☎ 634-6920; Paseo de los Héroes 1501; mains US$5-8) If you're feeling tropical, head here for Tijuana's best *mole*-based dishes served in a glass-roofed jungle setting. Mole is one of several delicious Oaxacan sauces made with chile, chocolate and plenty of spices. You can eat and drink well here for under US$12.

Cien Años (☎ 634-3039; Av José María Velasco 1407; mains US$12-20) One of Tijuana's temples of *alta cocina* (haute cuisine), Cien Años is well worth a splurge. The chefs have dug deep into a box of ancient Mexican recipes, some going back to the Aztecs and Mayans, and have come up with some rather unusual – but by all accounts, delicious – concoctions (how does 'spinal-cord soup' sound?). It's a formal place, so dress well.

La Cantina de los Remedios (☎ 634-3065; Av Diego Rivera 19; mains US$6-10) This massive hacienda-style place takes classic *mexicanismo* way over the top. It has an energetic vibe and good Mexican favorites; try the

---

THOSE WERE THE (CAESAR) SALAD DAYS

Though certainly worthy of kings, the Caesar salad was named not after old Julius, but for the Italian immigrant and restaurateur who invented it in – of all places – Tijuana. Plenty of myth surrounds the origin of the Caesar salad, but the following is the general consensus among food historians.

On the night of July 4, 1924, a small group walked into Caesar Cardini's restaurant at the **Hotel Caesar** (p61) and asked for something light to finish off their night of drinking. Late at night and low on ingredients, Cardini whipped together a salad with what he had: hearts of romaine, garlic-infused olive oil, croutons, parmesan cheese, coddled egg, lemon, Worcestershire sauce and salt. He did not use anchovies. Some stories have it that a similar salad *with* anchovies preceded the Caesar, called the 'aviators salad.' If this salad did exist, it was likely the creation of Cardini's brother, Alex, who named it for American fighter pilots stationed in San Diego, and Caesar adopted the salad.

Whoever invented it, Caesar's creation that night was an immediate hit and, before long, Southern Californians were driving down to Tijuana to sink their teeth into the original. In her cookbook, Julia Childs recalls being a young girl and making the trip in the mid-1920s with her parents, who were elated to finally sample the salad.

Caesar Cardini went to Los Angeles after the repeal of Prohibition in 1933, and in 1948 he patented his dressing under the name *Cardini's, The Original Caesar Dressing*. The Hotel Caesar still claims title to being the original location, and its **Caesar's Sports Bar & Grill** (p61) still prepares the salad tableside just as Cardini did. Nearly every restaurant on La Revo serves a version of the Caesar salad, but many feel the best in town is prepared at **Victor's** (p63). With Tijuana, who needs Rome?

ucculent fajitas. This is also a good place or just a drink.

Victor's (☎ 634-3309; Blvd Sánchez Taboada 9848; mains US$6-15) Caesar's restaurant may have invented it, but many feel that the honor of best Caesar salad goes to Victor's. The restaurant is divided into a cafeteria and a more formal steakhouse, where prices are higher and live piano jazz may accompany your meal.

Gypsy's (☎ 683-6006; Pueblo Amigo Mall; mains US$8-11; Tue-Sun) This lively tapas bar has an eclectic decor inspired by Spanish artists Miró, Gaudí and Dalí. Its menu of more substantial main courses includes *paella valenciana* (Valencia paella) for US$9, and there's live flamenco music after 10pm on Fridays.

La Diferencia (☎ 634-3346; Blvd Sánchez Taboada 10611-A; mains US$12-14) Behind a tuxedo shop, La Diferencia specializes in alta cocina, serving exotic Mexican dishes like crocodile fajitas, *crepes de huitlacoche* (corn fungus crepes) and *ensalada de nopal y chicharron* (cactus paddle and pork crackling salad).

Pampas do Brasil (☎ 686-3941; Blvd Sánchez Taboada 4499, Plaza Guadalupe; buffet US$15) Satiate your meat cravings at this excellent all-you-can-eat Brazilian meat-and-salad buffet.

For the cheapest restaurants in the Zona Río, and perhaps the city, visit the **Mercado Hidalgo** (p57), bordering Av Independencia and Blvd Sánchez Taboada; one recommendation is **Rincón del Oso**. Also near here is the **Tacos El Gordo** (cnr Blvd Sánchez Taboada & Mina; 10am-5am Mon-Thu, 10am-6am Fri-Sun), which enjoys cult status among night owls. The quality of the tacos, which are perhaps a tad too authentic for most gringos, is high, and the lines get long in the wee morning hours.

BLVD AGUA CALIENTE
Although Blvd Agua Caliente (and its eastern spin-off, Blvd Salinas) is a bit distant for pedestrians, it has many eateries worth trying.

El Rincón de Achimilco (☎ 686-2491; Privada Valencia Rivera 157) In a residential area just north of Blvd Agua Caliente, this family eatery serves a range of delicious antojitos, including flautas, *sopes*, *huaraches* and *gorditas* (all variations on the meat- and cheese-loaded tortilla) prepared Mexico City-style. A huge plate of food, including rice and beans, costs about US$3.50.

El Rodeo (☎ 686-5640; Blvd Salinas 10332; mains US$9-20) El Rodeo is a fine-beef restaurant with eccentric ranch decor – antique gas pumps, Coke machines and a shrine to assassinated PRI presidential candidate Luis Donaldo Colosio.

La Leña (☎ 686-4752; Blvd Agua Caliente 11191; mains US$10-25) Serving some of the city's best wood-fired Sonoran beef, La Leña is just east of the Grand Hotel Tijuana.

El Potrero (☎ 686-3826; Blvd Salinas 4700; mains US$6-12) El Potrero deserves a look not so much for its fairly straightforward food as for its oddball architecture – it's literally in the shape of a classic Mexican sombrero.

Saverio's (☎ 684-3604; Calle Carlos Robirosa 250; mains US$8-15; Tue-Sun) Saverio's is an outstanding Italian restaurant serving pizza, pasta and seafood from throughout the Boot with prices to match.

Entertainment
Map pp58-9

DRINKING & DANCING
If you want to down Jell-O shots while waiters blow whistles in your ear and strip-club touts beckon you in with 'free naked ladies!,' hang out on La Revo. If you're after something more 'cultured,' more sophisticated and more Tijuana-as-the-locals-do-it, hit the Zona Río or Agua Caliente area. Few if any bars on La Revo have a cover charge. The bigger clubs of Zona Río and Agua Caliente may charge US$3-10 depending on the night.

La Revo
Rowdy Av Revolución vibrates with venues for earsplitting live and recorded music. Picking your party is as easy as walking along and listening to what's pumping out the sound system. Classic haunts include the **Hard Rock Café** (☎ 685-0706; Av Revolución 520), **Iguanas-Ranas** (Av Revolución at Calle 3a) and **El Torito Pub** (☎ 685-1636; Av Revolución 643). Pop in the earplugs and grab a dance partner at **Las Pulgas** (☎ 688-1368; cnr Av Revolución & Calle 8a/ Hidalgo), which has live and recorded *banda* (raucous brass-band) and *norteña* (country style) music.

Zona Río & Agua Caliente
Plaza Fiesta Mall (Independencia at Guadalupe Victoria) What La Revo is to gringos, Plaza Fiesta mall is to locals. The dozen or so bars and restaurants here are great places

to knock back a few tequilas and hear the local rock and DJ talent thrash (or spin) it out. It's unique because you can take your pick simply by walking door to door. The bars include **Sambuca** (a Brazilian-themed place), **Monte Picacho** (live *rock en español* – Spanish-language rock – Sunday through Thursday, DJs Friday and Saturday), **Callejón del Ambiente** (great for '80s music and the diverse crowd), **Bar Sótano Suizo**, **El Bunker**, **Indestruckt** (for the industrial and garage scene) and **Pancho Villas** ('tequila, tacos & rock-n-roll!').

Tangaloo (www.tangaloo.com; Blvd Agua Caliente) Perhaps the hottest (and biggest) disco in town, Tangaloo gets big-name DJs who work Tijuana's hippest dance set into a frenzy. It also has live music on occasion.

Pueblo Amigo, between Paseo de Tijuana and Via Oriente, is another outdoor mall with more fun, local nighttime stomping grounds. Here you'll find the following:

Danzeterías (☎ 973-2391) Tango on Wednesdays, salsa and merengue on Thursdays and Fridays, and *carnaval* night on Saturdays. Best part: free dance lessons 8pm-9pm!

La Casa de Trova (☎ 683-4900; closed Sun & Mon) Live rock en español and *trova* (folk music) starting at 8pm.

Paparazzi Lounge (✆ from 6pm Tue & Thu-Sun) Start the night out at this formal cocktail lounge (complete with luxurious sofas) before heading next door to Balak.

Balak (✆ 9pm-late Thu-Sat) Hugely popular disco masquerading as a giant Mayan temple.

LIVE MUSIC & ART

Several of the clubs listed in the previous section feature live music, but the following café-cum-bars are dedicated to live music and art as much as a good time. If you only have one night out in Tijuana, try to hit one of the following.

El Lugar de Nopal (☎ 685-1264; Callejón 5 de Mayo 1328) This sophisticated café-bar-cum-restaurant-cum-cultural center is a fervent supporter of local artists and an enchanting place at that, especially in the garden patio. El Lugar de Nopal is tucked away in a residential area and is a bit hard to find but well worth the effort.

Antigua Bodega de Papel (☎ 633-9174; Calle 11a at Av Revolución) Another great place to hang out on the edge and tap the local music and

arts scene, this place has a small deli and live Latin jams, trova and more.

Voodoo House (☎ 685-5361; www.voodoo.mx.kz; Calle 8a 530 near Av Revolución) Have your brains rattled or your soul soothed, depending on the night. From Afro-Cuban and bossa nova to metal bands and home-spun trance, Voodoo does it all. The video nights are a hit as well.

GAY & LESBIAN VENUES

The only city in Baja with any significant gay and lesbian scene – more specifically gay than lesbian – is Tijuana. There are plenty of places to hit downtown, most of which build their evenings around drag-show fun. Locals, as much or more than foreigners, hang out at all these places, giving them a Tijuana vibe that you won't find at La Revo's standard gringo haunts. Also pick up a copy of *Arte de Vivir* for more on what's happening.

Club Extasis (☎ 526-682-8339; www.clubextasis.com; Plaza Viva Tijuana; ✆ Thu-Sun) Tijuana's biggest and best gay dance club – complete with male strippers and karaoke – is right on the border. Thursday is designated *noche lesbiana* (lesbian night).

Mike's Disco (Av Revolución 1220) One of the longest-running gay bars in town, Mike's has everything from drag shows and dancing to strippers and pajama parties.

Los Equipales (☎ 688-3006; Calle 7a/Galeana 8236 at Av Revolución) Slightly seedy but definitely energetic, Los Equipales has two drag shows every night except Wednesday.

El Callejón de Ambiente (www.callejon.cjb.net; Plaza Fiesta 8a, Zona Rio) Gay, straight, bi and freaky all rip up the dance floor to '80s dance tunes, electronica, synth-pop and more at this club in the Plaza Fiesta (p63). Great mix of people.

El Taurino (cnr Av Constitución & Calle 1a) On the flanks of the Zona Norte, this is the granddaddy of Tijuana's gay bars. It's in a new location, but the establishment has been around forever.

SPORTS
Bullfights

Bullfights (*corridas*) take place on Sunday afternoons every two or three weeks from the last weekend in April to late September/early October. For schedules and information in English, see www.bullfights.org.

DEATH IN THE AFTERNOON

It's said that Mexicans arrive on time for only two events – funerals and bullfights. To many others, *corridas de toros* (bullfights) hardly seem to be sport or, for that matter, entertainment, but Mexicans see it as both and more: It's as much a ritualistic dance as a fight.

The corrida begins promptly at 4, 4:30 or 5pm on a Sunday. To the sound of music – usually a Spanish *paso doble* – the matador, in his *traje de luces* (suit of lights), and the *toreros* (matador's assistants) give the traditional *paseillo* (salute) to the fight authorities and the crowd. Then the first of the day's bulls (there are usually six in an afternoon) is released from its pen for the first of the ritual's three *suertes* (acts) or *tercios* (thirds).

The cape-waving toreros tire the bull by luring him around the ring. After a few minutes two *picadores*, on heavily padded horses, enter and jab *picas* (long lances) into the bull's shoulders. This is usually the most gruesome part of the whole process, as it instantly weakens the bull from the sudden pain and blood loss.

After the picadores leave the ring, the *suerte de banderillas* begins, as two toreros take turns sticking three pairs of elongated darts (the *banderillas*) into the bull's shoulders without getting impaled on his horns. After that, the *suerte de muleta* is the climax, in which the matador, alone with his red cape, has exactly 16 minutes to kill the bull.

Starting with fancy cape work to tire the animal, the matador then exchanges his large cape for the smaller *muleta* and takes sword in hand, baiting the bull to charge before delivering the fatal *estocada* (lunge) with his sword. The matador must deliver the estocada into the neck from a position directly in front of the animal.

If the matador succeeds, and he usually does, the bull eventually collapses and dies. If the applause from the crowd warrants, he will be awarded an *oreja* (ear) or two and sometimes the tail. The dead bull is dragged from the ring to be butchered for sale.

A 'good' bullfight depends not only on the skill and courage of the matador but also on the spirit of the bulls. Animals lacking heart for the fight bring shame on the ranch that bred them. Very occasionally, a bull that has fought outstandingly is *indultado* (spared) – an occasion for great celebration – and will then retire to stud.

Tijuana's two bullfighting arenas are the most famous in Baja California, but there's also one in Mexicali.

Of the town's two bullrings, the larger, more spectacular venue is the **Plaza de Toros Monumental** (www.monumental.com.mx), the renowned bullring-by-the-sea in Playas de Tijuana, only a short distance from the border fence. The other is **El Toreo de Tijuana** (Blvd Agua Caliente), between central Tijuana and the Hipódromo de Agua Caliente (racetrack; see below). Spring bullfights take place at El Toreo, which has room for 12,000 spectators. In July or August, corridas move to the ring in Playas, which holds up to 25,000 people.

Tickets are available at the bullrings daily from noon to 6pm and from 10am on the day of the corrida. In the USA you can also purchase tickets through **Five Star Tours** (☎ 619-232-5049; 800-553-8687; www.tjbullfight.com) online or at the San Diego office (in the Amtrak station, at Broadway and Kettner Blvd). Prices range from US$8 for general admission to US$45 for prime seats in the shade.

Greyhound Races

Ever since the owner of **Hipódromo de Agua Caliente** (☎ 681-7811 ext 637), Tijuana multimillionaire Jorge Hank Rhon, refused to give in during a sustained labor dispute several years ago, the ponies no longer circle this landmark racetrack, and the place has literally gone to the dogs. In fact, it would be more accurate to call it a *galgódromo* (*galgo* means greyhound), because greyhound races with wagering take place at 7.45pm daily and also at 2pm weekends. Just beyond the Club Campestre Tijuana on Blvd Agua Caliente, the Hipódromo de Agua Caliente is open all year; admission is free and parking is cheap.

Rodeos

Charreadas (rodeos) usually take place Sunday afternoons from May to September at one of four venues in the Tijuana area – ask Secture or Cotuco (p56) for the latest details. One popular rodeo ground is the **Cortijo San José** in Playas de Tijuana, just south of Plaza de Toros Monumental.

Shopping   Map pp58-9
Av Revolución is the main tourist-oriented shopping street. Local handicrafts – especially jewelry, wrought-iron furniture, baskets, silver, blown glass, pottery and leather goods – are plentiful. Bargaining is the rule in smaller stores. Av Constitución, one block west, has shoe stores, flower shops, hardware stores and other places catering primarily to locals.

Tequila, Kahlua and other liquors are popular buys, but you can save a couple of dollars by buying in supermarkets rather than liquor stores.

Markets are fun places to shop. The **Mercado Municipal** (Municipal Market; Av Niños Héroes btwn Calles 1a & 2a), and the sprawling **Mercado de Artesanías** (Artisans' Market; Calle 1a & Av Ocampo), near the border, are both good for browsing. The **Mercado Hidalgo** (p57) is where the locals shop.

Getting There & Away
AIR
Mexico's fourth-busiest airport, **Aeropuerto Internacional Abelardo L Rodríguez** (Map p74; ☎ 683-2418) is in Mesa de Otay, east of downtown. It has become a popular departure and arrival point, and fares to/from other cities in Mexico may be cheaper than in the USA.

Aeroméxico (Map pp58-9; ☎ 684-8444, at the airport ☎ 683-2700, in the USA ☎ 800-237-6639) and its commuter subsidiary, **Aerolitoral**, share an office in Plaza Río. Aerolitoral flies to Tucson (Arizona) and La Paz via the mainland Mexican city of Hermosillo (Sonora). Aeroméxico has one daily direct flight each to La Paz and to Mazatlán, and up to 10 flights to Mexico City; it also serves numerous other destinations throughout Mexico.

Mexicana (at the airport ☎ 682-4183, in the USA ☎ 800-531-7921) has an office in the Zona Río (Map pp58-9; ☎ 634-6566; Av Diego Rivera 1511) and offers direct flights to Guadalajara, Zacatecas and Mexico City.

Aero California (☎ at the airport ☎ 682-8754, in the USA ☎ 800-237-6225) also has an office in the Plaza Río (☎ 684-2876; Av Independencia near Via Poniente) and flies daily to La Paz and Los Cabos. It also serves many mainland destinations from Mexico City northward.

BUS
Just about every town in Mexico is served from Tijuana, but there is a bewildering number of stations and companies. For more on bus travel in Baja California and beyond, see the Transportation chapter.

Border Bus Terminal
The **border bus terminal** (Central Camionera de La Linea; Map pp58-9; ☎ 683-5681) is on the southern edge of Plaza Viva Tijuana and is used by **ABC** (☎ 686-9010), **Estrellas del Pacifico** (☎ 683-5022) and **Turi-Mex** (☎ 682-9434). ABC leaves every 30 minutes to Ensenada (US$8, 1½ hours), where there are easy connections south to San Quintín. It departs almost hourly to Mexicali (US$13, 3 hours) and twice daily to San Felipe (US$27, 5½ hours).

Downtown Bus Terminal
The **downtown bus terminal** (Antigua Central Camionera; Map pp58-9; ☎ 688-0752) is at Av Madero and Calle 1a (Comercio), a short taxi ride or 10-minute walk from the border. It offers services by **ABC** (☎ 621-2424) (local buses only), **Greyhound** (☎ 688-1979, in the USA ☎ 800-231-2222; www.greyhound.com) and others. Greyhound serves San Diego and Los Angeles. ABC also offers Servicio Plus to some destinations. ABC goes to Tecate (US$3.50, 1½ hours) every 20 minutes and Ensenada (US$8, 1½ hours) every half hour or so.

La Mesa Long Distance Bus Terminal
Tijuana's **main station** (Central Camionera La Mesa; Map p54; ☎ 621-7640) for long-distance buses is about 3 miles (5km) southeast of the city center at Blvd Lázaro Cárdenas and Río Alamar. Companies include **ABC** (☎ 621-2982) and **Elite** (☎ 621-2602). **Transportes Norte de Sonora** runs buses to Tecate, Mexicali and mainland Mexico.

To reach Camionera La Mesa from downtown, take any 'Buena Vista,' 'Centro' or 'Central Camionera' bus (US$0.50) from Calle 2a (Juárez) east of Av Constitución; these buses also stop at the border bus lot.

For the same price, the quicker and more convenient gold-and-white *taxis de ruta* (route taxis; marked 'Mesa de Otay') stop on Av Madero between Calles 2a (Juárez) and 3a (Carrillo Puerto). A private taxi costs about US$12. ABC serves the following destinations regularly every day:

CROSSING THE BORDER

One of the world's busiest border crossings, the **San Ysidro–Tijuana** port of entry is open 24 hours a day. If you are crossing the border on foot, take the pedestrian bridge and go through the turnstile into Mexico. To reach Av Revolución, walk through the Plaza Viva Tijuana shopping mall to the pedestrian bridge over the river, cross the street and proceed along Calle Comercio. The entire walk takes about 15 minutes.

For drivers, there are usually no delays coming into Mexico, but returning can be a nightmare, especially at the end of holiday weekends. Lanes 9 to 12 are reserved for carpools of at least three passengers, but only on weekdays from 5am to 10pm. Be sure to arrange vehicle insurance (p241) either before crossing the border or at the border (Mesa de Otay is much quicker than San Ysidro).

If Tijuana is your only destination, it may be better to leave your car on the northern side of the border and either walk or take a shuttle across. Parking lots include **Border Station Parking** (4570 Camino de la Plaza; parking US$10/day); to get there turn right at the last exit off the I-5 before the border. Also here is a small tourist information kiosk with maps and other information.

This parking lot also doubles as the northern terminus of the **Mexicoach shuttle** (☎ 685-1470, in the USA ☎ 619-428-9517) connecting to the Terminal Turístico (p000) on Av Revolución. Buses depart at 15- to 30-minute intervals from 9am to 9pm daily. One-way fares are US$2.50.

The alternative crossing at **Mesa de Otay**, east of downtown near the airport, is open 6am to 10pm daily. Remember that it takes time to drive to Otay and return to US I-5 after crossing the border.

Destination	Fare	Duration
El Rosario	US$21	8 hrs
Ensenada	US$8	1½ hrs
La Paz	US$92	22-24 hrs
Loreto	US$72	20 hrs
Mexicali	US$13	2½ hrs
Mulegé	US$65	15 hrs
San Felipe	US$27	6 hrs
San Quintín	US$18	5-6 hrs
Santa Rosalía	US$54	11-13 hrs
Tecate	US$3.50	1½ hrs

Turminal Turístico (Mexicoach)

From Friday to Sunday, **Mexicoach** (Map pp58-9; ☎ 685-1470; Av Revolución at Calle 6a) operates its Rosarito Beach Express with departures at 11am and 1, 3 and 5pm (US$8 roundtrip; 40 minutes) from its terminal on Av Revolución. Buses stop outside the Rosarito Beach Hotel in Playas de Rosarito. It also runs between here and the US border (see Crossing the Border, above.)

TO/FROM THE USA

Several companies offer services between Los Angeles, San Diego, San Ysidro and Tijuana.

Bus

Greyhound (☎ 800-231-2222; www.greyhound.com) runs regular buses from both its **Los Angeles terminal** (☎ 213-629-8401; 1716 E 7th St; US$18; 4-5 hrs) and the **San Diego terminal** (☎ 619-239-3266; 120 W Broadway; US$5; 1 hr). Buses stop first at Tijuana's downtown terminal, then continue on to the Central Camionera La Mesa (same fare), adding about 20 minutes to the journey.

Also from San Diego, bus No 932, operated by **ATC/Vancom** (☎ 619-427-6438), goes from various stops along Broadway in downtown San Diego to San Ysidro on the US side of the border (US$2.25, 90 minutes).

Trolley

The **San Diego Trolley** (in the USA ☎ 619-233-3004, 800-266-6883) travels from San Diego's Amtrak station at Broadway and Kettner Blvd to the US side of the San Ysidro border in about 45 minutes (maximum fare is US$2.25). Trolleys depart every 15 minutes or so from about 5am to midnight.

From San Diego International Airport (Lindbergh Field), bus No 992 goes directly to the trolley stop at Plaza America in San Diego, across from the Amtrak station, at 15-minute intervals (US$2.25). If you're making the bus-trolley connection, be sure to request a free transfer.

Getting Around
TO/FROM THE AIRPORT

Taxicabs to the Tijuana airport from downtown or the border cost between US$10 and US$20, depending on your bargaining skills.

You can save a bundle by using public transportation. From the border, take any bus (about US$0.50) marked 'Aeropuerto' from the bus stop on the southeastern edge of Plaza Viva Tijuana.

From downtown or the Zona Río, catch the airport bus or a blue-and-white route taxi on Calle 4a between Av Constitución and Paseo de los Héroes.

BUS

From the border, you can take any bus (about US$0.50) marked 'Centro' to go downtown. The bus stop is on the southeast side of Plaza Viva Tijuana.

CAR

Rental cars may be cheaper in San Diego, and several of the large companies permit their cars to be taken across the border if you buy supplemental insurance. Companies in Tijuana include the following:

Avis (☎ 683-0603, 683-2310; Blvd Cuauhtémoc 406, Colonia Aeropuerto)

Alamo (Map pp58-9; ☎ 686-4040; Blvd Sánchez Taboada 10401, Zona Río; airport ☎ 683-8084)

Budget (Map pp58-9; ☎ 634-3304; Av Paseo de los Héroes 77, Zona Río; airport ☎ 683-2905)

Dollar (☎ 681-8484; Blvd Sánchez Taboada 10285, Zona Río)

National (Map pp58-9; ☎ 686-2103; Blvd Agua Caliente 10598)

TAXI

Tijuana has numerous types of taxis. In general, expect to pay from US$2 to US$6 for most city rides. The cheapest of the private taxis are the white ones with **Taxi Libre** painted in big orange letters on the sides. These taxis have *taxímetros* (taximeters), and the drivers are required to use them; make sure they do to avoid overcharging.

The **yellow taxis** at the border often try to overcharge; the fare should not be more than US$5 per car. A ride to the Central Camionera from the border costs about US$14.

Route taxis are an efficient and inexpensive way to get around town. They are station wagons that operate along designated routes. You can board them at their designated route terminus or by flagging them down. Fares depend on the distance

traveled but are usually about US$0.60 within town. The driver will stop wherever you want to get off.

From Av Madero and Calle 3a (Carrillo Puerto), brown-and-white route taxis (marked 'Mesa de Otay') go to the Zona Río, the Central Camionera La Mesa (La Mesa Long Distance Bus Terminal) and the airport along Paseo de los Héroes. Red-and-black cabs travel along Blvd Agua Caliente to the El Toreo bullring, the country club and the Agua Caliente racetrack. You can pick them up at Calle 4a and Av Niños Héroes in downtown. Yellow-and-blue route taxis to Rosarito (US$1, 30 minutes) depart from Av Madero and Calle 4a (Díaz Mirón).

TIJUANA TO ROSARITO
☎ 664

Traveling south from Tijuana via the toll road (Mex 1D), the urban sprawl quickly gives way to open coastal road and unrestricted ocean views. The first toll booth for México 1D is at Km 9. About 8 miles (13km) south of here is the village of **San Antonio del Mar** with the hilltop **KOA Trailer Park/Campground** (☎ 631-3305; site US$20). About 7 miles (11km) offshore are the **Islas de los Coronados**, a popular diving destination for Southern Californians. There is no boat service to the islands, but charter companies such as **Horizon Charters** (p39) offer diving tours.

Another 2 miles (3.2km) south, at Km 25, is the Moorish-architecture-inspired **Oasis Beach Resort & Convention Center** (Map p74; ☎ 631-3250, in the USA ☎ 800-818-3133; RV midweek/weekend US$49/59, d US$123), a luxurious beachfront hotel/RV park resort. It has 55 paved sites with small patios, brick barbecues and full hookups, including cable TV. Facilities include a tennis court, pools, Jacuzzis, a market, mini-golf and a clubhouse with bathrooms, sauna, TVs, laundry and weight room. Rates are for two people; each extra guest pays US$10 in the RV sites, US$15 in rooms.

PLAYAS DE ROSARITO
☎ 661 / pop 63,420

Since its 'discovery' in the 1990s, Rosarito has transformed from a modest fishing village into a weekend party-town destination with a plethora of restaurants, souvenir shops, hotels and bars. From April

MÉXICO 1 OR MÉXICO 1D?

Free road or toll road? That's the question you'll have to ask yourself when driving south from Tijuana to Ensenada.

México 1D, the divided toll road, is faster and more easily accessed, and it offers spectacular coastal views over its entire length. From the border at San Ysidro, simply follow the (slyly manipulative) 'Ensenada Scenic Road' signs along Calle Internacional. Paralleling the border fence, the road turns south in Playas de Tijuana, just before plunging into the ocean, and passes through the first of three tollgates.

Tolls for the entire 68-mile (110km) stretch, which takes about 1½ hours, are about US$6.60 for an ordinary passenger vehicle or motorcycle and twice that for any larger vehicle. One-third of the toll (24 pesos) is charged at each of three gates – Playas de Tijuana, Playas de Rosarito and San Miguel – though there are several other exits along the route. Watch out for livestock jumping the fences to graze on the irrigated median strip.

Two-lane, toll-free México 1 (the Transpeninsular) passes through equally spectacular scenery, but heavier traffic makes it slower. From the Tijuana border crossing, follow the signs to central Tijuana and continue straight (west) along Calle 3a (Carrillo Puerto), turning left (south) at Av Revolución. Follow Av Revolución to the end, where it veers left (east) and becomes Blvd Agua Caliente. Turn right just before the twin towers of the Grand Hotel Tijuana and head south.

México 1 hits the coast just north of Playas de Rosarito. From here, the free road and the toll road run parallel for several miles. Just past La Fonda, the Transpeninsular turns inland and zigzags through the countryside for 21 miles (34km) before returning to the coast and crossing the toll road again near San Miguel.

---

to October, North Americans pour in by the thousands and fill their weekends with horseback riding, beach-bumming, shopping, fishing, dining and – in the raucous bars that line southern Blvd Juárez – partying until the wee morning hours.

Rosarito's population nearly doubled in the 1990s, and it continues to be the fastest-growing community in Baja California (Norte). In recognition of the town's increased size and importance, the state government granted Rosarito *municipio* (county) status in 1995. Both the municipio and the town are now known formally as Playas de Rosarito.

Hollywood also did its part to anchor Rosarito even more prominently on the map and in people's minds. In 1996 Twentieth Century Fox opened its Fox Studios Baja (p75) just a few miles south of town in Popotla. Originally built just for the filming of *Titanic*, it is now a permanent facility, bringing a touch of glamour to this part of northern Baja.

Orientation

Rosarito's main artery, Blvd Benito Juárez, is a segment of the Transpeninsular and is lined by hotels, restaurants, shops and businesses. On most weekends it becomes

a two-way traffic jam, as hordes of visitors stream in.

Rosarito's 'downtown' is toward the southern end, around the Rosarito Beach Hotel. This is where most of the tourist-oriented places are located, while northern Rosarito has a more local flair.

Most places do have street addresses, but the numbering system is maddeningly erratic. Whenever possible, this section uses cross streets to help you locate a particular place, but you may still find that you'll need to refer to the map a little more often than usual.

Information

EMERGENCIES & MEDICAL SERVICES

Cruz Roja (Red Cross; ☎ 132 or ☎ 612-0414) Call for ambulance.

Hospital Santa Lucía (☎ 612-0440; Av Mar del Norte 557)

Police station (☎ 612-1110/1; Blvd Juárez at Rene Ortiz)

IMMIGRATION

Immigration office (☎ 613-0234; Acacias at Blvd Juárez) Located directly behind the police station.

INTERNET ACCESS

Bajachat (Blvd Juárez at Cleofas Arreola; US$2 75/hr; ☺ 9am-11pm)

NORTHERN BAJA

PLAYAS DE ROSARITO

0 —————————— 500 m
0 —————————— 0.3 miles

A B C D

1

To Tijuana (51km)
To Tijuana (51km)

Blvd Juárez

MEX 1D (toll)

29

MEX 1

42

33

31 8
18 7 Mexicali
Av de las Playas

27 Tijuana
La Fuente

21
Villa del Mar Rosarito

17
Villa de las Olas Ensenada

Calzada del Mar La Paz

41
34 J Amaro

16 E Zapata

35
Cárdenas

Quinta 26 46
Plaza 32
Shopping 25
Center

44
Laurel

MEX 1

Sauce

Ebano Cedro
15 Abeto

11 12 Alamo
20 47
45 Ciprés
2
37

Rene Ortiz
7 4
5 8 Acacias

Parque
Municipal 3 6
Abelardo
L. Rodríguez Oceana Plaza

Roble
5 13
30 43 24
28 38
39 40
Eucalipto

Nogal 14 Blvd Juárez
36 19

23 Cleofas Arreola
1 48
10
MEX 1

PACIFIC
OCEAN

Playa

Playa

To Ensenada (27km)

To Secture (500m)
& Ensenada (51km)

INFORMATION
American Express.............................. (see 9)
Bajachat... **1** D6
Banamex.. **2** C5
Banca Serfin.. **3** D5
Hospital Santa Lucía........................... **4** D5
Immigration Office............................. **5** D5
Lavamática.. **6** D5
Police Station...................................... **7** D5
Post Office... **8** D5
Rosarito Beach Convention & Visitors
  Bureau... **9** D5
Viajes Carousel................................... (see 9)

SIGHTS & ACTIVITIES (p71)
Museo Wa Cuatay............................. **10** D6

SLEEPING (pp71-2)
Alamo Hostel...................................... **11** C4
Hotel Brisas del Mar........................... **12** C4
Hotel del Sol...................................... **13** D5
Hotel Festival Plaza............................ **14** D6
Hotel Los Pelicanos............................ **15** C4
Motel Colonial.................................... **16** B3
Motel El Portal.................................... **17** C2
Motel Marsella's.................................. **18** B2
Motel Sonia... **19** D6
Motel Villa de Lis................................ **20** C5
Posada Don Luis.................................. **21** C2
Pueblito Inn... **22** C2
Rosarito Beach Hotel.......................... **23** D6

EATING (pp72-3)
Bistro Le Cousteau............................. **24** D5
Casa de la Longosta............................ **25** C3
Comercial Supermarket...................... **26** C3
Dragon del Mar.................................. **27** C2
El Jardín Bohemio............................... (see 21)
El Nido.. **28** D5
La Fachada.. **29** C1
La Flor de Michoacan **30** D5
La Flor de Michoacán #2.................... **31** C2
La Leña.. **32** C3
Los Pelicanos Restaurant & Bar........ (see 15)
Ortega's Place..................................... **33** C1
Palacio Royal...................................... **34** C3
Panificadora La Espiga....................... **35** C3
Rock & Roll Taco................................ **36** D6
Vince's.. **37** C5

ENTERTAINMENT (p73)
El Museo de Tequila........................... (see 14)
Macho Taco.. **38** D5
Papas & Beer....................................... **39** C5
Señor Frogs... **40** D5

SHOPPING (pp73-4)
Apisa.. **41** C3
La Misión Viejo.................................. **42** C1
Mercado de Artesanías....................... **43** D5
Mercado Sobre Ruedas....................... **44** C4

TRANSPORT (p74)
Mexicoach Bus Stop........................... (see 23)
Pemex.. **45** C5
Pemex.. **46** C3
Route Taxis to La Misión.................... **47** C4
Route Taxis to Tijuana........................ **48** D6

LAUNDRY
Lavamática (Blvd Juárez btwn Acacias & Roble; US$5/load)

MONEY
Nearly all merchants in Playas de Rosarito accept US dollars. **Banamex** (Blvd Juárez at Ciprés) and **Banca Serfin** (Blvd Juárez at Acacias) have ATMs and change money and cash traveler's checks.

POST
Post office (Acacias at Av Mar del Norte) Located east of the police station.

TOURIST INFORMATION
Secture (☎ 612-5222; ☼ 9am-7pm Mon-Fri, 10am-4pm Sat & Sun) The state-run tourist office is south of downtown at Km 28 on México 1 (Blvd Juárez). It has brochures, and the English-speaking staff will deal with tourist hassles and try to answer questions.
Cotuco (Rosarito Beach Convention & Visitors Bureau; ☎ 612-0396, 612-3078, in the USA ☎ 800-962-2252; Blvd Juárez at Roble, Oceana Plaza Mall; ☼ 9am-6pm Mon-Fri, 9am-3pm Sat). The most convenient tourist office has helpful staff.

TRAVEL AGENCIES
Viajes Carousel (☎ 613-0832; Blvd Juárez at Roble, Oceana Plaza Mall) Full-service travel agency.

Sights & Activities
Rosarito's long, wide, unsheltered beach can be windy and cool (and rather unappealing) in winter. In summer it's pleasant for a horseback ride, but it's hardly the tranquil sandy paradise offered by beaches on the Sea of Cortez. One popular activity among young foreigners is blowing off the fireworks sold throughout town.

MUSEO WA CUATAY
The name of Rosarito's small **historical and anthropological museum** (☎ 613-0687; Blvd Juárez 18; admission free; ☼ 8am-5pm), near the Rosarito Beach Hotel, translates as 'Place of the Waters,' the indigenous Kumiai name for the area. It is lovingly maintained by its caretakers and offers a good introduction to the area from pre-Columbian times to the present. Subjects include the missions, the creation of the *ejidos* (communal land holdings) and the beginnings of tourism. Admission is free but donations are greatly appreciated.

PARQUE MUNICIPAL ABELARDO L RODRÍGUEZ
The **amphitheater** at Rosarito's beachfront plaza contains the impressive 1987 mural *Tierra y Libertad* (Land and Liberty) by Juan Zuñiga Padilla, proof that Mexico's celebrated muralist tradition is still alive and well. Traditional motifs include the eagle and plumed serpent and Emiliano Zapata and his followers.

HORSEBACK RIDING
Horses can be hired at several locations on the western side of the Transpeninsular in Rosarito and on the beach by the Rosarito Beach Hotel. Rates vary widely, from US$7 per half-hour to US$5 per hour. Bargain, if you can.

Sleeping
Because it's a resort town and so close to the border, Rosarito lacks consistent budget accommodations. Rates vary both seasonally and between weekdays (Monday to Thursday) and weekends (Friday to Sunday). Given this fickle market, prices in the following sections are intended only to give you an idea of what to expect.

BUDGET
Alamo Hostel (☎ 613-1179, in the USA ☎ 888-772-1393; www.alamo-hostel.com; Alamo 15; dm/tent/RV US$15/10/18) For cheap sleeps and camping, try this friendly German-owned hostel. It's basic and cramped but very convivial, and it's only half a block from the beach. Bunks are in coed dorms, and a motley crew of permanent RV residents keeps everyone in high spirits.
Motel Marsella's (☎ 612-0468; Calle del Mar 75; r US$20-40; ℗) This 24-room motel has clean, carpeted and spacious rooms with wood paneling, large beds and cable TV.

MID-RANGE
Hotel Los Pelicanos (☎ 612-0445; Cedro 115; r US$50-72) In a quiet location down on the beach, Los Pelicanos is one of the best options in town. The restaurant has a great balcony right over the sand, and the whole place exudes a laid-back feel. Room rates are for two people, plus US$7.50 each additional person. Those with ocean views and balconies cost US$72.

Posada Don Luis (☎ 612-1166; Blvd Juárez 272; midweek r US$28-75, weekend r US$35-95; P 🛏 🎖) On the northern end of town, Posada Don Luis offers rooms varying from cramped and stuffy with plywood walls to spacious and comfortable with flowered bedspreads and Formica tables. There's also a Jacuzzi and sauna on the premises.

Pueblito Inn (☎ 612-2516, 800-027-5196, in the USA ☎ 888-203-8368; Blvd Juárez 286; r midweek/weekend US$45/100; P 🎖) This 47-room well-kept motel has its swimming pool in the parking lot; it's not scenic, but it's still a pool. Rooms are comfortable and have cable TV and telephones.

Motel Colonial (☎ 612-1575; Calle 1a at Calle de Mayo 71; r midweek/weekend US$30/45, ste midweek/weekend US$60/80; P) Close to the beach, Motel Colonial offers decent but aging rooms. Most are suites with separate living and dining areas, kitchenettes, double beds and enough space for cots and sleeping bags.

Motel El Portal (☎ 612-0050; Blvd Juárez at Vía de las Olas; r US$30-50) The brightly painted El Portal is probably the best choice in this part of town. Rooms are modest but spotless, and it's very friendly.

Motel Villa de Lis (☎ 612-2320; Alamo at Costa Azul; r midweek/weekend US$55/65; P) Quiet and clean, three-story Villa de Lis is popular for its clean rooms with cable TV. The upper rooms have ocean views and balconies. Rates drop US$10 in winter.

Hotel Brisas del Mar (☎ /fax 612-2547, in the USA ☎ 888-871-3605; Blvd Juárez 22; r US$67-101; P 🛏 🎖) A bit farther from the action, Hotel Brisas del Mar has 71 carpeted, contemporary rooms with air-con, heater and cable TV. There's secured parking, a heated pool and volleyball courts.

Hotel del Sol (☎ 612-2552/53/54; Blvd Juárez 32; r midweek/weekend US$40/50; P) Right in downtown Rosarito, Hotel del Sol offers good rooms with cable TV, telephones, carpet and tables. The newer rooms are better but slightly more expensive.

Motel Sonia (☎ 612-1260; Blvd Juárez 781; r midweek/weekend US$35/40; P 🍴) It may be basic but it's central and a good value, and the rooms are all clean and nonsmoking. Reservations are not accepted.

TOP END

Rosarito Beach Hotel (☎ 612-0144, in the USA ☎ 800-343-8582; www.rosaritobeachhotel.com; Blvd Juárez 31; r US$169-199, ste US$499; P 🛏 🎖) Opened in the late 1920s during Prohibition, this beachside hotel quickly became a popular watering hole and gambling haven for Hollywood stars like Orson Welles and Mickey Rooney. Larry Hagman (of *Dallas* fame), Vincent Price and several Mexican presidents have also been guests. Facilities include two pools, a fishing pier, a gym, two restaurants and the Casa Playa Spa, offering a full menu of treatments, massages, facials and body wraps. The best rooms are pricier ones in the new building closest to the beach.

Hotel Festival Plaza (☎ 612-2950, in the USA ☎ 800-453-8606; www.festivalplaza.info; Blvd Juárez 1207-1; r midweek US$86-130, r weekend US$108; P 🛏 🎖) This high-rise hotel, just north of the Rosarito Beach Hotel, looks like a colorful children's playground – for adult 'children,' that is. This place is party central, and any illusions of a quiet night's sleep quickly disappear when you discover that all rooms face the outdoor plaza, where live concerts take place! Some 10 clubs and restaurants, a tequila 'museum' and even a small Ferris wheel are part of the complex.

Eating

CENTRAL ROSARITO

Vince's (☎ 612-1253; Blvd Juárez 97-A; mains US$3-9) It's hard to beat the seafood here, especially in terms of value. The dining room stinks like fish, but hey! that's because it's also a fish market, meaning the food is *fresh*.

Rock & Roll Taco (Blvd Juárez at Magnolia; mains US$3-9) Allegedly a favorite hangout of Leonardo di Caprio and Kate Winslet during the filming of *Titanic*, R&R Taco is built on the site of a former mortuary, which may explain the numerous skeletons in the splashy decor. This is more a place for drinking and partying than eating, but it does serve decent tacos and other antojitos.

El Nido (☎ 612-1430; Blvd Juárez 67) One of the best places in downtown Rosarito, El Nido enjoys a good reputation for its prime cuts of meat, solidly prepared seafood dishes and hearty breakfasts.

La Flor de Michoacán 2 (Blvd Juárez 306; mains US$5-7) Although it's a bit pricey for *carnitas* (slow-roasted pork), it's excellent. A half-kilo order with tortillas, guacamole, beans, rice and salsa (US$15) will feed two or three, and you won't need to eat for hours.

Bistro Le Cousteau (☎ 612-2655; Blvd Juárez 184; mains US$12-22) Drop in here for owner-chef Philippe Chauvin's delicious French menu. His rack of lamb, veal cutlets and duck in orange sauce are proof that the French really *can* cook. The wine list is long, and the US$10 daily special is a good deal.

NORTHERN ROSARITO
La Flor de Michoacán (☎ 612-1858; Blvd Juárez 291; mains US$5-7) The beloved Flor de Michoacán serves authentic carnitas at the same prices as its branch in central Rosarito, albeit in a nicer setting.

La Fachada (☎ 612-1785; Blvd Juárez 317; US$8-20) Upscale La Fachada gets rave reviews from almost everyone for grilled specialties like steak and lobster.

Ortega's Place (☎ 612-1757; Blvd Juárez 200) Popular with families for its festive atmosphere, Ortega's serves tasty lobster dinners; its weekly Sunday champagne brunch (US$10) is also a big attraction.

El Jardín Bohemin (☎ 612-1166; Blvd Juárez 272) Part of Posada Don Luis, El Jardín serves Caribbean food with an emphasis on Cuban fare, and often has live music.

Los Pelicanos Restaurant & Bar (mains US$7-12) At its namesake hotel, Los Pelicanos serves juicy steaks and solid Mexican fare. It's not cheap, but its oceanview deck is a great place to watch the sunset.

La Leña (☎ 612-0826; Quinta Plaza shopping center, Blvd Juárez) Specializes in beef.

Casa de la Langosta (☎ 612-0924; Quinta Plaza shopping center, Blvd Juárez; mains US$8-17) This seafood restaurant has some of the best Puerto Nuevo–style lobster in town.

Good Chinese restaurants are the **Palacio Royal** (☎ 612-1412; Centro Comercial Ejido Mazatlán btwn J Amaro & E Zapata; mains US$5-8) and the banquet-style **Dragon del Mar** (☎ 612-0604; Blvd Juárez 283; mains US$5-9). Both have the usual wallet-friendly lunch specials.

To stock up on produce, cookies, drinks, cheese and the like, head to the giant **Comercial supermarket** in the Quinta Plaza shopping center. The best bakery is **Panificadora La Espiga**, with several branches around town, including one at Blvd Juárez and Cárdenas.

Entertainment
On weekends, throngs of college students, soldiers and young Mexican-Americans descend on Rosarito from Southern California

for a dose of serious partying. Many of the most raucous haunts are in or near the Hotel Festival Plaza complex. The Rosarito Beach Hotel presents performances by mariachis, singers and gaudy cowboys doing rope tricks on weekends.

El Museo de Tequila (☎ 612-2950; Blvd Juárez 1207-1) Competes with Pancho's in Cabo San Lucas for having the world's biggest tequila collection. There's often live mariachi music.

Rock & Roll Taco (Blvd Juárez at Magnolia; see Eating) An imaginatively decorated bar extends outdoors to a wooden deck and a small swimming pool. It's party central.

Señor Frogs (Blvd Juárez at Nogal) This Mexican chain, in its classic club-cum-restaurant style, offers a rowdy mix of music, drinking and dancing.

Papas & Beer (☎ 612-0444) Down by the beach, Papas & Beer is part of another national chain of dedicated watering holes. There's usually a small cover charge.

Macho Taco (Blvd Juárez at Nogal) For something a little mellower but definitely fun, hit Macho Taco, where the tacos are as good as the beer is cold and cheap.

From June to October, *charreadas* (Mexican rodeos) often take place on Saturday afternoon. Check with the tourist offices for details.

Shopping
Rosarito has a reputation for being the best place in northern Baja for quality rustic furniture, which can be handmade to order for a fraction of what it would cost north of the border. Several businesses are on Blvd Juárez in Rosarito proper, but you'll find the biggest concentration – and lower prices – on the Transpeninsular a few miles south of town.

Mercado de Artesanías (Artisans' Market; Blvd Juárez 306; ☒ 9am-6pm) Located downtown, the 150-stall Mercado de Artesanías offers a huge selection of curios, crafts and souvenirs.

Apisa (☎ 612-0125; Blvd Juárez 2400) For better quality and more unique items than the artisans' market, browse the 18,000 sq feet of this crafts warehouse in northern Rosarito. It has an astonishing assortment of colonial-style furniture, sculptures and crafts.

La Misión Viejo (☎ 612-1576; Blvd Juárez 139) Prices are good at the oldest of Rosarito's fine crafts stores.

TIJUANA TO ENSENADA

SIGHTS & ACTIVITIES	(pp75-6; 91)
Baja Country Club	1 C4
Chateau Camou	2 C3
Fox Studios Baja	3 A2
Foxploration	(see 3)
Inner Reef Surf Shop	4 B2
La Bufadora	5 C4
LA Cetto	6 C3
Misión del Descanso Site	7 B2
Misión Nuestra Señora de	
Guadalupe	8 C3
Misión San Miguel de la	
Frontera	9 B3
Monte Xanic	10 C3
Vides de Guadalupe Domecq	11 C3
Viña de Liceaga	12 C3
Vinos Bibayoff	13 C3

SLEEPING	(pp68; 75-7; 88-9)
Baja Beach Resort	14 C4
Baja Seasons RV & Villas Beach	
Resort	15 B3
Del Mar Suites	16 B2
Estero Beach Resort	17 C4
Hotel Calafia	18 B2
Hotel La Misión	19 B2
La Jolla Beach Camp	20 C4
Las Rocas Resort & Spa	21 B2
Oasis Beach Resort & Convention	
Center	22 A1
Villarino RV Park	23 C4

EATING	(p76)
Halfway House Restaurant	24 B2

TRANSPORT	
Tollgate	25 B3
Tollgate	26 A2
Tollgate	27 A1

From early morning to late afternoon on Sundays, the **Mercado Sobre Ruedas**, a produce-cum-flea market, takes place just south of the Quinta Plaza shopping center.

Getting There & Around

From Friday to Sunday, **Mexicoach** operates its Rosarito Beach Express from its Terminal Turístico in downtown Tijuana. It stops in front of the Rosarito Beach Hotel.

ABC buses between Tijuana and Ensenada stop at the tollgate at the southern end of Rosarito but do not enter the town itself. ABC's commuter line, Subur Baja, comes through about every 20 minutes from 6am to 8pm (US$1) and goes to Tijuana's downtown terminal near the border.

Yellow **route taxis** leave from a stand near the Rosarito Beach Hotel, connecting Rosarito with Tijuana (US$1; 30 minutes); flag one down anywhere on Blvd Juárez. White taxis with yellow/green stripes, running to points as far south as La Misión, leave from the southern side of Hotel Brisas del Mar at Alamo and Blvd Juárez.

Because all taxicabs travel along Blvd Juárez, Rosarito's main commercial drag, they are also a good way to travel from one end of town to the other; simply flag one down.

SARITO TO ENSENADA
▸potla
☎ 661

Until 1996 Popotla – about 3 miles (5km) south of Rosarito, at Km 33 on the Transpeninsular – was a rustic fishing village. Then Fox Studios Baja moved in. Planned as a temporary facility built for the filming of *Titanic* (1997), the site has evolved into a permanent studio. Its giant water tank has been used for scenes from several other movies, including *Tomorrow Never Dies* (1997) and *Deep Blue Sea* (1999). In 2000, parts of *Pearl Harbor*, starring Ben Affleck, were filmed here.

Visitors may wander the grounds of the new **Foxploration** (☎ 614-9000; www.foxploration. com; adult/child US$12/9; ☑ 9am-5:30pm Wed-Fri, 10am-6pm Sat & Sun), an outdoor movie-set-cum-theme-park. Its attractions include the Titanic Expo exhibit hall, loaded with sets and props from the movie; a replica of Canal Street, New York; an amphitheater; and Cinemágico, where you can witness all sorts of special effects in action.

To Baja insiders, Popotla was a favorite destination long before Hollywood arrived. The main attraction was – and still is – the super-fresh fish and seafood served at prices much lower than in Rosarito, Ensenada or Puerto Nuevo. Most places are informal, family-run affairs that don't serve alcohol (bring your own), take only cash and are open for lunch only.

SLEEPING
At Km 34 on the Transpeninsular, **Popotla Trailer Park** (☎ 612-1502; tent/RV US$17/20) caters to long-term campers. About 30 spaces are available to short-termers. The park has an oceanview restaurant, a clubhouse, showers, toilets and easy beach access.

At Km 35.5 on the Transpeninsular, **Hotel Calafia** (☎ 612-1580/81, in the USA ☎ 877-700-2093; www.hotel-calafia.com) is a rather curious open-air museum showcasing important moments in Baja history. The ground's Plaza de las Misiones presents replicas of the facades of several of the peninsula's missions. The hotel itself has an attractive oceanfront setting with spring and summer rates of US$67/160 midweek/weekend for rooms with ocean or garden views or US$88/173 for oceanfront rooms with balconies. Prices (lower in winter and fall) include dinner for two. On weekends the restaurant does a famous brunch for US$10; the best tables are right above the waves.

The nicest hotel along the Tijuana-Ensenada corridor is the Mediterranean-style **Las Rocas Resort & Spa** (☎ 612-2140, in the USA ☎ 619-234-9810, 888 527-7622; lasrocas@telnor.net; r US$99, ste US$133-183), at Km 38.5 on the Transpeninsular. Its 34 luxury suites and 40 standard rooms all have private, oceanview balconies, satellite TV and telephones. Suites are appointed with stylish furniture and have microwaves, coffeemakers and fireplaces. Guests relax by the free-form 'infinity' pool or luxuriate at the first-rate hotel spa, where the long menu of treatments ranges from a regular facial to the more exotic basalt-rock massage. Two restaurants serve delicious seafood and Mexican dishes. Spa packages are available.

Puerto Nuevo
☎ 661

If tectonic uplift were not raising this section of the coastline from the sea, the

---

SURF'S UP

The entire coast south of Rosarito to Ensenada is legendary with the surf crowd, including Cantamar (p76), La Fonda (p76) and San Miguel (p77).

A good place to get information is the **Inner Reef Surf Shop** (☎ 661-615-0841; Transpeninsular Km 34.5), about 6 miles (10km) south of Rosarito. The owner, Roger, has been surfing these shores for four decades. He also rents surfboards for US$2/20 per hour/day. Boogie boards rent for US$1.50/10 per hour/day and wetsuit cost US$1.50/10 per hour/day. Roof racks are available for rent as well. There's a three-hour minimum on all hourly rates.

Many surfers camp out at **Surfpoint Camping** (at 'Ollob Benny's Point'), a small campground at Km 38, just past the Las Rocas Resort & Spa. Full hookups for RVs up to 25 feet (7.5m) cost US$17; tent sites cost US$7.50. There are hot showers, and a restaurant is nearby.

village of Puerto Nuevo, at Km 44 on the Transpeninsular, might sink beneath the weight of its 35 or so seafood restaurants. They all specialize in lobster, usually cooked in one of two manners: *ranchera* (simmered in salsa) or *frito* (buttered and grilled) and served with flour tortillas, beans, rice, butter, salsa, chips and limes. All have similar prices: about US$15 for a full lobster dinner and US$10 for a grilled fish dinner.

The Ortega family opened the first lobster restaurant in Puerto Nuevo, and their restaurant, **Ortega's Patio**, at Km 49, is one of the nicest places in town, especially if you get to sit on the outdoor terrace. They have several other branches here and two more in Playas de Rosarito.

For the best deals, go to the smaller places on the southern edge of the village, which get less foot traffic and often outdo each other with amazing specials.

Within steps from Puerto Nuevo, at Km 44.5, the **Grand Baja Resort** (☎ 614-1493, in the USA ☎ 877-315-1002; www.grandbaja.com) offers junior suites for two with ocean views from US$69 off-season (October to March) and US$79-89 the rest of the year. Studios with kitchenette are slightly more expensive. One- and two-bedroom apartments (sleeping four people) start at US$99 and US$150, respectively.

Cantamar

At about Km 47 on the Transpeninsular stands this blip of a village, with a few small grocery stores, a bakery, tire store, taco stands, a Pemex station and an interchange to the toll road. The spectacular **Cantamar Dunes**, immediately south of here, are regularly subjected to assaults by ATVs and other off-road vehicles. Admission is US$5 and there's primitive camping.

South of Cantamar the **Halfway House** (México 1D; mains US$3-6) is a popular restaurant serving Mexican combinations for less than US$5 and steak and seafood dinners for around US$15. Well known among mainland Californians who surf the reef breaks at nearby **Punta Mesquite**, the restaurant is about 3 miles (5km) south of Puerto Nuevo on the Transpeninsular.

Misión del Descanso

The Dominican Misión del Descanso was one of the last missions founded in Cali-

fornia. A large marker commemorates original mission, but there are no ru. Instead, another church built in the ea. 20th century occupies the site.

To get to the site, turn east onto a sand road about 1½ miles (2.4km) south of Cantamar on the Transpeninsular (look for the sign of Vivero La Central nursery), which passes beneath the toll road and reaches the church after about half a mile (1km).

La Fonda

☎ 646

La Fonda is a tiny beach community presiding over a broad, sandy beach between Kms 58 and 60 on the Transpeninsular. Excellent surfing is nearby. At Km 58.5, **Del Mar Suites** (☎ 155-0392; r from US$50) offers spacious oceanview studios with private patios, full kitchens and couches. Its owner also rents tents for beach camping (US$20).

Next door, **Hotel La Misión** (☎ 155-0333, in the USA ☎ 562-420-8500; s/d US$45-55, ste US$80) has regular doubles with king-size beds, fireplaces and ocean views. Suites are more spacious and have Jacuzzis and refrigerators. Rates drop in winter. Its restaurant/bar has cheap dinner specials and margaritas, plus live music on weekends.

If you're traveling on the toll road, take the Alisitos exit (from the south) or La Misión (from the north) to get to any of these places.

La Misión

The village of La Misión, on the Transpeninsular's inland turn, is most notable as the site of the Dominican **Misión San Miguel de la Frontera**, also known as San Miguel Encino and San Miguel Arcángel. Founded in 1787 at a site unknown today, the mission moved up the valley of the Río San Miguel when the spring it depended on dried up. The few remaining ruins are behind the Escuela Primaria La Misión (the elementary school) at Km 65.5, about 1 mile (1.6km) south of the bridge over the Río San Miguel.

Bajamar

☎ 646

Continuing on México 1D will take you to this rambling resort development and residential complex at Km 77.5, built around an 18-hole golf course and a newer nine-holer. Both are open to the public; greens

or 18 holes are US$74/89 midweek/
.ends. Club rentals are US$30.

he resort's **Hacienda Bajamar** (☎ 615-
1/52, in the USA ☎ 888-311-6076; www.golfbajamar.
om) charges summer rates of US$112/136
midweek/weekends for standard rooms
and US$160/180 for suites. Golf packages
are available.

At Km 72, the ultra-deluxe **Baja Seasons
RV & Villas Beach Resort** (☎ 155-4015, in the USA
☎ 800-754-4190; www.bajaseasons.com; RV site off/on
beach US$30/40, r US$56, villa US$80-177) has 154
landscaped RV spaces with full hookups
on a lovely stretch of beach.

Free camping is possible on an attractive
beach at Km 71 on México 1D.

El Mirador

El Mirador, a roadside viewpoint at Km
84 on México 1D, is spectacularly situated
above the ocean. There are a few picnic tables and a children's playground, but no
food or beverage services.

San Miguel

☎ 646

San Miguel is a small beach community
about 7 miles (11km) north of Ensenada,
just south of the third tollgate, which
consists mostly of US retirees in mobile
homes. Its main claim to fame, however, is
a famous right-point break with waves that
draw in hordes of surfers, especially in the
cooler months.

Ramona Beach Motel & Trailer Park (☎ 174-
6045; RV/r US$14/20) at Km 104, has 50 RV sites
with full hookups and no-frills rooms.

Down by the beach, **San Miguel Village
RV Park** (☎ 174-6225; RV US$10) offers 100 sites
with full hookups, tent camping, hot showers and rustic toilets. There is also a small
seafood restaurant at the entrance to the RV
park.

El Sauzal

The seafood cannery at sedate El Sauzal,
about 2 miles (3km) north of Ensenada,
gives off a powerful fishy odor. However,
there are several **trailer parks** and **campgrounds**
here that charge only US$4 to US$10 a
night (though it's difficult to find one that
doesn't cater mostly to long-term RVers).
You can also try camping for free on any
unclaimed stretch of beach. For hotels, see
Ensenada.

ENSENADA

☎ 646 / pop 370,730

Ensenada may be a party town for weekenders from the USA, but it's also a sophisticated, wealthy city with great civic pride.
Generously designed public areas – rather
than hotels – line the waterfront, including
the Plaza Cívica, known as 'Plaza de las Tres
Cabezas' (Three Heads Plaza) for its massive busts of historical icons Benito Juárez,
Miguel Hidalgo and Venustiano Carranza.
The circular Plaza Ventana al Mar is anchored by a gigantic Mexican flag. Lining
the harbor is a tranquil *malecón* (waterfront
promenade), which culminates at the historic Riviera del Pacífico, perhaps the most
beautiful building in northern Baja.

Some four million tourists descend upon
Ensenada each year, including 350,000 arriving by cruise ship from Southern California. Most are drawn to Av López Mateos,
a clean, nicely landscaped and pedestrian-
oriented artery lined with shops, cafés and
restaurants with sidewalk seating, and
many hotels. Along its western reaches
music pounds out of the bars, which cater
to tourists and locals alike.

While downtown has no beaches, a full
menu of water sports awaits a few miles
south at Punta Banda, also the site of La
Bufadora (the blowhole). Ensenada is also
the capital of Baja's wine production and
the gateway to the vineyards and wineries
in nearby Valle de Guadalupe.

History

Located on the harbor of Bahía de Todos
Santos, Ensenada has sheltered explorers,
freighters and fishing boats for more than
four centuries. Juan Rodríguez Cabrillo,
searching for the Strait of Anián (the mythical Northwest Passage), entered the bay
in September 1542, encountering a small
group of Indian hunter-gatherers.

In 1602 Sebastián Vizcaíno named Ensenada de Todos los Santos after All Saints'
Day, November 1. During colonial times
the harbor was an occasional refuge for
Spanish galleons returning to Acapulco
from Manila; the last one sailed through
in 1815.

Ensenada's first permanent settlement
was established in 1804, but it wasn't until
1869, with the discovery of gold at Real del
Castillo, 22 miles (35km) inland, that this

ENSENADA

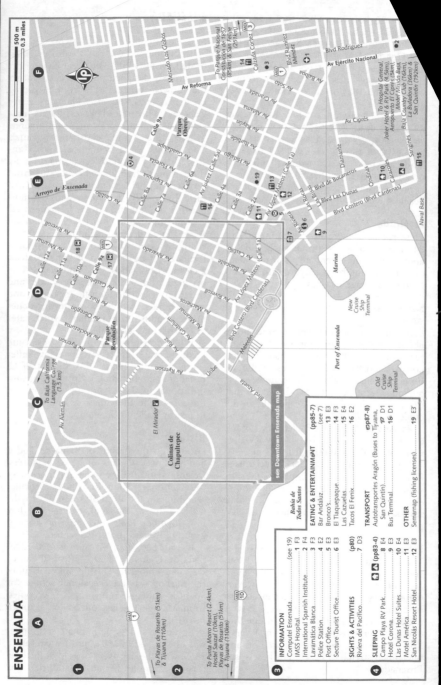

0   500 m
0   0.3 miles

INFORMATION
Computel Ensenada.........................(see 19)
IMSS Hospital..1 F3
Internacional Spanish Institute..............2 F4
Lavamática Blanca.................................3 F3
Police Station..4 E2
Post Office...5 E3
Secture Tourist Office............................6 E3

SIGHTS & ACTIVITIES (p80)
Riviera del Pacífico...............................7 D3

SLEEPING (pp83-4)
Campo Playa RV Park............................8 E4
Hotel Corona...9 E3
Las Dunas Hotel Suites.........................10 E4
Motel América.......................................11 E3
San Nicolás Resort Hotel......................12 E3

EATING & ENTERTAINMENT (pp85-7)
Bar Andaluz.......................................(see 7)
Bronco's...13 E3
El Tlaquepaque....................................14 F3
Las Cazuelas..15 E4
Tacos El Fenix..16 E2

TRANSPORT (pp87-8)
Autotransportes Aragón (Buses to Tijuana,
   San Quintín).......................................17 D1
Bus Terminal..16 D1

OTHER
Semarnap (fishing licenses)..................19 E3

backwater grew up. Because Bahía
Todos Santos was the closest harbor,
Ensenada boomed with an influx of miners,
merchants and hangers-on. In 1882 the city
became the capital of Baja territory. Closure
of the mines in the 1880s ended the boom,
and in 1915 status of territorial capital was
shifted to Mexicali.

After the Revolution, Ensenada, like
Tijuana, began to cater to the 'sin' indus-
tries of drinking, gambling and sex during
US Prohibition. As more visitors came to
Ensenada, entrepreneurs built more hotels
and restaurants, and the town became a
tourist resort and weekend getaway, as it
remains today.

Orientation
Ensenada, 68 miles (110km) south of
Tijuana and 119 miles (192km) north of
San Quintín, is a major fishing and com-
mercial port on sheltered Bahía de Todos
Santos. Most hotels and restaurants line Av
López Mateos (also known as Calle 1a),
which is one block inland from the water-
front Blvd Costero, also known as Blvd
Lázaro Cárdenas.

Five blocks inland, Av Benito Juárez
has shops and businesses catering to the
local population. On the western end of
downtown is Ensenada's 'party district,'
centered on Av Ruiz. Farther west, the hills
of Colinas de Chapultepec are an exclusive
residential zone.

Just north of town, México 3 heads east
and then north through the wine-growing
country of the Valle de Guadalupe to the
border at Tecate. From the southern end of
Ensenada, México 3's southern continuation leads to Ojos Negros, Laguna Hanson
in Parque Nacional Constitución de 1857
and San Felipe.

Heading southbound, the Transpeninsular (México 1) leads to the military
checkpoint at Maneadero, beyond which
foreigners must have a tourist card (see
Visas & Documents in the Directory chapter, p233).

Information
BOOKSTORES
The Bookseller (Map p81; ☎ 178-8964; Calle 4a 240;
⏰ 10am-6pm Tue-Sat) Used English-language magazines
and books.
Libros Libros Books Books (Map p81; ☎ 178-8448;

Av López Mateos 690; ⏰ 9am-8:30pm Mon-Sat, 10am-
7pm Sun) English-language magazines, newspapers and a
few Lonely Planet guidebooks.

EMERGENCIES & MEDICAL SERVICES
Cruz Roja (Red Cross; ☎ 066) Call for ambulance.
Hospital General (☎ 176-7800; Transpen-insular,
Km 111)
IMSS Hospital (Map p78; emergency ☎ 172-4500; Av
Reforma at Blvd Ramírez Méndez)
Police station (Map p78; ☎ 060; Calle 9a at Espinosa)

IMMIGRATION
Immigration Office (Servicios Migratorios; Map p81;
☎ 674-0164; Blvd Azueta 101; ⏰ 9am-5pm) Issues
tourist cards required for travel south of Maneadero.

INTERNET ACCESS
Compunet (Map p81; Av Riveroll at Calle 2a; US$1.35/hr;
⏰ 9am-11pm Mon-Fri, 9am-9pm Sat, 10am-9pm Sun)
Equinoxio Café (Map p81; Blvd Cárdenas 267; US$1.80/
hr; ⏰ 8am-10pm Tue-Sat, 9am-10pm Sun & Mon) Fast
computers, espresso drinks, laptop stations, WiFi access.

INTERNET RESOURCES
Ensenada Gazette (www.ensenadagazette.com)
Thorough Web-based English-language newspaper about
Ensenada and surroundings.
Enjoy Ensenada (www.enjoyensenada.com) Website of
the Ensenada Tourism Board.

LAUNDRY
Lavamática Blanca (Map p78; cnr Av Reforma & Calzada
Cortez) Self-service washers and dryers.

MONEY
Most businesses accept dollars, but if
you're traveling farther south you will need
pesos. Ensenada has plenty of banks that
have ATMs and also change money. **Banco
Santander**, **Banco Serfin** and **Bancomer** are all
on Av Ruiz (Map p81). **Banamex** (Map p81) is on
Av Ryerson at Calle 3a. **Cambio Yesan** (Map
p81; Av Ruiz 201; ⏰ 9am-7pm Mon-Fri, 9am-2pm Sat)
keeps longer hours, but rates may not be
as favorable.

POST
Post office (Map p78; Av López Mateos at Av Riviera;
⏰ 8am-6pm Mon-Fri, 9am-1pm Sat)

TELEPHONE
Telnor public telephones are widespread in
Ensenada, but the **Computel Ensenada office**
at the bus terminal (Map p78; Av Riveroll 1075)

conveniently allows payment by Visa or MasterCard. Definitely avoid the extortionate non-Telnor street phones when calling outside of Mexico.

TOURIST INFORMATION

Cotuco (Map p81; ☎ 178-2411; Blvd Costero 540; 9am-7pm Wed-Thu, 9am-5pm Sat-Tue) Across from the Pemex station, this office has friendly, informed bilingual staff and lots of free maps and brochures.

Secure (Tourist Assistance Office; Map p78 ☎ 172-3022/81; www.enjoyensenada.com; Blvd Costero 1477; 8am-5pm Mon-Fri, 10am-3pm Sat & Sun) Has less information than Cotuco but can help with legal problems.

TRAVEL AGENCIES

Viajes Damiana (Map p81; ☎ 174-0170; www.viajesdamiana.com; cnr Calle 2a & Av Obregón; 8am-9pm Mon-Fri, 9am-5pm Sat, 10am-2pm Sun) Reputable, full-service travel agency.

Sights

EL MIRADOR

Atop the Colinas de Chapultepec, **El Mirador** (Map p78) offers panoramic views of the city and Bahía de Todos Santos. Climb or drive up Av Alemán from the western end of Calle 2a in central Ensenada to the highest point in town.

BODEGAS DE SANTO TOMÁS

Founded in 1888 near the vineyards of the Valle de Santo Tomás south of Ensenada, Bodegas de Santo Tomás is one of Baja's premier vintners. The **Santo Tomás warehouse and tasting room** (Map p81; ☎ 178-3333, 178-2509; www.santotomas.com.mx; Av Miramar 666; 9am-5pm) is located in Ensenada and offers 30-minute tours (10am, 11am, noon, 1pm and 3pm). The US$5 tour includes a tasting of four table wines; for US$10, you can sample up to 15 wines and get a souvenir glass.

Varietals include pinot noir, chardonnay, cabernet, chenin blanc, barbera, tempranillo and merlot. Up to 150,000 cases are shipped annually throughout Mexico and to Western Europe, Japan and the USA.

RIVIERA DEL PACÍFICO

An extravagant waterfront complex with Spanish-Moorish architectural touches, the **Riviera del Pacífico** (Map p78; grounds 9am-7pm) opened in 1930 as the Playa Ensenada Hotel & Casino. The second casino in northern Baja (after the Agua Caliente in Tijuana),

this lavish facility was once the hau Hollywood figures including ex-Oly swimmer Johnny Weissmuller ('Tarza Myrna Loy, Lana Turner, Ali Khan and L lores del Río. Briefly managed by US boxe Jack Dempsey, the facility closed in 1938 when President Lázaro Cárdenas outlawed casino gambling.

Rescued from the wrecking ball in the early 1990s, the building was reborn as the **Centro Social, Cívico y Cultural de Ensenada** and now hosts cultural events, weddings, conventions and meetings.

Open to the public, the Riviera del Pacífico – framed by splendid gardens – is well worth exploring. The lobby (which is entered from the Jardín Bugambillias courtyard on the parking-lot side behind the building) contains an impressive **relief map** of the mission sites throughout Baja and Alta California. Most rooms feature carved and painted ceilings, elaborate tile work, giant wrought-iron chandeliers and creaky parquet floors. The Dining Room and the circular Casino Room are especially impressive, as is the elegant **Bar Andaluz** (p87), with its arched wooden bar.

The complex also contains the **Museo de Historia** (US$1; 9am-2pm & 3-5pm Tue-Sun, Mon from 10am), which traces northern Baja history from the indigenous inhabitants to the mission period. One wing features changing themed exhibits and an art gallery. On the building's basement level, the **Galería de la Ciudad** (admission free; 9am-6pm Mon-Fri) features Baja California artists.

MUSEO HISTÓRICO REGIONAL

This modest **museum** (Map p81; ☎ 178-3692; Av Gastelum near Av López Mateos; US$2.10; 10am-5pm) featuring the 'People and Cultures of Meso-America' is housed in an 1886 military barracks that served as the city's jail until as recently as 1986.

Perhaps more intriguing than the exhibit is the cell block where several of the tiny, windowless concrete cubicles sport some rather accomplished murals by the former inmates.

MUSEO EX-ADUANA MARÍTIMA

Built in 1887 by the US-owned International Company of Mexico, the former Marine Customs House is Ensenada's oldest public building. The **Maritime Museum**

DOWNTOWN ENSENADA

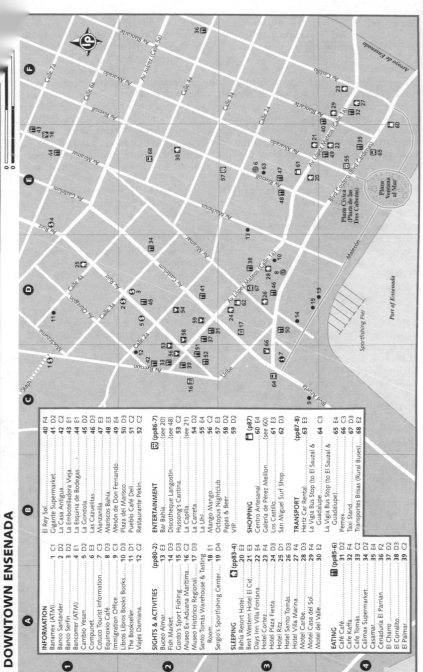

(Map p81; Av Ryerson 99 at Uribe; admission by donation; 10am-5pm Tue-Sun) houses rotating exhibitions with a cultural or historical angle.

MARKETS

Ensenada's largest outdoor market, the **Mercado Los Globos** (Map 78; Wed-Sun) is heaven on earth for collectors of bric-a-brac. Sprawled over an area of eight square blocks on Calle 9a east of Av Reforma, vendors sell everything from old radios and typewriters to fruit and vegetables. Weekends are the best time to visit.

By the sportfishing piers is the colorful **Fish Market** (Map p81; off Blvd Costero; 6:30am-7pm), where you can admire – and purchase – the day's catch daily. The *taquerías* (taco stalls) and food stalls are crowded with locals on weekends, but most places are only mediocre.

Activities

FISHING

Sportfishing is very popular in Ensenada. Catches include albacore, barracuda, bonito, halibut, white sea bass and yellowtail, depending on the season. Most people join an organized fishing trip for about US$40 per person, plus US$10 for a Mexican fishing license. Groups traveling together can also charter an entire boat. Rates depend on the vessel, but figure on about US$600 to US$850 for a 12-passenger cruiser or around US$250 for a four-person *panga* (fiberglass skiff); prices are lower during the week.

The two main operators are **Gordo's Sport Fishing** (Map p81; 178-3515; www.gordos.8m.com; Malecón) and **Sergio's Sportfishing Center** (Map p81; /fax 178-2185; www.sergios-sportfishing.com; Malecón), both with offices right next to the sportfishing piers near the Fish Market. Organized trips leave year-round at 7am and return at 3pm.

If you're taking your own boat, fishing licenses are available from **Semarnap** (Map p78; 176-3837; Calle 2a at Av Guadalupe).

DIVING

Buceo Almar (Map p81; 178-3013; Av Macheros 149) is the local dive shop with equipment for sale and rent. The owners custom-make high-quality wetsuits for about two-thirds of what an equivalent suit would cost in the USA.

WHALE-WATCHING

Between December and March, Calife gray whales pass through Bahía de To Santos on their way to southern Baja ca ing sites at **Laguna Ojo de Liebre** (Scammon Lagoon; p133), **Laguna San Ignacio** (p140) and **Bahía Magdalena** (p157). In addition to observing whales swimming, breaching and diving, you'll be able to see pelicans, gulls, cormorants and other seabirds skimming the ocean's surface. Sea lions and harbor seals dot the buoys and guano-covered rocks in the harbor and around the islands.

Both Gordo's and Sergio's operate four-hour weekend whale-watching trips for about US$30 per person.

GOLF

Two golf courses are within easy reach of Ensenada. About 10 miles (16km) to the south, at the end of a canyon, is the 18-hole **Baja Country Club** (Map p74; 177-5523; green fees including cart weekday/weekend US$45/55, club rental US$15; 7am-7pm). Golf packages through the Las Dunas Hotel Suites (p84) cost US$108/145 single/double occupancy, including lodging and unlimited golf.

The other golf course, on the ocean and generally considered nicer, is at **Bajamar** (p76), about 22 miles (35km) north of town.

Courses

Aside from La Paz, Ensenada is the best place in Baja to study Spanish. **Baja California Language College** (Colegio de Idiomas de Baja California; 174-5688, in the USA 619-758-9711, 877-444-2252; www.bajacal.com; Barcelona y Belgrado) offers Spanish immersion programs at its campus in the hills about 1 mile (1.6km) from the coast. One-week programs (30 hours) cost US$245/495 group/private; summer rates (June through August) for private instruction go up to US$529 per week. Twelve-hour weekend courses cost US$198 or, during summer, US$220.

International Spanish Institute (178-2101, in the USA 888-308-9048; www.sdro.com/spanishinstitute; Blvd Rodríguez 377) offers instruction at its campus southeast of downtown. Class size is limited to five students. The cost here is US$125 per week (30 hours) or US$80 for a weekend (eight hours), plus a one-time US$125 registration fee.

Both schools can help arrange hotel

ommodations or, even better, a stay with Mexican family (US$25 a day, including ree meals). Weeklong classes start on Monday.

Festivals & Events

More than 70 sporting, tourist and cultural events take place in Ensenada each year; the ones listed below are only a sample. Dates are subject to change, so contact one of the tourist offices or event organizers for specifics.

Carnaval (Carnival or Mardi Gras) February. Ensenada's biggest truly Mexican celebration.

Bicycle Ride Rosarito-Ensenada April and September. For details, see www.rosaritoensenada.com.

Fiesta de los Viñedos en Flor (Flowering Vines Festival) Early to mid-May. One-day festival at the beginning of the vintners' season. Held at selected winery, usually in nearby Valle de Guadalupe. Very intimate and tickets go fast. For details and ticket information, email fiestasvendimia@hotmail.com.

Fiesta La Misión Late May. Two days of dancing, food and music at Misión San Miguel de la Frontera.

SCORE Baja 500 Early June. Off-highway race; for details see www.score-international.com.

Fiesta de la Vendimia (Wine Harvest Festival) Early August. Weeklong wine festival kicking off harvest season with cultural events in Valle de Guadalupe and Ensenada. It's a great party, and tickets always sell out. For details and ticket information, email fiestasvendimia@hotmail.com.

International Seafood Fair Mid-September. Seafood-cooking competition judged by chefs from San Diego; for details, call ☎ 174-0448.

SCORE Baja 1000 Mid-November. Classic off-highway race from Ensenada to Cabo San Lucas. For details, see www.score-international.com.

Sleeping

Most hotels line downtown Ensenada's Av López Mateos, the main tourist strip. The cheapest ones are on the west end of the strip and, to match the neighborhood, are seedier than those to the east. Anywhere on Av López Mateos, request a room away from the street if you hope to get some shuteye while those outside tear up the night. Reservations are advisable on weekends and in summer. Unless specified, rates listed below are for weekends and may fall midweek.

BUDGET
Hostels & Camping

Hostel Sauzal (☎ 174-6381; 344 Av L; dm US$15) One of the few hostels in Baja, Hostel Sauzal is

a friendly, alcohol-free place in the suburb of El Sauzal, about 6 miles (10km) north of Ensenada. The bunks are in four-person rooms with ocean views, and the price includes breakfast. To get there, take the local bus (US$0.60) called 'El Vigia' from the corner of Costero and Gastelum (near the Cotuco tourist office).

Campo Playa RV Park (Map p78; ☎ 176-2918; Blvd Las Dunas at Sanginés; camping per vehicle US$18, hookups US$20) At the southern end of downtown, Campo Playa has 90 small, grassy campsites with shade trees for pitching a tent or parking a camper or motor home. Fees include access to hot showers.

Joker Hotel & RV Park (☎ 176-7201, in the USA ☎ 800-256-5372; site/r US$17/45) On the Transpeninsular, south of downtown, the Joker offers shaded sites with full hookups and barbeque pits. Guests can use the pool at the castle-like hotel, which has comfortable and clean rooms.

Hotels

Hotel Ritz (Map p81; ☎ 174-0501; explotur@telnor.net; Calle 4a 381; s US$26-30, d US$26-36) When it comes to security, character and cleanliness, you can't beat Hotel Ritz. Recently remodeled, its rooms are spacious and carpeted and have TVs and telephones. Its only drawback is the lack of off-street parking.

Motel América (Map p78; ☎ 176-1333; Av López Mateos 1309; s/d US$25/30; P) Clean and secure Motel América has small, tidy rooms with TVs; some have kitchenettes.

Motel Caribe (Map p81; ☎ 178-3481; Av López Mateos 628; r US$25-35; P) Though it's likely the best bargain downtown, Motel Caribe can feel pretty seedy some nights. A florescent-lit hallway links the rooms, and industrial size garbage cans sit outside the doors. That said, it has off-street parking and clean rooms with cable TV.

Hotel Plaza Fiesta (Map p81; ☎ 178-2715; Av López Mateos 542; s/d US$22/32) The Plaza Fiesta is an architectural gem that has sadly been allowed to decay. Rooms are clean but thick with air freshener and the scent of nights past. It's fine for a couple nights' cheap sleep if you don't mind the hourly-rate customers.

MID-RANGE
Motel del Valle (Map p81; ☎ 178-2224; Av Riveroll 367; s/d $40/44; P) Those who can stretch their

wallets outside the budget category but still want to be frugal should try the modern, well-kept Motel del Valle. Its 21 carpeted rooms have cable TV, and the friendly management keeps a watchful eye over the premises, making sure the communal coffee pot is always full.

Motel Misión Baja (☎ 176-6551; Av Topacio 287; s/d/t US$40, with kitchenette US$45; P 🗷) A bit south of town, this one offers good-value rooms with satellite TV, telephones and air-con. Rooms with kitchenettes are pricier but lack air-con.

Hotel Cortez (Map p81; ☎ 178-2307, in the USA ☎ 800-303-2684; Av López Mateos 1089; r US$78 Sun-Thu, US$90 Fri & Sat; P 🗷 🗐) For those seeking character and comfort, this is the spot. Rooms spread out over three structures and come with air-con, heaters and color TVs. Free coffee, newspaper, bottled water and room service are available as well. This is a popular place and often booked solid on summer weekends, so make reservations.

Bahía Resort Hotel (Map p81; ☎ 178-2101/03, in the USA ☎ 888-308-9048; www.hotelbahia.com.mx; Av López Mateos 850-A; r US$59-125, ste US$115-170; P 🗷 🗐) Centrally located Bahía Resort boasts 64 clean, carpeted rooms with balconies, heaters and small refrigerators. The bar here serves up tasty margaritas, and the pool is a hit on hot days.

Days Inn Villa Fontana (Map p81; ☎ 178-3434, in the USA 800-422-5204; www.villafontana.com.mx; Av López Mateos 1050; r weekdays US$46-58, weekends US$65-76, ste US$115-134; P 🗷 🗐) This spotless, comfy hotel has a bar, coffee shop, swimming pool, Jacuzzi and parking. The cheaper rooms are an excellent value, and all have carpeting, air-con and cable TV.

Best Western Hotel El Cid (Map p81; ☎ 178-2401, in the USA 800-352-4305; www.hotelelcid.com.mx; Av López Mateos 993; r US$58-123, ste US$84-168; P 🗷 🗐) Service is tops at this handsome hotel, not to mention the swimming pool, a great restaurant and secure parking. Prices vary monthly and seasonally, and they rise on weekends; prices listed here are about the highest. The Jacuzzi suites are the most expensive. All around, it's excellent.

Hotel Villa Marina (Map p81; ☎ /fax 178-3321/51; Av López Mateos at Alvarado; r US$77; P 🗷 🗐) This is Ensenada's only high rise, so if you want a bird's eye view of the harbor and sea, this is the place. Name a service – bar, pool, room service, disco, laundry, shops – the

Villa Marina's got it. Prices are che... midweek.

Motel Casa del Sol (Map p81; ☎ 178-1570; López Mateos 1001; s/d US$53/58; P 🗷 🗐) Speci... touches here include a welcome cockta... and free HBO cable TV. Rooms are spotless and have air-con, heat and telephones, and a bar and restaurant are on the premises.

Las Dunas Hotel Suites (Map p78; ☎ 176-2771; Calle Caracoles 169; r US$66-77; P 🗷 🗐) South of the downtown area, the pleasant Las Dunas offers family suites with bedroom, living room with sofabed, dining area and full kitchen for US$77. The standard rooms are comfortable but don't have kitchens. There's also a pool, Jacuzzi and barbecue area. Golf packages can be arranged with the Baja Country Club (p82) and cost US$79 per person for one night and a day's golf.

TOP END

Hotel Santo Tomás (Map p81; ☎ 178-1503; Blvd Costero 609; r US$89; P 🗷) There's plenty of free parking, coffee and newspapers at the comfy Santo Tomás, as well as a small range of business services. It's a relaxing place but comparatively pricey for what's on offer.

San Nicolás Resort Hotel (Map p78; ☎ 176-1901; www.sannicolas.com.mx; Av López Mateos 1534; r US$76-98, ste US$146-179; P 🗷 🗐) This beauty is popular with groups and has a coffee shop, bar, nightclub and restaurant. There's a fabulous outdoor pool and an indoor pool for those cold days. Standard rooms with all mod cons, including coffeemaker, are an excellent value at this end of the spectrum.

Hotel Corona (Map p78; ☎ 176-0901; www.hotel-corona.com.mx; Blvd Costero 1442; r US$145, US$58 low season weekdays; P 🗷 🗐) Facing the harbor near the Riviera del Pacífico, the tile-roofed Hotel Corona has 93 rooms, all with balconies, TVs, heaters and air-con. Get your money's worth by soaking in the Jacuzzi and sauna and working out in the gym.

Punta Morro Resort (☎ 178-3507, in the USA ☎ 800-526-6676; www.punta-morro.com; Hwy Tijuana-Ensenada Km 106; r US$121-151, ste US$229-325; P 🗷 🗐) This is a stylish, quiet and relaxing oceanside resort about 1½ miles (2.4km) northwest of Ensenada. Beautifully appointed suites have kitchens and terraces with views of the waves. The restaurant is among the best in the area. Rates drop by about 20% from Sunday to Thursday.

...ng

...senada has long been known for its ...od, and dining here is one of the city's ...ighlights. Its eateries run the gamut from ...corner taco stands and family restaurants – where antojitos are prepared in big, open kitchens – to busy seafood restaurants, sophisticated Mediterranean hideaways and stylish trendsetters with creative menus.

SEAFOOD

Tacos El Fenix (Map p78; cnr Av Espinoza & Av Juárez; tacos US$0.75-1; 8am-8:30pm) Tacos this good at these prices are simply a steal. A local institution and always thronged by regulars, the taco stand is clean, fresh and friendly.

Mariscos Bahía (Map p81; ☎ 178-1015; Av Riveroll 109; mains US$6-11; 10am-10pm) This restaurant is another local favorite for seafood, and portions are generous, prices reasonable and service friendly. The sautéed garlic shrimp for US$10 is a great value, and there's a nice sidewalk terrace from which to observe the action.

El Palmar (Map p81; ☎ 178-8788; Av López Mateos 328; mains US$6-10; 7am-10pm) Canopied by a giant palapa, El Palmar is another casual place to enjoy the day's catch. There's live *banda* (raucous brass-band music with vocals) on Friday and Saturday to help you digest your food.

Punta Morro Restaurant (☎ 178-3507; Transpeninsular Km 106, Punta Morro Hotel; mains US$16-22) For a special treat, book a table at this cliffside restaurant at the resort of the same name, just northwest of Ensenada. You'll be seated above crashing waves that will compete for your attention with the impeccably prepared and tasty seafood and meat dishes.

Casamar (Map p81; ☎ 174-0417; Blvd Costero 987; mains US$13-20) Casamar specializes in dishes like lobster salad, Filet Manila (a broiled fish filet smothered in mango sauce), a variety of shrimp dishes, fried frog legs and octopus. It's pricey but delicious.

Plaza del Marisco (Map p81; Blvd Costero near Uribe; tacos US$0.70-1.50) Near the Fish Market, this cluster of seafood taco stands has more reliable quality than those adjacent to the market itself.

MEXICAN

Manzanilla (Map p81; ☎ 175-7073; Av Riveroll 122; mains US$10-15; 6pm-midnight Wed-Sun) With a wonderful staff, outstanding regional and Italian cuisine and an atmosphere you'll melt into, Manzanilla is simply tops. The rib-eye steaks – nothing less than orgasmic – come from a select ranch in Sonora, the state famous for its beef. The server will start you off with Baja-grown manzanilla olives and house-baked bread before explaining each of the dishes, from fresh local oysters to lamb shank and exquisitely prepared fish. Make sure to leave room for dessert.

Cenaduría El Parrian (Map p81; cnr Av Castillo & Calle 4a; mains US$2-4; noon-midnight Fri-Wed) If you want to eat well for cheap, blow off the gringo traps along Av López Mateos and join the locals at El Parrian. It's spotless, and the small menu of enchiladas, tacos, tamales and tostadas is outstanding. Try the *pozole* (a hearty pork and hominy soup) and polish it off with a hot mug of *champurrado* (a chocolate corn drink).

El Tlaquepaque (Map p78; Calzada Cortez 327; mains US$2-4; noon-midnight Tue-Sun) Offering similar fare to El Parrian, this is an excellent family-style eatery concerned more with cooking up good, wholesome food than making bank off cruise-ship casualties in town for the day.

Las Cazuelas (Map p78; ☎ 176-1044, Blvd Sanginés 6; US$8-12) Though it serves standard antojitos, Las Cazuelas has a chef whose repertoire is more creative than most. Choices may include stuffed squid, quail in orange sauce and abalone with lobster sauce, and prices are reasonable. It's also famous for its breakfast omelets.

Bronco's (Map p78; ☎ 176-4900; Av López Mateos 1525; mains US$8-14) Vaquero culture is alive in the decor as well as in the hearty and humongous fare coming from the steamy kitchen. Bronco's mesquite-grilled steaks are top quality, and it's open for breakfast, lunch and dinner.

El Charro (Map p81; ☎ 178-4045; Av López Mateos 454; chicken dishes US$6-8; 9am-11pm). This is *the* place for marinated Mexican-style chicken, grilled or roasted over an open flame. Freshly made tortillas, salsa and other condiments accompany all orders.

La Gondola (Map p81; ☎ 174-0316; Av Ruiz 254; mains US$3-5; 8am-8pm Mon-Sat) This place is great for inexpensive, down-home cooking. Three-course *comida corrida* (set meal) costs US$3.25. Definitely qualifies as 'cute.'

Las Cazuelitas (Map p81; Costero 609-12; mains US$4-8; 🕙 7am-10pm Mon-Sat, 7am-3pm Sun) Mix diner with Mexican restaurant and you get Las Cazuelitas. Tie-clad waiters serve tasty, basic Mexican food to a mostly middle-class Mexican clientele. Great for breakfast.

Mesón de Don Fernando (Map p81; ☎ 174-0155; Av López Mateos 627; mains US$6-12) This tourist-oriented restaurant has adequate, if slightly pricey, fare. The best reason to come is for the excellent margaritas.

El Corralito (Map p81; ☎ 178-2370; Av López Mateos 627; mains US$4-7; 🕙 24hrs) This place serves OK antojitos but really shines on weekends, when the nighttime crowd arrives for refueling sessions between bar visits.

INTERNATIONAL

The Santo Tomás winery complex (p80), on Av Miramar between Calles 6a and 7a, features two outstanding dining establishments. **La Esquina de Bodegas** (Map p81; ☎ 178-7557; mains US$8-12, 7-course meal US$45; 🕙 lunch & dinner Mon-Sat) is worth a look for its decor alone. It metamorphosed from a former brandy distillery, integrating the ancient drums, vats and pipes into a hip industrial environment. En route to the dining area, you'll pass a wine boutique and an art gallery. The menu is Mediterranean with Mexican inflections.

The more formal of the two, **La Embotelladora Vieja** (Map p81; ☎ 174-0807; Miramar 666; appetizers US$5-10, mains US$16-18; 🕙 noon-10pm Mon-Sat) is set in a dimly lit wine cellar with giant, old French barrels looming over an elegant dining room. A full meal will run about US$35. The fare is 'Mexi-terranean.'

El Rey Sol (Map p81; ☎ 178-2351; Av López Mateos 1000; mains US$16-20) Venerable El Rey Sol is an elegant but relaxed French-Mexican restaurant, where full dinners start around US$35. Drinks are excellent. Leave room for the killer pastries.

Restaurante Pekín (Map p81; ☎ 178-1158; Av Ruiz 98; mains US$3.50-6) Local families flock to this established Chinese favorite, where huge plates cost as little as US$3.50.

CAFÉS

La Casa Antigua (Map p81; Av Obregón 110; 🕙 8am-11pm) Occupying one of Ensenada's oldest little houses, this friendly café serves great coffee, croissants, bagels (bagels!), sandwiches and homemade cakes and cookies.

Pueblo Café Deli (Map p81; Av Ruiz 96; 🕙 8am-night) Pasta, salads and sandwiches are ser in addition to delicious coffee drinks.

Café Café (Map p81; Av López Mateos 496; 🕙 9an-5pm) Artsy café where most of the owner's paintings are for sale.

Cafe Kaffa (Map p81; Av López Mateos near Av Blancarte; 🕙 6:30am-10pm) Good espresso drinks and decent snacks.

Cafe Tomás (Map p81; Av López Mateos at Ryerson; 🕙 7am-midnight) Delicious espresso drinks, but pastries are sometimes stale.

GROCERIES

Supermarkets in the downtown area include **Gigante** (Map p81; Gastelum at Calle 2a; 🕙 7am-11pm) and **Calimax** (Map p81; Gastelum at Calle 3a; 🕙 7am-11pm).

Entertainment

BARS

Potent, tasty and inexpensive beer, margaritas and other liquors are prime attractions for gringos, especially those under the mainland California drinking age of 21. On weekends, most bars and cantinas along Av Ruiz – which might more accurately be called 'Av Ruido' (Avenue Noise) – are packed from midday to early morning.

Tourists pack the bars along Av López Mateos on weekends, and locals fill them midweek.

HUSSONG'S CANTINA

Spit-and-sawdust **Hussong's Cantina** (Map p81; ☎ 178-3210; Av Ruiz 113; 🕙 10am-1am) is probably the best-known – and some say oldest – watering hole in the Californias. After arriving from Germany in the late 19th century, the Hussong family used their knowledge of traditional German brewing to establish one of Ensenada's first cantinas in 1892. Initially a stagecoach stop frequented by miners and ranchers, it later hosted Hollywood glam queen Marilyn Monroe, rough rider Steve McQueen and a host of other celebs. These days it's the 'mecca of margaritas and mariachis' for a motley crowd of locals (especially midweek), tattooed bikers, college students, honeymooning cruise-ship couples and retirees. Tables – and even spots at the bar – are at a premium after mid-afternoon.

SEARCH OF THE BEST MARGARITA

Hordes of gringos descend on Ensenada in search of the perfect margarita, and many become derailed as a result – the victims of their successful 'research.' Decide for yourself, but these places are arguably the top three on the 'margie' list.

Margaritas at **Hussong's Cantina** look small and innocent but pack a mean and sneaky punch. They're also a good value at US$2.50. At **Mesón de Don Fernando** you'll need both hands to hoist the 'bird-bath' glasses – ask for it 'on the rocks' and expect to fork over about US$5. Another convincing contender is dimly lit **Bar Bahía**, inside the Bahía Resort Hotel (p84), whose heady concoctions keep the karaoke crowd howling like coyotes in heat.

Please note: Lonely Planet accepts no responsibility for the behavior of those who wake up with racy tattoos or lost articles of intimate apparel.

Papas & Beer (Map p81; ☎ 174-0145; Av Ruiz 102; ☺ 10am-3am) Caters mostly to rowdy college students, and a small army of bouncers keeps things under control. Roaring music drowns out conversations, but the margaritas are tasty.

Mango Mango (Map p81; cnr Av Ruiz & Av López Mateos) Mellower than Papas & Beer.

VIP (Map p81; Av López Mateos at Gastelum) Live rock on weekends; popular with locals and tourists alike.

La Carreta (Map p81; Calle 2a near Gastelum; ☺ Wed-Sun) To brave the local *norteño* (country style) music scene, pop into the ranchoesque La Carreta, complete with wagon wheels out front and dancing inside. Thursday is ladies-only night.

Bar Andaluz (Map p78; ☎ 177-1730; ☺ 10am-5pm Tue-Sun) For a change in ambience, visit the cultured Bar Andaluz inside the Riviera del Pacífico (p80), where having a drink is an exercise in nostalgia. You can almost visualize Lana Turner sipping a martini at the polished walnut bar.

CLUBS

Discotheque Langostín (Map p81; ☎ 174-0318; Av Riveroll 109; cover US$3) Above the Mariscos Bahía restaurant, Langostín is where low-key locals take to the dance floor to disco, banda and rock, depending on the day.

Octopus (Map p81; Av Riveroll at Calle 2a; cover women/men US$10/15) Trendy Octopus caters to a youngish (18 to 25) crowd.

La Uh! (Map p81; cnr Alvarado & Cárdenas; ☺ Fri-Sun) Currently the hottest weekend disco. At 10:30pm on Fridays it hosts a women-only show with bare male dancers on stage.

La Capilla (Map p81; ☎ 178-2401; Av López Mateos 993) Smallish, popular club inside the El Cid Motor Hotel.

Shopping

Many items sold in Tijuana stores are available here at slightly lower prices, but the selection is smaller. Liquors and beers from all over Mexico are also available at discount prices. Wine prices are fairly reasonable due to the nearby wineries in the Guadalupe and Santo Tomás Valleys. Wine bought at the Santo Tomás tasting room (p81) is about 15% cheaper than in the stores.

Stores along Av López Mateos are tourist-oriented but fairly classy. Most of the stores sell crafts from throughout Mexico, including woven blankets, leather goods, wood carvings, wrought-iron candlesticks and margarita glasses. **Los Castillo** (Map p81; Av López Mateos 815) is a reputable store for silver jewelry.

Galería de Pérez Meillon (Map p81; ☎ 174-0394; Blvd Costero 1094, Local 39), in the Centro Artesanal, sells first-rate indigenous pottery and other crafts from Baja California's Paipai, Kumiai and Cucupah peoples, as well as the famous Mata Ortiz pottery from mainland Mexico.

Eduardo Echegaray, owner of **San Miguel Surf Shop** (Map p81; ☎ 178-1008; Av López Mateos 560), has been shaping surfboards (long and short) for some twenty years, and his prices are much lower than equivalent boards in the USA.

Getting There & Away

AIR

Aerolinea Aerocedros (☎ 177-3534) is a private company operating flights to Isla Cedros on Tuesdays and Fridays for about US$100 each way from the military **Aeropuerto El Ciprés** (Map p74), south of town. Contact Elvia or Rosa Irene for details.

BOAT

Carnival Cruises (in the USA ☎ 888-227-6482) and **Royal Caribbean** (☎ in the USA ☎ 800-327-6700) both offer three- and four-night luxury cruises to Ensenada from Long Beach, California. Seven- and eight-day cruises continue to mainland Mexican ports. See the Transportation chapter (p236) for more information.

BUS

Ensenada's main **bus terminal** (Central de Autobuses; Map p78; Av Riveroll 1075 at Calle 11a) is 10 blocks north of Av López Mateos.

ABC (☎ 178-6680) is the main peninsular carrier, with numerous buses from Ensenada to Playas de Rosarito and Tijuana as well as points south. **Estrella Blanca** (☎ 178-6770) operates from the same counter at the bus terminal, with buses to mainland Mexican destinations like Mazatlán and Guadalajara.

From its terminal, two blocks south of the main bus terminal, **Autotransportes Aragón** (Map p78; ☎ 177-0909; Av Riveroll 861) serves Tijuana and San Quintín regularly between 6am and 7pm. Note that Tijuana-bound buses drop Rosarito passengers at the toll-gate rather than in Rosarito proper.

There are at least two departures daily to the following destinations and hourly departures to Tijuana:

Destination	Fare	Duration
La Paz	US$68	23 hrs
Loreto	US$52	16 hrs
Mexicali	US$19	4 hrs
Playas de Rosarito	US$8	1½ hrs
San Felipe	US$17	4 hrs
San Quintín	US$10	4 hrs
Tecate	US$7-8	2 hrs
Tijuana	US$8.50	1½ hrs

Getting Around

Local bus services are provided by La Vigia's blue-and-white minibuses and by **Transportes Brisas** (Map p81; ☎ 178-3888; Calle 4a 771 near Av Miramar), whose buses are yellow. Both travel within Ensenada and as far as outlying farming communities like El Sauzal or Francisco Zarco (Guadalupe) to the north or Maneadero to the south. There are several stops along Blvd Costero, Av Reforma and Blvd Azueta. The destination

usually appears on the windshield. Th is about US$0.50.

Renting a car is cheaper in Tijuana or Diego, even with additional daily charg for Mexican insurance, than it is in Ens nada. The only agency in town is **Hertz** (Map p81; ☎ 178-2982; Av Riveroll 143-13).

Taxis are available 24 hours a day at several corner stands along Av López Mateos – one major stand is at the corner of Av Miramar (Map p81).

AROUND ENSENADA
☎ 646

The following sites appear on the Tijuana to Ensenada map, p74.

Estero Beach

So sprawling that it actually issues its own map, **Estero Beach Resort** (☎ 176-6235; www.hotelesterobeach.com) is a luxurious gringo enclave immediately south of Playa El Faro (see below). Besides a luxury hotel and RV park, it includes tennis courts, a convention center and a restaurant. Road signs are in English only.

RV sites cost US$35 with full hookups for two people; extra persons are US$5. Rates drop US$10 during midweek from October to March. Hot showers and clean toilets are available, and horses can be hired nearby. Hotel doubles range from US$95 to US$400 and are slightly cheaper midweek October through March.

Islas de Todos Santos

Professional surfers frequent these two islands, about 12 miles (19km) west of Ensenada, especially when winter storms bring towering surf to the smaller Isla Norte. In early 1997 the islands hosted the Torneo Mundial de Surfing, the world surfing championships. A Japanese-sponsored mari-culture project on the larger Isla Sur is cultivating abalone for the Asian market. While there's no scheduled transportation to the islands, it's possible to hire a launch. To do so, ask around the Ensenada sportfishing piers. You can dive here as well.

Playa El Faro

Playa El Faro, accessible from Km 14.8 on the Transpeninsular (follow signs for the Estero Beach Resort), has the small **El Faro**

ach Motel & Trailer Park (☎ 177-4620; site US$7,
/ US$12-15, s/d US$50/60). The motel has eight
clean, simple rooms with bath and shower,
but proximity to the beach is its only attraction. Camping is available on a sandy
lot next to the beach, with electricity, water,
showers and toilets.

Nearby are the **Corona Beach Trailer Park** (no
☎ ; site US$10), where sites have water and
electrical hookups, and the more elaborate
Rancho Mona Lisa Trailer Park (no ☎ ; site w/hookups
US$15-18). Look for the signs.

Punta Banda & La Bufadora

La Bufadora is a tidal blowhole that spews
water and foam through a V-shaped notch
in the headlands of the Punta Banda peninsula. Hope to arrive on a day when the
sea is rolling heavy and you'll see one hell
of a spectacle. It's the area's most popular
weekend destination for tourists and locals
alike, and has endless souvenir stands and
food stalls.

BCN-23, the paved road to La Bufadora
and Punta Banda, leaves the Transpeninsular at Maneadero and passes several campgrounds and roadside stands that sell chile
peppers and olives. Beyond the Baja Beach
Resort are a few isolated campsites and, past
a gaggle of taco stands and dozens of souvenir stalls at the end of the road, La Bufadora
itself roars – or sighs tiredly.

DIVING

Probably the best reason to visit the area,
Dale's La Bufadora Dive Center (☎ 154-2092; www.
labufadora.com/dales/dales.html) offers underwater
excursions to view sea anemones, sea urchins, sponge colonies, nudibranchs and
dozens of fish species.

The Canadian operator has three boats
and charges US$25/35 per person, with
three/four people on the boat. Full sets of
dive and snorkeling gear cost US$30/18,
respectively. Tanks are US$5. Dale also
rents kayaks for US$20/30 single/double
for a half-day and US$30/40 for a full day.
Oceanside camping is possible too.

SLEEPING & EATING

You can camp at the clifftop **Rancho La Bufadora** (☎ 178-7172; site US$5), which has nice
views, outhouses and a few fire rings.
There's electricity, but it's best to bring in
your own water. Local *ejidos* (communally
owned land) rent slightly cheaper sites
above La Bufadora.

Punta Banda has two other main campgrounds. Both places have clean bathrooms
with hot showers and small grocery stores.
All are on the road to La Bufadora.

La Jolla Beach Camp (☎ 154-2005) has about
400 spaces without hookups for US$11 for
two people; extra people cost US$2.50 each.
Hot showers are available.

Next door **Villarino RV Park** (☎ 154-2045;
RV site without/with hookups US$20/25) is markedly
shadier, but many spaces are occupied with
permanent mobile-home residents.

Many stalls at La Bufadora serve fish
tacos, shrimp cocktails and *churros* (deep-
fried dough dipped in sugar and cinnamon).
There are also a few seafood restaurants
with ocean views. One long-time favorite is
Los Panchos (☺ 9am-sunset Fri-Wed); the octopus
in *ranchero* sauce is a popular dish, but the
'Siete Mares' (Seven Seas) soup – loaded
with shrimp, octopus, fish, crab claws and
other fresh seafood – is superb.

Near the entrance to Rancho La Bufadora
is **Los Gordos**, where photographs, memora-
bilia and graffiti exude an Old Baja ambience. Specialties include a Mexican combo,
deep-fried calamari, lobster and shrimp in
garlic butter. The bar is a favorite watering
hole for US expatriates.

Celia's has a good, inexpensive Sunday
breakfast buffet, while **El Dorado**, with its
palapa-covered patio, is the place for a romantic seafood dinner.

GETTING THERE & AWAY

Taxicab rides to La Bufadora from downtown Ensenada cost about US$12. **Trans-
portes Brisas** in Ensenada offers regular
bus service as far as Maneadero; from the
turnoff to La Bufadora, you can probably
hitch a ride.

Maneadero

The farm settlement of Maneadero, 10 miles
(16km) south of Ensenada and just beyond
the turnoff to Punta Banda, contains little
of note. You are required to have a tourist
card for travel south of here. A military
guns-and drugs checkpoint south of town
checks for these; if yours are not in order,
you'll have to return to Ensenada.

VALLE DE GUADALUPE

Valle de Guadalupe (Map p74) is Baja California's premier wine-producing region, as rich in history as it is in wine. Located at Km 73, about 20 miles (32km) northeast of Ensenada, the town of **Francisco Zarco** is the valley's main population cente right smack in the heart of wine country México Hwy 3 (the Ensenada-Tecate road) makes for a lovely drive through the valley. Alternatively, buses from Ensenada to Tecate will drop passengers at the turnoff

WINE COUNTRY

Mexican wine? Who'd a thought? But it's true. Less than an hour's drive from Ensenada, the Valle de Guadalupe is Mexico's premier wine-producing region, with over 15 wineries turning out premium wines in some of the most peaceful countryside in northern Baja. As a wine-tasting destination, Valle de Guadalupe is still young and its wineries are small, meaning you'll often meet the winemakers themselves, and you'll encounter an intimacy in the tasting room that will delight anyone who's used to the Disneyland experience of Napa Valley.

Wine production in Baja California began with the Spanish missionaries, who planted grapes to supply themselves with wine for religious services. Jesuit missionary Father Juan Ugarte is credited with planting Baja's first vineyard at **Mision San Francisco Javier** (p154) around 1701.

Dominican missionaries planted Valle de Guadalupe's first vineyard when they founded a mission near the village of Guadalupe in 1834. After the church was destroyed in 1840 during an indigenous revolt, wine production stagnated until a group of Russian religious refugees, the Molokans, immigrated to the valley in the early 1900s.

The peninsula's first *commercial* winery – Bodegas de Santo Tomás – was founded in 1888 in the Valle de Santo Tomás, south of Ensenada. Still in operation, its **tasting room** (p81) is in downtown Ensenada. In the 1930s the winery expanded its operations by planting grapes in Valle de Guadalupe.

In 1960 the Cetto family (originally from Italy) began cultivating grapes here, and in 1972 Pedro Domecq built the valley's first commercial winery. Vinos LA Cetto and Vides de Guadalupe Domecq are now two of Valle de Gualdpe's largest wineries.

The tourist offices in Ensenada and Tecate offer a free excellent *Wine Country* brochure, which lists every winery in the valley. Be sure to pick one up for its excellent map.

Pack a lunch for a picnic at one of the wineries or stop at one of the taco stands around Francisco Zarco. Unless specified, the wineries listed here are open for drop-in tasting.

LA Cetto (☎ 646-155-2264; www.lacetto.com; México Hwy 3, Km 73.5, Francisco Zarco; ☿ 10am-5pm) One of the valley's premier wineries, LA Cetto is known for its Nebiollo (a red from Italy's Piedmont region), cabernet sauvignon and its reserve chardonnay. It also produces petite sirah, zinfandel, chenin blanc and sauvignon blanc.

Vides de Guadalupe Domecq (☎ 155-2249/54; México Hwy 3, Km 73.5, Francisco Zarco; tasting US$1; ☿ 10am-4pm Mon-Fri, 10am-3pm Sat) This huge winery produces merlot, chardonnay and blanc de blanc. cabernet sauvignon, tempranillo and barbera are used in blends.

Monte Xanic (☎ 646-174-6769; www.montexanic.com; Francisco Zarco; ☿ 9am-4pm Mon-Fri; Reservations required) Modern winery producing Monte Xanic and Calixa label wines. Worth a visit if you're real enthusiast.

Vinos Bibayoff (Bodegas Valle de Guadalupe; ☎ 646-176-1008; bibayoff@telnor.net; San Antonio de las Minas) Producing only about 1500 cases per year, this small winery is the only one in Valle de Guadalupe whose owners are descendents of the Russian Molokan immigrants. It's well worth a visit. To get there, turn north onto a dirt road from México Hwy 3 at Km 92. Otherwise take the road from Francisco Zarco.

Chateau Camou (☎ 646-177-2221; www.chateau-camou.com.mx; Francisco Zarco; tour US$5-40/person; ☿ 8am-3pm Mon-Sat, 9am-2pm Sun) This winery offers several varietals and excellent tours. Call in advance if you want the US$40 'Magnum tour,' which includes a sumptuous lunch.

Viña de Liceaga (☎ 646-155-3091, 646-684-0126; www.vinosliceaga.com; México Hwy 3, Km 93; ☿ 11am-5pm Sat & Sun, by appointment Mon-Fri) This small, family-operated winery in San Antonio de las Minas produces merlot, cabernet franc and chenin blanc, and several blends.

to the town on México 3, from where it's a short walk.

Settled by Russian immigrants in the early 20th century, the village contains ruins of the Dominican **Misión Nuestra Señora de Guadalupe**, the last mission built in the Californias, founded in 1834 and destroyed by Indians only six years later. Set in a fertile zone for grain farming and grazing, it was a powerful and important mission during its brief existence. There are Indian pictographs on a huge granite boulder known as Ojá Cuñúrr, where the canyon of the Río Guadalupe narrows, but almost nothing remains of the mission.

The Russians, pacifist refugees from the area of present-day Turkey, first arrived in Los Angeles but found the lands not to their liking and chose to head south across the border in 1905. They first lived in Indian dwellings known by their Kumiai name of *wa* but soon built adobe houses that the Kumiai later emulated; the present museum (see below) is a Russian adobe. Across from the site of the former Dominican mission are the arches of the former Russian school, demolished some years ago. The nearby Russian cemetery still contains headstones with Cyrillic inscriptions.

Sights

Only a handful of families of demonstrably Russian descent remain in the area. In Francisco Zarco the private **Museo Comunitario de Guadalupe** (☎ 155-2030; donations requested; ✆ 10am-7pm Tue-Sun) keeps alive their heritage with photographs and artifacts like samovars, a Russian bible and traditional clothing. In addition to the interior exhibits, antique farming machinery and a Kumiai tribal dwelling (wa) decorate the museum grounds.

Part of the house is still inhabited by the family of Franziska San Marín, herself married to a descendant of the early Russian settlers (ask to see the authentic sauna in the back of the house). The owners bake and sell fresh Russian-style breads and cakes on weekends. To reach the museum from Ensenada, turn left off México 3 (about 38km from Ensenada) toward Francisco Zarco; the museum will be on your left as you roll through town.

Opposite the Museo Comunario is the **Museo Histórico Comunitario** (☎ 178-2531; donations requested; ✆ 10am-5pm Tue-Sun), which tells the story of the local mission and also has an exhibit about the Russian settlers.

Festivals & Events

Two wine festivals – the **Fiesta de los Viñedos en Flor** (Flowering Vines Festival) in early to mid-May and the **Fiesta de la Vendimia** (Wine Harvest Festival) in August – are well worth attending. Both are held at different wineries each year, and you should purchase advance tickets because both sell out quickly. For more information, see p83.

PARQUE NACIONAL CONSTITUCIÓN DE 1857

☎ 646

In the Sierra de Juárez southeast of Ensenada and north of the highway to San Felipe, a striking plateau of ponderosa pines comprises most of Parque Nacional Constitución de 1857 (US$5/vehicle), a 12,350-acre (5000-hectare) park whose shallow and marshy but pleasant and solitary **Laguna Hanson** abounds with migratory birds – ducks, coots, grebes and many others – in fall. Hunting is prohibited, so bird-watchers will find the park an exceptional destination at this time of the year. Check the dying pines for woodpeckers. Anglers may hook catfish, bluegills and large-mouth bass.

The low granite outcrops north and west of Laguna Hanson offer stupendous views but require difficult ascents through dense brush and over and beneath massive rockfalls – watch for ticks and rattlesnakes. The easiest view route is to take the abandoned road northwest from near the ruined cabins and pit toilets to the first dry watercourse, and then follow it toward the peaks. Expect dead ends that are too steep to climb, but follow tunnels through the rockfalls before emerging on a saddle below the two main peaks. This short climb, which should take only about an hour, is nevertheless very tiring.

Technical climbers will find challenging **rock climbing** routes up the open granite despite the limited relief – most pitches do not exceed 200 to 300 feet (60 to 90m). The terrain resembles mainland California's Joshua Tree National Park.

On the eastern side of the park at the base of the Sierra de Juárez are several beautiful desert palm canyons, the most accessible of which is Cañón de Guadalupe – but unfortunately only from the eastern side. For more information, see Around Mexicali.

Near Laguna Hanson you'll find a visitor center/ranger station where you can pick up information about hiking, climbing, flora and fauna, and pay the admission fee.

Information

Primitive but well-maintained **campsites** with pit toilets, barbecue pits and picnic tables are on the western shore of the lake at an approximate elevation of 4000 feet (1200m).

Because livestock is plentiful, the water is suitable only for dousing your campfire, so bring your own to drink. Fuel wood is scarce and better left unburnt, but dried cow patties are everywhere. Expect hordes of mosquitoes in late spring.

Southeast of Ensenada at Km 39 on México 3 toward San Felipe, a paved lateral reaches the village of **Ojos Negros**, whose decent **Restaurant Oasis** has an English-speaking owner who's happy to provide tourist information.

Getting There & Away

As there is no public transportation to the park, visitors must drive. From Ojos Negros, a 27-mile (43km) dirt road, passable for almost any passenger car despite its frequent washboard surface, climbs eastward onto the plateau and into the park. Another

access road lies about 10 miles (16km) east of Ojos Negros at Km 55.

Approaching from the north, the best route into the park is from the El Cóndor turnoff, west of La Rumorosa at about Km 83 on México 2 (the Tijuana-Tecate-Mexicali highway). Drivers with low-clearance vehicles will undoubtedly prefer the Ojos Negros road, although the road from Km 55 should be passable for most, especially after the first 4.4 miles (7km); the total distance is about 20 miles (32km).

EL ALAMO & VALLE DE TRINIDAD
☎ 646

From Ojos Negros, México 3 continues south to a marked junction with a dirt road leading west to the once-bustling mining town of El Alamo. After the discovery of gold here in 1888, El Alamo boomed with thousands of gold-seekers, but the ore gave out quickly and now it's almost deserted.

From the junction, the highway leads south into the verdant Valle de Trinidad before crossing the San Matías pass toward San Felipe. Just south of the junction with El Alamo, but 5 miles (8km) east of the highway, is the site of the former **Misión Santa Catarina de los Paipais**, one of two Dominican missions in the peninsula's northern interior, now known officially as **Santa Catarina**. Parts of the adobe walls are the only remaining ruins, on a hill above the present village cemetery. An easily identifiable circular

---

DETOUR: PUERTO SAN ISIDRO

Take the paved lateral from the Transpeninsular at about Km 78 to the beachside **Ejido Eréndira**, a small farming community, reached after about 10½ miles (17km). Stock up on basic supplies before trippin' down to the isolated fishing cove of Puerto San Isidro, another mile or so north along the coast via a rough dirt road. (Many backpackers hitch a ride in from the Transpeninsular, where buses from Tijuana or other points north make dropoffs.)

For some serious relaxation, head out to **Castro's Fishing Place** (☎ 646-176-2897; cabins US$25-30, camping free), where Fernando Castro Ríos rents rustic but fully equipped ocean-facing *cabañas*. (Toilets are outside.) Ask around for Jorge Arballo, who leads all-day (7am to 2pm) fishing trips in *superpangas* (large fiberglass skiffs) for US$35 per person.

About a mile or so past Castro's Fishing Place is **Coyote Cal's** (☎ 646-154-4080, in the USA 888-670-2252; www.coyotecals.com; tent/RV/dm/r US$10/10/15/30; 🖭), the area's only hostel. Run by a young team of energetic surfers, this is a great and remote place to hang for a few days. The Crow's Nest – for an intimate twosome on the top floor – offers spectacular 360-degree views. Dorms sleep four to 10 people and face the ocean. Amenities include a well-equipped communal kitchen, guest laundry, swimming pool and ping-pong tables. A prime sandy beach is about a quarter-mile north, and there's good surfing everywhere. Prices include breakfast, and free beans and rice at dinner time.

mound marks the remains of the mission watchtower.

The village is a sprawling hodgepodge of wrecked cars and a few adobe houses, trailers and abandoned greenhouses (remnants of a federal government scheme to raise jojoba). The Catholic and Pentecostal churches, both emphasizing the term *indígena* (indigenous) in their formal titles, compete for the souls of the remaining Paipai, who still speak their native language as well as Spanish and continue to collect piñon nuts in the fall.

EJIDO URUAPÁN
☎ 646

Approximately 10 miles (16km) south of Maneadero, near Km 41, Ejido Uruapán is known for sea urchins, strawberries and quail – which draw hunters from north of the border in the winter months. The sea urchin processing plant, established with Japanese aid, exports countless *erizos* (sea urchins) across the Pacific Ocean. The Japanese have also built greenhouses for cultivating strawberries, mostly for export north to California.

The well-shaded and well-maintained **campground** right at the turnoff from the Transpeninsular has brick barbecue pits and is a fine site for primitive camping and picnicking. A sign mentions a fee of US$5, but often no one is there to collect it. From inside the village more signs direct you to a hot spring about 2km via a dirt road. This is primarily where the townspeople come to bathe and do their laundry, but it's open to visitors as well.

SANTO TOMÁS
☎ 646 / pop 400

The Dominican mission village of Santo Tomás at Km 51, some 6½ miles (10.5km) south of Ejido Uruapán, takes its name from the surrounding Valle de Santo Tomás, one of Baja's key wine-producing areas. Founded in 1791 as the last link in the chain connecting Alta and Baja California, Misión Santo Tomás de Aquino soon moved upstream from its original site to escape infestations of gnats and mosquitoes, which made it both uncomfortable and unhealthy. Winter rains bring forth hordes of harmless toads that stage Darwinian sprint trials across the Transpeninsular in

reckless defiance of the thundering 18-wheelers passing north and south.

The wine industry is a legacy of the Dominicans, who planted thousands of vines and other crops, most notably olives. At the mission's peak, in 1824, neophytes may have exceeded 400. Abandoned in 1849, it was the last Dominican mission to maintain a priest. A few crumbling ruins of the original mission remain on an alluvial fan where the river canyon narrows west of the Transpeninsular. But only a few faint foundations denote the upstream site, just south of El Palomar's campground/RV park behind the new church.

For modern visitors Santo Tomás' key institution is venerable **El Palomar**, a cluster of businesses including a Pemex station, a general store, a restaurant, a motel, an RV park/campground and a picnic area.

El Palomar's **campground and RV park** (☎ 153-8002; tent/RV US$10/16) sits among a grove of olive trees and bamboo; the olives are harvested, bottled and sold in the general store. In summer the park's two tennis courts, volleyball court, children's playground, swimming pool, **restaurant**, waterslides and 100 barbecue pits attract up to 2000 visitors daily. There are 30 RV spaces with full hookups.

On the slope behind the restaurant, **Motel El Palomar** (☎ 153-8002; s/d US$35-45) offers clean, simple rooms with hot water and heating.

SAN VICENTE
☎ 646 / pop 3500

The agricultural community of San Vicente bustles on its namesake arroyo at Km 90, about 7 miles (11km) south of the Ejido Eréndira junction. **Misión San Vicente Ferrer**, one of the few Dominican missions that never moved from its original site, was founded here in 1780. Substantial foundations and some walls of the fort and mission are in a state of arrested decay in a gated park northwest of the town. San Vicente boasts a small **Museo Comunitario** (admission free; ☼ 9am-3pm Mon-Sat) on the northern side of the plaza.

To get to the ruins by car, follow the well-signed, graded dirt road west across from the *llantera* (tire repair shop), at about Km 88 just north of town. Look for the northbound sign that says 'Santo Tomás 37, Ensenada 80.' The ruins are about 1 mile (1.6km) away from the road. Buses running between Tijuana and points south stop at the terminal in San Vicente.

At Km 90 on the eastern side of the Transpeninsular, **La Estrella del Sur** (☎ 165-6676; r US$25) has good, reasonably priced meals and four rooms with private baths and hot showers. Bicyclists should ask for special rates.

SAN TELMO
☎ 646

The village of San Telmo is 4 miles (6.5km) east of the Transpeninsular on the graded dirt road to Rancho Meling and Parque Nacional Sierra San Pedro Mártir.

San Telmo's most notable cultural feature is the very faint remains of a Dominican chapel, built between 1798 and 1800. What it's better known for, however, is **Rancho Meling** (Map p52; ☎ 177-5897; www.melingguestranch. com; s/d US$75/145, child US$45), a beloved Baja institution also known as Rancho San José. Some 27 miles (43km) east of San Telmo, Rancho Meling is a 10,000-acre (4000-hectare) cattle ranch established by Norwegian immigrant Salve Meling in the early 1900s. It was run by his daughter, Aida, as a guesthouse until she passed away in 1998.

Aida's children renovated the cozy ranch house and reopened with 12 rustic, spacious and clean rooms (more are still under renovation). All have private baths with hot showers and a fireplace or pot-bellied stove; rates include three hearty family-style meals. Horseback riding and pack trips into Parque Nacional Sierra San Pedro Mártir are available. Reservations are a must.

PARQUE NACIONAL SIERRA SAN PEDRO MÁRTIR
☎ 646

Baja California's most notable **national park** (US$7/vehicle) consists of 236 sq miles (614 sq km) of coniferous forests and granitic peaks reaching above 10,000 feet (3000m), plus deep canyons leading down into their steep eastern scarp. Major native tree types include several species of pines, plus incense cedar, Douglas fir and quaking aspen, while the most conspicuous fauna includes raccoon, fox, coyote and mule deer. The rare desert bighorn sheep inhabits some remote canyon areas.

Unlike Parque Nacional Constitución de 1857, this park has no major bodies of water. Westward-flowing streams like the Río San Rafael, Arroyo Los Pinos and Arroyo San Antonio support the endemic San Pedro Mártir rainbow trout, but wildfowl no longer breed here, as they did a century ago, because of a history of grazing and timber cutting.

Among the typical breeding land birds are the mountain quail, pinyon jay, mountain chickadee, pygmy nuthatch, western bluebird, Cassin's finch, pine siskin, red crossbill and dark-eyed junco.

The **ranger station** at the park entrance has maps and information.

Maps
The best map of the area is Centra Publications' Parque Nacional San Pedro Mártir, with an area map at a scale of 1:100,000 and details at a scale of 1:31,680.

Determined hikers and climbers should also obtain the latest edition of Walt Peterson's *The Baja Adventure Book,* which includes decent maps and describes several routes up Picacho del Diablo. The Mexican government topographic maps San Rafael H11B45 and Santa Cruz H11B55 may be useful too, see p229.

Climate
The Sierra San Pedro Mártir has a temperate climate similar to the mountains of southern mainland California; most precipitation falls in winter, when the snow depth at higher altitudes can be 3 feet (1m) or more, but snow is possible any time from October to May. In summer the area gets a lot of rainfall in the form of thunderstorms.

The average annual temperature is around 59°F (16°C), with highs around 68°F (22°C), but winter temperatures can drop well below freezing. At higher elevations, even in summer, changeable weather is a potential hazard. The best time to visit is in spring, when days are getting longer, temperatures are still moderate, the wildflowers are in bloom and there's plenty of water following the snow melt.

Sights & Activities
The Sierra San Pedro Mártir is an underappreciated area for hiking, camping and backpacking, in part because access is awkward and it's a little far for weekend trips

from mainland California. Still, most visitors are from the USA – usually families or small groups of college students. Anyone seeking the solitude that only total wilderness can offer will be rewarded, especially since off-road vehicles are not allowed in the park.

Within the park are many suitable car-camping areas and hiking trails, though trail maintenance is minimal. Hikers should carry a compass (or GPS) along with the usual cold- and wet-weather supplies, canteens and water purification tablets. Below about 6000 feet (1800m) or even a bit higher, beware of rattlesnakes. A detailed topographic map will be essential.

The **Observatorio Astronómico Nacional** (in Ensenada ☎ 646-174-4580 ext 302), Mexico's national observatory, features an 84-inch diameter telescope but may be visited only by prior arrangement, which can be difficult. Even if you don't get inside, you'll enjoy the stupendous views from up here, which extend all across the forest and over to the Pacific, the Sea of Cortez and the Mexican mainland.

To get to the observatory, follow the park access road to the end, then walk the final 1½ miles (2km).

The 10,154-foot (3046m) summit of **Picacho del Diablo**, also known as Cerro Providencia, draws climbers from throughout the Californias, but only a handful actually reach the summit because finding the route is so difficult.

Getting There & Away

There is no public transportation to Sierra San Pedro Mártir, and all access roads are dirt and in various conditions. Check road conditions locally before heading out.

TO/FROM SAN TELMO

From San Telmo de Abajo, south of Km 140 on the Transpeninsular, a graded dirt road climbs eastward through San Telmo de Arriba past Rancho Meling to the park entrance, about 50 miles (80km) from the highway. The road is passable for most passenger vehicles – and usually even small RVs – despite two major fords of the Río San Telmo. Spring runoff may cause problems for cars with low clearance, and drivers should probably avoid the road immediately after snowfall, when the warm sun can melt the snow very quickly. The

one-way trip from Ensenada can take as long as six to seven hours.

TO/FROM SAN FELIPE

The summit of Picacho del Diablo – and the network of trails at its foot – can also be accessed from the eastern edge of the park via a difficult climb along Cañón del Diablo. Access is through **Rancho Santa Clara**.

To get to the mouth of the canyon from San Felipe, take the sandy road northwest to Laguna Diablo, a dry salt lake, and Rancho Santa Clara. The road is reportedly safe and the surface mostly hard and dry, but ask for up-to-date information in San Felipe before attempting it.

Another route to Rancho Santa Clara is a good graded road that leaves México 3 (the Ensenada-San Felipe highway) just east of Km 164; rather than going down the middle of Laguna Diablo, the road keeps to high ground along its eastern shoreline. A roadside tire marks the turnoff to Rancho Santa Clara, which also is marked by a tire.

From Rancho Santa Clara, pick up the dirt road that leads west for about 5½ miles (9km) to Cañón Diablito. This is where you must park the car. The mouth of Cañón del Diablo is another 2 miles (3km) west.

Once in the canyon, you'll come upon a striking waterfall after about half a mile (800m). This is also the biggest obstacle on the trail, but cables should be there to help you across. At about the 8-mile (13km) point you reach **Campo Noche**, a good campsite before starting the ascent the next day.

MIKE'S SKY RANCHO

On the northwestern edge of Parque Nacional Sierra San Pedro Mártir, Mike's Sky Rancho is the beloved haunt of off-roaders, set in a small valley framed by the pine-covered foothills of the Sierra. The ranch offers worn but tidy motel-style rooms with kerosene stove and private bath, plain but hearty meals and a large swimming pool. Rooms cost around US$22 per person, breakfast and lunch US$7 each, dinner US$12 and full board US$50. Those seeking quiet and solitude should know that it's a popular destination with the off-road crowd. Motorcycles by the pool are a common sight, and the lounge is decorated with racing posters.

The turnoff from México 3 to the ranch is at Km 138, 37 miles (60km) west of the junction with Highway 5. It's 22 miles (35km) from the turnoff to the ranch. The graded dirt road makes it accessible to most passenger vehicles, though it's steep and tricky for ordinary passenger cars at a few points.

For information and reservations, write to Mike's Sky Rancho, PO Box 5376, San Ysidro, CA 92073.

CAMALÚ

Back on the Transpeninsular, at about Km 157, this little town has a Pemex station, a few stores and cafés, and a smattering of other infrastructure. About 4 miles (7km) before town, at Km 150, is the turnoff to **Punta San Jacinto**, reached after a (usually) easy 6-mile (11km) dirt road. This is a great **surf** beach where Baja Surf Adventures (p42) runs surf resorts. Primitive oceanfront campsites cost US$5. Nearby is the wreck of a stranded freighter.

COLONIA VICENTE GUERRERO

☎ 616

This booming agricultural center straddles the Transpeninsular, the town's main street. It has a single traffic light, a **bank** and a **casa de cambio**. Otherwise, there's little of interest to visitors except its shady plaza, Parque General Vicente Guerrero, a small community **museum** and nearby Misión Santo Domingo (see below). However, the long sandy beaches west of town are well worth a visit; in the summer months, surf fishing is excellent.

The bus terminal is in the center of town on the Pacific side of the highway.

Misión Santo Domingo

Founded in 1775 by Manuel García and Miguel Hidalgo at the mouth of the canyon of the Río Santo Domingo, Misión Santo Domingo de la Frontera was the second of nine Dominican missions in Baja California. The ruins are the best preserved of any Dominican frontier mission: many of the walls are still standing!

Every year in the first week of August at the site of the ruins, the Fiesta de Santo Domingo features horseracing, rodeos, dancing and food stalls. A short distance west is a pleasant private park with a swimming pool and café – a good spot for a picnic, accessible for a very modest admission.

To reach the site, go east on the dirt road on the northern side of the Río Santo Domingo, at the northern entrance to town. Note the massive landmark **Peñón Colorado**, the reddish bluff that rises out of the sediments at the entrance to the canyon.

Sleeping & Eating

Colonia Vicente Guerrero has only two motels, but at the southwestern end of town are two RV parks/campgrounds. The turnoff for both campgrounds is near Km 173 on the western side of the highway, but their signs are visible only for southbound travelers. If you're traveling north, look for the Fagro Shipping building, which leads to Don Pepe's; the turnoff to Don Diego's is a few hundred feet (100m) before here.

Mesón de Don Pepe RV Park & Restaurant (☎ 166-2216; tent/RV US$6/10), which suffers from the noise of trucks on the highway, offers RV sites with full hookups. The tent sites are on a pleasant grassy area. Hot showers are available, and the restaurant serves reasonably priced seafood and typical Mexican meals.

Spacious sites with full hookups can be had at **Posada Don Diego RV Park** (☎ 166-2181; tent/RV US$8/11). Only a few of its sites are in the shade, but it has hot showers, a laundry room, a **restaurant** (mains US$4-8) and a bar. The restaurant has a good reputation. This campground is a little closer to the beach, but the often-muddy road beyond the RV park can be difficult for ordinary passenger vehicles. Hiking to the beach, which offers great clamming (respect size limits), takes 30 to 45 minutes.

Motel Sánchez (☎ 166-2963; s/d US$18/24), in the town center by the traffic light, has large, fairly clean rooms and a friendly staff.

Las Maderas is a steakhouse at the northern end of town, easily spotted for its Wild West decor. There are numerous **taco stands** and a few small **stores** selling fruit, vegetables, bread and other staples.

SAN QUINTÍN

☎ 616 / pop 60,000

San Quintín is the focus of an increasingly important agricultural region on the Llano de San Quintín (San Quintín Plain), but attractive Pacific beaches at the foot of a group of cinder cones also make it an ideal area for camping, clamming, beachcombing and

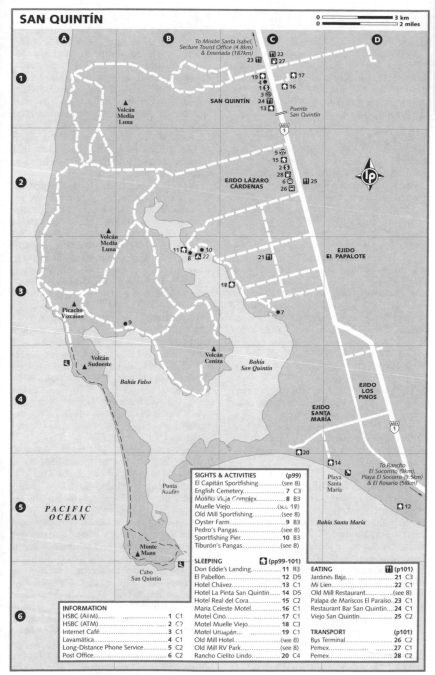

SAN QUINTÍN

0 — 3 km
0 — 2 miles

To Misión Santa Isabel,
Secture Tourist Office (4.8km)
& Ensenada (187km)

SAN QUINTÍN

Puente
San Quintín

Volcán
Media
Luna

EJIDO LÁZARO
CÁRDENAS

Volcán
Media
Luna

EJIDO
EL PAPALOTE

Picacho
Vizcaíno

Volcán
Sudoeste

Volcán
Ceniza

Bahía
San Quintín

Bahía Falso

EJIDO
LOS
PINOS

EJIDO
SANTA
MARÍA

PACIFIC
OCEAN

Punta
Azufre

Monte
Mazo

Cabo
San Quintín

To Rancho
El Socorrito (9km),
Playa El Socorro (9.5km)
& El Rosario (58km)

Playa
Santa
María

Bahía Santa María

SIGHTS & ACTIVITIES (p99)
El Capitán Sportfishing	(see 8)
English Cemetery	**7** C3
Molino Viejo Complex	**8** B3
Muelle Viejo	(see 10)
Old Mill Sportfishing	(see 8)
Oyster Farm	**9** B3
Pedro's Pangas	(see 8)
Sportfishing Pier	**10** B3
Tiburón's Pangas	(see 8)

SLEEPING (pp99–101)
Don Eddie's Landing	**11** R3
El Pabellón	**12** D5
Hotel Chávez	**13** C1
Hotel La Pinta San Quintín	**14** D5
Hotel Real del Cora	**15** C2
Maria Celeste Motel	**16** C1
Motel Cirio	**17** C1
Motel Muelle Viejo	**18** C1
Motel Uruapán	**19** C1
Old Mill Hotel	(see 8)
Old Mill RV Park	(see 8)
Rancho Cielito Lindo	**20** C4

INFORMATION
HSBC (ATM)	**1** C1
HSBC (ATM)	**2** C2
Internet Café	**3** C1
Lavamática	**4** C1
Long-Distance Phone Service	**5** C2
Post Office	**6** C2

EATING (p101)
Jardines Baja	**21** C3
Mi Lien	**22** C1
Old Mill Restaurant	(see 8)
Palapa de Mariscos El Paraíso	**23** B3
Restaurant Bar San Quintín	**24** C1
Viejo San Quintín	**25** C2

TRANSPORT (p101)
Bus Terminal	**26** C2
Pemex	**27** C1
Pemex	**28** C2

fishing. It's impossible to get around the place, however, without your own transportation.

Offshore Isla San Martín is part of the volcanic cordon that protects the plain from the ocean's erosive power. Plans to develop San Quintín into a major tourist resort are, so far at least, still confined to the drawing board.

History

Several briny coastal lagoons near San Quintín provided salt for the nearby Dominican missions in colonial times; 19th-century Russian settlements north of San Francisco Bay in the USA also acquired their salt here. The Russians and Americans hunted sea otters nearly to extinction, bringing Northwest Indians and their canoes along for the venture.

In the late 19th century San Quintín was the focus of settlement schemes by the English-based Mexican Land & Colonization Company, which introduced English colonists and established a steam-powered flour mill, a customs house, a pier, schoolhouses, fertilizer plants and, after a few years, a cemetery. Today only the remains of the Molino Viejo (Old Mill), the Muelle Viejo (Old Pier) and the cemetery testify to the English presence.

The San Quintín area is the world's largest producer of tomatoes, plus many other crops. However, fields west of the Transpeninsular are suffering because growers have extracted so much fresh water that brackish seawater has contaminated the aquifers on which they rely.

Recent years have seen an influx of Mixtec Indians from impoverished rural Oaxaca. During peak picking season, up to 60,000 farm workers work the fields. Many are here on a permanent basis, but others move on at the end of the harvest. Some unscrupulous contractors pay these Indians horrific wages, and child-labor violations and inadequate housing are commonplace. Farm laborers also suffer serious health problems because local agriculture relies heavily on chemical fertilizers and pesticides, with almost no protective equipment or instruction for those who apply them.

Orientation

San Quintín sits on a sheltered harbor 116 miles (187km) south of Ensenada on the Transpeninsular. The name San Quintín commonly refers to an area that includes not only San Quintín proper but also *ejidos* (communally owned land) and *colonias* (residential areas) to the south: Lázaro Cárdenas, El Papalote, Los Pinos and Santa María. San Quintín and Lázaro Cárdenas stretch out along the Transpeninsular for about 3 miles (5km), while the Ejido El Papalote is about 4 miles (6.5km) south of Lázaro Cárdenas. Santa María, another farming area, surrounds Hotel La Pinta San Quintín and Motel Cielito Lindo.

Because none of the streets (except for the highway) is named, and there are no street addresses whatsoever, it can be difficult to find anything in the San Quintín area. Refer to the map in this book, but trust your own eyes as well. Because San Quintín is so spread out, it's much better to drive than to rely on public transportation – off the highway, transportation is basically nonexistent.

Information

The local branch of the state-run **Secure tourist office** (☎ /fax 166-2788; ☼ 8am-5pm Mon-Fri, 10am-3pm Sat & Sun) is in a sparkling new building at Km 178, about three miles (4.8km) north of San Quintín. The friendly, English-speaking staff can help with information about the area from San Vicente all the way south to the Parallelo 28, which marks the boundary between Baja California (Norte) and Baja California Sur.

Opposite the plaza in Lázaro Cárdenas, half a block off the highway, **HSBC** bank has an ATM and cashes traveler's checks. There's another HSBC in San Quintín proper, just past Puente San Quintín on the west side of the road.

The **post office** is in Lázaro Cárdenas, and you'll find pharmacies, **Pemex** stations and grocery stores along the Transpeninsular in both Lázaro Cárdenas and San Quintín.

A **long-distance phone service** is adjacent to the Hotel Real del Cora at Km 193, and an unnamed **Internet café** (US$1.35/hr; ☼ 9am-9pm) is just north of Hotel Chávez.

Wash your clothes at the **Lavamática** in San Quintín, on the western side of the highway.

Warning: The San Quintín area has seen an increasing number of vehicle break-ins and the occasional robbery; especially vulnerable are those camping in remote areas. It's not cause for paranoia, but do take precautions. In an emergency, contact **Secure's tourist assistance** (☎ 078 or ☎ 163-3833).

Sights

San Quintín has a few modest cultural landmarks from the period of the early English settlement. The old wheat mill, the **Molino Viejo**, established in the early 20th century, was turned into a cannery by the Mexican government in 1940 and remained in operation until the 1970s. The mill was originally set up here because the local tides came through the narrow channel with such force that they could easily power the millwheel – both ebbing and flowing. You can still see the phenomenon of these surging waters by simply walking to the shore.

The mill's last manager started a modest hotel on the premises, which has evolved into a comprehensive tourist site. The former cannery is now a restaurant that's the center of local nightlife (such as it is), and also featured a couple of good hotels and an attractive waterfront area for hanging out.

Pilings alone now remain of the **Muelle Viejo** (old pier), but it's a good place to watch wildlife, especially birds. The motel restaurant here has good bay views.

From November to February tens of thousands of black Brant geese descend upon Bahía San Quintín. In those months the area also attracts hunters from around the world. Hunting is allowed only from Friday to Sunday and must be done with a guide; hunting licenses and gun permits are also required.

At the **English Cemetery**, south of the Muelle Viejo, the single identifiably English headstone is a recent construction memorializing Francis Barthemelon Henslowe of Wermigley, Norfolk and Santa María, who died July 24, 1896.

The **oyster farm** on Bahía Falsa is another popular destination, although it's rather remote and the drive here is rough.

Activities

Activities in the region center around the **beaches** and the ocean; the best easily accessible beaches are near Hotel La Pinta San Quintín in the Santa María area. North of town, at Km 183, in the Ejido Leandro

Valle, is a turnoff to **Playa San Ramón**, which – year-round, during low tide – offers the best **clamming** in the area. Yields are limited to 12 clams per person, and no clams under four inches (10cm) may be taken.

Breaks at the southern end of Cabo San Quintín, southwest of town, are good for **surfing**, but getting there can be a problem without a 4WD vehicle or a boat. Always inquire locally about road conditions before heading out.

Fishing licenses are necessary for both clamming and boat-fishing; the tourist office and sportfishing guides are both authorized to issue licenses to anyone over 16 years of age.

Daily rates for **fishing**, including guide and panga, start at around US$160 per boat for up to three people. Larger superpangas and cruisers are more expensive. The day starts early, around 6 or 6:30am, and ends before 2pm: the winds make the water too choppy later in the day. Surf fishing is also a favorite here.

Tiburón's Pangas (☎ 165-2760, 170-0821), **Pedro's Pangas** (☎ 171-1874, in the USA ☎ 888-568-2252) and **Old Mill Sportfishing** (☎ 619-585-0244, in the USA ☎ 888-828-2628) are all based at the Molino Viejo complex. They enjoy excellent reputations, but locals also recommend **El Capitán Sportfishing** (☎ 162-1716, 171-3087) – also at Molino Viejo – whose captain, Kelly Catian, goes out on a custom-built superpanga. **Don Eddie's Landing** (p100) also has a fleet of fishing boats. All fishing trips leave from the sportfishing pier.

Kelly provided the following list, indicating which fish are most common each month in the San Quintín area:

Albacore	June to October
Bluefin tuna	July to October
Cabrilla	year round
Corvina	year-round
Dorado	July to October
Halibut	January to June
Marlin	July to October
Rock cod	January and February
White sea bass	March to June, November and December
Yellowfin tuna	June
Yellowtail	April to June

Sleeping

Lodging choices in the San Quintín area consist of the quiet hotels on the beautiful but beachless Bahía San Quintín (great if you're fishing), the two hotels on the sandy beach and open ocean of Bahía Santa María, and the cheapest but also noisiest motels along the Transpeninsular.

If you're planning to stay at any place on Bahía San Quintín, try to arrive in daylight – the maze of dirt roads west of the Transpeninsular is poorly signed and difficult to negotiate in the dark.

BAHÍA SAN QUINTÍN

Old Mill Hotel (☎ 165-6030, in the USA ☎ 800-479-7962; oldmill@telnor.net; s US$25, d US$30-40). One of the best around, American-owned Old Mill Hotel sits on the site of the former wheat mill, 3 miles (5km) west of the highway. The motel has a range of attractive rooms, the grounds are pleasant, and the ocean's a clam shell's-throw away.

Don Eddie's Landing (☎ 165-6061/62; www.doneddies.com; r US$45-65; ste US$80) Just north of the Molino Viejo, Don Eddie's motel and sportfishing center boasts 17 clean and spacious rooms with tile floors, TVs and oceanview patios. A restaurant-bar with sweeping bay windows serves seafood and Mexican fare. Fishing pangas for four people start at US$180.

Motel Muelle Viejo (☎ 613-4206; r US$25-35) About 2½ miles (4km) south of the Old Mill complex is the friendly motel also known as Motel San Carlos. It has eight modest but shady **campsites** too, with hot showers and toilets for US$5 per night. The grounds are about 2 miles (3.2km) west of the Transpeninsular in the Ejido El Papalote; look for the wooden sign.

Old Mill RV Park (no ☎ ; r/RV/tent US$10/15/10) This spot has tent and RV sites with full hookups and a few basic rooms. It's in the Molino Viejo complex and hooked into the local grid for reliable electricity, but it's still windy, barren and close to breeding mosquitoes in summer. Overall, it's a good deal.

BAHÍA SANTA MARÍA

Hotel La Pinta San Quintín (☎ 165-9008, in the USA 800-336-5454; www.lapintahotels.com; r US$84) Farther south, in Ejido Santa María, La Pinta falls short of the standards of its sister hotels elsewhere on the peninsula, but its desirable beachfront location is great for clamming, surf fishing and other beach activities. Balconies face a wide sandy beach.

Rancho Cielito Lindo (in the ☎ USA 619-593-2252; cielitolindo@bajasi.com) South of town near Hotel La Pinta, Rancho Cielito Lindo occupies attractive grounds near the beach. Rooms all have two queen-size beds and a shower/bath for US$45; it also has a bar, a **restaurant** (try the cracked-crab dinner) and a full sportfishing fleet. Formal **campsites** with pleasant palapas – tents, vans and pickups only – and access to hot showers are also available for US$5. To get here, turn west off the Transpeninsular near the packing plant. The road is paved except for the final mile or so.

Free beach camping is theoretically possible but can be dangerous (theft is common) in the area near Hotel La Pinta San Quintín. If you do decide to camp, stay well above the water line.

TRANSPENINSULAR

Motel Uruapán (☎ 165-2058; Km 190; s/d US$18/22) Offering 50 pleasant, clean rooms, the Motel Uruapán is definitely the best budget deal in town.

Hotel Real del Cora (☎ 166-8576; Km 193; s/d US$27/32) A surprising island of charm in gritty San Quintín, this hotel has 25 rooms with telephone and TV, tall ceilings and sparkling baths.

Hotel Chávez (☎ 165-2005; Km 194; s/d US$22/27) Just before the Puente San Quintín bridge, Hotel Chávez is a friendly, comfortable motel-style place; the modern rooms have TV, heat and fans.

Maria Celeste Motel (☎ 165-3999; s/d US$30/33) Amenities at this comfy hotel include bottled water, spic-and-span bathrooms, full carpeting, TVs and phones.

Motel Cirio (☎ 165-3015; s/d US$27/30) Turn east off the highway just north of the Maria Celeste Motel to find this place. Rooms are small but quieter than those on the main road. It also has a communal kitchen and a barbecue area.

SOUTH OF SAN QUINTÍN

About 10 miles (16km) south of San Quintín and 1 mile (1.6km) west of the Transpeninsular, **El Pabellón** (no ☎ ; site US$5) has basic facilities for tents and RVs – with access to showers and toilets – on a lovely sandy beach. A grocery store is a 20-minute walk away, and clamming and surf fishing are superb.

Another 6 miles (9km) or so farther south, **Rancho El Socorrito** (no ☎; US$5/vehicle) has primitive beachfront camping. Playa El Socorro has **free camping** about another half-mile (800m) south.

Eating

The San Quintín area is famous for its clams, and cursed are they who pass through without sampling. They're sold at numerous stands and restaurants, but for reliable quality, go to the casual **Palapa de Mariscos El Paraíso** (☎ 165-2906) near Km 192. It has a great menu of *cocteles* (seafood cocktails), fish tacos, ceviche tostadas, abalone (in season) and, of course, clams.

Mi Lien (Transpeninsular) Across from Palapa de Mariscos El Paraíso, this is the area's lone Chinese restaurant.

Jardines Baja (☎ 165-6060; mains US$7-10; ☯ Tue-Sun) Accessed via the signed road to the Old Mill Hotel, this family-run restaurant is great for its casual atmosphere and delicious seafood, chicken and steak dishes.

Viejo San Quintín (Transpeninsular) This expatriate hangout makes good Mexican combinations in addition to American-style burgers and sandwiches.

Restaurant Bar San Quintín (☎ 165-2376; Km 193; mains US$4-10; ☯ 7:30am-11pm) Alongside Motel Chávez in San Quintín proper, this diner-style restaurant has good breakfasts, filet mignon (about US$9) and burgers (from US$4).

Misión Santa Isabel (☎ 165-2309; Transpeninsular; mains US$4-7) North of the Pemex station, Misión Santa Isabel is a favorite locals' hangout and is always full. The portions here are huge and cheap, and breakfasts are excellent.

Old Mill Restaurant (☎ 165-6034; mains US$8-20) This is the area's most expensive restaurant, located in the Molino Viejo complex. You're paying for the atmosphere of an adapted seaside cannery and beautiful views as much as for the food.

Getting There & Away

The long-distance **bus terminal** (☎ 165-3050) is in Ejido Lázaro Cárdenas on the western side of the Transpeninsular. ABC is the main carrier, with scheduled service to points north and south.

There are regular daily departures to the following destinations:

Destination	Fare	Duration
El Rosario	US$4	1 hr
Ensenada	US$10	3½ hrs
Guerrero Negro	US$22	6 hrs
La Paz	US$60	18-20 hrs
Loreto	US$48	12 hrs
Mexicali	US$25	8 hrs
Mulegé	US$36.50	10 hrs
San Ignacio	US$23	7½ hrs
Santa Rosalía	US$33	8½ hrs
Tijuana	US$18	5½ hrs

Getting Around

Transportes Ejidales vans shuttle between Camalú and Ejido El Papalote to the south, roughly every 15 minutes. You can flag them down anywhere en route. Their primary clientele is farm workers; fares range from US$0.80 to US$1.50.

EL ROSARIO

☎ 616 pop 3500

About one hour (36 miles or 58km) south of San Quintín, El Rosario is regarded by seasoned Baja travelers as the terminus of the 'civilized' part of Baja and the gateway to the untamed stretches of the central peninsula. The few tourist services, including a 24-hour Pemex station, are all right on the highway.

Historically El Rosario forms the southern border of the Dominican mission frontier. Known in pre-Spanish times as the Cochimí Indian ranchería of Viñadaco, it was officially founded in 1774 as Misión Nuestra Señora del Rosario Viñadaco. An abundant water supply permitted cultivation of wheat, corn and fruit, including almonds and peaches; missionaries also directed the harvesting of lobster, abalone and clams. After relocating once (when the major spring dried up), the mission closed in 1832 because epidemics had so ravaged the Cochimí population that no laborers remained for the mission fields.

Only limited remains of the **Misión Nuestra Señora del Rosario's** two sites are still standing. The initial mission site is at the end of a short dirt road above the highway, about 150 yards (137m) west of Motel Sinai, but only the outlines of the foundations are still visible. Across the Río del Rosario, in the lower half of town (Rosario de Abajo), several standing walls make up the ruins of the later mission.

Sleeping & Eating

With the completion of the Transpeninsular in late 1973, **Mamá Espinosas** (☎ 165-8770; mains US$5-10; ⏲ 6am-10pm), near the Pemex, became a favorite stop for a variety of travelers. In the early days of Baja road races, celebrities Steve McQueen, James Garner and Parnelli Jones sampled Doña Anita Espinosa's lobster burritos here. The restaurant has expanded, and the walls are covered with autographed off-road posters and family photos.

Motel La Cabaña (☎ 165-8615; r US$14) is part of Mamá Espinosas. Rooms are clean, comfy and simple, and they open onto the small parking area. It's perfect for a night's sleep before continuing south.

At Km 56.5 at the eastern end of town, **Motel Sinai** (☎ 165-8818; RV US$16; r US$20-30) has a range of rooms plus an RV park. Electricity and water are available, and campers may use the shower in the motel office. The **laundromat** next door is part of the motel and can wash clothes for guests.

Getting There & Away

Buses stop at El Rosario's terminal on a schedule similar to that of San Quintín's terminal. Southbound buses depart about an hour later than those leaving San Quintín; northbound buses depart about an hour earlier.

AROUND EL ROSARIO

At the end of a good but sometimes rough road that leads west 10½ miles (17km) from El Rosario, the fish camp of **Punta Baja** also attracts surfers and sea kayakers to a good right-point break in the winter, but no tourist services are available.

From the hill overlooking the camp, arriving tourists and local goatherds can see the five volcanoes of the San Quintín area to the north.

Some 46 miles (74km) south of El Rosario by a series of decent graded and not-so-decent dirt roads, **Punta San Carlos** is one of the best windsurfing spots on the Pacific side of the peninsula.

TECATE

☎ 665 / pop 77,800

Sleepy Tecate, proud home of the Tecate Brewery, more closely resembles a mainland Mexican *pueblo* (town) than does any other locality in northern Baja California. Town life revolves around the delightfully shaded *zócalo* (central plaza), known as Parque Hidalgo, which is a favorite gathering spot for locals and visitors. On weekends, mariachi bands stroll the plaza, and fiestas take place throughout the year.

Tecate sits in a bowl-shaped valley surrounded by mountains. The most famous of them is Mt Cuchumá (3885 feet or 1165m), which is sacred to the Kumeyaay tribe, whose surviving elders and shaman still hold occasional ceremonies atop the summit. Cuchumá offers numerous opportunities for nature lovers and recreationists, and it's especially nice in spring when the wildflowers are in bloom. There's also abundant birdlife. At the foot of the mountain is Rancho La Puerta, one of the oldest and most exclusive health spas in North America.

History

Tecate's origins derive from an 1831 land grant to a Peruvian named Juan Bandini (who became the mayor of San Diego immediately before the US takeover of Alta California), but the establishment of early businesses and the development of agriculture in the 1880s really put the town on the map. The surrounding countryside yielded both grains and fruit crops such as grapes and olives.

After 1919 the railroad linked Tecate with Tijuana and Arizona. Completion of México 2, the last link on the Tijuana-Mexico City highway, was a further boost to the economy.

Tecate's onetime whiskey factory, a major employer, folded with the repeal of US Prohibition. Businessman Alberto Aldrete's malt factory, founded in 1928, expanded into a major brewery by 1944 but soon went bankrupt. Acquired later by a Mexican conglomerate, it became the Cervecería Cuauhtémoc Moctezuma (Tecate Brewery) and now produces Tecate, Carta Blanca, Sol and XX beers.

Maquiladoras (assembly plants), however, are the major employers; the largest is Schlage Locks, employing over 3000 people. Since its opening in 1986, the Universidad Autónoma de Baja California's extension center has enhanced the town's cultural environment.

TECATE

INFORMATION		
Banamex	1	C1
Bancomer	2	C1
Cruz Roja	3	A2
HSBC (ATM)	4	C1
Long-Distance Telephone/Fax	(see 28)	
Mexican Customs & Immigration	5	C1
Multi-Servicio Cox	6	B1
Police Station	7	D1
Post Office	8	C1
Secure Tourist Office	9	C2
US Customs & Immigration	10	C1

SIGHTS & ACTIVITIES	(p104)	
Iglesia Nuestra Señora de Guadalupe	11	C2
Instituto de Cultura de Baja California	12	C2
Universidad Autónoma's Centro de Extensión	13	C2

SLEEPING	(pp104-5)	
Hotel Tecate	14	C2
Motel El Dorado	15	A1
Motel Paraíso	16	B1
Okakopa Iwa Hotel	17	C1

EATING	(p105)	
Calimax Supermarket	18	B2
El Jardin	19	C1
La Peña de Losa	20	C1
La Placita	21	D1
La Tradición	22	C2
Mariscos Chemel	23	C1
Panadería El Mejor	24	D1
Taquería Los Amigos	25	D2

ENTERTAINMENT	(p105)	
Ricky's	26	B2

SHOPPING	(p105)	
Mercado de Artesanías	27	D2

TRANSPORT	(pp105-6)	
Bus Terminal	28	D1

Orientation

Tecate is about 34 miles (55km) east of Tijuana and 90 miles (145km) west of Mexicali. México 2 – the east-west route linking Tijuana and Mexicali – divides into Av Benito Juárez to the north and Av Hidalgo, two blocks south, as it enters town.

Av Juárez runs past Parque Hidalgo, the main town square and the bus terminal, while Av Hidalgo runs past the Tecate brewery. Lázaro Cárdenas runs north from Av Hidalgo up to the border crossing. Ortiz Rubio runs south one block east of Cárdenas and then becomes México 3 to Ensenada (105km).

Information

The **Customs & Immigration** posts on both sides of the border are open 6am to midnight daily. Saturday is the busiest day; Sunday, surprisingly, is relatively quiet.

The small **Secure tourist information office** (☎ 654-1095; Callejón Libertad, Parque Hidalgo; ☑ 8am-8pm Mon-Sat) is on the southern side of Parque Hidalgo, but English-speaking staff are not always available.

Most businesses accept US dollars, but Tecate has banks on Av Juárez and around Parque Hidalgo, including **Banamex**, **Bancomer** and **HSBC**. Exchange at **Multi-Servicio Cox** (Av Juárez near Santana; ☑ 9am-7pm Mon-Sat).

Tecate's **post office** (cnr Ortiz Rubio & Callejón Madero) is three blocks north of Parque Hidalgo. Tecate has plenty of public telephones, but the best place to make a long-distance call is the bus terminal, which has several **phone booths**.

For medical service, the **Cruz Roja** (Red Cross; ☎ 132) is at the western end of Av Juárez. The **police station** (☎ 654-1177, emergency ☎ 134) is on México 2, east of downtown.

Sights & Activities

The joy of Tecate is hanging out in **Parque Hidalgo**, the main plaza, where cowboy-hatted old-timers play checkers on cement tables, children run around with balloons, and mariachi bands stroll bench to bench selling songs of love and death. The park is anchored by a band gazebo and ringed by well-tended gardens and café tables. Unlike in most Mexican cities, Tecate's main church, the **Iglesia Nuestra Señora de Guadalupe** (cnr Cárdenas & Av Hidalgo) is not on the plaza but one block south, at the corner of Cárdenas and Av Hidalgo.

The **Instituto de Cultura de Baja California** (☎ 654-1483; ◷ 8am-8pm Mon-Fri, 9am-1pm Sat) is on the southern side of Parque Hidalgo. It offers art exhibits, films and other cultural events. The **Universidad Autónoma's Centro de Extensión**, just south of the bridge over the Río Tecate, hosts occasional traveling exhibitions of *bajacaliforniano* art.

Tecate's other main landmark, the **Tecate Brewery** (Cervecería Cuauhtémoc-Moctezuma; ☎ 654-1111; visitastecate@ccm.com.mx; Av Hidalgo; beer garden ◷ 10am-5pm Mon-Fri Mar-Sep, 11am-4pm Mon-Fri Oct-Feb, 10am-2pm Sat year-round) offers brewery tours by reservation only, preferably for at least 10 people. The brewery, Tecate's largest building, produces some of Mexico's best-known beers, including Carta Blanca, XX, Bohemia and the town's namesake, Tecate. The Jardín Cerveza (beer garden) is open to the public, and you should definitely stroll in for your free beer (one per visit)! The garden closes to the public for community events, so call ahead if this is your main reason to visit Tecate.

Behind the brewery, the 1915 **Estación Ferrocarril Tijuana-Tecate** (train station) served the San Diego & Arizona Railway that ran along and across the border for more than 60 years (see also p106). The inside is closed to the public.

On selected dates throughout the year, the **Pacific Southwest Railway Museum** (in the USA ☎ 619-478-9937, 619-465-7776; Hwy 94, Campo, CA) runs excursions to Tecate aboard historic trains. Occasional day trips from Tijuana include a three-hour stay in Tecate; fares are about US$100 and usually include lunch. The trains chug downhill from 2500 feet on their way from Campo, passing three tunnels on the way. Contact the museum about occasional train rides from San Diego.

Festivals & Events

While less extroverted than Tijuana and Ensenada, Tecate holds several festivals that draw in locals from throughout the region. Those listed below are in addition to regular Mexican holidays. Double-check with the tourist offices, as event dates sometimes change.

Nacional de Bicicleta de Montaña Late June. National Mountain-Biking Championships. For details call ☎ 654-2246.

Feria Tecate en Marcha Mid-July, sometimes in September. Celebrated with parades and rodeos. Takes place in Parque Adolfo López Mateos. For details call ☎ 654-1319.

Romería de Verano Early August. Popular local summer festival in Parque Hidalgo, including food stalls, artisanal goods and regional music and dance.

Fundación de Tecate Early October. Two-week celebration of Tecate's anniversary.

Día de Nuestra Señora de Guadalupe December 12. Tecate's Festival of Our Lady of Guadalupe is one of the peninsula's most interesting celebrations of this holiday, with groups from all over Baja coming to display their costumes and to dance.

Posadas de Tecate Throughout December. Annual Pre-Christmas parades.

Sleeping

Low-key Tecate has a fair number of accommodations in the budget and mid-range price brackets.

CAMPING

About 13 miles (21km) east of Tecate, the pleasant **Tecate KOA Kampground** (☎ 655-3014; www.koa.com, rojai@telnor.net; tent/RV US$15/25, cabins US$40-55) is part of Rancho Ojai, a working ranch. A heated pool, mini-golf and nature trail are among the many assets. Guests can also rent horses. It's by the side of México 2, the free road to Tijuana (look for the Rancho Ojai sign).

MOTELS & HOTELS

Okakopa Iwa Hotel (☎ 654-1144; okakopa@todito. com; Callejón Madero 141; s/d US$45/52; P) For location, price and friendliness, this is Tecate's winner. It's sort of a miniature motel, and cars are practically parked *in* the downstairs rooms. But it's quiet, and the brown-carpet rooms are spotless and have TVs and telephones. The parking is secure and the management friendly.

Motel La Hacienda (☎ 654-1250, 654-0953; Av Juárez 861; P 🐾) Except for its removed location on the outskirts of town, La Hacienda is great: a flower-festooned (and secure) parking area gives way to clean, carpeted, air-conditioned double rooms with TVs.

Motel Paraíso (☎ 654-1716; Calle Aldrete 83; s/d US$16/23) This is the best budget option, but rooms are ragged around the edges.

Motel El Dorado (☎ 654-1333; Eldorado_ 1971@yahoo.com.mx; Av Juárez 1100; s/d US$54/59, US holidays US$71/77; P 🐾) This 40-room motel has giant, comfortable rooms with cable TV, telephones and carpeting.

Hotel Tecate (☎ 654-1116 ; w/out/with TV US$18/25). From the courtyard entrance on Cárdenas, follow the arrows inside and upstairs to this well-worn hotel with cheap, unattractive rooms. The main perks are the hot showers are dependable and the toilets are clean.

Eating

Tecate has some great eats, despite its small-town feel.

Taquería Los Amigos (cnr Hidalgo & Ortiz Rubio; mains US$1-2) Join the locals for superb (and massive) flour quesadillas with beans, cheese, excellent guacamole and *carne asada* (grilled beef). The tacos are tasty too.

La Peña de Losa (☎ 655-7648; Libertad 201; mains US$4-7) The mix of Mexican and international food is good, but the best bet is the US$5 comida corrida, which includes drink, soup, main course and desert.

La Tradición (☎ 654-8040; Libertad 200; mains US$6-10) Likely Tecate's slickest eatery, this family favorite serves delicious Mexican food in an attractive dining room.

El Jardín (Libertad 274; mains US$4-6; 🕑 8am-late) Sitting at plastic tables on the plaza and watching the action over a plastic mug of Tecate is the main attraction here. The food's decent too.

La Placita (Ortiz Rubio 30; tacos US$0.90-2.25) Pop in for delicious taco concoctions as well as standard antojitos and tortas (sandwiches).

Mariscos Chemel (☎ 654-4112; Obregón 250) Locals swarm this taquería for succulent, inexpensive fish and shrimp tacos.

Self-caterers may find the assortment at the **Calimax supermarket** (Av Juárez btwn Aldrete & Carranza) useful. Locals swear that **Panadería El Mejor** (☎ 654-0040; Av Juárez 331; baked goods US$0.20-1; 24hrs), near the bus terminal, bakes the best bread and pastries in Baja – and they may well be right. They even serve free coffee.

Entertainment

Cowboy hats outnumber tables three to one at **Taconazo** (no ☎ ; Calle 15 at Av México; cover US$8-15), where big name *norteño* bands play Mexican country-style music every other Saturday night to a packed house. Chest to chest and legs entwined, couples rip up the dance floor and pay no attention to the occasional gringo who strolls in to join 'em. It's well worth checking out.

Otherwise, join the rock-and-rollers and blow out your eardrums at **Ricky's** (cnr Av Juárez & Aldrete; cover US$3; 🕑 Thu-Sat).

Shopping

Hand-painted clay tiles and Tecate beer are the town's specialties, but shopping is not as good as in Tijuana or the beach towns. A small **Mercado de Artesanías** (☎ 654-1750; Piedra del Sol at México 3; 🕑 weekends) is just south of Parque Adolfo López Mateos.

Getting There & Away

Tecate's **bus terminal** (☎ 654-1221; cnr Av Juárez & Rodríguez) is one block east of Parque Hidalgo. ABC's Subur Baja buses go to Tijuana's Central Camionera La Mesa at least hourly (US$3.50; 1½ hours) and more frequently to the downtown terminal (US$3; 1 hour).

ABC also goes to Mexicali (US$10.25; 3 hours) hourly from 6:30am to 10pm. Ten buses leave daily for Ensenada (US$7-8; 2 hours). To Santa Rosalía, La Paz and Los Cabos, you have to go through Tijuana.

If you're driving from San Diego, take Hwy 94 to the Tecate turnoff. Coming from Arizona, take the I-8 and switch to Hwy 94 just east of Jacumba. From Tijuana you can choose between the free México 2 or the toll road México 2D, which starts just east of Mesa de Otay. The latter is easier to find

RAILS ACROSS THE BORDER

The Tijuana & Tecate Railway was originally part of the San Diego & Arizona Railway and an extensive cross-border route system, built by Southern Pacific and completed in 1919. The line actually began in Lakeside, a northeastern suburb of San Diego, linked up just south of Chula Vista with a spur from Coronado and entered Mexico at Tijuana. It reentered the USA at Tecate before descending the rugged eastern scarp of the Jacumba Mountains, including the difficult Carrizo Gorge, via a series of switchbacks and tunnels. At El Centro, it joined another route (the Inter-California line), recrossed the border at Mexicali and reentered the USA just beyond Los Algodones.

The San Diego & Arizona Railway continued to operate (carrying freight in its later years) until 1970, when Southern Pacific sold the Tijuana & Tecate segment to the Mexican government. In 1976 Hurricane Kathleen demolished several trestles on the route, ending operations between San Diego and El Centro. In 1997, during the privatization of the Mexican railroad, the segment was bought by the Texas-based Railtex company, which hauls freight along here and through San Diego County under the name San Diego & Imperial Valley Railroad.

Currently no passenger service is available, except on the occasional trips aboard historic trains offered by the Southern Pacific Railroad Museum between Campo and Tecate.

and faster once you're on it. The downside is the exorbitant fee of US$6 per vehicle for what amounts to a 20-mile (32km) drive on the actual toll road. From Mexicali follow México 2 all the way west to Tecate.

AROUND TECATE

☎ 665

Rancho Tecate Resort & Country Club

On México 3, about 6 miles (10km) south of Tecate in the Tanama Valley, **Rancho Tecate Resort & Country Club** (☎ 654-0011; www.ranchotecateresort.com; r US$75-87, f US$110; 🖭) features a hotel, tennis courts, restaurant, two artificial lakes, swimming pool and Jacuzzi. There's also a golf course, but because only three of the nine holes are operating, you have to play three rounds. The greens fee is US$10 per person, and the course is open to the public.

Rancho La Puerta

If restoring body, mind and soul is your foremost concern, a stay at the exquisite health spa and resort of **Rancho La Puerta** (☎ 654-9155, in the USA ☎ 800-443-7565, worldwide ☎ 760-744-4222; www.rancholapuerta.com; weekly room & board s US$2460-3090, d US$2380-3500; P ✗ 🞀 🖭) may be what you need. Founded in 1940 by self-improvement gurus Deborah and Edmund Szekely, the lushly landscaped resort snuggles up against the foot of Mt Cuchumá, also known as 'Holy Mountain.'

The one-week stay (Saturday to Saturday) at this nonsmoking facility is anchored

in a low-fat diet and lots of exercise. Days start with a sunrise hike before breakfast, then continue with as many classes as you like, all included in the price; choose from about 50 different ones, including African dance, cardio boxing, Pilates, t'ai chi and postural alignment. In addition, there are tennis courts, swimming pools, Jacuzzis and saunas. Meals are served three times daily.

Accommodations range from *rancheras* (studio bedrooms) to larger villas, all decorated with folk art, handcrafted furniture and tiles, and vibrant weavings. Guest capacity is limited to 160, and vacancies fill up as much as a year in advance. Cancellations do happen, though, so it's worth calling or checking the website.

Rates also include transportation to and from San Diego International Airport (Lindbergh Field). The rancho is on México 2, about 3 miles (5km) west of Tecate.

Hacienda Santa Verónica

Climbing to a high plateau, México 2 passes through a zone of small farms and ranches. **Hacienda Santa Verónica** (no ☎ ; tent/RV/d US$10/28/53; P 🖭), about 15 miles (24km) southeast of Tecate, can be reached via a lateral off the main highway. The 5000-acre Spanish-colonial-style resort is on a former bull-breeding ranch and offers roomy cabins with fireplaces and patios, a large swimming pool, six tennis courts, volleyball and basketball courts. Horseback riding is available too. Visitors seeking peace and quiet should know that the ranch also has an off-road racing track.

Camping fees include access to restrooms, showers, laundry, and sports and fossil-fuel facilities.

La Rumorosa

East of Tecate, for about 40 miles (64km), México 2 passes through an imposing panorama of immense granite boulders to **La Rumorosa**. Here it descends the precipitous Cantú Grade, with extraordinary views of the shimmering Desierto del Colorado. At Km 83 the village of El Cóndor gives access to a northern route into the Parque Nacional Constitución de 1857. For details, see p91.

MEXICALI

☎ 686 / pop 764,600

Most foreigners blow through Mexicali on their way south to San Felipe or east to the Mexican mainland, stopping only to refuel, stock up on cheap liquor, shop or hit the strip clubs. But they're missing the hip, cultured, interesting city Mexicali has blossomed into while shedding its stereotypical border-town image.

Admittedly, it isn't an easy city to explore: Its streets are wide and its best restaurants, bars and nightclubs (of which there are many) are spread among soccer field-size parking lots in the sprawling areas around the Centro Cívico-Comercial and Zona Hotelera. The city doesn't pander to tourists like San Felipe and Los Cabos, but with determination and a couple nights' stay, you'll find a modern Mexico rivaled in Baja only by Tijuana and La Paz. After a night of dining and dancing, switch gears and hit the historic core of the old town (near the border), where you can take in the seedy bars, crowded shops, decrepit old buildings and bustling street life the Centro Civico lacks. Then you'll know Mexicali.

Orientation

On the eastern bank of the intermittent Río Nuevo, most of Mexicali's main streets run east-west, paralleling the border. From Mexican Customs & Immigration, Av Francisco Madero heads east past Parque Niños Héroes de Chapultepec, running through Mexicali's central business district of mod-

est restaurants, stores, bars and budget hotels. The other streets that run parallel to Av Madero are also key shopping areas. Madero finally hits the north-south artery of Calzada Justo Sierra (which becomes Calzada Benito Juárez), along which lie the city's best restaurants and hotels. The city's designated hotel area, the *zona hotelera*, is in the triangle formed by Calzadas Independencia, Montejano and Benito Juárez.

Unfortunately, much of Mexicali is no longer pedestrian-friendly, mostly because local, state and federal authorities have consciously shifted government services to the new Centro Cívico-Comercial and discouraged commercial development near the border zone. Walking isn't so bad when the weather is cool, but the lack of trees or any other shade is almost lethal in summer heat.

If you're heading south from the USA, follow the broad southeast diagonal Calzada López Mateos, which heads through Mexicali's relatively new industrial and commercial section before dividing into México 5 (to San Felipe, 195km) and México 2 (to Hermosillo, Sonora, 604km).

Information

BOOKSTORES

Librería INAH (Map p112; ☎ 557-1104; Av Reforma 1310, Local 3) Small selection of high-quality history and anthropology books.

Librería Universitaria (Map p108; Calzada Benito Juárez at Calzada Independencia) Across from the Universidad Autónoma. Good selection of books (mostly in Spanish) on Mexican history, archaeology, anthropology and literature.

CULTURAL CENTERS

Instituto de Cultura de Baja California (☎ 553-5874) Presents film series at the Teatro del Estado (p114) Café Literario on Calzada López Mateos.

Universidad Autónoma de Baja California (Map p108; www.uabc.mx) Main campus located on Calzada Benito Juárez, south of Calzada Independencia. Has a theater hosting cultural events, including live drama and lectures.

INTERNET ACCESS

Internet (Map p108; Calzada Independencia; US$1.35/hr; ⊙ 8am-10pm Mon-Sat)

Direct Net (Map p108; Calzada Justo Sierra 820 L-3; US$2 per hr; ⊙ 8am-midnight Mon-Sat, 10am-10pm Sun)

EMERGENCIES & MEDICAL SERVICES

Cruz Roja (Red Cross; Map p108; ☎ 066, 561-8101; Blvd Cárdenas 1492)

MEXICALI

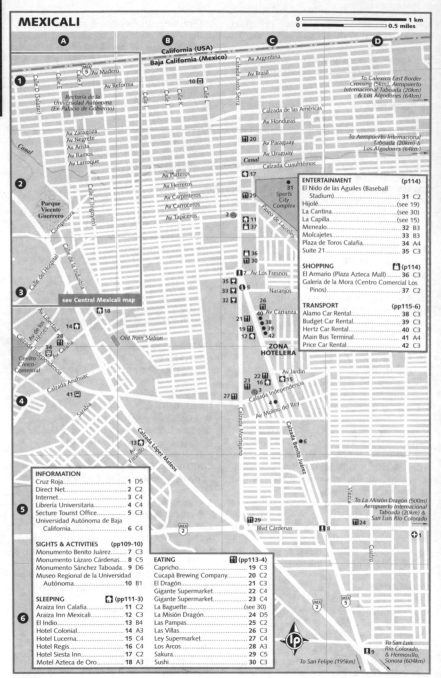

0 — 1 km
0 — 0.5 miles

California (USA)
Baja California (Mexico)

see Central Mexicali map

Old Train Station

ZONA HOTELERA

To Calexico East Border
Crossing (5km), Aeropuerto
Internacional Taboada (20km)
& Los Algodones (64km)

To Aeropuerto Internacional
Taboada (20km) &
Los Algodones (64km)

To La Misión Dragón (500m)
Aeropuerto Internacional
Taboada (20km) &
San Luis Río Colorado

To San Luis
Río Colorado,
& Hermosillo,
Sonora (604km)

To San Felipe (195km)

ENTERTAINMENT (p114)
El Nido de las Aguiles (Baseball Stadium)	31 C2
Hijolé	(see 19)
La Cantina	(see 30)
La Capilla	(see 15)
Menealo	32 B3
Molcajetes	33 B3
Plaza de Toros Calafia	34 A4
Suite 21	35 C3

SHOPPING (p114)
El Armario (Plaza Azteca Mall)	36 C3
Galería de la Mora (Centro Comercial Los Pinos)	37 C2

TRANSPORT (pp115-6)
Alamo Car Rental	38 C3
Budget Car Rental	39 C3
Hertz Car Rental	40 C3
Main Bus Terminal	41 A4
Price Car Rental	42 C3

INFORMATION
Cruz Roja	1 D5
Direct Net	2 C2
Internet	3 C4
Librería Universitaria	4 C4
Secture Tourist Office	5 C3
Universidad Autónoma de Baja California	6 C4

SIGHTS & ACTIVITIES (pp109-10)
Monumento Benito Juárez	7 C3
Monumento Lázaro Cárdenas	8 C5
Monumento Sánchez Taboada	9 D6
Museo Regional de la Universidad Autónoma	10 B1

SLEEPING (pp111-3)
Araiza Inn Calafia	11 C2
Araiza Inn Mexicali	12 C3
El Indio	13 B4
Hotel Colonial	14 A3
Hotel Lucerna	15 C4
Hotel Regis	16 C4
Hotel Siesta Inn	17 C3
Motel Azteca de Oro	18 A3

EATING (pp113-4)
Capricho	19 C3
Cucapá Brewing Company	20 C2
El Dragón	21 C3
Gigante Supermarket	22 C4
Gigante Supermarket	23 C4
La Baguette	(see 30)
La Misión Dragón	24 D5
Las Pampas	25 C2
Las Villas	26 C3
Ley Supermarket	27 C4
Los Arcos	28 A3
Sakura	29 C5
Sushi	30 C3

~~spital General~~ (Map p112; ☎ 556-1123; cnr Calle
~~1~~ Hospital & Calzada Independencia)
~~L~~ospital México-Americano (Map p112; ☎ 552-
2749; Av Reforma 1000) Caters to US visitors.
Police (☎ 060)

MONEY

Cambios (currency exchange offices) are especially abundant in the immediate border area; they do not charge commission on exchanges. Downtown banks with ATMs include **Bancomer** (Map p112; Azueta near Av Madero), **HSBC** (Map p112; corner Av Madero & Morelos) and **Banamex** (Map p112; Madero near Morelos). Many other banks in both Mexicali and Calexico have 24-hour ATMs.

Travelers passing through Calexico can change money (cambios here usually offer slightly better rates than their Mexicali competitors) and buy car insurance along Imperial Ave (Hwy 111), which leads straight to the border.

POST
Central post office (Map p112; cnr Av Madero & Morelos)

TOURIST INFORMATION
Calexico Chamber of Commerce (Map p112; ☎ 760-357-1166; staff@calexicochamber.ca.gov; 1100 Imperial Ave/Hwy 111; ☺ 8:30am-5pm Mon-Fri) Good source of information on the US side of the border.
Cotuco Tourist Office (Comité de Turismo y Convenciones, Conventions and Visitors Bureau; Map p112; ☎ 551-9800/01; cnr Calzada López Mateos & Camelias; ☺ 8am-6pm Mon-Fri) Very helpful; 1¾ miles (3km) southeast of the downtown border crossing.
Secure Tourist Office (Secretaría de Turismo del Estado; Map p108; ☎ 566-1116, 566-1277; www.mexicaliturismo.com; Calzada Benito Juárez; ☺ 8am-8pm Mon-Fri, 9am-1pm Sat) An English-speaker is always on duty, and Secture's city map is very useful.

TRAVEL AGENCIES
Mexicali has many downtown travel agencies, among them:
Aero Olímpico Tours (Map p112; ☎ 552-5025; Av Madero 621)
Viajes Ana Sol (Map p112; ☎ 553-4787; Av Madero 1324-A) Near the rectory of the university.

Sights
LA CHINESCA
Mexicali's **Chinatown**, mostly centered along Av Juárez and Altamirano south of Calzada López Mateos, has its origin in the labor

shortages experienced in the early 20th century, when the Colorado River Land Company began agricultural operations in the Valle de Mexicali. From its beginnings, La Chinesca was a center of commerce and social interaction for the immigrant community, peaking around the 1920s. Today the neighborhood is no longer what it once was, but it still contains many Chinese restaurants, other businesses and typically Sino-Mexican architecture (also see p110).

Near the corner of La Chinesca's Altamirano and Av Zuazua, a concentration of rehearsal halls for banda groups has developed. The groups proclaim their presence by displaying their names and telephone numbers on bass drums on the sidewalk. In late afternoon, after band members finish their day jobs, it's possible to hear them practice -- or hire them for a gig.

CENTRO CÍVICO-COMERCIAL
The highlights of Mexicali's modern **civic center** (Map p108), all located along Calzada Independencia, are the state government's **Poder Ejecutivo** (Governor's Office), **Cámara de Diputados** (Legislature) and **Poder Judicial** (Supreme Court). The plaque on the monument between them describes Mexicali as 'La Ciudad Cuyo Cielo Capturó Al Sol' (The City Whose Sky Captured the Sun).

MUSEUMS & GALLERIES
Local artists display their paintings, sculptures and photographs (for sale at reasonable prices) at **Galería de la Ciudad** (Map p112; ☎ 553-5044; Av Obregón 1209; ☺ 9am-7pm Mon-Fri, 9am-1pm Sat), just east of Calle D (Salazar).

Permanent displays at the **Museo Regional de la Universidad Autónoma** (Map p108; ☎ 554-1977; cnr Av Reforma & Calle L; US$1; ☺ 9am-6pm Mon-Fri, 10am-4pm Sat & Sun) cover subjects like geology, paleontology, human evolution, colonial history and photography. Traveling exhibitions inclue themes such as indigenous textiles from mainland Mexico.

Sol del Niño (Map p112; ☎ 553-8383; Parque Vicente Guerrero; US$3; ☺ 8:30am-5pm Mon-Fri, 10am-7pm Sat & Sun) is a science and technology museum for children with lots of hands-on exhibits, including working TV and radio stations.

HISTORIC BUILDINGS
The **Catedral de la Virgen de Guadalupe** (Map p112; cnr Av Reforma & Morelos) is Mexicali's major

THE STORY OF LA CHINESCA

Near Mexicali's main border crossing, a pagoda gracing the Plaza de la Amistad (Friendship Plaza) is the first visitors see of La Chinesca, one of Mexico's largest Chinatowns.

Chinese immigrants came to the Valle de Mexicali largely because the onset of WWI left companies like the Colorado River Land Company and other landowners in short supply of cheap labor. Trying to meet the increasing worldwide demand for American agricultural products, these companies looked to immigrants to prepare the land for cultivation. The Colorado River Land Company leased areas of land of up to 1000 acres (400 hectares) to individuals who then assumed complete responsibility for management and production. Many lessees were wealthy Chinese from California who imported contract labor from China. Eventually some of the imported workforce formed cooperatives to work the land, pooling resources and sharing profits.

After the war ended in 1918, Mexicans from mainland Mexico flocked to the valley, attracted by the fervor of development. As the area started to experience a surplus of labor, resentment against the hard-working and entrepreneurial Chinese grew quickly, culminating in 1937 when President Lázaro Cárdenas ordered the confiscation of large landholdings, forcing thousands of Chinese off the land and into Mexicali city or back to China.

Meanwhile, in the mid-'20s, Mexicali's economy was booming, thanks in large part to US Prohibition. Americans flooded into Mexicali for boozing binges, gambling and sex: Most of the action was centered in and around La Chinesca. A huge fire in 1923 revealed a series of tunnels leading to underground bars, brothels and opium dens. At least one tunnel burrowed under the international border to surface in Calexico, undoubtedly for the transportation of contraband to the dry USA.

Today's Chinese population in Mexicali is around 2000, originating from Canton. It's the largest Chinese population in Mexico. The Asociación China de Mexicali, set up in 1918 to unify the Chinese laborers, is still going strong, providing representation, support and advice to the community. It also organizes cultural events, the big one being Chinese New Year. Preservation of the Chinese culture is most apparent in the Chinese language school, which runs Cantonese language classes for children on weekends.

Unfortunately La Chinesca itself is pretty run-down, but it retains a buzz that leaves the newer parts of town feeling a bit soulless.

religious landmark. One block north, on Av Madero between Altamirano and Morelos, the former Escuela Cuauhtémoc is a neoclassical building that now serves as the city's **Casa de la Cultura** (Map p112; ☎ 552-9630; admission free; ✆ 9am-8pm Mon-Fri, Sat hrs vary), which hosts rotating art exhibitions.

Now housing the rectory of the Universidad Autónoma, the grounds of the former 1922 **Palacio de Gobierno** (Government Palace; Map p112) interrupt Av Obregón just east of Calle E. Just north of this imposing building, at the intersection of Av Reforma and Calle F (Irigoyen), the former headquarters of the **Colorado River Land Company** (1924; Map p112) is now used for offices, but its attractive patio fountain and restored balcony murals merit a visit.

Two blocks southwest of the rectory, the former **Cervecería Mexicali** (Mexicali Brewery; Map p112; cnr Av Zaragoza & Calle E) sits vacant but in a good state of preservation despite fire

damage in 1986. Opened in 1923 under a German master brewer, it satisfied local demand for half a century and even managed to export some of its production.

MONUMENTS

Mexicali's monuments, which appear on its *glorietas* (traffic circles), are dedicated to past presidents, peasants, the fishermen of San Felipe and various other luminaries. Some notable figures honored in stone and steel are **Benito Juárez** (Map p108), where Calzada Justo Sierra meets Calzada Benito Juárez; **Lázaro Cárdenas** (Map p108), at the intersection of Blvd Cárdenas and Calzada Benito Juárez; **Vicente Guerrero** (Map p108), on Calzada López Mateos; and **Rodolfo Sánchez Taboada** (Map p108), also on Calzada López Mateos.

Festivals & Events

Mexicali hosts a multitude of annual festivals and events, ranging from dog shows and golf tournaments to off-highway races. Most are less gringo-oriented than those in other parts of the peninsula.

The list below is a sample of the more important events.

Aniversario de Mexicali March 14. Celebration of the city's founding in 1903.

Triatlón Campo Mosqueda May 18. Mexicali's triathlon.

Festejos de Independencia September 16. Celebration of Mexico's Independence Day.

Feria del Libro Late September. Annual book fair

Fiesta del Sol Late September to mid-October. Festival of the Sun commemorating the city's founding; pop-music concerts, art exhibits, theatrical performances and parades.

Paseo Ciclista Mexicali-San Felipe Late October. Mexicali-San Felipe Bicycle Race.

Feria de Muestra Gastronómica Early November. Gastronomic Fair featuring a cooking competition among Mexicali chefs.

Día de Nuestra Señora de Guadalupe December 12. Festival of Our Lady of Guadalupe, with nightly processions from December 1 through 12.

Sleeping

Accommodations are less expensive here than in Tijuana, but adequate budget places are hard to find. If you don't fancy sleeping in a hotel whose reception has iron bars on the windows, you're going to have to pay for it.

Ordinary accommodations are better and no more expensive in Calexico, just across the border; most motels on 4th St charge US$30 to US$40.

BUDGET

In and around La Chinesca are several places, including the following.

Hotel Nuevo Pacífico (Map p112; ☎ 552-9430; Áv Juárez 95; r US$15) Offers cheap but noisy doubles in dubious surroundings.

Hotel México (Map p112; ☎ 554-0669; Av Lerdo de Tejada 476; s/d US$22/30) Central Mexicali's best bargain may be the family-oriented Hotel México, where rooms are small but clean.

Close to the Central de Autobuses, **El Indio** (Map p108; ☎ 557-2277; Av Fresnillo 101; s/d US$32/42), off Blvd López Mateos, offers good and clean standard rooms set in a flowered courtyard.

MID-RANGE

Motel Azteca de Oro (Map p108; ☎ /fax 557-1433; Calle de la Industria 600; s/d US$35/45; P 🕱) Slightly isolated, and across from the train station, Azteca de Oro equips all rooms with telephones, TVs and air-con.

Hotel del Norte (Map p112; ☎ 552-8101, 800-027-3230, in the USA ☎ 888-221-8504; Melgar 205; s/d US$39/44; P 🕱) Conveniently close to the border crossing, this landmark art-deco-style hotel has 52 comfortable rooms, some with color TVs and air-con. Its downstairs restaurant serves moderately priced Mexican dishes, lunch and dinner specials, and huge margaritas.

Hotel Regis (Map p108; ☎ 566-3435; Calzada Benito Juárez 2150; r US$34; P 🕱) Friendly Hotel Regis is close to good restaurants and nightspots in the zona hotelera. Rooms are clean and comfy, and there's a restaurant on site.

Araiza Inn Calafia (Map p108; ☎ 568-3311, in the USA ☎ 877-727-2492; www.araizainn.com.mx; Calzada Justo Sierra 1495; r US$69-110; P 🕱) This slick 173-room hotel is located about 1½ miles (2.5km) southeast of central Mexicali. Rooms are simple but comfortable and have air-con and cable TV.

Hotel Colonial (Map p108; ☎ 556-1312, in the USA ☎ 800-437-2438; colonial@mv.net.mx; Calzada López Mateos 1048; r US$68; P 🕱 🕱) This small but highly regarded hotel offers clean comfy rooms with air-con and TVs.

Hotel Siesta Inn (Map p108; ☎ 568-2001; 800-026-5466, in the USA ☎ 800-426-5093; Calzada Justo Sierra 899; r US$50-68; P 🕱 🕱) The very comfortable Siesta Inn is more motel than hotel, with modern carpeted rooms and secure parking. There's a coffee shop next to the lobby.

TOP END

Many, though not all, of Mexicali's upscale hotels are in the zona hotelera.

Araiza Inn Mexicali (Map p108; ☎ 564-1100, in the USA ☎ 877-727-2492; www.araizainn.com.mx; Calzada Benito Juárez 2220; r US$09-110; P 🕱 🕱) This very posh hotel offers excellent service and spacious comfortable rooms. There's a pool, Jacuzzi and gym to keep you relaxed as well. Better deals are available if you book online.

Holiday Inn Crowne Plaza (Map p112; ☎ 557-3600, in the USA ☎ 800-227-6963; cnr Calzada López Mateos & Av de los Héroes; r from US$155; P 🕱 🖳 🕱) This deluxe high rise boasts every service imaginable, from CD players in the rooms to free Internet access. It's geared to business folks and very comfortable. Prices include a buffet breakfast.

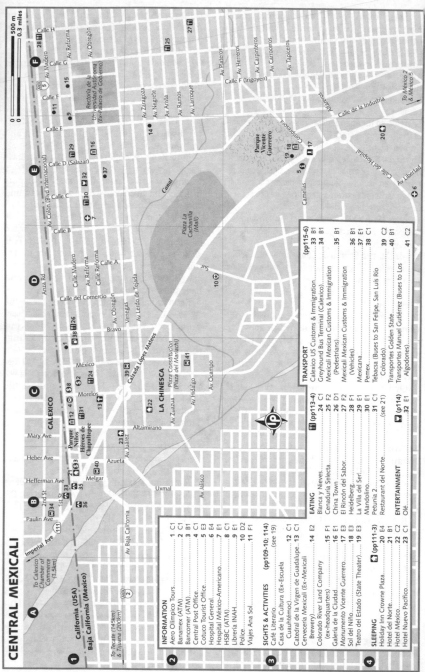

Hotel Lucerna (Map p108; ☎ 564-7000, in the USA ☎ 800-582-3762; Calzada Benito Juárez 2151; r US$95-137 Mon-Fri, US$78-120 Sat & Sun; ☐ ☒ ☒) After its popular nightclub, the best thing about this deluxe hotel is the palm-lined swimming pool. In an idyllic setting of fountains and colonial-style courtyards, its 192 rooms have color TVs and air-con; those overlooking the pool usually have balconies.

Eating

Mexicali has a variety of quality restaurants throughout the city. However, the city lacks small general stores and fresh produce markets, so you'll have to head to one of the big chain supermarkets. **Gigante** (Map p108) has two locations downtown (one on Calzada Montejano, one on Calzada Benito Juárez) and sells everything, as does **Ley** (Map p108; cnr Calzada Montejano & Calzada Independencia). The bakery **La Baguette** (Map p108; Calzada Benito Juárez; ⊙ 7am-9pm), nearly opposite the Benito Juárez monument, sells excellent empanadas and muffins.

CENTRAL MEXICALI   Map p112
Mandolino (☎ 522-9544; Reforma 1070; mains US$9-15) Hit this great hideaway for delicious pizza and pasta, and a bar upstairs that doesn't quit until the last punter staggers out the door. Spot the building by the broken Vespa dangling from the roof.

Cenaduría Selecta (☎ 552-4047; Av Arista 1510; mains US$4-9) This family-run diner is a Mexicali institution specializing in antojitos like beef tacos and burritos. The US$4.50 set meals are a bargain.

Blanca y Nieves (☎ 522-9485; Reforma 515; mains US$2-6) Join the families and old-timers enjoying ice cream and burgers at this air-conditioned ice cream parlor.

El Rincón del Sabor (☎ 554-0888; Av Larroque 1500; mains US$4-8) Good air-conditioned diner serving Mexican food at reasonable prices.

Restaurant del Norte (cnr Madero & Melgar; mains US$5-12) Part of the Hotel del Norte, this US-style coffee shop has large and inexpensive, but rather ordinary, specials all day.

Petunia 2 (Av Madero at Altamirano; mains US$3-4) This tiny juice-bar-cum-restaurant serves delicious *liquados* (blended fruit drinks) and cheap Mexican food all day long.

China Town (Av Madero 701; mains US$6-8) This spotless Chinese restaurant serves whopping portions of (you guessed it) Chinese food.

La Villa del Seri (☎ 553-2677; cnr Av Reforma & Calle D; mains US$8-15) Meat-lovers will love this place specializing in Sonoran beef. The seafood and antojitos are excellent too, and portions are huge. Check out the stuffed deer adorning the piano.

Heidelberg (☎ 554-2022; cnr Av Madero & Calle H; mains US$7-12) Mexicali's lone German restaurant serves hearty Middle European–style food, in addition to Mexican specialties, in a very Germanic setting.

ZONA HOTELERA & AROUND   Map p108
Capricho (☎ 556-0700; Calzada Benito Juárez 1840; mains US$6-10; ⊙ noon-1am, bar until 3am) Fill up on tasty, reasonably priced Italian fare (pizzas, pastas, salads) and hang out with the trendy crowd when you're done. The bar is as popular as the restaurant. Good lunch specials plus ridiculous Wednesday night karaoke.

Las Villas (Av Venustiano Carranza 1199; mains US$6-12) Great if you can't agree with each other, Las Villas is two restaurants and a bar around one big pretty patio. Villa Vittorio (☎ 553-5503) serves Italian food, Villa Rufinos (☎ 568-1314) serves Mexican, meats and *mariscos* (seafood), and Villa Champs (☎ 568-1314) is the sports bar. It's very popular.

Las Pampas (☎ 565-6558; Calzada Justo Sierra 1049; mains US$8-15; buffet men/women US$14/12) This little yellow house, dwarfed by its parking lot, serves delicious Brazilian food: beef and salads. The buffet is a deal.

Cucapá Brewing Company (☎ 568-4205; Calzada Justo Sierra at Panamá; mains US$7-11; ⊙ Mon-Sat) The ultimate cure for the Mexican light-beer blues, Mexicali's new microbrewery has six excellent brews on tap (four lagers, two ales) and good, hearty bar meals to go with them. No shorts after 6pm.

El Dragón (☎ 566-2020; Calzada Benito Juárez 1830; mains US$6-10) This highly regarded Chinese restaurant serves top-notch food. The owners also operate **La Misión Dragón** (☎ 566-4320; Blvd Cárdenas 555; mains US$6-12), which is set among lovely gardens complete with pagoda and miniature lake, a quarter-mile (0.5km) east of Calzada Benito Juárez.

Sakura (☎ 566-4848; Blvd Cárdenas 200; mains US$7-15; ⊙ Mon-Sat) Intimately lit by lanterns hung over an indoor pool, Sakura serves sushi and other Japanese dishes. Karaoke nights run from Wednesday to Saturday.

Sushi (☎ 568-3636; Calzada Justo Sierra 1515-5; sushi US$7-9) If the well prepared sushi doesn't get you pumped, the live music (Wednesday through Saturday nights) should. Indoor and outdoor bar seating adds an interesting touch.

Los Arcos (☎ 556-0903; Av Calafia 454; mains US$7-15) Perhaps Mexicali's most popular seafood restaurant, Los Arcos is near the Plaza de Toros in the Centro Cívico-Comercial.

Entertainment
DRINKING & DANCING

Mexicali has a dynamic nightlife. Most bars and clubs are along Calle Madero and in the area known as *'la cuchilla'* (the knife), named for the pointed shape created by the meeting of Calzadas Benito Juárez and Montejano (formally, it's the zona hotelera).

Hijolé (Map p108; Calzada Benito Juarez at Av Carranza; ◷ 5pm-4am) This hipster hangout brings 'em in with US$0.50 draft beers on Monday, karaoke on Thursday, and live music Sunday and Tuesday.

Molcajetes (Map p108; ☎ 556-0700; Calzada Montejano 1100; cover US$3 Fri-Sun; ◷ from 5pm Wed-Sun) Molcajetes gets packed on weekends, when making it to the yellow school bus (that's the bar) can be tough. Big fun.

Olé (Map p112; Av Reforma 1150; ◷ noon-3am Fri, 8pm-2am Sat) Converted from a two-story house into a café-bar, Olé has DJs (inside) and live rock (out back) on Saturday nights. If it's too loud, go upstairs.

Mandolino (see Eating, p113) Above its namesake Italian restaurant, Mandolino is the spot for kicking off the night. The bar is smaller than others in the zona hotelera and it has a great vibe.

For weekend dancing, head to **Menealo** (Map p108; Calzada Montejano; ◷ Thu-Sat), behind Molcajetes. You can warm up first at **Suite 21** (Map p108; Calzada Montejano), a stylish lounge-moderne next door. For something mellower try **La Cantina** (Map p108; Calzada Justo Sierra 1515), near Sushi. It looks plain, but it's relaxed but busy inside. **Sushi** (p113) itself has live *trova* (folk music) and *rock en español* (Spanish-language rock) on weekends.

Especially popular with university students, **La Capilla** (Map p108; ☎ 566-1100, Calzada Benito Juárez 2151; ◷ 8pm-2am) is a music and dance club at Hotel Lucerna.

THEATER

A variety of theatrical and musical performers, such as Cuba's La Tropicana dance troupe, appear throughout the year at the state theater, **Teatro del Estado** (State Theater; Map p112; ☎ 554-6418; Calzada López Mateos at Av Tapiceros), an ultramodern building seating 1100 and equipped with the 'latest acoustical technology.' Its Instituto de Cultura de Baja California also presents retrospective film series in the **Café Literario**. The theater is opposite the Cotuco tourist office.

SPORTS

Corridas de toros (bullfights) take place once a month from October to May in the **Plaza de Toros Calafia** (Map p108; ☎ 557-3864; cnr Av Calafia & Calzada Independencia; tickets US$6-20), next to the Centro Cívico-Comercial. Tickets are available at the gate.

Mexicali's professional baseball team, Las Aguilas (The Eagles), plays in the Liga Mexicana del Pacífico, which begins its official season in October shortly after the World Series in the USA. The regular season ends in early January, when a series of playoffs determines the league's representative to the Caribbean Series, which rotates among Mexico, Puerto Rico, the Dominican Republic and Venezuela.

Mexicali's baseball stadium (Map p108; ☎ 567-5129), nicknamed 'El Nido de las Aguilas' (Eagles' Nest), is on Calzada Cuauhtémoc (also known as Av Cuauhtémoc) about 3 miles (5km) east of the border post. Games begin at 7:30pm on weeknights, at 6pm on Saturday and at noon on Sunday. Tickets range from US$2 to US$8.

Shopping

Curio stores selling cheap leather goods and kitschy souvenirs are concentrated on Melgar and Av Reforma, a short walk from the border. For a more sophisticated selection, try **El Armario** (Map p108; ☎ 568-1906; Calzada Justo Sierra 1700, Ste 1-A), in the Plaza Azteca mall, or **Galería de la Mora** (Map p108; ☎ 568-1255; Calzada Justo Sierra 1515, Locales 2 & 3), in the Centro Comercial Los Pinos.

Mexican beer and hard liquor are cheaper than in the USA, but duty-free quantities permissible by customs are limited to one liter.

Pharmaceuticals and medical services are much cheaper on the Mexican side of the border. Many clinics and hospitals are located on the streets that parallel the US border, including Av Reforma and Av Obregón.

Getting There & Away
AIR
Aeropuerto Internacional General Rodolfo Sánchez Taboada (Map p108; ☎ 553-5158, 553-4023) is about 12 miles (20km) east of town via Carreterra Aeropuerto Algodones. **Mexicana** (Map p112; ☎ 553-5920, at the airport ☎ 552-9391; Av Obregón 1170) flies all over Mexico and daily to Guadalajara and Hermosillo.

BUS
National
Major intercity bus companies have offices at the **main bus terminal** (Map p108; ☎ 557-2420, 557-2450; Calzada Independencia near Calzada López Mateos). **ABC** (☎ 552-6548; www.abc.com.mx) operates exclusively on the peninsula to as far south as La Paz, via Tijuana.

The following companies serve mainland Mexico (for information on travel to mainland Mexico, see Lonely Planet's *Mexico* guidebook):

Autotransportes Estrellas del Pacífico (☎ 557-1830) Around the corner from the main terminal at Calzada Anahuac 553. Buses go to Guadalajara and intermediate points every two hours daily from 11am and to Tijuana every two hours daily from 5am.

Transportes del Pacífico (☎ 557-2461) Goes to many Mexican mainland destinations along the Sea of Cortez before turning inland at Tepic and continuing to Mexico City.

Transportes Norte de Sonora/Elite (☎ 556-0110) Serves northern Mexican destinations such as Ciudad Juárez, Chihuahua, Monterrey and San Luis Potosí. Elite offers slightly more expensive 1st-class services. Also goes daily to Guadalajara and Mexico City.

ABC fares and approximate travel times to destinations within Baja California are as follows.

Destination	Fare	Duration
Ciudad Constitución	US$81	21hrs
Ensenada	US$19	4hrs
Guerrero Negro	US$51	12hrs
La Paz	US$91	24hrs
Loreto	US$73	19hrs
Mulegé	US$66	17hrs
San Quintín	US$24	8hrs
Santa Rosalía	US$63	16hrs
Tijuana	US$13	3hrs
Vizcaíno	US$55	14hrs

ABC offers an hourly service to San Luís Río Colorado (US$5.50, 1 hour) on the Sonora/Arizona border.

Tebacsa (Map p112; ☎ 555-7011, 554-0454; Calzada López Mateos near Calle México) runs buses to San Luís Río Colorado every 90 minutes (US$1.60).

Transportes Manuel Gutiérrez (Map p112; ☎ 554-6822/26) runs hourly buses to Los Algodones (only 8 miles/13km from Yuma, Arizona) from Av Hidalgo between Aldana and Morelos at the southern end of Plaza Constitución (Plaza del Mariachi).

To/From the USA
Across the border in Calexico, **Greyhound** (Map p112; ☎ 760-357-1895, 800-229-9424; www.greyhound.com; 121 1st St) is directly opposite the pedestrian border crossing. It has 12 buses daily to Los Angeles (US$30; 6-7 hours). From its **Los Angeles terminal** (☎ in the USA ☎ 213-629-8401, 213-629-8536, 800-229-9424; 1716 E 7th St), there are 14 buses daily to Calexico.

There are frequent daily buses between Calexico and the mainland California cities of El Centro (US$3, 20 minutes), Indio (US$23, 2-3 hours), El Cajon (US$23, 2½ hours), San Diego (US$23, 3 hours), Riverside (US$35, 4-5 hours), San Bernardino (US$29-35, 4-5½ hours), Phoenix (US$42, 5-7½ hours), Yuma (US$18, 1 hour) and a few others.

From near the border, **Transportes Golden State** (Map p112; ☎ 553-6159; cnr Calzada López Mateos 234 & Melgar) has services to the mainland California destinations of Indio and Mecca (US$18) and El Monte and Los Angeles (US$30).

Calexico-Mexicali's **main border crossing** (Map p112) in downtown is open 24 hours, but drivers should avoid the northbound afternoon rush hour. To relieve congestion, US and Mexican authorities have opened a new border complex, **Calexico East**, in the industrial-park area east of downtown, at the junction of Av República Argentina and Blvd Abelardo L Rodríguez. This one is open 6am to 10pm daily.

If you're traveling east to mainland Mexico or south beyond Ensenada or San Felipe, obtain a tourist card. If you're driving to mainland Mexico, you need a vehicle permit and a tourist card; both are available from Mexican Customs & Immigration at either crossing (also see p234). For more on vehicle permits and travel to mainland Mexico, consult Lonely Planet's *Mexico* guidebook.

US Customs & Immigration officials at Calexico often x-ray the luggage of pedestrians crossing into the USA, so it's wise to remove photographic film from bags and backpacks.

Getting Around

Most city bus routes start from Av Reforma just west of Calzada López Mateos, two blocks from the border crossing. The 'Justo Sierra' bus goes to the museum and the Secture tourist office. Any 'Centro Cívico' bus goes to the Cotuco tourist office and the bullring. The 'Central Camionera' bus goes to the Centro Cívico-Comercial and the bus terminal. Local bus fares are about US$0.50.

International car rental agencies include:
Alamo (Map p108; ☎ 568-2020; Calzada Benito Juárez 1004)
Budget (Map p108; ☎ 568-2400/01; Calzada Benito Juárez 1050)
Hertz (Map p108; ☎ 582-5222, 582-5678; Calzada Benito Juárez 1223; airport 552-3494)
Price (Map p108; ☎ 565-6262; Calzada Benito Juárez 1014)

A taxi ride from the border to the central bus station or zona hotelera costs about US$5. Try bargaining, but agree on the fare before accepting the ride. A reliable alternative is to call **Ecotaxi** (☎ 562-6565), which has slightly cheaper fares. Taxis are the only method of transport to the airport (about US$15).

AROUND MEXICALI

South of Mexicali, México 5 proceeds through a prosperous farming region en route to the Gulf resort of San Felipe, 120 miles (193km) south.

Some 17 miles (27km) south of Mexicali and 2 miles (3km) east of the highway, rising clouds of steam mark the **Cerro Prieto** geothermal electrical plant, whose 620-megawatt capacity makes it the largest of its kind in North America. It is not open to the public.

Cerro El Chinero (Chinese Hill), just east of México 5 and north of the junction with México 3, on the way to San Felipe, memorializes a group of Chinese immigrants who died of thirst in the area.

At Km 56, 35 miles south of Mexicali, the Indian village **Cucapá El Mayor** has the **Museo Comunitario** (☼ 10am-5pm), with exhibits on subsistence life and indigenous artifacts; outside are examples of traditional Cucupah nomadic dwellings. A small store within sells a selection of crafts, including attractive bead necklaces.

Another 23 miles (37km) south, around Km 93, is the edge of the vast, desolate **Laguna Salada** – 500 sq miles (1300 sq km) of salt flats when dry (as is usual). Although these flats were part of the Gulf of California four centuries ago, today they constitute one of Baja's most arid regions. Unusually heavy rains in the mid-1980s, however, swelled the nearby Colorado and Bravo Rivers, turning the landscape into an ephemeral marsh. Southeast of the lake is the Río Colorado delta, a 60-mile (97km) expanse of alluvium (soil deposited by floodwaters).

LOS ALGODONES

☎ 658 / pop 12,000

Settled by ranchers from Sonora in the mid-19th century, the border town of Los Algodones, next to Andrade, California, was a stagecoach stop on the route from Yuma (Arizona) to San Diego when the Río Colorado was navigable. Named for the surrounding cotton fields, Los Algodones is about 40 miles (64km) east of Mexicali but only about 8 miles (13km) west of Yuma across the Río Colorado.

Nearly deserted in the brutally hot summer, Los Algodones bustles in winter, when more than a million foreigners cross the border. Many of these are retirees from Yuma who find prescription drugs, eyeglasses and dental work much cheaper here than in the USA. So many 'snowbirds' frequent Los Algodones town that Mexican professionals organize bus charters from Yuma for their benefit.

The border is open 8am to 10pm daily, but Mexican authorities will process car permits from 8am to 3pm only. There's a **tourist information office** (☎ 517-7635; Av B 261; ☼ 8am-4pm Mon-Fri). There are many cambios, but US dollars are accepted widely here.

Besides its pharmacies, dentists and opticians, Los Algodones is virtually a wall-to-wall assemblage of kitschy souvenirs, but resolute shoppers may find attractive textiles from mainland Mexico.

Sleeping & Eating

There's one unnamed **motel** (no ☎; s/d

DETOUR: CAÑÓN DE GUADALUPE

Southwest of Mexicali and descending the eastern scarp of **Parque Nacional Constitución de 1857** (p91), palm-studded Cañón de Guadalupe is a delightful hot-springs area superb for hiking, swimming and car camping. Because it's in the rain shadow of the coast range, it's dry and pleasant (except in summer, when it's brutally hot). The best time to visit is from November to late May. In addition to the cold canyon pools and small waterfalls, there are rock art sites in the vicinity.

Take México 2 about 22 miles (35km) west of Mexicali, where a smooth graded road (signed and passable for high-clearance passenger vehicles in dry weather) leads 27 miles (43km) south to a junction that leads another 8 miles (13km) west to Cañón de Guadalupe. For northbound travelers from San Felipe, the canyon is also accessible by a difficult sandy road (4WD recommended, though not essential) leading northwest from the southern end of Laguna Salada, at the turnoff from México 5 to Ejido José Saldaña No 2. This road is slow, tiresome, sometimes difficult to follow and not really worth doing unless there's no alternative.

The **Guadalupe Canyon Hot Springs & Campground** (☎ in the USA 949-673-2670; www.guadalupe-canyon.com; US$25-35/vehicle Mon-Thu, w/ 2-night min US$75-170 Fri-Sun) has comfortable camping facilities starting at US$20 per site from June to mid-October but rising to US$70 for two nights the rest of the year, including use of hot tubs with water temperatures up to 110°F (43°C). The larger sites cost US$120 to US$170 for two nights for up to four vehicles. There's a restaurant (which may run out of food) and a swimming pool. The campground gets crowded on weekends. The owner requires a two-night minimum stay on weekends and three-night minimum stay during holiday periods.

If you can't get into this site, there are other, more modest sites up here – with thermal baths – that aren't tied into the online reservation loop. Hence, they're cheaper.

US$20/35) in town. Its entrance is not particularly inviting, but it's the only choice.

On the US side of the border, the Quechan Indians of Fort Yuma Reservation operate the spacious but basic **Sleepy Hollow RV Park** (☎ 760-572-5101; with/without hookups US$15/25), in Andrade.

Los Algodones' most popular eateries are **Carlota's Bakery**, mobbed by snowbirds at breakfast, and **Restaurant Tucán** (☎ 517-7689), just off the main street. Opposite, **El Gourmet** (☎ 517-7009) is a quieter choice with a stylish bar area.

Getting There & Away

There is no public transportation across the border at Los Algodones. Hourly bus service from Los Algodonesto Mexicali exists, but not from Andrade to Yuma. California State Route 186 is now paved to US Interstate 8, which leads east to Yuma.

SAN FELIPE

☎ 686 / pop 25,000

Beautifully located between the desert and the Sea of Cortez, San Felipe is perfect kick-back territory. The clean, safe white-sand beach is the town's main pulling card for visitors, who can rent paddleboats on the beach.

San Felipe has somewhat of a split personality. Normally tranquil to the extreme, the town's noise levels rise and accommodations are hard to find during national holidays and US spring break, when visitors stream in. However, the action doesn't last long and can be easily avoided with a bit of preplanning. If you can't avoid the busy times, don't worry: the margaritas at sundown, fresh shrimp tacos and generous nature of the locals will make the frenzy more than bearable. Try to visit between November and April, before temperatures soar as high as 120°F (49°C).

History

In 1721 Jesuit missionary Juan de Ugarte landed at the port of San Felipe de Jesús. Seventy-six years later, Fray Felipe Neri, a Dominican priest from Misión San Pedro Mártir, established a small supply depot and settlement here in the hope of replenishing his struggling mission, located in an isolated, mile-high valley about 45 miles (72km) to the west. Both the depot and the mission failed in the early 19th century, in part because of water shortages.

In 1925 San Felipe's population was only about 100, but by 1948, when the improved highway to Mexicali made travel much easier, it reached nearly 1000.

Today half a dozen fishing cooperatives operate out of San Felipe, exporting shrimp and various fish species to the USA, Canada and elsewhere. The San Felipe fleet has 41 boats, several of which can remain at sea for as long as 40 days.

Sportfishing and warm winters have attracted hundreds of North American retirees, while large hotels and sprawling trailer parks have sprung up to accommodate growing numbers of visitors. Many houses, subdivisions and condominiums are under construction.

Orientation

San Felipe hugs the shoreline of its namesake bay, a curving inlet of the northern Gulf of California, 120 miles (193km) south of Mexicali. North-south *avenidas* (avenues) bear the names of seas around the world, while east-west *calles* (streets) bear the names of Mexican ports. Av Mar de Cortez is the main north-south drag, while Calzada Chetumal leads west to a junction with México 5, the highway north to Mexicali. Downtown along the beach is San Felipe's attractive *malecón* (waterfront promenade).

Northwest of San Felipe is the eastern approach to Parque Nacional Sierra San Pedro Mártir (p94) and the famous peak of Picacho del Diablo, via a turnoff from México 3.

Information

INTERNET ACCESS
Computer & Satellite Installation (Av Mar de Cortez Sur; US$5/hr) Office space by the hour with US telephone lines.
Thrifty Ice Cream & Internet (Av Mar de Cortez; US$2/hr) Fast and cheap.

INTERNET RESOURCES
San Felipe website (www.sanfelipe.com.mx) The expat operated 'official' site is packed with information.

LAUNDRY
Speedy Wash (cnr Av Camino del Sur & Manzanillo; ☙ 8am-4:30pm Mon-Sat) Drop-off service available.

MEDIA
San Felipe Newsletter (www.jetiii.biz/sanfelipe/sfnews) English-language monthly; available free around town.

EMERGENCIES & MEDICAL SERVICES
Centro de Salud (☎ 577-1521; Av Mar Bermejo at Ensenada)
Cruz Roja (Red Cross; ☎ 24hr emergency ☎ 066, nonemergency ☎ 577-1544; cnr Av Mar Bermejo & Puerto Peñasco)
Saint James Infirmary (☎ 577-0117, 577-2976, 577-2965; Av Mar Negro Sur 1285) Best in area; caters to North Americans.

MONEY
Nearly all merchants accept US dollars.
Bancomer (Av Mar de Cortez near Acapulco) Has an ATM.
Curios Mitla (Calzada Chetumal at Av Mar de Cortez) Changes dollars for pesos.

POST
Post office (Av Mar Blanco btwn Calzada Chetumal & Ensenada; ☙ 8am-3pm Mon-Fri, 9am-1pm Sat)
Yet Mail (☎ 577-1255; Av Mar del Cortez) A quick way of sending post. Daily collections take the post over the border to San Diego and mail it from there.

TELEPHONE
Telnor public telephones are available throughout San Felipe.

TOURIST INFORMATION
Secture (☎ 577-1155, 577-1865; cnr Av Mar de Cortez & Manzanillo; ☙ 8am-8pm Mon-Fri, 9am-3pm Sat, 10am-1pm Sun) Staff is extremely helpful, and usually there's someone who speaks English.

Sights & Activities

CAPILLA DE LA VIRGEN DE GUADALUPE
The local shrine of the Virgen de Guadalupe, Mexico's great national symbol, is a small monument atop a hill north of the malecón. The climb to the top offers panoramic views of town and bay.

CLAMMING
Clamming is popular, particularly when very low tides reveal wide expanses of firm, wet sand. The best beaches for clamming are south of town beyond Playa El Faro and north of town beyond Campo Los Amigos. Small, tasty butter clams can be found around rocks, while the larger, meatier white clams are just beneath the wet sand. Check with locals about minimum acceptable sizes and per-person limits – clammers caught with undersized specimens are subject to hefty fines.

SAN FELIPE

0 ———— 500 m
0 ———— 0.3 miles

INFORMATION	
Bancomer (ATM)..................... 1	D3
Centro de Salud........................ 2	C3
Computer & Satellite Installation.. 3	C4
Cruz Roja................................... 4	D2
Curios Mitla.............................. 5	D3
Post Office................................. 6	C3
Saint James Infirmary................ 7	B4
Secture Tourist Office................ 8	C3
Speedy Wash............................. 9	B3
Thrifty Ice Cream & Internet.... 10	C3
Yet Mail.................................. 11	D2

SIGHTS & ACTIVITIES	(pp118-20)
Capilla de la Virgen de	
Guadalupe.......................... 12	D2
Casey's Baja Tours.................. 13	C4
Tommy's Sport Fishing........... 14	D2
Tony Reyes Sport Fishing 15	C3

SLEEPING	(pp120-1)
Campo San Felipe Trailer Park.. 16	C3
Chapala Motel........................ 17	C3
Departamentos Peña............... 18	C3
El Capitán Motel..................... 19	C3
Hacienda de la Langosta Roja.. 20	C3
Hotel Costa Azul...................... 21	C3
Hotel El Cortéz....................... 22	C3
Hotel Riviera.......................... 23	C4
La Jolla Trailer Park................ 24	B3
Marco's RV Park..................... 25	D1
Motel El Pescador................... 26	D3
Motel Las Palmas.................... 27	C4
Playa Bonita Trailer Park........ 28	D1
Playa de Laura Trailer Park...... 29	C4
Rubén's Trailer Park............... 30	D1

EATING	(pp121-2)
Arthuro's................................ 31	C3
Baja Java................................. 32	D3
BajaMar.................................. 33	D3
Chencho's............................... 34	D2
El Nido................................... 35	C4
George's................................. 36	C4
La Langosta Roja................ (see 20)	
Los Mandiles.......................... 37	D3
Petunia's................................ 38	D2
Restaurant El Capitán........ (see 19)	
Rice & Beans.......................... 39	D3
Rosita Patio & Grill................. 40	D2
Soporte Comercial.................. 41	C3

ENTERTAINMENT	(p122)
Beachcomber.......................... 42	D3
Club Bar Miramar.............. (see 40)	
Rockodile............................... 43	D3

SHOPPING	(p122)
The People's Gallery............... 44	C4

TRANSPORT	(p122)
Pemex.................................... 45	B2
Terminal ABC (Bus Terminal).... 46	B4
Thrifty Car Rental................... 47	D2

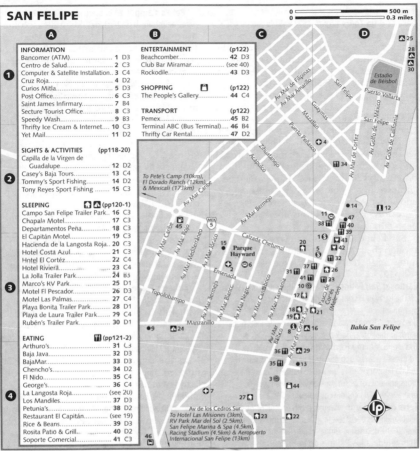

FISHING

Fishing draws many visitors to San Felipe, and Bahía San Felipe has become a parking lot of *pangas* (fiberglass skiffs), shrimpers, trawlers and tuna clippers. Fishing licenses are obligatory for any type of fishing, including surf fishing.

Tommy's Sport Fishing (☎ 577-1120, 577-0446), at the north end of the malecón, just past Rosita Patio & Grill, rents out local 25-foot (7.5m) pangas. A whole day's fishing, including license equipment and bait, costs US$40 per person. The boats fit up to five people.

Travelers with their own boats will find several launching ramps, including a convenient one at Hotel El Cortez. **Tony Reyes Sport Fishing** (☎ 577-1120; Av Mar Bermejo 130) is another option.

The following list indicates when the various species are most common in the vicinity of San Felipe:

Albacore	July to August
Barracuda	May to October
Bonefish	June to August
Cabrilla	year-round
Corvina	July to November
Halibut	January to April
Marlin	June to September
Rockfish	year-round
Sea bass	May
Yellowtail	March to November

Tours

Casey's Baja Tours (☎ /fax 577-1431; www.sanfelipe.tv; Mar y Sol near Av Mar de Cortez Sur) runs excursions to Puertecitos (US$55); Valle de los Gigantes (US$25), home to the giant cardón cactus; a petrified forest (US$35); and waterfalls (US$50). Prices do not include tax.

Festivals & Events

Carnaval is celebrated in San Felipe with much vigor during the week before Lent. On holidays like Thanksgiving, Christmas and New Year's, San Felipe's population practically doubles. The main street becomes a surge of motorcycles, dune buggies and other ATVs, and noise levels rise significantly. Do as the locals do: if you can't beat 'em, join 'em.

San Felipe also hosts many special events, though the hot summer months are usually quiet and event-free. For race-car events, see p122.

Carnaval San Felipe Early March. This celebration starts off the party year with a parade of floats and general merriment.

US Spring Break Mid-March. University students from north of the border flock here to party.

Día de la Marina Nacional June 1. National Navy Day.

La Fiesta Maristaco August. A festival celebrating the fishing industry; San Felipe's chefs gather to make enormous amounts of *ceviche*, a seafood cocktail made – in this case – with 150 kilos of vegetables and 250 kilos of fish.

Feria del Camarón November. This Shrimp Festival celebration has become a tourist and gastronomic success despite the decreasing shrimp population in the Gulf.

Bienvenida a los Pájaros de la Nieve December. Perhaps the antithesis of spring break, this event acknowledges the annual arrival of snowbird retirees from the frozen north.

Sleeping

Rates in San Felipe, as in other coastal resorts, vary both seasonally and between weekdays and weekends. A budget hotel during the week may well be a mid-range place on the weekend or during spring break.

CAMPING & RV PARKS

Campgrounds and RV parks are abundant in San Felipe itself and also dot the beaches to the north and south. The quality of sites varies considerably; prices range from US$7 to US$28 per night. Most places have drinkable water, electricity and hot showers.

Pete's Camp (☎ in the USA 909-676-4224; www.petescamp.com; US$12/vehicle) Six miles (10km) north of San Felipe at Km 177 of México 5, Pete's has 83 basic campsites on the beach, a bar, restaurant and some 300 long-termers.

El Dorado Ranch (☎ 550-0157, in the USA ☎ 800-404-2599; www.eldoradoranch.com; ☒) San Felipe's cushiest trailer park – a town in itself – is 7 miles (12km) north of town. It has 200 RV sites (100 on the beach) with full hookups for US$30 per night. Its extensive amenities include a pool, Jacuzzi, tennis courts, restaurant, bar, laundry and grocery store.

Marco's RV Park (☎ 577-1875; Av Golfo de California 868; site US$10) At the northern end of town, Marco's has small but well-equipped campsites and RV sites.

Playa Bonita Trailer Park (☎ 577-1215, in the USA 626-967-4250; playabonita@aol.com; site US$25, additional person $10) Across the street from Marco's, Playa Bonita has 35 sites with hookups, as well as toilets, showers and a restaurant. Prices rise slightly on holidays.

Rubén's Trailer Park (☎ 577-2021; Av Golfo de California 703; site US$15) Rubén's has 54 shaded sites with full hookups. There's a boat launch, restaurant, toilets, showers and a patio.

La Jolla Trailer Park (☎ 577-1222; cnr Av Mar Bermejo & Manzanillo; site US$15, additional person US$3) Near the center of town, La Jolla offers 50 fully equipped sites, toilets, showers and laundry facilities.

Playa de Laura Trailer Park (☎ 577-1128; site from US$20, additional person US$3) Between Av Mar de Cortez and the beach, Playa de Laura has 40 sites, half with full hookups and the rest with water and electricity only. Hot showers and rental boats are also available.

Campo San Felipe Trailer Park (☎ 577-1012; camposanfelipe@hotmail.com; site US$15-20, additional person $2) In town but still on the beach, San Felipe has 39 fully equipped sites with showers and toilets. Rates depend on beach proximity; reservations are not accepted.

RV Park Mar del Sol (☎ /fax 577-1088, in the ☎ USA 800-336-5454; Av Misión de Loreto 149; ☒) About 1½ miles (2.5km) south of town, the Mar del Sol has 84 RV sites with full hookups for US$20 (US$5 for each additional person) and 30 tent sites for US$12 per night for two people (US$3 for each additional person). Amenities include access to hotel facilities (October to June), showers, toilets, a small grocery store, laundry room and swimming pool.

HOTELS

Chapala Motel (☎ 577-1240; Av Mar de Cortez 142; r US$48; P ⚡) Two-story Chapala offers clean, straightforward rooms that open onto a parking lot in traditional motel style. All have air-con, some have kitchenettes, and the staff is very friendly. It's a great deal for San Felipe.

Hacienda de la Langosta Roja (Red Lobster; ☎ 557-0483, in the ☎ USA 800-967-0005; redlobstersf@yahoo. com.mx; Calzada Chetumal 125; P ⚡) One of the most upscale places in the town center, the Langosta Roja is also home to one of San Felipe's best restaurants.

Motel Las Palmas (☎ 577-1333; palma@wotw.com; Av Mar Báltico 1101; r US$62 Sun-Thu, US$73 Fri & Sat; ⚡ ⚡) The three-star Las Palmas boasts 45 clean, air-conditioned rooms. It has a lovely pool area with plenty of lounge chairs, a poolside bar and a view of the Gulf of California.

Hotel Riviera (☎ 577-1185; Av de los Cedros Sur near Av Mar Báltico; r US$57 Sun-Thu, US$72 Fri & Sat; P ⚡ ⚡) Overlooking the town, the Riviera has air-conditioned rooms with private bath and shower. Its two bars and small swimming pool are shelters from the summer heat.

El Capitán Motel (☎ 577-1303; Av Mar de Cortez 298; r US$45 Sun-Thu, US$73 Fri & Sat; P ⚡ ⚡) This two-star, 40-room motel is a good value considering the spotless rooms have air-con and satellite TV. There's a restaurant and swimming pool too.

Departamentos Peña (☎ 577-1827; Av Mar de Cortez 238; r US$35) Behind the owners' little supermarket is this small, friendly and clean mini-motel. It's one of the cheapest in town, doors from the 2nd-floor rooms open onto a shared balcony.

Hotel Costa Azul (☎ 577-1548/49; Av Mar de Cortez at Ensenada; r US$60 Sun-Wed, US$82 Thu-Sat; ⚡) With 140 rooms, the Costa Azul dwarfs nearly every hotel in town and is extravagantly landscaped. Amenities include a pool, satellite TV, bar, restaurant and coffee shop. It's also the main destination for spring-breakers, so it can get noisy.

Motel El Pescador (☎ 577-2648; cnr Calzada Chetumal & Av Mar de Cortez; s/d US$40/45; ⚡) This small, one-star motel has 24 rooms basic but definitely acceptable rooms with air-con.

Hotel El Cortéz (☎ 577-1055, in the USA ☎ 800-800-9632; cortezho@telnor.net; Av Mar de Cortez Sur; s/d US$73/90, bungalows US$110-180; P ⚡ ⚡) This

110-room beachfront place, near the center of town, boasts rooms with sea views, air-con and TVs. A few smaller rooms have beachfront patios, and the pricier bungalows come with kitchens. Amenities include a restaurant/bar (with satellite TV), a swimming pool and a boat ramp.

Hotel Las Misiones (☎ 577-1708, in the USA ☎ 858-454-7166; Av Misión de Loreto 148; r US$66 Sun-Thu, US$88 Fri & Sat; P ⚡ ⚡) Two miles (3km) south of San Felipe, this 190-room hotel has extensive facilities including a trailer park, two tennis courts, restaurants, bars, cafeterias and swim-up bars in two of its three swimming pools. Rooms have air-con, color TVs, telephones and showers/baths. There's a 10% AAA discount.

San Felipe Marina Resort & Spa (☎ 577-1435, in the USA ☎ 800-291-5397; snmarina@telnor.net; r US$145-550; P ⚡ ⚡) Located at Km 4.5 on the road to the airport, this is a luxurious facility with a wide range rooms, from standards to suites and villas. The pool area is stunning with its views of the bay.

Eating

As a popular tourist destination, San Felipe has a good selection of restaurants serving the usual antojitos as well as outstanding seafood specialties. For excellent, inexpensive tacos, try the numerous stands along the malecón, most of which specialize in fish and shrimp.

Chencho's (☎ 577-1058; Puerto Peñasco 233; mains US$3-7; ☽ Wed-Mon) Since 1967 this little family eatery has been serving wholesome Mexican dishes at good prices. Breakfasts (French toast, pancakes and all types of egg dishes) are all under US$4.

La Langosta Roja (Calzada Chetumal 125; mains US$12-20; ☽ 7am-11pm) Upscale but relaxed, Langosta Roja is extremely popular for its delicious seafood, pastas, seafood cioppino, and reasonably priced wine list (Baja wines, of course).

Rosita Patio & Grill (☎ 577-1770; Malecón at Zihuatanejo; mains US$6-12) Rosita's has a large and varied menu, emphasizing seafood at moderate prices.

El Nido (☎ 577-1028; Av Mar de Cortez Sur 348; mains US$8-15; ☽ 2-9pm Thu-Tue) This is the perfect place for a romantic meal. Choose from various seafood dishes and steaks cooked over mesquite charcoal; the chicken tacos are excellent.

Rice & Beans (☎ 577-1770; Malecón; mains US$6-11) Gringos love this place for the balcony over the malecón as much as for the food (though that's good too).

BajaMar (Av Mar de Cortez 101; mains US$5-13) Add the big patio to the marina-style decor, the bar and the great food, and you get one of the best restaurants in town. The seafood cocktails and ceviches are delicious.

Restaurant El Capitán (mains US$3-7; ☉ Thu-Tue) In front of its namesake motel, El Capitán gets very busy and serves delicious burritos and cheap breakfasts.

George's (☎ 577-1057; Av Mar de Cortez Sur 336; mains US$4-7) This US-style coffee shop and breakfast joint is a favorite among local expats.

Los Mandiles (☎ 577-1168; cnr Calzada Chetumal & Av Mar de Cortez; mains US$5-10; ☉ Thu-Tue) This Mexican family-style restaurant specializes in seafood and steak.

Baja Java (☎ 577-2465; cnr Calzada Chetumal & Av Mar de Cortez; mains US$3-6; ☉ Thu-Tue) Upstairs, Baja Java is a great spot for breakfast and lunch – and one of the only places in town where you can get a cappuccino.

Soporte Comercial (Av Mar de Cortez near Calzada Chetumal; pastries US$0.20-.50; ☉ 7am-10pm) Pop in here for delicious Mexican pastries.

Arthuro's (Av Mar Báltico 148) Just south of Calzada Chetumal, Arthuro's serves Mexican and US-style dishes.

Petunia's (Av Mar de Cortez 241) Good for cheap Mexican food.

Entertainment

There are several clubs on and around the malecón. **Rockodile** (Av Mar de Cortez) is a bar/disco attracting the party crowd on weekends with thumping music and the obligatory whistle blowing. Just south of here, at the corner of Calzada Chetumal, the **Beachcomber** (☎ 577-2122) is a combination bar/grill.

Club Bar Miramar (☎ 577-1192; Av Mar de Cortez 315) fills up with leather-skinned expats who sit around watching the pool tables while the party crowd fills up the front room. It's a cool place.

A preferred destination for fossil-fuel fanatics, San Felipe boasts Mexico's only **racing stadium**, which serves as both the start and finish of some off-highway races, though most start and finish at the arches on the approach to town. The stadium is about 5 miles (8km) south of town, the main annual events are the SCORE San Felipe 250 in mid-March, San Felipe Grand Prix in early April, mid-June's Corp San Felipe 200 and Carrera Mexicali–San Felipe, which takes place at the beginning of December.

Shopping

The entire length of Mar de Cortez is lined with stores packed with souvenirs from around Mexico. For arts and crafts by local and expatriate artists, as well as crafts classes, visit **The People's Gallery** (Av Mar de Cortez Sur 5; ☉ Thu-Tue).

Getting There & Away

Aeropuerto Internacional San Felipe (☎ 577-1368, 577-1858) is 8 miles (13km) south of town via a spur off México 5, but presently there are no commercial flights.

San Felipe's bus terminal, **Terminal ABC** (☎ 577-1516), is on Av Mar Caribe, just south of Av de los Cedros Sur. Buses to Mexicali (US$13, 2½ hours) leave at 6am, 7:30am, noon, 4 and 8pm. Buses leave for Ensenada (US$17, 4 hours) at 8am and 6pm daily. The Tijuana service (US$27, 5½ hours) leaves five times daily. Buses to Puertecitos (US$4, 2 hours), south of San Felipe leave at 10:30am and 7pm daily. Buses leave Puertecitos for San Felipe at 7am and 5pm.

Rental cars are pricey but are available at **Thrifty** (☎ 577-1277; Av Mar de Cortez 75-B), inside the Century 21 office.

PUERTECITOS

As paved México 5 gradually extends southward, access to the once-isolated string of communities stretching to Puertecitos and beyond is becoming easier. The road to Puertecitos is very good despite numerous *vados* (fords) and potholes, which require slowing down; the last 14 miles (22.5km) are still slow going.

On the way to Puertecitos, it's well worth visiting the **Valle de los Gigantes** (Valley of the Giants), home to huge cardón cacti (some supposedly 100 years old), about 12 miles (20km) from San Felipe. You'll feel like you've just stepped into the movie set of a spaghetti western.

Puertecitos itself, 52 miles (84km) south of San Felipe, is popular with North American retirees who festoon their driveways with street signs pilfered from their hometowns.

There is a **Pemex** station (rarely open), one public telephone, two small shops and decent sportfishing in the area. Camino Compadre takes you to several warm, spring-fed pools near the point just south of town. They make for good bathing, but be careful: the water can nearly boil at certain times of the day.

Fishing

The following list indicates when the various fish species are most common around Puertecitos:

Cabrilla	October to May
Corvina	January to August
Grouper	year-round
Marlin	June to September
Rockfish	June and September
Roosterfish	August
Sierra	May to October
White sea bass	November to March
Yellowtail	May to October

Sleeping & Eating

Playa Escondida Trailer Park charges about US$10 per site. Remodeled **Puertecitos Motel & Restaurant** has four double rooms for US$40, plus four RV sites (US$8) with cold water. The restaurant is closed on Thursday. Puertecitos has electricity for only four hours a day, from 6pm to 10pm.

At nearly every beach both north and

south of Puertecitos, you'll find primitive **beach camps**, all of which charge less than US$5.

SOUTH OF PUERTECITOS

Though there's been talk for years of paving the road south of Puertecitos to its intersection with the Transpeninsular, the laying of pavement still looks a long way off. Always ask about conditions, because much of the road is very rough and subject to washouts as far as Bahía San Luis Gonzaga, about 50 miles (80km) south. While vehicles with high clearance and short wheelbase are desirable, they are not absolutely essential, and 4WD is not necessary. Allow at least five hours to Bahía San Luis Gonzaga, and drive slowly to avoid punctures of tires or oil pan.

Trailers and large RVs, with luck and skill, can go as far as La Costilla, approximately 5 miles (8km) south of Puertecitos. **Punta Bufeo** is 91 miles (147km) from San Felipe. The mountains meet the water here, making this small resort mostly steep and rocky. There are cabins for rent, a restaurant, dirt landing strip and boat anchorage.

Beyond Punta Bufeo, the road becomes easier but still requires caution as far as Rancho Grande. For more details on the highway, see **Bahía San Luis Gonzaga** (p126) in the Central Baja chapter.

Central Baja

CONTENTS

CENTRAL BAJA

Central Baja – the area between Baja's Desierto Central (Central Desert), roughly starting at El Rosario, to Llano de Magdalena (Magdalena Plain), northwest of La Paz – is one of the least frequented parts of the peninsula. Yet its vast, wild landscapes are some of the most unique and spectacular you'll see. Visitors roll through to fish its hidden coves or explore its isolated beaches – ideal for camping, clamming and lounging in the sun. The region is also home to the peninsula's best whale-watching: Laguna San Ignacio, Laguna Ojo de Liebre and Bahía Magdalena are all nurseries for the California gray whale, where you can board a skiff and get within touching distance of mothers and their calves.

The sinuous 76-mile (122km) stretch of the Transpeninsular between El Rosario and Cataviña traverses a surrealistic landscape of huge boulders among stands of the *cardón* cactus (resembling the saguaro of the southwestern USA) and the twisted, drooping *cirio* (nicknamed 'boojum' for its supposed resemblance to an imaginary creature in Lewis Carroll's *The Hunting of the Snark)*. Beyond Guerrero Negro, the Desierto de Vizcaíno is a harsh, desolate expanse, but the oasis of San Ignacio reflects the semitropical environment of the Gulf coast.

On the Sea of Cortez, Loreto, and especially Mulegé, are relaxed little towns more resembling their counterparts in mainland Mexico than their Baja brethren, and make excellent bases for exploring the spectacular Gulf coast between Santa Rosalía and Loreto. Be sure to stop in Santa Rosalía, where French colonial clapboard buildings and a prefabricated Eiffel church make it one of the strangest sights on the peninsula.

TOP FIVE

- Get up close and friendly with majestic California gray whales and their calves at **Laguna Ojo de Liebre** (p133), **Laguna San Ignacio** (p140) and **Bahía Magdalena** (p157).
- Fish, kayak and relax on one of Baja's most beautiful bays, **Bahía de Los Angeles** (p128).
- Gape in awe at the pre-Columbian rock art of **Sierra de San Francisco** (p138).
- Camp on the beach along the spectacular island-studded **Bahía Concepción** (p147), south of Mulegé.
- Dive and kayak to your heart's content in the national park waters off **Loreto** (p149).

- MULEGÉ JANUARY AVERAGE HIGH: 80°F/27°C   - WATER TEMP OFF LORETO: 62-83°F/17-28°C

MISIÓN SAN FERNANDO

About 35 miles (56km) southeast of El Rosario, near the site of the Franciscan mission of San Fernando Velicatá, the roadside settlement of Rancho El Progreso offers simple food and cold drinks. From Km 121 on the Transpeninsular, just west of the rancho, a dirt spur leads west about 3 miles (5km) to the **mission ruins**. Despite a couple of sandy spots, the road is passable for anything but a low rider.

The famed Franciscan Padre Junípero Serra founded the mission in 1769, but the Dominicans assumed control four years later when Serra decided to concentrate his efforts in Alta California. A few years later, epidemics nearly obliterated the native population, and the mission closed in 1818.

Some of the mission church's adobe walls are still standing, but of greater interest are the **petroglyphs** on a conspicuous granite outcrop a few hundred yards down the arroyo. They date from about AD 1000 to 1500. Unfortunately, vandals have damaged some paintings and others have weathered poorly, but together with the mission ruins they make the trip worthwhile.

CATAVIÑA

☎ 646

Set in a landscape of massive granite boulders, the isolated oasis of Cataviña, roughly midway between El Rosario and Bahía de Los Angeles, is a good place to fill the tank and trip out on the scenery. There's no Pemex station, but you can buy gas next to the RV park; the next Pemex station on the Transpeninsular is at **Villa Jesús María**, 123 miles (198km) south. South of town, at Km 211, fix your sights on the boulder field of **El Pedregoso**, a giant pile of granite boulders that seems to have simply fallen from the sky.

For great **free camping**, follow any of the sandy tracks off into the desert north of the arroyo, which runs to the north of Cataviña and west of the Transpeninsular among the boulders and towering *cardones* (cardón cacti). Firewood is plentiful (keep it small), but bring food and water. A bonus is a series of Cochimí **cave paintings** east of the highway, just beyond the arroyo. (There's a dirt road that leads from the highway at the arroyo. Once you drive in a short distance, there is a sign leading to the paintings.)

Those who prefer to stay in Cataviña proper can use the **Parque Natural RV Park** (site US$7). It lacks showers but has full hookups. Economical rooms are available at **Cabañas Linda** (no ☎; r US$20) on the eastern side of the highway. Fatigued visitors with a bigger budget can stay at **Hotel La Pinta** (☎ 176-2601, in the USA ☎ 800-800-9632; www.lapintahotels.com; r midweek/weekend US$72/84). It features an attractive cactus garden, a swimming pool and a children's playground.

On the eastern side of the highway is reasonably priced **Café La Enramada**, successful enough to have built a pleasant new *palapa* (palm-leaf shelter) with cardón walls and glass windows to keep out the wind. The cafe offers quality *antojitos* (Mexican snacks or light meals), seafood specialties and traditional Mexican chocolate (ask for 'chocolate Ibarra' or you may get instant). It's a much better value than the more elaborate restaurant at Hotel La Pinta and has a small grocery store.

Rancho Santa Inés (d US$10, site US$5), a fourth-generation ranch, at the end of a paved road half a mile (1km) south of Cataviña, permits camping and has toilets and hot showers. It also has very clean dormitory accommodations. A **restaurant** provides good meals, and the proprietors can arrange excursions to the isolated ruins of **Misión Santa María**, which Walt Peterson's *The Baja Adventure Book* called 'Mission Impossible.' The ruins are 17 miles (27km) east of the highway by a road difficult even for 4WD vehicles – the trip takes about three days out and back.

BAHÍA SAN LUIS GONZAGA

About 32 miles (52km) south of Cataviña, near Laguna Chapala and across from the **Lonchería Los Cirios** (a basic restaurant between Km 234 and Km 235), a graded but rough road, passable even for large RVs, cuts northeast to Bahía San Luis Gonzaga, Puertecitos and the popular Gulf resort of San Felipe. Bahía San Luis Gonzaga is a quiet, beautiful area now experiencing increased but not overwhelming tourist development, primarily attracting **fishing** enthusiasts. It is one of the most beautiful bays in Baja. Except for a few large vacation homes, accommodations are fairly basic, though good food is available.

The road to Bahía San Luis Gonzaga is one of the worst in Baja, so before

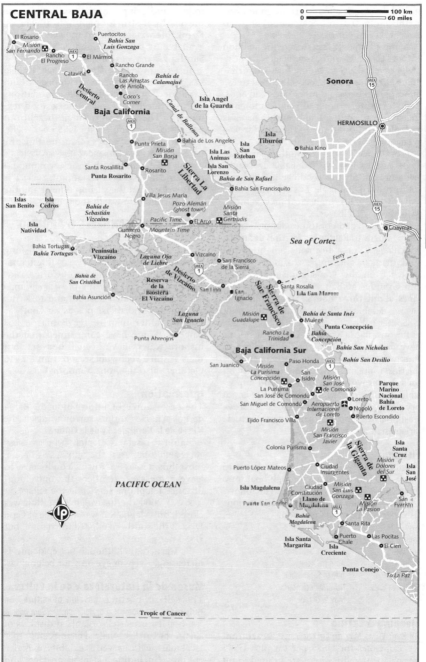

CENTRAL BAJA

0 _____ 100 km
0 _____ 60 miles

El Rosario
Misión
San Fernando
Rancho
El Progreso
Cataviña

Puertocitos
*Bahía San
Luis Gonzaga*
MEX 1
El Mármol
Rancho Grande
Rancho
Las Arrastas
de Arriola
*Bahía de
Calamajué*
Coco's
Corner

*Desierto
Central*

Baja California
MEX 1

Canal de Ballenas

Isla Angel
de la Guarda

Sonora
MEX 15

HERMOSILLO

Punta Prieta
Misión
San Borja
Bahía de Los Angeles
Isla Las
Animas
Isla San
Lorenzo
Isla San
Esteban
Isla
Tiburón
Bahía Kino

Santa Rosalillita
Rosarito
Punta Rosarito

*Sierra La
Libertad*

Bahía de San Rafael
Bahía San Francisquito

Islas
San Benito
Isla
Cedros
Villa Jesús María
Pozo Alemán
(ghost town)
Misión
Santa
Gertrudis

Isla
Natividad
*Bahía de
Sebastián
Vizcaíno*
Pacific Time
El Arco
Guerrero
Negro
Mountain Time

Sea of Cortez

Bahía Tortugas
Bahía Tortugas
**Península
Vizcaíno**
*Laguna Ojo
de Liebre*
Vizcaíno
San Francisco
de la Sierra
Ferry
Guaymas

Bahía de
San Cristóbal
**Reserva
de la
Biósfera
El Vizcaíno**
*Desierto
de Vizcaíno*
San Lino
MEX 1

Bahía Asunción
San
Ignacio
Santa Rosalía
Isla San Marcos

*Laguna
San Ignacio*
Misión
Guadalupe
*Sierra de
San Francisco*
Bahía de Santa Inés
Mulegé
Punta Concepción

Punta Abreojos
Rancho La
Trinidad
*Bahía
Concepción*
Bahía San Nicholas

Baja California Sur
Paso Honda
MEX 1
Bahía San Desilio

San Juanico
Misión
La Purísima
Concepción
San
Isidro
Misión
San José
de Comondú
La Purísima
San José de Comondú
San Miguel de Comondú
Aeropuerto
Internacional
de Loreto
Loreto
Nopoló
**Parque
Marino
Nacional
Bahía
de Loreto**
Puerto Escondido

Ejido Francisco Villa
Misión
San Francisco
Javier

Colonia Purísima
Misión
Dolores
del Sur
Isla
Santa
Cruz
Isla
San
José

Puerto López Mateos
Ciudad
Insurgentes
*Sierra de
la Giganta*

Isla Magdalena
Ciudad
Constitución
**Llano de
Magdalena**
Misión
San Luis
Gonzaga
Misión
La Pasión
San
Evaristo
MEX 1

Puerto San Carlos
*Bahía
Magdalena*
Santa Rita

Isla Santa
Margarita
Isla
Creciente
Puerto
Chale
Las Pocitas
El Cien

PACIFIC OCEAN

Punta Conejo
To La Paz

Tropic of Cancer

starting out, ask about current conditions at the *llantera* (tire-repair shop) next to Lonchería Los Cirios.

About 13 miles (21km) east of the junction is **Coco's Corner**, a wild assemblage of ready-made objets d'art, including beer-can ornaments, a cactus garden, ocotillo 'street trees,' hubcaps, fan belts and other odds and ends. Radiator water, motor oil and automatic transmission fluid are all available here, as are cold drinks and modest meals. **Camping** is encouraged (free, with pit toilets).

From Coco's Corner, another dirt road leads east to little-visited **Bahía de Calamajué**; a branch off this road eventually leads south toward Bahía de Los Angeles but is suitable only for high-clearance vehicles with short wheelbases.

The main road continues about 4 miles (6km) north to **Rancho Las Arrastras de Arriola**, which has water, a mechanic, a llantera and cold drinks. The entire 20-mile (32km) stretch from the Transpeninsular to Rancho Grande (at Bahía San Luis Gonzaga) takes about three hours. Magna Sin **gasoline** is available at Rancho Grande for about US$5 per gallon.

Beyond Bahía San Luis Gonzaga, storms have damaged sections of the roadway to Puertecitos and San Felipe. For more details on this route, which is now very difficult for vehicles with low clearance and impossible for RVs, see p123. While 4WD is not necessary, the road is often steep, narrow, washboarded and difficult for any vehicle larger than a camper van.

Fishing

Anglers usually bring their own boats to Bahía San Luis Gonzaga, though boats and guides may be locally available. The following list indicates at what times the various fish species are most common:

Bass	April to June
Cabrilla	July
Corvina	March to September
Grouper	April to October
Sierra	July to September
White sea bass	November to March
Yellowtail	May to October

Sleeping & Eating

RV Park Villas Mar de Cortez rents beachfront RV campsites for US$5 per car plus US$5 per palapa; facilities here are limited to pit toilets, and gringo morons sometimes use the nearby airstrip for nighttime drag races. Drinkable water and cold showers are both available at Rancho Grande's Minimarket San Luis, across the highway.

Just to the north, **Alfonsina's** (r US$40) also has its own airstrip, much improved and expanded motel-style accommodations with private baths, and a fine seafood restaurant. There's also a single beachfront palapa for car campers for US$5 per night.

Two and a half miles (4km) north is the turnoff for **Papá Fernández** (tent site US$10), a popular fish camp with basic accommodations and an excellent restaurant. Service is a little slow, but the shrimp omelet and the fresh tortillas are worth the wait.

BAHÍA DE LOS ANGELES & AROUND
☎ 200 / pop 600

Bahía de Los Angeles is a popular fishing village on the shore of its sparkling namesake bay, an inlet of the Sea of Cortez. People come here to fish the offshore islands and nearby isolated beaches and to kayak among the Midriff Islands as far south as Loreto, rather than to see Bahía de Los Angeles. Some have complained that the inshore waters have been fished out, but there is still a yellowtail season from May to October (also the hottest months).

Information

The best source of information on Bahía de Los Angeles and its surroundings is the **Museo de la Naturaleza y de la Cultura**.

Bahía's **caseta telefónica** (telephone office; ☎ 124-9101/02/05/08) is the only way to reach most businesses in town. You'll have to leave a message. It offers the only long-distance telephone service in the village.

As of 2004 the local Pemex station was closed, but Magna Sin was available at Casa Díaz at the southern edge of town for about US$5 per gallon.

Be warned: theft, though not epidemic, is increasing. Keep an eye on your belongings.

Museo de la Naturaleza y de la Cultura

The self-supporting **museum of nature and culture** (no ☎; admission by donation; ☖ 9am-noon & 2pm-4pm) features well-organized displays of shells, sea turtles, whale skeletons and other local marine life as well as exhibits on native cultures (including Cochimí artifacts and rock art displays), mining, and horse gear and *vaquero* (cowboy) culture. Also on the grounds are a desert botanical garden and a good reconstruction of a mining site. The volunteers here, mostly resident gringos, are a good source of information.

Programa Tortuga Marina

Bahía de Los Angeles was once the center of the turtle fishery on the Gulf and, unfortunately, the now illegal practice has not completely disappeared. In a modest facility just north of town, the **Sea Turtle Program** conducts research on sea turtle biology, ecology and conservation. In 1996 the program released a loggerhead turtle named Adelita at Santa Rosalillita on the Pacific side of the peninsula and tracked her by radio transmitter across the ocean to Japan (read all about Adelita's voyage at www.adelitas-journey.com). The modest program's tanks offer the opportunity to see endangered sea turtle species such as the leatherback, the green and the hawksbill.

Fishing

Casa Díaz (p130) and a few other outfitters arrange full-day (6am to 1pm) fishing excursions for US$100 to US$120.

Those with their own boats can use the launch ramps at Villa Vitta Trailer Park or **Guillermo's** (p130) for about US$10 per day (use is free if you're staying at either place).

The following list indicates when gamefish species are abundant in the vicinity of Bahía de Los Angeles:

Cabrilla	April to January
Corvina	February to June
Grouper	year-round
Halibut	April
Marlin	June to August
Roosterfish	November to April
Sailfish	May to September
Sierra	March
Yellowtail	year-round

Sea Kayaking

Bahía de Los Angeles has become a prime kayaking destination, and paddling to the islands around the bay can be one of the most challenging adventures in the Sea of Cortez. Northeasterly winds of up to 35 knots can suddenly appear and churn the water into a nasty mess, so expect some excitement.

Isla Coronado, northeast of town, is the most popular local destination for kayakers. To get there, follow the dirt road north out of town for about 5 miles (8km) to Punta La Gringa; in winter there are usually plenty of campers around to watch your vehicle while you paddle. Many kayakers continue north from Punta La Gringa to Punta Remedios and **Isla Angel de la Guarda**.

Those exploring offshore islands should take care to avoid disturbing wildlife; careless visitors have scared many birds, most notably pelicans, from their nests, exposing eggs and chicks to predators and the hot sun.

Daggett's Beach Camping, Camp Gecko (see below) and a couple other places rent kayaks for US$15 to US$20 per day.

Sleeping & Eating

For those hotels without telephone numbers, you can usually reserve by calling the caseta telefónica and leaving a message.

Bahía de Los Angeles has several motels, RV parks and other campsites north and south of town, plus a handful of decent restaurants. Punta La Gringa, a beautiful beach area to the north, has several rugged **campsites** with choice views of offshore islands, but the road is a bit hard to follow, the trash cans are overflowing and toilet facilities are nil.

Daggett's Beach Camping (no ☎ ; site US$10) Just north of the Programa Tortuga Marina, Daggett's has hot showers, and it's much cleaner and tidier than most other area campgrounds. It's also possible to rent kayaks or to arrange fishing tours.

Camp Gecko (no ☎ ; www.campgecko.com; cabin US$15-25) Congenial Camp Gecko, in a quiet shoreline location 3½ miles (6km) south of town on the Bahía San Francisquito road, offers a variety of cabins, all with flush toilets, firewood and regular trash collection. The pricier ones have their own hot showers, while the others have separate hot showers. Camping or palapa rental is US$3 per night with access to the same amenities.

Hotel Las Hamacas (☎ 124-9114; d US$50-60; 🛏) In town, Las Hamacas has clean and spacious doubles; the pricier rooms have TVs and air-con. Its **restaurant** is a good choice and a bit cheaper than others in town.

Costa del Sol (☎ 124-9110, in Ensenada ☎ 646-178-8167; costadelsolhotel@hotmail.com; s/d US$50/75; 🛏)

Just south of Las Hamacas, this is the most upscale of any accommodations options. Its large rooms have TVs and air-con.

Hotel Villa Vitta (☎ 124-9103; r US$25-50; ☒) Villa Vitta offers clean, comfortable, air-conditioned rooms; rates depend on the number and size of beds you need. Its **restaurant** specializes in moderately priced seafood.

Guillermo's Trailer Park & Restaurant (☎ 124-9104; tent/RV without hookups/RV with hookups/r US$4/4/12/65) Next door to Hotel Villa Vita and separated from the beach by an unsightly row of trailers and fishing shanties, Guillermo's has about 40 spaces for tents and RVs, some with limited shade and a few with full hookups. The baths are less than immaculate, but the hot water is reliable. Its motel annex has good rooms with private baths, while meals at **Guillermo's Restaurant** cost about US$7-10. The food here is tasty, and the margaritas are large but expensive (go for the 4 to 5pm happy hour).

Casa Díaz (☎ 124-9112; r US$22-25) This family-run motel has a grocery store, a **restaurant** and 14 cozy stone cabins with hot showers.

Getting There & Away

There is no bus service to Bahía de Los Angeles; without your own wheels (or wings), you'll have to hitch from the junction on the Transpeninsular. The turnoff from the Transpeninsular is about 65 miles (105km) south of Cataviña. It's an easily spotted paved road whose potholed surface leads another 42 miles (68km) to the bay.

SANTA ROSALILLITA

Twenty-four miles (39km) south of the Bahía de Los Angeles junction on the Transpeninsular, a road leads 10 miles (16km) west to Santa Rosalillita, an overgrown fish camp on the Pacific coast. The road is graded but unrelentingly washboarded. The exit off the Transpeninsular is signed southbound but not northbound. For **surfing** enthusiasts, beaches north of Punta Santa Rosalillita, reachable by a difficult 7½-mile (12km) dirt road that requires high clearance, are renowned for exceptional breaks, while Punta Rosarito to the south, known among surfers as 'The Wall,' may be the most consistent break on the entire peninsula.

Santa Rosalillita has made big headlines in recent years as the starting point of the Escolera Náutica, a 'land bridge' that would connect the village to the Sea of Cortez via a paved road wider than the Transpeninsular itself. It would allow yachters to bypass the cape and hit planned upscale marinas along the gulf.

PARALELO 28

☎ 615

Marked by a 140-foot (42m) steel monument ostensibly resembling an eagle, the

---

DETOUR: MISIÓN SAN BORJA

The extensive ruins of Misión San Borja de Adac, founded in 1762, are the best preserved of all the Jesuit adobes in Baja California. The few remaining local families still cultivate grapes, olives and other crops.

To get to the mission, take the well-signed lateral off the Transpeninsular from the truck stop of Rosarito (not to be confused with the Playas de Rosarito resort town between Tijuana and Ensenada), 8½ miles (14km) south of the Santa Rosalillita junction and 32 miles (52km) south of the Bahía de Los Angeles junction. The 21-mile (34km) road is rough in spots, but any vehicle with a short wheelbase and the clearance of a small pickup can handle it.

The route passes through a spectacular Wild West valley landscape of cirio, cardón, torote (elephant tree), datilillo (yucca) and cholla beneath broad volcanic mesas. The road forks about 2 miles (3km) before San Borja; a sign indicates that both forks go to the mission, but the left (northern) fork is easier on both car and driver.

Dominicans built the now-restored landmark church, made of locally quarried volcanic stone with many outstanding details, well after the Jesuits' expulsion. See the custodian before climbing the spiral staircase to the chorus, and leave a small (or large) donation. On October 10, the local saint's day, devotees from throughout the region converge on the tiny *ranchería* (settlement) to pray and party.

28th parallel marks the border between the states of Baja California (Norte) and Baja California Sur. The time zone changes here: Pacific Time (to the north) is one hour behind Mountain Standard Time (to the south).

Hotel La Pinta Guerrero Negro (☎ 157-1304, in the USA ☎ 800-800-9632; www.lapintahotels.com; r US$77-88), part of the Baja chain of La Pinta hotels, sits precisely on the 28th parallel. It has a **restaurant**, a bar and 28 comfortable rooms. **Trailer Park Benito Juárez**, alongside the hotel, has a few palapas and spacious RV sites for US$10 per night.

GUERRERO NEGRO
☎ 615 / pop 10,000

Guerrero Negro, the first settlement south of the 28th parallel, is a company town that owes its existence to the world's largest evaporative saltworks. Most travelers, however, come here to visit famous **Laguna Ojo de Liebre** (better known in English as Scammon's Lagoon; p133), the mating and birthing site for California gray whales. The Exportadora de Sal (ESSA) dominates the local economy, but the tourist trade is an important supplement, especially during the winter whale-watching season. A more recent economic factor is the Mexican army, which has a new camp at the Paralelo 28 monument, north of town.

Named for the Black Warrior, a Massachusetts whaler wrecked nearby in the mid-19th century, Guerrero Negro capitalizes on tourism through its annual **Festival Cultural de la Ballena Gris** (Gray Whale Cultural Festival), lasting three weeks in early February. It includes events such as environmental talks, films, bicycle races and a book fair. Although the town continues to improve its streets, Guerrero Negro is still the least appealing of the whale-watching bases – it's just a drab, no-frills place.

Orientation
Guerrero Negro comprises two very distinct sectors: a disorderly strip along Blvd Emiliano Zapata west of the Transpeninsular, and ESSA's orderly company town, with a standard grid pattern that begins shortly after Blvd Zapata curves southwest near the airfield. Most of the town's accommodations and restaurants are in the former area on Blvd Zapata.

Information
Banamex (Blvd Emiliano Zapata), at the entrance to the ESSA sector, will change US dollars and traveler's checks between 8:30am and 3pm weekdays. The town's **post office** is in the ESSA sector. Check email at **IntecNet** (Blvd Emiliano Zapata at Quintana Roo; US$2.50/hr), about three blocks south of the Pemex station.

The town's **Clínica Hospital IMSS** (☎ 157-0433) is on the southern side of Blvd Zapata where the road curves southwest.

Guerrero Negro is one of the main gas stops along the Transpeninsular, so the gas station tends to run out of gas on a regular basis during high season. Fill up your tank as soon as you get to town, on the off-chance that there won't be gas when you head back to the station.

Campers and RVers can obtain purified drinking water at a reasonable cost at **Fresk-Pura**, on the southern side of Blvd Zapata.

Saltworks
ESSA's saltworks consists of about 70 sq miles (182 sq km) of evaporative ponds, each about 110 sq yards (100 sq meters) in area and about a yard deep, just south of Guerrero Negro. In the intense desert sunlight and high winds, water evaporates quickly, leaving a saline residue that is dredged from the pools, hauled to nearby quays and barged to Isla Cedros for transshipment by freighter. The works produces more than five million tons of salt annually.

Whale-Watching
Guerrero Negro is the northernmost of Baja's whale-watching locales and has the most abundant accommodations of any of them. Tours from Guerrero Negro, however, are usually briefer than tours elsewhere because they require traveling some distance to the whale-watching sites.

Three-hour tours usually start at 8am and 11am, and cost around US$40, including transportation to Laguna Ojo de Liebre and a box lunch. Local operators include **Mario's** (☎ 157-0120) and **Malarrimo Ecotours** (☎ 157-0250; www.malarrimo.com), both at their namesake establishments (see Sleeping & Eating).

Note that whale-watching excursions at Guerrero Negro and more southerly points conform to Mountain Standard Time; southbound visitors who forget to change their watches at the state border will literally miss the bus.

Sleeping & Eating

Accommodations in Guerrero Negro are fairly abundant and reasonably priced, but the winter whale-watching season can put a strain on these resources. For this reason, reservations are advisable from January through March.

Malarrimo Motel & RV Park (☎ 157-0100; www. malarrimo.com; Blvd Emiliano Zapata; tent/van/RV/s/d US$10/12/14/40/45; **P**) Also known as Cabañas Don Miguelito, this is one of the cushiest places in town. Rooms are large and comfortable, and the grounds are attractively landscaped. For RVers, hot water is plentiful and the toilets are clean. Motel rates drop by US$5 outside whale-watching season. Its highly regarded **restaurant** (mains US$7-18) specializes in seafood in both traditional antojitos and more sophisticated international dishes. It's not cheap, but portions are abundant.

Motel Las Ballenas (☎ 157-0116; s/d US$19/25; **P**) Clean and with a TV in every room, this friendly motel is likely the best value in town. It's just your basic motel with industrially carpeted rooms and a bare parking area, but something about the pink paint job and the staff's friendliness give it a welcoming feel. It's off the main drag (behind El Morro) but signed.

Hotel El Morro (☎ 157-0414; Blvd Emiliano Zapata at Victoria Sanchez; s/d US$28/31; **P**) Easily spotted on the northern side of Blvd Zapata, El Morro has 35 clean, pleasant rooms with cable TV and hot showers. The attached diner-style **restaurant** (mains US$6-9) serves reliable chicken, meat and seafood.

Motel Brisa Salina (☎ 157-1795; s/d US$20/25, RV US$12 **P**) On the northern side of Blvd Zapata, this is a no-frills motel where small rooms have TV and hot water. At press time, the owners were finishing up RV spaces with full hookups in the back.

Motel Don Gus (☎ 157-1611; dongushotrest@prodigy. net.mx; s/d US$28/35; **P**) Around the corner from the bus terminal, just off Blvd Zapata, Motel Don Gus has huge, spotless rooms around a large off-street parking area. It's definitely upscale by Guerrero Negro standards, and the attached **restaurant** (mains US$5-10) serves good Mexican food and pastas.

Motel San Ignacio (☎ 157-0270; s/d US$21/24; **P**) The rooms are clean and spacious here, but because they're close to the boulevard, they tend to be noisy.

Guerrero Negro's best food bargains are the numerous taco stands along Blvd Zapata, which keep erratic hours but maintain high standards. The three near the Pemex, including delicious **Carnitas Michoacan** (full meal US$3-5), are great.

On the main drag, near Hotel El Morro, **Restaurant Puerto Viejo** (Blvd Zapata; mains US$3-5) serves good, cheap breakfasts. For similar fare, check out **Cocina Económica Letty** (mains US$3-8) on the southern side of Blvd Zapata, which also serves very fine antojitos and seafood at friendly prices. **Mario's** (☎ 157-0808; US$5-9), just south of town on the

---

SCAMMON & THE WHALES

Laguna Ojo de Liebre takes its English name, **Scammon's Lagoon**, from Captain Charles Melville Scammon, an American whaler who frequented the area in the 1850s. Born in Maine, Scammon yearned to captain a trading ship but had to settle for command of less lucrative whalers, such as the *Boston* out of San Francisco. In 1857, upon learning from some Mexicans that an estuary near Bahía de Sebastián Vizcaíno was the breeding ground of the gray whale, he headed south.

For whalers, the density of whales in constricted, shallow lagoons meant almost literally shooting fish in a barrel, but Scammon's first attempts were disastrous: Whales crushed two of his small whaleboats and seriously injured half the crew. Resorting to 'bomb lances' – bombs fired into a whale from a hand-held gun – instead of harpoons, Scammon and his crew managed to get 740 barrels of oil, filling virtually every container on board, which was later sold in San Francisco as lubricant.

By the end of 1859 Scammon and other whalers had nearly eliminated the gray whale from the lagoons. Whaling did not cease until 1935, and it took many decades for the population to recover. Today the US and Mexican governments have effective laws, in addition to international agreements, that protect the gray whale and its habitat.

Transpeninsular, serves excellent, moderately priced seafood.

Getting There & Away

AIR

Aeropuerto Guerrero Negro is 1¼ miles (2km) north of the state border, just west of the Transpeninsular. Guerrero Negro also has an airfield near the ESSA sector in town.

The Aeroméxico connector airline **Aerolitoral** (☎ 157-1745) flies Monday through Saturday to Hermosillo, with connections to Ciudad Juárez, Ciudad Obregón, Chihuahua, Mexico City, Phoenix and Tucson. Its offices are on the northern side of Blvd Zapata near the Pemex station.

You can fly north to Isla Cedros (US$55) continuing to Ensenada (US$103) with **Aerocedros** (☎ 157-1626; Blvd Zapata) on Tuesday and Friday at 1:30pm.

BUS

From Guerrero Negro's **bus terminal** (☎ 157-0611), on the southern side of Blvd Zapata, Autotransportes de Baja California (ABC) and Autotransportes Aguila offer services throughout the peninsula. There are five or six daily departures to the destinations in the following table and one daily to Mexicali (US$62, 15 hours).

Destination	Fare	Duration
Cabo San Lucas	US$60	11 hrs
Ciudad Constitución	US$35	9 hrs
Ensenada	US$37	8-9 hrs
La Paz	US$50	10 hrs
Loreto	US$28	6-7 hrs
Mulegé	US$19	4-5 hrs
San Ignacio	US$9	3 hrs
San Quintín	US$20	5-6 hrs
Santa Rosalía	US$17	4 hrs
Tijuana	US$45	10-12 hrs
Vizcaíno	US$6	1 hr

AROUND GUERRERO NEGRO

Laguna Ojo de Liebre

Also known in part as **Parque Natural de la Ballena Gris** (Gray Whale Natural Park), Laguna Ojo de Liebre (Scammon's Lagoon) has the greatest number of whales of any of Baja's main whale-watching sites. It is part of the massive 9833-sq-mile (25,566-sq-km) **Vizcaíno Biosphere Reserve** (Reserva de la Biosfera El Vizcaíno), which sprawls from Laguna San Ignacio, Guerrero Negro, Isla Natividad and Isla Cedros across to the Sea of Cortez, taking in part of the Sierra de San Francisco. The reserve is the joint responsibility of **Semarnap** (in Guerrero Negro ☎ 157-1777) and **Ejido Benito Juárez** (☎ 157-1733), whose lands the reserve occupies.

At the lagoon, local *pangueros* (fishermen with skiffs) take visitors for 1½-hour **whale-watching** (US$25-30/person) excursions on its shallow waters. It's also possible, and sometimes preferable, to organize whale-watching tours through hotels or operators in Guerrero Negro. Whale-watching now officially begins December 15 and lasts until April 15, but whales are few at the earliest dates. Late-season trips, those from mid-February on, are likelier to encounter friendly whales.

Camping is possible at the lagoon, where savvy visitors choose sites above the sometimes flooded tidal flats; the more remote sites are also closer to the maternity channel, so you can hear the whales up close and personal. The ejido charges US$5 per vehicle for camping or day use. Its **Restaurant Palapa** (mains US$5-9) has superb food at very reasonable prices – don't miss the tasty *almejas rancheras* (clams with salsa).

Five miles (8km) southeast of the Guerrero Negro junction, at Km 208 of the Transpeninsular, a smooth, graded road leads 15 miles (24km) southwest to Laguna Ojo de Liebre. All vehicles must register with the guard at ESSA's checkpoint, which controls the access road.

El Arco, Pozo Alemán & Misión Santa Gertrudis

About 17 miles (27km) south of Guerrero Negro, a once paved but now gravel 26-mile (42km) lateral leads eastward to El Arco, a 19th-century gold-mining town that now serves as a supply center for surrounding ranchos. The area's real highlight, however, is the nearby **ghost town** of Pozo Alemán, a few miles east on a sometimes rugged dirt road. Its ruins include caves, several residences, the smelter, a blacksmith's shop, a still-functioning windmill and water system, and a company store with items still on the counter. A caretaker oversees the ruins and shows visitors around; a small tip is appropriate.

The dirt road continues east to Bahía San Francisquito (see Detour, p133) on the

Sea of Cortez. Just west of Bahía San Francisquito, a graded road leads north to Bahía de Los Angeles – the drive takes about three hours – and can be pretty rough at times.

About 23 miles (37km) east of El Arco via an unpaved road, you'll find the isolated Misión Santa Gertrudis, founded by the famous Jesuit Fernando Consag in 1751. After the Spanish government expelled the Jesuits in 1767, Dominicans took over and finished the small stone church, now undergoing restoration, which bears a ceiling date of 1796.

The church **museum** contains a selection of Guaycura, Cora and Cochimí artifacts, as well as *ofrendas* (offerings) left by pilgrims for Santa Gertrudis. Every November 16, pilgrims jam the village for the **Fiesta de Santa Gertrudis**.

Another landmark is **El Camino Real**, the royal road (really a trail), which still leads 29 leagues (100 miles or 161km) from San Ignacio to San Borja via Santa Gertrudis. Most travelers prefer the improved road from El Arco, passable for any passenger vehicle and even small RVs. The entire trip from Guerrero Negro takes 2½ to three hours.

ISLA CEDROS

Isla Cedros is a mountainous northward extension of Península Vizcaíno, separated from the mainland by Canal de Kellet, the much smaller Isla Natividad and Canal de Dewey. Reaching altitudes of nearly 4000 feet (1200m) above sea level, this desert island is a rewarding, off-the-beaten-track destination for adventurous travelers.

Early Spanish explorers found surprisingly large numbers of Cochimí Indians on the island, whose intransigence led to their forcible relocation to the mainland mission of San Ignacio by the Jesuits. Manila galleons later used Isla Cedros as a port of refuge on their return across the Pacific. The island supports unusual vegetation, including native tree species and coastal wildlife such as elephant seals and sea lions. Cedros mule deer, an endangered subspecies, still inhabit the rugged backcountry. The island is known for its abalone and lobster.

Most of the island's 1465 inhabitants live in the tiny port of **Cedros** on the sheltered eastern shore, but many also live at ESSA's company town at Punta Morro Redondo at the southern tip of the island, which is the site of the airfield and the transshipment point for salt barged over from Guerrero Negro.

The ramshackle village of Cedros faces Bahía de Sebastián Vizcaíno from the slopes beneath towering Cerro Vargas, also called Cerro Cenizo, whose summit (3950 feet or 1185m) is usually hidden by clouds. It's definitely not a stereotypical tourist destination. Cedros has no bank or any other place to change money, and you can't even get a margarita, but there is **phone service**, an **IMSS hospital/clinic** and a Capitanía del Puerto (port authority).

Several two-story buildings with porches or balconies facing the bay add a touch of vernacular architectural interest. Electricity is available only 6am to noon and 5 to 11pm. Running water is available mornings only, though most houses have storage tanks. Prices are high on the island because nearly everything is shipped in – including salt, despite the mountains of it at Punta Morro Redondo.

In Cedros' tidy hillside church, murals in the curious **Capilla de la Reconciliación** (Chapel of Reconciliation) depict events in Mexican

---

DETOUR: BAHÍA SAN FRANCISQUITO

About 52 miles (84km) east of El Arco and 80 miles (129km) south of Bahía de Los Angeles, Bahía San Francisquito is one of the most beautiful, isolated beaches in Baja. Here you'll find the remote, rustic fishing resort **Punta San Francisquito** (no ☎), many of whose guests arrive by private plane. Beachfront **camping** is possible at the resort for just US$5 per site with access to hot showers, while cabañas cost US$15 per person or US$30 with full board. The restaurant is open all year and offers excellent, if pricey, food.

A short distance north of the resort, **Puerto San Francisquito** (no ☎) has equally attractive beachfront camping for about US$3 per person with a saltwater flush toilet, but no fresh water.

The road from Bahía de Los Angeles is passable for just about any vehicle, but drive with caution because it has washed away at certain points. The total drive takes about 2½ hours.

and Baja Californian history, such as the expulsion of the Jesuits, in a comic-book style.

Sleeping & Eating

Accommodations in Cedros are very basic, and there are only a few places to eat. **Casa de Huésped Aguilar**, on the waterfront, charges US$10 for rooms with shared bath (no hot water) or US$15 with private bath. To find the unmarked building, walk straight downhill from the church; before entering the grounds of the fishing cooperative, look for the two-story house on your left. If no one is on duty, you'll have to hike up the hill to Manuel Aguilar's house, a brown stucco next to the elementary school and the power plant, to check in.

Getting There & Away

Isla Cedros' airfield is at Punta Morro Redondo, about 5 miles (8km) south of the village. Taxis charge about US$5 per person, but locals will sometimes offer you a ride there. Flights from Guerrero Negro and Ensenada serve Isla Cedros.

Return flights from Isla Cedros to Guerrero Negro (US$55) ostensibly leave at 1pm (Pacific Time), but travelers should arrive at least an hour ahead of time to avoid being left at the airstrip. See the Getting There & Away sections under Guerrero Negro and Ensenada for more information.

ISLAS SAN BENITO

This tiny archipelago consists of three small islands 30 nautical miles (55km) west of Isla Cedros. The westernmost island, the largest of the three, supports a large winter camp of abalone divers and their families, as well as a substantial breeding colony of northern elephant seals. The seals begin to arrive in December but are most numerous in January and February. Sea turtles and whales are visible offshore (the islands are just off the gray-whale migration route).

Unless you bring camping equipment and enough food and water to stay overnight, expect to spend no more than an hour on shore.

Passing yachts often anchor here, and sailors come ashore to see the seals, but budget travelers can catch a lift on the *Tito I*, which carries daily supplies to the abalone divers and returns to Isla Cedros with the day's catch. For a (free) passage on the

Tito I, visit the Sociedad Cooperativa de Producción Pesquera in the village of Cedros before it closes to the public at 1pm.

The crew of the *Tito I* is exceptionally friendly and will probably offer breakfast to passengers, but travelers prone to seasickness should refrain from eating too heavily. The four-hour voyage to the San Benitos, against the wind and the northwestern swell, is generally rougher than the voyage back.

PENÍNSULA VIZCAÍNO

One of Baja's most thinly populated areas, Península Vizcaíno is a sparsely vegetated, mountainous extension of the Desierto de Vizcaíno. While you may not need a rugged 4WD vehicle everywhere – roads are generally passable – conditions are terrible in certain areas. Even the best roads are pretty rough, so driving can be very slow.

Vizcaíno
☎ 615 / pop 2350

About 40 miles (64km) south of Guerrero Negro, the crossroads town of Vizcaíno is the gateway to the peninsula and has a Pemex station. Excellent rooms and a good **restaurant** are available at **Motel Kadekaaman** (☎ 156-4112; s/d US$28/34 Jun-Oct, US$28/35 Nov-May; P ⊠). The adjacent RV park charges US$10.

From Vizcaíno's **bus terminal** (☎ 154-0771), Aquila buses run north five times daily and south four times daily. Buses also go to Bahía Tortugas (US$15; 3 hours) on Monday, Tuesday, Wednesday and Saturday at 5am.

SAN IGNACIO
☎ 615 / pop 4000

After the scrub and cacti forests of the Desierto de Vizcaíno, the palm oasis of San Ignacio is a soothing sight. With its lingering colonial atmosphere and its laurel-shaded central plaza backed by a beautifully preserved mission, San Ignacio makes the perfect place to chill out. But there's more: It's also the jumping-off point for two of Baja's premier attractions: whale-watching excursions to Laguna San Ignacio – probably the best spot for contact with so-called friendly whales – and trips to the spectacular pre-Columbian rock art sites in the Sierra de San Francisco.

DETOUR: BAHÍA TORTUGAS

Bahía Tortugas (pop 2600) is 107 miles (172km) west of Vizcaíno via a paved, and then gravel, road.

The town is appealing more for its barren, windswept setting and the drive out here through some seriously desolate stretches than the town itself is for any postcard-perfect scenery. Passing yachts usually anchor at Bahía Tortugas because it's the only port between San Diego and Cabo San Lucas that has direct refueling facilities, making it a good spot for lifts south despite its remoteness. Hang out on the pier near the tuna cannery. Anglers cruise the offshore kelp beds for bass, mackerel and barracuda, while farther offshore they find bonito and yellow tail. You can hire a guide to take you fishing in a *panga* (skiff) for about US$50 per day.

Bahía Tortugas has a few hotels, a bank, a Pemex and a long-distance telephone office in town. **Motel Nancy** (☎ 615-158-0100; Av Independencia; s/d US$18/27) is a friendly, family-run place. Or try the **Motel Rendon** (☎ 615-158-0232; s/d US$18/23), on Altamirano. The decent restaurant next door, **El Moroco**, is run by the same family.

In 1728 the Mexican Jesuit Juan Bautista Luyando located Misión San Ignacio de Kadakaamán here, planting dense groves of date palms and citrus in the Arroyo El Carrizal surrounding the town. After the Jesuits' expulsion, Dominican missionaries supervised construction of the lava-block church (finished in 1786) that still dominates the town's plaza.

San Ignacio has several grocery stores, a handful of restaurants, lodging and modest trailer parks. San Ignacio's Fiesta Patronal (festival in honor of San Ignacio's patron saint) takes place the last week of July.

Orientation & Information

San Ignacio is 88 miles (142km) south of Guerrero Negro. The town proper is about 1 mile (1.6km) south of the Transpeninsular; a paved lateral leads from the highway junction (known as San Lino) past a small lagoon and through groves of date palms into the town. Parking is easy, and the town invites walking.

Most services are found around the plaza, including the post office and Ladatel pay phones. For Internet access, go to **Café Intro** (US$1.50/hr), across from Hotel Posadas.

Casa Leree has a superb selection of books on Baja California, and its amiable North American owner, Juanita Ames, can tell you about hiking in the area.

Sights & Activities
MISIÓN SAN IGNACIO

With lava-block walls nearly 4 feet (1.2m) thick, the former Jesuit **Misión San Ignacio de Kadakaamán** (admission free; ☼ 9am-6pm daily Oct-Mar, 8am-3pm Mon-Sat Apr-Sep) is one of

Baja's most beautiful churches. It has been in continuous use since its founding in 1728. Opposite the plaza, occupying the site of a former Cochimí ranchería and initiated by the famous Jesuit Fernando Consag, the church was completed in 1786 under the direction of Dominican Juan Crisóstomo Gómez. Epidemics reduced the Cochimí population from about 5000 at contact to only 120 by the late 18th century, but the mission lasted until 1840.

MUSEO SAN IGNACIO

Just south of the mission church, the Instituto Nacional de Antropología y Historia (INAH) has built an impressive new **museum** (☎ 154-0222; admission free; ☼ 9am-6pm daily Oct-Mar, 8am-3pm Mon-Sat Apr-Sep) that has elaborate displays on the Desierto Central's rock art, including a replica cave-mural site that's the next best thing to descending into Cañón San Pablo (see Sierra de San Francisco, p138). You must request permission at the **INAH office** here to visit any rock art site in the area.

Tours

Kuyima (☎ 154-0070; www.kuyima.com; ☼ 8am-8pm daily Dec 15-Apr 15, 8am-1pm & 3pm-6pm Mon-Fri, 9am-1pm Sat Apr 16-Dec 14), a local cooperative on the plaza, arranges whale-watching trips ($40/person) in season as well as visits to rock art sites in the surrounding area year-round.

You can hire guides directly through INAH (see Museo San Ignacio, above) to take you to rock art sites throughout the Sierra de San Francisco. Hotel Posadas arranges both whale-watching trips and excursions to Sierra de San Francisco.

Sleeping & Eating

Casa Lereé (☎ 154-0158; janebames@yahoo.com. mx; r US$35-65) Historic Casa Lereé has three lovely rooms, a huge bougainvillea-shaded backyard and a delightfully friendly North American host who is full of information about the area. Formerly a residence, two of the rooms have private bath, and the third shares the house bathroom. Each is adorned with wall hangings, rugs and paintings (some verging on psychedelic) by a local artist. There's a wee bookstore attached and a cozy common area that was once the barn.

Chalita (☎ 154-0082; r US$18) This family-owned place, facing the southern side of the plaza, has a few comfy but basic rooms around a backyard filled with fruit trees. The **restaurant** serves good cheap Mexican food.

Ignacio Springs Bed & Breakfast (☎ 154-0333; www.ignaciosprings.com; yurt US$50-70; 🕱 💻) These are some serious yurts! We're talkin' *deee-* luxe. All four have air-con, one has its own bathroom, and the other three share an immaculate bathroom. It's right on the water (the local lagoon, not the ocean), and the owners provide kayaks for your paddling pleasure. There's free Internet, and tours can be arranged onsite.

Hotel Posadas (☎ 154-0313; r US$25; [P]) On the road to Laguna San Ignacio, motel-style Posadas is clean, comfy and straightforward. Doors open onto the bare parking area. It's very friendly.

Hotel La Pinta San Ignacio (☎ 154-0300, in the USA ☎ 800-800-9632; www.lapintahotels.com; r US$77-84; 🏊) San Ignacio's big daddy hotel is part of the La Pinta chain and on the main road into town, northwest of the plaza. It sports colonial-style architecture, a tiled courtyard, swimming pool and groves of date palms and citrus.

ROCK ART OF CENTRAL BAJA

When Jesuit missionaries inquired about the creators and meaning of the giant rock paintings of the Sierra de San Francisco, the Cochimí Indians responded with a bewilderment that was, in all likelihood, utterly feigned. The Cochimí claimed ignorance of both symbols and techniques, but it was not unusual, when missionaries came calling, to deny knowledge of the profound religious beliefs that those missionaries wanted to eradicate.

At sites like **Cueva Pintada**, Cochimí painters and their predecessors decorated high rock overhangs with vivid red-and-black representations of human figures, bighorn sheep, pumas and deer, as well as more abstract designs. It is speculated that the painters built scaffolds of palm logs to reach the ceilings. Postcontact motifs do include Christian crosses, but these are few and small in contrast to the dazzling pre-Columbian figures surrounding them.

Cueva de las Flechas, across Cañón San Pablo, has similar paintings, but the uncommon feature of arrows through some of the figures here is the subject of serious speculation. One interpretation is that these depict a period of warfare. Similar opinions suggest that they record a raid or a trespass upon tribal territory, or perhaps constitute a warning against such trespass. One researcher, however, has hypothesized that the arrows represent a shaman's metaphor for death in the course of a vision quest. If this is the case, it is no wonder that the Cochimí would claim ignorance of the paintings and their significance in the face of missionaries, unrelentingly hostile to such beliefs.

Such speculation is impossible to prove, since the Cochimí no longer exist. However, the Instituto Nacional de Antropología y Historia (INAH) has undertaken a survey of the Cochimí, the largest systematic archaeological survey of a hunter-gatherer people yet attempted in Mexico. INAH has discovered that, in addition to rock art and grinding stones, the Cochimí left evidence of permanent dwellings. In recognition of its cultural importance, the Sierra de San Francisco has been declared a **Unesco World Heritage Site**. It is part of the Reserva de la Biosfera El Vizcaíno, which includes the major gray-whale calving areas of Laguna San Ignacio and Laguna Ojo de Liebre.

The Sierra de San Francisco remains an INAH-protected archaeological zone, which means that visitors need entry permits to conduct research. Research permits are issued through the INAH office in Mexico City only, not the one in San Ignacio. INAH has also instituted regulations for tourists, in the interest of preserving the paintings.

San Ignacio has several basic RV parks at San Lino on the approach to town. On the eastern side of the road into San Ignacio, just north of the Hotel La Pinta San Ignacio, is the very basic **Martín Quesada RV Park** (site US$3). On the western side, free camping is available at **Camping La Muralla**. Across the road, **Don Chon** (site US$4) has plenty of shade and a nice riverside location but, like La Muralla, lacks showers and toilets.

Just south of Hotel La Pinta on the western side of the road, **El Padrino RV Park** (☎/fax 154-0089; tent/RV US$8/15) lacks shade in some areas despite handsome stands of date palms. There are around 100 sites, 15 of which have full hookups; four good showers have a dependable hot water supply. The restaurant here, **Flojos**, serves good, fresh seafood.

The **Rice & Beans RV Park** (☎ 154-0283; RV without/with hookups US$15/5, tent US$10), on the road to San Lino, just off the Transpeninsular west of town, has 30 spaces, 24 with full hookup.

Tota's (mains US$4-8), on the road to the lagoon (about a five minute walk from the plaza), serves delicious Mexican standards, made daily by the loving hands of Tota herself.

On the Transpeninsular, west of the San Lino junction, **Quichuley** serves good antojitos at moderate prices.

Getting There & Away

Transpeninsular buses pick up passengers opposite the Pemex station at the San Lino junction. There are at least five northbound buses daily between 6am and 3pm and as many southbound between 6am and 10:30pm.

AROUND SAN IGNACIO
Sierra de San Francisco

To date, researchers have located about 500 pre-Columbian **rock art sites** (p137) in an area of roughly 4300 sq miles (11,200 sq km) in the Sierra de San Francisco north of San Ignacio. Reached by a graded road from a conspicuously signed junction at Km 118 of the Transpeninsular, 28 miles (45km) north of San Ignacio, the village of San Francisco de la Sierra is the gateway to the area's most spectacular manifestations of Baja's unique cultural heritage.

About 1½ miles (2.5km) west of San Francisco de la Sierra, **Cueva del Ratón** is the most accessible site, featuring typical representations of *monos* (human figures), *borregos* (desert bighorn sheep) and deer, but they are not as well preserved as paintings elsewhere in the area. The site is well worth seeing for day visitors, who must obtain INAH permission at San Ignacio (see Museo San Ignacio, p136). The INAH staff will also help to arrange for a guide to show you the paintings, which are protected by a chainlink fence and locked gate. Visiting hours are 6am to 5pm daily.

The area's most rewarding excursion is a descent into the dramatic Cañón San Pablo to see its famous **Cueva Pintada**, **Cueva de las Flechas** and other magnificent sites. Cueva Pintada, really an extensive rock overhang rather than a cave, is the single most imposing site. Among English-speakers, it is known as Gardner's Cave; the popular American novelist Earle Stanley Gardner wrote several well-known books about his own adventures in the area. Mexicans, however, intensely resent the identification with Gardner and strongly prefer the Spanish term.

Exploring **Cañón San Pablo** requires a minimum of two days, preferably three. Visitors must obtain permission and contact guides from INAH in San Ignacio, as well as agree to a series of INAH guidelines and other restrictions in the interest of preserving the paintings. Visitors may not touch the paintings, smoke at the site or take flash photographs – 400 ASA film easily suffices even in dim light. Campfires and alcoholic beverages are prohibited.

Excursions to Cueva del Ratón can take about three hours in a 4WD car. You must hire a guide, and each guide can take four people. The cost ranges from US$4 for one person to US$8 for four people. Excursions to Cañón San Pablo involve hiring a guide for US$15 per day, a mule for each individual in the party for US$12 per day, plus additional pack animals, either mules or burros, to carry supplies such as tents and food. Visitors must also provide food for the guide; San Francisco de la Sierra has a small market, but it's better to bring food from Guerrero Negro or San Ignacio.

Backpacking is permitted, but backpackers still must hire a guide and mule. Most visitors will find the steep volcanic terrain much easier to manage on muleback, which leaves more time to explore the canyon and enjoy the scenery. The precipitous mule-back descent into the canyon takes about five or six hours, the ascent slightly less; in winter this means almost an entire day devoted to transportation alone. Perhaps the best time to visit is in late March or April, when days are fairly long but temperatures are not yet unpleasantly hot.

San Francisco's residents, descendants of the early *vaqueros* (ranchers or cowboys) who settled the peninsula along with the missionaries, still maintain a distinctive pastoral culture, herding mostly goats in the surrounding countryside. They also re-

tain a unique vocabulary, with many terms surviving from the 18th century, and produce some remarkable **crafts** – look at the guides' *polainas* (leather leggings) for riding in the bush, for instance. Such items are generally made to order, but occasionally villagers will have a pair of men's *teguas* (leather shoes) or women's open-toed *huaraches* (sandals) for sale.

GETTING THERE & AWAY
The road from the Transpeninsular is regularly graded, but, because parts of its surface are poorly consolidated at times, there

NO SALT, POR FAVOR

Having survived and recovered from the brutality of commercial whaling, the California gray whale still faces contemporary challenges in Baja California. Recently it was an innocent bystander in a tug-of-war between Mexican government agencies with dramatically different visions of the future of Laguna San Ignacio.

The point of contention was a 203-sq-mile (520-sq-km) saltworks, which Exportadora de Sal (ESSA) wanted to establish at the 184-sq-mile (470-sq-km) lagoon. Those statistics deceptively understate the scale of the project, since ancillary works would have directly affected 819 sq miles (2100 sq km) and indirectly affected up to 5850 sq miles (15,000 sq km) of El Vizcaíno Biosphere Reserve. ESSA, a Guerrero Negro–based and state-owned enterprise with a large holding (49%) by the Japanese multinational Mitsubishi Corporation, proposed a 1-mile (1.6km) canal to pump water continuously from Laguna San Ignacio to a 300-sq-km system of dikes and ponds. A 15-mile (25km) conveyor belt would have shifted the salt to a 1¼-mile (2km) pier near Punta Abreojos, northwest of the lagoon. Projected production was 7 million tons of salt yearly, which would have made ESSA the world's largest salt producer.

Mexico's powerful Secretaría de Comercio y Fomento Industrial (Secofi, Secretariat of Commerce and Industrial Development) backed the project, but the resolute Instituto Nacional de Ecología (INE, National Ecology Institute) vigorously objected because of the potential impact on the gray whale, the endangered peninsular pronghorn antelope and the mangrove wetlands that serve as incubators for fish and shellfish. The impact on the whales was the biggest, literally and figuratively, and most controversial issue.

Nobody really knows how much disruption the whales can tolerate during courtship and during the birth and raising of their young. ESSA claims that whale numbers have doubled in its three decades of operations at Laguna Ojo de Liebre, but conservationists are skeptical of the company's data. In addition, less than half of the narrower and shallower Laguna San Ignacio is suitable for whales. It might also suffer more from turbulence caused by pumping, which could reduce salinity and temperature in areas frequented by newborn calves. While gray whales have adapted to some human activities at Ojo de Liebre, studies have shown that noises such as oil drilling seriously disturb the big creatures.

The proposed saltworks became an environmental cause célèbre, and Mitsubishi was the target of a vigorous letter-writing and boycott campaign. Organizations such as the US-based Natural Resources Defense Council (NRDC) and the International Fund for Animal Welfare made stopping the project their number-one environmental priority in Mexico.

In March 2000, environmentalists finally won a major victory when President Ernesto Zedillo unexpectedly announced that the Mexican government was canceling the project in order to preserve the entire Vizcaíno Biosphere Reserve. Speaking at a meeting on national environmental policy, President Zedillo said, 'We're dealing with a unique place in the world both for the species that inhabit it and for its natural beauty, which we should preserve.'

are spots that are difficult for vehicles with poor traction and low clearance (4WD is not necessary, however). It can be very difficult after a rain.

Laguna San Ignacio

Along with Laguna Ojo de Liebre and Bahía Magdalena, Laguna San Ignacio is one of the major winter **whale-watching** sites on Baja's Pacific coast, with probably the highest concentration of 'friendly' whales of any location. For a general discussion of whale-watching in Baja, see p35.

Whale-watching excursions take place from December 15 to April 15, but whales are most abundant in January, February and March. In other seasons, the area is an outstanding site for bird-watching in the stunted mangroves and at offshore **Isla Pelícanos**, where about 150 ospreys and as many as 5000 cormorants nest (landing on the island is prohibited, but *pangas* – skiffs – may approach it). Sea kayaking is allowed but only in the mangroves, not in the main lagoon.

At La Laguna and La Fridera fish camps on the southern shore of the lagoon, whale-watching excursions of about three hours cost around US$30 per person. Camping at the fish camps costs US$5 to US$10. **Free camping** is permitted in some areas as well.

Kuyima (p136), based in San Ignacio, operates a whale-watching camp consisting of 20 tent spaces and 10 cabañas. Reservations are required for the cabañas. Rates are about US$165 per night per person, which includes all meals and the whale-watching boat excursion. Single-night camping is available in tent spaces and RV sites for US$10 per night.

Camp guests have access to solar shower bags and very clean flush toilets using seawater; the camp itself is spotless and the English-speaking staff is friendly. Meals are available in the **restaurant** (mains US$5-10; ☼ 6am-10pm), where the food is excellent and abundant. Kuyima's cozy solar-powered dining room, out of the prevailing winds, has whale and natural history videos, as well as a library of natural history books.

GETTING THERE & AWAY

The road from San Ignacio has deteriorated in recent years; most passenger cars need at least two hours to cover the 40 miles (65km) to La Fridera fish camp (assuming no rain

has fallen recently) without wrecking their suspension. The first half of the road from the village is spine-wrenching washboard, but the second half is notably better.

SANTA ROSALÍA

The former French mining town of Santa Rosalia is truly a Baja anomaly. Wandering its narrow historic streets, lined with weather-beaten balconied houses, immediately sets you wondering: 'Wait a minute, where *am* I?' Not only have you stepped back in time, you've seemingly stepped into…colonial France?

The town dates from the 1880s, when the French-owned Compañía del Boleo (one of the Rothschild family's many worldwide ventures) built it under a 99-year concession from the government of Mexican President Porfirio Díaz. Nearly all of the buildings downtown were constructed from timber imported from Oregon and British Columbia. French-style colonial homes still stand along the main streets. The Compañía also assembled a prefabricated, galvanized-iron church designed by Alexandre Gustave Eiffel for the 1889 World Fair in Paris (see boxed text, p143). The church is still in use, while balconies and porches along the tree-lined streets encourage a spirited street life contrasting with the residential segregation of the mining era.

The French left by 1954, but a palpable legacy remains in the town's atypical architecture, a bakery that sells Baja's best baguettes and building codes decreeing that new construction must conform to the town's unique heritage.

Orientation

Santa Rosalía is on the Gulf coast 45 miles (73km) east of San Ignacio and 38 miles (61km) north of Mulegé. Most of central Santa Rosalía nestles in its namesake arroyo west of the Transpeninsular, while residential areas occupy plateaus north and south of the canyon. French administrators built their houses on the northern Mesa Francia, now home to municipal authorities, the museum and many historic buildings, whereas Mexican officials occupied the southern Mesa México.

The town's narrow *avenidas* (avenues) run northeast-southwest; its short *calles* (streets) run northwest-southeast. One-way traffic is the rule. Large RVs will find it

SANTA ROSALÍA

0 — 300 m
0 — 0.2 miles

INFORMATION
Banamex (ATM).....................1 B3
Bancomer (ATM)...................2 A3
Cruz Roja.............................3 B3
Hospital General...................4 B2
IDS.....................................5 B2
Post Office...........................6 B2
Sistemas de Computación y
Comunicación....................7 B3

SIGHTS & ACTIVITIES (pp141-2)
Benemérito Sociedad Mutualista..8 A3
Biblioteca Mahatma Gandhi........9 C2
Ex-Copper Foundry.................10 C1
Iglesia Santa Bárbara..............11 B2
Monumento de Marineros.........12 D3
Museo Histórico Minero de Santa
Rosalía (Ex-Fundición del
Pacífico)..........................13 B2

SLEEPING (p142)
Hotel del Real........................14 C2
Hotel Francés.........................15 B2
Hotel Olvera..........................16 C2
Motel San Víctor.....................17 A3

EATING (pp142-3)
Angel Cafe.............................18 A3
Cenaduria Gaby (de Pedro García)..19 A3
Panadería El Boleo...................20 B2
Restaurant El Muelle.................21 B3

TRANSPORT (p143)
Bus Terminal..........................22 D3
Pemex..................................23 C3

To San Ignacio (73km)

To San Lucas RV Park (500m),
Hotel El Morro (1.5km),
Hotel Las Casitas (3km) &
Mulegé (61km)

MESA FRANCIA
(RESIDENTIAL AREA)

MESA MÉXICO
(RESIDENTIAL AREA)

Harbor

Santa Rosalía Ferry
& Immigrations Office

Ferry to
Guaymas

Plaza
Juárez

CENTRAL BAJA

---

difficult to navigate around town and should
park along or near the Transpeninsular.

Plaza Benito Juárez, about four blocks
west of the highway, is the focus of the
town. The Andador Costero, overlooking
the harbor south of downtown, is an attractive *malecón* (waterfront promenade) with
good views of offshore Isla Tortuga.

Information
Most tourist-oriented services are on or
near Av Obregón, but there is no official
information office.

The **immigration office** (☎ 152-0313) is in the
ferry terminal.

Internet access is available at **Sistemas
de Computación y Comunicación** (cnr Calle 3 & Av
Constitución; US$2.50/hr; ⊙ 8:30am-2pm & 4-8:30pm
Mon-Sat) and at **IDS** (cnr Calle 1 & Av Obrégon; US$2/hr,
⊙ 9am-2pm & 4-9pm Mon-Sat).

Santa Rosalía has the only banks between
Guerrero Negro and Loreto; Mulegé-bound
travelers should change US dollars or traveler's checks here. **Banamex** and **Bancomer** are
on opposite corners of Av Obregón and
Calle 5; both have ATMs.

The **post office** is at the corner of Av Constitución and Calle 2.

The **Hotel del Real** (p142) has long-distance telephone services, but there are also
many Ladatel public phones around town.

The **Hospital General** (☎ 152-0789; Av Cousteau)
is in Mesa Francia, and there's a **Cruz Roja**
(Red Cross; ☎ 152-0640; Av Carranza near Calle 2) near
Plaza Juárez.

Sights
HISTORIC SITES
Due to its origins as a 19th-century company
town, Santa Rosalía's architecture is fascinat-
ingly atypical for a Mexican town. Its most
famous landmark is the **Iglesia Santa Bárbara**
(cnr Av Obregón & Altamirano; ⊙ daily). Designed
and erected in Paris, then disassembled and
stored in Brussels, the structure was originally
intended for West Africa but finally shipped
to Mexico. Here, a director of the Compañía
del Boleo stumbled upon it by chance, and
in 1895 Alexandre Gustave Eiffel's prefabricated church finally reached Santa Rosalía; it
was reassembled by 1897 and adorned with
attractive stained-glass windows.

On the eastern side of Playa near the Transpeninsular, the **Biblioteca Mahatma Gandhi** (Playa at Av Constitución) was another Compañía del Boleo project. The **Benemérito Sociedad Mutualista** (1916; cnr Av Obregón & Calle 7) features an interesting clock tower.

Many buildings on Mesa Francia also deserve a visit, most notably the **Fundición del Pacífico**, now the mining museum, and the Hotel Francé as well as the ruins of the **copper foundry** along the Transpeninsular. Most of the original plant is intact; the highway passes beneath its old conveyor belt north of the turnoff into town. Lined with numerous French colonial houses, **Av Cousteau** runs between the Fundición and the hotel; it also displays a wealth of antique mining equipment, including steam locomotives, mine cars and cranes.

MUSEO HISTÓRICO MINERO DE SANTA ROSALÍA

Once the business offices of the Compañía del Boleo, this **mining museum** (US$1.25; 8am-7pm Mon-Sat) includes accountants' offices (now filled with scale models of historic buildings like the Benemérito Sociedad Mutualista, the Panadería El Boleo and the Cine Trianon, destroyed by fire some years ago), the purchasing office (filled with maritime memorabilia), the pay office (complete with safe) and the boardroom. The museum overlooks downtown from Mesa Francia at the southern end of Av Cousteau.

Festivals & Events

Celebrations of Santa Rosalía's **Fundación de la Ciudad** (Founding of the City) last four days in mid-October.

Sleeping

Hotel Francés (152-2052; Av Cousteau 15; r US$50; P) Up on Mesa Francia, the historic Hotel Francés once provided all the 'necessary services' (as the INAH paper on the door says) to lone French employees (men) of the Compañía del Boleo. Probably more fun then, it now offers an atmospheric restaurant, a small swimming pool, wonderful views of the rusting copper foundry and air-conditioned period-style rooms.

Hotel Olvera (152-0267; cnr Av Montoya & Playa; r US$15-18) 'Rickety' is an understatement for this creaky old hotel, but the place is definitely endearing (and atmospheric) once

you're settled in. Rooms are worn but c and the best ones open onto the big balc overlooking the streets below. Careful that staircase.

Motel San Víctor (152-0116; Av Progreso 36 Calle 9; r US$15; P) Basic but quiet, this pleasant, family-run operation on a shady street is more than fine for a good night's rest. The secure parking is comforting if you're driving.

Hotel del Real (152-0068; Av Montoya 7; r US$23-27;) In yet another historic building, the Hotel del Real offers US$23 rooms in the wood building in front and US$27 rooms in the air-conditioned rooms in the add-on in back. Unfortunately its unappealing location is a bit noisy.

Hotel Las Casitas (152-3023; www.santarosalia casitas.com; Transpeninsular Km 3; r US$45; P) Santa Rosalía's newest hotel, 3km south of town, has only five rooms, but each is beautifully tiled has a private balcony with sublime views of the sea from the queen-sized bed. A hot tub completes its allure.

Hotel El Morro (152-2390; s/d 30/35; Transpeninsular Km 1.5; P) About 1 mile (1.5km) south of town, just off the Transpeninsular, this is another excellent cliffside hotel. Along with sea views and a relaxed atmosphere, it offers a swimming pool, restaurant and bar.

About half a mile (1km) west of the Transpeninsular between Km 181 and Km 182, spacious **San Lucas RV Park** (no ; site US$6) has a good beach and boat launch sites, flush toilets and hot showers. Bird-watching is good in the area.

Eating

Panadería El Boleo (152-0310; Av Obregón between Calles 3 & 4; 8am-9pm Mon-Sat, 9am-1pm Sun) Started by the French when mining operations were in full swing at the turn of the 20th century, this is one of the best (if not coolest) bakeries in Baja California. For many travelers, it's an obligatory stop for its delicious Mexican and French breads and pastries. Baguettes usually sell out by about 10am.

Restaurant El Muelle (cnr Av Constitución & Plaza; mains US$4-10) El Muelle is great both for its crispy-crust pizzas and its outdoor patio. The margaritas are darn good, too. It's one of the best eateries in town.

Taco stands are numerous along Av Obregón, but most of them serve nothing

EIFFEL BEYOND THE TOWER

Few know that French engineer Alexandre Gustave Eiffel (1832-1923), so renowned for his tower in Paris, also played a significant role in the New World. New York's Statue of Liberty is his most prominent transatlantic landmark (he was the structural engineer), but his constructions also dot the Latin American landscape from Mexico to Chile. Santa Rosalía's **Iglesia Santa Bárbara** is only one of many examples.

In 1868, in partnership with the engineer Théophile Seyrig, Eiffel formed G Eiffel et Compagnie, which later became the Compagnie des Etablissements Eiffel. Among their notable creations in South America were the Aduana de Arica (Customs House, 1872; Arica was part of Peru and is now part of Chile), Arica's Iglesia San Marcos, the gasworks of La Paz (Bolivia) and the railroad bridges of Oroya (Peru). Most of these were designed and built in Eiffel's workshops in the Parisian suburb of Levallois-Perret and then shipped abroad for assembly.

What might have been his greatest Latin American monument effectively ended his career. In the late 19th century, Eiffel had argued strongly in favor of building a transoceanic canal across Nicaragua, but a few years later, he obtained the contract to build the locks for Ferdinand de Lesseps' corruption-plagued French canal across Panama. Implicated in irregular contracts, Eiffel was sentenced to two years in prison and fined a substantial amount. Though his conviction was overturned, he never returned to his career as a builder.

but beef. For standard antojitos at good prices, try **Cenaduría Gaby (de Pedro García)** (Calle 5 near Av Obregón; mains US$4-7). **Angel Cafe** (cnr Av Obregón & Calle 5; US$4-7) serves sandwiches and hamburgers in a nice, open patio.

The restaurant at **Hotel Francés** (6am-11pm), enjoying the same resurgent popularity as the hotel, is well worth a stop, though the service can be slow.

Getting There & Away

BOAT

Santa Rosalía's small marina offers some possibilities for catching a ride by private yacht north or south along the Gulf coast or across to mainland Mexico.

The new **Santa Rosalía Ferry** (152-1246, in Mexico 800-672-9053; www.ferrysantarosalia.com; ticket window 9am-6pm Mon, Wed & Thu; 10am-3pm Tue, Fri & Sun; 10am-2pm Sat) to Guaymas, Sonora, in mainland Mexico, leaves Tuesday, Friday and Sunday at 8pm. The journey is nine hours. The boat departs Guaymas Monday, Thursday and Saturday at 8pm.

One-way standard/first-class passenger fares are US$45/59. It's US$23/27 for children under 11. Fares for cars and pickups up to 5.4m are US$135; vehicles 5.5m to 7m cost US$293; vehicles 7m to 10m cost US$450. These fares do *not* include passengers. Cars with trailers, total length up to 15m, will cost you US$720, which includes one passenger. Advanced reservations are recommended.

BUS

Autotransportes Aguila and ABC buses between Tijuana and La Paz stop at Santa Rosalía's **bus terminal** (152-0150), on the western side of the Transpeninsular opposite the malecón. Sample fares for northbound buses are listed in the table here; departures are at midnight, 4am, 5am, 3pm, 5pm and 6pm. There's one night bus to Mexicali (US$72, 14-16 hrs).

Destination	Fare	Duration
Ensenada	US$54	12 hrs
Guerrero Negro	US$14	3-4 hrs
San Ignacio	US$6	1 hr
San Quintín	US$37	9 hrs
Tijuana	US$58	14 hrs
Vizcaíno	US$9	2 hrs

Southbound buses to La Paz (US$34, 8 hours) pass five times daily and will drop you in Mulege (US$6.30, 1 hour), Loreto (US$13, 3 hours), Ciudad Constitución (US$24, 5 hours). There are also daily departures to Cabo San Lucas (US$44, 10 hours) and San Jose del Cabo (US$46, 11 hours).

MULEGÉ

 615 / pop 3170

Anyone who's traveled the peninsula will likely agree: Mulegé is the prettiest little town in Baja. At the eastern scarp of the Sierra de la Giganta, Mulegé is bathed in a blissful (if you like the heat) subtropical weather. Old adobe and stone buildings hem in its narrow streets, and the verdant Arroyo Santa Rosalía (also known as the Río Mulegé) runs alongside town, making for a lovely 3km stroll out to the rock-strewn beach of Playa El Farito. Scrawny mangroves extend along the lower reaches of the river's estuary, frequented by large numbers of birds, while date palms line its banks farther inland. Mulegé's restored mission is one of the finest in Baja, and the townspeople are laidback and friendly. South of town, islands of deep brown and amber hues shelter the Bahía Concepción, where spectacular beaches are tucked into some seriously gorgeous coves. You'll much prefer swimming here than near the polluted mouth of the arroyo.

Orientation & Information

Mulegé has no formal tourist office. The bulk of visitor services are on the northern side of the river, on or near Jardín Corona, the town plaza.

Get your Internet fix at **Internet Café Cuesta** (Madero; US$2/hr; ⌚ 9am-9pm Mon-Sat) or **Servicio Internet Minita** (Madero; US$2/hr; ⌚ 10am-9pm Mon-Sat, 2-6pm Sun, closed 1-3pm daily May-Sep).

Efficient **Lavamática Claudia** (☎ 153-0057; cnr Zaragoza & Moctezuma; ⌚ 8am-7pm Mon-Sat) charges US$5 for a full load of laundry.

For medical needs, Mulegé's **Centro de Salud** (☎ 153-0298; Madero) is opposite Canett Casa de Huéspedes.

Mulegé has no banks, ATMs or exchange services; the nearest places to get cash are Santa Rosalía and Loreto, so load your wallet before arriving in Mulegé. Many Mulegé merchants will change US dollars or accept them as payment.

Mulegé's **post office** (Av General Martínez) is almost across from the Pemex station.

Long-distance telephone services are available at **Mini Super Padilla** (Zaragoza at Av General Martínez), and there are plenty of Ladatel phones around town.

Drivers of large RVs (or anything bigger than a van conversion) should not even consider entering downtown Mulegé's narrow, irregular and sometimes steep streets.

Sights

MISIÓN SANTA ROSALÍA DE MULEGÉ

Across the Transpeninsular and near the southern bank of the river, Mulegé's re-

stored mission (⌚ 10am-2pm) stands atop a hill southwest of town. Founded in 1705 and completed in 1766, the mission functioned until 1828, when the declining Indian population led to its abandonment. Remodeled several times, the church is less architecturally distinguished than its counterparts at San Ignacio and San Borja; it's imposing but utilitarian, with fewer enticing details. The exterior alone is still faithful to the original.

Behind the church, a short footpath climbs a volcanic outcrop to an overlook with soothing views of the palm-lined Arroyo Santa Rosalía and its surroundings. This is one of the visual highlights of the area, well worth a detour even for travelers not intending to stay in town.

MUSEO MULEGÉ

Federal inmates from Mulegé's 'prison without doors,' a strikingly whitewashed neocolonial building on Cananea, overlooking the town, traditionally enjoyed a great deal of liberty. Except for the most serious felons, who were confined in its inner compound, prisoners usually left at 6am for jobs in town, returning at 6pm. They could even attend town dances, and a number of them married locally.

Now the town museum (Cananea s/n; admission by donation; ⌚ 9am-3pm Mon-Fri), the building houses some eclectic artifacts: archaeological and religious materials, cotton gins, antique diving equipment, firearms and – most curious of all – the massive shell of a Star 48B space-launch motor, which dropped out of the sky in 2000, landing on a nearby ranch.

Activities

There's some great **diving** around Mulegé, the best spots being around the **Santa Inés Islands** (north of town) and just north of Punta Concepción. There is excellent beach diving and snorkeling at Punta Prieta, near the lighthouse at the mouth of Arroyo Santa Rosalía.

Swiss-owned **Cortez Explorers** (☎ 153-0500; www.cortez-explorer.com; Moctezuma 75A; ⌚ 10am-1pm & 4-7pm Mon-Sat) offers diving excursions and instruction (resort course only), snorkel equipment rental and bike rental. A four-hour scuba course costs US$90, including all equipment and a guided underwater dive. Diving excursions (including a boat,

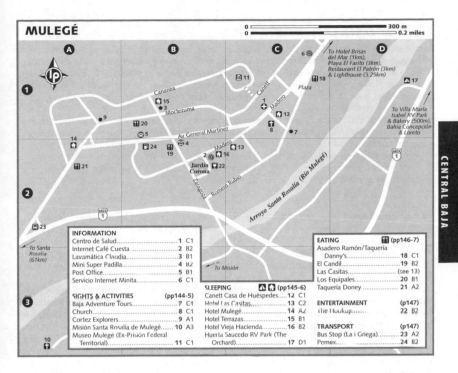

MULEGÉ

INFORMATION	
Centro de Salud	1 C1
Internet Café Cuesta	2 B2
Lavamática Claudia	3 B1
Mini Super Padilla	4 B2
Post Office	5 B1
Servicio Internet Minita	6 C1

SIGHTS & ACTIVITIES	(pp144-5)
Baja Adventure Tours	7 C1
Church	8 C1
Cortez Explorers	9 A1
Misión Santa Rosalía de Mulegé	10 A3
Museo Mulege (Ex-Prisión Federal Territorial)	11 C1

SLEEPING	(pp145-6)
Canett Casa de Huéspedes	12 C1
Hotel Las Casitas	13 C2
Hotel Mulegé	14 A2
Hotel Terrazas	15 B1
Hotel Vieja Hacienda	16 B2
Huerta Saucedo RV Park (The Orchard)	17 D1

EATING	(pp146-7)
Asadero Ramón/Taquería Danny's	18 C1
El Candil	19 B2
Las Casitas	(see 13)
Los Equipales	20 B1
Taquería Doney	21 A2

ENTERTAINMENT	(p147)
The Hookup	22 B2

TRANSPORT	(p147)
Bus Stop (La Griega)	23 A2
Pemex	24 B2

a dive-master guide, two tanks and a weight belt) cost US$80, minimum two persons or you pay US$120. Snorkeling trips cost US$30 to US$35 per person, with a US$80 minimum. Dive equipment is also rented on a daily basis.

For **mountain biking**, Cortez Explorers offers bike rentals for US$15 the first day, US$10 the following days.

Two excellent local guides offer trips to see **cave paintings** in Cañón La Trinidad for US$40 to US$45, as well as trips to San Borjita, local ranches and **bird watching** tours: **Salvador Castro** (☎ 153-0232), who can be contacted through Hotel Las Casitas (see Sleeping), and **Ciro Cuesta**, owner of **Baja Adventure Tours** (☎ 153-0481; cirocuesta@prodigy.net. mx; Romero Rubio).

Mulegé is a popular **fishing** destination as well. Game-fish species available all year in the area include bonito, cabrilla, corvina, crevallo, grouper, pargo, sierra and skip-jack. Seasonal species include dorado (May to November), needlefish (June to November), roosterfish (April to October), sailfish

(July to October), striped marlin (June to October) and the especially popular yellow-tail (November to May). Wahoo make rare appearances. Cortez Explorers will take you fishing for US$150 for up to four people.

Bahía Concepción, south of Mulegé, is the main destination for **sea kayaking** in the area. **El Candil** (p146) rents kayaks for US$30 per day.

Sleeping

Mulegé lacks upscale accommodations, yet it has a couple very appealing family hotels; you won't be dowsed in all the mod-cons but you'll be comfortable.

HOTELS

Hotel Las Casitas (☎ 153-0019, 153-0681; lascasitas1962@hotmail.com; Madero; s/d US$25/30; ☒) Colorful bougainvilleas and tropical plants shade the two patios of this welcoming hotel in an attractive historic building. The attached restaurant is excellent, the management is friendly, and the rooms, while small and a bit dark, are perfectly adequate.

DETOUR: CAÑÓN LA TRINIDAD

In Cañón La Trinidad, 18 miles (29km) southwest of Mulegé, adventure lovers can get a serious fix during a hike-and-swim excursion to several pre-Columbian **rock art** sites set in impressive volcanic overhangs. The setting is spectacular, and the rock paintings themselves are multicolored Cochimí depictions of human figures and wildlife, including fish and sea turtles. Those at a lower site, visited prior to the swim up the canyon, are more vivid and better preserved, thanks to their more sheltered location.

The rough drive to the canyon from Mulegé involves taking several unmarked junctions from the westbound (San Estanislao) road and can be difficult for a first-timer. Therefore, the best way to get out here is by contacting Salvador Castro or Ciro Cuesta in Mulegé (p145), both highly recommended local guides. Otherwise, get precise directions at your hotel.

All visitors must check in with the INAH caretakers at Rancho La Trinidad (on the way to the canyon), who also lead hikes for a very modest fee.

Something about it just *feels* like you're in Mexico.

Hotel Vieja Hacienda (☎ 153-0021; hotel hacienda_mulege@hotmail.com; Madero 3; r US$35-40; P ✗ ⚑). Great if you want a pool, the Vieja Hacienda offers two floors of good-size rooms at the northeastern corner of the plaza. Rooms themselves are straightforward and clean, and there's an outdoor bar beside the big sunny patio.

Hotel Mulegé (☎ 153-0090; s/d US$27/32; ✗) Near the Y-intersection at the entrance to town, this is Mulegé's 'modern' hotel. Rooms are spotless and have satellite TV, but character is nil.

Hotel Terrazas (☎ 153-0009; Zaragoza; r US$32-54) Named for its giant rooftop terraces, Hotel Terrazas is long past its prime but still decent. Guests can use the ramshackle kitchen area in the rooftop palapa, though it's so old and dry it could spontaneously combust (or blow off the roof) any time.

Hotel Brisas del Mar (☎ 153-0889; s/d US$27/32) This palatial new hotel, on the road to Playa El Farito and the lighthouse, seems a bit big for its britches, but definitely has good views. For Mulegé, its *huge*.

Baja Adventure Tours (see Activities; r US$23; ✗) rents three new rooms with air-con and private baths.

Cheapest of Mulegé's several guesthouses is the plain, eight-room **Canett Casa de Huéspedes** (☎ 153-0272; Madero; s/d US$11/14). It's not a bad place, but late sleepers should know that the church bells across the street make morning mincemeat of your brain.

CAMPING

Eastbound Madero and Romero Rubio merge into a single dirt road leading to **beach camping** areas at Playa El Farito near the lighthouse, 2 miles (3km) northeast of town. This is also a popular party spot for local youth, so there's no guarantee of any sleep, at least on weekends.

Abounding with palms, mangoes and citrus, friendly **Huerta Saucedo RV Park** (The Orchard; ☎ 153-0300) is half a mile (1km) east of town on the river side of the Transpeninsular. RVs driving from central Mulegé should take the highway or the road that passes beneath the Transpeninsular bridge. Spaces with full hookups cost US$16; those without are US$5 for two people, plus US$2 for each additional person. Hot (sometimes lukewarm) showers, decent toilets and a boat ramp are available. Canoe rentals are US$4 per hour.

Just beyond Huerta Saucedo, **Villa María Isabel RV Park** (☎ 153-0246) charges US$6 per person for sites without hookups, US$15 with full hookups, but the real reason to stop here is the fabulous bread and cinnamon rolls at its first-rate **bakery** – well worth a stop.

Eating & Entertainment

El Candil (Zaragoza; mains US$6-10) Just off the plaza, popular El Candil serves filling meat and seafood dishes and mediocre Mexican fare. Gringos regularly fill the bar for international sports on satellite TV.

Asadero Ramón/Taquería Danny's (cnr Romero Rubio & Madero; tacos US$1) The outstanding Saturday *carnitas* (slow-roasted pork) make up for the fact that no one can decide what this place is called. The *carne asada* (grilled beef) tacos are delicious too.

Los Equipales (☎ 153-0330; Moctezuma; mains US$6-12) Specializing in Sonoran beef, Los Equipales serves outstanding meals that, if pricier than most in town, are worth the money.

Las Casitas (☎ 153-0019, 153-0681; Madero; mains US$4-9) In its namesake hotel, Las Casitas is especially good for breakfast, as the birds chirp you awake over a bottomless cup of coffee. Typical antojitos, daily specials, a few seafood dishes and unusual drinks like mango daiquiris make the lunch and dinner menus enticing.

Restaurant El Patrón (☎ 153-0284; Playa El Farito; mains US$5-10) El Patrón's fabulous setting right on the water (on the beach out near the lighthouse) makes for an unforgettable meal. It's a casual place, making it that much better. The tiny **bar** comes alive with *norteño* bands on weekends.

At the western end of Mulegé just before the Transpeninsular, **Taquería Doney** serves up some of the region's best tacos.

Even though *you* might not, **The Hookup**, facing the central plaza, is often the liveliest bar in town.

Getting There & Away

Mulegé has no formal bus terminal, but buses running from Tijuana to La Paz stop daily at the Y junction (called 'la i griega') on the Transpeninsular at the western edge of town. Buy tickets at the store up the hill from the stop.

Fares and approximate travel times are in the following table.

Destination	Fare	Duration
Ciudad Constitución	US$17	4 hrs
Ensenada	US$56	13 hrs
La Paz	US$26	7 hrs
Loreto	US$9	2 hrs
Santa Rosalía	US$6.30	1 hr
Tijuana	US$65	15 hrs

BAHÍA CONCEPCIÓN

☎ 615

More than 50 miles (80km) of pristine beaches dot the coastline of Bahía Concepción, south of Mulegé. The most accessible (and most crowded) run along the western edge of the bay, but few people travel the dirt road to Punta Concepción at the peninsula's northern tip. Camping is possible on almost every beach in the area, but most of the best sites charge for the privilege.

EcoMundo-Baja Tropicales

Established in 1989, the EcoMundo kayaking and natural history center is an extension of Roy Mahoff and Becky Aparicio's long-running **Baja Tropicales** (☎ 153-0320; http://home.earthlink.net/~rcmathews; ecomundo@aol.com) company. Baja Tropicales offers local kayak trips from its facilities, south of Mulegé at Km 111 of the Transpeninsular. In addition to accommodations (see Sleeping & Eating), the EcoMundo project includes an educational center and a gallery-bookstore.

Baja Tropicales' guided **kayaking** daytrips on Bahía Concepción cost US$49 per person, including meals and beverages, for a minimum of four people. Experienced kayakers may rent kayaks for US$25 per day. Snorkeling gear can be rented for US$5. For more information, inquire at Hotel Las Casitas in Mulegé or contact Baja Tropicales directly.

Sleeping & Eating

EcoMundo (above) has accommodations, including bungalows (with hammocks or cots and lights) for US$12 and tent sites for US$6. Hot showers and outhouses are available, and the **restaurant** offers breakfast and lunch.

At **Playa Santispac**, 13 miles (21km) south of Mulegé, there are 35 campsites (US$7) with palapas at water's edge available for US$7 apiece. Amenities are limited, but there are cold showers; bring drinking water. Also here is **Ray's Place** (mains US$9-13; ☒ 2-9pm Tue-Sat); you can't miss the sign boasting the best food 'between Tijuana and Cabo.' As long as they don't include Cabo Pulmo (where Nancy's will give them some serious competition) the sign might just be right – it's that good! Both the seafood and the burgers are sublime.

Playa El Burro is just south of EcoMundo. Consisting of a large stretch of beach, this is a very pleasant place to camp (site US$7). Outhouses and showers are available. **Bertha's Restaurant**, on the beach, offers some of the best breakfasts in the area.

RV Park El Coyote (US$7/vehicle), 18 miles (29km) south of Mulegé, is a fine area for beach camping, although it's close to the highway and often unpleasantly crowded.

South, at Km 94.5 of the Transpeninsular, the area's cushiest accommodations are at **Resort Hotel San Buenaventura** (☎ 153-0408; r US$69-99). It's an attractive stone building and each room boasts its own shaded patio. It is also possible to camp on the beach for US$10. There's a boat launch at the beach, and kayaks are available for rent. Also on site is **George's Olé Sports Bar & Grill** (❤ 8am-10pm; mains US$4-8), which makes a good lunch stop.

El Requesón, 28 miles (45km) south of Mulegé, once made a *Condé Nast Traveler* list of Mexico's top 10 beaches, but its scanty services keep it suitable – fortunately – for short-term camping only. One attractive feature is the *tombolo* (sandspit beach) that connects it to offshore Isla El Requesón except during very high tides. Despite its proximity to the highway, it's relatively quiet; camping here is free.

A short distance south of El Requesón is **La Perla**, where camping sites are US$5. It's a small beach but doesn't tend to get as crowded as some of the other beaches in the area.

Free camping is possible at **Playa Armenta**, just south of La Perla. It has a short but sandy beach, and although it's more exposed to the highway than El Requesón, it's less crowded.

SAN ISIDRO & LA PURÍSIMA

South of Bahía Concepción, the paved Transpeninsular continues to Loreto, but at Km 60 a graded alternative route crosses the Sierra de la Giganta to the twin villages of San Isidro and La Purísima, both also accessible by a very good paved highway from Ciudad Insurgentes (see San José de Comondú, below). Travelers who prefer not to retrace their steps may wish to take the graded road either north- or southbound. Drivers with high-clearance vehicles will find it more enjoyable, whereas those with RVs or trailers will find it difficult; 4WD is unnecessary, however.

This area was the site of **Misión La Purísima Concepción**, founded in 1717 by Jesuit Nicolás Tamaral, but only foundations remain. The major landmark is the steep-sided volcanic plug of **El Pilón**, a challenge for technical climbers, which lies between the two villages. From La Purísima, a graded road goes northwest to San Juanico, one of the

Pacific coast's prime surfing spots, and to Laguna San Ignacio, a very popluar whale-watching destination.

Neither San Isidro nor La Purísima has a Pemex station, but private gasoline sellers offer both Nova and Magna Sin at about a 25% markup – look for hand-painted signs. San Isidro's simple **Motel Nelva** (s/d US$6/12) provides accommodation.

San Isidro and La Purísima offer bus service to La Paz (US$9; 5 hours; daily at 6:30am & 3pm) with Autotransportes Aguila, which picks up most of its passengers in Ciudad Constitución. Buses leave from San Isidro and pass through La Purísima.

SAN JOSÉ DE COMONDÚ

South of San Isidro, a bumpy, rocky, undulating road (which is never really difficult, at least for high-clearance vehicles) crosses a volcanic upland before dropping steeply into San José de Comondú, site of the Jesuit **Misión San José de Comondú**. The temple dates from the 1750s, although the mission proper began in 1707.

Only part of the mission temple remains intact, but there are extensive walls surrounding it. Restoration is lagging, but the building contains good examples of traditional religious art, though the canvases are deteriorating badly. Note the historic photos, dated 1901, when a major *recova* (colonnade) and two short *campanarios* (bell towers) still existed. Ask for the key to the temple at the bright-green house 30 yards to the east.

West of San José de Comondú is its almost equally picturesque twin, **San Miguel de Comondú**. Most inhabitants of the area are fair-skinned descendants of early Spanish pioneers, in contrast to later mestizo arrivals from mainland Mexico.

For vehicles without high clearance, access to San José de Comondú is easier by a graded lateral from Ejido Francisco Villa that leaves the paved highway about 40 miles (64km) north of Ciudad Insurgentes. Note that one tricky stream ford may present problems for vehicles with low clearance.

Driving north from San José de Comondú to San Isidro, the steep climb over loose rock may cause some vehicle problems. At the crest of the hill, take the left fork to San Isidro.

SAN JUANICO

About 30 miles (48km) northwest of La Purísima and 60 miles (97km) south of Laguna San Ignacio, the village of San Juanico is well known among surfers for nearby **Punta Pequeña**, at the northern end of Bahía San Juanico. Its right-point breaks, some believe, provide the highest-quality surf on the peninsula in a southern swell. September and October are the best months for surfing. Other area activities include windsurfing, sea kayaking, diving and sportfishing.

Scorpion Bay (☎ 138-2850; www.scorpionbay. net; site US$5/person, cabaña US$30) is a well-run campground operated by an American in cooperation with the local *ejido* (communal land holding). The palapa **restaurant** serves excellent food.

San Juanico is most easily accessed by a good graded dirt road heading north from La Purísima. Unfortunately, despite depiction as a graded surface on the AAA map, the road south to San Juanico from Laguna San Ignacio is potentially hazardous, even for high-clearance vehicles.

The road from Laguna San Ignacio veers off from the graded road approximately 8 miles south of Laguna San Ignacio. This is the Baja 1000 road – and passable by most trucks – as long as drivers know how to drive dirt roads. The road passes through a number of sand dunes and seems to be in the middle of nowhere, which means it's very easy to get lost and you'll be isolated if you happen to break down. If you're lucky, the drive will take about four hours.

LORETO

☎ 613 / pop 11,800

Like Mulegé, Loreto's subtropical climate makes it particularly inviting for those of us who like to sweat over our beers in summer and be warm enough to *want* beer in winter. Loreto's spectacularly restored mission underscores its role in the history of the Californias, and the church's adjacent plaza gives downtown a distinctly Mexican feel. Topping things off, the long malecón makes for lovely walks right along the Gulf. The town remains a modest fishing port with cobblestone streets, though some of its historic past has now fallen beneath developers' onslaughts.

Loreto is an ideal base for all types of outdoor activities, and a number of outfitters cover the range, from kayaking and diving along the reefs around Isla del Carmen to horseback riding and hiking in the Sierra de la Giganta. The town sits within the **Parque Marino Nacional Bahía de Loreto**, one of Baja's two national marine parks, composed of 799 sq miles (2077 sq km) of shoreline and offshore islands.

History

In 1697 the Jesuit priest and explorer Juan María Salvatierra established the Misión Nuestra Señora de Loreto on the Gulf coast as the first permanent Spanish settlement in the Californias. In concentrating local Indians at mission settlements instead of dispersed *rancherías* (indigenous settlements) and converting them to Catholicism, the Jesuits directly extended the influence and control of the Spanish crown in one of the empire's most remote areas.

It was a convenient staging point for missionary expansion even after the official expulsion of the Jesuits in 1767 – in 1769, Franciscan Padre Junípero Serra trekked northward to found the now-famous chain of missions in mainland California. Also the first capital of the Californias, Loreto served that role until its near destruction by a hurricane in 1829.

Orientation

Between the Transpeninsular and the shores of the Sea of Cortez, Loreto is 218 miles (351km) north of La Paz and 84 miles (135km) south of Mulegé. It has a slightly irregular street plan, but the colonial mission church on Salvatierra is a major landmark; most hotels and services are within easy walking distance of it.

The Plaza Cívica, as the *zócalo* (central plaza) is known, is just north of Salvatierra between Madero and Davis. Salvatierra itself is a de facto pedestrian mall (vehicle access is limited and inconvenient), lined with topiary laurels, between Independencia and the beach. Stroll east along Salvatierra and you'll hit the malecón and its rocky beach.

Information
IMMIGRATION

Loreto's **Immigration and Customs Office** (☎ 135 1254) is at the airport, south of town. Its in-town office is in the **Casa de la Cultura** (☎ 135-1266, Paseo Tamaral).

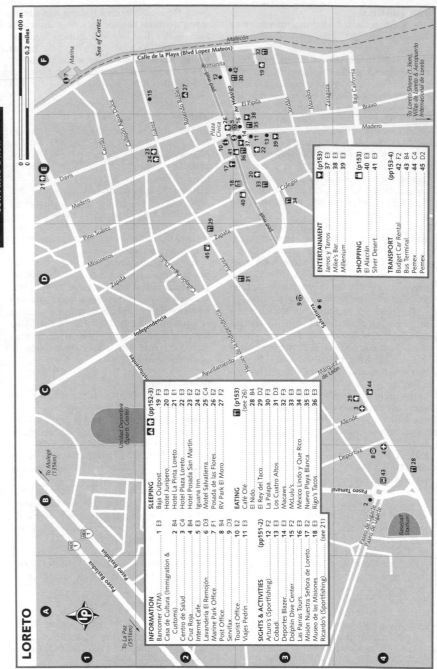

LORETO

INTERNET ACCESS
Internet cafe (Madero; US$2.50/hr; ☻ 9am-1pm & 4-7pm Mon-Fri, 9am-2pm Sat) Just off the Plaza Cívica.

LAUNDRY
Lavandería El Remojón (Salvatierra btwn Independencia & Ayuntamiento; ☻ closed Sun)

MEDICAL SERVICES
Centro de Salud (☎ 135-00-9; Salvatierra 68)
Cruz Roja (Red Cross; ☎ 135-1111; Salvatierra near Allende)

MONEY
Bancomer (cnr Salvatierra & Madero) Changes US dollars and traveler's checks from 8:30 to 11:30am and has an ATM. The majority of stores in Loreto do not accept US dollars.

POST
Post office (Deportiva btwn Juárez & Salvatierra)

TELEPHONE
Servifax (Salvatierra 75) Long-distance phone office; closes around 7pm.

TOURIST INFORMATION
Tourist Office (☎ 135-0411; cnr Madero & Salvatierra; ☻ 8am-8pm Mon-Fri) In the Palacio de Gobierno on the western side of the Plaza Cívica, this office provides little more than brochures.
Marine Park Office (☎ 135-0477; ☻ 9am-3pm Mon-Sat) Next to the marina, this is a good source of information for all water activities in the Gulf (including kayaking, fishing and camping on the islands). Because Loreto's shoreline and offshore islands are protected, by registering with the Marine Park you will ensure that you know all the guidelines for traveling in the park. In addition, the staff provides information about such things as fish populations, dive locales and campsite occupancy.

TRAVEL AGENCIES
Viajes Pedrín (☎ 135-0204; Av Hidalgo; ☻ closed Sun) Full-service travel agency; sells airline tickets.

Sights
MISIÓN NUESTRA SEÑORA DE LORETO
Above the entrance to this **mission** (Salvatierra at Pino Suárez; ☻ daily), the inscription 'Cabeza y Madre de las Misiones de Baja y Alta California' (Head and Mother of the Missions of Upper and Lower California) aptly describes its role in the history of the Californias. Featuring a floor plan in the shape of a Greek cross, the mission

suffered serious damage when the ceiling and bell tower collapsed during the 1829 hurricane; it has been restored only over the last 25 years.

It's polite to take off your hat when you enter the mission. During mass, you should sit down and resist the urge to shoot photos.

MUSEO DE LAS MISIONES
Alongside the mission church, INAH's **museum** (☎ 135-0441; US$3; ☻ 9am-1pm & 1:45-6pm Tue-Sun) recounts the European settlement of Baja California in a generally chronological manner. It pays attention to the peninsula's indigenous population, honoring the accomplishments of the Jesuits and their successors without ignoring the native demographic collapse caused by the missions. It also displays a fine selection of the implements of daily ranch life of the early European settlers. The museum **bookstore** sells a variety of Spanish-language books about the archaeology, anthropology and history of Mexico and Baja California.

Activities
FISHING
Many guides are available for all-day **fishing** trips, but fishing near Loreto is poorer than it once was. The creation of the offshore national park is beginning to have a positive impact on the fish population (in part because professional shrimpers are no longer allowed in the park area).

Bonito, cabrilla, corvina, crevalle, grouper, pargo, sierra and skipjack are all-year game species. Dorado swarm offshore from April to October, but striped marlin, needlefish, roosterfish and sailfish also inhabit these waters. From November to May, yellowtail is the main attraction.

For about US$100, you can hire a local guide at the marina to take you out for a day trip. Outfitters that arrange all-day fishing trips include **Arturo's** (☎ 135-0766; www.arturosport.com; Av Hidalgo at Romanita) and **Ricardo's** (☎ 135-0025; Davis near Romanita) at Hotel La Pinta Loreto (p152). Both charge around US$130 to US$175 depending on the size of the boat and number of people.

DIVING & SNORKELING
Reefs around Isla del Carmen, Isla Coronado and other sites are superb for water

sports. From April to November, the water temperature is 75° to 85°F (24° to 29°C) and visibility is 60 to 80 feet (18 to 24m). From December to March, the water temperature is 60° to 70°F (15° to 21°C); visibility is 30 to 50 feet (9 to 15m).

Diving and snorkeling excursions can be arranged at Baja Outpost (see below); Cobadi (☎ 104-2468, 135-1222; Madero near Av Hidalgo; www.loretours.com) or Dolphin Dive Center (in the USA ☎ 626-447-5536; www.dolphindivebaja.com; Juárez near Blvd López Mateos). Two-tank diving excursions cost between US$85 and US$125 per person, depending on the amount of gear you need and the dive destination. Deportes Blazer (☎ 135-0911; Av Hidalgo 23) sells scuba gear.

Tours

Baja Outpost (☎ 135-1134, in the USA ☎ 888-649-5951; off Blvd Lopez Mateos btwn Av Hidalgo & Jordán), a well-run outfitter based in the hotel of the same name, offers a wide array of exciting tours including diving (US$90) and snorkeling (US$52) trips, whale-watching (US$185), mountain biking (US$75), horseback riding (US$85), kayaking, and excursions to nearby rock art sites (US$135). All prices are per person.

Las Parras Tours (☎ 135-1010; www.lasparrastours.com; Madero 16) also offers hiking, cycling, horseback riding and sea kayaking tours at similar prices. It makes an effort to involve local people in its business. Las Parras also rents bikes for US$5/25 per hour/day.

Festivals & Events

Loreto's main fiestas are early September's Día de Nuestra Señora de Loreto and mid-October's Fundación de la Ciudad, which celebrates the city's founding in 1699.

Sleeping

HOTELS

Iguana Inn (☎ 135-1627; www.iguanainn.com; Juárez at Madero; r US$40-45; P ⊠) The three modern courtyard bungalows here, equipped with coffeemakers, microwaves and fridges, are a superb value. US owners Mike and Julie are wonderfully friendly and allow you to watch movies from their video library. The rooms are behind their small house, two blocks north of the plaza.

Baja Outpost (☎ 135-1134, in the USA 888-649-5951; off Blvd Lopez Mateos btwn Av Hidalgo & Jordán; r/palapa US$65/86; P ⊠) Cabañas don't get much more deluxe than those at Baja Outpost, and the hotel-style rooms are almost as slick. The former are small but cozy, and cushy queen beds dominate the rooms. Best of all, it's right off the malecón – great for those evening walks. The rates include breakfast.

Hotel Junípero (☎ 135-0122; Av Hidalgo; s/d US$30/36) Although it's a bit worn around the edges, Hotel Junípero is still a great deal, offering large rooms with king-size beds, bathrooms, fridges, TVs and fans. Some rooms open onto the mission site while others have balconies over the street.

Posada de las Flores (☎ 135-1162, in the USA ☎ 877-245-2860; www.posadadelasflores.com; Plaza Cívica; r US$158-259; P ⊠) Loreto's most upscale hotel occupies a historical building with an elegant interior courtyard complete with fountain and dreamy background music. The spacious suites overlook the plaza, and every room has a very nouveau-Mexican flare.

Hotel Plaza Loreto (☎ 135-0280; Av Hidalgo 2; s/d US$45/55; ⊠) This attractive colonial-style hotel near the mission offers comfortable rooms with air-con.

Hotel La Pinta Loreto (☎ 135-0025; in the USA ☎ 800-800-9632; www.lapintahotels.com; Davis at Constituyentes; r US$88-111; ⊠ ⊠) On Davis about 1 mile (1.6km) north of the plaza, La Pinta has a swimming pool (not always filled), restaurant, bar and easy beach access. Its 48 rooms have TVs, showers and private balconies facing the Gulf, but some guests have complained that the lack of heating makes winter nights chilly.

Very basic Hotel Posada San Martín (☎ 135-0792; cnr Juárez & Davis; r US$15-20) is the best of the local cheapies, but the cheapest rooms are stuffy. Motel Salvatierra (☎ 135-0021; Salvatierra 123; s/d US$20/22; ⊠) has clean but small rooms with air-con and hot showers.

CAMPING

RV Park El Moro (☎ 135-0542; Rosendo Robles 8; tent/RV/s/d US$5/12/30/40; P ⊠) Only half a block from the beach and a few blocks from the mission, El Moro has about 13 sites with full hookups, and a few tent spaces. It's very friendly and tidy, with clean baths and hot showers, but has limited shade. The eight rooms available have air-con and TVs.

Loreto Shores (☎ 135-0629; RV US$15) On the beach across the Río Loreto, spacious Loreto hores has full hookups, clean bathrooms, hot showers and a laundry room but very little shade.

Villas de Loreto (☎ 135-0586; www.villasdeloreto. com; RV US$15, d US$78-112; P ⛵) If you don't mind being a good walk south of downtown, this is one of the best options for camping *and* lodging. The spacious rooms are decorated with Mexican crafts and have beautifully thatched roofs. Immaculate and comfortable *casitas* (small houses), with full kitchens and dining areas, are also for rent for US$156 to US$172. This is a non-smoking resort. There are kayaks available to rent, and use of their bikes is free for guests.

Eating

Nuevo Playa Blanca (☎ 135-1176; cnr Av Hidalgo & Madero; mains US$5-10) This long-time favorite serves good fish and lobster dishes, but the seafood cocktails and ceviches are the real treat.

 Macaws (Blvd López Mateos near Jordán; appetizers US$4-6, mains US$5-10) Sun-beaten fishing fanatics line Macaws' bar during happy hour (4-6pm) partly because the drinks are two-for-one, but mostly for the mellow music, relaxed vibe and outstanding appetizers (try the oven-baked clams with melted cheese). Meals are pretty good too.

 La Palapa (☎ 135-1101; Av Hidalgo at Romarita; mains US$6-12) Locals start to drool when you bring up this place, obviously having devoured the excellent seafood in the past.

 Café Olé (☎ 135-0496; Madero 14; mains US$3-6) Near the Plaza Cívica, Café Olé serves good, inexpensive breakfasts (with especially tasty hotcakes) and antojitos. Order at the counter and sit outside.

 Los Cuatro Altos (cnr Juárez & Independencia; mains US$6-12; ⛵ closed Tue) Named after the four-way stop where it's located, Cuatro Altos is a well-liked seafood restaurant and grill, with everything from burgers and steaks to ceviche and salad.

 México Lindo y Que Rico (Av Hidalgo at Colegio; mains US$4-7) Big glasses of juice, friendly service, a casual setting and tasty, reasonably priced Mexican food make this a winner. Try the *fillet empapelado en salsa de chipotle* (fish cooked in foil with chipotle chili sauce).

 El Nido (☎ 135-0027; Salvatierra 154) Across from the bus terminal, this is the local branch of the Baja steakhouse chain.

Three of Loreto's several taco stands stand out above the rest:

El Rey del Taco (Juárez at Zapata; tacos US$1-2) The first fish taco stand in Loreto; there's a reason this place is still around.

McLulu's (Hidalgo at Colegio; tacos US$1-2) Whips out fish tacos that are nothing less than *delicioso*.

Rigo's Tacos (Hidalgo at Madero; tacos US$0.80-1) Specializes in carne asada and quesadillas; feels like you're eating on mom's front porch.

Entertainment

Nightlife in Loreto usually means hanging out late at one of the restaurant bars. **Mike's Bar** (Av Hidalgo at Madero; ⛵ 10am-3am), below Nuevo Playa Blanca (see Eating), offers nightly music after 10pm. If you're thirsty before that, drop in for the delectable appetizers to go with your drinks. **Jarros y Tarros** (Mugs and Jugs; Av Hidalgo; ⛵ 8pm-3am) is a good place for playing pool. **Millenium** (Madero near Jordán; ⛵ Fri & Sat) is the local dance club.

Shopping

Loreto has several handicrafts stores on the streets closest to the plaza. For quality items from throughout Mexico, try **El Alacrán** (☎ 135-0029; Salvatierra & Misioneros). **Silver Desert** (☎ 135-0684; Salvatierra 36) sells silver jewelry, local handicrafts and clothing. Prices are reasonable, and the owners are very helpful and friendly.

Getting There & Away
AIR

Aeropuerto Internacional de Loreto (☎ 135-0454) is reached by a lateral off the Transpeninsular, just across the Río Loreto. To get there from town, head south on Madero. **Aero California** (☎ airport 135-0500, 135-0555) flies direct to/from Los Angeles (about US$200) on Wednesday, Saturday and Sunday.

 Aerolitoral (☎ airport 135-1837), represented by Viajes Pedrín (p151), flies daily from La Paz to Loreto, continuing to Hermosillo and Los Angeles (about US$280). It returns daily as well. **Aeroméxico** (☎ airport 135-1837) flies daily to/from San Diego (US$210).

BUS

Loreto's **bus terminal** (☎ 135-0767) is near the traffic circle where Salvatierra, Paseo de Ugarte and Paseo Tamaral converge. The following are some of the main schedules and fares:

CENTRAL BAJA

Destination	Fare	Duration
Guerrero Negro	US$19	5-6 hrs
La Paz	US$21	5 hrs
Mexicali	US$86	19 hrs
San Ignacio	US$18	4 hrs
San José del Cabo	US$32	8 hrs
Santa Rosalía	US$13	3 hrs
Tijuana	US$72	18 hrs

Getting Around

Taxi rides to or from the airport cost about US$9. **Budget Rent A Car** (☎ 135-1090; Hidalgo near Blvd López Mateos) has an office downtown and at the airport (☎ 135-0937). The cheapest rate quoted at the time of research was US$70 per day, all included.

Las Parras Tours (p152) rents mountain bikes.

AROUND LORETO

☎ 613

Isla Coronado

About 3 miles (5km) northeast of Loreto, opposite Punta Tierra Firma, Isla Coronado is one of the Gulf's most accessible islands and the northernmost island in the Parque Marino Nacional Bahía de Loreto. The turquoise waters along its sparkling sandy beach, facing the mainland, are ideal for **snorkeling**. There are also many seabirds, mostly pelicans, and the rocky eastern shore has a small sea lion colony.

Many kayakers make the trip to Coronado, where **camping** is possible, and several palapas offer shade. Las Parras Tours and Baja Outpost in Loreto offer **kayaking** tours to this and other nearby islands, as well as drop-off and pickup so you can paddle independently.

Nopoló

In the 1980s Fonatur, the federal tourist development agency also responsible for mainland Mexican debacles like Cancún and Ixtapa, plopped this incongruous resort complex onto an erstwhile goat ranch 4 miles (6.5km) south of Loreto.

Despite construction of an international airport and an elaborate street plan off a single palm-lined avenue, Nopoló remains a cluster of largely vacant and weedy lots except for its single upscale hotel, the lighted tennis courts, and sprawling 18-hole golf course, and a handful of private houses.

The **Campo de Golf Loreto** (☎ 133-0554) features a cart bridge that many isolated rural communities might start a revolution to get. Greens fees are US$44, while cart/club rentals are US$35/22.

The **Whales Inn** (☎ 133-0700; reservaciones @whalesinn.com; d US$230-300; P ☒ ☒) is an adults-only, all-inclusive facility featuring two swimming pools (sometimes heated), tennis courts (sometimes with nets), a nightclub, a bar, two restaurants and a nude beach. Drinks, food, golf and all activities are included in the rates.

Puerto Escondido

An ostensibly Mediterranean-style marina in a scenic natural port 16 miles (26km) south of Loreto, Puerto Escondido was the site of yet another ambitious Fonatur scheme. It was intended as a resort complex with five-star hotels, luxurious homes, condominiums, stores, a fitness center and moorings for 300 yachts. The paved but potholed access road off the Transpeninsular beyond the full-service **Tripui Resort RV Park** (☎ 133-0818; RV US$16) aptly symbolizes the ragged results.

Misión San Javier

Built from blocks of volcanic stone in the Sierra de la Giganta west of Loreto, Misión San Francisco Javier de Viggé-Biaundó is one of the Californias' best-preserved mission churches, in perhaps the most spectacular setting of any of them. Founded in 1699 at nearby Rancho Viejo by the famous Jesuit Francisco María Piccolo, the Californias' second mission moved to this site in 1720 but was not completed until 1758.

The church itself is in very good condition, with original walls, floors and venerable religious artworks, but visitors may no longer climb the spiral staircase to the chorus. Irrigation canals of Jesuit vintage, the first on the peninsula, still water the local fields. Every December 3, hundreds of pilgrims celebrate the saint's fiesta here.

Just over a mile (1.6km) south of Loreto is the junction for the spectacular 22-mile (35km) mountain road to the mission and village of San Javier, which takes about 1½ hours, not counting photo stops. The dirt surface is graded only to Rancho Viejo but is passable for most passenger cars despite a few bumpy spots and arroyo crossings. Rancho Las Parras, in a verdant canyon way to San Javier, grows figs, dates, olives, and citrus, but livestock have contaminated most of the water along the route – do not drink without treating it. A spring just before Km 20 westbound should be potable, and there are a couple of potential swimming holes.

With an early start, this would be a good daytrip on a mountain bike, but parts of the road are steep enough that even the strongest cyclist will probably have to walk for short stretches. The village's only tourist facility is **Restaurant Palapa San Javier** (mains US$3-4; ☺ lunch & dinner), where the owner serves simple meals, cold beer and sodas under a shady palapa alongside his house. Ask about camping; there may even be rustic accommodations available.

The road leading southwest from San Javier, passing a series of remote ranchos before reaching the intersection with the paved Ciudad Insurgentes-San Isidro highway just north of Colonia Purísima, is much improved and passable for any vehicle with good clearance. While this interesting road is slower than the paved Transpeninsular, a big plus is it allows drivers to avoid the unpleasant Judiciales checkpoint south of Nopoló.

PUERTO ESCONDIDO TO CIUDAD INSURGENTES

Beyond Puerto Escondido, the Transpeninsular twists and climbs through the Sierra de la Giganta before turning westward into the **Llano de Magdalena** (Magdalena Plain), a major agricultural zone, stretching south nearly to La Paz.

A bronze monument to pioneer agriculturalists graces the road north from the highway junction at **Ciudad Insurgentes**, an increasingly prosperous town with restaurants, groceries and a **Pemex** station, but still no accommodations. If you're planning to continue west to Puerto López Mateos or north to San José de Comondú, stock up on supplies here.

CIUDAD CONSTITUCIÓN

☎ 613 / pop 45,000

Constitución is primarily an agricultural service center, and most travelers find little of interest here, except the faraway feeling of hanging around the main drag (the Transpeninsular as it rolls through town)

watching people shop, sell, eat tacos, hawk newspapers, cruise, and dodge the little maniacs whizzing around on skateboards and bikes. Touristy it ain't, but it is very convenient to the major whale-watching centers of Puerto San Carlos and Puerto López Mateos, which have only limited accommodations.

Having grown dramatically with the Llano de Magdalena's rapid expansion of commercial agriculture, Ciudad Constitución bears all the marks of a 'progressive' city: clean, broad paved streets (at least in the center), several banks and even high culture – state and national cultural organizations visit the local Teatro de la Ciudad (City Theater) on their tours.

At the northern entrance to town, at the turnoff to Puerto San Carlos, is a monument to General Agustín Olachea Avilés, a Todos Santos native who participated in the famous Cananea copper strike in Sonora. Olachea Avilés joined the revolutionary forces in 1913, became a general in 1920 at the age of 28 and put down a Yaqui Indian rebellion in Sonora in 1926. Later, as governor of Baja California's Territorio Sur, he promoted agricultural development in Ciudad Constitución.

Fresh water for cultivation was a serious problem before the exploitation of huge aquifers beneath the plain. Israeli technicians have since advised farmers on water conservation and crop substitution to take advantage of newly drilled wells. Water-efficient crops like garbanzos (chickpeas) and citrus are superseding thirsty, pesticide-dependent cotton.

Orientation

The city is 134 miles (216km) northwest of La Paz, 89 miles (143km) southwest of Loreto and 36 miles (58km) east of Puerto San Carlos on Bahía Magdalena. The north-south Transpeninsular is the main street, known as Blvd General Agustín Olachea Avilés and more commonly as Blvd Olachea, but the city has matured beyond the strip-development phase (unlike such northern Baja towns as San Quintín). Still, most important services are within a block or two of Blvd Olachea, where passing delivery trucks have clipped, bent and twisted the city's once shiny Banamex street signs; traffic seems to cross Olachea at every corner. The other major street is the parallel Av Juárez, one block east.

Information

Constitución has no *cambios* (money exchanges), but three banks on Blvd Olachea change US dollars or traveler's checks and have ATMs: **Banca Serfín** (cnr Galeana), **Banamex** (cnr Mina) and **Bancomer** (at Pino Suárez).

The **post office** (Galeana 236) is toward the north end of town, just west of Blvd Olachea.

SuperCom Internet Café (US$1.50/hr) is on the north end of Olachea (between Guadalupe Victoria and Guerrero) near the Hotel Oasis sign.

Sleeping

Hotel Oasis (☎ 132-3919; hoasis01@prodigy.net.mx; Guerrero 284; r US$27-31; P 🞮) At the north end of town, three blocks west of Blvd Olachea, the Oasis is an excellent little hotel with spacious, spotless, air-conditioned rooms with satellite TV. Spot it by the big rusty sign on Olachea.

Hotel Maribel (☎ 132-0155; Guadalupe Victoria 156; s/d US$28/36; 🞮) Just off Blvd Olachea, at the north end of town, Hotel Maribel is quieter than most, featuring clean, nondescript rooms with telephones and TVs. The attached **restaurant** offers basic Mexican dishes.

Hotel El Conquistador (☎ 132-2745; Bravo 161; s/d US$30/40; P 🞮) A conquistador in armor guards the lobby of this comfortable three-star hotel run by an attentive staff. The pleasant attached **café** serves decent meals. It's half a block west of Blvd Olachea, one block south of the plaza.

Hotel Conchita (☎ 132-0266; Blvd Olachea 180; s/d US$16/18) Three blocks south of the plaza, Hotel Conchita is big and impersonal but clean and secure. It's also smack in the center of town.

Hotel Reforma (☎ 132-0988; Obregón 125; r US$12-16; P) Though it's pretty dilapidated and adorned with sun-drying laundry and a broken down car, Hotel Reforma has a nostalgic motel charm to it. Perhaps it's the trees over the dirt parking lot.

The RV park **Campestre La Pila** (☎ 132-0562; site US$10 for 2 people, additional person US$5; 🞮) is south of town and about a half mile (1km) west of the highway. Turn right off Olachea at the large factory. There are hot showers, electrical outlets, toilets and a swimming

pool. The park proper is a pleasant, gr**ʌ** area surrounded by a farm land and a f**◌** shade trees.

At the northern end of town near the junction with the highway to Puerto López Mateos, Austrian-run **Manfred's RV Trailer Park** (☎ 132-1103; 🞮) has spacious sites for US$13 to US$20. There's plenty of shade, hot showers, a swimming pool, an Austrian restaurant and a spacious apartment with private bath for US$30 per night.

Eating

There are more **taquerías** on Blvd Olachea than you can shake a tortilla at, and they all make for great people-watching. For more cheap eats, hit the **Mercado Central** (Av Juárez btwn Hidalgo & Bravo).

For good, cheap antojitos and sandwiches, look for the place on the west side of Olachea with the palapa roof, no walls, makeshift kitchen, dirt floor and five oil-cloth-covered tables inside called **Lonchería La Pequeña** (cnr Blvd Olachea & Bravo; mains US$2-4, 🕑 5am-10pm) It's a real deal.

Café Cactus (☎ 138-3501; cnr Blvd Olachea & Morelos; mains US$5-9; 🕑 5pm-midnight Tue-Thu, 6pm-1am Sat & Sun) is a bit more upscale and good for Mexican dinners, coffee and deserts.

The iced 'mochaccinos' at **Coffee Star** (Blvd Olachea near Mina), on the west side of Olachea, are a godsend when you're rolling through this heat.

Getting There & Away

North-south ABC and Autotransportes Aguila buses on the Transpeninsular stop at Constitución's **bus terminal** (☎ 132-0376; cnr Av Rosaura Zapata & Pino Suárez), two blocks east of Blvd Olachea.

Buses depart daily from Constitución for destinations north and south; see the following table. There are 12 daily to La Paz.

Destination	Fare	Duration
Guerrero Negro	US$56	9 hrs
La Paz	US$11.50	2½ hrs
Loreto	US$10	2 hrs
Mexicali	US$96	19 hrs
Puerto López Mateos	US$3.50	1 hr
Puerto San Carlos	US$3	1 hr
San Isidro	US$12	3 hrs
San Jose del Cabo	US$13-23	5 hrs
Santa Rosalía	US$19	5 hrs
Tijuana	US$81	19 hrs

BAHÍA MAGDALENA

☎ 613

'Mag Bay,' as those with the North American penchant for diminutives like to call it, is one of Baja's three main winter calving grounds for California gray whales. Puerto López Mateos and Puerto San Carlos are the main population centers on the lagoon. The latter has the best accommodations and the most whale-watching operators.

Puerto López Mateos

pop 3200

Protected by the barrier island of Isla Magdalena, Puerto Adolfo López Mateos, 20 miles (32km) west of Ciudad Insurgentes by a good paved road, is one of Baja's best **whale-watching** sites. The bay is narrow here, so you don't have to travel as far by boat to see the whales. Boca de Soledad, only a short distance north of the port, boasts the highest density of whales anywhere along the peninsula.

The annual Festival del Ballenato, celebrating the birth of gray-whale calves, takes place in early February.

The cooperative **Unión de Lancheros** (☎ 131-5178) and the **Sociedad Cooperativa Aquendi** (☎ 131-5115) run whale-watching trips from the pier near their headquarters by the lighthouse. Trips cost US$50 per hour for up to six persons. Because people begin to arrive the night before for early-morning departures and camp at nearby Playa Soledad, it's easy to form groups to share expenses.

Free **camping**, with pit toilets only (bring water), is possible at **Playa Soledad**. López Mateos' only other accommodations are at the small and simple but tidy **Posada Ballena López** (s/d US$10/15), within easy walking distance of the whale-watching pier.

Besides a few so-so taco stands, López Mateos has several decent seafood restaurants, including **Restaurant California** (☎ 131-5208) and **Cabaña Brisa**.

Autotransportes Aguila provides daily buses to/from Ciudad Constitución (US$3.75). The bus stop is next to the Restaurant California.

Puerto San Carlos

pop 3600

Increasingly popular for some of southern Baja's best **whale-watching**, Puerto San Carlos is a dusty and windy but friendly deep-water port on Bahía Magdalena, about 36 miles (58km) west of Ciudad Constitución (watch for livestock, including cattle and even pigs, on the paved highway). Puerto San Carlos ships cotton and alfalfa from the fields of the Llano de Magdalena, and a minor building boom has given it the best accommodations of any of Baja's whale-watching destinations. Nearby beaches on Bahía Magdalena are fine for camping, clamming and sportfishing.

The new **Museo Ballena Sudcaliforniana** (Southern Baja Whale Museum) is very rudimentary, displaying only a single gray-whale skeleton and a few rusting artifacts from 19th-century whaling days, but mid-February's Festival de la Ballena Gris (Gray Whale Festival) is becoming a big-time event.

ORIENTATION & INFORMATION

All Puerto San Carlos' streets are named for Mexican port cities. Gasoline, including Magna Sin and diesel, is available at the Pemex station. There's an **Internet cafe** (cnr Puerto La Paz & Puerto Benito Juárez; US$2.50/hr) near the *parque central* (main plaza). Puerto San Carlos lacks a tourist office but has a **post office**, long-distance **telephone** service and an **IMSS clinic**.

WHALE-WATCHING

From mid-January through March, local *pangueros* (fishermen with skiffs) take up to six passengers to view friendly whales in Bahía Magdalena for US$60 per hour per boat. The minimum time for a good trip is about 2½ hours. Some people come for the day from Loreto or La Paz (both about 2½ hours away by car) or even fly in from Cabo San Lucas, but early morning is the best time to see whales.

Among the local operators are **Ulysturs** (☎ 136-0017) and **Mar y Arena** (☎ 136-0076; bajamagbay@hotmail.com), on the right as you enter town. Most hotels in town can arrange for tours as well.

SLEEPING & EATING

San Carlos has some surprisingly good hotels, but be sure to make reservations during whale-watching season. Prices quoted are for whale-watching season and usually drop for the rest of the year. The following are all in town and easy to find.

CENTRAL BAJA

Hotel Alcatraz (☎ 136-0017; hotelalcatraz@prodigy. net.mx; Calle Puerto La Paz s/n; s/d US$32/41) A large patio filled with plants, tables and chairs makes this the most relaxing place in town. Rooms are spacious and have TVs, and the gracious owner is full of information and sets up whale-watching tours for guests. Be sure to make reservations in season. The Alcatraz's shady **Restaurant Bar El Patio** is by far the best in town.

Hotel Brennan (☎ 136-0288; www.hotelbrennan. com.mx; s/d US$36/45) This is another gem, with modern, immaculate rooms and friendly owners.

Molly's Suites (☎ 136-0131; turismo@balandra. uabcs.mx; Puerto La Paz; s/d US$45/54) Owned by the same family as hotel Brennan, Molly's Suites offers equally pleasant rooms.

Motel Las Brisas (☎ 136-0498; Puerto Madero; s/d US$12/15; **P**) Rooms here open onto a parking area and are shaded by trees. It's a well-worn motel, but friendly and perfectly fine for the price.

Mariscos Los Arcos (☎ 136-0347; Puerto La Paz 170; mains US$4-8) This little brick-front restaurant has a big bar, and excellent shrimp tacos and seafood soup.

Free **camping** is possible on the fairly clean public beach north of town, but the aging palapas are falling into disrepair and there are no toilets. South of town, people often camp among the mangroves near the whale-watching launch sites; it's messier here, but there's a good selection of bird life, perhaps suggesting that aesthetics are more important to humans than to wildlife.

RV Park Nancy (☎ 136-0195; site US$5) has nine small, shadeless spots.

GETTING THERE & AWAY

Based in a small house on Puerto Morelos, **Autotransportes Aguila** (☎ 136-0453) offers buses to Ciudad Constitución (US$3, 1 hour) and La Paz (US$13, 4 hours) at 7:30am and 1:45pm daily. This is the only public transportation.

PUERTO CHALE

About 36 miles (58km) south of Ciudad Constitución, a 15-mile (24km) graded dirt road leads west from the village of Santa Rita on the Transpeninsular to Puerto Chale, a tiny Pacific coast fish camp popular for **windsurfing**.

MISIÓN SAN LUIS GONZAGA

Founded back in 1737 by German Jesuit Lambert Hostell, the date-palm oasis of Misión San Luis Gonzaga, southeast of Ciudad Constitución, closed with the Jesuits' departure in 1768, after an original Indian population of 2000 had fallen to only 300.

San Luis' well-preserved church, dating from the 1750s but lacking the embellishments of the San Borja and San Francisco Javier churches, is not one of the mission system's gems, but its twin bell towers are unusual. Besides the church, there are ruins of more recent vintage with elaborate neoclassical columns. The village's only facilities are a school and a Conasupo (small store).

At Km 195, about 9 miles (14km) south of Ciudad Constitución on the Transpeninsular, a graded lateral good enough even for low riders or mammoth RVs leads 25 miles (40km) east to the edge of the Sierra de la Giganta and San Luis Gonzaga. Keep watching for the sign reading 'Presa Iguajil.'

Southern Baja

CONTENTS

Also called the Cape Region, southern Baja is home to some of the peninsula's most enticing attractions. La Paz, arguably the finest city in all of Baja, sits on the largest bay in the Sea of Cortez, and its *malecón* (waterfront promenade) pulls tourists and locals out of their abodes for gorgeous sunsets, relaxed socializing and upbeat civic events. Kayakers and divers base themselves here to explore the offshore islands, especially Espíritu Santo. Windsurfers head south to the Eastern Cape, where Los Barriles draws wind-seekers from around the world. Folks pickier about their beaches head farther south along the Eastern Cape to beaches around Cabo Pulmo for snorkeling and swimming among the only living coral reef in western North America.

On the Western Cape you'll find the wave-pounded beaches of the Pacific and the historic town of Todos Santos. Resident expats have successfully transformed it into an upscale yet subdued artist colony, where sprays of bougainvillea and newly painted adobe buildings conjure images of Taos and Santa Fe, New Mexico. Surfers take to the waves around here, especially Playa Los Cerritos, and help keep the town anchored to its humble roots.

Both México 19 and the Eastern Cape Road lead to Los Cabos, as does the Transpeninsular as it passes through the Central Cape and the tiny towns of El Triunfo, San Antonio and Santiago. Los Cabos, true enough, is part of southern Baja, but as a tourist mecca in and of itself, the region receives its own chapter.

TOP FIVE

- Watch azure waters slide beneath your kayak as you paddle the narrow inlets of **Espíritu Santo island** (p167).

- Let **La Paz** (p161) cast its spell on you with sunsets, seafood tacos and its wonderful *malecón*.

- Swim with tropical manta rays and tropical fish at the coral reef of **Cabo Pulmo** (p180).

- Rip up the waves at **Playa Los Cerritos** (p186), south of Todos Santos.

- Learn (or master!) kite surfing at **Los Barriles** (p177), the wind-sport capital of Baja California.

■ LA PAZ JANUARY AVERAGE HIGH: 73°F/23°C ■ WATER TEMP OFF CABO PULMO: 68-83°F/20-28°C

LA PAZ

☎ 612 / pop 196,900

There's something special about La Paz that's difficult to pinpoint: the pinkish light of sundown over the bay, the progressive atmosphere created by its university and cultural center, the crooked sidewalks, its status as a free port, its palpable cultural links to mainland Mexico, the abundance of restaurants and cafés, the eccentric and friendly *Paceños* themselves and a lively street life that has and will seemingly forever refuse to cave in to tourism. It all conspires to keep plenty of return visitors swearing that this is the best city in Baja. To top it all off, La Paz is an excellent base for all sorts of ocean activities. Kayaking, diving, sportfishing, whale-watching and beach bumming can all be done as daytrips from town. Best of all, you get to return to La Paz at the end of the day.

History

In 1535 on Península Pichilingue, Hernán Cortés established Baja's first European settlement. But despite the discovery of pearls in the Gulf of California, it was soon abandoned due to Indian hostility and food and water shortages.

By the late 16th century, England and Holland were disputing Spain's maritime hegemony, and buccaneers were raiding Spanish ships throughout the world; the treasure-laden galleons that sailed from Manila to Acapulco were especially popular targets. After the turn of the century, in response to incursions by Northern Europeans, Viceroy Gaspar de Zuñiga y Acevedo of New Spain granted Sebastián Vizcaíno a license to exploit the pearl fisheries of the Cape Region and establish settlements to discourage privateers.

Though Vizcaíno renamed Bahía de la Santa Cruz as Bahía de La Paz (Bay of Peace), he abandoned the idea of a settlement there because of the shortage of supplies and the area's limited agricultural potential.

In 1720 the Jesuits established a mission, but epidemics and Indian uprisings led to its abandonment 29 years later. La Paz was briefly occupied by US Marines during the Mexican-American War, then attacked by William Walker during his preposterously incompetent attempt to annex Baja California to the USA.

THE DUTCH IN THE PACIFIC

New World piracy was largely the province of the English, but other Northern European countries eagerly joined in the battle against Spanish wealth and hegemony in the Americas. The French and especially the Dutch were most active in the Caribbean and on the coast of Brazil, but the Dutch had Pacific ambitions as well.

Since the late-16th-century voyage of Sir Francis Drake, British buccaneers had frequented the Pacific coasts of North and South America, despite the distances between their homes and their convenient, well-watered island bases in the Caribbean. Thomas Cavendish's capture of the *Santa Ana* off Cabo San Lucas in 1587 attracted privateers' interest to New Spain (Mexico) and Baja California; British pirates lay in wait for treasure-laden galleons returning from Manila and sometimes took other major prizes.

The Netherlands, having rebelled against Spanish domination in 1566, was eager to make its mark on the seas. The Dutch became rivals of the Spaniards in the Caribbean and the Portuguese in Brazil, and they soon rounded the Horn to the Pacific. Though they lurked at Cabo San Lucas in hopes of emulating Cavendish's windfall, their earliest voyages had limited success. Profit was not the only motive that spurred the Dutch; they were fanatical Protestants who resented the reactionary Catholicism the Spaniards had imposed on them in Europe.

In 1615 the surprisingly genteel occupation of Acapulco by the Dutch privateer Joris van Spcilbergen induced the Spaniards to build the famous port's landmark castle, the Fuerte de San Diego. For decades, though, the menace of Dutch privateers forced the Spaniards to send patrols from the mainland to the Cape Region. Península Pichilingue, north of La Paz, even takes its name from the Dutch privateers whom the Spaniards called 'Flexelingas,' after their home port of Vlissingen, just north of the modern Belgian border.

SOUTHERN BAJA

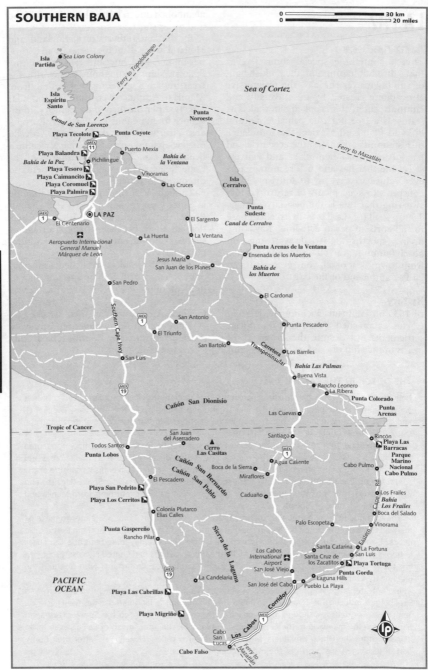

SOUTHERN BAJA

0 [========] 30 km
0 [========] 20 miles

Isla Partida • Sea Lion Colony

Isla Espíritu Santo

Sea of Cortez

Canal de San Lorenzo

Ferry to Topolobampo

Punta Noroeste

Ferry to Mazatlán

Playa Tecolote
Punta Coyote
MEX 11
Playa Balandra
Bahía de la Paz
Pichilingue
Puerto Mexia
Bahía de la Ventana
Playa Tesoro
Playa Caimancito
Vinoramas
Playa Coromuel
Playa Palmira
Las Cruces
Isla Cerralvo

Punta Sudeste

MEX 1
El Centenario
LA PAZ
El Sargento
Canal de Cerralvo

Aeropuerto Internacional General Manuel Márquez de León
La Huerta
La Ventana
Punta Arenas de la Ventana
Jesus Maria
Ensenada de los Muertos
San Juan de los Planes
Bahía de los Muertos

San Pedro

El Cardonal

Southern Cape Hwy
MEX 1
San Antonio
El Triunfo
Punta Pescadero
San Bartolo
Carretera Transpeninsular
Los Barriles
San Luis
Bahía Las Palmas
Buena Vista
MEX 19
Rancho Leonero
La Ribera
Cañón San Dionisio
Punta Colorado
Punta Arenas
Las Cuevas

Tropic of Cancer
San Juan del Aserradero
Santiago
Rincón
Todos Santos
▲ Cerro Las Casitas
Playa Las Barracas
Punta Lobos
Cañón San Bernardo
Boca de la Sierra
Agua Caliente
MEX 1
Parque Marino Nacional Cabo Pulmo
Cabo Pulmo
Cañón San Pablo
Miraflores
Playa San Pedro
El Pescadero
Caduaño
Los Frailes
Playa Los Cerritos
Bahía Los Frailes
Boca del Salado
Colonia Plutarco Elias Calles
Vinorama
Punta Gaspereño
Rancho Pilar
Palo Escopeta
Santa Catarina
La Fortuna
Sierra de la Laguna
San Luis
Los Cabos International Airport
Santa Cruz de los Zacatitos
Playa Tortuga
PACIFIC OCEAN
MEX 19
La Candelaria
San José Viejo
Punta Gorda
San José del Cabo
Laguna Hills
Playa Las Cabrillas
Pueblo La Playa

Playa Migriño
Los Cabos Corridor
MEX 1
Cabo San Lucas
Ferry to Mazatlán
Cabo Falso

SOUTHERN BAJA

Mining at nearby El Triunfo, along with pearling and fishing in the Gulf, contributed to the city's postindependence growth. Its political status advanced with the grant of statehood to Baja California Sur in 1974.

Orientation

As the Transpeninsular approaches the city, it runs parallel to Bahía de La Paz and becomes Calzada (Calle) Abasolo. To continue to Cabo San Lucas without visiting downtown La Paz, turn right (south) on 5 de Febrero and follow the signs to Carretera al Sur (the southbound Transpeninsular) and Cabo San Lucas.

Four blocks east of 5 de Febrero, Abasolo becomes Paseo Alvaro Obregón, running along the malecón and on to Península Pichilingue. On weekend nights, Paseo Obregón is a mile-long traffic jam, while the malecón attracts hordes of teenyboppers.

Most of La Paz has a regular grid pat tern that makes orientation easy, although the city center's crooked streets and alleys change their names almost every block. In this area, locals occasionally use different street names as well – the official name of block-long Lerdo de Tejada, for instance, is usually ignored in favor of Santos Degollado, the name of its longer extension. Note also that the numbering system along Paseo Obregón is so irregular that it seems completely improvised.

On Av Independencia, four blocks from the Muelle Turístico (tourist pier) on the malecón, Plaza Constitución is the traditional heart of the city. Both Plaza Constitución, known officially as Jardín Velasco, and the Muelle Turístico have attractive bandshells. Many tourist activities take place on the Muelle Turístico on weekends.

Information

BOOKSTORES

Librería Agora de La Paz (☎ 122-6204; cnr Altamirano at 5 de Mayo) Carries a great selection of Spanish-language books on Baja and mainland Mexico. Inside Museo Regional de Antropología e Historia.

Librería Contempo (☎ 122-7875; Agustín Arreola 25-A) Stocks English-language newspapers and magazines.

Libros Libros Books Books (☎ 122-1410; Constitución 195) Stocks English-language newspapers and some books and magazines.

IMMIGRATION

On weekends, immigration officials staff the ferry terminal at Pichilingue and the **airport** (☎ 124-6349), but tourist-card extensions are available only at the Paseo Obregón **immigration office** (Servicios Migratorios; ☎ 125-3493; Paseo Obregón 2140, Edificio Milhe; ☒ 9am-6pm Mon-Fri).

INTERNET ACCESS

Galería Internet Café (Espacio Don Tomás, cnr Paseo Obregón & Constitución; US$1.50/hr) Snacks, coffee and fast computers.

Geo Imagen Internet (Revolución 1450; $1.50/hr; ☒ 9am-9pm)

Internet (Paseo Obregón 1665, inside Plaza Cerralva; US$1/hr; ☒ 9am-9pm Mon-Fri)

LAUNDRY

La Paz Lava (Ocampo at Mutualismo; US$5/load) Full service.

Lavandería Yoly (5 de Mayo btwn Verdad & Rubio; US$5/load) Opposite the baseball park (Estadio Arturo C Nahti); full service.

MEDICAL SERVICES

Hospital Salvatierra (☎ 122-1496, 122-1596; Bravo btwn Verdad & Domínguez)

Cruz Roja (Red Cross; ☎ 122-1111, 122-1222) Call for ambulance.

MONEY

Most banks and *cambios* (currency exchange houses) are on or around 16 de Septiembre (see map for locations), and all banks have ATMs.

Shopping centers such as **Centro Comercial Californiano** (General Ortega at Rosales) and **Centro Comercial Colima** (Abasolo at Colima) will change a traveler's check if you make a purchase worth at least 10% of the check's face value. There are also ATMs here.

POLICE

The **tourist police** office is inside the tourist office (see Tourist Information).

POST

Post office (cnr Constitución & Revolución)

TELEPHONE

Telmex/Ladatel payphones are abundant, so it's easy to make long-distance calls with Telmex cards or credit cards, or by reversing charges (remember to avoid the predatory

SOUTHERN BAJA

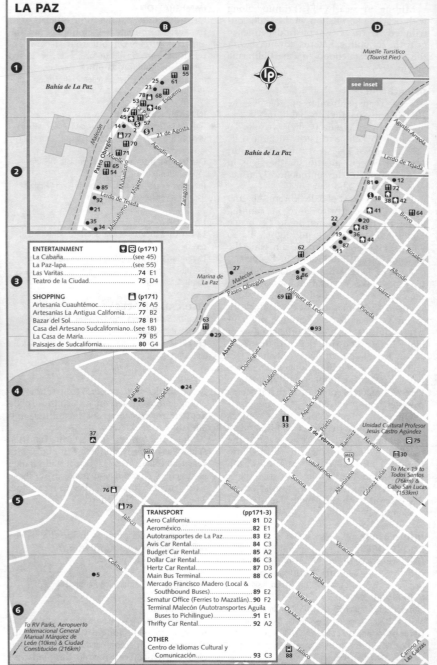

LA PAZ

ENTERTAINMENT (p171)
La Cabaña.....................................(see 45)
La Paz-lapa...................................(see 55)
Las Varitas...74 E1
Teatro de la Ciudad............................75 D4

SHOPPING (p171)
Artesanía Cuauhtémoc........................76 A5
Artesanías La Antigua California........77 B2
Bazar del Sol......................................78 B1
Casa del Artesano Sudcaliforniano..(see 18)
La Casa de María.................................79 B5
Paisajes de Sudcalifornia....................80 G4

TRANSPORT (pp171-3)
Aero California....................................81 D2
Aeroméxico...82 E1
Autotransportes de La Paz..................83 E2
Avis Car Rental....................................84 C3
Budget Car Rental...............................85 A2
Dollar Car Rental.................................86 C3
Hertz Car Rental..................................87 D3
Main Bus Terminal...............................88 C6
Mercado Francisco Madero (Local &
   Southbound Buses).........................89 E2
Sematur Office (Ferries to Mazatlán)..90 F2
Terminal Malecón (Autotransportes Aguila
   Buses to Pichilingue).......................91 E1
Thrifty Car Rental................................92 A2

OTHER
Centro de Idiomas Cultural y
   Comunicación..................................93 C3

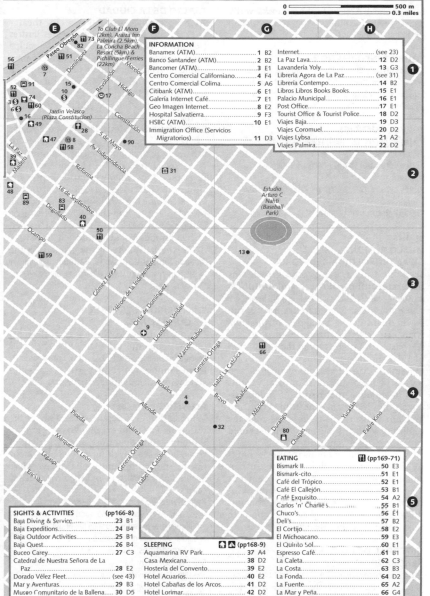

0 — 500 m
0 — 0.3 miles

INFORMATION
Banamex (ATM)................................**1** B2	Internet................................(see 23)
Banco Santander (ATM).................**2** B2	La Paz Lava..............................**12** D2
Bancomer (ATM)............................**3** E1	Lavandería Yoly.........................**13** G3
Centro Comercial Californiano........**4** F4	Librería Agora de La Paz............(see 31)
Centro Comercial Colima................**5** A6	Librería Contempo....................**14** B2
Citibank (ATM)................................**6** E1	Libros Libros Books Books..........**15** E1
Galería Internet Café......................**7** E1	Palacio Municipal......................**16** E1
Geo Imagen Internet......................**8** E2	Post Office...............................**17** E1
Hospital Salvatierra.......................**9** E2	Tourist Office & Tourist Police.....**18** D2
HSBC (ATM)..................................**10** E1	Viajes Baja...............................**19** D3
Immigration Office (Servicios	Viajes Coromuel.......................**20** D2
Migratorios).............................**11** D3	Viajes Lybsa............................**21** A2
	Viajes Palmira..........................**22** D2

SIGHTS & ACTIVITIES (pp166-8)
Baja Diving & Service....................**23** B1	
Baja Expeditions...........................**24** B4	
Baja Outdoor Activities..................**25** B1	
Baja Quest...................................**26** B4	
Buceo Carey.................................**27** C3	
Catedral de Nuestra Señora de La	
Paz..**28** E2	
Dorado Vélez Fleet......................(see 43)	
Mar y Aventuras...........................**29** B3	
Museo Comunitario de la Ballena...**30** D5	
Museo Regional de Antropología o	
Historia....................................**31** F2	
Palacio de Gobierno......................**32** G4	
Santuario de la Virgen de	
Guadalupe...............................**33** C4	
Scuba Baja Joe.............................**34** A3	
Sea Scuba...................................**35** A2	
The Fishermen's Fleet.....................**36** D3	

SLEEPING (pp168-9)
Aquamarina RV Park......................**37** A4	
Casa Mexicana..............................**38** D2	
Hostería del Convento....................**39** E2	
Hotel Acuarios..............................**40** E2	
Hotel Cabañas de los Arcos............**41** D2	
Hotel Lorimar...............................**42** D2	
Hotel Los Arcos............................**43** D3	
Hotel Mediterrané........................**44** D3	
Hotel Perla..................................**45** B2	
Hotel Plaza Real...........................**46** B1	
Hotel Yeneka...............................**47** E2	
Pensión California.........................**48** E2	
Posada Luna Sol.........................(see 29)	
Posada San Miguel.......................**49** E2	

EATING (pp169-71)
Bismark II....................................**50** E3	
Bismark-cito................................**51** E1	
Café del Trópico...........................**52** E1	
Café El Callejón............................**53** B1	
Café Exquisito..............................**54** A2	
Carlos 'n' Charlie's........................**55** B1	
Chuco's......................................**56** E1	
Deli's..**57** B2	
El Cortijo....................................**58** E2	
El Michoacano.............................**59** E3	
El Quinto Sol...............................**60** E1	
Espresso Café..............................**61** B1	
La Caleta....................................**62** C3	
La Costa.....................................**63** B3	
La Fonda....................................**64** D2	
La Fuente....................................**65** A2	
La Mar y Peña..............................**66** G4	
La Pazta...................................(see 44)	
La Terraza...................................**67** B1	
Le Bistrot Francais.........................**68** B1	
Rancho Viejo...............................**69** C3	
Super Taquería Hermanos González..**70** B2	
Taquería El Muelle.........................**71** B2	
Tequila Bar & Grill.........................**72** D2	
Tex Burger..................................**73** E1	

SOUTHERN BAJA

blue phones). At private phone kiosks, verify charges before calling, as rates can vary up to 50% between offices.

TOURIST INFORMATION
Tourist office (☎ 122-5939; cnr Paseo Obregón & Bravo; ☯ 8am-10pm Mon-Fri, 8am-midnight Sat & Sun) Moderately helpful, English spoken; tourist police also here.

TRAVEL AGENCIES
Viajes Baja (☎ 122-3660, 122-4130; Paseo Obregón 2110 at Allende)
Viajes Coromuel (☎ 122-8006; cnr Paseo Obregón & Rosales)
Viajes Lybsa (☎ 122-6001; cnr Paseo Obregón near Tejada)
Viajes Palmira (☎ 122-4030; Malecón at Allende)

Sights
MUSEO REGIONAL DE ANTROPOLOGÍA E HISTORIA
Set behind an attractive cactus garden, this first-rate anthropological and historical **museum** (☎ 122-0162; cnr 5 de Mayo & Altamirano; admission free; ☯ 9am-6pm Mon-Fri, 9am-1pm Sat), run by the Instituto Nacional de Antropología y Historia (INAH), chronicles the peninsula's past, from prehistory to the Revolution of 1910 and its aftermath.

Exhibits cover pre-Columbian rock art, native peoples, the mission era, various mining booms, the arrival of independence, the Mexican-American War and William Walker's invasion (don't miss the replica of Walker's flag and the bonds used to finance his adventures).

A small gallery contains rotating exhibits by local artists and photographers or seasonal displays on topics like November's Day of the Dead, Mexico's most famous informal holiday. The museum also contains a bookstore with a good selection on both Baja California and Mexico in general.

CATEDRAL DE NUESTRA SEÑORA DE LA PAZ
Nothing remains of La Paz's first cathedral, built in 1720 under the direction of Jesuit missionaries Jaime Bravo and Juan de Ugarte near the site of present-day Jardín Velasco. The present structure dates from 1861 but mimics the style of California mission architecture.

TEATRO DE LA CIUDAD
At the entrance to La Paz's city theater (p171), the **Rotonda de los Hombres Ilustres** (Rotunda of Distinguished Men) is a sculptural tribute to figures who fought against filibuster William Walker's invasion of La Paz in 1853 and the French mainland intervention of 1861.

A sprawling concrete edifice, the theater is the most conspicuous element of the **Unidad Cultural Profesor Jesús Castro Agúndez** (☎ 125-1917), a cultural center that takes up most of the area bounded by Altamirano, Navarro, Héroes de la Independencia and Legaspi. Other units within the center include the Galería Maestro José Carlos Olachea, exhibiting works by contemporary Mexican artists; and the Archivo Histórico Pablo L Martínez, a research archive named after a famous Baja California historian.

On the periphery of the grounds is the **Museo Comunitario de la Ballena** (Community Whale Museum; Navarro near Altamirano; admission free; ☯ 1am-1pm).

SANTUARIO DE LA VIRGEN DE GUADALUPE
Paying homage to Mexico's greatest religious icon, the **Santuario** (5 de Febrero btwn Revolución & Aquiles Serdán) is La Paz's biggest religious monument, built partly in a mission style with various modernistic touches.

Activities
When it comes to fun in, on and under the water, La Paz is an excellent base. Many of the city's tour operators offer a variety of trips, from sea kayaking and whale watching to snorkeling and scuba diving. Here are La Paz's outfitters and the services they offer:
Baja Diving & Service (☎ 122-1826; www.clubcantamar.com; Paseo Obregón 1665, Local 2) La Paz's best-established dive operator and shop has gleaming reports and great staff, and offers courses.
Baja Expeditions (☎ 125-3828, in the ☎ USA 800-843-6967; www.bajaex.com; 585 Sonora at Abasolo) The somewhat legendary Tim Means runs one of the first operators in Baja, where everything is top-notch: outstanding kayaking trips, diving and snorkeling tours, and whale-watching.
Baja Outdoor Activities (☎ 125-5636; www.kayactivities.com; Paseo Obregón s/n) Highly regarded and offering all types of kayaking trips and rentals, this

place offers three-day whale-watching tours for US$250 including two nights' hotel, food and drinks.

Baja Quest (☎ 123-5320; www.bajaquest.com; Rangel 10 at Sinaloa) Diving, snorkeling, kayaking, whale-watching trips and all types of packages are available, as are weeklong kayaking and marine ecology clinics.

Buceo Carey (☎ 123-2333; cnr Topete & Legaspi, La Paz Marina) Runs diving, kayaking, fishing, whale-watching, hiking and multiday land trips.

The Cortez Club (☎ 121-6120, in the USA ☎ 800-999-2242; www.cortezclub.com) At La Concha Beach Resort (p169), Cortez Club specializes in diving but also rents kayaks, windsurfing equipment, Hobie cats and the like.

Mar y Aventuras (☎ 122-7039; www.kayakbaja.com; Topete 564) This excellent kayaking operator has all types of paddling tours, full kayak and gear rentals, and professional staff.

Scuba Baja Joe (☎ 122-4006; Paseo Obregón 460 at Ocampo) Offers diving and snorkeling trips.

Sea Scuba (☎ 123-5233; 460 Paseo Obregón, Ste 208, cnr Ocampo) Runs dive trips and rents equipment.

SEA KAYAKING

La Paz is one of Baja's premier kayaking destinations, luring paddlers from around the world to the azure waters and shallow, finger-like inlets of nearby **Isla Espíritu Santo** and surrounding islands. From north to south, the three main island groups are: tiny Los Islotes (actually three islands), Isla Partida and Isla Espíritu Santo.

Several operators (see above) in town offer a variety of tours, from easy one-day paddles to multiday trips that allow you to camp on the islands by night and explore the spectacular coves by day.

Daytrips may be combined with a snorkeling stop at a resident **sea lion colony** at Los Islotes. You can do multiday trips with a guide or have one of the operators listed here drop you off and pick you up at a specified time. You can even set up meeting points to have food prepared for you so you can squeeze in max paddling time (and not wear yourself out flipping tortillas).

Full-day trips cost around US$80. One-way shuttles to the north end of Isla Espíritu Santo (so you can paddle back down) cost around US$125 for two people. A week-long kayaking/camping trip with guides and full food service costs from US$850 to US$1050 per person in a group of 12 to 16. Prices for custom trips vary. Most companies that offer kayaking excursions also rent kayaks for US$25 to US$50 per day. Nearly everyone speaks English.

DIVING & SNORKELING

The main diving and snorkeling destinations in Bahía de La Paz (beware of contaminated water) and the Gulf are **Isla de las Focas**, an island just north of Península Pichilingue's Punta Coyote renowned for its beaches and sea lion colony; **Los Islotes**, a group of islets just north of Isla Partida with various shipwrecks, underwater caves, reefs and sea lion colonies; and **Isla Cerralvo**, east of Península Pichilingue.

Snorkeling trips to Isla de las Focas cost about US$45, whereas two-tank scuba trips to Los Islotes run around US$92. Prices usually include food and drinks, but clarify what's included before booking a trip.

WHALE-WATCHING

La Paz ranks lower than the Baja whale-watching destinations of Laguna Ojo de Liebre, Laguna San Ignacio and Bahía Magdalena, but these gentle giants definitely ply the waters off La Paz, especially January to April. During these times you have a good chance of sighting gray whales as well as a possibility of spotting blue, finback, mink, orca and/or humpback whales. Many of the operators mentioned above offer whale-watching trips by boat for about US$125 per person. Some go out from La Paz and others go overland to Bahía Magdalena. Go for the latter.

FISHING

Game-fish species available all year in the vicinity of La Paz include bonito, corvina, crevalle, grouper, needlefish, pargo, rock bass, sierra and skipjack. Seasonal species include black and blue marlin (both July to October), dorado (April to December), roosterfish (May to January), sailfish (June to October), snook (December to June, but rare), striped marlin (May to October), yellowfin tuna (July to November, sporadically) and yellowtail (December to May).

The Fishermen's Fleet (☎ 122-1313; www.fishermensfleet.com; Paseo Obregón at Allende) is very professional, offering both daytrip boat charters and three- to four-night fishing packages that include lodging (US$525 and US$670, respectively).

SOUTHERN BAJA

The Hotel Los Arcos lobby contains an information desk for the **Dorado Vélez Fleet** (☎ 122-2744 ext 608), which offers trips on boats ranging from 22 to 30 feet and provides all equipment, licenses and transportation. Most of La Paz's other major hotels and travel agencies can also arrange trips.

Courses

Centro de Idiomas, Cultura y Comunicación (☎ 125-7554; www.cicclapaz.com; Calle Madero 2460) offers introductory, intermediate and advanced Spanish lessons and a total-immersion program. The school charges about US$18 per hour for private lessons and US$99 to US$220 for weeklong classes. **Se Habla...La Paz** (☎ 222-7763; www.sehablalapaz. com; Madero 540) offers language instruction, cultural programs and homestays. Rates are US$220 for a week (20 hours) in small classes or for a ten-hour private course.

Special Events

Carnaval is in February or March. These pre-Lenten celebrations are probably the peninsula's (and among the country's) best.

Fundación de la Ciudad is from May 1 to 7, when *Paceños* (people of La Paz) celebrate the founding of La Paz in 1535. Events include a dramatization of Hernán Cortés' landing, sports events like a half-marathon and a commercial exhibition.

The city also comes alive September 15 and 16 for **Día de la Independencia**, when Mexico celebrates its independence from Spain. **Día de los Muertos** (p227) is another good holiday to be in town for. **Día de la Marina** (Navy Day) is June 1, and **Festival de las Artes** (Arts Festival) is held in late November.

Sleeping

La Paz has good accommodations at all budget levels. Only two hotels are actually on the waterfront, while the rest are a block or more inland (still only a short walk from the malecón).

BUDGET

Pensión California (☎ 122-2896; pensioncalifornia @prodigy.net.mx; Degollado 209; s/d US$13/17) Faded paintings and dusty bric-a-brac adorn the interior courtyard walls of this longtime budget favorite. Rooms are dark, but the blue and yellow concrete walls give them a

cheerful feel. Each has a ceiling fan, fluorescent light, adjustable blinds and a shower.

Hotel Yeneka (☎ 125-4688; Madero 1520; s/d US$22/28) Quirky Hotel Yeneka has 20 dark but clean rooms with firm beds (mattresses set over concrete) and a lobby covered in hubcaps, car bumpers, mud-splattered license plates, hats and other trinkets that threaten to spill into the street.

Hostería del Convento (☎ 122-3508; Madero 85; s/d US$12/16) This is Pensión California's disheveled sister hotel, featuring the same blue and yellow paintjob but much less character.

Posada San Miguel (☎ 122-8888; Domínguez 1510; s/d US$12/15) Built around a central patio, the 14-room Posada San Miguel is a pleasant, pseudocolonial place whose dark but clean rooms each have a private bath and hot water.

El Cardón Trailer Park (☎ 124-0078; car/RV US$10/12, tent US$3-4; 🖳 🖳) At Km 4 on the Transpeninsular, just before town in a partly shaded area distant from the beach, this well-organized park has 90 spaces, each with full hookups, electric light and a small *palapa* (palm-leaf shelter). Facilities include a laundry room, a swimming pool, hot showers, clean toilets, a small paperback book exchange, a travel agency and an Internet cafe.

RV Park Casa Blanca (☎ 124-0009; Transpeninsular; site US$15; 🖳) Just west of El Cardón, the shady, secure and well-kept Casa Blanca has a pool, a restaurant and sites with full hookups.

La Paz Trailer Park (☎ 122-8787; Brecha California 120; vehicle/tent US$20/12; 🖳) Facilities at this deluxe park include immaculate bathrooms and showers, a fine restaurant, a Jacuzzi, a swimming pool and a book exchange. It's about 1 mile (1.6km) south of downtown.

Aquamarina RV Park (☎ 122-3761; Rangel at Nayarit; site US$20; 🖳) Resembling a bayside fortress (thanks to its heavy-duty and slightly intimidating security), Aquamarina is the closest RV park to town. It's highly regarded and has full hookups.

MID-RANGE

Posada Luna Sol (☎ 123-0559; Topete 564; s US$35-45, d $40-50; 🅿 🕱) This fabulous new hotel-cum-guesthouse has immaculate rooms with colorful Mexican sinks, tile floors and air-con. There's a rooftop terrace with hammocks above and a kitchen (coffee and fridge only) below. It's in a quiet spot and owned by Mar y Aventuras (see Activities, p167), which is especially convenient if you plan to kayak.

Hotel Mediterrané (☎ 125-1195; www.hotelmed. com; Allende 36; r US$50-75; 🖳) Each spacious (nay, *giant*) room in this gay-friendly hotel is immaculate, comfortable and named for a Greek island. Free Internet access, a video library (for your en-suite VCR), bikes and kayaks are all on offer. An Italian restaurant, La Pazta (p170), is located in the hotel.

Club El Moro (☎ 122-4084; Carretera Pichilingue Km 2; r US$62-123; P 🍽 🛋) With a gorgeous pool and landscaping to match, this is one of the nicest places to stay in La Paz, if you don't mind being a bit out of town. The suites are a particularly good deal, offering spacious rooms with kitchenettes and living rooms. It's located on the road to Pichilingue.

Hotel Lorimar (☎ 125-3822; Bravo 110; r without/with air-con US$25/33; 🍽) An attractive interior courtyard, bright and immaculate rooms and a very helpful, English-speaking staff make the Lorimar one of the best values in town. Staff can arrange for shuttle service out to Tecolote Beach (p173).

Casa Mexicana Inn (☎ 125-2748; www.lapacenalapaz.com; Bravo 106; s US$55-75, d US$65-85) All five rooms at this cozy little place are uniquely decorated with Mexican and Guatemalan handicrafts and Talavera tile. The Vista Paz room has a terrace and excellent views over the bay. Breakfast is included.

Hotel Acuarios (☎ 122-9266; Ramírez 1665; s/d US$45/50; P 🍽 🛋) The 60-room Acuarios has a restaurant, a swimming pool and a modern (albeit impersonal) feel. Rooms with air-con, full carpeting, TVs and telephones are definitely comfortable, however.

Hotel Perla (☎ 122-0777; Paseo Obregón 1570; r US$68-79; P 🍽 🛋) One of two hotels on the malecón, this historic hotel (if they came, they stayed here) has a swimming pool, a restaurant, a bar and a laidback open-air nightclub on the 2nd floor. Some rooms offer bay views, while others overlook the pool; all have air-con, TVs and private baths.

Hotel Plaza Real (☎ 122-9333; cnr Calle La Paz & Esquerro; r US$35) This one's friendly and has an appealing location on the pedestrian

Calle La Paz, but its circa-1972 vibe gives it a somewhat cold feel.

TOP END

Araiza Inn Palmira (☎ 121-6200; www.araizainn. mx; Blvd Alberto Alvarado Aramburo s/n; r from US$90; P 🍽 🛋) About 1½ miles (2.5km) north of downtown on the Pichilingue road, the Araiza Inn is a modern hotel appealing to vacationing families and small conventions, with a swimming pool, tennis courts, a restaurant and a nightclub.

Hotel Cabañas de los Arcos (☎ 122-2744, in the USA ☎ 800-347-2252; www.bajahotels.com; Mutualismo near Paseo Obregón; cabañas US$65-90, d US$85-110; P 🍽 🛋) Set among lush tropical gardens, this highly regarded establishment boasts cabaña-style rooms with fireplaces, tiled floors, thatched roofs, TVs, air-con and minibars. The double rooms and suites are in the nearby **Hotel Los Arcos** (Paseo Obregón 498), which has two swimming pools, a sauna, a restaurant and a coffee shop. All rooms have air-con, telephones, color TVs and showers.

La Concha Beach Resort (☎ 121-6161, in the USA ☎ 800-999-2252; www.laconcha.com; r/ste US$107/140; P 🍽 🛋) At Km 5 on the road to Pichilingue stands this 107-room beachfront hotel. It's adorned with palm trees, a swimming pool with poolside bar, a fine Mexican restaurant and a water-sports center (though the water is very shallow). Rooms are all air-conditioned and have balconies overlooking the bay.

Eating
RESTAURANTS

La Mar y Peña (☎ 122-9949; 16 de Septiembre at Albañez; US$7-15) Choose from nearly 60 seafood dishes while mariachi bands kick out the tunes at this casual local favorite. It's part of a seafood co-op so the fish is always fresh.

La Fonda (☎ 125-4700; Bravo at Revolución; mains US$4-8) The outdoor patio is great, but the real reason to come is the cheap and excellent *comidas corridas* (set meals) served from 1 to 7pm. Choices include *chochinita pibil* (pork in a rich sauce) and *machaca de marlin* (cured, shredded marlin), and are served with soup, drink and dessert.

Bismark II (☎ 122-4854; cnr Degollado & Altamirano; mains US$7-12) Long ago, a woman opened a taco stand that later grew into this favorite seafood restaurant with good prices and great fish. There's also a branch called **Bismark-cito** (Paseo Obregón at Constitución) with the same fare.

El Quinto Sol (☎ 122-1692; cnr Av Independencia & Domínguez; mains US$4-8) Besides its bean specialties, this vegetarian landmark and health-food market offers large breakfast servings of yogurt (plain or with fruit, granola or muesli), *licuados* (fruit shakes), fresh-baked breads and pastries.

Le Bistrot Francais (☎ 125-6080; 10 Calle Esquerro; mains US$7-16) This is another good restaurant offering vegetarian options, and the courtyard tables provide a pleasant atmosphere.

Café El Callejón (Callejón La Paz; mains US$5-8) One of downtown's best values, touristy El Callejón has outdoor tables and cheap, tasty *antojitos* (Mexican snacks or light meals) accompanied by cheesy live keyboard music.

La Pazta (☎ 125-1195; Allende 36-B; mains US$5-10) Just south of the malecón in the Hotel Mediterrané, La Pazta serves good Italian specials at reasonable prices.

Carlos 'n' Charlie's (☎ 122-9290; Paseo Obregón near 16 de Septiembre) Serving a predominantly Mexican crowd, this branch of the national chain is more noted for drinking than for dining, but the food is definitely reliable.

Tex Burger (☎ 125-5184; Paseo Obregón at Morelos; burgers US$4-5, mains US$4-10) These are some of the best burgers in town, and you'll have 22 concoctions to choose from. Chicken, seafood and pasta are also on the menu.

Chuco's (Malecón at 16 de Septiembre; mains US$6-12) Chuco's is the best place to eat dinner and watch the sun go down. The margaritas are especially good.

La Caleta (☎ 123-0287; Malecón at Pineda; mains US$6-11) Also on the waterfront, La Caleta is very popular for its reasonably priced meals and drinks, which you can slurp down to live jazz and mellow sunset tunes.

Tequila Bar & Grill (☎ 122-5217; cnr Mutualismo & Ocampo; mains US$6-10) This is a favorite for antojitos (and a popular meeting place for local politicos). The margaritas are excellent.

La Costa (☎ 122-8808; Topete at Navarro) Simply put, La Costa serves the best lobster in La Paz.

El Cortijo (☎ 122-2532; Revolución 1460; mains US$4-8) The good food and cheap prices explain why this popular Mexican place has been around since 1960.

La Terraza (cnr Paseo Obregón & La Paz) Part of Hotel Perla, La Terraza has good food and an attractive, open terrace.

TAQUERÍAS
La Paz has some of the best tacos on the peninsula, from stand-while-you-eat taco stands to quasi-restaurants that pack 'em in every night. Eat at any of the following and you'll forever measure tacos by your memory of them.

Super Taquería Hermanos Gonzalez (no ☎ ; Mutualismo near Arreola; tacos US$1-1.50; ☽ 8am-5pm) Sidewalk snacking has never been better, and folks stand around in the shade of a big tree while they fill up on these legendary deep-fried fish and shrimp tacos. Choose fried or soft tortillas and load 'em up with plenty of delicious salsas.

Rancho Viejo (☎ 128-4647; cnr Domínguez & Márquez de León; tacos US$0.80-2; ☽ 24hrs) When it comes to meat, there's no competition; the melt-in-your-mouth *tacos de arrachera* (skirt steak) are to die for. Also try the delicious *tacos al pastor* (rotisserie pork) and the *gringas* (flour tortillas with meat, salsa and melted cheese). Veggie-heads can go for the *papas asadas* (grilled potatoes stuffed with mushrooms, corn, onions and cheese); just tell them to hold the meat.

Taquería El Muelle (Muelle at Paseo Obregón; tacos US$1; ☽ 7pm to late) The *carne asada* (grilled beef) tacos themselves are good, but the real reason to stop by this stand is to try the salsas. There are a dozen big bowls to choose from, including spicy *cacahuete* (peanut) and two so hot the cook calls them 'salsa Jennifer Lopez' and 'salsa Janet Jackson.' Yeow!

El Michoacano (cnr Bravo & Prieto; carnitas US$3-5/person; ☽ 8am-2pm) It's technically not a taquería, but you do wrap the *carnitas* (slow-roasted pork) in corn tortillas, so it's close enough. Buy the pork by the kilo, sit at the outdoor tables and chow down. Wednesdays are two-for-one, and it's cheaper if you buy your own tortillas at the *tortilleria* next door and take it all to the beach.

CAFÉS & ICE CREAM
Espresso Café (Paseo Obregón 10) Frequented more by Mexicans than gringos, this is a popular coffee bar that also serves drinks and light meals.

La Fuente (Paseo Obregón at Muelle) La Fuente Scoops up La Paz's best ice cream; home-made flavors include *elote* (corn), guava and tequila-with-almond. Spot it by the big polka-dot tree out front.

Family-run **Café del Trópico** (16 de Septiembre near Paseo Obregón) serves excellent fresh-roasted coffee at its sidewalk countertop. Both **Deli's** (cnr Callejón La Paz & Mutualismo) and **Café Exquisito** (Paseo Obregón near Muelle) serve good coffee and espresso drinks; Deli's has pastries too.

Entertainment
CLUBS & LIVE MUSIC
Most of La Paz's nightlife is concentrated on and around Paseo Obregón, but it never gets as raucous as Cabo San Lucas. Most fun of all is getting home: La Paz's uneven sidewalks and mismatched steps are virtual minefields for tipsy walkers.

Las Varitas (☎ 125-2025; Av Independencia 111; cover US$3) The local rock-n-roll scene is fun to check out here; angst-ridden bands rip out loud tunes to a small but often packed house.

La Paz-lapa (Paseo Obregón at 16 de Septiembre; ☾ 10pm-4am Tue, Fri & Sat; cover US$4) This is downtown's dance club, and Tuesday night is ladies' night (no cover for the gals) It's above Carlos 'n' Charlie's.

La Cabaña, in Hotel Perla (p169), is an open-air nightclub with a mellow, local vibe and musical leanings toward salsa, merengue and tropical.

THEATER
The **Teatro de la Ciudad** (City Theater; ☎ 125-0004) offers performances by musical and theatrical groups such as Guadalajara's Ballet Folklórico, as well as occasional film series. The giant theater is within the Unidad Cultural Profesor Jesús Castro Agúndez (p166).

Shopping
Peter Gerhard, in his classic *Lower California Guidebook* of the 1960s, tells of a tourist who bought a black pearl in La Paz only to learn that it was an exquisitely burnished ball bearing! Few visitors are so gullible, but local stores have plenty of junk alongside the good stuff. Most are along the waterfront Paseo Obregón.

Casa del Artesano Sudcaliforniano (☎ 125-8802; cnr Paseo Obregón & Bravo) Next to the tourist office, this large store sells jewelry, handi-crafts, paintings, sculptures and clothes made in La Paz and Baja California Sur.

Artesanías La Antigua California (Paseo Obregón near Arreola) Features a wide selection of quality crafts from throughout the country.

Bazar del Sol (☎ 122-3626; Paseo Obregón 1165) Loaded with kitsch.

La Casa de María (☎ 122-5606; cnr Abasolo & Jalisco) Good choice for handicrafts and es-pecially furniture.

Artesanía Cuauhtémoc (☎ 122-4575; Abasolo 3315) Weavers' cooperative.

Paisajes de Sudcalifornia (☎ 123-3700; Bravo 1890) Specializes in southern Baja art and crafts.

On weekends during the Christmas season, countless baubles change hands at the Mercado Navideño, which turns downtown Madero and Av Independencia into pedestrian malls.

Getting There & Away
AIR
Aeropuerto Internacional General Manuel Márquez de León (☎ 122-1466/67), more commonly known as La Paz International Airport, is just 6½ miles (10km) southwest of downtown, at the end of a short lateral off the Transpeninsular.

Aeroméxico (☎ 122-0091; Paseo Obregón btwn Hidalgo & Morelos) flies daily between La Paz and Los Angeles, Tucson, Tijuana, Culiacán, Durango, Guadalajara, Guaymas, Mazatlán and Mexico City. Its subsidiary, **Aerolitoral**, at the same address, flies daily to/from Loreto continuing to/from Los Angeles.

Aero California (☎ 125-1023, in the USA ☎ 800-237-6225; Paseo Obregón 550) has offices at the airport and downtown. It operates two daily flights between La Paz and Los Angeles, daily flights to Tucson via Hermosillo and one daily nonstop to Tijuana. It also offers many flights to mainland Mexican destinations. Most flights have onward national and international connections.

BOAT
Ferry
The major terminal for ferries to the mainland towns of Topolobampo and Mazatlán is in **Pichilingue**, about 14 miles (22km) north of central La Paz. For all sailings, you must arrive at the terminal two hours before departure.

Sematur (☎ 125-4440; www.sematur.com.mx; cnr Prieto & 5 de Mayo) runs the Mazatlán ferry and has an office in La Paz; tickets can be purchased here. **Baja Ferries** (☎ 123-1313, 125-2346, in Mexico ☎ 800-122-1414; www.bajaferries.com.mx; cnr Isabel La Católica & Navarro) runs the Topolobambo line and also has a ticket office in La Paz.

Before they will ship your vehicle to mainland Mexico, ferry officials require you to show a tourist permit; for details, see p234.

Weather permitting (high winds often delay winter sailings), the Topolobampo ferry leaves at 4pm Monday through Friday and 11pm Saturday. The journey takes five hours. The return ferry from Topolobampo departs at 10pm daily.

The 18-hour ferry to Mazatlán departs at 3pm daily, arriving at 9am the following morning. The return ferry leaves Mazatlán at 3pm, arriving at 8am in La Paz.

Approximate one-way fares from La Paz are as follows:

Class	To Topolobampo	To Mazatlán
Salón	N/A	US$63
Turista	US$53	US$82-161
Cabina	US$129-299*	US$101-198
Especial	N/A	US$107-203

* rate for 1-4 people

Vehicle rates are as follows:

Vehicle length	Topolobampo	Mazatlán
Up to 5.4m*	US$87	US$182
Auto with trailer	US$333	US$350
Motor home	US$390	US$410
Motorcycle	US$50	US$100

* 1m = 3 feet 3 inches

Private Yacht

Between November and March, La Paz is a good place to catch a lift on a private yacht to mainland Mexico. The most frequent trip is La Paz to Puerto Vallarta with stops at Bahía de los Muertos, Los Frailes (great coral snorkeling), then Isla Isabél and Puerto Vallarta. Allow about one week, with two to three nights at sea.

At the **Marina de La Paz**, the Dock Restaurant, the Penthouse Racing Club and the Club Cruceros (www.clubcruceros.org) are the best places to hang out. Club Cruceros also has a bulletin board where you can get information about people looking for help crewing their yachts.

BUS

Autotransportes de Baja California (ABC; ☎ 122-3063), **Autotransportes Aguila** (☎ 122-4270) and **Autotransportes de La Paz** (☎ 122-2157) operate long-distance buses. ABC and Aguila use the **Main Bus Terminal** (Central Camionera; cnr Jalisco & Héroes de la Independencia), whereas Autotransportes de La Paz uses the **Autotransportes de La Paz terminal** (cnr Degollado & Prieto).

There are three to five departures daily to the following northbound ABC/Aguila destinations:

Destination	Fare	Duration
Ciudad Constitución	US$11.50	2½ hrs
Ensenada	US$88	23 hrs
Guerrero Negro	US$50	10-12 hrs
Loreto	US$21	5 hrs
Mexicali	US$102	24 hrs
Mulegé	US$26	7 hrs
Puerto López Mateos	US$14	4 hrs
Puerto San Carlos	US$13	4 hrs
San Ignacio	US$35	9 hrs
San Quintín	US$57	17 hrs
Santa Rosalía	US$30	8 hrs
Tijuana	US$92	22-24 hrs

Southbound ABC/Aguila buses depart several times daily for El Triunfo (US$3, 1 hour), San Antonio (US$4, 70 minutes), Buena Vista (US$6, 1½ hours), Miraflores (US$9, 2½ hours) and San José del Cabo via the Transpeninsular (US$14, 3 hours).

Aguila buses take the Southern Cape Highway (México 19) from La Paz to Cabo San Lucas (US$13, 2½ hours) and to Todos Santos (US$8, 1½ hours) at least five times daily between 7am and 7pm.

Autotransportes de La Paz operates buses to Todos Santos (US$7) and Cabo San Lucas (US$14) eight times daily between 6:45am and 7:45pm.

Getting Around
BUS

The government-regulated **Transporte Terrestre** (☎ 125-3274, 125-6229) minivan service charges US$14 per person to/from the airport, while private taxis cost US$15 to US$18, depending on your bargaining.

Autotransportes Aguila buses leave the **Terminal Malecón** (☎ 122-7898; cnr Paseo Obregón &

Av Independencia) for Península Pichilingue and the ferry terminal (US$2, 1 hour) hourly between 7am and 6pm.

Most local buses leave from the front of the **Mercado Francisco Madero** (cnr Degollado & Revolución).

CAR

Car rental rates start around US$45 per day, including 300km of travel; taxes and insurance are extra. International rental agencies include the following:

Avis (☎ 122-2651, airport 124-6312; Paseo Obregón 820)

Budget (☎ 123-3622, airport 124-6433; Paseo Obregón btwn Muelle & Tejada)

Dollar (☎ 122-6060; Paseo Obregón at Pineda)

Hertz (☎ 122-5300, airport 124-6330; Paseo Obregón btwn Juárez & Allende)

Thrifty (☎ 125-9696, airport 124-6365; cnr Tejada & Paseo Obregón)

AROUND LA PAZ
Beaches

There are several small but pleasant beaches north and west of La Paz. To the west are the bayside **Playa El Comitán** and **Playa Las Hamacas**, but no public transportation serves them. El Comitán has deteriorated in recent years and swimming is no longer advisable there.

On Península Pichilingue, to the north, the beaches nearest to La Paz are **Playa Palmira**, **Playa Coromuel** and **Playa Caimancito**. Playa Palmira has the Araiza Inn Palmira, a marina and a few condominium complexes with restaurant and bar, while Coromuel and Caimancito have restaurants and bars, toilets and shady palapas. Playa Coromuel also has a big Plexiglas

waterslide, and its seafood restaurant is good. **Playa Tesoro**, the next beach north, also has a restaurant and shade.

Camping is possible at **Playa Pichilingue**, 110 yards (100m) north of the ferry terminal; it has a restaurant and bar, toilets and shade. The road north of Pichilingue is paved to the exceptional beaches of **Playa Balandra** (whose sheltered location is not good for camping because of mosquitoes in its mangroves) and **Playa Tecolote** (where, across the Canal de San Lorenzo, Isla Espíritu Santo looks like a chunk of southern Utah's canyon country floating on the sea). **Playa Coyote**, on the Gulf side of the peninsula, is more isolated.

Surprisingly uncrowded even in ideal winter weather, Playa Tecolote's wide, sandy beach lacks potable water and other amenities. However, it does have the nearby steak-and-seafood **Restaurant El Tecolote**, where the fish is excellent but the drinks are watery.

Most hotels can arrange shuttles to the beaches for about US$8. Aguila buses also leave from the Malecón terminal to Tecolote (US$2.50 one way) at noon and 2pm, with return buses leaving the beach at 5:30pm.

Beware: Local expats warn that stealthy thieves break into campers' cars at Tecolote and other isolated beaches.

La Ventana & Ensenada de los Muertos

Southeast of La Paz (about a 45-minute drive), just before the village of **San Juan de los Planes**, a paved spur off highway BCS-286 turns north toward La Ventana, on its namesake bay opposite Isla Cerralvo. This is one of the best sites for windsurfing and kite surfing in Baja.

DETOUR: EL CENTENARIO TO SAN EVARISTO

West of La Paz, just beyond the village of El Centenario, a paved but potholed bumpy spur off the Transpeninsular leads north along the western shore of Bahía de La Paz to the small phosphate-mining port of **San Juan de la Costa**. It's a beautiful drive out, right along the cliffs of the bay. San Juan has one passable restaurant. North of here, the graded road continues along the eastern escarpment the Sierra de la Giganta, whose multicolored mountains – especially impressive in the morning sun – resemble a cutaway of Arizona's Grand Canyon. The road ends at **San Evaristo**, a small fish camp opposite Isla San José, on a sparkling inlet of the Gulf of California.

In April and May San Evaristo swarms with boaters and campers who enjoy bountiful fishing for snapper and cochinito. Most of the beaches along the San Juan-San Evaristo route are rocky or gravelly, but determined campers will find a few pleasant, sandy and isolated spots.

La Ventana Campground (US$5) is a large campground with basic services. The campground gets very crowded during the prime windsurfing months (November to February). There are also a couple of unnamed **RV parks** (site US$5-7) in town. The pleasant **Baja Joe's** (in La Paz ☎ 126-2322; www.bajajoe.com; r US$35-60 Mar 16-Nov 14, US$65-95 Nov 15-Mar 15) offers some stunning rooms on the water. Bikes and kayaks are available to guests, and windsurfing rentals are US$25/40 per hour/day (lessons are also available). There are a few **restaurants** in town and a market as well.

About 32 miles (51km) southeast of La Paz, BCS-286 turns northeast just beyond San Juan de los Planes, where the paved road surface ends, and continues to Ensenada de los Muertos, on its own namesake bay, with plenty of places to **camp**. The bay is a popular **fishing** area; it's one of the main destinations for fishing packages organized in La Paz.

From a junction just southeast of San Juan de los Planes, an unpaved lateral climbs the **Cuesta de los Muertos** (Slope of the Dead) and continues south to Los Barriles. Though unsuitable for RVs of any sort, this route is an interesting alternative for visitors with high-clearance vehicles. For more details, see North of Los Barriles (p178).

CENTRAL CAPE

The Central Cape begins about 15 miles (24km) south of La Paz, roughly where México 19 (the Southern Cape Highway) splits off from the Transpeninsular. The Transpeninsular continues through several picturesque villages, which had their heyday during the 19th-century mining era and retain an old-time small town feel. Most of them are agricultural centers that export much of their crop (including cherry tomatoes, basil and peppers) to the USA. Between the two highways is the scenic Sierra de la Laguna, an ecological wonderland.

EL TRIUNFO & SAN ANTONIO
☎ 612
El Triunfo (population 350), on the Transpeninsular, is the first town beyond the junction of the two highways, followed by San Antonio (population 600), about 5

miles (8km) to the east. Both towns were part of a large cattle ranch under the Jesuits in the early 18th century, but the population quickly swelled after gold and silver strikes in 1748. At its peak, San Antonio counted a population of more than 10,000 and was the largest settlement in the Cape Region, mostly home to *mestizo* (mixed indigenous and European) miners and Yaqui laborers from the state of Sonora.

When Loreto was obliterated by a hurricane in 1829, San Antonio briefly became the capital of the Californias; a year later, the capital was moved to La Paz. The boom revived after the discovery of even higher quality ore at El Triunfo in 1862, but the mines ran dry in the late 19th century; by 1925 both settlements were virtual ghost towns.

These days, small-scale mining has resumed in El Triunfo, and San Antonio is a modest farming community in a picturesque canyon. Both warrant a brief stop. Places worth a look in El Triunfo include the **old smelter**, the **Casa Municipal** and the small, pretty **church**. Local **artisans** sell colorful handwoven baskets, and there's a small **restaurant** for refreshments. Cobbled streets and restored buildings give San Antonio a more prosperous appearance.

Opposite San Antonio's Pemex station, a graded 14-mile (22km) road follows Arroyo San Antonio to a junction with BCS-286, the paved highway between San Juan de los Planes and La Paz. This is a particularly good mountain-bike route, winding gradually downhill through the arroyo.

Just about 8 miles (14km) east of San Antonio, at Km 141, is the **Rancho Verde RV Park** (☎ 126-9103, in the USA ☎ 888-516-9462; ranchoverde@mexonline.com; tent/RV US$7/11), nicely located on a 3000-acre ranch in a lush valley. RV rates include full-hookups (except electric). An informative natural trail explains the dense vegetation.

SANTIAGO
☎ 624 / pop 2500
Tranquil Santiago, a charming village about 6 miles (10km) south of Las Cuevas and 1 mile (1.6km) west of the Transpeninsular, was the site of one of the bloodiest episodes in Baja's history. Pericú Indians revolted and murdered the Jesuit Lorenzo Carranco and several other Spaniards here

before being subdued by Spanish soldiers and European epidemics. No trace remains of the mission, which closed in 1795, but a lovely little church has been built near the original site.

Although landlocked, Santiago has grown considerably since tourism came to the area. Many locals are employed in construction, fishing and general services. Santiago is also an important supplier of palm fronds used in thatched-roof construction.

Prosperity and pride led the residents to establish Baja's only zoo in 1983. The tidy **Zoológico Santiago** (admission by donation; 🕑 8am-6pm) contains a variety of animals, including a Bengal tiger, a black bear, emus and ostriches, deer, monkeys, native reptiles, peccaries and a collection of colorful macaws. Many families enjoy Sunday barbecues here.

Friendly **Hotel Palomar** (☎ 142-0604; s/d US$30/60), downhill from the plaza, has modest rooms with hot showers; you can set up tents on the fruit-tree-covered grounds for US$5. The **restaurant** (mains US$5-11), which gets customers from as far away as San José del Cabo, is noted for its fine seafood. The English-speaking owner, Sergio Gómez, is a good source of information on the Sierra de la Laguna.

There's also a small **taquería** on the plaza, next to the Pemex station.

AROUND SANTIAGO

Just past the zoo, a dirt road reaches the village of **Agua Caliente** after about 5 miles (8km). Another 2½ miles (4km) farther west by another dirt road is **El Chorro**, where natural hot-spring water is being piped into a concrete reservoir. The amount of water, its cleanliness and temperature vary widely every year, depending on rainfall and other conditions. There are other **hot springs** in San Jorge and Santa Rita, both at the end of a dirt road north of Agua Caliente. Ask in Santiago about road conditions and for detailed directions. Also contact **Pepe's Outdoor Activity Center** (p181) in Cabo Pulmo; owner Pepe takes folks out to some remote hot springs in a spectacular canyon.

Sol de Mayo

If hot springs don't do it for you, how about a cool **swimming hole** fed by a 30-foot waterfall? Getting there requires a bit of

scouting, but it's worth the effort. From Santiago, turn right onto a dirt road just before reaching the plaza. At the store, take the road to San Dionisio (signed), then keep left at the junction (you should see the palm-studded valley below). After three-quarters of a mile (1.2km), turn right just before the air field, then continue for 1½ miles (2.5km) until the road forks. Take the right fork (a sandy, narrow dirt road). It dead-ends after about 3¾ miles (6km), with the trail starting right past the gate. You'll see the waterfall after a minute or two, but getting down to it requires a challenging scramble that should be attempted only by the physically fit. The last 20 feet are real ankle-busters, so use absolute caution. You'll certainly have earned your dip in the pool.

Tropic of Cancer

Precisely at latitude 23.5°N, just south of Santiago, a concrete sphere on the Transpeninsular marks the Tropic of Cancer, which also passes through Hawaii, Taiwan, central India, Saudi Arabia and the Sahara Desert. Locals have built an elaborate shrine to the Virgin of Guadalupe – and a bar – right next to it.

SIERRA DE LA LAGUNA

South of where the Transpeninsular and México 19 intersect, the precipitous heart of the Cape Region begins. This is one of the most rugged and inaccessible areas of the entire peninsula, with top elevations around 7000 feet (2100m). It is traversed – east to west – by a succession of steep canyons, the larger of which double as backpacking routes. The Sierra receives more water than any other area in southern Baja, which accounts for its extraordinary lushness.

The area's complete wilderness and isolation make for adventurous **backpacking**. The terrain is difficult and unpredictable, and should be attempted only by experienced hikers. Trails are not marked and are often hard to find. Water sources are not dependable, and weather conditions can change suddenly. Be prepared for anything.

Several foothill villages provide access to these unique mountains of the interior, which are also accessible from Todos Santos on their Pacific slope. Hikers should plan on spending several days crossing the Sierra; the best time is from November to February after the fall rains have filled the canyons with fresh water. However, days are short at this time of year, and the mercury can drop below freezing at night in January and February.

Those not wanting to go it alone should consider hiring a local **guide**. Ask around in Santiago or check with Señor Gómez of the Hotel Palomar (p175). **Pepe Murietta**, at Pepe's Outdoor Activity center (p181) in Cabo Pulmo, and **Cuco Moyron**, at Rancho Pilar (p186), south of Todos Santos, both offer full guide services for one-day to multiday trips into the Sierra de la Laguna; prices vary depending on number of people, duration, etc.

The best guidebook for hiking in the Sierra de la Laguna is Walt Peterson's *The Baja Adventure Book*.

Cañón San Dionisio

The northernmost of the east-west routes through the Sierra de la Laguna is the most popular, perhaps because of its unique ecology – cacti, palms, oaks, aspens and pines grow virtually side by side. A route highlight is La Laguna, a flat meadow at 5600 feet (1700m) that was once a lake.

Most people start the crossing from the Todos Santos side, where a steep trail climbs into the mountains from near San Juan del Aserradero (La Burrera), about 15 miles (24km) northeast of Todos Santos. From the trailhead, it's about 7 miles (11km) to La Laguna. From here it's another 8 miles (13km) to the eastern trailhead at the town of San Dionisio. The entire crossing can be negotiated in about five to six days. Going the other way, San Dionisio can be reached from Santiago (12 miles, 19km) via a dirt road passable for any passenger vehicle driven with caution. You can also try to hitch a ride or hire a taxi (about US$30).

Cañón San Bernardo

The central route across the Sierra is considered a bit easier and is also popular with day hikers. The trailhead is near the village of Boca de la Sierra, at the end of a dirt road about 4 miles (6km) west of Miraflores. Miraflores itself, accessible by paved road from the Transpeninsular at Km 71, is a dusty town of little interest.

After about 14 miles (22.5km) the trail comes out at Santo Domingo, from where it's connected to México 19 by a series of signed dirt roads. The entire trip across takes about five days.

Cañón San Pablo

The southernmost route traverses the Sierra via Cañón San Pablo and picks up at the town of El Salto, about 5 miles (8km) west of Caduaño, terminating at El Güerivo after about 10½ miles (17km). From here dirt roads lead northwest to San Andrés and El Pescadero back to México 19. The turn-off to Caduaño is at about Km 68 on the Transpeninsular. You sould budget about five days to cross the Sierra on this route.

EASTERN CAPE

Still among the less developed coastal areas in the Cape Region, the East Cape is where you're most likely to catch a glimpse of the Old Baja magic. It was wealthy American fishermen and adventurers who first 'discovered' the area – which stretches from Bahía Las Palmas, about 75 miles (120km) south of La Paz, all the way to San José del Cabo – in the 1940s and '50s. Hollywood celebrities such as John Wayne, Bing Crosby and Errol Flynn flew here in their private aircraft, making perilous landings on improvised airstrips. Deep-sea fishing and white-winged-dove hunting were favorite pastimes of this testosterone-driven crowd. The original fly-in resort, the Rancho Buena Vista Hotel, where many of them stayed, is still in operation today.

Fishing in these rich waters continues to be the East Cape's main draw. But other outdoor enthusiasts will find plenty to do as well. Remote beaches and clear waters are great for swimming and lounging. There's world-class windsurfing at Los Barriles. Diving off Cabo Pulmo, the only coral reef on the west coast of North America, may yield encounters with huge manta rays and schools of tropical fish.

For the most part, the infrastructure of the East Cape is still relatively basic; most roads are unpaved and there are many places without phone connections. In recent years, however, small-scale development has begun to encroach upon the area's pristine beauty, especially south of Los Barriles. Real estate prices have surged as North Americans have snapped up beachfront lots for their vacation homes, and 'towns' like Buena Vista and Los Barriles, until a few years ago little more than dusty outposts, are growing at a steady clip.

Getting There & Around

The Transpensinsular brushes the coast at Los Barriles from where a rough dirt road leads north to Punta Pescadero and El Cardonal. At Las Cuevas, near Km 93, a paved road leads to the coastal village of La Ribera. After about 6 miles (10km) on this road, another paved road veers off to the right. This is the Eastern Cape Road to Cabo Pulmo, Los Frailes and beyond, culminating at San José del Cabo after about 60 miles (100km).

Just before reaching Cabo Pulmo, after about 17 miles (27km), pavement abruptly gives way to a tooth-clattering dirt road. Most 2WD vehicles can usually get through, but it may become impassable after any sort of rain. Always check conditions locally before heading out. Under favorable conditions, smaller RVs should be able to make it through to San José as well.

About 12 miles (19km) south of Los Frailes, at Vinorama, another dirt road called Palo Escopeta Rd heads west and joins back with the Transpeninsular just south of Los Cabos International Airport. This road is usually in a fair state.

Aguila buses from La Paz to Los Cabos travel along the highway, stopping for pickups and dropoffs along the way (there are no bus terminals). Check the La Paz and San José del Cabo sections for details.

LOS BARRILES

☎ 624 / pop 600

November through March is high-wind season, and Baja's windsurfing capital booms when the wind is up. The town is also sailing toward becoming another big-time Cape development. Houses and time-shares are going up like sails on a windy day, and resident gringos buzz around town on ATVs. If you windsurf, kite surf or fish, you'll surely love it here If you don't, you might want to save your pesos and blow off toward Cabo Pulmo.

Orientation & Information

All tourist services are along the main drag, 20 de Noviembre, into which you'll dead-end from the road leading off the Transpeninsular; turn left on 20 de Noviembre for the center of town. Everything is easy to find.

There is no tourist office. Internet access is available at **The Office** (20 de Noviembre s/n; US$4.50/hr; ⌣ daily) on the left as you're heading down 20 de Noviembre. Beside it is an **HSBC** ATM. **Baja Money Exchange** (⌣ closed Sun), in Plaza del Pueblo (on the left on the way into town), changes cash and traveler's checks. A modern self-service **laundry** (⌣ closed Sun) is across from Mañanas restaurant.

There's also a **post office** (just inland from 20 de Noviembre) and a **Cruz Roja** (Red Cross; near 20 de Noviembre).

Windsurfing

Brisk 'El Norte' winds averaging 20 to 25 knots descend the 6000-foot (1800m) *cordillera* (mountain range) toward the mid-morning launch site at **Playa Norte**, about 2 miles (3km) north of Los Barriles. The wind picks up around 11am at more southerly locations. The wind direction and curving shoreline, running south and then east into the Gulf, make it possible to sail 20 miles (32km) out to sea without losing sight of the shore.

San Francisco Bay Area–based **Vela Windsurf Resorts** (in the USA ☎ 831-461-0820, 800-223-5443; www.velawindsurf.com) operates its **Baja Highwind Center** out of Los Barriles' Hotel Playa del Sol from mid-November to the first week in March. These world-class instructors teach seminars using state-of-the-art equipment.

Packages include accommodations at either the Playa del Sol or Hotel Palmas de Cortez, all meals, unlimited use of equipment, daily seminars, and activities like mountain biking, snorkeling and kayaking. Weeklong trips start around US$930 per person, double occupancy. Reservations are essential: space is limited to 32 sailors, and the resort is usually completely booked from December 1 to January 31. Note that seminars are best suited for intermediate to advanced sailors. Drop-in lessons cost US$65, and three-day kite surfing lessons start at US$350.

Mountain Biking

The people of Vela Windsurf Resorts have built a 30-mile trail network around Los Barriles. Trails are generally paved in thorns, making 'slime tubes' (self-sealing puncture tubes) essential. You'll also need fairly wide tires to ride safely on sandy trails. A good long-distance trip is the triangular circuit up the Transpeninsular to San Antonio, continuing north through the arroyo to San Juan de los Planes and back down the coast to Los Barriles (72 miles, 115km). You can also head north from Los Barriles to Bahía de los Muertos, a spectacular ride.

Sleeping

Martín Verdugo's Beach Resort (☎ 141-0054; 20 de Noviembre; tent/RV US$11/15, r US$50-56) This convivial resort accommodates 61 RVs with full hookups and an additional 15 tents. Facilities include hot showers, laundry rooms and spotless bathrooms. It also offers large and nicely decorated beachfront motel rooms. Fishing boats rent for US$130 for a 22-foot *panga* (skiff) to US$190 for a 23-foot superpanga and US$300 for a 28-foot super-cruiser.

Hotel Playa del Sol (☎ 141-0212; www.bajaresorts.com; 20 de Noviembre; s/d US$70/100) Playa del Sol has 26 clean, recently remodeled rooms, and rates include full board.

Hotel Palmas de Cortez (☎ 141-0050, in the USA ☎ 800-368-4334; www.bajaresorts.com; s/d US$90/140, ste s/d US$120/180, condo US$350; P ✖ ♈) A traditional favorite among fisherfolk, the luxurious Palmas de Cortez is a beautiful hotel with 31 rooms, 15 suites and 10 condominiums, all of them with ocean views. Nice touches include an aviary with parrots and cabaña suites with private hammocks. The swimming pool, which blends seamlessly with the ocean, is one of the best on the Cape. Rates include all meals, unless you rent a condominium (all of which have kitchens). You'll dead-end into the hotel as you come down the road into town from the highway.

Eating

Taquería Los Barriles ('Blue Tarp Taquería'; tacos US$1.10; ☯ 8am-3pm Wed-Mon) Locals swear by this makeshift taquería, whose owner, Sylvia, puts up an especially mouthwatering display of condiments to complement your fish, shrimp or meat tacos. Its on the road into town.

La Parillada (20 de Noviembre; ☯ 5-10pm Fri-Sun) On weekends, big appetites flock to La Parillada, a little shack serving succulent charbroiled chicken for US$4/7 per half/whole, along with french fries, salsa and tortillas.

Tío Pablo (☎ 141-0330) Another place known for its gut-busting portions is the ever-popular Tío Pablo, just inland from 20 de Noviembre (the main drag). Most people come for the pizza and burgers, but it's famous for the 28oz (840g) 'beltbuster steak.' There's also an all-you-can-eat salad bar.

Otra Vez (☎ 141-0249; 20 de Noviembre; mains US$5-10) This indoor eatery has an ambitious menu featuring Thai, Mexican and American dishes, as well as low-fat and vegetarian choices.

NORTH OF LOS BARRILES

☎ 612

North of Los Barriles, a mostly graded but rough and potentially dangerous road, not suitable for large RVs, hugs the coast to Punta Pescadero and El Cardonal, and even crosses the very difficult Cuesta de los Muertos en route to San Juan de los Planes and La Paz. Conditions get worse the farther north you go, with narrow, steep and curvy sections quite common. While most beaches north of Los Barriles are rocky or gravelly, some are suitable for free **camping**. Check locally about road conditions before heading out.

After about 8 miles (13km), you'll reach remote **Hotel Punta Pescadero** (☎ 141-0101, in the USA ☎ 800-426-2252; www.punta-pescadero.com; r US$196). A consummate getaway, the resort hugs a narrow but long ribbon of sandy beach. Each of the 21 rooms has an ocean-view terrace, lounge area, fridge, satellite TV and coffeemaker. Rates include all meals for two people. Sportfishing trips per boat cost US$110 on a panga, US$140 to US$200 on a superpanga and US$220 to US$400 on a cruiser. Scuba rentals, surf-fishing equipment and horses are also available.

It takes determination to continue for 6 miles (10km) to reach the Canadian-run **El Cardonal Hide-A-Way** (☎ 141-0040, in the USA & Canada ☎ 514-467-4700; www.elcardonal.net; r night/week US$60/400), but you'll be rewarded with a spectacular, remote setting and the sense that you've really made it off the beaten path. Beachfront suites feature two double beds and full kitchenettes. Tents and small campers are charged US$10, while RVs pay US$13 for full hookups. Children stay free, and the restaurant is open all day. Activities include diving and snorkeling, horseback riding, kayaking and fishing, all fee-based. You can also play volleyball, badminton and horseshoes. **Rock-art excursions** to Rancho Boca del Alamo can be arranged.

BUENA VISTA
☎ 624 / pop 300

What windsurfing is to Los Barriles, sportfishing is to tiny Buena Vista. This small village, about 1 mile (1.6km) south of Los Barriles, grew up around the East Cape's first fly-in fishing resort, the Rancho Buena Vista Hotel, once frequented by Hollywood hotshots. There are a few other hotels now but little infrastructure otherwise.

Hikers will be rewarded with fine bay views from the top of Flat Top Mountain, reached via an easy 30- to 45-minute trail. Ask for directions at Rancho Leonero (p180); they're the people who built the trail. Less ambitious folk can walk, drive or bike up to the Flag Monument for equally impressive views. Look for the turnoff around Km 105.5 off the Transpeninsular.

Mountain bikers can take the Pemex Ridge Trail from behind the Pemex station at Km 109, which runs through a cactus forest and offers great bay views.

Fishing
The following list indicates the prime seasons for the various fish species on the East Cape. Many of the hotels and resorts listed under Sleeping have their own fishing fleet, open to guests and nonguests.

Blue marlin	June to November
Cabrilla	March to May
Dorado	March to November
Roosterfish	April to June
Sailfish	June to November
Sierra	December to March
Striped marlin	March to June
Yellowfin	May to November
Yellowtail	February to May
Wahoo	June to November

Diving & Snorkeling
North American–owned **Vista Sea Sport**

(☎ 141-0031; www.vistaseasport.com) offers dive tours to Cabo Pulmo (US$110), Los Frailes (US$110), Punta Pescadero (US$100), Isla Cerralvo (US$120) and the Gorda Banks (US$140), as well as snorkeling tours (US$25 to US$50) in the Los Barriles area. It also offers PADI Discover courses (US$60-120) and certification courses (US$395/person, two-person minimum, or US$500 for private lesson).

Sleeping & Eating
La Capilla Trailer Park (no ☎ ; site US$10) This rustic park lies about a half-mile (800m) south of Hotel Buena Vista Beach Resort (see below). The dirt road to Rancho Leonero (turnoff at Km 103.5; see below) also provides access. Sites hug the beach and have full hookups. Bathrooms are rather grimy, but hot showers are usually available. Vacancies are rare in winter, when the place fills with 'snowbirds' from the north.

Casas Ramada (☎ 141-0038; cabin US$25) These are the East Cape's most original digs, featuring a quartet of Afghani style huts overlooking the beach. Made from local materials, each round hut comes complete with refrigerator, small gas stove, fans, bathroom and private outdoor hot tub. The office is in the house with the painted portraits at the southern edge of town.

Hotel Calafia (☎ 141-0028; r US$31-36) Mexican-owned Calafia, at Km 107 on the Transpeninsular, has seven small, simple but clean rooms as well as a **restaurant**.

Rancho Buena Vista Hotel (☎ 141-0177, in the USA ☎ 800-258-8200; www.ranchobuenavista.com; s/d US$109/195; ⓧ) This historic hotel remains the sentimental favorite of anglers and their families, although the Hollywood glamour has decidedly worn off. Facilities include a swimming pool, a bar, a restaurant, tennis courts and a fleet of 15 fishing cruisers (US$286 to US$434). Rooms are ultra-comfortable, and rates include full board. Combination hotel and fishing packages are available (which will save you some cash). The entrance is opposite the Flag Monument at around Km 105.5.

Hotel Buena Vista Beach Resort (☎ 141-0033, in the USA ☎ 800-752-3555; www.hotelbuenavista.com; s/d US$110/170, ste s/d US$146/207; ⓧ) Located half a mile (800m) south of Rancho Buena Vista Hotel, this resort has a pretty garden setting, a hot mineral spa and swim-up pool bar. Its extensive menu of activities ranges from kayaking, horseback riding and bird-watching to tours to Indian rock paintings and mineral hot springs. The resort's sportfishing fleet includes a 23-foot super-panga (US$264), a 28-foot deluxe cruiser (US$385) and a 29-foot luxury cruiser (US$451). Room rates include all meals.

Rancho Leonero (☎ 145-3636, in the USA 800-646-2252; www.rancholeonero.com; ⌕) For a special treat, ensconce yourself at Rancho Leonero, an isolated resort on a spectacular beach-front location reached by taking a turnoff at Km 103.5. Manly fisherfolk mix with gregarious families, and stories of marlins that got away (or not) fly fast and furiously at the bar each night. Their famed dining room, overlooking the sea, often serves up the day's catch sushi-style, in delicious ceviche or grilled over a wood fire. Leonero's fishing fleet consists of well-maintained cruisers, superpangas and pangas costing US$300/220/160, respectively. Nonanglers can relax poolside or in the soft sand, glide over the ocean in a sea kayak, tone biceps in the outdoor gym, or go diving or horseback riding. There's even a rock reef right off the beach for great snorkeling. Remnants of an Indian midden and marine fossil beds are steps away along the beach.

Spotless, spacious rooms have thatched roofs, stone walls, tiled floors and some of the best showers on the East Cape. Standard rooms, including tax and service charge and full board costs US$134/171; deluxe rooms and bungalows are US$189/226. Even larger oceanview bungalows are US$232/268. Off-season rates are US$25 less.

There are a few **taco stands** around the Pemex station, but outside the resorts the only restaurants are **La Gaviota** and **Calafia** (see p179), both serving standard Mexican seafood and antojitos.

LA RIBERA & AROUND

From Rancho Leonero, the dirt road continues south to tiny La Ribera, also accessible via a paved lateral from Las Cuevas, about 8 miles (13km) south of Buena Vista on the Transpeninsular. La Ribera is the last point for supplies southbound on the Eastern Cape Road, so stock up here if you're headed to Cabo Pulmo or beyond.

There are no hotels, but the **Correcaminos Trailer Park** (☎ 145-9900; tent/RV US$8/12), close

to the beach, has 25 mostly shady sites in a mango orchard with hookups as well as tent spaces.

About 4 miles (6km) farther south is **Hotel Punta Colorada** (☎ 141-0050, in the USA ☎ 800-368-4334; www.bajaresorts.com; s/d US$96/132, ste s/d US$144/192), another anglers' favorite. Day rates for fishing trips range from US$220 to US$350, depending on the boat.

CABO PULMO
☎ 624 / pop 111

The Eastern Cape Road leads to what many consider the most spectacular site on the East Cape, the secluded Cabo Pulmo. It is home to the only coral reef on the west coast of North America, estimated to be 25,000 years old. On the cusp of tropical and temperate waters, it harbors 220 species of colorful tropical fish and a dozen species of petrified coral. The reef and 27 sq miles (71 sq km) of ocean surrounding it constitute the **Parque Marino Nacional Cabo Pulmo**, a legally protected area founded in 1995. The marine park is bounded by Playa Las Barracas in the north and Bahía Los Frailes in the south.

The coral reef consists of seven fingers jutting into the sea right from the shoreline. The reef system is very fragile and especially susceptible to pollution. Planned on-shore resort and housing developments pose the biggest threats, as does petrochemical pollution from two-stroke outboard motors. The University of La Paz is developing an Integrated Area Management Plan (IAMP) to determine the level of impact with which the park can cope.

Fishing is not permitted in the park but is possible in areas outside the boundaries. Diving, snorkeling and sea kayaking are extraordinary. Green turtles nest at Playa Las Barracas, about 15 minutes north of Cabo Pulmo, in August and September. Three miles (4.8 km) south of Cabo Pulmo is the exquisite beach of **Playa Arbolito,** with outstanding snorkeling, beachcombing and basic free **camping**.

The village of Cabo Pulmo has a few hotel facilities, restaurants and dive centers but no other infrastructure. It's entirely solar-powered. Pepe, at Pepe's Outdoor Activity Center (see Activities), also operates his **Internet Café Mejiama** (US$5/hr) via the satellite on his trailer.

Activities

Optimal conditions for **diving** and **snorkeling** are found in June and July, when glassy waters allow for visibility up to 100 feet. It's lower in May, August and September, but the greater amount of plankton attracts more and different marine life, including many pelagics and manta rays. From December to March, heavy winds often make diving impossible.

There are 14 dive sites in the national park, of which **El Bajo** has the highest concentration of fish, including the gigantic and rare whale shark and ore fish. **El Cantil** is the largest reef and has good coral, plus bat rays, hammerhead sharks and manta rays. **El Vencedor**, a tuna boat sunk in 1981, is a good place to spot baby eels and sea cucumbers; it was even featured in a Jacques Cousteau video. **Rock Island/El Islote** has the best sea fans, plus frog fish, sea horses and big groupers. To the south, **Los Frailes** is a submarine canyon whose walls are home to manta rays and turtles. Water depths range from 25 to 100 feet. There's also a sea lion colony in Bahía Los Frailes.

There's snorkeling right off the beach, but the best place is at **Playa La Sirenita** (Mermaid Beach), about a 10-minute boat ride away.

Affable and English-speaking José Luis Murietta, better known as Pepe, runs a full-service dive shop at his **Pepe's Outdoor Activity Center** (Pepe's Dive Center; ☎ 141-0001; www.cabopulmo.com.mx). Guided dives cost US$45 for one tank, US$65 for two; night dives cost US$55. His resort courses, which get you down to about 40 feet, cost US$75; four-day full PADI certification runs US$350; referral courses are US$180. Pepe also leads three-hour snorkeling excursions for US$45 per person, gear included. Pepe also offers full-day hikes to hot springs near Santiago for US$60, excursions by horseback (US$45 per person), kayaking tours (US$45 per person) and surfing trips to nearby Punta Perfecta. In fact, when it comes to activities around here, you'll be hard pressed to find something Pepe doesn't have his hands in.

The dive center at the **Cabo Pulmo Beach Resort** has diving packages and prices similar to Pepe's.

Rock climbers will find challenging sea view routes on the nearby granite (there is also some basalt and other volcanic rock).

For **hikers**, the Vista Trail is a two-hour loop around Pulmo Mountain.

Sleeping & Eating

Cabo Pulmo's most formal accommodations are US-owned **Cabo Pulmo Beach Resort** (☎ 141-0244, in the USA ☎ 888-997-8566; pulmo@caboworld.com; r from US$40), where spic-and-span hotel-style rooms cost US$40. Larger rooms cost US$85. Small bungalows cost around US$60, and *casitas* (cottages) sleeping up to four people cost US$120. The beach house, for up to six people, rents for US$175. All but the hotel rooms have kitchens. The resort also operates a PADI dive center and offers sea kayaking, climbing, hiking and snorkeling excursions.

Pepe, of Pepe's Outdoor Activity Center also has a basic palapa for rent (US$35), and if he's full he can sure figure out *something* for you.

For gourmet quality and possibly the best food and wine anywhere on the Cape, go to American-run **Nancy's** (mains US$13-16; ☺ 8am-10pm Thu-Tue), where you'll have an unforgettable outdoor dining experience. All the recipes are Nancy's creations, including delicacies such as scallop ceviche, lobster salad over greens with avocado and tomato, shrimp *guajillo* (a type of chili sauce) and scallops caramelized in butter and garlic. Vegetarians will love the vegetable enchiladas. The bread is homemade and the margaritas (blammo!) are knockouts.

Nancy also rents two **casitas** (☎ in the USA ☎ 617-242-9019 for reservations; US$40-50) and offers cooking classes (US$20 per person).

El Caballero (mains US$4-8) has a large menu with straightforward Mexican fare; it's the best value in 'town.' At the relatively basic **Tito's**, you can dine on a patio deck made from a local shipwreck.

BAHÍA LOS FRAILES TO SAN JOSÉ DEL CABO

About 5 miles (8km) south of Cabo Pulmo, Bahía Los Frailes is a beautiful crescent-shaped bay with free beach **camping** on its northern end. **Hotel Bahía Los Frailes** (in the ☎ USA 624-145-1332, 800-934-0295; www.losfrailes.com; r from US$286) is a serene luxury hideaway with lovely rooms right on the beach. The rooms, all facing the beach and decorated with hand-carved headboards and Mexican handicrafts, start at US$286 for two.

SOUTHERN BAJA

The suites cost US$349, and the deluxe two-room suite goes for US$635. Rates include three utterly delicious meals, as well as fresh muffins and a thermos of coffee brought to your door each morning.

Past Los Frailes, the road gets rougher, but it's regularly graded and passable for most vehicles all the way to San José del Cabo. It's a spectacular drive, hugging the cliffs above the ocean or dropping to the shore as it meanders south. Plans are underway to completely pave this road, in large part to accommodate the new part-time residents in their vacation homes. About 8 miles (13km) south of Los Frailes, the road reaches **Rancho Boca del Tule** and, after another 3½ miles (5.5km), **Rancho Boca La Vinorama**, where some extravagant housing development has already occurred.

A short distance south, a graded dirt road heads west to the village of **Palo Escopeta**, hitting the Transpeninsular just north of the Los Cabos International Airport after about 22 miles (35km). This is an alternate route to San José and offers a smoother and faster ride compared to the rest of the coastal road. These days, except after storms, they're about the same.

For additional information about the stretch of the Eastern Cape Road as it approaches San José del Cabo, see p199.

WESTERN CAPE

The Western Cape, from Todos Santos south along the Southern Cape Highway (México 19), has so far been spared the development of Los Cabos, but subdivision signs continue to sprout along its sandy Pacific beaches. The near absence of potable water may yet save the area.

TODOS SANTOS
☎ 612 / pop 4000

In recent years, the placid historical village of Todos Santos has seen a major influx of North American expatriates, including artists for whom Santa Fe and Taos have grown too large and impersonal. In 1985 the completion of the paved Southern Cape Highway (México 19) through Todos Santos created a straighter and quicker western alternative to Cabo San Lucas than the serpentine Transpeninsular, improving access

to beaches south of town. Nevertheless, Todos Santos proper remains a charming destination.

History

Founded in 1724 as a Jesuit *visita* (outstation) dependent on La Paz, Misión Santa Rosa de Todos Los Santos became a full-fledged mission a decade later, but a two-year Pericú rebellion nearly destroyed it. When the La Paz mission was abandoned in 1749, it became Misión Nuestra Señora del Pilar de Todos Santos. Epidemics killed Indians relocated from San Luis Gonzaga and La Pasión, and Todos Santos then limped along until its abandonment in 1840.

In the late 19th century, the former colonial village became a prosperous cane-milling town with four red-brick *trapiches* (mills) producing the dark sugar known as *panocha*. The first mill was shipped from San Francisco to Cabo San Lucas and then overland to Todos Santos. The depleted aquifers eliminated most of the thirsty sugar industry, though mills still operate in nearby Pescadero and San Jacinto. Some farmers have instituted multicropping methods to grow fruits and vegetables with less reliance on chemical fertilizers.

Despite its small size, Todos Santos has produced many notable historical figures for the peninsula and Mexico at large. Among them are General Manuel Márquez de León (who fought against the French intervention of 1861 and later, less heroically, led a Sinaloa rebellion against Porfirio Díaz), Colonel Clodomiro Cota Márquez (also active against the French intervention), General Agustín Olachea Avilés and General Melitón Albañez (notable participants in the Mexican Revolution) and Dionisia Villarino Espinoza (a heroine of the Revolution).

Orientation

Like many Mexican towns, Todos Santos, 47 miles (76km) south of La Paz, has a fairly regular grid plan, but local residents rely more on landmarks than street names for directions (though street names do exist).

Information

The English-language bookstore **El Tecolote Libros** (☎ 145-0295; cnr Juárez & Av Hidalgo) functions as Todos Santos' de facto **tour-**

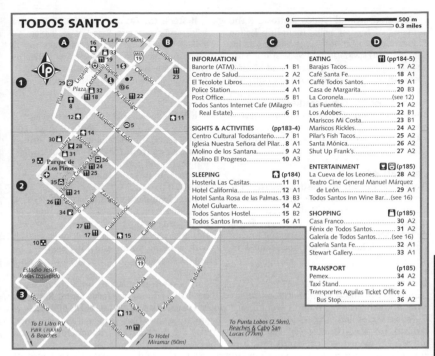

TODOS SANTOS

INFORMATION	
Banorte (ATM)........................1	B1
Centro de Salud....................2	A2
El Tecolote Libros.................3	A1
Police Station.......................4	A1
Post Office............................5	B1
Todos Santos Internet Cafe (Milagro	
Real Estate)..........................6	A1

SIGHTS & ACTIVITIES	(pp183-4)
Centro Cultural Todosanteño......7	B1
Iglesia Nuestra Señora del Pilar..8	A1
Molino de los Santana............9	A2
Molino El Progreso................10	A3

SLEEPING	(p184)
Hostería Las Casitas...............11	B1
Hotel California.....................12	A1
Hotel Santa Rosa de las Palmas..13	B3
Motel Guluarte.....................14	A2
Todos Santos Hostel...............15	B2
Todos Santos Inn...................16	A1

EATING	(pp184-5)
Barajas Tacos.......................17	A2
Café Santa Fe.......................18	A1
Caffé Todos Santos................19	A1
Casa de Margarita.................20	B3
La Coronela.....................(see 12)	
Las Fuentes.........................21	A2
Los Adobes..........................22	B1
Mariscos Mi Costa.................23	B1
Mariscos Rickles...................24	A2
Santa Mónica.......................25	A2
Pilar's Fish Tacos...................25	A2
Santa Mónica.......................26	A2
Shut Up Frank's....................27	A2

ENTERTAINMENT	(p185)
La Cueva de los Leones...........28	A2
Teatro Cine General Manuel Márquez	
de León............................29	A1
Todos Santos Inn Wine Bar....(see 16)	

SHOPPING	(p185)
Casa Franco.........................30	A2
Fénix de Todos Santos............31	A2
Galería de Todos Santos........(see 16)	
Galería Santa Fe...................32	A1
Stewart Gallery.....................33	A1

TRANSPORT	(p185)
Pemex................................34	A2
Taxi Stand...........................35	A2
Transportes Aguilas Ticket Office &	
Bus Stop...........................36	A2

ist office. Available here is a very detailed (some might say cluttered) town map and a sketched map of nearby beach areas. El Tecolote maintains an outstanding selection of books and magazines specializing in Baja California, and carries a small selection of Lonely Planet guides. It also sells Lee Moore's thorough *Todos Santos Book,* with up-to-date local information on everything from the best restaurants and art galleries to how to contact a local *curandero* (Mexican folk healer). A two-for-one paperback book exchange is available.

Look around town for a copy of *El Calendario de Todos Santos,* a free English-language monthly publication that will tune you into life in Todos Santos.

Banorte (cnr Juárez & Obregón), changes foreign currencies and has an ATM.

The **post office** is on Heróico Colegio Militar, between Av Hidalgo and Márquez de León.

Inside Milagro Real Estate is **Todos Santos Internet Cafe** (Juárez at Topete; US$2.50/hr; 9am-5pm Mon-Sat). The restaurant **Los Adobes** (p184)

has three computers at the bar where you can down a margarita while checking your email.

For medical or emergency services contact Todos Santos' **Centro de Salud** (145-0095; cnr Juárez & Degollado). The **police station** is on Legaspi near Av Hidalgo.

Sights & Activities
Murals at the **Centro Cultural Todosanteño** (Juárez near Topete), Todos Santos' former schoolhouse and current cultural center, date from 1933; their nationalist and revolutionary motifs depict missionaries and Indians, the Spanish *conquistadores*, Emiliano Zapata, cooperativism, rural laborers, industry, athletics ('vigor in mind and muscle') and 'emancipation of the rural spirit.'

Todos Santos has a plethora of **art galleries**, all of which are open to the public. The Stewart Gallery, owned by artist Charles Stewart, who essentially kicked off the Todos Santos art scene, is a good place to start. See Shopping for more information.

Scattered around Todos Santos are the remains of former **mills**, including **Molino El Progreso** (Rangel at Progreso) and **Molino de los Santana** (Juárez btwn Zaragoza & Degollado), opposite the clinic. Molino Cerro Verde and Molino Jesús Amador are on the northern outskirts of town.

The most accessible **beaches** are south of town and about 6½ miles (10km) northwest of town. The **surfing** at Playa Los Cerritos (p186), where you can rent boards, is often excellent.

Festivals & Events

Todos Santos' annual **Festival de Artes** (art festival) lasts two days in February (dates vary). In late February, Todos Santos holds a tour of local historic homes. The **Fiesta de Todos Santos**, which celebrates the town's patron saint, La Virgen de Pilar, is held on October 12.

Sleeping

Todos Santos has a small but good selection of hotels.

Todos Santos Inn (☎ 145-0040; www.todos santosinn.com; Legaspi 33; r US$106-151, ste US$240; ✖ ✆) US-owned Todos Santos Inn is by far the most beautiful and relaxing hotel in town. Fashioned from a restored 19th-century brick building, it has a tropical interior courtyard with a tiny but very appealing swimming pool. The six rooms (with two more on the way) all have four-poster beds and a luxurious air. It all makes leaving the hotel itself very difficult.

Motel Guluarte (☎ 145-0006; cnr Juárez & Morelos; r US$20; Ⓟ ✖ ✆) If you're driving and looking for a good deal with a parking lot, this is the place. It's no-frills but spotless. Being a motel, the rooms open over the pool area. Try to get a room on the 2nd floor.

Hotel California (☎ 145-0525; hotelcalifornia reservations@hotmail.com; Juárez at Morelos; r US$106-196; ✖) The newly reopened Hotel California (which you *can* leave, if you wish) is a stunning creation of its US owners, who completely remodeled the place, giving it a very artsy edge. The rooms are all decorated with paintings of local artists and the attached restaurant is excellent. The hotel has long held the mythical status ('mythical' being the key word here) of being the lodging that inspired the Eagles' hit *Hotel California*.

Hostería Las Casitas (☎ 145-0255; www.mex online.com/lascasitas.htm; Rangel at Av Hidalgo; s/d US$52/67) The rolled palapa roof edges, rarely seen nowadays, add authentic detail to this comfortable five-room Canadian-run B&B. A filling gourmet breakfast is included in the price. The owners' artwork livens up the place.

Hotel Miramar (☎ 145-0341; cnr Verduzco & Pedrajo; s/d US$15/20; Ⓟ) Southwest of the town center, the Miramar has only limited ocean views from the 2nd-floor balconies, but that's still more ocean view than anything else in town. It's clean and reasonably priced, if basic.

Hotel Santa Rosa de las Palmas (☎ 145-0394; Olachea at Villarino; r US$40; ✆) Set among verdant gardens on the south side of town, this pleasant hotel has eight rooms, each with a living room and kitchenette. The hotel lacks air-con but has fans and a swimming pool.

If you're really achin' for a cheap sleep, try the ramshackle **Todos Santos Hostel** (no ☎ ; Degollado near Cuauhtémoc; bed US$5), which, if anything, has beds and a friendly owner. You can pitch a tent here, too, for the same price.

Located southwest of the baseball park, **El Litro RV Park** (☎ 146-5713; tent/RV US$7/13) offers spacious camping sites and RV sites with hookups. The toilets are spotless and there are three bathrooms, two with showers.

Eating

Todos Santos has an astounding number of good restaurants considering the size of the town.

Barajas Tacos (Degollado at Cuauhtémoc; tacos US$1-3; ⏰ closed Tue) This excellent palapa-roofed taquería serves delicious tacos, carnitas, and *papas asadas* (stuffed grilled potatoes).

Mariscos Mi Costa (Colegio Militar at Ocampo; mains US$5-9) This little family-style place serves 11 varieties of outstanding seafood cocktails, plus a delicious *sopa de mariscos* (seafood soup) and huge plates of tacos.

Los Adobes (☎ 145-0203; Av Hidalgo near Colegio Militar; mains US$12-16) For some seriously good *alta cocina* (haute cuisine) try this upscale but casual new restaurant. Dishes include *mole poblano* (a Puebla-style mole, a spicy chili sauce flavored with chocolate and spices), Cornish game hen in 'Jamaica sauce' and several mouthwatering seafood dishes.

Casa de Margarita (☎ 145-0184; Pedrajo btwn Progreso & Villarino; mains US$6-12) This family-run restaurant attracts a devoted following for its fine, reasonably priced antojitos and seafood. It also offers a Sunday champagne brunch.

Las Fuentes (☎ 145-0257; cnr Degollado & Colegio Militar; mains US$6-10) Las Fuentes serves excellent Mexican dishes (the chicken with mole sauce is exceptional) and seafood specialties in a shady patio among colorful bougainvillea and three refreshing fountains.

La Coronela (Juárez at Morelos; mains US$6-10) Part of Hotel California, La Coronela serves big breakfasts, including French toast, eggs benedict with smoked marlin, and homemade muffins, cinnamon rolls and banana bread. For lunch and dinner, choose from sandwiches, pizza and other items.

Café Santa Fe (☎ 145-0340; cnr Centenario & Márquez de León; mains US$14-18) In a class all by itself, Café Santa Fe entices patrons from as far away as La Paz and Cabo San Lucas. The grub here is Italian and prices are high, but service is excellent and it's well worth a splurge. Reservations are a good idea during holiday periods.

Shut Up Frank's (Degollado near Rangel; mains US$4-9) Get your north-of-the-border fix at this restaurant and sports bar where the menu – painted in blue on the walls outside – includes burgers, ribs, steak, pancakes and big egg breakfasts.

Caffé Todos Santos (☎ 145-0300; Centenario 33; mains US$5-10) The espresso drinks here will make you caffeine junkies bug-eyed. It also offers savory pastries, big breakfasts and enticing fruit salads. The deli-style sandwiches are outstanding.

Mariscos Ricklos (Colegio Militar near Morelos; mains US$6-9) Specializes in seafood and has reasonable prices.

Santa Mónica (☎ 145-0204; Degollado at Colegio Militar; mains US$5-9) Well-regarded Santa Mónica is Todos Santos' oldest restaurant and serves seafood, lobster and steak dishes in a casual atmosphere.

For fine food at bargain prices, try any or all of the **taco stands** along Heróico Colegio Militar between Márquez de León and Degollado; each has its own specialty, be it fish, chicken, shrimp or beef. **Pilar's Fish Tacos** (cnr Zaragoza & Colegio Militar; tacos US$1-2) is somewhat legendary for its – you guessed it – fish tacos.

Entertainment

The **wine bar** (☻ 5-9pm) in the Todos Santos Inn is a good place to kick off the evening by tasting wines from Baja California. Over at **Shut Up Frank's**, colloquially known as 'Callate Pancho,' expat sport fanatics crowd the bar and shout at the games on the TV.

Proud of its tranquility, Todos Santos is no party town, but **La Cueva de los Leones** (Juárez btwn Morelos & Zaragoza) features live *norteña* (Mexican country style music) and *banda* (raucous brass-band music) on weekends. **La Coronela** has live music on weekend nights, sometimes ending with lots of dancing.

The restored theater **Teatro Cine General Manuel Márquez de León** (☎ 145-0122), on the northern side of the plaza, hosts occasional live concerts and other performances.

For live sports action, enthusiastic amateur baseball teams from Todos Santos and other nearby communities play several nights weekly (plus daytime games on weekends) at **Estadio Jesús Rosas Izquierdo** (cnr Rangel & Villarino).

Shopping

As an artists' colony, Todos Santos has numerous stores and galleries open to the public, displaying samples of local crafts and artwork. For jewelry, artwork and clothes, try **Casa Franco** (Juárez near Zaragoza) or **Fénix de Todos Santos** (cnr Juárez & Zaragoza).

Galería de Todos Santos (cnr Topete & Legaspi) features imaginative artwork by Mexican and North American artists, with regular openings. **Galería Santa Fe** (Centenario), alongside its namesake restaurant on the southern side of the plaza, is well worth a visit, as is the **Stewart Gallery** (Obregón btwn Legaspi & Centenario).

Getting There & Away

Buses stop outside the **Transportes Aguilas ticket office** (☎ 120-9448; Colegio Militar near Morelos). From 7:30am to 9pm, they go hourly to Cabo San Lucas (US$5, 1¼ hours), San José del Cabo (US$7, 2 hours) and La Paz (US$5, 1¼ hours). A 6pm bus goes to Tijuana (US$110; 24 hours), stopping at all major towns en route.

AROUND TODOS SANTOS

At the **Punta Lobos** beach, about 1½ miles (2.5km) south of Todos Santos, *pangueros* (skiff operators) sell their catches in the late afternoon, offering a cheaper, better selection than local markets.

Farther south on México 19, across from a botanical garden, a 2½-mile (4km) dirt road leads to **Playa San Pedrito**, a sandy crescent beach with surfable breaks.

Spacious **San Pedrito RV Park** (☎ 108-4316; 🖳) charges US$4 per person for camping without hookups, US$15 for RV sites with all hookups and US$45 for two people in modest cabañas. It's still recovering from the last hurricane, but it also still attracts hundreds of people November through February, when there can be up to 150 people camped on the beach and some 40 RVs in the park. During this time a reggae band plays every Saturday night in the restaurant. There's a swimming pool and a laundry on site. The gates are closed from 10pm to 7am.

In a northern swell, the crescent beach at **Playa Los Cerritos** has a good right break but has become more crowded in recent years. There is also good fishing from the rocky headland to the north. A hut at the north end of the beach rents surfboards (US$15/day), and the owner repairs boards and will set up surf lessons.

At Km 65, **Los Cerritos RV Park** operates on a shoestring budget, but the toilets flush and the cold showers work (water is expensive because it's trucked in – consider a 'sea shower' to conserve this precious commodity). There is some shade but no electricity. Ejido Pescadero keeps the area weed-free, charging US$4 to park outside

the fence, US$5 to park inside. There have been reports of thefts, so secure your possessions at night.

At Km 74, near a giant (and blank) billboard, a dirt road heads seaward; after about 300 yards (273m), the left fork leads to **Rancho Pilar** (www.ranchopilar.com), owned by artists Pilar and Cuco Moyron. Cuco custom-makes traditional Baja style *huaraches*, cutting the sole out of an old tire and tying up the leather straps while you wait. As he tells his guests, 'they're guaranteed for 2000 miles.' Pilar makes and sells 'beach jewelry' and woven palm-frond hats to adorn your other appendages. While you wait for your sandals, you can browse other crafts, such as Cuco's ceramic candleholders, which cast light figures onto the wall.

Cuco also offers one-day and multiday hikes into the Sierra de La Laguna (p175) for US$150 to US$300 for a group of up to four people. Ask about beach **camping**, which Cuco will probably be offering by the time this book hits the shelves.

At an unmarked turnoff at about Km 83, **Playa Las Cabrillas** features a long but steep sandy beach unsuitable for surfing. However, there are many good rustic **campsites** just off the highway.

At Km 97, a dirt road (actually more like a sand trail – suitable only for 4WD) leads half a mile (1km) west among mangroves to **Playa Migriño** and Estero Migriño, a good bird-watching site that also has a right break in the winter months. Cow patties and insects are both abundant, so watch your step and bring bug repellent.

Los Cabos

LOS CABOS

Between the azure waters of the Sea of Cortez and the mighty Pacific Ocean, Los Cabos boasts one of the most spectacular resort settings imaginable. Here, at the southern tip of the world's third longest peninsula, the towns of San José del Cabo and Cabo San Lucas hang suspended in a salty paradise, attracting over 800,000 visitors each year who come to fish, snorkel, scuba dive, party and sun their buns on the region's breathtaking beaches.

The region has three distinct personalities. San José is a traditional yet refined Mexican town. Its central plaza, hemmed in by small historic buildings, the municipal market and the narrow streets remind you that yes indeed, this is Mexico. If San José is the older brother who clings to the traditions of its Mexican past, Cabo San Lucas is the wily younger upstart, bent more on partying and flaunting its fashionable good looks than maintaining any sort of tradition or planning for the future.

Linking the two towns is Los Cabos Corridor, an 18-mile (29km) stretch of beautiful beaches, some of the world's most beautiful championship golf courses, sandy coves and Los Cabos' most expensive resorts (we're talking *Lifestyles of the Rich and Famous* here). The Corridor is developed end-to-end, but it's still possible to hunker down in an untouched stretch of sun-baked sand and take in the rays.

TOP FIVE

■ Snorkel the crystal-clear waters off **Playa del Amor** (Lover's Beach, p208) and sleep off your buzz in the sand.

■ Fill your belly with fabulous seafood and Mexican haute cuisine in one of historic San José del Cabo's many superb **restaurants** (p195).

■ Dance, dance, dance the night away in Cabo San Lucas, where **partying** (p219) is taken to dizzying heights.

■ Send your little balls sailing down the fairway of Cabo del Sol's **Ocean Course** (p202), one of Los Cabos' six world-famous signature courses.

■ Test your angler's luck in the legendary big-game **sportfishing** (p208) waters off Cabo San Lucas.

■ CABO JANUARY AVERAGE HIGH: 79°F/26°C   ■ WATER TEMP OFF CABO: 70-80°F/21-27°C

HISTORY

Baja's southern tip has been, in succession, a sleepy haven for Pericú Indians, a sheltered hideaway for pirates and a string of sedate fishing communities. The Pericú inhabited the foothills of the Sierra de la Laguna to the north, never settling around the Cape proper because fresh water was scarce there. The majority of them died soon after the arrival of Europeans and their deadly diseases.

When Europeans first saw the peninsula in the 16th century, water shortages made the southern Cape an unappealing place for permanent settlement, but its secluded anchorages offered privateers an ideal base for raiding Spain's Manila galleons.

By the early 17th century, the Spanish had lost enough gold and silver to prompt the establishment of a small presidio (military outpost) at Cabo San Lucas. Around 1730 the Jesuits established Misión San José del Cabo, which became a more permanent settlement. The presidio deterred the pirates and, eventually, both encampments became villages whose inhabitants relied on fishing and fish-canning for their livelihood. During the Mexican-American War, US troops occupied the area, as did the eccentric William Walker's forces a few years later.

After WWII, US private pilots brought tales of the area's big game fish and magnificent beaches to listeners north of the border. As more North Americans arrived, upscale hotels and restaurants sprouted, and the federal government built an international airport near San José del Cabo. Cruise ships soon included Cabo San Lucas on their itineraries, and a ferry service (since discontinued) began to operate to and from the mainland city of Puerto Vallarta. In recent years, hordes of North American tourists and retirees have frequented the area, downtown Cabo San Lucas lost its village ambience and a string of multistory luxury resort hotels – not to mention several golf courses – has disfigured the coastline between Cabo San Lucas and San José del Cabo.

GETTING THERE & AROUND

Los Cabos International Airport (p198) is 6½ miles (10.5km) north of San José del Cabo. Shuttle services and taxis link the airport with both towns and the resorts along the Corridor. Both forms of transport are expensive (US$75 for a cab or US$15 for a shuttle to Cabo San Lucas), and taking a public bus entails walking for 25 minutes in the pounding sun out to the Transpeninsular. Public buses (US$1.50) run along the Corridor linking San José with Cabo San Lucas.

SAN JOSÉ DEL CABO

☎ 624 / pop 60,000

San José is the sophisticated side of Los Cabos, with numerous gourmet restaurants and upscale shops tucked into a lovely little historic center. Compact and pedestrian-friendly, it charms its visitors with century-old, colonial-style brick and adobe buildings and is anchored by a shady plaza and a pretty church. As the capital of the *municipio* (county) of Los Cabos, the town is well maintained, clean and sedate. Unlike in Cabo San Lucas, a quiet, laid-back atmosphere prevails. About 1 mile (1.6km) south of downtown lies the modern part of San José, primarily along the beachfront's *zona hotelera* (hotel zone), where giant resorts line the long, wide beach.

Orientation

San José del Cabo is 20 miles (32km) east of Cabo San Lucas and 119 miles (192km) south of La Paz. The historic downtown is linked to the zona hotelera by manicured Blvd José Antonio Mijares; the zona hotelera hugs the beaches of Playa de California & Playa del Nuevo Sol, which together makes one long beach. San José's commercial center orbits Plaza Mijares, the northern terminus of Blvd Mijares.

About 1½ miles (2.5km) east of downtown is Pueblo La Playa, a tranquil fishing village that is also the starting point of the unpaved Eastern Cape Road (p199).

Information

BOOKSTORES

Libros Libros Books Books (☎ 142-4433; Mijares near Coronado) Decent selection of English-language magazines and novels; some Lonely Planet guidebooks; maps.

EMERGENCY

Cruz Roja (Red Cross; ☎ 066 ambulance, 142-0316; Mijares near Benito Juárez)

LOS CABOS

SAN JOSÉ DEL CABO

A   **B**   **C**   **D**

To Huerta Verde
B&B (3.5km),
Los Cabos International
Airport (10.5km) &
La Paz (192km)

INFORMATION
Banca Serfin..............................**1** F1
Bancomer...................................**2** G6
Canadian Consulate....................**3** G2
Corre Caminos............................**4** G3
Cruz Roja...................................**5** G2
IMSS Hospital.............................**6** F2
Lavamática San José....................**7** E3
Lavandería Laundry Mat...............**8** G6
Libros Libros Books Books.............**9** F2
Municipal Tourist Office..............**10** D4
Police Station...........................**11** G2
Post Office...............................**12** G2
Telecomm................................**13** G3
Trazzo Digital...........................**14** G6
Viajes Damiana.........................**15** G6

SIGHTS & ACTIVITIES (pp192-3)
Iglesia San José.........................**16** H6
Killer Hook Surf Shop..................**17** F2
Nomadas de Baja California..........**18** E1
Victor's Sportfishing.............(see 19)

SLEEPING (pp193-5)
Best Western Hotel Posada Real.....**19** E6
Casa Natalia.............................**20** F1
El Encanto Inn...........................**21** F1
El Encanto Suites.......................**22** F1
Hotel Colli................................**23** H6
Hotel Diana..............................**24** G6
Hotel Fiesta Inn.........................**25** D6
Hotel La Palmita........................**26** F5
Nuevo Hotel San José..................**27** F1
Posada Señor Mañana.................**28** F1
Posada Terranova......................**29** E1
Presidente InterContinental..........**30** H5
Tropicana Inn............................**31** G2

EATING (pp195-7)
Almacenes Goncanseco................**32** F1
Ándale Bistro............................**33** G6
Baan Thai.................................**34** F1
Damiana...................................**35** F1
El Ahorcado..............................**36** D1
Fandango..................................**37** G6
French Riviera............................**38** H6
Helados Bing.............................**39** G2
Iguana Bar................................**40** F2
Jazmín's...................................**41** G6
La Cenaduría del Pancho..............**42** H6
La Picazón................................**43** E3
Morgan's Encore........................**44** G6
Pan del Triunfo..........................**45** G6
Pica Grill..................................**46** E3
Taquería El Fogón.......................**47** D2
Taquería Erica............................**48** D2
Tequila.....................................**49** F1
Tropicana Bar & Grill.............(see 31)
Xochimilco................................**50** G6

ENTERTAINMENT (p197)
Cactus Jacks.............................**51** G2
Rodeo Mix................................**52** G6
Sim Pecao.................................**53** G6

SHOPPING (pp197-8)
Antigua Los Cabos......................**54** H6
Arte Diseño Decoración................**55** H6
Copal......................................**56** F1
Dulcería Delicia.........................**57** E2
Fruitlandia...............................**58** G2
La Mina....................................**59** F2
Veryka.....................................**60** F1

TRANSPORT (pp198-9)
Advantage Car Rental..................**61** H6
Alamo Car Rental.......................**62** D4
Dollar Car Rental.......................**63** D3
Main Bus Terminal......................**64** E3
Mexicana..................................**65** D6
National Car Rental...............(see 19)
Pemex.....................................**66** E1
Thrifty Car Rental......................**67** D4
Thrifty Car Rental......................**68** G2

Marinos

Castro

Paseo Los Cabos

To Los Cabos Corridor
& Cabo San Lucas (32km)

LOS CABOS

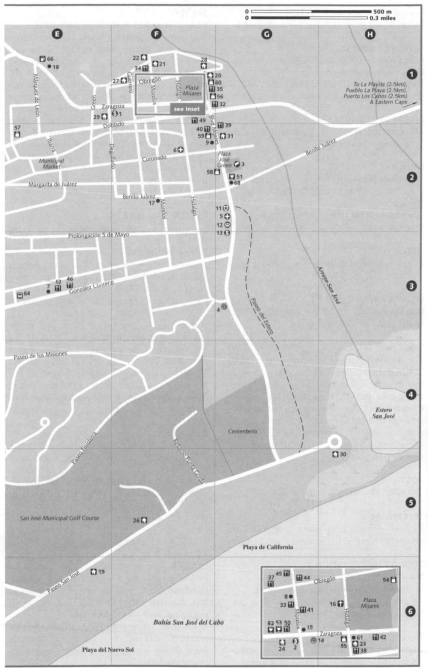

0 _____ 500 m
0 _____ 0.3 miles

E   **F**   **G**   **H**

66
18

22
34   21

28

27   Obregón

20
60
35
56
32

Plaza
Mijares

see inset

Green

Zaragoza
29   1

Márquez de León

Doblado

Ibarra

57

49
40   39
59   31
9

6

Municipal
Market

Degollado

Coronado

Plaza
José
Green   3
58
51
68

To La Playita (2.5km),
Pueblo La Playa (2.5km),
Puerto Los Cabos (2.5km)
& Eastern Cape

Benito Juárez

Margarita de Juárez

Benito Juárez
17

Morelos

Hidalgo

Prolongación 5 de Mayo

11
5
12
13

7   10   46
64   González Cunrero

4

Paseo del Estero

Arroyo San José

Paseo de los Misiones

3

1

2

Estero
San José

4

Cementerio

Federico Paula Gesta

Paseo Finisterra

30

LOS CABOS

San José Municipal Golf Course

26

5

19

Playa de California

Paseo San José

Bahía San José del Cabo

Playa del Nuevo Sol

37   45
   44

Obregón

8
33
  41

16

54

Plaza
Mijares

Hidalgo

52 53 50
  15

Morelos

Zaragoza

24   2   14

61
39
38

42

55

6

Fire (☎ 068)
Police (☎ 060, 142-0361; Mijares near Benito Juárez)

INTERNET ACCESS
Corre Caminos (Blvd Mijares; US$6/hr) Coffee served; south of downtown on way to beach
Trazzo Digital (☎ 412-0303; Zaragoza 24; US$4/hr; ⓨ Mon-Sat) Fastest cafe downtown.

INTERNET RESOURCES
For Internet resources pertinent to all of Los Cabos, see p206.

LAUNDRY
Lavamática San José (González Conseco s/n; self service/full service US$3/4.80; ⓨ 8am-8pm Mon-Sat, 9am-3pm Sun)
Lavandería Laundry Mat (Morelos at Obregón; self service/full service US$2.80/5; ⓨ 8am-8pm Mon-Sat)

MEDIA
For a list of the local English-language publications, see p206.

MEDICAL SERVICES
IMSS hospital (☎ 142-0180 emergency, ☎ 142-0076 nonemergency; cnr Hidalgo & Coronado)

MONEY
The *cambio* (money exchange) at Los Cabos International Airport offers poor rates. In town, several cambios keep long hours, but banks pay better rates. Downtown's **Bancomer** (cnr Morelos & Zaragoza) and **Banca Serfin** (cnr Degollado & Zaragoza) cash traveler's checks and have ATMs. **Telecomm** (Blvd Mijares), next to the post office, can arrange international money transfers.

POST
Post office (Mijares near González Conseco)

TELEPHONE
Ladatel public telephones are plentiful everywhere, especially around Plaza Mijares.

TOURIST INFORMATION
Municipal tourist office (☎ 146-9628; www.loscabos.gob.mx, turismoloscabos@prodigy.net.mx; Transpeninsular near González Conseco; ⓨ 8:30am-3pm Mon-Fri) Stacks of brochures, helpful staff, lousy location.

TRAVEL AGENCIES
Viajes Damiana (☎ 142-0752, 142-3752; cnr Zaragoza & Morelos) Widely respected full-service travel agency.

Sights
PLAZA MIJARES & IGLESIA SAN JOSÉ
San José's central plaza is far more traditional than anything found in San Lucas. In the evening, tourists mill around, local families wander down with the kids, and the plaza turns into a small kickball-court-cum-tricycle-track, with oblivious wandering toddlers thrown in for suspense. On weekends, bands (for better or worse) take to the stage. The plaza is surrounded by colorful, historical buildings and anchored by the Iglesia San José, an imposing replica of the original mission church. Note the mosaic above the front portal depicting a 1734 local Indian uprising.

ESTERO SAN JOSÉ
San José's most delightfully peaceful spot is the estuary adjacent to the Hotel Inter-Continental in the zona hotelera. In colonial times, between raids on Spanish galleons, pirates took refuge in what is now a protected wildlife area replenished by a subterranean spring. It's a bird-watcher's delight, with frigate birds, sparrow hawks, white herons, red-tailed hack and other species making their home here. From the corner of Benito Juárez, a palm-lined **pedestrian trail** (Paseo del Estero) parallels Mijares all the way to the zona hotelera. This is a delightful alternative to the boulevard, but it may not always be passable because of high water levels, especially after rains.

BEACHES
San José's long, white sandy beaches are a major attraction for visitors, but they're a good twenty-minute walk from the center of town. **Playa del Nuevo Sol** and its eastward extension, **Playa de California** (at the southern end of Blvd Mijares), are both good for swimming. Together, they make an incredibly long beach – a great morning walk if you head east away from the hotels. After half a mile (1km) or so, you'll reach **La Playita**, the beach adjacent to Pueblo La Playa (p199). La Playita has always had excellent surf fishing and a more local feel than the other beaches, but this is all changing with the development of Puerto Los Cabos. Unfortunately, until the project is complete (a date that's anybody's guess), giant dump trucks will continue to pound down the beach.

Activities
FISHING
Fishing is not as big a pastime in San José as it is in Cabo San Lucas and on the East Cape, but several operators do offer excursions. For a fish calendar, see p212.

Victor's Sportfishing (☎ 142-1092, 142-2255), at the Best Western Hotel Posada Real (p194), organizes six-hour *superpanga* (fast outboard skiffs) trips from Playa Palmilla for US$185 (maximum three people) and eight-hour cabin-cruiser trips from US$330 (maximum four people) to US$395 (maximum six). Two people in a *panga* (skiff) costs US$150.

Panga trips cost about the same with **Gordo Banks Pangas** (☎ 142-1147, in the USA ☎ 800-408-1199; www.gordobanks.com), based at nearby La Playita (p199), whose cabin-cruiser trips cost US$350 to US$480.

If your Spanish is up to it, you might try negotiating a deal with one of the independent panga owners you'll see hanging around the beach, who are usually a few dollars cheaper. With the development of Puerto Los Cabos to the east, however, the fishermen may soon be required to park their pangas in the marina rather than down on the sand.

SURFING
In town, **Killer Hook Surf Shop** (☎ 142-2430; cnr Morelos & Benito Juárez) is a good source for surfing information, wax, rash guards and the like (no boards, though).

The closest surfing beach, and the best in the Los Cabos area, is Zipper's Beach (Playa Costa Azul), at Km 28.5 on the Transpeninsular. Experienced surfers claim that summer reef and point breaks match the finest in Hawaii. Above Zipper's, on the north side of the highway, **Costa Azul Surf Shop** (Map p201; ☎ 147-0071; Transpeninsular) has rental equipment (surfboards, snorkels and body boards) and also does repairs. Stop here for the latest surf report and to pick up their free surf-break map.

At nearby Playa Acapulquito, Cabo Surf Hotel (p202) also rents surfboards for US$15/30 per hour/day. A concession at Brisa del Mar Trailer Park rents surfboards too.

Nomadas de Baja (see Tours) offers full-day surfing lessons for US$95 per person, gear included.

GOLF, TENNIS & BICYCLING
The nine-hole, par-35 course at **San José Municipal Golf Course** (San José Campo de Golf; ☎ 142-0905) charges a very reasonable US$30, making it by far the cheapest course in Los Cabos. Tennis courts rent for US$15/30 per hour during the day/night. If you want to swing with the big wigs, head out to one of the Corridor courses (p202).

Brisa del Mar Trailer Park (p202) rents mountain bikes for US$20 per day.

Tours
Nomadas de Baja (☎ 146-9612, mobile ☎ 044-624-151-1874; www.nomadasdebaja.com; Zaragoza near Márquez de León) is an ecologically minded adventure tour company that offers a wide range of explorations along the coast, the Los Cabos hinterlands and the Sierra de la Laguna. Options include trips to waterfalls and hot springs (US$65), a sunrise hike (US$45) and biking through the desert (US$85). The very popular Cabo Pulmo excursion can be tailored to kayakers, snorkelers or divers (or any combination; US$105 to US$155).

Nomadas' bilingual owner, Marco Hernandez, can also customize guided hiking treks to the Sierra de la Laguna for individuals or groups. His standard two-day/two-night trips cost US$350, including mules, food, guides and transport.

Festivals & Events
March 19 marks the **Fiesta de San José**, a celebration of the town's patron saint. Festivities last four or five days and include folk dancing, parades, lots of food and horse races.

Sleeping
Downtown San José has several sophisticated boutique hotels within its historical core. The town is a bit tight on budget hotels, but there are a couple. The nearest camping is at La Playita. The most expensive hotels are the all-inclusive luxury resorts down on the beach. Be sure to make reservations everywhere during the peak winter months.

DOWNTOWN SAN JOSÉ
Hotel Colli (☎ 142-0725; Hidalgo near Zaragoza; r US$42; ❄) One of the best values in town, family-run Hotel Colli has immaculate rooms

LOS CABOS

(flowered bedspreads, painted furniture), free bottled water and a tiny patio out back. It has a perfectly preserved circa-1963 look to it. Best of all, the owners are wonderfully friendly.

El Encanto Inn (☎ 142-038; www.elencantoinn.com; Morelos 133; r US$75, ste US$85-125; ✗ ⊑) Time seems to move slowly at this sun-yellow, colonial-style hotel. Rooms with tile floors, firm beds and wrought-iron furniture open onto a small flower-festooned courtyard. The poolside suites in the new annex across the street – **El Encanto Suites** – are stunning. They surround an open grass-covered garden replete with lawn chairs for your sunning delight. Rates for both places include breakfast at the poolside tables in the annex.

Tropicana Inn (☎ 142-1580; www.tropicanacabo. com; Blvd Mijares near Coronado; r US$70-110; ✗ ⊑) With its spacious outdoor patio, tropical foliage and poolside bar (complete with underwater chairs) it's hard to believe this pretty hotel is right downtown. Entrance is through its namesake restaurant and bar (p196). Rooms are spacious and have satellite TV.

Casa Natalia (☎ 142-5100, in the USA ☎ 888-277-3814; www.casanatalia.com; Blvd Mijares 4; s US$198-275, d US$396-412; ✗ ⊑) On the northeastern corner of Plaza Mijares, Casa Natalia is an ultra-chic yet homey retreat run by a European couple. Each of the 18 rooms gets its character from a mix of modern architecture and interesting art objects. All rooms come with a private patio (where your breakfast is served each morning) and a sunken shower/tub. Special touches include embroidered robes and a hammock, and monstrous wooden chessboards in the lounge. Its popular restaurant serves gourmet-quality fare.

Posada Terranova (☎ 142-0534; www.hterranova. com.mx; Degollado at Doblado; s/d/ste US$55/60/65) This central hotel is friendly and straightforward, with spacious, spotless rooms equipped with cable TV. The enormous suites, with kitchen and dining room, are the real value. The attached restaurant makes breakfast convenient.

Hotel Diana (☎ 142-0490; Zaragoza 30; r US$30) The clean, plain rooms here stay pretty cool, despite their lacking windows, and the family that runs the place is very friendly. Enter through a small lobby, and

a linoleum-floor hallway takes you back to the rooms.

Posada Señor Mañana (☎ 142-0462; www. srmanana.net; Obregón 1; r US$34-56; ⊑) Run by a friendly Swedish woman, this rambling and slightly dilapidated hotel is a block off the plaza near a swampy stretch of the Arroyo San José. Rooms are simple but clean with cold cement walls and private baths. They open onto a courtyard with a half-full (or half-empty) swimming pool. It's a bit pricey for what's on offer, but the communal kitchen will help you keep your costs down.

Nuevo Hotel San José (☎ 142-2464; Obregón at Guerrero; r US$17-20) The street-facing rooms at San José's cheapest hotel are giant, while those in back are smaller and darker. Special touches include exposed electrical wires (that do indeed shock), pipes masquerading as shower heads, seatless toilets, industrial toilet paper holders and a motley (burp) clientele. Hey, it's cheap.

BEACH HOTELS

San José's closest beachfront hotels are at Playa de California and Playa del Nuevo Sol, a 20-minute walk from downtown. All but Hotel La Palmita are on the beach.

Hotel La Palmita (☎ 142-0434; Paseo San José; r US$66; P ✗ ✗ ⊑) Overlooking the golf course and across the road from the beach, this hotel is a handsome, modern inn with nicely decorated rooms. There are plenty of poolside lounge chairs for soaking up the sun, plus a deli and small store are right outside.

Best Western Hotel Posada Real (☎ 142-0155, in the USA ☎ 800-780-7234; www.posadareal.com. mx, www.bestwestern.com; Playa de California; r US$99-223; P ✗ ✗ ⊑) After a US$2 million makeover, this beachfront hotel sparkles once again. Oceanview rooms occupy a three-floor structure wrapped around a beautiful cactus garden. It's a good choice if you're looking for something in the resort vein without the Roll's Royce price tag.

Hotel Fiesta Inn (☎ 142-9300, in the USA ☎ 800-343-7821; www.fiestainn.com; r US$147-221, ste US$234-297; P ✗ ✗ ⊑) The Hotel Fiesta Inn is an all-inclusive resort (meaning all meals, drinks and most activities are included in the price) right on the beach. The pool area, with the requisite swim-up bar, and the shuffleboard court (most fun after a few margaritas) are the hotel's main draws. It's popular but a bit low on charm.

Presidente InterContinental (☎ 142-0211, in the USA ☎ 888-567-8725; www.loscabos.interconti. com; r US$125-800; P ⊠ ☒ ☒) This is the big daddy of San Jose's beach resorts: all three pools are big, the grounds are big, the buffets are big, the rooms are big and, yep, the price tag's big. It's quite handsome for a resort, without the imposing multifloor heights of some of its counterparts up the coast. Both standard and all-inclusive rates are available.

PUEBLO LA PLAYA

Pueblo La Playa is about 15 minutes by car from downtown San José. Accommodations are much closer to the beach here than they are in downtown San José and cost less than the luxury resorts on Playas California and Nuevo Sol. However, due to the massive development of Puerto Los Cabos, Pueblo La Playa was not the most peaceful place to stay at the time this book went to press. The following hotels were once some of the best values around – and with the completion of the project may well be again – but at press time they weren't conducive to a quiet, romantic stay near the beach (unless you like dodging dump trucks during your stroll down the sand).

If you're in Los Cabos to fish, surf or engage in other activities that draw you out of Pueblo La Playa for the day, it's still a great place to stay. Just be sure to call ahead of time and be certain to ask the owners how quiet things are when you call. These are all small hotels, and the owners will give you an honest assessment of their changing slice of paradise.

La Fonda del Mar/Buzzard's Bar (in the USA ☎ 909-303-3918, 702-255-0630; www.buzzardsbar.com; r shared bath US$75, private bath US$90) Owned by a friendly US couple, this four-room B&B is just the spot for low-key relaxation. Three of the rooms have their own sinks and toilets but share a shower-room (which is immaculate), and a fourth has its own shower. They're all set within a small garden, just off the fabulous outdoor restaurant. The beach is a shell's throw away. Prices drop US$10 May 16 to October 31.

El Delfín Blanco (☎ 142-1212; www.eldelfinblanco. net) Facing La Playita beach, this Swedish-run accommodation sits in a garden filled with palm and banana trees. Amenities include a barbecue area and outdoor kitchen. Tent sites cost US$10 to US$15. Otherwise you stay in the neatly decorated, thatch-roof cabañas with shared bath for US$34/44 for one/two people. Larger casitas with private bath cost US$56 for two people.

La Playita Resort (☎ 142-4166, in the USA ☎ 626-962-2805, 888-242-4166; r US$50-80) Almost in the sand at La Playita beach, this modest and wonderfully friendly American-owned resort has large, comfortable rooms and three penthouses. Rates – which are flexible when business is slow or for multiday stays – include continental breakfast. The owners have lowered their rates to about US$50 during construction of Puerto Los Cabos.

ELSEWHERE

Huerta Verde B&B (☎ 148-0511, in the USA ☎ 303-877-1395; www.lovemexico.com; r US$140-171) About 2 miles (3.5km) toward the airport, Huerta Verde is an enchanting B&B tucked into a terraced hillside. There are seven suites, some with kitchenettes, all set in a lush garden (the name translates as 'Green Orchard'). Numerous species of land and sea birds make their home here, so it's a real treat for bird watchers. It's also a bit remote, so phone ahead for availability and directions.

Eating

The main restaurant scene is concentrated around Plaza Mijares and its side streets, and the overall quality is very high. If your wallet isn't too thick, look for more casual eateries along González Conseco and Doblado.

PLAZA MIJARES & BLVD MIJARES

Damiana (☎ 142-0499; Blvd Mijares at Plaza Mijares; mains US$8-20) Popular Damiana occupies a restored 18th-century house with wood-beam ceilings and traditional decorations. At night the courtyard, canopied with bougainvillea, is especially romantic. If you pick and choose carefully you can make a meal for about US$20, although it's easy to spend twice as much. Reservations are recommended.

La Cenaduría del Pancho (☎ 145-5470; Zaragoza 10; lunch US$4-7.50, dinner US$9-15) La Cenaduría serves up honest-to-goodness food at some of the best prices in town (for sit-down dining, anyway). The vast menu ranges from *antojitos* (light snacks or small meals) like tamales and ceviche tostadas to more substantial seafood and grilled dishes. Check out the rooftop terrace with a view of the plaza and church. It's open for breakfast, lunch and dinner.

Tropicana Bar & Grill (☎ 142-0907; Blvd Mijares near Coronado) Tropicana has a large, open sports bar, sidewalk seating and a rather imposing inside dining room (due to the skirted chairs and ornate silverware). No-nonsense Mexican-American main courses like baby-back ribs and a lobster-steak combination characterize the mid- to top-priced menu.

Almacenes Goncanseco (Mijares at Doblado) is a good-size supermarket. Almost next door, **Helados Bing** (Blvd Mijares near Doblado) has tasty ice cream, *paletas* (ice cream bars), milkshakes and other refreshing concoctions.

SOUTH OF THE PLAZA

Tequila (☎ 142-1155; Doblado near Hidalgo; mains US$12-20; ☾ dinner only) The main drawing card for this classy joint is the 90 varieties of its namesake swill. Aside from the excellent Mexican cuisine, the menu is Mediterranean with Mexican and Asian touches; dining takes place beneath ancient fruit trees on the breezy patio.

Morgan's Encore (☎ 142-4737; cnr Obregón & Morelos; mains US$12-20; ☾ 6-11pm) Set in a beautifully remodeled heritage building, Morgan's specializes in gourmet Mexican and international food. Follow the staircase to the open-air terrace upstairs for a fabulous setting.

French Riviera (☎ 147-7198; cnr Hidalgo & Doblado; snacks US$1-3) This French-owned bakery whips out superb croissants, baguettes and pastries fresh daily. The ham-and-cheese croissants are sublime. Espresso is served in the back.

Iguana Bar (☎ 142-0266; Blvd Mijares; mains US$6-10) This is the stomping ground of gregarious expats chowing down on moderately priced Mexican and US staples. After dark it morphs into a throbbing nightclub.

WEST OF THE PLAZA

Ándale Bistro (☎ 142-4114; Morelos near Obregón; mains US$11-18; ☾ Mon-Sat) Andalé does inspired pasta dishes in the US$10 range, as well as meat (filet mignon, veal medallions) and fish main courses topping out around US$17. Artsy decor and a secluded upstairs patio add to the relaxed ambience.

Jazmín's (☎ 142-1760; Morelos near Obregón; breakfast US$3.50-5, mains US$9-20) Jazmín's serves Mexican, seafood and vegetarian meals in a peaceful setting with excellent, unobtrusive service and, incongruously, a paperback book exchange. Breakfasts are excellent.

Xochimilco (☎ 142-5432; Zagoza at Morelos) Sophisticated decor and a small but distinctive mid-priced menu of specialties from around Mexico make this a great choice.

Fandango (☎ 142-2226; Obregón 19; mains US$13-18; ☾ noon-10pm Mon-Sat) Fandango does Pacific Rim cuisine in a casual setting accented by brightly pigmented murals.

Baan Thai (☎ 142-3344; Morelos near Obregón; mains US$10-20; ☾ noon-10pm Mon-Sat) For a change of pace, try the flavorful and spicy concoctions at this upscale Thai restaurant. Both the tom kha ghai soup (US$4.50) and the fish wrapped in banana leaf (US$13.50) are excellent.

Pan del Triunfo (Morelos at Obregón; ☾ 7am-9pm Mon-Sat, 7am-2pm Sun) Drop in for lip-smacking Mexican breads, cookies, pastries and donuts, all baked daily on the premises.

ELSEWHERE

For cheap eats, you'll have to remove yourself from the touristy area of downtown and venture west toward the Mercado Municipal, the highway and the bus terminal.

La Picazón (González Conseco; mains US$3-8) Next to the bus terminal, La Picazón is a super-friendly, outdoor eatery with possibly the town's best margaritas, US$1 tacos and excellent fish burgers. The affiliated **Pica Grill**, next door, specializes in *carne asada* (grilled beef) meals.

Municipal Market (Ibarra at Coronado; ☾ 6am-4pm) The numerous *loncherías* (lunch stalls) alongside San José's municipal market offer simple, inexpensive and good meals. A bowl of *menudo* (tripe and hominy stew) or a plate of enchiladas will set you back only about US$3.

Strolling west along Doblado will turn up several cheap taquerías, the two best being **Taquería Erica** (Doblado near México 1; tacos US$1-2; ☾ 10am-4am) and **Taquería El Fogón**

DINING WITH THE HANGMAN

It's hard to beat a name like El Ahorcado (the hangman or, literally, the hung man). And even with San José's blossoming culinary scene, it's hard to beat The Hangman's food. This is the one restaurant in San José you shouldn't miss. The best part: it's cheap.

West of the highway, in the Colonia Chamizal neighborhood, **El Ahorcado** (no ☎ ; cnr Pescadores & Marinos; ☾ 6pm-1am Tue-Sun) is easy to spot. Just look for the cowboy dangling in a hangman's noose. Why the morbidity? It all started in the town of Tamazula de Gordiano, in the mainland Mexican state of Jalisco, when owner Sergio Velasco opened up a taquería beneath a giant eucalyptus tree – apparently a tree with a history. During the Mexican Revolution, General Gordiano Guzmán, after whom the town is named, used the tree to string up counterrevolutionaries and outlaws by their undesired necks. So decades later, even though Sergio Velasco named his taquería 'Sergio's,' everyone who ate there said they were 'going to eat with the hangman.' And the name stuck.

In 1996 Velasco moved his family and the restaurant to San José and, as at the original, filled every inch of the patio with junk: ranch paraphernalia, carousel horses, devil heads, license plates, broken surf boards, dolls, masks, bumpers. His wife and four kids (and a handful of friends) all help run the place, carefully explaining (in English, if you wish) the menu's imaginative tacos and quesadillas, all stuffed with traditional ingredients you won't easily find around here.

At no more than US$1.40 a pop, choices include quesadillas made with *huitlacoche* (a black fungus that grows on corn), *flor de calabaza* (squash flower) and *nopal* (cactus paddles). The tacos are equally imaginative, and every table has 11 varieties of salsa with which to garnish your food. And the Velasco family is so friendly, you'll find yourself hanging around all night.

(Doblado near México 1; items US$1-3; ☾ 8am-2am). The latter serves a wider variety (including quesadillas, fajitas and grilled chicken) and has a pleasant, breezy patio.

Entertainment

San José is pretty *tranquilo* (mellow) after dark. If you're really looking to party, head over to Cabo San Lucas (p219). There are a few places in San José, however. **Tropicana Bar & Grill** and **Iguana Bar** are two restaurants whose bars have happy hours popular with gringos.

Sim Pecao (Zaragoza near Morelos) For cold beer, a mellow vibe and live jazz, *trova* (folk) and *rock en español* (Spanish-language rock), drop by this hip, laid-back bar. It's a good place to mingle with locals and tourists alike.

Cactus Jacks (Mijares near Benito Juárez) Cactus Jacks does karaoke Wednesday through Saturday nights and hosts the occasional live band. Pool tables and a large-screen TV (showing sporting events) help bring in the night owls.

Rodeo Mix (Zaragoza near Guerrero; cover men/women US$2.50/free) For a taste of the local scene, try this spot. Live *banda* (raucous brass band music) sets the eardrums throbbing Thursday and Saturday, and recorded dance pop pours over the dance floor Tuesday and Friday.

Shopping

As if in rhythm with the town's restaurants, shopping in San José has become excellent, with plenty of high-quality interior design items and crafts. You'll find ceramics, woven rugs, lamps, glassware, vases, small furniture, wall decorations and – never fear – plenty of cheap souvenirs. Following are some of the stores worth a visit.

Arte Diseño Decoración (☎ 142-2777; Zaragoza at Hidalgo) Excellent selection of Talavera (Puebla) ceramics; high-end silverware.

Antigua Los Cabos (☎ 146-9933; Blvd Mijares 5 at Obregón) Small selection of women's handbags, fine tequilas and gourmet sweets.

Copal (☎ 142-3070; Blvd Mijares near Doblado) Great for lacquered boxes from Olinalá, Guerrero; fine Yucatecan hammocks, Oaxacan wool blankets, fancy glassware and interesting Christmas decorations.

Veryka (☎ 142-0575; Blvd Mijares 6-B) Wide selection of crafts from all over Mexico.

La Mina (Blvd Mijares near Doblado) This is the better of three high-end silver shops on this stretch of Blvd Mijares. Most of the silver is from the mainland town of Taxco, known for its beautiful silver jewelry.

Don't leave Mexico without sampling some of its unique sweets. And after spending all your money on yourself, this stuff makes great gifts for the folks back home:

Fruitlandia (Blvd Mijares near Coronado) This long stall is the place for fresh traditional sweets such as ground, sweetened *semilla de calabaza* (squash seeds), *tamarindo con chile* (tamarind paste with chile), *pepitorias* (brittle sesame and peanut bars), candied limes, and *jamoncillo* (milk fudge) and *chilacayote* (candied squash). Be sure to try the bright green *biznaga* (candied cactus).

Dulcería Delicia (Doblado west of Márquez de León) Stocks piñatas and every kind of Mexican factory candy and kitschy party favor imaginable.

Getting There & Away

AIR

Serving both San José del Cabo and Cabo San Lucas, **Los Cabos International Airport** (☎ 142-2111, 146-5013) is 6½ miles (10.5km) north of town. **Mexicana** (☎ 142-1530) has an office at Plaza Los Cabos between the beachfront Paseo San José and Paseo Los Cabos. It's also at the airport along with the following airlines:

Alaska Airlines (☎ 146-5106, 146-5210) Flies to/from Los Angeles, San Diego, San Francisco, San Jose (California, USA), Portland and Seattle.

Continental Airlines (☎ 142-3840, 146-5040, 146-5050) Flies daily to/from Houston.

America West (☎ 142-2880, 146-5380) Flies twice daily to/from Phoenix.

American Airlines (☎ 142-2735, 146-5300) Flies daily to/from Los Angeles and Dallas/Fort Worth, and November 1 to April 31 to/from Chicago.

Aeroméxico (☎ 142-0341, 146-5097/98) Flies daily to/from San Diego. Serves mainland Mexican destinations, with international connections via Mexico City.

Aero California (☎ 142-0943, 413-3700) Flies daily to/from Los Angeles.

Mexicana (☎ 142-0606, 146-5001/02) Flies twice daily to/from Los Angeles and daily to Mexico City.

BUS

The **main bus terminal** (☎ 142-1100) is on González Conseco just east of the Transpeninsular. Autotransportes Aguila goes to La Paz (US$10) at least 14 times daily between 6am and 7:30pm; seven buses travel straight north *(via corta;* 3 hours) and the other seven go via Cabo San Lucas and Todos Santos *(via larga;* 3½ hours). The fare to

Todos Santos is US$6 (1½ hours). There are also daily buses to Loreto (US$32, 8-9 hours) and Tijuana (US$105, 24-27 hours).

Getting Around

San José is small enough to be pedestrian-friendly; even from the zona hotelera the walk into town takes only about half an hour. Outside town, buses, taxis or bicycles may be necessary.

TO/FROM THE AIRPORT

Taxis from the airport to downtown San José or the zona hotelera cost about US$50 and hold up to five people; they cost about US$75 to Cabo San Lucas. Heading the opposite direction, they're about US$30 from downtown San José to the airport and around US$40 from Cabo San Lucas. Top-end hotels often arrange transportation for their guests.

Much cheaper are the shuttle services at the airport, which charge US$8 to US$11 to San José and about US$14 to Cabo San Lucas.

You can take a bus from the airport into town, but it entails a 20- to 30-minute walk past the car rental agencies and out the airport access road to the Transpeninsular. There you can flag a bus to either San José (US$0.50) or Cabo San Lucas (US$1.75). From downtown San José, buses leave the terminal on González Conseco to the airport junction on the Transpeninsular.

BUS

Aguila buses go from San José to Cabo San Lucas (US$1.50, 30 minutes), but far more frequent are the local buses departing from the Transpeninsular (México 1) just west of downtown; the price is the same (also see p222). These will also drop you anywhere along the Corridor.

CAR & TAXI

A taxi anywhere in town costs US$3 to US$5, and a ride to Cabo San Lucas costs about US$30.

All major car rental agencies have offices at the airport; some also have branches downtown. The car rental scene on the Southern Cape is more competitive than elsewhere on the peninsula, and some good deals with unlimited mileage are available. Agencies include the following:

Advantage (☎ 142-3990, cnr Hidalgo & Zaragoza; ☎ 146-0004 airport)
Alamo (☎ 146-0626, Transpeninsular)
Avis (☎ 142-1180 airport)
Dollar (☎ 142-0100, Transpeninsular; ☎ 146-5060 airport)
Hertz (☎ 146-5088 airport)
National (☎ 142-3020, Best Western Hotel Posada Real; ☎ 146-5020/22 airport)
Thrifty (☎ 142-2380, Transpeninsular s/n; ☎ 142-3656, cnr Blvd Mijares & Benito Juárez; ☎ 146-5030 airport)

AROUND SAN JOSÉ DEL CABO

Drive east on Benito Juárez, and in 15 minutes you'll hit the village of **Pueblo La Playa**, also known as La Playita. Here you'll find delicious food, cold beer and great atmosphere at friendly **Buzzard's Bar** (mains US$5-10; ◷ 8am-8:30pm Mon-Sat, 9am-2pm Sun); it's part of La Fonda del Mar (p195). There are several other good places to stay, but at the time this book went to press, Pueblo La Playa was much less tranquil than it was in the past.

A massive 2000-acre (800-hectare) resort community called **Puerto Los Cabos** (www.puertoloscabos.com) is underway here, which will include a 535-slip marina, an ecopark, two new 18-hole golf courses, luxury hotels, condominiums and several gated subdivisions with deluxe vacation homes. The development will essentially engulf the once tiny fishing village of Pueblo La Playa and transform the surrounding coastline for good. The marina is slated to open in 2005, but predicting the completion of a resort in Mexico (where hurricanes and changing presidencies can drop anchor on progress in a single day) is palm-reading at best. Until the entire development is complete, construction of the area will detract significantly from its allure. Drive out and check it out, but think twice about staying out here before talking to the hotel owners or investigating for yourself.

There has been plenty of controversy over the development because of its environmental impact on the area and because numerous town residents were forced to relocate. Because the area is changing rapidly and detours come and go as construction progresses, you'll likely make a wrong turn here or there while exploring.

Pueblo La Playa also marks the southern terminus of the spectacular **Eastern Cape Road** (p177), a graded dirt road leading northeast toward Bahía Los Frailes, Cabo Pulmo and La Ribera. This is a spectacular drive and possible for nearly all vehicles, except after heavy storms. Most vehicles can make it all the way to Buena Vista, experiencing, at worst, serious tooth-chatter from the washboard. The worst part of the road is the stretch south of Bahía Los Frailes.

Leaving Pueblo La Playa, the road turns inland to skirt the beachfront development of **Laguna Hills**, (which successfully closed this stretch of the coastal road to the public). After Laguna Hills the road hits the coast again, and you'll pass **Punta Gorda** and the increasingly populated **Santa Cruz de los Zacatitos**, the site of the original construction assault on this part of the East Cape. Most of the homes here are largely self-sufficient, producing their own solar energy and obtaining water through desalination. From here on up the scenery is astounding, and you'll find yourself stopping to snap photos at nearly every turn. About 6 miles (10km) off Zacatitos are the famous **Gorda Banks**, two seamounts that are prime fishing grounds for marlin and other big-game fish; they are also popular with divers.

Back on land, a few miles farther east is **Playa Tortuga**, named for the turtles who nest here, and then **San Luis**, another new vacation-home hotspot. Another 8 miles (13km) farther is the turnoff to the Palo Escopeta Road back to the Transpeninsular. The turnoff will give you the short loop back to San José. Otherwise you can take the Eastern Cape Road all the way through Cabo Pulmo and La Ribera where it rejoins the Transpeninsular at Buena Vista.

LOS CABOS CORRIDOR

☎ 624
The 18-mile (29km) stretch of the Transpeninsular between San José del Cabo and Cabo San Lucas is commonly referred to as 'The Corridor.' This state-of-the-art, divided four-lane highway parallels the most beautiful stretch of coast in the Los Cabos area. It's a visual feast of secluded coves, jutting points, generous sandy beaches, teeming tidal pools, rolling desertscape and drop-dead-gorgeous ocean views.

LOS CABOS

Naturally it's also the arena for the area's most aggressive developers, who have snapped up the choice beachfront properties to build sprawling resorts and condo complexes. Practically all of them are of the sophisticated and posh variety, intended to appeal to upscale (read: filthy rich) travelers. Interspersed between the hotels are world-class golf courses – seven at last count – with more in the planning stages. Most locals seem to welcome all this expansion, primarily for its job- and income-creating potential. Meanwhile, old-time travelers lament the area's loss of charm and natural beauty. Still, whether you stay on the Corridor or not, exploring its beaches is one of the highlights of Los Cabos.

Sights & Activities
BEACHES

All along the Transpeninsular you'll see blue beach-access signs sporting pictographs of the types of activities available (snorkeling, fishing, diving, surfing, etc) at the particular beach. Parking is along the highway or in parking lots. If you're using the bus, ask the driver to drop you off at your beach of choice. By law, all Mexican beaches are open to the public, but access from the highway is becoming increasingly restricted because of developments. If you look like a tourist, you'll have no problem walking through the lobbies of the bigger resorts, strolling past the pool area and out to the beach.

The Corridor beach closest to San José is **Playa Costa Azul**, at Km 28, also known as **Zipper's Beach**, which is quite popular with surfers. Access is through Zipper's Bar & Grill (p204). Surfers also hang out at the much smaller adjacent **Playa Acapulquito**, accessible at Km 28 just before the lookout. Cabo Surf Hotel (p202) rents surfboards for US$15/30 per hour/day. Also see p193 for more on surfing.

Next up is **Playa Palmilla**, at Km 27, a long crescent of fine sand popular with swimmers and water-sports enthusiasts. Facilities include a dive shop, equipment concession and restaurant.

The Hotel Meliá Cabo Real, at Km 19.5, sits on a lovely cove known as **Playa Cabo Real**, which is protected by a breakwater, making it safe for swimming and water sports. The hotel also provides access to **Playa La Concha**, a beach club (admission is charged). East of here is **Playa Bledito**, sought out by beachcombers.

One of the largest open stretches of beach is at **Playa El Tule**, at Km 15, reached through the arroyo at Puente Los Tules. Surfers come here, as do the occasional beach campers. There are zero facilities.

Next up is **Playa Chileno** at Km 14, which offers good swimming and snorkeling and fresh-water showers. Cabo Acuadeportes rents kayaks, snorkeling and dive equipment (see Diving & Snorkeling). The beach is easily accessible from the road and just a short walk from a large parking lot. On weekends it fills up with local families.

Perhaps the nicest Corridor beach is **Playa Santa María** on its namesake **Bahía Santa María**, a sheltered cove teeming with underwater creatures. Numerous snorkeling excursions from San José and Cabo San Lucas come here, so waters may occasionally get crowded. Snorkeling gear and beach chairs are available for rent, but there's no infrastructure otherwise. It's reached via a sandy road near Km 12 and there's a guarded parking lot (free).

Access to **Playa Las Viudas**, also known as Dolphin Beach, is via a sandy road next to the Hotel Twin Dolphin turnoff at Km 12. Depending on road conditions, it may be advisable to walk the quarter-mile (400m) to the beach, which is secluded and good for swimming.

Playa Barco Varado now fronts the mega-sized Cabo del Sol development and is better for diving and snorkeling than for swimming. Access is through the Cabo del Sol entrance at Km 10. The closest surf beach to Cabo San Lucas is **Playa Cabo Bello**, right below the Da Giorgio restaurant (p204) and reached via the Misones del Cabo turnoff at Km 5.

DIVING & SNORKELING

The best snorkeling along the Los Cabos Corridor is at Playa Santa María. From Playa Chileno, **Cabo Acuadeportes** (☎ 143-0117; www.cabowatersports.com) runs two-hour snorkeling trips for US$25 – though you can do much the same on your own by going right to the cove. Its dive excursions cost US$43/71 for one/two tanks and take you to various dive sites. Other dive operators based in Cabo San Lucas offer trips to sites off the Corridor and elsewhere.

LOS CABOS CORRIDOR

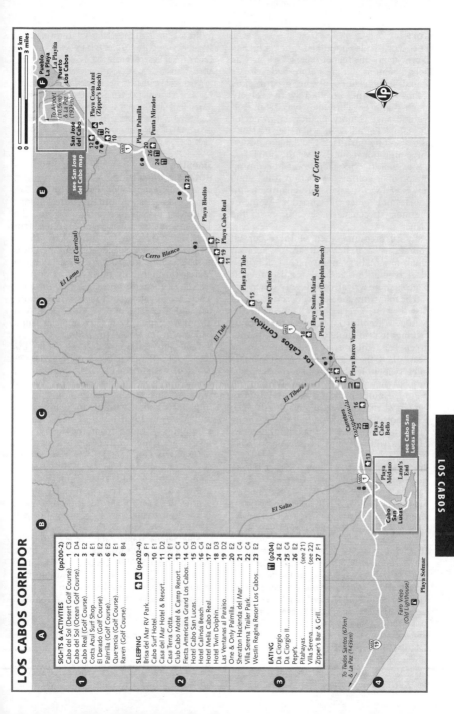

SIGHTS & ACTIVITIES (pp200-2)
Cabo del Sol (Desert Golf Course)	1 C3
Cabo del Sol (Ocean Golf Course)	2 D4
Cabo Real (Golf Course)	3 E2
Costa Azul Surf Shop	4 E1
El Dorado (Golf Course)	5 E2
Palmilla (Golf Course)	6 E2
Que'encia (Golf Course)	7 E1
Raven (Golf Course)	8 B4

SLEEPING (pp202-4)
Brisa del Mar RV Park	9 F1
Cabo Surf Hotel	10 E1
Casa del Mar Hotel & Resort	11 D2
Casa Terra Cotta	12 E1
Club Cabo Motel & Camp Resort	13 C4
Fiesta Americana Grand Los Cabos	14 C4
Hotel Cabo San Lucas	15 D3
Hotel Calinda Beach	16 C4
Hotel Meliá Cabo Real	17 D3
Hotel Twin Dolphin	18 D3
Las Ventanas al Paraíso	19 D2
One & Only Palmilla	20 E1
Sheraton Hacienda del Mar	21 C4
Villa Serena Trailer Park	22 C4
Westin Regina Resort Los Cabos	23 E2

EATING (p204)
Da Giorgio	24 E2
Da Giorgio II	25 C4
Pepe's	26 E2
Pitahayas	(see 21)
Villa Serena	(see 22)
Zipper's Bar & Grill	27 F1

Playa Costa Azul (Zipper's Beach)
Playa Palmilla
Punta Mirador
Playa Bledito
Playa Cabo Real
Playa El Tule
Playa Chileno
Playa Santa María
Playa Las Viudas (Dolphin Beach)
Playa Barco Varado
Playa Cabo Bello
Playa Médano
Land's End

San José del Cabo
see San José del Cabo map

Cabo San Lucas
see Cabo San Lucas map

Sea of Cortez

Los Cabos Corridor

Carretera Transpeninsular

El Lomo (El Currizal)
Cerro Blanco
El Tule
El Tibutú
El Salto
Faro Viejo (Old Lighthouse)
Playa Solmar

To Airport (10.5km) & La Paz (193km)

Pueblo La Playa
Puerto Los Cabos
La Plavita

To Todos Santos (67km) & La Paz (143km)

LOS CABOS

5 km
3 miles

GOLF

The worldwide popularity of golf has skyrocketed in recent years, so it was only a matter of time before a developer would have visions of the pristine Los Cabos coastline covered with velvety green blankets. This man was Don Koll from Orange County, California, owner of the Hotel Palmilla. So when he, in 1990, asked golfing guru Jack Nicklaus to design three nine-hole courses near the hotel, Los Cabos took the first step toward becoming the premier golfing destination it is today: no fewer than six signature championship courses now grace the Corridor – some of the most spectacularly set courses on the planet.

By all accounts, each of these coastal courses is a golfer's dream – and an environmentalist's nightmare – although local regulations at least require all golf courses to be irrigated with gray water.

The following courses are described from east to west. Green fees change with the season, with winter rates (generally, mid-October to mid-June) the highest. Summer green fees (the rest of the year) can be nearly half the winter rate. Most courses offer 'twilight fees' (more like 'roaster fees') for play after anytime between 10:30am and noon in summer and 1:30pm and 3pm in winter, when it can be brutally hot. All green fees quoted here include golf cart, driving range, bottled water and tax. Renting a set of clubs will set you back another US$45 or US$50.

Querencia (private course) Tom Fazio-designed; 18 holes, plus nine-hole short course; members only.

Palmilla (One & Only Palmilla; ☎ 144-5250; www.palmillaresort.com; US$214/187) Jack Nicklaus signature course; 27 holes, 6900 yards, par 72. Cabo's first signature course, with 27 holes between the Arroyo nine, Mountain nine and Ocean nine.

El Dorado (☎ 144-5450/51; www.caboreal.com; green fees winter/summer US$242/169) Jack Nicklaus signature course; 18 holes, 7050 yards, par 72. Six oceanfront holes.

Cabo Real (☎ 144-0040; www.caboreal.com; green fees winter/summer US$276/190) Robert Trent Jones signature course; 18 holes, 6988 yards, par 72. Front nine considered toughest in Los Cabos. Host of two Senior Slams. Three oceanfront holes.

Cabo del Sol Ocean Course (☎ 145-8200; www.cabodelsol.com; green fees winter/summer US$250/158) Jack Nicklaus signature course; 18 holes, 7103 yards, par 72. Nearly two miles of oceanfront course and often referred to as the 'Mexican Pebble Beach.' Listed by *Golf Magazine* as one of top 100 courses in the world.

Cabo del Sol Desert Course (☎ 145-8200; www.cabodelsol.com; green fees winter/summer US$218/126) Tom Weiskopf signature course; 18 holes, 7097 yards, par 72. Inland course with views of Sea of Cortez at every hole.

Raven Golf Club (Country Club Cabo San Lucas; ☎ 143-4653; www.golfincabo.com; green fees winter/summer US$176/121) Roy Dye signature course; 18 holes, 7220 yards, par 72.

Sleeping

HOTELS & CAMPING

Brisa del Mar Trailer Park (☎ 142-3999; brisarv@hotmail.com) About 2 miles (3km) southwest of San José, at Km 28.5 on the Transpeninsular, Brisa del Mar has tent sites for US$37 on the beach and US$30 off the beach. RV spaces with full hookups cost US$37/27 on/off the beach. From March through November, prices drop to US$22/12 for tents and US$30/20 for RVs. There are hot showers, toilets, a restaurant/bar and a guest laundry. Also beachfront but more expensive are its small cabañas, which rent for US$60 to US$90.

Cabo Surf Hotel (☎ 142-2666, in the USA ☎ 858-964-5117; www.cabosurfhotel; r US$180-670; P ⊠ ⊠) Right on Playa Acapulquito, at Km 28, this is a deluxe surfers' favorite with an oceanview restaurant and 16 impressive rooms with ocean-facing patios and Mexican furnishings. The waves are stumbling distance from the lobby, and boards are rented at the shop below.

Casa Terra Cotta (☎ 142-4250; www.terracottamex.com; casitas US$85-125 Dec-Apr, US$65-90 May-Nov) Clinging to a hillside near Zipper's Beach at Km 28.5 on the Transpeninsular, this is a snug B&B set in a tropical garden. Each of the four casitas has a private patio with hammock and view of the Sea of Cortez.

Villa Serena Trailer Park (☎ 143-0509, in the USA ☎ 800-932-5599; www.grupobahia.com; site US$21; ⊠) At Km 7.5, Villa Serena has 54 sunny sites with full hookups and a great blufftop restaurant (p204). Facilities include a pool, Jacuzzi, laundry, showers and bathrooms.

RESORTS

All the resorts on the Corridor fall into the five-star luxury category with amenities and prices to match. Breathtaking bay views, gorgeous landscaping and top-rated service are *de rigueur*, as are facilities like swimming pool(s) with swim-up bars, lighted tennis courts, multiple restaurants and bars, fitness centers and room service.

Rooms usually have ocean views and private terraces, minibars, TVs, air-con, direct phones, in-room safes and other amenities. Rarely do they cost less than US$200 per night. Some hotels enforce minimum stays (especially around holidays and on weekends) of three or more nights.

All resorts can arrange for a wide range of activities from sportfishing to horseback riding to diving. Size, location and architecture are the main elements that set properties apart. Even if you have no intention of staying here, drop in for a drink, meal and sweeping ocean views.

The following rates are all per night and include 10% sales tax, 2% lodging tax and the resort hotels' compulsory 15% service charge. The Corridor's resorts include those here, listed from east to west.

One & Only Palmilla (Hotel Palmilla Resort; ☎ 146-7000, in the ☎ USA 800-637-2226, 866-829-2977; www.palmillaresort.com; Transpeninsular Km 7.5; d US$595-1080; P ⊠ ⊠ ⊠) Built in 1956 by Rod Rodríguez, son of a former Mexican president, this is the Corridor's original Hollywood hideaway. It's on Playa Palmilla and includes a golf course. There's a three-night minimum on weekends.

Westin Regina Resort Los Cabos (☎ 142-9000, in the USA ☎ 888-625-5144; relos@westin.com; Transpeninsular Km 22.5; d US$181-2231; P ⊠ ⊠ ⊠) This mega-resort boasts daring, modern architecture and landscaping designed to complement the desert colors and surroundings. You can literally fall out of the swimming pool into the sand; it's proximity to the beach makes it one of the hotel's most alluring features. And the beach itself is to die for.

Hotel Melía Cabo Real (☎ 144-0000, in the USA ☎ 800-336 3542; www.solmelia.com; Transpeninsular Km 19.5; d US$270-795; P ⊠ ⊠ ⊠) At Playa Bledito, this 302-room resort is easily recognized by its glass and marble pyramid lobby. The resort sits on a lovely, breakwater-protected cove next to the Cabo Real golf course.

Las Ventanas al Paraíso (☎ 144-0300, in the USA ☎ 888-525-0483; www.lasventanas.com; Transpeninsular Km 19.5; d US$730-5080; P ⊠ ⊠ ⊠) In a class by itself, the exclusive Ventanas oozes Zen-like serenity, and charms with deceptively

simple landscaping and architecture. A luxurious spa and golf course are adjacent. A minimum stay of four or seven days is required in January, February and around most holidays. If you can afford to stay here, please participate in the adopt-an-author program by contacting the Lonely Planet author at the front of this book.

Casa del Mar Hotel & Resort (☎ 144-0030, in the USA ☎ 888-227-9621; www.casadelmarmexico.com; Transpeninsular Km 19.5; d US$502-787; P ⊠ ⊠ ⊠) Comparatively intimate (24 rooms and 36 suites), the Casa del Mar, like the Melía, is part of the Cabo Real development that also includes the Ventanas, a condo complex and a golf course. And holy hot-tubs, Batman, you should see the spa!

Hotel Cabo San Lucas (☎ 144-0014/17/18, in the USA ☎ 800-733-2226; cabotravel@earthlink.net; Transpeninsular Km 14; d US$318-838; P ⊠ ⊠ ⊠) Set on a bluff amid 2500 acres (1000 hectares) of luxuriant tropical gardens at Playa Chileno, this is another of the Corridor's old-timers, dating to 1962.

Hotel Twin Dolphin (☎ 145-8190, in the USA ☎ 800-421-8925; www.twindolphin.com; Transpeninsular Km 12; d US$235-545; P ⊠ ⊠ ⊠) Also an original Corridor resort, the Twin Dolphin is built on a more intimate scale (50 rooms and suites) at Playa Las Viudas. Assets include a jogging trail and free shuttle to Cabo. Another of its wildcards is its proximity to Playa Santa María, one of the most beautiful beaches on the Corridor.

Fiesta Americana Grand Los Cabos (☎ 145-6200, in the USA ☎ 800-343-7821; www.fiestamericana.com; Transpeninsular Km 10.3; d US$310-4562; P ⊠ ⊠ ⊠) Neighboring the Hacienda del Mar (next), the colorful Fiesta Americana is part of a Mexican chain and has 330 rooms, three restaurants, a beautiful pool area and an expansive beach.

Sheraton Hacienda del Mar (☎ 145-8000, in the USA ☎ 888-672-7137; www.sheratonhaciendadelmar.com; Transpeninsular Km 10; d US$304-2856; P ⊠ ⊠ ⊠) Part of the Cabo del Sol development, which also encompasses two golf courses, the all-suites Hacienda del Mar is distinguished by its dramatic, riverlike pool and original colonial artworks.

Hotel Calinda Beach (☎ 145-8044, in the USA ☎ 877-441-9944; www.hotelescalinda.com.mx; Transpeninsular Km 6.5; d US$125-198; P ⊠ ⊠ ⊠) The closest resort to Cabo San Lucas, the cliffside Calinda Beach has some of the best views of Land's End. It also has the best Corridor rates, especially considering they include three meals per day. Keep yourself busy in three swimming pools, two tennis courts, three bars, Jacuzzis and more.

Eating

Eating along the Corridor takes place mostly at the resort hotels, where you should figure on spending at least US$40 per person for a full meal, including wine.

Pitahayas (☎ 145-8010; Sheraton Hacienda del Mar; ♥ 5:30-10pm) Pitahayas, one of the most notable resort restaurants, specializes in Pacific Rim cuisine, including vegetarian selections. The dining is set beneath a giant palapa with fabulous ocean views.

Notable eateries outside the resorts include the following.

Zipper's Bar & Grill (Transpeninsular Km 28, Zipper's Beach; mains US$7-15) Zipper's caters to surfers (meaning big portions of pub grub) and specializes in mesquite-grilled beef and classic rock. The hamburgers and fish and chips are both excellent, but it hurts every time 'Free Bird' rolls around (again) on the stereo.

Pepe's (☎ 144-5040; Transpeninsular Km 7; mains US$10-20) Almost alongside Hotel Palmilla, Pepe's is deservedly popular for its delicious Mexican seafood, casual setting and views over Palmilla beach.

Da Giorgio (☎ 142-1988; Transpeninsular Km 25.5) West of the Palmilla, Da Giorgio offers various Italian-style seafood dishes, pizza and pasta at mid- to top-range prices. There's also another branch, **Da Giorgio II** (☎ 145-8160), at the Misiones del Cabo development at Km 5.5. Its dramatic, terraced clifftop setting makes it one of the best Corridor places to watch the sun set over Land's End.

Villa Serena (☎ 145-8244; Transpeninsular Km 7.5; mains US$9-26) Popular both for its reasonable prices and fabulous views, Villa Serena is known for its daily lobster specials, surf-and-turf plates and wonderful Sunday paella feasts.

Getting There & Around

Public buses running between San José and Cabo San Lucas will drop you anywhere along the Corridor for US$1.50. Taxis from either town cost US$8 to US$30, depending on where you want to go.

CABO SAN LUCAS

☎ 624 / pop 90,000

Welcome to Land's End. If you drove down the peninsula, you've hit the end of the road (and after all that desolation, you're in for some serious culture shock). If you're flying in, it's but the beginning. From downtown Cabo San Lucas you can hop in a rental car and beat it out the dirt roads into spectacular desert scenery, wee ranch villages or empty beach paradises all in less than an hour. Gary Morton, owner of Cabo Inn, puts it like this: 'I'll have guests in town for a few days, and then they rent a car to get out of Cabo. They come back all wild-eyed and shaking, and when I ask them where they went, they say, "I don't know. But it was *amazing!*"'

With its vast array of excellent restaurants, bars that stay open practically 'round the clock, night clubs, strip joints, stunning beaches, luxury hotels and activities ranging from parasailing to banana boating, it's easy to whip through four days in Cabo without leaving the city limits. But do it. Rent a car, read the 'Cabo San Lucas In...' box (p207), flip through the Southern Baja chapter and blow out of town for the day. When you return to Cabo, those icy margaritas, four-course meals and sunset cruises will be all the more enjoyable.

Orientation

At the southernmost tip of the Baja peninsula, Cabo San Lucas is 1059 miles (1694km) from Tijuana and, via México 1, 137 miles (221km) from La Paz; via México 19, it's 95 miles (153km) from La Paz. After splitting south of La Paz, the paved Transpeninsular and the Southern Cape Highway (México 19) rejoin at Cabo, making a fine driving or bicycle circuit. The Transpeninsular is also called 'Carretera a San José del Cabo,' whereas México 19 is referred to as 'Carretera a Todos Santos.' A bypass road skirting Cabo's northeastern edge connects the two.

The town's main drag, Blvd Lázaro Cárdenas, is essentially a continuation of the Transpeninsular. Past the intersection with Zaragoza, it peters out into a minor shopping street while most of the action continues along Blvd Marina, culminating at Land's End. Tourist-oriented shops,

CABO SAN LUCAS

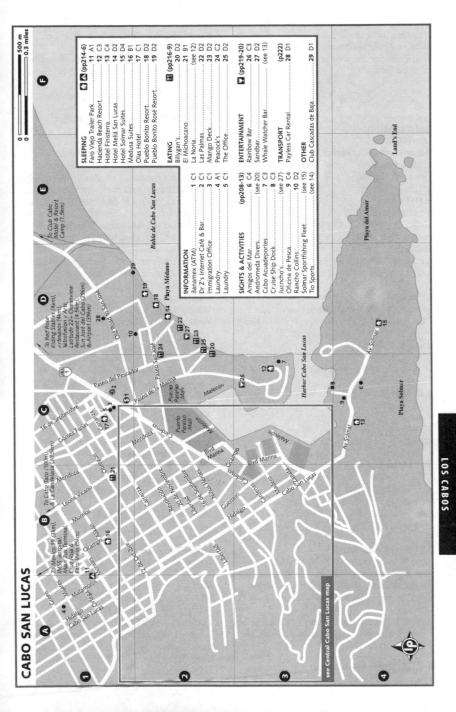

LOS CABOS

SLEEPING	🏠🛏 (pp214-6)
Faro Viejo Trailer Park	11 A1
Hacienda Beach Resort	12 C3
Hotel Finisterra	13 C4
Hotel Meliá San Lucas	14 D2
Hotel Solmar Suites	15 D4
Medusa Suites	16 B1
Olas Hotel	17 C1
Pueblo Bonito Resort	18 D2
Pueblo Bonito Rosé Resort	19 D2

EATING	🍴 (pp216-9)
Billygan's	20 D2
El Michoacano	21 B1
La Noria	22 D2
Las Palmas	23 D2
Mango Deck	24 C2
Peacock's	25 D2
The Office	(see 12)

ENTERTAINMENT	🎭 (pp219-20)
Rainbow Bar	26 C3
Sandbar	27 D2
Whale Watcher Bar	(see 13)

TRANSPORT	(p222)
Payless Car Rental	28 D1

OTHER	
Club Cascadas de Baja	29 D1

INFORMATION	
Banamex (ATM)	1 C1
Dr Z's Internet Café & Bar	2 C1
Immigration Office	3 C1
Laundry	4 A1
Laundry	5 C1

SIGHTS & ACTIVITIES	(pp208-13)
Amigos del Mar	6 C4
Andromeda Divers	(see 20)
Cabo Acuadeportes	7 C3
Cruise Ship Dock	8 C3
Juancho's	(see 27)
Oficina de Pesca	9 C4
Rancho Collins	10 D2
Solmar Sportfishing Fleet	(see 15)
Tio Sports	(see 14)

0 ——— 500 m
0 ——— 0.3 miles

To Red Rose
Riding Stables (4km),
Tesoros (4km),
Vitrofusion / Arte,
Latitude 22+ Oceanview
Restaurant (4.5km),
San José del Cabo (29km)
& Airport (39km)

To Club Cabo
Hotel & Resort
Camp (1.5km)

Bahía de Cabo San Lucas

Playa Médano

Harbor Cabo San Lucas

Playa del Amor

Land's End

Playa Solmar

To México 19 (3km),
IMSS Hospital,
Main Bus Terminal,
Cruz Roja &
Faro Falso (6km)

To Cabo Taco (100m)
& La Candelaria (30.5km)

see Central Cabo San Lucas map

restaurants, bars, a post office, police and other infrastructure are all along this road. The commercial area just north of here has a more local flair.

Cabo does not use street numbers, so addresses always specify the nearest cross streets.

Information

BOOKSTORES

Libros Libros Books Books (Map p210-11; ☎ 143-3172; Blvd Marina s/n) Good selection of English-language novels and magazines.

EMERGENCY

Fire (☎ 068, 142-3577)
Police (Map pp210-11; ☎ 060 emergency, 143-3977 nonemergency; cnr Old Road to San José and Cárdenas) Next to the McDonald's.
Cruz Roja (Red Cross; Map p205; ☎ 066 ambulance, 143-3300; México 19, Km 121)

IMMIGRATION

Immigration office (Map p205; Servicios Migratorios; ☎ 143-0135; cnr Cárdenas & Farías; ☽ 9am-2pm Mon-Fri)

INTERNET ACCESS

Using the Internet in San Lucas can put a serious dent in the wallet if you are not careful.

Café Cabo Mail (Map pp210-11; cnr Cardenas & Zaragoza, Plaza Arámburo; US$6/hr) Air-conditioned, big booths, fast computers.
The Corner (Map pp210-11; cnr Cárdenas & Matamoros; US$7/hr; ☽ 7am-midnight) Full bar, great for drinking while pecking.
Dr Z's Internet Café & Bar (Map p205; Cárdenas near 16 de Septiembre; US$4/hr; ☽ 8am-8pm Mon-Sat) Full bar, plus coffee and great atmosphere.
Internet Express (Map pp210-11; Cárdenas near Matamoros; US$2.50/hr; ☽ 10am-10pm Mon-Fri, 10am-9pm Sat & Sun) Cheap.

INTERNET RESOURCES

Cabo Bob's (www.cabobob.com) Great site, for Cabo Bob's humor as much as for his trove of information.
Los Cabos Guide (www.loscabosguide.com) Hands down, the most comprehensive guide to Los Cabos on the Internet.
Los Cabos Tourism Board (www.visitcabo.com) Tidbits on everything from hotels and restaurants to events and activities.

LAUNDRY

Self-service *lavanderías* (laundries) are

sprinkled throughout town. Locations include the following:
(Map p205) Near the Olas Hotel on Revolución and Farías
(Map pp210-11) On Mendoza between Revolución and 16 de Septiembre
(Map pp210-11) In the Hotel Santa Fe, on Zaragoza at Obregón
(Map p205) On Matamoros just north of Mijares

MEDIA

The following local publications – wholly or partly in English – contain plenty of useful information to help you navigate around town. Look for them in restaurants, bars, hotel lobbies and shops. Almost all are free.

Baja Sun – Los Cabos Monthly all-English edition catering mostly to residents but still featuring the occasional useful article.
Destino: Los Cabos Quarterly, partly bilingual paper without much advertising and with good articles about lesser-known area attractions as well as hotel and restaurant profiles. Not widely available.
Gringo Gazette (www.gringogazette.com) English-language biweekly publication with an offbeat but surprisingly informative editorial approach, despite the preponderance of real estate–related articles. Geared toward both the visitor and resident.
Los Cabos Magazine Published twice yearly, the most useful and informative of the local publications, packed with hotel and restaurant reviews, details about beaches, golfing and other activities, plus several good maps. Cover price of US$4.95 but may also be available some places for free.
Los Cabos News Mostly Spanish biweekly, with some articles in English, covering general and tourism-related news in the Los Cabos area.

MEDICAL SERVICES

Cruz Roja (Red Cross; Map p205; ☎ 143-3300) Located at Km 121, México 19.
IMSS Hospital (Map p205; ☎ 143-1194 emergency, 143-1589 nonemergency) Just north of the Pemex station on México 19.
Farmacia Arámburo (Map pp210-11; Cárdenas near Ocampo) Well-stocked pharmacy.

MONEY

US dollars are widely accepted at stores, restaurants and hotels, but the exchange rate may not be favorable. Banks with 24-hour ATMs and exchange services (usually until 1 pm only) include:

Banca Serfin (Map pp210-11; Plaza Arámburo; Cárdenas near Zaragoza)
Banamex (Map p205; Cárdenas & Paseo de la Marina)

CABO SAN LUCAS IN...

Two Days
Start off the morning by renting snorkel gear and taking a water taxi to **Playa del Amor** (p208) for some beach and underwater fun. Return for lunch at **Las Palmas** (p218) on **Playa Médano** (p208) to maximize beach time. Take a sunset pirate cruise aboard the 19th-century **Sunderland** (p213). Return to land for a late dinner at **Mi Casa** (p217) and get wild with the tourists at **El Squid Roe** (p219). On your second day rent a car and drive to **Cabo Pulmo** (p180), stopping in **Pueblo La Playa** (p199) for a massive breakfast burrito at **Buzzard's Bar** (p199). Snorkel at Cabo Pulmo, have lunch at **Nancy's** (p181) and, on your way back to Cabo San Lucas, stop at **El Ahorcado** (p197) in San José del Cabo for dinner. After this, you'll surely sleep the whole flight home.

Four Days
Follow the two-day plan but hang on to your rental car so you can drive to **La Candelaria** (p221) for traditional ceramics and a taste of ranch life. Go from *ranchos* to riches by dining at fabulous **Sancho Panza** (p218) upon your return to Cabo San Lucas. On day four, head to San José del Cabo in the morning for Los Cabos' best **shopping** (p197); hit the **Mercado Municipal** (p196) for local action and a cheap lunch. Spend the afternoon on **Playa Santa María** (p200) and return to Cabo for more nighttime merrymaking.

One Week
To the four-day plan add an overnight trip to historic **Todos Santos** (p182) or to vibrant **La Paz** (p161) for a spectacular sea kayaking trip to **Isla Espíritu Santo** (p167).

Banco Santander (Map pp210-11; Cárdenas at Av Cabo San Lucas)

Cambios such as **Baja Money Exchange** (Map pp210-11; Blvd Marina near Plaza Las Glorias) have longer hours but poorer exchange rates, not to mention commission fees. **American Express** (Map pp210-11; ☎ 143-5766; Morelos near Cárdenas) cashes its own traveler's checks for free and can arrange instant international cash transfers, as can **Telecomm/Western Union** (Map p210-11; cnr Cárdenas & Old Road to San José), by the post office.

POST
Mail Boxes Etc (Map pp210-11; ☎ 143-3032; Plaza Bonita, Local 44-E)
Post office (Map pp210-11; Cárdenas near 16 de Septiembre; ☒ 8am-4pm Mon-Fri, 9am-noon Sat)

TELEPHONE & FAX
Telmex/Ladatel pay phones are located on nearly every street corner in Cabo. You can send faxes from the Telecomm office, Mail Boxes Etc (see above) and most Internet cafes.

TOURIST INFORMATION
Cabo San Lucas does not have an official tourist office, but there are several free publications with more or less useful information available around town.

Signs saying 'Tourist Information' are usually time-share booths. If you can ignore the aggressive come-ons, ask for free maps and other information and then make your getaway. Your best bet for information is the staff at your hotel. The nearest official tourist office is in San José del Cabo (p192), but it's rarely worth trekking all the way over for general questions.

TRAVEL AGENCIES
Los Delfines (Map pp210-11; ☎ 143-1396, 143-3096; Morelos at 16 de Septiembre) Well-established travel agency with an English-speaking staff.
American Express (see Money) Full-service travel agency.

Dangers & Annoyances
A major annoyance is the gauntlet of time-share salespeople lined up along Blvd Marina like buzzards on a fence. They will try to entice you with free meals, drinks or rounds of golf if you attend a 'short' tour and presentation, which usually ends up taking up half of your vacation day. Because nearly their entire income comes from sales commissions, they will put serious pressure on you to take advantage of the 'unique

opportunity' offered by buying into their properties. The best advice is, of course, to ignore them, but this may be hard to do.

If you're not used to Mexican resort beaches, the many wandering beach vendors – often poor immigrants from mainland Mexico – can be abrasive. They are especially prevalent along Playa Médano but also work more remote Corridor beaches like Playa Chileno and Playa Santa María. A simple 'no gracias' will usually send them on their way, but it can get to you after the 30th time. However, if you *are* inclined to buy something, you'll probably pay less than in stores.

Sights

Built into the solitary hill in downtown Cabo, the **Casa de la Cultura** (Map pp210-11; entrance on Niños Héroes) has a theatre, a small park and a *mirador* (lookout point). The mirador is surrounded by landscaped gardens and offers a view of all of Cabo. It is a peaceful retreat from the craziness of downtown.

BEACHES

Cabo San Lucas has three main beaches. The most popular is **Playa Médano** (Dune Beach; Map p205), which runs northeast for about 2 miles (3km) from the Hacienda Beach Hotel. Calm waters make it ideal for swimming, although you'll need to watch out for jet skis. Bars and restaurants abound, as do ambulant souvenir vendors. It's also action central for all water sports. If you want greater peace and quiet, head to the stretch past the Club Cascadas de Baja development.

Flanked by towering rocks, quiet **Playa del Amor** (Lover's Beach; Map p205) – with access to both the Pacific and the bay waters – is by far Cabo's most scenic beach. Swimming near the arches should be avoided, but snorkeling on the bay side is excellent. Water taxis from Playa Médano or the Plaza Las Glorias docks are the only way to access the beach. They charge anywhere from US$7 to US$12 depending on who you ask and how many people are in your group. Cabo Acuadeportes (p212) charges US$7. Some days the waves are too rough for the taxis to land, in which case you'll have to hit a different beach. Aside from the water taxis, you can arrange a drop-off (and pickup) with a glass-bottom boat (US$10;

see p213). The only other access is via a Class 3 scramble over the rocks from Hotel Solmar (not recommended).

Playa Solmar, on the Pacific side of the point, is quieter and well suited for sunbathing, but has a reputation for unpredictable breakers that drown several unsuspecting tourists every year. Locals jokingly call it 'Divorce Beach.'

For beaches between Cabo San Lucas and San José del Cabo, see p200.

AROUND CABO SAN LUCAS

About 3 miles (5km) northwest of town is Cabo San Lucas' historic lighthouse, **Faro Viejo** (Map p205), perched high above Cabo Falso (False Cape), so named because it was once erroneously thought to be the southernmost point on the Baja peninsula.

Surrounded by a spectacular dunescape, the lighthouse was in operation from 1895 to 1961, when it was replaced by a candy-striped cousin on a hillside above. The latter is worth a visit for extraordinary 360-degree views of the ocean, city and sierras. Most likely, it will be just you and the wind – unless, of course, a herd of 'dune warriors' on ATVs happens to be tearing through the countryside below (usually in the late afternoon). We recommend that you consciously avoid ATV tours, which tear up the delicate dune ecology.

If you're traveling by car or mountain bike, follow México 19 for about 2½ miles (starting from the Pemex station), and then turn left about half a mile (800m) past the Km 120 sign onto a dirt road just in front of the Coca-Cola distributorship. Turn right when you get to a T-junction, then left at Smokey's Bar and straight on up to the lighthouse.

Daytrips to **San José** (p189) and up the **Eastern Cape Road** (p177) to **Cabo Pulmo** (p180) both make excellent daytrips from Cabo San Lucas. You could also drive up the **Western Cape** (p182) to the historic town of **Todos Santos** (p182), where gringos and art galleries are fast becoming the town's defining characteristics.

Activities
FISHING

Cabo's claim as Marlin Capital of the World may be hyperbole, but there's no doubt that the Cape Region is one of the world's best places for game fishing. Fishing is best during hurricane season (July to early October), when rougher seas bring out the marine life.

Competition among the sportfishing charters is fierce, but quality varies. Always ask what's included in a boat charter. Most rates for eight-hour trips include fishing licenses and permits, tackle, crew and ice. Sometimes they also include beer and soda, cleaning and freezing, and tax. Live bait is usually available at the docks, but good charters will take care of that for you. Things to bring on your own include a hat, sunscreen, sunglasses and anti-seasickness medication. Boats usually leave between 6am and 7am and return between 3pm and 4pm.

Prices depend entirely on the size and type of boat, and the reputation of the operator and skipper. Figure on spending about US$100 per person for a good charter, all included. Boats range from US$300 for a 26-foot cruiser (for up to three passengers) to US$450 for a 29-footer (four people). Cruisers 40 to 42 feet (which generally accommodate eight to 10 people, often more) will cost anywhere from US$700 to US$1400, but figure on around US$900 if you don't need all the luxury bells and whistles.

If you need to obtain your own fishing license, you can do so at the **Oficina de Pesca** (Map p205; 8:30am-2pm Mon-Fri), right by the cruise ship docks (US$11/27 per day/week).

The most professional place in town to stock up on rods, reels, line, leaders, lures, etc is **Minerva's Baja Tackle** (Map pp210-11; 143-1282; minerv@allaboutcabo.com; Madero at Blvd Marina). Serious fisherfolk swear by the store's quality and selection, and give high marks to the friendliness and know-how of the staff. Minerva is a real Cabo character who also operates her own fishing fleet. Contact the store to set up a boat.

Other operators with very professional crews and captains and good reputations include **Pisces Sportfishing Fleet** (Map pp210-11; 143-1288; www.piscessportfishing.com), by the Plaza Las Glorias docks; **Solmar Sportfishing Fleet** (Map p205; 143-0646, in the USA 800-344-3349; www.solmar.com), at the Hotel Solmar (p216); and **Picante Bluewater Sportfishing** (Map pp210-11; 143-2474, in the USA 714-572-6693; www.picantesportfishing.com; Puerto Paraíso 39-A), located in Puerto Paraíso Mall, facing the water.

Another possibility is a fishing trip aboard a *panga* (skiff). Rates start around US$30 per hour, with a six-hour minimum for three people. You almost always have to rent your own gear and buy your own fishing license. The operators listed here may be able to set you up on a panga, but the best place to do this is at La Playita (p199), the beach at Pueblo La Playa near San José del Cabo. The panga owners may be forced to bring their skiffs into the Puerto Los Cabos marina when it's finished (supposedly in 2005), so ask around.

The following list indicates the prime months for the various fish species, but most species actually inhabit Cabo's waters year-round. For more fishy information, see p39.

CATCH & RELEASE

More than 40,000 marlin are caught annually off Los Cabos alone, but most of them are returned to the ocean to fight another day. Although each boat is legally allowed to kill one billfish (marlin, swordfish, sailfish) per daily outing, most fisherfolk follow the advice of the Sportfishing Association of Los Cabos and opt to catch and release. Billfish releases are reported to the Billfish Foundation, which will send the proud angler a Release Certificate. Fish need not be killed in order to be taxidermied. Experts can make replica mounts from photographs taken of the fish.

Unless done correctly, fish can be so seriously injured in the release process that they die anyway after being returned to the sea. Avoid treble or stainless steel hooks; instead use long-shank, unplated iron hooks that can be more easily removed. Dragging a fish overboard and holding it in an upright position can lead to internal damage. Try to remove the hook with the fish still in the water. If possible, avoid touching the animal, as this can damage the skin, subjecting it to bacterial infections. If a fish's gills are damaged, or it is already bleeding, it will likely succumb to its injuries.

CENTRAL CABO SAN LUCAS

Ⓐ **Ⓑ** **Ⓒ** **Ⓓ**

INFORMATION
American Express.............................. 1 H3
Baja Money Exchange...................... 2 G5
Banca Serfin (ATM)........................... 3 G3
Banco Santander (ATM)................... 4 F5
Café Cabo Mail................................. 5 G3
Farmacia Arámburo.......................... 6 G3
Internet Express................................7 F4
Laundry.. 8 G1
Laundry.. (see 32)
Libros Libros Books Books............... 9 G5
Los Delfines................................... 10 G2
Mail Boxes Etc............................. (see 1)
Police Station................................ 11 H1
Post Office..................................... 12 H1
Telecomm/Western Union.............. 13 H1
The Corner..................................... 14 F4
US Consulate.................................. 15 G5

SIGHTS & ACTIVITIES (pp208-13)
Baja Dive International................... 16 G6
Casa de la Cultura.......................... 17 F3
Dos Mares....................................... 18 G6
Land's End Divers........................... 19 G6
Minerva's Baja Tackle..................... 20 G4
Neptune Divers.......................... (see 19)
Pez Gato I & Pez Gato II................. 21 G6
Picante Bluewater Sportfishing........ 22 H3
Pisces Sportfishing Fleet................. 23 G6
Sportfishing Dock........................... 24 G6

SLEEPING 🏠 (pp214-6)
Bungalows Breakfast Inn................. 25 D4
Cabo Inn.. 26 G1
Hotel Dos Mares............................ 27 G5
Hotel El Dorado.............................. 28 F1
Hotel Los Milagros......................... 29 F4
Hotel Mar de Cortez....................... 30 F4
Hotel Mélida...................................31 F3
Hotel Santa Fe................................32 F1
Las Margaritas Inn.......................... 33 G3
Siesta Suites Hotel.......................... 34 G5

EATING 🍴 (pp216-9)
Antojitos Doña Lolita...................... 35 F3
Arámburo Supermarket................... 36 G3
Cabo Coffee Co.............................. 37 F5
El Pescador.................................... 38 G3
El Pollo de Oro............................... 39 G2
Hard Rock Café.............................. 40 G3
La Palapa....................................... 41 G3
La Trattoria.................................... 42 G3
Los Paisas...................................... 43 G1
Mama's Royal Café......................... 44 F5
Margaritavilla................................. 45 G3
Mariscos Mazatlán.......................... 46 H2
Mariscos Mocambo......................... 47 G2
Mi Casa.. 48 F5
O Mole Mio.................................... 49 G4
Pane, Pizza e Vino.......................... 50 G4
Pastelería Suiza...............................51 F5
Sancho Panza................................. 52 G5
Sanliz Supermarket......................... 53 G5
Spencer's.................................... (see 30)
Stoplight.. 54 G3
The Fish House............................... 55 G5
The Shrimp Factory......................... 56 G5

ENTERTAINMENT 🍷(pp219-20)
Again & Again................................ 57 G2
Cabo Wabo Cantina........................58 F4
El Squid Roe.................................. 59 G3
Jungle Bar...................................... 60 G4
Kaboo.. 61 G3
Nowhere Bar.................................. 62 H3
Pancho's...63 F5
Slim's... 64 G4
TangaTanga................................ (see 55)
The Giggling Marlin........................ 65 G4
What's Up? Karaoke Bar................. 66 G2

SHOPPING 🛍 (p220)
Cortes.. 67 G3
Dos Lunas...................................... 68 G3
Faces of Mexico............................. 69 F4
Flea Market.................................... 70 G3
Galerías Zen-Mar............................ 71 F4
Tierra Huichol................................ 72 G3

TRANSPORT (pp220-2)
Advantage Car Rental..................... 73 G2
Aero California............................... 74 G5
Alamo Car Rental........................... 75 H2
Avis Car Rental.............................. 76 G4
Buses to San José........................... 77 H2
Dollar Car Rental........................... 78 H2
National Car Rental........................ 79 G4

12 de Octubre

Libertad

🏠 25

Miguel Ángel Herrera

Constitución

LOS CABOS

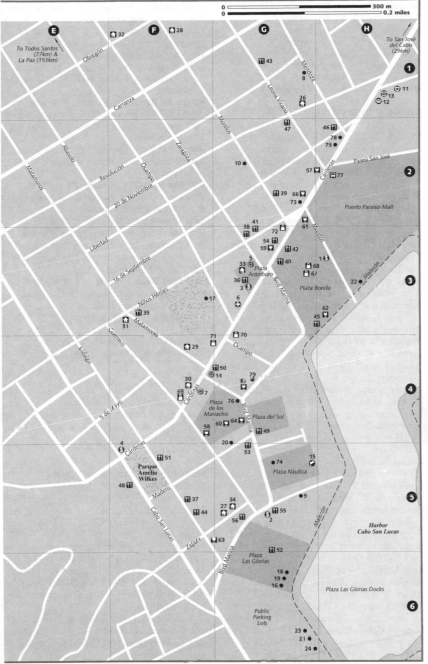

Blue marlin	July to October
Dorado	July to November
Roosterfish	July to December
Sailfish	August to October
Shark	January to May
Striped marlin	November to June
Tuna	June to October
Wahoo	August and September

DIVING & SNORKELING

Underwater explorations around Los Cabos may yield encounters with manta rays, sea lions, turtles, hammerhead sharks, marlin and an entire aquarium's worth of colorful tropical fish. Best of all, some of the finest diving sites are just a five-minute boat ride away from the marina.

Roca Pelicano (Pelican Rock, 25 to 80 feet) is perfect for beginners and has lots of tropical and schooling fish, while nearby **Land's End** (50 to 60 feet) gives intermediate to advanced divers a chance to frolic with sea lions. Even more experienced types won't want to miss the **Sand Falls** (30 to 100 feet), where steep sand banks plunge into a submarine canyon just 30 yards offshore. (Jacques Cousteau made a documentary on this spectacular place.) Another challenge is **Neptune's Finger** (80 to 100 feet), an amazing canyon-wall dive. Snorkelers can hit the water right off Playa del Amor (on the bay side only).

Dive shops cluster near the Plaza Las Glorias docks and on Playa Médano. Two-hour snorkeling tours cost about US$25 (gear included); one-tank dives cost US$35 to US$45; two-tank dives cost US$60 to US$70; one-tank night dives go for US$45 to US$50. Introductory (resort) courses cost US$75 to US$100. Open water certification costs around US$400 and full PADI dive master certification costs about US$600. Rescue courses average US$300.

Rates usually include tanks and weights. Regulators, buoyancy compensator jackets and full wetsuits rent for about US$10 each; airfills and weight belt cost US$12 and US$5, respectively. Mask, fins and snorkel average US$12. Some places rent underwater cameras for about US$25.

Most operators also organize tours to sites farther afield, including all-day trips to Cabo Pulmo (US$125 to US$140; see p180) or Gorda Banks (US$125 to US$160; see p199). These usually require

a minimum of four people. Two- to three-hour snorkeling excursions to Playa Santa María (p201) cost US$25 to US$50. Most companies mentioned under Cruises also run snorkeling trips in the mornings.

Reputable dive outfitters – all of which have English-speaking staff – include the following:

Amigos del Mar (Map p205; ☎ 143-0505, in the ☎ USA 800-344-3349; www.amigosdelmar.com) Near the cruise-ship dock, south of Blvd Marina off Av Solmar. PADI. Long in the business.

Andromeda Divers (Map p205; ☎ 143-2765; www.scubadivecabo.com; Playa Médano, at Billigan's) All PADI courses available.

Baja Dive International (Map pp210-11; ☎ 143-3830; www.baja-dive.net; Plaza Las Glorias, Local 1-4) PADI. All rentals and courses available.

Cabo Acuadeportes (Map p205; ☎ 143-0117; www.cabowatersports.com; Playa Médano at Hacienda Beach Resort) PADI Five Star dive center, NAUI (Nautical Association of Underwater Instructors) Pro facility and SSI (Scuba Schools International).

Land's End Divers (Map pp210-11; ☎ 143-2200; www.mexonline.com/landsend.htm; Plaza Las Glorias, Local A-5) All courses, tours available.

Neptune Divers (Map pp210-11; ☎ 143-7111; Plaza Las Glorias)

Tio Sports (Map p205; ☎ 143-3399; www.tiosports.com; Playa Médano at Hotel Meliá San Lucas)

GOLF

With its six signature championship golf courses along the Los Cabos Corridor, Cabo San Lucas has become one of the world's premier golfing destinations. The courses are described in the Corridor section (p202).

HORSEBACK RIDING & BICYCLING

Rancho Collins (Map p205; ☎ 143-3652, 148-5956), based just off the driveway to the Hotel Meliá San Lucas (p216), offers one- to 1½-hour beach rides for US$25 to US$35 and longer sunset rides to the Faro Viejo (p208) for US$50. The owner – quite a cowboy – is a great guy, but may be forced (by the nearby luxury hotel) to move his operation, so call beforehand. **Red Rose Riding Stables** (Map p205; ☎ 143-4826), at Km 4 on the Transpeninsular, has similar rates.

Tio Sports (see Diving & Snorkeling) rents mountain bikes for US$5/20 per hour/day. Guided tours cost US$30 per person. It also rents horses.

WATER SPORTS

For water sports and fun, head to Playa Médano, where you'll find rentals for just about every sort of beach activity and water sport imaginable. **Cabo Acuadeportes** (see Diving & Snorkeling, above) has the largest stable of toys. Kayaks rent for US$15/20 single/double per hour. The two-hour snorkeling tour (US$25 per person) will take you by boat to some great spots you can't otherwise access. Snorkel gear without the tour costs US$12 per day. Parasailing flights cost US$30. **Tio Sports** (see Diving & Snorkeling) has similar equipment but slightly higher prices.

Another option is to set up shop on the sand and rent **wave-runners** for about US$80 an hour so you can scare the hell out of unsuspecting swimmers. There are also plenty of opportunities to hire a speedboat to drag you and your friends across the bay on a **banana boat**. At US$8 per person they're cheaper than wave-runners.

For something a little more *tranquilo*, try renting and **sailing** a catamaran, sailboat (Lasers and Sunfish) or a sailboard. They're all available for about US$35 per hour from **Cabo Acuadeportes**, as well as in front of the bigger hotels.

Farther down the beach, **Juancho's** (Map p205; ☎ 144-4252; Playa Médano) pledges an 'airgasmic experience' with its parasailing operation, and the sign promises 10% off for women who sail naked. Sorry guys, no way out of the normal US$30 fee. But a woman out front offers a pitcher of margaritas and a massage for US$25. Her slogan is 'get hammered while you get nailed.' Plenty of fun for everyone. Juancho's is part of the **Sandbar** (p220), in case you need more beer.

Cabo San Lucas for Children

Most of Los Cabos' top-end hotels – primarily those on Playa Médano and along the Corridor – offer daycare services and supervised activities that allow you bigger kids to make off and play on your own for a while. Other than that, little is geared specifically toward children, per se, but there's plenty for the kids to do. Children old enough to swim, snorkel and participate in activities like horseback riding will be the most easily entertained. The pirate cruise aboard the *Sunderland* is always a hit with the young'ns.

Tours

GLASS-BOTTOM BOAT TOURS

Dos Mares (Map pp210-11; ☎ 143-1057; Plaza Las Glorias) operates 45-minute bay tours aboard its glass bottom boats for US$10. Departures are hourly from the **Plaza Las Glorias docks** (Map p210-11) and from Playa Médano. Drop-offs and pickups at Lover's Beach (p208) can be arranged at no extra charge.

SUNSET & SNORKELING CRUISES

Capping off a day at the beach with a sunset cruise is a popular pastime among Cabo vacationers. They're a great way to suck down all the free booze you want (which is why they call them 'booze cruises'), meet some strangers (hey baby!) and take in some fabulous views. Sunset cruises depart around 5pm in winter and 6pm in summer, and are usually segregated into 'romantic cruises' or the aforementioned booze cruises. Daytime snorkeling trips are a little mellower, departing between 10am and noon, and head to Bahía Santa Maria (p200) for the dip.

Trips last two to three hours, and prices almost always include drinks and snacks; snorkeling trips include lunch. Boats depart from the Plaza Las Glorias docks (Map p210-11), and children under age 13 usually pay half-price or less.

The 42-foot catamarans **Pez Gato I** and **Pez Gato II** (☎ 143-3797) offer booze cruises at sunset (US$35) and snorkeling cruises to Bahía Santa Maria (US$45) by day. The bars are open on both, and the latter includes snorkeling equipment and lunch. The 36-foot trimaran **Jungle Cruise** (☎ 148-7674), another wild party boat, departs daily at 10:30am for snorkel cruises on Bahía Santa Maria and nightly at 5pm for its sunset cruises. The much tamer **Encore** (☎ 143-2015), a 60-foot ocean-racing yacht with capacity for 25 people, charges US$30.

Sun Rider (☎ 143-2252) and **Vancouver Star** (☎ 143-2188) both offer morning snorkeling cruises (departing about 11am) and sunset cruises (departing around 5:30pm). Both cost US$40 and include dinner, drinks and, in the case of the latter, dancing. **Kaleidoscope** (☎ 148-7318) is a 100-foot catamaran with adults-only cruises for US$40.

For something a little different, take a 'pirate cruise' aboard the **Sunderland** (☎ 143-2714; www.pirateshipcabo.com; ☾ mid-Oct–mid-May), eautiful 19th-century four-masted tall p that lets you glide into the sunset with t noisy engine sounds. The crew dresses pirates' garb, and the captain himself will hower you with tales of Cabo's sordid corsair past. The cost is US$40 or US$20 for kids under 12.

WHALE-WATCHING CRUISES

During the peak of the gray whale migration, from January to March, you can easily spot whales right from the shore. You can get even closer by jumping aboard a whale-watching cruise. Many of the cruise ships listed earlier also run whale-watching trips from January through April (April being the tail end of the season). They cost between US$30 and US$40 and usually last three hours.

Festivals & Events

Cabo San Lucas has several popular annual events, including many **fishing tournaments**. The most prestigious is the Bisbee's Black & Blue Marlin Jackpot Tournament, held in late October. A week before is the Gold Cup Sportfishing Tournament, and late November sees the Los Cabos Billfish Tournament. The **Festival San Lucas**, which celebrates the town's patron saint, kicks off on October 18 or 19.

Sleeping

Cabo San Lucas has loads of accommodations, from the monolithic luxury resorts along Playa Médano and Playa Solmar to small B&B-type places and mom-and-pop budget hotels in central San Lucas. Farther afield, the Corridor is home to Los Cabos' most expensive resorts. Where you stay depends on your budget and what you want out of your visit.

Staying on the Corridor makes getting to downtown for shopping, dining and partying a bit of a trudge, but you have the best beaches and biggest swimming pools only steps from your room.

Playa Médano gives you the best of both worlds, while the hotels downtown are less expensive and, in many cases, more charming. Campgrounds and RV parks are just east of town.

Prices fluctuate significantly by season. Rates quoted below apply to peak season (usually November to May), so expect to

pay 25% to 50% less at other times. Almost all of the big resorts, B&Bs and boutique hotels charge a compulsory service charge of 10% to 15% in lieu of tipping, included in these quoted prices. Note that many smaller, family-run establishments don't accept credit cards.

No hotel in Cabo San Lucas is cheap enough to be considered 'budget'; this is about the priciest place to stay on the peninsula.

Unlike the Mexican resorts of Cancún and Mazatlán, Cabo San Lucas lacks any spark of a gay scene, and there are no specifically gay hotels. But most luxury hotels are so large and anonymous – and the smaller hotels friendly enough – that sexuality is generally a nonissue.

DOWNTOWN

Hotel Los Milagros (Map pp210–11; ☎ 143-4566, in the USA ☎ 718-928-6647; www.losmilagros. mx; Matamoros 116; r US$65-75; ☒ ☒) This US-owned boutique hotel is an oasis of good taste and style. Rooms feature scalloped brick ceilings and Mexican manor–style furniture. All have air-con but lack phones or TVs to emphasize the desert-retreat atmosphere. Some have kitchenettes. Ambient music spills softly over the cactus- and bougainvillea- filled patio, and the miniature, tiled pool nails the point home that you're here to relax.

Cabo Inn (Map pp210–11; ☎ 143-0819; www. caboinnhotel.com; 20 de Noviembre at Leona Vicario; s/d US$58, r for 6 US$120; ☒) Perhaps the best value in town, the Cabo Inn is quiet and has the character of a big, old Mexican house. Its courtyard bursts with foliage, and Mexican tapestries adorn the walls. There are plenty of tables outside the rooms and a barbecue grill to cook your day's catch. Bathrooms are a bit small, but the charm more than makes up for this. Coffee and advice are both free. The rooftop 'Love Palace' (US$90) comes with a private patio for sleeping under the stars.

Bungalows Breakfast Inn (Map pp210–11; ☎ 143-0585, in the USA ☎ 800-424-2226; www.cabobungalows. com; near cnr Libertad & Herrera; bungalow US$110-151, ste US$84-151; ☒ ☒ ☒) Inside Cabo's most secluded hideaway, a palm-fringed pool gives way to 16 light-flooded studios and two-bedroom bungalows with Mexican furnishings, fridges and beds you simply melt into. Everything has been decorated with love, including the private patios, which make venturing outside the hotel difficult. The en-suite TVs all have VCRs for watching movies from the in-house video library. The gourmet breakfasts garner rave reviews. The hotel is just off Calle Libertad (follow the signs from Constitución).

Hotel Mar de Cortez (Map pp210-11; ☎ 143-0032, in the USA ☎ 800-347-8821; www.mardecortez. com; Cárdenas near Guerrero; r US$46-56; 🅿 🖳) This Cabo faithful is the town's oldest hotel, though you'd never know it sleeping in one of the plush rooms in the newer wing. All are sparse but spotless, with tiled floors and, depending on what you pay, a terrace or garden view. The cheapest rooms are in the older sector. There's a good, affordable restaurant attached (great breakfasts), and the staff is particularly adept at setting up fishing and scuba tours.

Hotel Santa Fe (Map pp210-11; ☎ 143-4401; santafe@go2mexico.com; Zaragoza at Obregón; r US$70 🅿 🖳) All of the 46 spacious and immaculate studios here have satellite TV, kitchenettes, air-con, telephones and sofa beds (plus the main bed, of course). Some have sliding doors that open onto the pool area. A small market, café and coin laundry are adjacent to the hotel.

Siesta Suites Hotel (Map pp210-11; ☎ 143-2773, in the USA ☎ 866-271-0952; Zapata near Guerrero; r US$62; 🖳) If you're bent on self-catering, try Siesta Suites, whose clean rooms all have fully equipped kitchenettes. The place is definitely showing some wear, and it's ground zero for Cabo nightlife. The full bar and raised swimming pool barely fit in the patio area outside the rooms. There's a barbecue, and free coffee in the morning.

Medusa Suites (Map p205; ☎ 143-3492; medusasuites@hotmail.com; Ocampo at Alikán; r US$45; 🅿 🖳) This is a cute Spanish-style cottage with nine compact suites around a pool and bar area. Each comes with fridge, TV, telephone and kitchenette.

Las Margaritas Inn (Map pp210-11; ☎ 143-6770; margaritas@real-turismo.com; Plaza Arámburo; s/d US$60/70; 🅿 🖳) En-suite kitchens and giant rooms are the main attractions here. Atmosphere? Not a lick. It's a modernish, three-story, motel-type place facing a big parking lot on a busy street. Its location in the heart of Cabo's nightlife strip may notch it up in appeal if you're here to party. It's definitely friendly.

Hotel Dos Mares (Map pp210-11; ☎ 14... 143-3870; Zapata btwn Guerrero & Hidalgo; r US$... 🖳 🖳) Someone went a little crazy with room freshener and the bathrooms are a... claustrophobic, but you can escape both diving into the tiny swimming pool in the middle of the big outdoor patio. The place is clean but slightly overpriced.

Hotel Mélida (Map pp210-11; ☎ 143-6564; Matamoros at Niños Héroes; s/d US$35/45; 🖳) The dozen or so rooms at this family-run property are spacious and spotless and have TVs. The downside is that some rooms have sliding doors that open onto a cement wall near the street, meaning they're a bit noisy.

Hotel El Dorado (Map pp210-11; ☎ 143-2810; Morelos btw Carranza & Obregón; r US$35-45; 🅿 🖳 🖳) The 36 large, clean rooms here wrap motel-like around a central parking area. All have TVs and plenty of room to spread out. Character is nil, but it's very friendly.

Olas Hotel (Map p205; ☎ 143-1780; Revolución near Farías; r US$36; 🅿 🖳) The hospitable and quiet Olas Hotel has spotless rooms with individual patios, TVs and comfortable king-size beds. A small supermarket and coin laundry are across the street, and there's a café on the premises.

PLAYA MÉDANO & PLAYA SOLMAR

Cabo San Lucas' luxury resorts line the beachfronts of both the bay side (Playa Médano) and the Pacific side (Playa Solmar). Facilities at each are similar and include beautiful swimming pools, Jacuzzis, tennis courts, restaurants, bars and all other amenities that come with luxury resorts. Prices for the following hotels swing greatly between seasons. November to mid-April is high season, with peak season (when prices are at their absolute highest) between December 20 and January 5. Low season is May to October. Prices quoted here include both 12% tax and gratuity, plus the 10% to 15% service charge they all tack on top. Room rates are for two adults, but often you'll get the same rate for two adults and two children or even four adults (all in the same room, of course).

Hacienda Beach Resort (Map p205; ☎ 143-0663, 143-0122, in the USA ☎ 800-733-2226; www. haciendacabo.com; r US$183-482, townhouse US$445 537; 🅿 🖳 🖳 🖳) This is the *grande dame* of Playa Médano, a glorious five-star Mission-

notel with fountains and tropical
...ns so lush that the complex blends
...erfectly with its natural surroundings.
...e of the original Cabo hotels, it oozes
...-time charm and tradition in its public
...eas. Rooms are comfortable, and all have
...cean views; some are right next to the sand.
Beachfront souvenir vendors and time-
share hawkers are kept off the premises.
The bar (which serves killer margaritas) and
restaurant are popular expat hangouts.

Hotel Meliá San Lucas (Map p205; ☎ 143-4444,
in the USA ☎ 800-336-3542; www.meliasanlucas.
solmelia.com; r US$245-495; P ✕ 🞩 🞰) The
Meliá San Lucas is a popular saffron-
colored behemoth whose main draw is
the beautifully landscaped pool area with
a palapa-roof swim-up bar – which is key
if you plan to spend much time poolside.
Spacious, nicely decorated rooms have
minibars, safes and TVs, and most also
have oceanview terraces.

Pueblo Bonito Resort (Map p205; ☎ 143-2900,
in the USA ☎ 800-990-8250; www.pueblobonito.
com; r US$245-2196; P ✕ 🞩 🞰) The Pueblo
Bonito's mega-proportions are mitigated
by Moorish-style blue-tiled domes. The
opulent lobby is another eye-catcher.
Rooms, of course, have all the usual perks.
The luxury suites (US$275 to US$360) are
definitely bigger than the junior suites
(US$245 to US$315), but the latter are just
as good, considering you'll be spending
most of your time outside. Executive,
presidential and penthouse suites kick the
price tag much higher.

Pueblo Bonito Rosé Resort (Map p205; ☎ 143-
5500, in the USA ☎ 800-990-8250; www.pueblobonito.
com; r US$238-1769; P ✕ 🞩 🞰) The Pueblo
Bonito's adjacent sister property is slightly
more sophisticated with its Greek statues
and imposing columns around the pool area.
The hotel itself is even bigger than Pueblo
Bonito and boasts a state-of-the-art spa.

Hotel Finisterra (Map p205; ☎ 143-3333, in the
USA ☎ 800-347-2252; www.finisterra.com; US$153-458;
P ✕ 🞰 🞰) On Playa Solmar, just off
Blvd Marina, the Finisterra commands an
impressive clifftop location. Some rooms
have fireplaces, while others have either
ocean or marina views.

Hotel Solmar Suites (Map p205; ☎ 143-3535, in
the USA ☎ 800-344-3349; www.solmar.com; r US$171-
403; P ✕ 🞩 🞰) East of the Finisterra, this
secluded beachfront resort boasts oceanview

studios, suites and condos. It's still a biggie,
but it's smaller than many of the Playa
Médano hotels, which gives it a more
romantic feel. The resort is also famous for
its sportfishing fleet (see p209), making it an
excellent choice if you plan to fish.

CAMPING

Cabo San Lucas only has one in-town
campground/RV park. The rest are east of
town along the Corridor.

Faro Viejo Trailer Park (Map p205; ☎ 143-4211;
Morales btwn Matamoros & Abasolo; site US$15) Cabo
San Lucas' only in-town campground,
Faro Viejo has full hookups and clean
bathrooms.

Club Cabo Motel & Camp Resort (Map p205;
☎ 143-3348; clubcabo@cabonet.net.mx; tent US$8-10,
RV US$16, cabaña US$55-65; 🞰) After Faro Viejo,
this Dutch-operated RV park is the closest
to town. It's also the most congenial and
has dependable services. The thatched-
roof cabañas have more than a modicum
of style. The grounds, which lie adjacent
to a migratory bird refuge, are quiet, well
maintained and feature a large swimming
pool, Jacuzzi and barbecue area. It's a bit
hidden but well signposted once you turn
toward the beach at the intersection of the
Transpeninsular (México 1) and the Cabo
bypass road; look for the Club Cascadas
sign. The resort is 1 mile (1.6km) east of
Club Cascadas de Baja (Map p205), just
before the Villas de Palmar development.

Eating

Cabo's culinary scene features everything
from American fast-food chains to gourmet
restaurants. Prices are high for Baja, but,
generally, so is the quality. Most places are
casual and feature outdoor seating.

MEXICAN

Calle Leona Vicario has been dubbed
'Taco Alley' for good reason. The street is
lined with taquerías offering good, cheap
authentic food (mostly tacos, of course) all
day, all night.

Los Paisas (Map pp210-11; Leona Vicario at
Revolución; tacos US$1; 🕑 6pm-6am) Renowned
for its beef tacos and stuffed potatoes,
both served always with a plate of grilled
onions, Los Paisas is *the* spot for the late-
night munchies.

El Michoacano (Map p205; ☎ 108-0713; Leona

Vicario at Obregón; 8am-6pm; meal US$5) This open-air branch of the renowned *carnitas* (slow-roasted pork) chain serves up some of the best cheap eats in Cabo – which is why locals flock here, especially on weekends. Three people can fill up on a half-kilo of carnitas (unless you're famished). Extra perk: orders are accompanied by chips, tortillas, *chicharrones* (pork cracklings), beans and salsa.

Cabo Taco (Map p205; Leona Vicario at 5 de Febrero; tacos US$1-2) Cabo Taco whips out delicious seafood tacos and usually has some bizarre thing on the menu (like manta ray tacos).

Antojitos Doña Lolita (Map p210-11; cnr Niños Héroes & Matamoros; mains US$4-9) This small eatery serves delicious homestyle Mexican fare from an outdoor kitchen of wood-burning stoves and black iron pots. The daily changing menu usually features four main dishes and a soup. It's open for lunch and dinner.

O Mole Mio (Map pp210-11; 143-7577; Blvd Marina at Madero, Plaza del Sol; mains US$11-20) With wrought-iron furniture, Mayan fertility figures adorning the walls and colorful lanterns for light, the decor is as creative as the food. Even standards like enchiladas and tamales are presented with a whole new twist. The seafood is outstanding.

Margaritavilla (Map pp210-11; 143-0010; cnr Malecón & Blvd Marina, Plaza Bonita; mains US$8-15) Famous for its gargantuan margaritas, roaming mariachis and good appetizers, Margaritavilla is an upscale, two-story Mexican restaurant catering to foreign palates. This means the plates are huge but tend to be a bit bland. Still, a marina-side table makes for great atmosphere at night.

Mi Casa (Map pp210-11; 143-1933; Av Cabo San Lucas btw Madero & Cárdenas; mains US$13-18) In a flower-festooned patio across from Parque Amelia Wilkes, Mi Casa serves excellent dishes from around Mexico, complete with warm tortillas made freshly on the premises. Dishes range from jumbo shrimp with tamarind sauce or *pulpo al ajillo* (baby octopus sautéed in garlic and butter) to *chile en nogada*, a Puebla specialty of poblano chiles stuffed with meat and smothered in a walnut cream sauce. You can't go wrong here.

La Noria (Map p205; 143-0663; Hacienda Beach Resort; mains US$15-20) For something special, treat yourself to dinner at this renowned restaurant in the Hacienda Beach Resort (p215). The place gets top marks from the locals for its gourmet takes on traditional dishes, superb service and reasonable prices. Dining takes place on the waterfront terrace or the high-ceilinged *comedor* (dining room).

El Pollo de Oro (Map pp210-11; Morelos near 16 de Septiembre) Drop in here for great grilled chicken. A quarter bird plus rice, beans and tortilla costs just US$3.50.

Playa Médano is home to a string of casual eateries where you eat with your toes dug into the sand. All serve the usual *antojitos* (Mexican snacks and light meals such as enchiladas and tamales), seafood and Mexican combos at mid-range prices and are open all day. They include the following:

Billygan's (Map pp210-11; 143-0402; Playa Médano) Big plates of good food; sandwiches, burgers and seafood; happy hour from 2 to 7pm.

Mango Deck (Map pp210-11; 143-0901; Playa Médano) Very casual place with rustic wood décor.

The Office (Map pp210-11; 143-3464; Playa Médano) Known for its raucous Mexican fiestas held several times weekly.

SEAFOOD

Seafood, of course, is a Cabo specialty, and there are numerous restaurants where you can get your fill.

The Fish House (Map pp210-11; 144-4501; Blvd Marina near Guerrero; mains US$7-11; 3-11pm) Although the airy dining room feels quite upscale, the prices are reasonable, especially considering the quality of the fare. The menu is small, which makes choosing one of the seafood specialties easier.

Mariscos Mazatlán (Map pp210-11; 143-8565; cnr Mendoza & 16 de Septiembre; mains US$7-12; 11am-

...m) Local families fill the big dining room ...re for the good prices and great seafood. ...unday afternoons are especially busy (and ...especially fun).

Mariscos Mocambo (Map pp210-11; ☎ 143-2122; cnr Leona Vicario & 20 de Noviembre; US$9-13) Touristy but renowned for its large portions of fresh fish and shellfish, Mariscos Mocambo is just the place for casual atmosphere and reasonably priced seafood.

The Giggling Marlin (Map pp210-11; ☎ 143-1182; Blvd Marina; mains US$9-24; ☑ 9am-1am) Seafood (as much as partying) may be the specialty at this restaurant-bar, but there's plenty more on the menu. If you're not feeling fishy, try the MOAB (Mother Of All Burgers) or one of many Mexican standbys.

The Shrimp Factory (Map pp210-11; ☎ 143-5066; Blvd Marina at Guerrero) Casual and popular, The Shrimp Factory dishes out boiled shrimp and lobster by the kilo or half-kilo. The lobster's good (though nothing near a good Maine tail), but the shrimp is where it's really at. A kilo of the latter serves two to three and costs US$16 for large shrimp and US$19 for jumbo. The lobster's pricier.

El Pescador (Map pp210-11; cnr Zaragoza & Niños Héroes; mains US$7-12) The menu at this modest and friendly eatery is an oceanic treasure trove: Shrimp, fish, oysters, snails, crab, octopus – you name it, it's served here. It's casual and prices are good.

Las Palmas (Map p205; ☎ 143-0447; Playa Médano) This cheerful place on the beach at Playa Médano serves great seafood, and they will prepare your catch of the day. It also has large salads and respectable sushi.

La Palapa (Map pp210-11; ☎ 143-0808; Niños Héroes near Zaragoza; mains US$7-12) This longtime Cabo favorite draws big crowds for its budget breakfasts and good-value seafood dinners. Its free tuna-dip appetizer is a treat.

INTERNATIONAL

Latitude 22+ Oceanview Roadhouse (☎ 143-1516; Transpeninsular, Km 4.5; mains US$5-10; ☑ 8am-11pm) Bring your sense of humor along with your appetite to this barbeque and burger joint northeast of town on the road to San José. Who knows where they pilfered all the maritime paraphernalia from, but it makes for great atmosphere. And the food? Wow! Appetizers include chicken wings, barbequed ribs, French onion soup and their delicious 'killa' burritos. Over a dozen burgers grace the menu along with mesquite grilled chicken, pork and beef ribs, roasted pork loin and grilled chops. Whatever you do, don't bring up Philadelphia.

Sancho Panza (Map pp210-11; ☎ 143-3212; off Blvd Marina, Plaza Las Glorias; mains US$20-30; ☑ 3-11pm) As much a visual as a culinary treat, Sancho Panza is one of San Lucas' most high-profile restaurants. The chef cleverly fuses Mediterranean and Latin tastes to create exquisite dishes such as tuna carpaccio, rack of lamb with a traditional Greek *tzatziky* sauce, and porcini mushroom fondue. The wine bar is superb, and Cuban art ardorns the walls. There's also live jazz most nights. Reservations are highly recommended after 7pm.

Peacock's (Map pp205; ☎ 143-1858; Paseo del Pescador s/n near Paseo San José; mains US$15-30; ☑ 6-10pm) Another Mecca for *alta cocina* (haute cuisine), Peacock's serves some of the best food in town. The chef mixes Mediterranean and Latin flavors into dishes like seafood-stuffed baked eggplant, yellowtail crusted with pecans and lemon butter, and roast duck in a mango-honey glaze. It's well worth the splurge, and reservations are recommended during high season. It's above Playa Médano near the road down to Hotel Melía San Lucas.

Hard Rock Café (Map pp210-11; ☎ 143-3806; Blvd Marina, Plaza Bonita) No surprises here, just the usual tasty Hard Rock fare like burgers, sandwiches, pastas, salads and steaks, plus a few Mexican specialties (which aren't HRC's strongpoint) thrown in for good measure. Oh, and then there's that rock 'n' roll atmosphere.

Pane, Pizza e Vino (Map pp210-11; ☎ 143-3090; Cárdenas at Matamoros; pizzas US$8-12) In conversations about who makes the best pizza in town, this favorite always seems to come up. Open for dinner nightly, its Neapolitan chef cranks out pie after pie, usually large enough to feed two.

La Trattoria (Map pp210-11; ☎ 143-0068; Cárdenas near Blvd Marina; mains US$12-18) This upscale, classic Italian restaurant is next to the Hard Rock Café. The menu is extensive, with numerous antipastos, soups, salads, two dozen pasta dishes and some great house specialties.

Stoplight (Map pp210-11; ☎ 143-4740; Cárdenas near Morelos; mains US$8-15) Hit the breaks, meat lovers. This festive restaurant on busy

Cárdenas serves some great beef dishes, including baby-back ribs, New York steak and a juicy rib eye. Mexican antojitos grace the menu as well.

OTHER

Mamá's Royal Café (Map pp210-11; Hidalgo near Zapata; breakfast US$6-10; ☻ 7:30am-9:30pm) Mexican decorations splash cheerful colors over the patio here, and breakfasts are the best reason to come. They're big and delicious and included several versions of eggs benedict, French toast and plenty of Mexican egg dishes.

Pastelería Suiza (Map pp210-11; Hidalgo btwn Cárdenas & Madero) Opposite Parque Amelia Wilkes, this bakery sells yummy bread, bagels, pastries and pies.

Cabo Coffee Co (Map pp210-11; Hidalgo near Madero; US$1-3; ☻ 6am-10pm) Organic Mexican coffees are roasted on the premises, so the coffee drinks rock. It's a great place to wake up to a light snack and a caffeine kick.

Spencer's (Map pp210-11; Cárdenas near Guerrero; breakfasts US$2.50-4; ☻ 7am-9pm) Inside Hotel Mar de Cortez (p215), this is one of the best breakfast values in town. US-style eggs and potato plates cost just US$2.50. Plenty more is on the menu, and it's all good and cheap.

The two largest and most centrally located supermarkets are **Arámburo Supermarket** (Map pp210-11; ☎ 143-1450; Cárdenas, Plaza Arámburo) and **Sanlíz Supermarket** (Map pp210-11; cnr Blvd Marina & Madero). Both are open until 11pm.

Entertainment

Cabo nightlife concentrates along Blvd Marina, which, flooded with neon, is beginning to resemble a miniature Las Vegas. This is where legendary watering holes like The Giggling Marlin and El Squid Roe pull in throngs of gregarious gringos in search of a good time. The scene is sort of frat party meets street carnival, with lots of audience participation, risqué floor shows and lost inhibitions. It's silly and frivolous, but everyone seems to be enjoying themselves.

Alcohol consumption is encouraged all day long, from the welcome margarita at your hotel to free-drink coupons in the newspapers to all-day happy hours.

DRINKING

El Squid Roe (Map pp210-11; Cárdenas at Morelos) Whether you can deal with the frat-like party crowd or not, legendary El Squid Roe is a mandatory stop for any serious night out. The music's loud, the margaritas flowing (available even in 'yards!') and the neon bright. You might even brave the elevated 'temporary pimp' stand, where solo revelers show their stuff as the night progresses.

The Giggling Marlin (see p218) Famous for its debauchery, this is where folks relive their frat-party days (or create the ones they never had), sucking Jell-O shots off strangers' bellies, shaking their booties in sexy dance contests, or simply hanging upside down like a hooked marlin from the in-house block-and-tackle (yes, it's how the men prove they're well hung).

TangaTanga (Map pp210-11; Blvd Marina near Guerrero) Sun-baked expats and return vacationers knock 'em back over fish stories and classic rock at this small outdoor bar.

Slim's (Map pp210-11; Blvd Marina, Plaza de los Mariachis) Cabo's smallest bar holds about 12 people, though this author crowded in with well over 20. You're guaranteed to make new friends.

What's Up? Karaoke Bar (Map pp210-11; Cárdenas at Morelos) If you can brave the horrendous singing, join the locals here in silliness and song.

Nowhere Bar (Map pp210-11; Malecón, Plaza Bonita) The mostly US crowd here spills out onto the malecón, drinks in hand, nearly every night of the week.

Rainbow Bar (Map p205; Malecón, Marina) This is Cabo's lone gay and lesbian haunt, though it generally draws a mixed crowd.

Jungle Bar (Map pp210-11; Plaza de los Mariachis) This small bar is a good place to escape

LOS CABOS

ONE TURTLE, NO GLASS

For the thirsty among us, Tecate and Pacifico beers are available in 1L bottles. Show you know what's up by using the proper slang: One-liter Tecates are called *caguamas* (sea turtles) while 1L Pacificos are called *ballenas* (whales). And forget about *cerveza* (beer) – call it a *chela* or a *cheve* (unless you're minding your manners). Chupar (to suck) is slang for drinking alcohol, but be careful in your combinations – laughter may follow an announcement that you're off to suck a sea turtle.

the afternoon sunshine while still being outside (sort of) or drown your sorrows in reggae and booze. At night, it's right in the action.

Pancho's (Map pp210–11; ☎ 143-0973; Hidalgo at Zapata) This brightly pigmented outdoor eatery competes with the Museo de Tequila in Rosarito for having the largest selection of tequila. Panchos has about 400 varieties.

Sandbar (Map p205; Playa Médano) A great place to escape the madness is this low-key bar on Playa Médano, next to the Hotel Meliá San Lucas. Here you can sip your drink snuggled into a comfy beach chair while toasting your tootsies beside a crackling bonfire right in the sand. There's live music on weekend nights to boot.

The best bars for watching the sun plop into the Pacific are at the Playa Solmar hotels, especially the Hotel Finisterra's **Whale Watcher Bar** (Map p205).

LIVE MUSIC

Cabo Wabo Cantina (Map pp210–11; ☎ 143-1188; Guerrero near Madero, Plaza de los Mariachis) With countless photos of himself adorning every wall, rock 'n' roller Sammy Hagar has erected a shrine to himself as much as a venue for local and international rock bands. Admittedly, it's a pretty cool space, with two stages and live music every night of the week. Buy a shirt for about US$20.

Hard Rock Café (p218) A perennial favorite, the Hard Rock has a dance floor and pop bands.

Kaboo (Map pp210–11; cnr Cárdenas & Morelos) One of the biggest clubs on the strip, Kaboo has mediocre DJs every night of the week who *will* get you dancing after a few shots.

Again & Again (Map pp210–11; Cárdenas at Leona Vicario) For a taste of the local pop-music scene, join the youthful crowd here, where gringos in shorts are rarely seen and live bands rock the house every Thursday and Saturday night. On Friday it's a disco, and the dance floor is packed.

Sancho Panza (p218) As well as a restaurant, Sancho Panza is a fabulous wine bar with live jazz most weekends.

Shopping

Downtown Cabo is teeming with souvenir shops hawking more or less the same cheesy trinkets, usually at inflated prices – so sharpen those bargaining skills. If you're

in the market for high-end Mexican crafts, consider heading over to San José del Cabo where the shopping is better.

Plaza Bonita has the most upscale shops, including **Dos Lunas** (Map pp210–11; ☎ 143-1969) which has reasonably priced resort wear made from natural fibers as well as some nice jewelry. **Cortes** (Map pp210–11; ☎ 143-1770) is worth a look for its high-quality Mexican-made furnishings and crafts.

The stretch of Cárdenas between Matamorros and Ocampo is especially thick with souvenir shops.

Flea Market (Map pp210–11; Cárdenas at Ocampo) This maze of crafts stalls is the easiest place to stock up on souvenirs. Picking through the stalls is fun.

Faces of Mexico (Map pp210–11; Cárdenas at Guerrero) Has a good selection of arts and crafts.

Galerías Zen-Mar (Map pp210–11; ☎ 143-0661; Cárdenas near Matamoros) Offers traditional Indian crafts, Zapotec weavings, bracelets and spectacular masks.

Tierra Huichol (Map pp210–11; ☎ 105-0857; Morelos at Cárdenas) The practically psychedelic beadwork of Jalisco's indigenous Huichol is available here.

Artesanos (Map p205; ☎ 143-3850) For the best selection in hand-painted ceramics and pottery, head to this large warehouse at Km 4.1 on the Transpeninsular.

Vitrofusión y Arte (Map p205; ☎ 143-0255, 143-0120) This is the place for margarita glasses, vases and other handblown-glass items. It's on the Cabo bypass, about a third of a mile (0.5km) past the intersection with the Transpeninsular (look for a small sign). Most days you can watch the glass blowers at work in the factory behind the store.

The **Puerto Paraíso Mall** (Cárdenas) is the newest edition to Cabo's shopping scene, providing a typically international mall-of-the-21st-century experience. A few shops do sell high-end Mexican crafts, but most everything else is available anywhere.

Getting There & Away
AIR

For information on air travel to and from **Los Cabos International Airport**, see p198. **Aero California** (☎ 143-3700, 143-4255) has an office in Plaza Náutica, off Blvd Marina.

BUS

For buses to San José del Cabo, see Getting

Around, next. Long-distance buses operated by **Autotransportes Aguila** (☎ 143-7880) leave from the **main bus terminal** (Map p205), at the junction of México 19 and the Cabo bypass (across from the Pemex). From here, it's a 20- to 30-minute walk south to downtown, which is also served by local bus.

Buses to Todos Santos (US$5, 1¼ hours) leave 12 times daily. Sixteen buses head to La Paz (US$13), taking either the *via corta*

(short route, via Todos Santos; 2½ hours) or the *via larga* (long route, via San José; 3½ hours). There are four daily buses to Loreto (US$32, 8 hours) and three daily to Tijuana (US$105, 24-27 hours).

Getting Around
TO/FROM THE AIRPORT

To or from the airport, a regular taxi costs US$60 to US$75 for up to four people,

---

DETOUR: LA CANDELARIA

A few days in Cabo San Lucas makes it easy to forget you're in Mexico. A bumpy drive through the cacti and mesquite to the village of La Candelaria (population 85) will take care of that. This small *rancho* (rural settlement) in the foothills of the Sierra de la Laguna is known for its traditional clayware and makes a perfect daytrip, not to mention an excellent excuse to buy some locally made pottery.

In many ways, life in La Candelaria is much as it was on the peninsula's ranchos generations ago, when livestock was slaughtered at home, and household items such as leather riding chaps, horse-hair ropes, *huaraches* (sandals) and pottery were all made by hand.

Many of these traditions have faded from Baja ranch life, but in the last decade, La Candelaria's pottery tradition has resurfaced, thanks in large part to the efforts of US expat Lorena Hankins, who helped rekindle the craft among a group of local women. Several houses in town, and especially Hankins', sell beautiful handmade clayware: *cazuelas* (cooking bowls), *tinajas* (water coolers), *ollas* (bean pots) and *tortilleras* (tortilla holders). They're all as functional as they are beautiful. The tinajas, for example, keep water cool through evaporation, even in the sweltering summer heat. No glazes are used on the pottery, so there's no lead to worry about. You simply season them yourself and cook away.

All the clayware is made from scratch, beginning with the arduous process of digging up the clay, grinding it with *mano y metate* (mortar and pestle) and sifting out the powder. Each piece is formed by hand without a wheel, burnished several times with stones and fired in the ground. The result is a beautiful, blackish-gray, totally functional work of art.

A few men in town also make exceptionally durable chairs from *palo chino* (a deciduous hardwood) and woven palm buds. From tree trunk to chair, they make everything by hand. Ask at the house at the end of the road through town, near Lorena Hankins'.

During La Candelaria's small sugarcane harvest (usually in March or April), residents fire up the old Cuban sugar press by belting the gears to the rear wheel of an old truck (when the tractor isn't working). Around this time, you can buy the finished product: delicious cones of unrefined sugar called *panocha*. If you're lucky a few women may be making *milcocha* (sticky taffy) near the press.

There are no restaurants out here. Either pack a lunch or ask around for Christina's house, where Christina usually has something tasty on hand.

From Cabo San Lucas, head north on Leona Vicario, cross México 19 highway (reset your odometer here) and continue straight until you hit a three-way fork just after the pavement ends. Take the right fork, and you'll shortly reach a guarded gate, which an old man in a cowboy hat will open for you. Immediately after the gate is another fork; stay left. At odometer reading 5.6, you'll reach another fork; stay right. At odometer reading 7.5 you'll pass the turn to El Zauzal (stay left). About odometer-reading 9km, you'll run across a sandy stretch through the settlement of Los Pozos. At 13km you'll reach another arroyo with a big fig tree on the left and a shrine beneath it. Leaving the arroyo you'll soon crest a hill and pass the junction to La Trinidad; veer left here and you'll drop down into La Candelaria. Note on your return the sign says 'Cabo San Lucas - 22km.' The entire drive is actually about 17 miles (27.5km) from the highway to La Candelaria. It takes about one to 1½ hours and is passable for most cars except after heavy rains.

whereas *collectivo taxis* (nine-passenger minivans) charge US$13 to US$14 per person.

There's also an airport shuttle service leaving from outside the Plaza Las Glorias Hotel (Blvd Marina at Hidalgo) six times daily (US$14 per person). Most hotels offer shuttle service at about the same rate.

BUS

A fleet of modern orange/blue or green/yellow buses run between Cabo San Lucas and San José del Cabo along the Corridor at approximately half-hour intervals from early morning to about 8pm.

In Cabo, the main bus stop is on the south side of Cárdenas at Leona Vicario. Upon request, the driver will stop at any of the hotels or beaches along the Corridor. The flat fare is US$1.50. Aguila buses departing from the main bus terminal on México 19 also stop in San José del Cabo on their way to La Paz.

CAR & MOTORCYCLE

Numerous places along Blvd Marina and Cárdenas rent motor scooters and ATVs, but usually you're not allowed to take either onto the highways. Figure on spending about US$20/30/60 per hour/half-day/day.

As Cabo San Lucas is growing, finding parking is becoming a problem. Street parking is scarce in the downtown, as are paid lots. However, there is free public parking in the dirt lot at the southern end of Blvd Marina, past Plaza Las Glorias (free, for now anyway). Some of the finer restaurants are now beginning to offer valet parking.

Major international car rental agencies have multiple branches downtown, mostly along Cárdenas and Blvd Marina. Some also have desks inside the major hotels, and nearly all have offices just outside the airport in San José.

Prices vary as much as US$10 per day between companies, so it does pay to shop around. Renting an economy car shouldn't set you back more than US$45 to US$55 a day, insurance included (and do get that insurance). You might get better rates by prebooking in your home country. Agencies include the following:

Advantage (Map pp210-11; ☎ 143-0909; cnr Niños Héroes & Cárdenas)

Alamo (Map pp210-11; ☎ 143-6060; Cárdenas near Leona Vicario)

Avis (Map pp210-11; ☎ 143-4607; Blvd Marina, Plaza de los Mariachis)

Dollar (Map pp210-11; ☎ 143-4166, 143-1250; cnr Cárdenas & Mendoza)

National (Map pp210-11; ☎ 143-1818; Blvd Marina near Ocampo)

Payless (Map p205; ☎ 143-5222; Old Road to San José s/n)

TAXIS & SHUTTLES

Taxis are plentiful but lack meters and are not cheap; fares for destinations within downtown should not exceed US$5. New to Cabo are pedicabs (passenger bikes), which charge US$1.50 per person per ride. They are based on the south side of Blvd Lázaro Cárdenas at Morelos, or you can flag them down.

Directory

CONTENTS

ACCOMMODATIONS

Baja has a vast array of accommodations, from Tijuana dives and free beach camping to five-star Cabo resorts. This book categorizes accommodations as budget (where a typical room for two people costs under US$30), mid-range (US$30 to $75) and top end (above US$75). Camping is almost always the cheapest way to go. To the best of our knowledge, prices throughout this book always include taxes, which, when charged, are usually 12% (10% value added tax plus 2% hotel tax). Top end hotels usually tag on an additional 12% to 15%

in gratuities, bringing the grand total to a whopping 27%.

B&Bs

Bed and breakfasts are not a traditional Mexican form of accommodations, which explains why most are run by North American expatriates. B&Bs are usually small, luxurious, favorably located and characterized by a personal atmosphere. Prices vary widely and may range from US$40 to US$120 a night.

Camping

Most organized campgrounds are actually trailer parks, set up for RVs (camper vans) and trailers (caravans), but many accept tent campers at lower rates. Some are very basic, others quite luxurious. Expect to pay about US$3 to US$7 to pitch a tent, and US$8 to US$20 for two people in an RV with full hookups and facilities. Some restaurants or guesthouses in small beach spots will let you pitch a tent on their land for a few (US) dollars per person.

PRACTICALITIES

- Mexicans use the metric system for weights and measures.

- Electrical current is 110V, 60Hz; most plugs have two flat prongs, as in the USA and Canada.

- Of the nine main dailies in Baja California, those with the highest circulations are Mexicali's *La Voz de la Frontera*, Tijuana's *El Mexicano* and Tijuana's *El Heraldo de Baja California*.

- Four television stations operate in Baja California (Norte). Cable and satellite services are widely available throughout the peninsula.

- Of Baja California's numerous radio stations, the majority broadcast from Tijuana, Mexicali and Ensenada. Tijuana's Radio Frontera (102.5 FM) offers the broadest mix of independent programs and music.

All Mexican beaches are public property. You can camp for free on most of them, but they can be risky places for your belongings.

Homestays

Opportunities for homestays are few in Baja, except for those arranged through Spanish schools in La Paz and Ensenada. They usually include room and board and are a great way to get to know the people and culture.

Hostels

There are no Hostelling International-affiliated hostels in Baja, however, hostel-style accommodations are offered in Playas de Rosarito, El Sauzal near Ensenada and in Puerto San Isidro.

Hotels & Motels

Most decent hotels start around US$30, but most towns and all cities have a handful that are cheaper and still tolerable. Don't judge a hotel by its facade: Go inside, ask to see a room, sniff around and test the mattress.

In the tourist areas – especially in the northern coastal areas and Los Cabos – seasonal price fluctuations are quite common, as are differences between weekend and midweek rates. While price differences between single and double occupancy are small or nonexistent, it does matter whether you're staying in a room with one or two double beds.

Room nomenclature can be a bit confusing, especially when you're trying to book a room over the phone. A *sencilla* is a room with one double, queen- or king-size bed meant for one or two people. Both the bed and the room are also called *matrimonial* (you can guess the meaning). If you want a room with two beds you need to ask for a *doble* (double). Dobles are for two or four people, yet are priced differently depending on the number of people in the room.

'Singles' (s) in this book refer to rooms with one bed (for one or two people). 'Doubles' (d) are rooms with two beds, and the price is for two people. Sometimes the prices are quoted by room (r), meaning the price is for a room, usually for two people. See the inside back cover for a key to symbols used in this book.

Resorts

Los Cabos is Baja's main resort destination, with international chains operating luxury resorts along the Los Cabos Corridor that can cost as much as US$700 to US$800 for the cheapest room, not including meals. That said, most hover around US$250 for a double. If you're researching prices online, remember they generally won't include the 27% taxes and gratuities charge mentioned earlier.

BUSINESS HOURS

Shops are generally open Monday to Saturday from 9am or 10am to 7pm. *Siesta* (break time), when shops close, is loosely between 2pm and 4pm, although it is not usually observed in big cities or tourist resorts, where businesses tend to be open even on Sunday. Siestas are most common in central Baja. In rural areas, some shops close Saturday afternoon and all day Sunday.

Chain supermarkets, such as Calimax and Gigante, are usually open 7am to 11pm daily. Government offices usually close at 2pm.

Typical restaurant and café hours are 8am to between 10pm and midnight. Bars are normally open daily, but each seems to have its own special pattern of hours. Nightclubs open around 9pm but stay dead until well after 10pm.

Banks are normally open 9am to 5pm Monday to Friday and 9am to 1pm or 2pm Saturday. In smaller towns they may close earlier or not open Saturday. *Casas de cambio* (money exchange offices) usually stay open from 9am or 10am to 6pm or 7pm daily, longer in Los Cabos. Post offices typically open from 8am or 9am to 4pm, 5pm or 6pm Monday to Friday, and 9am to 1pm Saturday.

In this book we include opening hours for establishments only where they do not fit the above parameters.

CHILDREN

Kids don't have to be very old to enjoy activities such as snorkeling, horseback riding, shell collecting, boating and watching wildlife, and Baja has plenty of opportunities for these. You can only imagine your child's reaction at seeing a gray whale and her calf surfacing right next to your skiff. Take the kids on a pirate cruise (p213) in Cabo San

Lucas, or let them swim to their hearts' content in the tranquil, shallow waters of Bahía Concepción (p147) or Bahía de Los Angeles (p128). If you're driving through Mexicali, promise them a stop at the Sol del Niño (p109), a science and technology museum for children. The big resorts of Los Cabos usually offer a myriad of activities to keep the kids busy during the day while you're off scuba diving or fishing.

Diapers (nappies) are widely available, but you may not easily find creams, lotions, baby foods or familiar medicines outside of larger cities and tourist towns. Bring what you need. Rarely, if ever, will you find a child's safety seat in a taxi, but most international car rental companies can arrange for one in the car, though you may have to pay extra. Larger hotels often have a baby-sitting service, and others may be able to help you make arrangements.

Lonely Planet's *Travel with Children,* by Cathy Lanigan, has lots of practical advice on the subject, as well as firsthand stories from many Lonely Planet authors and others who have done it.

Parental consent forms are required for people under 18 traveling with one or no parents; see p234 for more information.

CLIMATE CHARTS

Baja California is famous for its sunny skies and warm temperatures, but the peninsula actually has a surprising range of climates. As a general rule, temperatures are higher in the south, along the Sea of Cortez coast and at lower elevations. In the tropical Cape Region from La Paz to Cabo San Lucas, the hottest months, May to October, are also the wettest. Tropical storms called *chubascos* occasionally pelt the area, which is also visited by hurricanes once in a while. Winter is generally warm and sunny. For tips on the best seasons to travel, see p9.

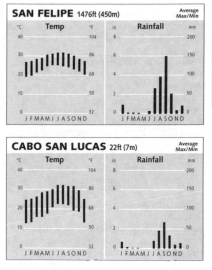

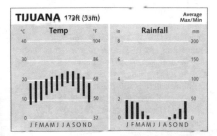

COURSES

Baja is less popular than mainland Mexico for studying Spanish, but Ensenada and La Paz both have good language schools for foreigners. Rates are about US$220 per week, and schools can arrange homestays.

CUSTOMS

Things that visitors are allowed to bring into Mexico duty-free include items for personal use such as clothing; a camera and video camera; up to 12 rolls of film or videocassettes; a cellular phone; a portable computer; a CD or cassette player; medicine for personal use, with prescription in the case of psychotropic drugs; 3L of wine, beer or liquor; 400 cigarettes; and US$300 worth of other goods (US$50 if arriving by land).

US residents returning to the USA from Baja may bring in duty-free items valued up to US$400, for personal use only. You're allowed 1 liter (33.8 fluid oz) of hard liquor (spirits), wine or beer into mainland California every 30 days. You may bring in 100 cigars (though not of Cuban origin) and 200 cigarettes duty free.

Fireworks, switchblade knives, products made from endangered species, plants, seeds, soil, pork, poultry and live birds are all prohibited from import into the USA. US Customs allows fish caught in Mexico to enter the USA as long as it conforms with

Mexican bag limits, the species is somehow identifiable and you can produce a Mexican fishing license (see p41).

DANGERS & ANNOYANCES

People new to Baja worry about two things: theft and military checkpoints. If you're driving, see p239 for more on both. If you don't have a car, your worries are few. But use common sense: avoid dark streets at night, don't leave items unattended on the beach, and don't flaunt your (monetary) goods. Generally, only the bigger hotels have *caja fuertes* (safes) for valuables, but rarely will things go missing when they don't.

Tourist police squads patrol most major destinations, keeping things pretty safe. Tijuana and Mexicali, like any big cities, warrant caution after dark. Tijuana is the only city where violent crimes occur frequently, though cases involving tourists are rare.

As for scams, perhaps the most prevalent of all are those by telephone companies charging extortionate prices through toll-free numbers (for details, see p232).

Recreational Hazards

Many of Baja's Pacific beaches have dangerous offshore rip currents, so ask before entering the water, and be sure someone on shore knows your whereabouts. Hire sports and aquatic equipment only from reputable sources, such as those listed in this book. Safety standards are generally lower than in countries like the USA or Australia, and the operator may not carry any accident liability insurance. Several tourists have been injured and even killed in jet ski and diving accidents, and have been subjected to dangerous landings when parasailing.

DISABLED TRAVELERS

Mexico makes few concessions to the disabled, though some hotels and restaurants (mostly toward the top end of the market) and public buildings are starting to provide wheelchair access. Mobility is easiest in the major tourist resorts, where dropped curbs are more common than elsewhere. Public transportation is mainly hopeless.

Mobility International USA (☎ 541-343-1284; www.miusa.org) advises disabled travelers on mobility issues and runs exchange programs (including in Mexico).

Official information can make Mexico sound more alarming than it really is, but you might still find advice from your country's foreign affairs department valuable:

Australia (☎ 1300-139-281; www.dfat.gov.au)
Canada (☎ 800-267-8376; www.dfait-maeci .gc.ca)
UK (☎ 0870-606-0290; www.fco.gov.uk)
USA (☎ 202-647-5225; http://travel.state.gov)

In the UK, **Radar** (☎ 020-7250-3222; www.radar .org.uk) is run by and for disabled people. Its excellent website has links to good travel and holiday-specific sites, as does Australia's **Acrod** (www.acrod.org.au).

Another excellent information source for disabled travelers is **Access-able Travel Source** (www.access-able.com).

DISCOUNT CARDS

The ISIC student card, the GO25 card for travelers 12 to 25, and the ITIC card for teachers can all help you obtain reduced-price airfare to or from Mexico at student and youth-oriented travel agencies. Once in Baja, however, these cards won't make much of a difference.

EMBASSIES & CONSULATES
Mexican Embassies & Consulates

The following are embassies unless otherwise noted. Updated details can be found at www .sre.gob.mx.

Some Mexican embassy and consulate websites are very useful information sources on visas and similar matters.

Australia Canberra (☎ 02-6273-3963; www.embassyof mexicoinaustralia.org; 14 Perth Ave, Yarralumla, ACT 2600)
Canada Ottawa (☎ 613-233-8988; www.embamexcan .com; 45 O'Connor St, Suite 1500, ON K1P 1A4) consulate in Montreal (☎ 514-288-2502; www.consulmex.qc.ca; 2055 rue Peel, bureau 1000, QC H3A 1V4); consulate in Toronto (☎ 416-368-2875; www.consulmex.com; Commerce Court West, 199 Bay St, Suite 4440, ON M5L 1E9); consulate in Vancouver (☎ 604-684-3547; www.consulmexvan .com; 710-1177 West Hastings St, BC V6E 2K3)
France Paris (☎ 01-53-70-27-70; www.sre.gob.mx/fran cia; 9 rue de Longchamp, 75116); consulate in Paris (☎ 01 42 86 56 20; 4 rue Notre Dame des Victoires, 75002)
Germany Berlin (☎ 030-269-323-332; www.embamex .de [in Spanish]; Klingelhöferstrasse 3, 10785 Berlin); consulate in Frankfurt-am-Main (☎ 069-299-8750; Taunusanlage 21, 60325)

Ireland Dublin (☎ 01-260-0699; www.sre.gob.mx/irlanda; 43 Ailesbury Rd, Ballsbridge, Dublin 4)
Japan Tokyo (☎ 3-3581-1131; www.sre.gob.mx/japon; 2-15-1 Nagata-cho, Chiyoda-ku, 100-0014)
New Zealand Wellington (☎ 04-472-0555; www.mexico.org.nz; Level 8, 111 Customhouse Quay)
UK London (☎ 020-7235-6393; www.embamex.co.uk; 8 Halkin St, SW1X 7DW)
USA Washington, DC (☎ 202-728-1600; www.sre.gob.mx/eua; 1911 Pennsylvania Ave NW, 20006); consulate in Washington, DC (☎ 202-736-1000; consulwas@aol.com; 2827 16th St NW, 20009)

Embassies & Consulates in Baja

Most of the foreign consulates in Baja are in Tijuana. Besides the countries listed below, Austria, China, Finland, Gambia, Honduras, Italy, Korea, Norway, Spain and Switzerland also have representations in this city.

Canada Tijuana (Map pp58-9; ☎ 664-684-0461; tijuana@canada.org.mx; German Gedovius 10411-101, Zona Río); San José del Cabo (Map pp190-1; ☎ 624-142-4333; loscabos@canada.org.mx; Plaza José Green No 9, Blvd Mijares) The Canadian consulate will also assist citizens of Australia and Belize.
France Tijuana (☎ 664-681-3133; Calle Fresno 10897 at Av del Bosque, Jardines de Chapultepec; www.consulfr.org.mx/honoraires/tijuana.htm); La Paz (☎ 612-122-1620; smmahieux@prodigy.net.mx; Zaragosa 30)
Germany Tijuana (Map p54; ☎ 664-680-1830, 664-680-2512; Cantera 400-305, Edificio Ole, Playas de Tijuana)
UK Tijuana (Map pp58-9; ☎ 664-681 7323, 664-686-5320; balnyan@telnor.net; Blvd Salinas 1500, Colonia Aviación, La Mesa)
USA Tijuana (Map p54; ☎ 664-622-7400; Tapachula 96, Colonia Hipódromo; nighttime assistance after 4:30pm in San Diego, CA ☎ 619-692-2154); Cabo San Lucas (Map pp210-11; ☎ 624-143-3566; Blvd Marina No 1, Local No C-4, Plaza Náutica)

FESTIVALS & EVENTS

Bajacalifornianos observe all major national and Catholic holidays (see p228), some of which involve public festivities, processions, music and food. Special festivities and fairs like Carnaval and saints' days usually take place only in major towns and cities. See regional entries for information on local events.

JANUARY
Día de los Reyes Magos (Three Kings' Day; Epiphany; January 6) Mexican children traditionally receive gifts this day, rather than at Christmas.

FEBRUARY
Día de la Candelaría (Candlemas; February 2) Processions, bullfights and dancing occur in many towns to commemorate the presentation of Jesus in the temple, 40 days after his birth.
Carnaval (Carnival; late February to early March) Celebrated in Ensenada (p83), San Felipe (p120) and La Paz (p168), usually the week before Lent, with parades, music, food and fireworks.

MARCH/APRIL
Día del Señor San José (St Joseph's Day; March 19) Residents of San José del Cabo (p193) celebrate the festival of St Joseph, the town's patron saint, with street dances, horse races, food fairs and fireworks.
Semana Santa (Holy Week; March/April) Starting on Palm Sunday, a week before Easter, this is celebrated in every church in Baja. It's also when Mexicans flock to the beaches to paaarty, so be ready.

AUGUST
Fiesta de la Vendimia (Wine Harvest Festival; early August) Ensenada and Valle de Guadalupe kick off the grape harvest season (p83).

SEPTEMBER
Día de Nuestra Señora de Loreto (Our Lady of Loreto; September 8) Loreto celebrates its founding with much vigor on this day (p152).
Día de la Independencia (September 15 to 16) Commemorates Mexican independence from Spain (1821). The biggest celebrations take place in Tijuana (p60) and La Paz (p168), with fireworks, horse races, folk dances and mariachi bands.

NOVEMBER
Día de Todos los Santos (All Saints' Day; November 1) & **Día de los Muertos** (Day of the Dead; November 2) Cemeteries throughout Mexico come alive as families visit graveyards to commune with their dead on the night of November 1 and the day of November 2, when the souls of the dead are believed to return to earth. The festivities are especially colorful in Tijuana (p60) and La Paz (p168).

DECEMBER
Día de Nuestra Señora de Guadalupe (Festival of Our Lady of Guadalupe; December 12) Tecate hosts one of the most interesting celebrations of this day (see p104).
Posadas (December 16 to 24) Children and adults parade with candles, reenacting the journey of Mary and Joseph to Bethlehem; this celebration is more common in small towns than big cities.
Navidad (Christmas Day; December 25) Marks the end of a week of posadas.

DIRECTORY

FOOD

Some of the Eating sections in the larger towns throughout this book are divided by type of cuisine, while others are divided by neighborhoods. The restaurant scene of each town dictates how the establishments are arranged, to make deciding on where to eat easier for the reader. For each restaurant, average prices are given for main courses. 'Mains' means a main dish, as opposed to an entire meal. If it's a taquería, average prices of tacos are given. For bakeries, ice cream stores and coffee shops, assume you can get a treat or two for under US$2 or US$3, depending on how many scoops or *pan dulces* (morning sweet breads) you decide to eat. For details on regional cuisine, see the Food & Drink chapter (p43).

GAY & LESBIAN TRAVELERS

Though it might appear to be one of the world's more heterosexual countries, Mexico is more broad-minded than visitors might expect. Gays and lesbians tend to keep a low profile but in general rarely attract open discrimination or violence. In Baja, Tijuana is the city with the liveliest scene, although smaller ones exist in Ensenada and Mexicali – though, perhaps surprisingly, not in Los Cabos.

A decent source of information (mostly in Spanish) on the Internet is **Frontera Gay** (www.fronteragay.com), which focuses on the border-town scene. The 'mother' of all Mexican gay websites, though, is **The Gay Mexico Network** (www.gaymexico.net), sort of the central clearinghouse for information on all things gay throughout Mexico. Its Tijuana section lists gay clubs in the city.

Based in San Diego, California, **Arco Iris Tours** (☎ in the USA 800-765-4370; www.arcoiristours.com) specializes in G&L travel to Mexico and offers tours to Tijuana.

HOLIDAYS

The chief Mexican holiday periods are Christmas-New Year's, Semana Santa (a week either side of Easter) and mid-July to mid-August. Transportation and tourist accommodations are heavily booked at these times. Banks, post offices and government offices throughout Baja are closed on the following national holidays:

Año Nuevo January 1 – New Year's Day
Día de la Constitución February 5 – Constitution Day

Día de la Bandera February 24 – Day of the National Flag
Día de Nacimiento de Benito Juárez March 21 – Anniversary of Benito Juárez' birth
Semana Santa – Business closures are usually from Good Friday to Easter Sunday
Día del Trabajo May 1 – Labor Day
Cinco de Mayo May 5 – Anniversary of Mexico's 1862 victory over the French at Puebla, where it is grandly celebrated. It's a normal, business-as-usual day in Baja California.
Día de la Independencia September 16 – Commemorates the start of Mexico's war for independence from Spain; the biggest celebrations are in Mexico City, the evening before.
Día de la Raza October 12 – Commemorates Columbus' discovery of the New World and the founding of the *mestizo* (mixed-ancestry) Mexican people
Día de la Revolución November 20 – Anniversary of the 1910 Mexican Revolution
Día de Navidad December 25 – Christmas Day

At Easter, businesses close from Good Friday (*Viernes Santo*) to Easter Sunday (*Domingo de Resurrección*). Many offices and businesses close during major national festivals (see p227).

INSURANCE

A travel insurance policy to cover theft, loss and medical problems is definitely a good idea. Some policies specifically exclude 'dangerous' activities such as scuba diving, motorcycling, and even trekking. For further information on medical insurance, see p244. For information on motor insurance, see p241.

INTERNET ACCESS

Visiting an Internet café is the easiest way to get online in Baja. Only the tiniest of villages lacks a café, so you'll rarely have trouble finding one. Prices are highest in Los Cabos (up to US$7 per hour), while prices on the rest of the peninsula are US$1 to US$2 per hour.

Mid-range and top-end hotels usually have phone lines in the rooms, though your portable's modem may not work once you leave your home country. The safest option is to buy a reputable 'global' modem before you leave home. Many B&B or boutique-type hotels have a computer where you can go online for free.

For more information on global connectivity, see www.teleadapt.com.

LEGAL MATTERS

Mexico's judicial system is based on Roman or Napoleonic law, presuming an accused person guilty until proven innocent. In all but the most minor car accidents, everyone involved is considered guilty and liable until proven otherwise. Without car insurance, you will be detained until fault has been established.

Drivers found with drugs or weapons on board are likely to have their vehicles confiscated and be detained in jail for months while their cases are investigated. Drinking on Mexican streets is illegal, as is fighting and disturbing the public order.

If arrested, you have the right to notify your embassy or consulate, but consular officials can't get you out of jail.

If you encounter minor legal hassles with public officials or local businesspeople in Baja California (Norte), you can contact **La Procuraduría de Protección al Turista** (Attorney General for Tourist Protection), now under the auspices of the state-run tourist office, Secture. The numbers to contact are as follows:

Ensenada (☎ 646-172-3022)
Mexicali (☎ 686-566-1116)
Playas de Rosarito (☎ 661-612-0200)
Tecate (☎ 665-654-1095)
Tijuana (☎ 664-688-0505)
San Felipe (☎ 686-577-1155)
San Quintín (☎ 616-163-3843)

The 24 hour national hotline maintained by **Secture** (☎ 01-800-903-92-00 toll-free anywhere in Mexico) also provides advice on tourist protection laws and where to obtain help.

MAPS

The *Baja California Road Map*, published by the Automobile Club of Southern California, an affiliate of AAA, is the best general map of the peninsula. It is available for free to AAA members and sold to everyone else for US$3.95 at AAA offices and in bookstores.

International Travel Maps & Books (ITMB; in Vancouver, Canada ☎ 604-879-3621; www.itmb.com) has the most recent (2003) map of Baja California (US$13.95) at a scale of 1:1,000,000.

The *Baja Almanac* (1997; US$24.95), by **Baja Almanac Publishing** (www.baja-almanac.com), contains topographical maps at a scale of 1:100,000 and is a good resource for off-road travel.

Essential for hikers and backpackers is the series of topo maps published by **INEGI** (Instituto Nacional de Estadística, Geografía e Informática; www.inegi.gob.mx) and available for US$6 each. There are INEGI offices in Tijuana (☎ 664-638-7931; Av Revolución 1046 between Calle 8 & 9), Mexicali (☎ 686-557-5883; Calzada Independencia 1086) and La Paz (☎ 612-123-3150; Altamirano 2790).

All of these maps may be ordered from the US-based companies **Map World** (☎ 888-849-6277; www.mapworld.com) and **Maplink** (☎ 805-692-6777; www.maplink.com). In the UK, a good place for Baja-related maps and books is **Stanfords** (☎ 020-7240-3611; www.stanfords.co.uk).

MONEY

Mexico's currency is the peso, which is divided into 100 centavos. Coins come in denominations of five, 10, 20 and 50 centavos and one, two, five, 10, 20 and 50 pesos, and there are notes of 10, 20, 50, 100, 200 and 500 pesos.

Both Mexican pesos and US dollars are commonly used in Baja, but US dollars may not be accepted in some small towns and villages. The $ sign refers to pesos in Mexico. The designations 'N$' and 'NP' (both for *nuevos pesos*) and 'MN' (*moneda nacional*) all refer to pesos. Prices quoted in US dollars will normally be written as 'US$5,' '$5 Dlls' or '5 USD.'

Because the peso's exchange value is unpredictable, prices in this book are given in US-dollar equivalents. Refer to the inside back cover for exchange rates and p11 for an idea of what things cost.

ATMs

Automated teller machines (ATMs) are the easiest way of obtaining cash pesos from a credit card or a bank account back home. They are common in nearly all significant towns, but not necessarily in all popular tourist destinations (such as Mulegé and San Ignacio). If a town has a bank, it almost always has an ATM. Cirrus and Plus are the most common networks. Despite the handling fee that may be charged to your account, ATMs offer a better exchange rate than banks and cambios.

Cash

Carrying wads of cash anywhere is inherently risky, but you will need it when paying bus and taxi drivers, making small purchases at convenience stores, eating at all but the fanciest restaurants, leaving tips and so on. It is definitely the preferred method of payment in smaller, remote parts of the peninsula.

Credit Cards

Major credit cards are accepted by virtually all airlines, car rental companies and travel agents in Baja and by many hotels, upscale restaurants and shops in the border zone and in the Cape Region. Outside of these major tourist hubs, however, few businesses will honor your credit cards. MasterCard and Visa are the most widely accepted, American Express is accepted to a lesser extent. Note that Pemex stations will not take credit cards.

Moneychangers

Money can be exchanged at banks, hotels and *casas de cambio* (exchange houses). Exchange rates vary a little from one bank or casa de cambio to another. Different rates are also often posted for *efectivo* (cash) and *documento* (traveler's checks). Cambios are usually quicker and less bureaucratic than banks. They also have longer hours and may be open evenings or weekends.

Banks rarely charge commissions, but cambios do. Hotels, especially at the top end of the scale, offer poor rates and often charge commissions as well.

Traveler's Checks

Traveler's checks are generally accepted in tourist areas, and most banks will cash them, but the bureaucracy involved can be tiresome. Some banks will not cash more than US$200 worth of checks at a time. Major-brand checks, denominated in US dollars, are best, and American Express is most widely accepted.

PHOTOGRAPHY & VIDEO

In tourist areas, print film is widely available at supermarkets, drugstores and tourist shops, but for slide film you usually have to go to a specialized photography store. Outside the cities, slide film is difficult to find, and even print film may not be widely available. Stock up before heading into the boondocks or bring your favorite film from home. Mexican Customs allows the duty-free import of up to 12 rolls of film, but enforcement is lax. Prices are generally slightly higher than what you'd pay in the USA and Canada.

In general, buy film for its planned usage. For proverbially sunny Baja, 100 ASA film is just about the most useful and versatile, as it gives you good color and enough speed to capture most situations on film. To avoid having harsh shadows, it's best to shoot during early morning and late afternoon, when the sun is low in the sky and the light is softer. If you plan to shoot brightly lit night scenes, or in dark areas, without a tripod, switch to 400 ASA.

A polarizing filter is a most useful piece of gear down here, as it deepens the blue of the sky and water, can eliminate reflections and makes clouds appear quite dramatic. It's best used to photograph nature.

Mexicans, especially in tourist areas, are normally very gracious about being photographed. No one seems to mind being photographed in the context of an overall scene, but if you want a close-up shot, you should ask first. It's not a good idea to photograph soldiers.

For more tips on travel photography, pick up a copy of Lonely Planet's *Travel Photography*.

PETS

Under Mexican law, travelers entering the country may bring a dog, cat or up to four canaries (!) with them, provided they can present the following certificates at the border: a pet health certificate signed by a registered veterinarian and issued not more than 72 hours before the animal enters Mexico and a pet vaccination certificate showing inoculation against rabies, hepatitis, pip and leptospirosis. Unless you have no alternative, it's probably better to leave your pet at home.

POST

The Servicio Postal Mexicano (the formal name for Mexico's national postal service) sells postage stamps and sends and receives mail at every *oficina de correos* (post office) in Baja.

Unfortunately, it is not distinguished by efficiency: letters from Tijuana, for instance, arrive in San Diego only after passing through Mexico City.

Sending Mail

Service is not always dependable, and packages in particular sometimes go missing. Mark all mail conspicuously with the phrase 'Vía Aérea' (air mail). Registered (certificado or registrado) service helps ensure delivery and costs just US$1.50 extra for international mail. An airmail letter from Mexico to the USA or Canada can take four to 14 days to arrive. Mail to Europe may take between one and three weeks, to Australasia a month or more.

An airmail letter or postcard weighing up to 20g costs US$0.80 to the USA or Canada, US$1 to Europe and US$1.10 to the rest of the world. Items weighing between 20g and 50g cost US$1.30, US$1.50 and US$1.80, respectively.

Receiving Mail

You can receive letters and packages care of a post office if they're addressed as in the following example:

Jane SMITH (last name in capitals)
Lista de Correos
Tijuana
Baja California 00000 (post code)
MEXICO

When the letter reaches the post office, the name of the addressee is placed on an alphabetical list, which is updated daily. To claim your mail, present your passport or other identification. There's no charge; the snag is that many post offices hold 'Lista' mail for only 10 days before returning it to the sender.

If you think you're going to pick up mail more than 10 days after it has arrived, change 'Lista de Correos' in the above address to 'Poste Restante.' Poste Restante may hold mail for up to a month. Inbound mail usually takes as long to arrive as outbound mail does.

SOLO TRAVELERS

The main drawback to traveling alone is accommodation. As a solo traveler, you'll pay more than twice what you would if splitting a room with another person. There are few hostels in Baja to cut prices, so camping is the cheapest way out of this dilemma. Also, with a majority of Baja's tourists being drivers from the USA and Canada, it's not as easy on the peninsula as in the rest of

Mexico to hook up with other travelers. Another bummer about traveling alone is having to leave your belongings on the beach when you go for a swim. The only solution is to take to the beach only things (cheap flip-flops, towel and hat) that you don't mind losing. You can always leave your key at the hotel desk.

On the upside, traveling alone can be a great way of getting into the local culture as well as improving your Spanish, because it makes communication with Mexicans essential.

Traveling alone as a woman implies inherent risks anywhere in the world; Baja is no exception, and it's certainly not more dangerous than other places. See p234 for more information for female travelers.

TELEPHONE
Calling Cards

If you have an AT&T, MCI or Sprint card, or a Canadian calling card, you can use it for calls from Mexico to the USA or Canada by dialing the appropriate access number; contact your long distance carrier for numbers and rates before leaving.

Call Offices

Cabinas (sometimes also called casetas de teléfono) are call stations, usually found in shops, where you take the call in a booth after an on-the-spot operator connects it for you. They are far fewer casetas in Baja than the rest of Mexico, but most towns have at least one. They can be more expensive than Telmex pay phones but not always so. You don't need a phone card to use them, and they eliminate street noise. Many offer off-peak discounts.

Collect Calls

A llamada por cobrar (collect call) can cost the receiving party much more than if they call you, so you may prefer to find a phone where you can receive an incoming call, then pay for a quick call to the other party to ask them to call you back.

If you do need to make a collect call, you can do so from pay phones without a card. Call an operator on ☎ 020 for domestic calls or ☎ 090 for international calls. Collect calls to the USA and Canada can be made with a calling card number by dialing your carrier's access number.

MEXICO COUNTRY CODE

To call a number in Mexico from another country, dial your international access code, then the **Mexico country code** (☎ 52), then the area code and number.

Mexican international operators can usually speak English. Some telephone casetas and hotels will make collect calls for you, but they usually charge for the service.

Mobile Phones

The most widespread mobile (cellular) phone system in Mexico is **Telcel** (www.telcel.com), with coverage virtually everywhere that has a significant population. You can buy a Telcel mobile for under US$200 and purchase prepaid minutes (in the form of cards from any Telcel store) in denominations starting at US$10. To dial any mobile telephone from a landline, you must dial ☎ 044 before the area code, giving you a total of 10 digits to punch. US cell phones work in major population centers throughout Baja, but check those rates before racking up the minutes. I paid US$1.50 per minute with my carrier without setting up any special plan.

Prefixes, Codes & Costs

When making a direct call, you need to know what *prefijo* (prefix) and *claves* (country or area codes) to include before the number. Since 1999, Mexican telephone numbers have gone through two major changes. All local numbers now have seven digits plus a three-digit area code, required when calling the area from another area code.

Calling within the same town, you don't need to add an area code to a number. Your call will cost about US$0.05/minute on a Telmex pay phone. To call another town in Mexico, add 01 + area code before the number, which will cost about US$0.40/minute. To call another country, add 00 + country code + area code. Calls will cost about US$0.50 per minute to the USA or Canada, US$2 per minute to Europe or South America, and about US$2.50 to Australasia.

When dialing Mexican toll-free numbers (☎ 800 followed by seven digits) always use the 01 prefix. You can call these numbers

from Telmex pay phones without inserting a telephone card. Some US and Canadian toll-free numbers can be reached from Mexico (dial ☎ 001 before the 800), but you will probably have to pay for the call.

To speak to a domestic operator, call ☎ 020; for an international operator, call ☎ 090. For Mexican directory information, call ☎ 040.

Public Pay Phones

Public pay phones are nearly everywhere, and most work well. Pay phones are operated by a number of different companies: The most common and reliable are those marked with the name of the country's biggest phone company, Telmex. Telmex pay phones work on *tarjetas telefónicas* or *tarjetas Ladatel* (both the generic way of saying 'phone card'), which come in denominations of 30, 50 or 100 pesos (about US$3, US$4.50 and US$9, respectively). These cards are sold at many kiosks and shops – look for the blue-and-yellow sign reading 'De Venta Aquí Ladatel.' Nortel owns the public phones in northern Baja.

Scams

In Baja's tourist areas, you'll notice a variety of other pay phones advertising that they accept credit cards or that you can make easy collect calls to the USA on them. You'll also see stickers with a toll-free number slapped all over Telmex and Telnor pay phones. Avoid using both like dirty Tijuana water! Charges for these operator-assisted calls are exorbitant: rates of US$7 to US$28 for the first minute, followed by US$4 to US$10 for each additional minute are not uncommon. The operator may quote you cheaper rates, but you won't know your final tally until it's posted on your next month's credit card bill – by then, it'll be impossible to prove that you were given a different rate.

TIME

The northern state of Baja California is on Pacific Standard Time (PST), while Baja California Sur is on Mountain Standard Time (MST), which is one hour ahead of PST. PST is eight hours behind Greenwich Mean Time (GMT), while MST is seven hours behind GMT.

In summer, PST is moved ahead one hour for Pacific Daylight Time (PDT) and thus becomes the same as MST. Northern Baja is always on the same time as mainland California.

Bus departures and opening hours are often given on the 24-hour clock ('military time').

TOILETS

Public toilets do exist, but never bank on finding one when you need it. Better yet, take advantage of facilities in places like hotels, restaurants, bars and bus stations. Toilet paper may not always be available, so carry some with you. If there's a basket beside the toilet, put paper, tampons, etc in it – it's there because the drains can't cope otherwise.

TOURIST INFORMATION

For tourist information before you leave home, contact the **Mexican Tourism Board** (☎ in the USA or Canada 800-449-3942; www.visitmexico.com).

Most of the major tourist towns in Baja California have tourist offices, especially in Baja California (Norte). They can be helpful with maps and brochures, and usually some staff members speak English.

Offices of the **Secretaría de Turismo del Estado** (Secture) are affiliated with the state governments of either Baja California (Norte) or Baja California Sur. Most sizable towns also have a tourist office associated with the **Comité de Turismo y Convenciones** (Cotuco; Committee on Tourism & Conventions).

TOURS

The following companies offer great ways to get to and around Baja, meet new people and see some of Baja's best attractions. For more specific activity-based tours, such as kayaking trips, see the Baja Outdoors chapter, p35.

Green Tortoise (☎ 415-956-7500, 800-867-8647; www.greentortoise.com) Based out of San Francisco. Operates its Baja Beach Daze tour from November to April. Sort of a hostel on wheels, Green Tortoise appeals to the young and adventurous who put camaraderie over comfort. Tours may be joined in San Francisco, Los Angeles or San Diego and run either nine or 15 days. Prices range from US$419 (plus US$91 for food) to US$549 (plus US$151 for food). Its 17-day whale-watching excursion costs US$599 plus US$151 for food.

Baja Discovery (☎ 619-262-0700, 800-829-2252; www.bajadiscovery.com) Operates out of San Diego and offers several tours around Baja, including its popular four- to eight-day walking excursions. Prices are US$1095 to US$1975.

Baja California Tours (☎ 858-454-7166, 800-336-5454; www.bajaspecials.com; 7734 Herschel Av, Ste O, La Jolla, California) Specializes in short-term guided tours to northern Baja, including Tijuana, Playas de Rosarito, Puerto Nuevo and Ensenada. Also offers themed tours, set around special events like wine festivals or bicycle races. A two-day wine country tour costs US$209. Its daytrip to Ensenada costs US$60.

VISAS & DOCUMENTS
Passport

Though it's not recommended, US and Canadian tourists can enter Baja without a passport if they have official photo identification, such as a driver's license, plus an original copy of their birth certificate or (for US citizens only) a certificate of naturalization. Citizens of other countries who are permanent residents in the USA have to take their passport and Permanent Resident Alien Cards (green cards). Naturalized Canadian citizens require a valid passport. Citizens from all other countries must have a valid passport and, in some cases, a tourist visa (see Visas, next).

Visas

Citizens of the USA, Canada, European Union countries, Australia, New Zealand, Norway, Switzerland, Iceland, Israel, Japan, Argentina and Chile are among those who do not require visas to enter Mexico as tourists. Nationals of most African, Asian and eastern European nations require visas. Some nationals will also require a roundtrip ticket to enter Mexico. Check well ahead of travel with your local Mexican embassy or consulate.

US and Canadian citizens visiting Mexico on business must complete form FM-N, authorizing the conduct of business for 30 days. This form is available from Mexican consulates or at the border. You will need a valid passport or original birth certificate plus a letter from your company stating the purpose of your trip and the source of your income. If your stay exceeds 30 days, you will need to apply for an FM-3 card. In addition to your passport and company letter, you will be required to provide two photographs and must pay US$150. This permit is good for multiple entries for one year.

Travel Permits & Tourist Fees

The Mexican tourist card – officially the Forma Migratoria para Turista (FMT) – is a small document that is stamped by Mexican immigration when you enter Mexico and which you must keep until you leave. It is available free of charge at border crossings, international airports and ports. At the US-Mexico border, you won't usually be given a tourist card automatically but must pick it up at the Instituto Nacional de Migración (INM, National Immigration Institute), which has offices at all the border crossings (p237).

The tourist card is not valid until you pay a tourist fee equivalent of 195 pesos (about US$18). If you're entering by air, the fee is already included in your ticket. If you're entering by land, you must pay the fee at a Banjercito bank, which has teller windows at all major border crossings. Bank hours at Tijuana-San Ysidro are 8am to 10pm weekdays, 8am to 6pm Saturday, and noon to 4pm Sunday; the bank at Otay Mesa is open 10am to 6pm daily. In Tecate, bank hours are 8am to 4pm daily, and in Mexicali it's open around the clock.

In Baja you do not need a stamped tourist card if you're entering by land and are staying north of Ensenada or San Felipe for visits of fewer than 72 hours. Everyone, regardless of age, must get a stamped tourist card for travel beyond Ensenada or San Felipe.

One section of the card deals with the length of your stay in Mexico. Normally you will be given the maximum 180 days if you ask for it. It's always advisable to put down more days than you think you'll need. The card is good for multiple entries.

Tourist Card Extensions & Lost Cards

If the number of days given on your tourist card is fewer than the 180-day maximum, its validity may be extended one or more times, at no cost, up to the maximum.

To get a card extended, you must apply to the Servicios Migratorios (immigrations), which has offices in many towns and cities. The procedure is free and usually quick. You'll need your passport, tourist card, photocopies of these documents and – at some offices – evidence of 'sufficient funds.' Most offices will not extend a card until a few days before it is due to expire.

If you lose your card or need more information, contact the **Sectur's emergency hotline** (☎ in Mexico City 55-5250-0123, toll-free in Mexico 01-800-903-9200).

Consent Forms for Minors

Every year numerous parents try to run away from the USA or Canada to Mexico with their children to escape legal entanglements with the other parent. To prevent this, minors (people under 18) entering Mexico without one or both of their parents are officially required to show a notarized consent form, signed by the absent parent or parents, giving permission for the young traveler to enter Mexico. A form for this purpose is available from Mexican consulates. In the case of divorced parents, a custody document may be acceptable instead. If one or both parents are dead, or the traveler has only one legal parent, a notarized statement to that effect may be required.

These rules are aimed primarily at visitors from the USA and Canada but apparently apply to all nationalities. Enforcement, however, is fairly lax.

WOMEN

In a land of machismo, women have to make some concessions to local custom – but don't let that put you off. In general, Mexicans are great believers in the difference (rather than the equality) between the sexes. Foreign women without male companions will inevitably be confronted with catcalls and attempts to chat them up. Many men may only want to talk to you, but it can get very tiresome. A good way to discourage unwanted attention is to avoid eye contact (sunglasses will help here) and, if possible, ignore the attention altogether. Otherwise, use a cool but polite initial response and a consistent, firm 'No.' Of course, it is possible to turn uninvited attention into a worthwhile conversation by making clear that you are willing to talk, but no more.

In general, you should be fine if you use common sense. Don't put yourself in peril by doing things Mexican women would not do, such as challenging a man's masculinity, drinking alone in a cantina, hitchhiking without a male companion or going alone to isolated places.

Although informal 'dress codes' are more permissive than in the recent past, avoid clothing that Mexican men may interpret as provocative to avoid unwanted come-ons.

Women must recognize the threat of rape, which is more of a problem in tourist than in rural areas. You're more vulnerable if you've been drinking or using drugs than if you're sober. At night, if you're going out with friends, take care not to become separated from the group. Don't hitchhike, especially when alone, and don't pick up hitchhikers when you're driving alone. Driving at night is not a good idea either.

WORK

Except for those directly involved in tourist specialties, like natural history tours or diving, paid work is not an attractive option in Baja. Wages are low by US or European standards, and permits are hard to obtain. English tutoring may be feasible in Tijuana or Mexicali, but competition is stiff because of the proximity to the border.

Transportation

GETTING THERE & AWAY

ENTERING THE COUNTRY

Immigration officers won't usually keep you waiting any longer than it takes to flip through your passport and enter the length of your stay on your tourist card. See p233 for further information on documents. Anyone traveling to Baja via the USA (be it by air, land or sea) should check US visa requirements.

AIR

The USA is the only country with direct international flights to Baja California. Most flights originate on the West Coast, from Los Angeles in particular, although there are also some from Phoenix, Tucson, Dallas-Fort Worth, Chicago and Denver. All Mexican airlines also operate flights to and from the Mexican mainland.

Most visitors to Baja California arrive at the international airport in Los Cabos (near San José del Cabo), although there are also direct flights from US and Mexican cities to Tijuana, Mexicali, Guerrero Negro, Loreto and La Paz.

Destinations throughout Baja California are served by the following list of airlines:

THINGS CHANGE...
The information in this chapter is particularly vulnerable to change. Check directly with the airline or a travel agent to make sure you understand how a fare (and ticket you may buy) works and are aware of the security requirements for international travel. Shop carefully. The details given in this chapter should be regarded as pointers and are not a substitute for your own careful, up-to-date research.

Aero California (no website; airline code JR; in the USA ☎ 800-237-6225, in Mexico ☎ 800-685-5500; hub Tijuana)
Aerolitoral (www.aerolitoral.com.mx; airline code 5D; in the USA & Canada ☎ 800-237-6639; hub Monterrey)
Aeroméxico (www.aeromexico.com; airline code AM; in the USA & Canada ☎ 800-237-6639, in Mexico ☎ 800-021-4050; hub Mexico City)
Alaska Airlines (www.alaskaair.com; airline code AS; in the USA ☎ 800-426-0233, in Mexico ☎ 800-252-7522; hub Seattle)
America West Airlines (www.americawest.com; airline code HP; in the USA ☎ 800-235-9292, in Mexico ☎ 800-235-9292; hub Phoenix)
American Airlines (www.aa.com; airline code AA; in the USA ☎ 800-433-7300, in Mexico 800-904-6000; hub Dallas)
Continental Airlines (www.continental.com; airline code CO; ☎ in the USA ☎ 800-231-0856, in Mexico ☎ 800-900-5000; hub Houston)
Delta Air Lines (www.delta.com; airline code DL; in the USA ☎ 800-221-1212, in Mexico ☎ 800-902-2100; hub Atlanta)
Horizon Air (www.horizonair.com; airline code QX; in the USA ☎ 800-547-7921, in Mexico ☎ 800-252-7522; hub Seattle)
Mexicana (www.mexicana.com.mx; airline code MX; in the USA ☎ 800-531-7921, in Mexico ☎ 800-502-2000; hub Mexico City)
Northwest Airlines (www.nwa.com; airline code NW; in the USA ☎ 800-225-2525, in Mexico ☎ 800-907-4700; hubs Detroit, Minneapolis/St Paul, Memphis)

Australia & New Zealand
The cheapest, most direct route across the Pacific is to fly to a US West Coast city (preferably LA) and make the short hop south.

Good websites for fares include:
Flight Centre Australia (www.flightcentre.com.au) New Zealand (www.flightcentre.co.nz)
STA Travel Australia (www.statravel.com.au) New Zealand (www.statravel.co.nz)
travel.com.au (www.travel.com.au)
travel.co.nz (www.travel.co.nz)

Canada
There are no direct flights from Canada to Baja California, but Alaska Airlines has direct flights to Los Cabos from Seattle. For online fares, try:
Expedia (www.expedia.ca)
Travel CUTS (☎ 800-667-2887; www.travelcuts.com) Canada's national student travel agency
Travelocity (www.travelocity.ca)

Continental Europe
Across Europe, many travel agencies have ties with STA Travel, where cheap tickets can be purchased and STA-issued tickets can be altered (usually for a small fee). Otherwise, searching online ticket fares is a good place to start.

Mainland Mexico
Mexico's two main airlines, Mexicana and Aeroméxico – as well as their subsidiaries and other smaller airlines – connect the airports at Tijuana, Mexicali, Loreto, La Paz and Los Cabos with mainland Mexico.

UK & Ireland
It's usually cheaper to fly to Los Angeles than to Mexico City, though the latter is an option. An excellent place to start your inquiries is **Journey Latin America** (☎ 020-8747-3108; www.journeylatinamerica.co.uk). In Ireland try **HolidaysOnline.ie** (www.holidaysonline.ie).

USA
Fares from the USA fluctuate wildly because of seasonal variations and advance purchase requirements. Many airlines offer

---

DEPARTURE TAX

A departure tax equivalent to about US$25 is levied on international flights from Mexico. It's usually included in your ticket cost, but if it isn't, you must pay in cash during airport check-in. Ask your travel agent in advance.

---

bargain packages – including air, hotel and sometimes meals, for short-term visitors – especially to resorts in the Los Cabos area.

The cheapest flights are the direct ones (for airline websites, see earlier): Alaska Airlines flies direct to **Los Cabos** from San Francisco, San Jose, Los Angeles, San Diego, Portland and Seattle. Continental flies direct from Houston. America West (whose radio call sign, by the way, is 'cactus') flies there from Phoenix, while American Airlines goes direct from Los Angeles and Dallas-Fort Worth. Aeroméxico flies direct from Los Angeles. Mexicana flies from San Diego.

Aeroméxico flies direct daily to **La Paz** from Los Angeles and Tucson.

Aero California flies direct to **Loreto** from Los Angeles three days a week. Aeroméxico flies direct from San Diego to Loreto.

From Phoenix and Houston, Aerolitoral stops in Hermosillo (Sonora) before continuing to **Guerrero Negro**. From Los Angeles the airline also bounces Hermosillo-Loreto-La Paz.

For online ticketing, try:
www.cheaptickets.com
www.expedia.com
www.lowestfare.com
www.onetravel.com
www.orbitz.com
www.smarterliving.com
www.travelocity.com

LAND
Border Crossings
From west to east, there are six official border crossings from the US state of California to Baja. At any crossing, Mexican Customs & Immigration will issue and stamp tourist cards (see p234).
Andrade-Los Algodones (☽ 8am-10pm) This crossing is about 7 miles (11km) west of Yuma, Arizona, via US Interstate 8 and California State Hwy 186.
Calexico-Mexicali (☽ 24hrs) This congested crossing is about 8 miles (13km) south of El Centro via California State Hwy 111.
Calexico East-Mexicali (☽ 6am-10pm) This crossing has relieved some of the pressure from the downtown crossing.
Mesa de Otay-Tijuana (☽ 6am-10pm) This crossing offers a far less congested port of entry than San Ysidro; it is east of downtown Tijuana near the airport.
San Ysidro-Tijuana (☽ 24hrs) This border crossing, 15 miles (24km) south of downtown San Diego, is one of the world's busiest.

Tecate (☼ 6am-midnight) The Tecate border crossing is about 30 miles (50km) southeast of San Diego via California State Hwys 94 and 188.

Bus & Trolley

For details about bus and trolley travel from US cities to Tijuana, see p66). To Mexicali and beyond, see p115.

Buses run regularly from major centers in Mexico to Mexicali and Tijuana.

Car & Motorcycle

Countless visitors drive their own vehicles into Baja California from the USA. The most important item to carry with you is proof of liability insurance purchased from a Mexican company (see p241). If you're traveling only on the peninsula, you do *not* need the vehicle permit required for mainland Mexico. If you plan to take your car to mainland Mexico, you *will* need a car permit. For more on driving in the mainland, see Lonely Planet's *Mexico*. For more on driving in Baja, see p239.

Train

Amtrak (☎ 800-872-7245; www.amtrak.com) has stations in San Diego (where you cross to Tijuana) and Calexico (where you can cross to Mexicali). The **Pacific Southwest Railway Museum** (office in La Mesa, California ☎ 619-465-7776; www.psrm.org) in Campo, California, occasionally fires up its historic trains for rides to Tecate (p106).

SEA
From the USA
CRUISE SHIPS

Both **Carnival Cruises** (☎ in the USA 888-227-6482) and **Royal Caribbean** (☎ in the USA 800-327-6700) offer three-night (Friday to Monday) and four-night (Monday to Friday) cruises to Ensenada with year-round departures from the port in Long Beach, California. Summer prices start around US$472/523, respectively, but vary widely between seasons and also depend on cabin location and amenities. Many cruise ships sail to Los Cabos as well. You'll find tons of options online.

PRIVATE YACHTS

If you know something about boats and sailing, try looking for a crew position on one of the many boats that sail south from Southern California. Marinas at Dana Point, Newport Beach, Belmont Shores and Marina del Rey are all good places to ask.

From October through February, sailboats converge on San Diego to make repairs and purchases and to change crews. A good way to get your name out to skippers seeking crew is to send a three-by-five card, for posting on the bulletin board, to **Downwind Marine** (☎ 619-224-2733; www.downwindmarine.com; 2804 Canon St, San Diego, CA 92106), a nautical chandler geared specifically toward cruising.

Any vessel traveling south along the Baja coast beyond Ensenada or staying more than three days in Ensenada must file a crew list with a Mexican consulate before entering Mexican waters.

Mexico's ministry of the environment, natural resources and fisheries, the **Comisión Nacional de Acuacultura y Pesca** (Conapesca; ☎ 619-233-6956; 2550 5th Ave, Suite 101, San Diego, CA 92103; ☼ 8am-2pm Mon-Fri) maintains an office in San Diego and can provide necessary forms and information.

From Mainland Mexico

An alternative to car travel between mainland Mexico and Baja is the ferry service (both passenger and vehicle) across the Sea of Cortez. Ferries sail between Santa Rosalía and Guaymas three times a week (p143), and between La Paz and Topolobampo (near Los Mochis), and La Paz and Mazatlán daily (p171).

GETTING AROUND

AIR

Subsidiaries of Aeroméxico and Mexicana, as well as smaller airlines, have direct flights within Baja California. For information on flights between Baja and mainland Mexico, see p236.

From Tijuana, Aero California flies daily to/from Los Cabos, and Aerolitoral flies daily to/from La Paz. You can also fly between Loreto and La Paz on Aerolitoral as it hops north or south on its route to/from Los Angeles.

For airline websites and toll-free numbers within Mexico, see Getting There & Away, earlier.

BICYCLE

Bicycling is an increasingly popular way to tour Baja. If you are bringing your bicycle to Baja California, fill your repair kit with every imaginable spare part.

Many cyclists ride the entire length of the peninsula, but such a trip requires a tent, sleeping bag, flashlight (torch), tools, spare tubes and tires, food, several water jugs, a first-aid kit and other supplies.

Cyclists should be in top physical shape, have excellent equipment and be prepared to handle their own repairs, even in the middle of nowhere. Small towns and villages often have bicycle mechanics, but they may lack parts.

Road bikes are suitable for paved roads like the Transpeninsular, but potholes are numerous and highway shoulders are very steep and narrow; even though most Mexican drivers are courteous to cyclists, there are likely to be anxious moments when an 18-wheeler blows by at 70mph (112km/h).

On the gravel or dirt roads that crisscross much of the peninsula, a *todo terreno* (mountain bike) is a much better choice, but even then thorns are a major hazard to bicycle tires. Tube sealant, tire liners and patch kits are imperative.

Bicycles can travel by air, but regulations change constantly. Expect to pay anywhere from US$45 (on Mexicana) to US$100 (on Continental) *each way* to check your bike as luggage.

Places to rent bikes in Baja are rare, except in the tourist resorts (noted throughout the book).

BOAT

Aside from ferries running across the Sea of Cortez to the mainland, boat travel in Baja is usually recreational. Fishing trips, snorkeling and diving excursions, and sunset cruises (such as those in Cabo San Lucas) are all boat based. Many people driving to Baja bring kayaks to paddle to and/or around islands in the Sea of Cortez and bays along the peninsular.

BUS

Air-conditioned buses operate daily between towns all along the Baja peninsula. Most have on-board toilets (bring your own toilet paper) and amenities like videos, drinks and snacks are common on long-distance carriers. Some companies offer *primera clase* (first class) services, which are more comfortable, faster and only slightly more expensive: Norte de Sonora's version is its Elite buses; ABC's similar first class buses are called ABC Plus.

Travel from top to bottom of the peninsula takes 24 to 27 hours (with a change in La Paz), as buses stop in almost every town to drop off and pick up passengers. A ticket from Tijuana to Los Cabos costs about US$105; Tijuana to Loreto will set you back about US$72, and Tijuana to San Quintín about US$18.

Baja's main long-distance bus companies are **Autotransportes de Baja California** (ABC; www.abc.com.mx) and, in the south, its subsidiary **Subur Baja** (www.abc.com.mx). **Norte de Sonora** operates principally in the north, and **Autotransportes Aguila** (in La Paz ☎ 612-122-2157) operates principally in the south.

For fares and details, see the Getting There & Away entries in the respective city sections.

CAR & MOTORCYCLE

Car travel is usually more convenient than bus travel and often the only way to reach isolated towns, villages, mountains and beaches, but it is more expensive due to fuel prices.

Bring Your Own Vehicle

Driving across the border into Baja California is about as complex as navigating a fast food drive-through. You need to stop only if you need a tourist permit (p234). The tough part begins as soon as you cross the border and it's time to start dodging taxis and spotting street signs on your quest for the highway or a hotel. But even that is fairly straightforward if you have a co-pilot plotting your route on the map. Once you're on the Transpeninsular or other highway, it's generally smooth sailing.

The auto insurance websites listed under Insurance are excellent resources for information on driving in Mexico.

FUEL

All *gasolina* (gasoline) and diesel fuel in Mexico is sold by the government-owned Pemex (Petrólcos Mexicanos) at gas stations

ROAD DISTANCES (MILES/KM)

	Cabo San Lucas	Cataviña	Ensenada	Guerrero Negro	La Paz	Loreto
Cataviña	761 / 1225					
Ensenada	991 / 1596	229 / 369				
Guerrero Negro	614 / 989	147 / 237	377 / 607			
La Paz	137 / 221	624 / 1005	853 / 1373	476 / 766		
Loreto	355 / 573	405 / 652	635 / 1022	258 / 415	218 / 351	
Tijuana	1061 / 1711	299 / 481	68 / 110	447 / 720	923 / 1486	705 / 1135

all along the Transpeninsular; in some towns and at remote junctions, private individuals also sell fuel out of drums, usually at a considerable markup. Almost all gas stations accept only cash.

All gasoline is *sin plomo* (unleaded) and comes in both Magna Sin, equivalent to US regular unleaded, and Premium, equivalent to US super unleaded. Diesel fuel is also widely available; regular diesel has a higher sulfur content than US diesel, but a newer 'Diesel Sin' has less sulfur than before. If diesel drivers change their oil and filter about every 3500km, they should have no problems.

In central Baja it's a good idea to top up your tank at every gas station you pass. Carrying at least a five-gallon (23-liter) spare can will also keep you out of trouble if you're planning on doing any off-road traveling.

SERVICE
The Mexican tourism ministry, Secture, maintains a network of Ángeles Verdes (Green Angels), bilingual mechanics in green uniforms and green trucks who patrol major stretches of highway daily during daylight hours looking for motorists in trouble. They make minor repairs, replace small parts, provide fuel and oil, and arrange towing and other assistance by radio if necessary. Service is free; parts, gasoline and oil are provided at cost. Patrols are most prevalent in the northernmost and southernmost stretches of the highway.

Contact them at following numbers:
24-hour toll-free hotline (☎ 800-903-9200)
Tijuana (☎ 664-624-3479; ☻ 8am-4pm Mon-Fri)
La Paz (☎ 612-124-1668, ☻ 8am-8pm daily; also
☎ 612-124-0100, 612-124-0199 Mon-Fri)

Most serious mechanical problems can be fixed efficiently and inexpensively by mechanics in Baja's towns and cities if the parts are available. On the other hand, don't expect miracles if your problems are linked to state-of-the-art computerized systems or other features foreign to Mexican mechanics. Volkswagens (without fuel-injection engines) and Toyotas are the easiest to have repaired in Baja.

Because Baja's notoriously bad roads take a heavy toll on tires, *llanteras* (tire-repair shops) are ubiquitous, even in many out-of-the-way spots.

Driver's License & Permits
To drive in Baja, you need a valid US or Canadian driver's license or an International Driving Permit. Always have your car registration papers. If you are from a country other than the USA or Canada, bring your International Driving Permit as well as your national license.

Police & Military Checkpoints
Having four rifle-toting 18-year-olds picking through your glove box is inevitably nerve wracking, but it's part of the Baja road experience. After a few times it becomes

clear that they're only doing their jobs and aren't out to hassle tourists. They're checking vehicles for drugs, weapons and illegal migrants (all largely because of pressure from the USA).

Heading south, the checkpoint soldiers usually just ask you where you're going and wave you on your way. It's the northbound traffic that gets the added pleasure of vehicular search, and you can bet on getting it. Always be cooperative and courteous, and, no matter what, keep a sharp eye on *everything* that's happening.

Insurance

Mexican law recognizes only Mexican *seguro* (car insurance), so a US or Canadian policy won't help. Driving in Mexico without Mexican insurance would be extremely foolish (see p229). At the very minimum, you should get liability insurance, which is often all you *can* get for cars older than 1991. If you can, we recommend obtaining full coverage (collision, liability, road-side assistance, fire, theft, glass, medical and legal).

Insurance offices are at every Baja border crossing, some of them open 24 hours a day. Rates are government controlled and thus fairly standard on both sides of the border. Most major US insurance companies and automobile clubs (which usually require membership) also can arrange coverage.

Prices depend on the age and make of your vehicle and the length of the insurance policy. For example, full coverage for a car valued between US$15,000 and US$20,000 is US$12/16 for liability/full-coverage and about US$4/14 for each additional day. In general, the longer your stay, the cheaper the per-day rate. If you're planning on spending a lot of time in Baja (two weeks or more), consider a six-month or annual policy, which works out much cheaper (as low as US$80 per year for liability or US$130 for full coverage).

Following is a list of reliable US-based companies offering Mexican insurance policies. Those with websites sell insurance online and most sell policies over the phone.
Baja Bound (☎ 619-437-0404, 888-552-2252; www.bajabound.com; 2222 Coronado Ave, Suite H, San Diego, CA 92154; ⊗ 8:30am-4pm Mon-Fri)
Borderline Insurance (☎ 619-428-0095, 800-332-2118; 2004 Dairy Mart Rd, Suite 103, San Ysidro, CA 92073; ⊗ 9am-5pm Mon-Fri)
Discover Baja Travel Club (☎ 800-727-2252; www.discoverbaja.com)
Instant Mexico Insurance Services (☎ 619-428-4714, 800-345-4701; www.instant-mex-auto-insur.com; 223 Via de San Ysidro, San Ysidro, CA 92173; ⊗ 24hrs)
Club Mex (International Gateway Insurance Brokers; ☎ 619-422-3028, 800-423-2646; www.clubmex.net; 3450 Bonita Rd, Suite 103, Chula Vista, CA 92013; ⊗ 8:30am-5pm Mon-Fri, 9am-noon Sat)
Mex-Insur San Ysidro (☎ 619-428 1121, US Interstate 5, Via de San Ysidro exit, San Ysidro, CA 92173); Chula Vista (☎ 619-425-2390; 99 Bonito Rd, Chula Vista, CA 91910)
Oscar Padilla Mexican Insurance San Ysidro (☎ 800-258-8600, 619-428-4406; www.mexicaninsurance.com; 120 Willow Rd, San Ysidro, CA 92173) ; Calexico (☎ 760-357-4883; 747 Imperial Av, Calexico, CA 92231)

TRANSPORTATION

LA MORDIDA

Officially no policeman is authorized to accept money, and all traffic fines should be paid at the police station or by mail. Historically, however, Mexico has been notorious for *la mordida* (literally 'the bite,' or bribe). The most frequent opportunity for the mordida is a traffic violation such as speeding or running a stop sign. Realists do not expect the mordida to disappear from Mexican life any time soon, but petty harassment of tourists for minor matters seems to be declining.

If you get pulled over, you can either try to pay the bribe and get on with your day, or you can argue the validity of the citation. Some people simply pretend not to understand, let alone speak, any Spanish in the hopes that the officers become exasperated enough to just let them go. Insisting on going to the police station to pay the fine can also be a deterrent, especially if you've been pulled over for no good reason. If you end up going to the station, be sure to get a receipt.

If, however, you are willing to pay the bribe, don't offer money to police officers directly; it's illegal. One strategy is to tell officers that, if they forgive you, you will be extremely grateful (*'Si me perdona, se lo podría agradecer'*). Another good one is asking if it's possible to pay the fine on the spot (*¿Sería posible pagar la multa ahora?*).

Sanborn's Insurance (☎ 956-686-3601, 800-222-0158; www.sanbornsinsurance.com; 2009 S 10th St, McAllen, TX 78503)

Purchase

New and used vehicles are cheaper to purchase in the USA than in Baja, so you're better off buying one there and driving it south.

Rental

Auto rental in Mexico is expensive by US or European standards, but worthwhile if you want to visit several places in a short time. A car is a must for getting off the beaten track, where public transport is scarce or nonexistent. Cars can be rented in most of Baja's cities and resorts and at airports.

Renters must have a valid driver's license (US and Canadian licenses are accepted; everyone else should bring International Driving Permits as well as their national licenses), passport and major credit card. You are usually required to be at least 23 (sometimes 25) years old.

Always ask exactly what the insurance covers – sometimes it covers only minimal liability insurance of, say, US$200, which would put you in big trouble in case of an accident. Most agencies offer a choice between a per-kilometer deal or *kilometraje libre* (unlimited kilometers). The latter is usually preferable if you intend to do some hard driving. The matchbox-size Chevy Pop has replaced the VW Beetle as the cheapest car on the list and will set you back about US$50 per day in places like Los Cabos. Elsewhere, bank on paying around US$60 to US$65 per day, all included.

Sometimes, booking a car from home through an international agency, or when buying your plane tickets, will get you a better deal. Following are the major firms operating in Mexico with the US telephone numbers first:

Alamo (www.alamo.com; ☎ 800-462-5266, in Mexico ☎ 800-849-8001)
Avis (www.avis.com; ☎ 800-230-4898, in Mexico ☎ 800-288-8888)
Budget (www.drivebudget.com; ☎ 800-527-0700, in Mexico ☎ 800-700-1700)
Dollar (www.dollar.com; ☎ 800-800-4000, in Mexico N/A)
Europcar (www.europcar.com; ☎ 877-526-8679, in Mexico ☎ 800-201-2084)

Hertz (www.hertz.com; ☎ 800-654-3001, in Mexico ☎ 800-654-3030)
Thrifty (www.thrifty.com; ☎ 800-847-4389, in Mexico ☎ 800-021-2277)

Road Rules

Mexicans drive on the right side of the road (except when they're passing you from behind, which will be often). The speed limit on the Transpeninsular is 80km/h (about 50mph). Stop signs in towns mean the same thing they do around the world but Mexicans seem to follow the 'no cop, no stop' rule, making the foreign driver feel like a fool when coming to a complete stop.

Road Conditions

The Transpeninsular is paved top to bottom, with occasional washouts in the southern reaches that are usually passable for all cars. The toll portion (México 1D) of the Transpeninsular between Tijuana and Ensenada is the best-maintained highway in Baja – four lanes wide, smooth and fast, with spectacular coastal views.

In towns and cities, beware of *alto* (stop) signs, potholes and *topes* (speed bumps). Wide one-way streets in Tijuana, for example, are infamous for stop signs placed on one street corner or the other, but not on both. Consequently, drivers in the far-left lane may not see a stop sign on the right corner until they are already in the intersection. Driving slowly and carefully should eliminate the danger of overlooking stop signs. Also see p256 about road signs.

OFF-HIGHWAY DRIVING

Thousands of miles of rough dirt roads and tracks crisscross Baja's backcountry. Many unpaved roads are graded and passable even for ordinary passenger vehicles, but others require a 4WD vehicle with high clearance. Sharp stones and other hazards can shred even heavy-duty tires, forcing wise drivers to travel at much slower speeds than on paved roads. In such circumstances, Mexican drivers regularly deflate their tires, to as little as 20 or 22lbs per square inch (psi), in order to avoid punctures and smooth out the rough surfaces. This obviously reduces fuel efficiency, but gas is cheaper than a set of new tires.

Make sure your vehicle is in excellent condition; some areas are so isolated that getting stuck can be dangerous. Heat, drought, rain, flash floods and snakes are among the hazards that may bedevil an unprepared driver. Essentials for excursions off paved highways include water, extra fuel, a first-aid kit, flashlight (torch), tools, flares, matches and a disposable lighter, and sleeping bags.

One way to avoid trouble is by checking conditions with the locals before setting out. Roads often deteriorate quickly, especially after rains, and what was an easy, if bumpy, ride last week may have become impassable. If you've already headed out and find conditions questionable, turn back. Some travelers may prefer to form an informal convoy with other vehicles.

Road Hazards

The Transpeninsular presents many tricky turns – so to speak – but it's a wonderful road trip if you keep a few things in mind.

First off, most of the highway is only the width of a country road, which provides little margin for error. Potholes can be real axle busters, and animals – including burros and cows – can pop up around any corner. Large debris is also a frequent menace, and many drivers will often signal this problem ahead of you by waving their hands downward, which means you should slow down.

When you approach a large, slow-moving truck from behind, the driver will frequently throw on the left-turn signal, indicating that it's safe for you to pass. Just remember that you're relying on someone else's judgment; when you accelerate to pass the driver, make sure the person is not actually signaling to turn left!

Night on the roads of Baja is ? witching hour – sinister and with am mayhem. Either don't drive at all or like a nun with a load of school childr

LOCAL TRANSPORTATION
Bus

Generally known as *camiones,* local buse are the cheapest way to get around cities and to nearby villages. In Baja California, they exist in Tijuana, Ensenada, San Quintín, Mexicali, La Paz and Los Cabos. They run everywhere, frequently, and are cheap (about US$0.50). Most buses are surprisingly modern, clean and uncrowded.

Taxi

Every large town and city in Baja California has taxi service. Most taxis are private, with government-regulated fares, though haggling over fares is still the rule. In Tijuana, Loreto, San José del Cabo and Cabo San Lucas, you will also find bright-yellow, government-run minivans called *Aeroterrestre taxis,* which provide transportation to and from major airports; fares are government-controlled and not subject to bargaining. Tijuana's new *taxis libres* (p68) are one of the few taxi services that use *taximetros* (taxi meters), and they invariably lead to savings.

Route taxis are an efficient and inexpensive way to get around town. They are station wagons that operate along designated routes, just like city buses, only slightly more expensive and much faster. You can board them at their designated route terminus or after flagging them down. The driver will stop wherever you want to get off.

:alth Dr David Goldberg

Travelers to Baja California need to be concerned chiefly about water- and food-borne diseases. Most of these illnesses are not life threatening, but they can certainly have an impact on your trip or even ruin it. Exercise great care in what you eat and drink.

BEFORE YOU GO

Bring medications in their original containers, clearly labeled. A signed, dated letter from your physician describing all medical conditions and medications, including generic names, is also a good idea. If carrying syringes or needles, be sure to have a physician's letter documenting their medical necessity.

INSURANCE

Mexican medical treatment is generally inexpensive for common diseases and minor treatment, but if you suffer some serious medical problem, you may want to find a private hospital or fly out for treatment. Travel insurance can typically cover the costs. Some US health insurance policies stay in effect (at least for a limited time) if you travel abroad, but it's worth checking exactly what you'll be covered for in Mexico. For people whose medical insurance or national health systems don't extend to Mexico – which includes most non-Americans – a travel policy is advisable. (Check the Subway section of the Lonely Planet website at www.lonelyplanet.com/subwwway for more information.)

You may prefer a policy that pays doctors or hospitals directly rather than requiring you to pay on the spot and claim later. If you have to claim later, keep all documentation. Some policies ask you to call collect to a center in your home country, where an immediate assessment of your problem is made. Check that the policy covers ambulances or an emergency flight home. Some policies offer lower and higher medical-expense options; the higher ones are chiefly for countries such as the USA, which have extremely high medical costs. There is a wide variety of policies available, so check the small print.

MEDICAL CHECKLIST

- Antibiotics
- Antidiarrheal drugs (eg loperamide)
- Acetaminophen/paracetamol (Tylenol) or aspirin
- Anti-inflammatory drugs (eg ibuprofen)
- Antihistamines (for hay fever and allergic reactions)
- Antibacterial ointment (eg Bactroban) for cuts and abrasions
- Steroid cream or cortisone (for poison ivy and other allergic rashes)
- Bandages, gauze, gauze rolls
- Adhesive or paper tape
- Scissors, safety pins, tweezers
- Thermometer
- Pocket knife
- DEET-containing insect repellent for the skin
- Permethrin-containing insect spray for clothing, tents and bed nets
- Sun block
- Oral rehydration salts
- Iodine tablets (for water purification)
- Syringes and sterile needles

IMMUNIZATIONS

The only required vaccine is yellow fever, and that's only if you're arriving in Mexico from a yellow fever–infected country in Africa or South America. However, you should be up to date with your diptheria and tetanus vaccines (if you haven't had a booster shot in 10 years) and consider getting a hepatitis A vaccine as well. Since most vaccines don't produce immunity until at least two weeks after they're given, visit a physician four to eight weeks before departure.

INTERNET RESOURCES

There is a wealth of travel health advice on the Internet. For further information, the Lonely Planet website at www.lonelyplanet.com is a good place to start. The World Health Organization publishes a superb book called *International Travel and Health*, which is revised annually and is available online at no cost at www.who.int/ith. Another website of general interest is MD Travel Health at www.mdtravelhealth.com, which provides complete travel health recommendations for every country, updated daily, also at no cost.

IN MEXICO

AVAILABILITY & COST OF HEALTH CARE

There are a number of hospitals in Baja (including Tijuana, p55, and Cabo San Lucas, p206). Almost every locale in Baja has either a hospital or medical clinic and Cruz Roja (Red Cross) emergency facilities, all of which are indicated by road signs showing a red cross. Hospitals are dependable for non-life-threatening ailments (like diarrhea or dysentery) and minor surgery (such as stitches, sprains). Medical bills are comparatively low, but both hospitals and doctors require payment at the time of service, regardless of whether you have travel health insurance. Doctors usually insist on cash payment. Only a few facilities accept credit cards.

If you develop a life-threatening medical problem, you'll probably want to be evacuated to a country with state-of-the-art medical care. Since this may cost tens of thousands of dollars, be sure you have

insurance to cover this be
You can find a list of med
and travel insurance compan
State Department website at
state.gov/medical.html.

Mexican pharmacies are ide
a green cross and a 'Farmacia' si
are well supplied and the pharmac
trained. Some medications requiring
scription in the US may be dispens
Mexico without a prescription. To find
after-hours pharmacy, you can look in
local newspaper, ask your hotel concierg
or check the front door of a local pharmacy,
which will often post the name of a nearby
pharmacy that is open for the night.

INFECTIOUS DISEASES

Dengue Fever

Dengue fever is a viral infection found throughout Central America. In Mexico, the risk is greatest along the Gulf Coast, especially from July to September. Dengue is transmitted by Aedes mosquitoes, which bite preferentially during the day and are usually found close to human habitations, often indoors. They breed primarily in artificial water containers, such as jars, barrels, cans, cisterns, metal drums, plastic containers and discarded tires. As a result, dengue is especially common in densely populated, urban environments.

Dengue usually causes flu-like symptoms including fever, muscle aches, joint pains, headaches, nausea and vomiting, often followed by a rash. The body aches may be quite uncomfortable, but most cases resolve uneventfully in a few days. Severe cases usually occur in children under age 15 who are experiencing their second dengue infection.

There is no specific treatment for dengue fever except to take analgesics such as acetaminophen/paracetamol (Tylenol) and drink plenty of fluids. Severe cases may require hospitalization for intravenous fluids and supportive care. There is no vaccine. The cornerstone of prevention is insect protection measures (see p247).

Hepatitis A

Hepatitis A occurs throughout Central America. It's a viral infection of the liver usually acquired by ingestion of contaminated water, food or ice, though it may also be acquired by direct contact with infected

ess occurs worldwide, but
s higher in developing na-
ns may include fever, malaise,
usea, vomiting and abdom-
nost cases resolve uneventfully,
patitis A occasionally causes se-
damage. There is no treatment.
accine for hepatitis A is extremely
d highly effective. If you get a booster
12 months later, it lasts for at least 10
s. You really should get it before you go
Mexico or any other developing nation.
ecause the safety of hepatitis A vaccine has
not been established for pregnant women or
children under age two, they should instead
be given a gammaglobulin injection.

Typhoid Fever

Typhoid fever is caused by ingestion of food
or water contaminated by a species of *Salmonella* known as *Salmonella typhi*. Fever occurs
in virtually all cases. Other symptoms may
include headache, malaise, muscle aches, dizziness, loss of appetite, nausea and abdominal pain. Either diarrhea or constipation may
occur. Possible complications include intestinal perforation, intestinal bleeding, confusion, delirium or (rarely) coma.

The drug of choice for typhoid fever is
usually a quinolone antibiotic such as ciprofloxacin (Cipro) or levofloxacin (Levaquin),
which many travelers carry for treatment
of travelers' diarrhea. However, if you self-
treat for typhoid fever, you may also need to
self-treat for malaria, since the symptoms of
the two diseases can be indistinguishable.

Yellow Fever

Yellow fever no longer occurs in Central
America, but many Central American
countries, including Mexico, require yellow
fever vaccine before entry if you're arriving
from a country in Africa or South America
where yellow fever occurs. If you're not arriving from a country with yellow fever,
the vaccine is neither required nor recommended. Yellow fever vaccine is given
only in approved yellow fever vaccination
centers, which provide validated International Certificates of Vaccination ('yellow
booklets').

The vaccine should be given at least 10
days before departure and remains effective for approximately 10 years. Reactions
to the vaccine are generally mild and may

include headaches, muscle aches, low-grade
fevers or discomfort at the injection site.
Severe, life-threatening reactions have been
described but are extremely rare.

Cholera

Cholera is an intestinal infection acquired
through ingestion of contaminated food
or water. The main symptom is profuse,
watery diarrhea, which may be so severe
that it causes life-threatening dehydration.
The key treatment is drinking oral rehydration solution. Antibiotics are also given,
usually tetracycline or doxycycline, though
quinolone antibiotics such as ciprofloxacin
and levofloxacin are also effective.

Only a handful of cases have been reported
in Mexico over the last few years. Cholera
vaccine is no longer recommended.

Other Infections

Gnathostomiasis is a parasite acquired by eating raw or undercooked freshwater fish, including ceviche, a popular lime-marinated
fish salad. Cases have been reported from
Acapulco and other parts of Mexico. The
chief symptom is intermittent, migratory
swellings under the skin, sometimes associated with joint pains, muscle pains or
gastrointestinal problems. The symptoms
may not begin until many months after
exposure.

Histoplasmosis is caused by a soil-based
fungus and acquired by inhalation, often
when soil has been disrupted. Initial symptoms may include fever, chills, dry cough,
chest pain and headache, sometimes leading
to pneumonia. An outbreak was recently
described among visitors to an Acapulco
hotel.

Coccidioidomycosis, also known as 'valley
fever,' is a fungal infection that is restricted
to semiarid areas in the American southwest, nearby areas in northern Mexico, and
limited foci in Central and South America.
Valley fever is acquired by inhaling dust
from contaminated soil. It begins as a lung
infection, causing fever, chest pain and
cough, and may spread to other organs,
particularly the nervous system, skin and
bone. Treatment requires high doses of antibiotics for prolonged periods and is not
always curative.

Brucellosis is an infection occurring in domestic and wild animals that may be trans-

mitted to humans through direct animal contact or by consumption of unpasteurized dairy products from infected animals. Symptoms may include fever, malaise, depression, loss of appetite, headache, muscle aches and back pain. Complications can include arthritis, hepatitis, meningitis and endocarditis (heart valve infection).

Tularemia, also known as 'rabbit fever,' is a bacterial infection that primarily affects rodents, rabbits and hares. Humans generally become infected through tick or deerfly bites or by handling the carcass of an infected animal. Occasional cases are caused by inhalation of an infectious aerosol. In Mexico, most cases occur in rural areas in the northern part of the country. Tularemia may develop as a flu-like illness, pneumonia or skin ulcers with swollen glands, depending upon how the infection is acquired. It usually responds well to antibiotics.

Typhus may be transmitted by lice in scattered pockets of the country.

HIV/AIDS has been reported from all Central American countries. Be sure to use condoms for all sexual encounters.

TRAVELERS' DIARRHEA

To prevent diarrhea, avoid tap water unless it has been boiled, filtered or chemically disinfected (iodine tablets); only eat fresh fruits or vegetables if cooked or peeled; be wary of dairy products that might contain unpasteurized milk; and be highly selective when eating food from street vendors.

If you develop diarrhea, be sure to drink plenty of fluids, preferably an oral rehydration solution containing lots of salt and sugar. A few loose stools don't require treatment, but if you start having more than four or five stools a day you should start taking an antibiotic (usually a quinolone drug) and an antidiarrheal agent (such as loperamide). If diarrhea is bloody or persists for more than 72 hours or is accompanied by fever, shaking chills or severe abdominal pain you should seek medical attention.

ENVIRONMENTAL HAZARDS & TREATMENT
Altitude Sickness

Altitude sickness may develop in travelers who ascend rapidly to altitudes greater than 2500m. Being physically fit does not lessen your risk of altitude sickness. It seems to be chiefly a matter of genetic pre[...] Those who have experienced alt[...] ness in the past are prone to future[...] The risk increases with faster ascen[...] altitudes and greater exertion. Sy[...] may include headaches, nausea, vor[...] dizziness, malaise, insomnia and loss [...] petite. Severe cases may be complicate[...] fluid in the lungs (high-altitude pulmon[...] edema) or swelling of the brain (high-[...] titude cerebral edema). Most deaths ar[...] caused by high-altitude pulmonary edema.

The standard medication to prevent altitude sickness is a mild diuretic called acetazolamide (Diamox), which should be started 24 hours before ascent and continued for 48 hours after arrival at altitude. Possible side effects include increased urination, numbness, tingling, nausea, drowsiness, nearsightedness and temporary impotence. For those who cannot tolerate acetazolamide, most physicians prescribe dexamethasone, which is a type of steroid. A natural alternative is gingko, which some people find quite helpful. The usual dosage is 100mg twice daily.

To lessen the chance of altitude sickness, you should also be sure to ascend gradually to higher altitudes, avoid overexertion, eat light meals and avoid alcohol.

The symptoms of altitude sickness develop gradually so that, with proper care, serious complications can usually be prevented. If you or any of your companions show any symptoms of altitude sickness, you should not ascend to a higher altitude until the symptoms have cleared. If the symptoms become worse or if someone shows signs of cerebral or pulmonary edema, such as trouble breathing or mental confusion, you must immediately descend to a lower altitude. A descent of 500m to 1000m is generally adequate except in cases of cerebral edema, which may require a greater descent. Supplemental oxygen is helpful if available. Acetazolamide and dexamethasone may be used to treat altitude sickness as well as prevent it.

Travel to high altitudes is generally not recommended for those with a history of heart disease, lung disease, or sickle cell disease. It is also not recommended for pregnant women.

Mosquito Bites

To prevent mosquito bites, wear long

HEALTH

g pants, hats and shoes (rather
als). Bring along a good insect
preferably one containing DEET,
would be applied to exposed skin
thing, but not to eyes, mouth, cuts,
s or irritated skin. Products contain-
ower concentrations of DEET are as
tive, but for shorter periods of time. In
eral, adults and children over 12 should
e preparations containing 25% to 35%
EET, which usually lasts about six hours.
Children between two and 12 years of age
should use preparations containing no more
than 10% DEET, applied sparingly, which
will usually last about three hours. Neuro-
logical toxicity has been reported from
DEET, especially in children, but appears
to be extremely uncommon and generally
related to overuse. Don't use DEET-containing compounds on children under age
two.

Insect repellents containing certain botanical products, including oil of eucalyptus
and soybean oil, are effective but last only
1 to 2 hours. Where there is a high risk of
malaria or yellow fever, use DEET-containing repellents. Products based on citronella
are not effective.

For additional protection, apply permethrin to clothing, shoes, tents and bed
nets. Permethrin treatments are safe and
remain effective for at least two weeks,
even when items are laundered. Permethrin
should not be applied directly to skin.

Don't sleep with the window open unless there is a screen. If sleeping outdoors
or in accommodation that allows entry of
mosquitoes, use a bed net treated with permethrin, with edges tucked in under the
mattress. The mesh size should be less than
1.5mm. Alternatively, use a mosquito coil,
which will fill the room with insecticide
through the night. Repellent-impregnated
wristbands are not effective.

Tick Bites

To protect yourself from tick bites, follow
the same precautions as for mosquitoes,
except that boots are preferable to shoes,
with pants tucked in. Be sure to perform
a thorough tick check at the end of each
day. You'll generally need the assistance of
a friend or mirror for a full examination.
Remove ticks with tweezers, grasping them
firmly by the head. Insect repellents based

on botanical products, described above,
have not been adequately studied for insects other than mosquitoes and at this
point cannot be recommended to prevent
tick bites.

Water

Tap water in Mexico is generally not safe to
drink. Agua purificada (purified water) and
hielo (ice from purified water) are available throughout Baja from supermarkets
and liquor stores. Restaurants are supposed
to make ice with purified water, and hotels
will generally make you aware of the quality of the water; finding a bottle of water
in the room is a good indication that the
agua from the tap is not the purest. Note
that most top-end hotels provide purified
tap water.

Licuados con leche (milkshakes) from
juice stands are usually safe because the
government requires the use of pasteur-
ized milk and purified water. Tea or coffee
should also be okay, since the water should
have been boiled.

Off the main roads, some sort of water
purification system is advisable, unless you
carry enough bottled water with you. Vigorous boiling for one minute is the most
effective means of water purification. At
altitudes greater than 2000m, boil for three
minutes.

Another option is to disinfect water
with iodine pills. Instructions are usually
enclosed and should be carefully followed.
Or you can add 2% tincture of iodine to
one quart or liter of water (five drops to
clear water, 10 drops to cloudy water) and
let stand for 30 minutes. If the water is cold,
a longer time may be required. The taste of
iodinated water can be improved by adding
vitamin C (ascorbic acid). Don't consume
iodinated water for more than a few weeks.
Pregnant women, those with a history of
thyroid disease and those allergic to iodine
should not drink iodinated water.

A number of water filters are on the
market. Those with smaller pores (reverse
osmosis filters) provide the broadest protection, but they are relatively large and are
readily plugged by debris. Those with somewhat larger pores (microstrainer filters) are
ineffective against viruses, although they
remove other organisms. Manufacturers'
instructions must be carefully followed.

Sun

To protect yourself from excessive sun exposure, you should stay out of the midday sun, wear sunglasses and a wide-brimmed hat, and apply sunscreen with SPF 15 or higher, providing both UVA and UVB protection. Sunscreen should be generously applied to all exposed parts of the body approximately 30 minutes before sun exposure and be re-applied after swimming or vigorous activity. Drink plenty of fluids and avoid strenuous exercise when the temperature is high.

Heat Stroke

Heat stroke may occur in those who are exposed to excessively high temperatures for a number of days. The elderly are at greatest risk, especially those with chronic medical problems. Heat stroke often occurs during physical exertion but, particularly in the elderly, may also occur at rest. The first sign may be an abrupt collapse, but there may be early, subtle findings, including dizziness, weakness, nausea, headache, confusion, drowsiness, and unreasonable behavior. If early symptoms of heat illness are observed, remove the victim from direct sunlight, loosen clothing, give cold fluids, and make sure the victim rests for at least 24 hours. In the event of heat stroke, the victim should be brought immediately to the nearest medical facility. To prevent heat stroke, drink plenty of fluids, eat salty foods, protect yourself from sun exposure, and avoid alcohol and strenuous exercise when the temperature is high.

Animal Bites

Do not attempt to pet, handle or feed any animal, with the exception of domestic animals known to be free of any infectious disease. Most animal injuries are directly related to a person's attempt to touch or feed the animal.

Any bite or scratch by a mammal, including bats, should be promptly and thoroughly cleansed with large amounts of soap and water, followed by application of an antiseptic such as iodine or alcohol. Contact the local health authorities immediately for possible postexposure treatment, whether or not you've been immunized against rabies. It may also be advisable to start an antibiotic, since wounds caused by animal bites and scratches frequently become infected. One of the newer quinolones, such

as levofloxacin (Levaqu...
travelers carry in case of d...
an appropriate choice.

Snake & Scorpion Bites

The most common venomous sn...
is the rattlesnake *(cascabel).* To...
the odds of being bitten, always we...
socks and long trousers when v...
through undergrowth where snakes m...
present. Keep your hands out of holes...
crevices, and be cautious when collect...
firewood.

Though painful, snake bites do no...
cause instantaneous death. Place the victim at rest, keep the bitten area immobilized, and move them immediately to the nearest medical facility. Avoid tourniquets, which are no longer recommended.

Scorpions are a problem in many states. If stung, you should immediately apply ice or cold packs, immobilize the affected body part and go to the nearest emergency room. To prevent scorpion stings, be sure to inspect and shake out clothing, shoes and sleeping bags before use, and wear gloves and protective clothing when working around piles of wood or leaves.

CHILDREN & PREGNANT WOMEN

In general, it's safe for children and pregnant women to go to Mexico. However, be particularly careful not to drink tap water or consume any questionable food or beverage. Also, when traveling with children, make sure they're up to date on all routine immunizations. It's sometimes appropriate to give children some of their vaccines a little early before visiting a developing nation. You should discuss this with your pediatrician. If pregnant, bear in mind that should a complication such as premature labor develop while abroad, the quality of medical care may not be comparable to that in your home country.

HEALTH

TRADITIONAL MEDICINE	
Problem	**Treatment**
jet lag	melatonin
motion sickness	ginger
mosquito bite prevention	oil of eucalyptus, soybean oil

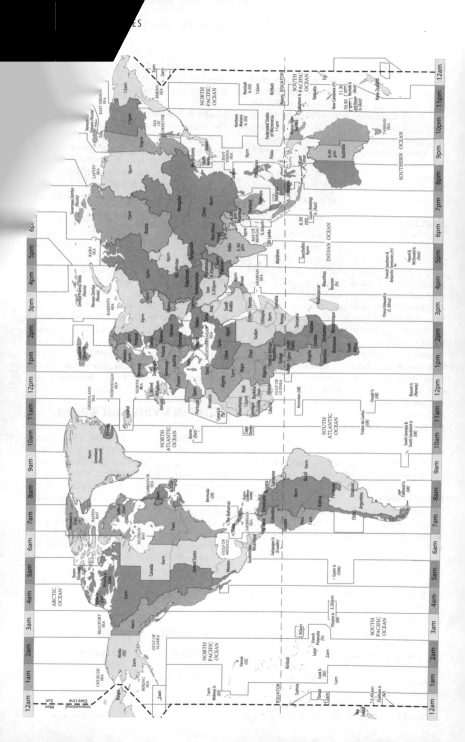

Language

CONTENTS

The predominant language of Baja California is Spanish. Mexican Spanish is unlike Castilian Spanish (the language of much of Spain) in two main respects: in Mexico the Castilian lisp has more or less disappeared and numerous indigenous words have been adopted.

Travelers in cities, resort areas like Los Cabos and larger villages can almost always find someone who speaks at least some English. All the same, it is advantageous and courteous to know at least a few words and phrases in Spanish. Mexicans will generally respond much more positively if you attempt to speak to them in their own language.

For words and phrases for use when dining, see Eat Your Words on p47. For a more comprehensive guide to the Spanish of Mexico, get a copy of Lonely Planet's *Mexican Spanish Phrasebook*.

PRONUNCIATION

Spanish spelling is phonetically consistent, meaning that there's a clear and consistent relationship between what you see in writing and how it's pronounced. In addition, most Spanish sounds have English equivalents, so English speakers shouldn't have too much trouble being understood.

Vowels

a	as in 'father'
e	as in 'met'
i	as in 'marine'
o	as in 'or' (without the 'r' sound)
u	as in 'rule'; the 'u' is not pronounced after **q** and in the letter combinations **gue** and **gui**, unless it's marked with a diaeresis (eg *argüir*), in which case it's pronounced as English 'w'
y	at the end of a word or when it stands alone, it's pronounced as the Spanish **i** (eg *ley*); between vowels within a word it's as the 'y' in 'yonder'

Consonants

As a rule, Spanish consonants resemble their English counterparts. The exceptions are listed below.

While the consonants **ch**, **ll** and **ñ** are generally considered distinct letters, **ch** and **ll** are now often listed alphabetically under **c** and **l** respectively. The letter **ñ** is still treated as a separate letter and comes after **n** in dictionaries.

b	similar to English 'b,' but softer; referred to as 'b larga'
c	as in 'celery' before **e** and **i**; otherwise as English 'k'
ch	as in 'church'
d	as in 'dog,' but between vowels and after **l** or **n**, the sound is closer to the 'th' in 'this'
g	as the 'ch' in the Scottish *loch* before **e** and **i** ('kh' in our guides to pronunciation); elsewhere, as in 'go'
h	invariably silent. If your name begins with this letter, listen carefully if you're waiting for public officials to call you.
j	as the 'ch' in the Scottish *loch* (written as 'kh' in our guides to pronunciation)
ll	as the 'y' in 'yellow'
ñ	as the 'ni' in 'onion'
r	a short **r** except at the beginning of a word, and after **l**, **n** or **s**, when it's often rolled
rr	very strongly rolled
v	similar to English 'b,' but softer; referred to as 'b corta'
x	usually pronounced as **j** above; in some indigenous place names it's

pronounced as an 's'; as in 'taxi' in
other instances
as the 's' in 'sun'

ord Stress

n general, words ending in vowels or the
letters **n** or **s** have stress on the next-to-last
syllable, while those with other endings
have stress on the last syllable. Thus *vaca*
(cow) and *caballos* (horses) both carry
stress on the next-to-last syllable, while
ciudad (city) and *infeliz* (unhappy) are
both stressed on the last syllable.

Written accents will almost always
appear in words that don't follow the rules
above, eg *sótano* (basement), *América* and
porción (portion).

GENDER & PLURALS

In Spanish, nouns are either masculine
or feminine, and there are rules to help
determine gender (there are of course some
exceptions). Feminine nouns generally end
with **-a** or with the groups **-ción**, **-sión** or
-dad. Other endings typically signify a
masculine noun. Endings for adjectives also
change to agree with the gender of the noun
they modify (masculine/feminine **-o/-a**).
Where both masculine and feminine forms
are included in this language guide, they
are separated by a slash, with the masculine
form first, eg *perdido/a*.

If a noun or adjective ends in a vowel, the
plural is formed by adding **s** to the end. If
it ends in a consonant, the plural is formed
by adding **es** to the end.

ACCOMMODATIONS

I'm looking for ...	*Estoy buscando ...*	e·stoy boos·kan·do ...
Where is ...?	*¿Dónde hay ...?*	don·de ai ...
a camping	*un área para*	oon a·re·a pa·ra
ground	*acampar*	a·kam·par
a guesthouse	*una pensión*	oo·na pen·syon
a hotel	*un hotel*	oon o·tel
a youth hostel	*un albergue*	oon al·ber·ge
	juvenil	khoo·ve·neel

Are there any rooms available?

¿Hay habitaciones	ay a·bee·ta·syon·es	
libres?	lee·bres	

I'd like a ...	*Quisiera una*	kee·sye·ra oo·na
room.	*habitación ...*	a·bee·ta·syon ...
double	*doble*	do·ble
(two beds)		

MAKING A RESERVATION
(for phone or written requests)

To ...	*A ...*
From ...	*De ...*
Date	*Fecha*
I'd like to book ...	*Quisiera reservar ...* (see the list under 'Accom— modations' for bed and room options)
in the name of ...	*en nombre de ...*
for the nights of ...	*para las noches del ...*
credit card ...	*tarjeta de crédito ...*
number	*número*
expiry date	*fecha de vencimiento*
Please confirm ...	*Puede confirmar ...*
availability	*la disponibilidad*
price	*el precio*

double	*matrimonial*	
(two people,		
one bed)		
single	*individual*	een·dee·vee·*dwal*
twin	*con dos camas*	kon dos *ka*·mas
How much is it	*¿Cuánto cuesta*	kwan·to kwes·ta
per ...?	*por ...?*	por ...
night	*noche*	*no*·che
person	*persona*	per·*so*·na
week	*semana*	se·*ma*·na
full board	*pensión*	pen·*syon*
	completa	kom·*ple*·ta
private/shared	*baño privado/*	ba·nyo pree·*va*·do/
bathroom	*compartido*	kom·par·*tee*·do
cheaper	*más económico*	mas e·ko·*no*·mee·ko
discount	*descuento*	des·*kwen*·to

Does it include breakfast?

¿Incluye el desayuno?	een·*kloo*·ye el de·sa·*yoo*·no

May I see the room?

¿Puedo ver la	pwe·do ver la
habitación?	a·bee·ta·*syon*

It's fine. I'll take it.

Está bien. La tomo.	es·*ta* byen la *to*·mo

I don't like it.

No me gusta.	no me *goos*·ta

CONVERSATION & ESSENTIALS

When approaching a stranger for information
you should always extend a greeting, and use
only the polite form of address, especially

with the police and public officials. Young people may be less likely to expect this, but it's best to stick to the polite form unless you're quite sure you won't offend by using the informal mode. The polite form is used in all cases in this guide; where options are given, the form is indicated by the abbreviations 'pol' and 'inf.'

Saying *por favor* (please) and *gracias* (thank you) are second nature to most Mexicans and a recommended tool in your travel kit.

Hi.	*Hola.*	o·la (inf)
Hello.	*Buen día.*	bwe·n dee·a
Good morning.	*Buenos días.*	bwe·nos dee·as
Good afternoon.	*Buenas tardes.*	bwe·nas tar·des
Good evening/ night.	*Buenas noches.*	bwe·nas no·ches
Goodbye.	*Adiós.*	a·dyos
Bye/See you soon.	*Hasta luego.*	as·ta lwe·go
Yes.	*Sí.*	see
No.	*No.*	no
Please.	*Por favor.*	por fa·vor
Thank you.	*Gracias.*	gra·syas
Many thanks.	*Muchas gracias.*	moo·chas gra·syas
You're welcome.	*De nada.*	de na·da
Apologies.	*Perdón.*	per·don
May I?	*Permiso.*	per·mee·so
(when asking permission)		
Excuse me.	*Disculpe.*	dees·kool·pe
(used before a request or when apologizing)		

How are things?
¿Qué tal? — ke tal
What's your name?
¿Cómo se llama usted? — ko·mo se ya·ma oo·sted (pol)
¿Como te llamas? — ko·mo te ya·mas (inf)
My name is ...
Me llamo ... — me ya·mo ...
It's a pleasure to meet you.
Mucho gusto. — moo·cho goos·to

SIGNS

Entrada	Entrance
Salida	Exit
Información	Information
Abierto	Open
Cerrado	Closed
Prohibido	Prohibited
Servicios/Baños	Toilets
Hombres/Varones	Men
Mujeres/Damas	Women

The pleasure is mine.
El gusto es mío. — el goos·to
Where are you from?
¿De dónde es/eres? — de don·de es/
I'm from ...
Soy de ... — soy de ...
May I take a photo?
¿Puedo sacar una foto? — pwe·do sa·kar oo·na

DIRECTIONS
How do I get to ...?
¿Cómo llego a ...? — ko·mo ye·go a ...
Is it far?
¿Está lejos? — es·ta le·khos
Go straight ahead.
Siga/Vaya derecho. — see·ga/va·ya de·re·cho
Turn left.
Voltée a la izquierda. — vol·te·e a la ees·kyer·da
Turn right.
Voltée a la derecha. — vol·te·e a la de·re·cha
Can you show me (on the map)?
¿Me lo podría señalar (en el mapa)? — me lo po·dree·a se·nya·la (en el ma·pa)

north	*norte*	nor·te
south	*sur*	soor
east	*este*	es·te
west	*oeste*	o·es·te
here	*aquí*	a·kee
there	*ahí*	a·ee
avenue	*avenida*	a·ve·nee·da
block	*cuadra*	kwa·dra
street	*calle/paseo*	ka·lye/pa·se·o

HEALTH
I'm sick.
Estoy enfermo/a. — es·toy en·fer·mo/a
I need a doctor.
Necesito un doctor. — ne·se·see·to oon dok·tor
Where's the hospital?
¿Dónde está el hospital? — don·de es·ta el os·pee·tal
I'm pregnant.
Estoy embarazada. — es·toy em·ba·ra·sa·da

I'm allergic to ...	*Soy alérgico/a a ...*	soy a·ler·khee·ko/a a ...
antibiotics	*los antibióticos*	los an·tee·byo·tee·kos
penicillin	*la penicilina*	la pe·nee·see·lee·na
I'm ...	*Soy ...*	soy ...
asthmatic	*asmático/a*	as·ma·tee·ko/a
diabetic	*diabético/a*	dya·be·tee·ko/a
epileptic	*epiléptico/a*	e·pee·lep·tee·ko/a

¡Socorro!		so·ko·ro
¡Fuego!		fwe·go
Me han robado.		me an ro·ba·do
¡Déjeme!		de·khe·me
¡Váyase!		va·ya·se
¡Llame a ...!		ya·me a
e police	la policía	la po·lee·see·a
a doctor	un médico	oon me·dee·ko
an ambulance	una ambulancia	oo·na am·boo·lan·sya

It's an emergency.
Es una emergencia.   es oo·na e·mer·khen·sya
Could you help me, please?
¿Me puede ayudar,   me pwe·de a·yoo·dar
por favor?   por fa·vor
I'm lost.
Estoy perdido/a.   es·toy per·dee·do/a
Where are the toilets?
¿Dónde están los baños?   don·de es·tan los ba·nyos

I have ...	Tengo ...	ten·go ...
diarrhea	diarrea	dya·re·a
nausea	náusea	now·se·a
a headache	un dolor de cabeza	oon do·lor de ka·be·sa

LANGUAGE DIFFICULTIES
Do you speak (English)?
¿Habla/Hablas (inglés)?   a·bla/a·blas (een·gles) (pol/inf)
Does anyone here speak English?
¿Hay alguien que hable   ai al·gyen ke a·ble
inglés?   een·gles
I (don't) understand.
(No) Entiendo.   (no) en·tyen·do
How do you say ...?
¿Cómo se dice ...?   ko·mo se dee·se ...
What does ...mean?
¿Qué significa ...?   ke seeg·nee·fee·ka ...

Could you please ...?	¿Puede ..., por favor?	pwe·de ... por fa·vor
repeat that	repetirlo	re·pe·teer·lo
speak more	hablar más	a·blar mas
slowly	despacio	des·pa·syo
write it down	escribirlo	es·kree·beer·lo

NUMBERS
1	uno	oo·no
2	dos	dos
3	tres	tres
4	cuatro	kwa·tro
5	cinco	seen·ko
6	seis	says
7	siete	sye·te
8	ocho	o·cho
9	nueve	nwe·ve
10	diez	dyes
11	once	on·se
12	doce	do·se
13	trece	tre·se
14	catorce	ka·tor·se
15	quince	keen·se
16	dieciséis	dye·see·says
17	diecisiete	dye·see·sye·te
18	dieciocho	dye·see·o·cho
19	diecinueve	dye·see·nwe·ve
20	veinte	vayn·te
21	veintiuno	vayn·tee·oo·no
30	treinta	trayn·ta
31	treinta y uno	trayn·ta ee oo·no
40	cuarenta	kwa·ren·ta
50	cincuenta	seen·kwen·ta
60	sesenta	se·sen·ta
70	setenta	se·ten·ta
80	ochenta	o·chen·ta
90	noventa	no·ven·ta
100	cien	syen
101	ciento uno	syen·to oo·no
200	doscientos	do·syen·tos
1000	mil	meel
5000	cinco mil	seen·ko meel

PAPERWORK
birth certificate	certificado de nacimiento
border (frontier)	la frontera
car-owner's title	título de propiedad
car registration	registración
customs	aduana
driver's license	licencia de manejar
identification	identificación
immigration	migración
insurance	seguro
passport	pasaporte
temporary vehicle import permit	permiso de importación temporal de vehículo
tourist card	tarjeta de turista
visa	visado

LANGUAGE

SHOPPING & SERVICES

I'd like to buy ...
Quisiera comprar ...   kee-*sye*-ra kom-*prar* ...

I'm just looking.
Sólo estoy mirando.   so-lo es-*toy* mee-*ran*-do

May I look at it?
¿Puedo verlo/la?   pwe-do *ver*-lo/la

How much is it?
¿Cuánto cuesta?   kwan-to *kwes*-ta

That's too expensive for me.
Es demasiado caro   es de-ma-*sya*-do *ka*-ro
para mí.   *pa*-ra mee

Could you lower the price?
¿Podría bajar un poco   po-*dree*-a ba-*khar* oon po-ko
el precio?   el *pre*-syo

I don't like it.
No me gusta.   no me *goos*-ta

I'll take it.
Lo llevo.   lo *ye*-vo

Do you   *¿Aceptan ...?*   a-sep-*tan* ...
accept ...?

American   *dólares*   do-la-res
   dollars   *americanos*   a-me-ree-*ka*-nos
credit cards   *tarjetas de*   tar-*khe*-tas de
   crédito   *kre*-dee-to
traveler's   *cheques de*   che-kes de
   checks   *viajero*   vya-*khe*-ro

less   *menos*   me-nos
more   *más*   mas
large   *grande*   gran-de
small   *pequeño/a*   pe-*ke*-nyo/a

I'm looking   *Estoy buscando ...*   es-*toy* boos-kan-do
for (the) ...

ATM   *el cajero*   el ka-*khe*-ro
   automático   ow-to-*ma*-tee-ko
bank   *el banco*   el *ban*-ko
bookstore   *la librería*   la lee-bre-*ree*-a
exchange house   *la casa de*   la *ka*-sa de
   cambio   *kam*-byo
general store   *la tienda*   la *tyen*-da
laundry   *la lavandería*   la la-van-de-*ree*-a
market   *el mercado*   el mer-*ka*-do
pharmacy/   *la farmacia*   la far-*ma*-sya
   chemist
post office   *la officina*   la o-fee-see-na
   de correos   de ko-*re*-os
supermarket   *el supermercado*   el soo-per-
      mer-*ka*-do
tourist office   *la oficina de*   la o-fee-*see*-na de
   turismo   too-*rees*-mo

What time does it open/close?
¿A qué hora abre/cierra?   a ke *o*-ra a-*bre*/s

I want to change some money/traveler
Quisiera cambiar dinero/cheques de viajero.
kee-*sye*-ra kam-*byar* dee-*ne*-ro/*che*-kes de vya-*kı*

What is the exchange rate?
¿Cuál es el tipo de cambio?   kwal es el *tee*-po de *kaı*

I want to call ...
Quisiera llamar a ...   kee-*sye*-ra lya-*mar* a ...

airmail   *correo aéreo*   ko-*re*-o a-*e*-re-o
letter   *carta*   *kar*-ta
registered (mail)   *certificado*   ser-tee-fee-*ka*-do
stamps   *timbres*   *teem*-bres

TIME & DATES

What time is it?   *¿Qué hora es?*   ke *o*-ra es
It's one o'clock.   *Es la una.*   es la *oo*-na
It's seven o'clock.   *Son las siete.*   son las *sye*-te
Half past two.   *Dos y media.*   dos ee me-dya
midnight   *medianoche*   me-dya-*no*-che
noon   *mediodía*   me-dyo-*dee*-a

now   *ahora*   a-*o*-ra
today   *hoy*   oy
tonight   *esta noche*   es-ta *no*-che
tomorrow   *mañana*   ma-*nya*-na
yesterday   *ayer*   a-*yer*

Monday   *lunes*   *loo*-nes
Tuesday   *martes*   *mar*-tes
Wednesday   *miércoles*   myer-ko-les
Thursday   *jueves*   *khwe*-ves
Friday   *viernes*   *vyer*-nes
Saturday   *sábado*   *sa*-ba-do
Sunday   *domingo*   do-*meen*-go
January   *enero*   e-*ne*-ro
February   *febrero*   fe-*bre*-ro
March   *marzo*   *mar*-so
April   *abril*   a-*breel*
May   *mayo*   *ma*-yo
June   *junio*   khoo-nyo
July   *julio*   khoo-lyo
August   *agosto*   a-*gos*-to
September   *septiembre*   sep-*tyem*-bre
October   *octubre*   ok-*too*-bre
November   *noviembre*   no-*vyem*-bre
December   *diciembre*   dee-*syem*-bre

TRANSPORTATION
Public Transportation

What time does   *¿A qué hora ...*   a ke *o*-ra ...
... leave/arrive?   *sale/llega?*   sa-le/*ye*-ga
   the boat   *el barco*   el *bar*-ko
   the bus (city)   *el camión*   el ka-*myon*

...ty)	el autobus	el ow-to-*boos*
	el avión	el a-*vyon*

SIGNS

...gh Mexico mostly uses the familiar ...rnational road signs, you should be ...epared to encounter these other signs ...s well:

Acceso	Entrance
Aparcamiento	Parking
Camino en Reparación	Road Repairs
Ceda el Paso	Give way
Conserve Su Derecha	Keep to the Right
Cuida Su Vida, Maneje Con Precaución	Protect Your Life, Drive with Caution
Curva Peligrosa	Dangerous Curve
Derrumbes	Landslides
Despacio	Slow
Desviación	Detour
Dirección Única	One-way
Escuela (Zona Escolar)	School (zone)
Hombres Trabajando	Men at Work
Mantenga Su Derecha	Keep to the Right
No Adelantar	No Passing
No Hay Paso	Road Closed
No Rebase	No Overtaking
No Rebase con Raya Continua	Don't Drive with Your Lights On
Pare/Stop	Stop
Peaje	Toll
Peligro	Danger
Por Su Seguridad Disminuye La Velocidad	Decrease Speed for Your Safety
Precaución Zona de Ganado	Careful: Cattle Zone
Prepare Su Cuota	Have Toll Ready
Prohibido Aparcar/ No Estacionar	No Parking
Prohibido el Paso	No Entry
Puente Angosto	Narrow Bridge
Salida de Autopista	Exit Freeway
Si Toma No Maneje	Don't Drink and Drive
Utilice Cinturón de Seguridad	Use Your Seatbelt
Topes/Vibradores	Speed Bumps
Tramo en Reparación	Road Under Repair
Vía Corta	Short Route (often a toll road)
Vía Cuota	Toll Highway

the airport	el aeropuerto	el a·e·ro·*pwer*·to
the bus station	la estación de autobuses	la es·ta·*syon* de ow·to·*boo*·ses
the bus stop	la parada de autobuses	la pa·*ra*·da de ow·to·*boo*·ses
a luggage locker	un casillero	oon ka·see·*ye*·ro
the ticket office	la taquilla	la ta·*kee*·ya

A ticket to ..., please.
Un boleto a ..., por favor. oon bo·*le*·to a ... por fa·*vor*
What's the fare to ...?
¿Cuánto cuesta hasta ...? kwan·to *kwes*·ta a·sta ...

student's	de estudiante	de es·too·*dyan*·te
1st class	primera clase	pree·me·ra *kla*·se
2nd class	segunda clase	se·*goon*·da *kla*·se
single/one-way	viaje sencillo	vee·*a*·khe sen·*see*·yo
return/round trip	redondo	re·*don*·do
taxi	taxi	tak·see

Private Transportation

I'd like to	Quisiera	kee·*sye*·ra
hire a/an ...	rentar ...	ren·*tar* ...
4WD	un cuator por cuatro	oon kwa·*tro* por kwa·*tro*
car	un coche	oon *ko*·che
motorbike	una moto	*oo*·na mo·to
bicycle	bicicleta	bee·see·*kle*·ta
hitchhike	pedir aventón	pe·*deer* a·ven·*ton*
pickup (ute)	pickup	*pee*·kop
truck	camión (or camioneta)	ka·myon

Where's a gas/petrol station?
¿Dónde hay una gasolinera? don·de ai oo·na ga·so·lee·*ne*·ra
How much is a liter of gasoline?
¿Cuánto cuesta el litro de gasolina? kwan·to *kwes*·ta el *lee*·tro de ga·so·*lee*·na
Please fill it up.
Lleno, por favor. ye·no por fa·*vor*
I'd like (20) pesos worth.
Quiero (veinte) litros. kye·ro (vayn·te) *pe*·sos

diesel	diesel	dee·sel
leaded (regular)	gasolina con plomo	ga·so·*lee*·na kon *plo*·mo
petrol (gas)	gasolina	ga·so·*lee*·na
unleaded	gasolina sin plomo	ga·so·*lee*·na seen *plo*·mo
oil	aceite	a·*say*·te
tire	llanta	yan·ta
puncture	agujero	a·goo·*khe*·ro

Is this the road to (...)?
¿Por acquí se va a (...)?
por a·*kee* se va a (...)
(How long) Can I park here?
¿(Por cuánto tiempo) Puedo estacionarme aquí?
(por *kwan*·to *tyem*·po) *pwe*·do ess·ta·syo·*nar*·me a·*kee*
Where do I pay?
¿Dónde se paga?
don·de se *pa*·ga
I need a mechanic/tow truck.
Necesito un mecánico/remolque.
ne·se·*see*·to oon me·*ka*·nee·ko/re·*mol*·ke
Is there a garage near here?
¿Hay un garaje cerca de aquí?
ai oon ga·*ra*·khe ser·ka de a·*kee*
The car has broken down (in ...).
El coche se se descompuso (en ...)
el *ko*·che se des·kom·*poo*·so (en ...)
I have a flat tire.
Tengo una llanta ponchada.
ten·go *oo*·na *yan*·ta pon·*cha*·da
I ran out of gas/petrol.
Me quedé sin gasolina.
me ke·*de* seen ga·so·*lee*·na
I had an accident.
Tuve un accidente.
too·ve oon ak·see·*den*·te

TRAVEL WITH CHILDREN
Are children allowed?
¿Se admiten niños?
se ad·*mee*·ten *nee*·nyos

I need ...
Necesito ...
ne·se·*see*·to ...
Do you have ...?
¿Hay ...?
ai ...
  a car baby seat
  un asiento de seguridad para bebés
  oon a·*syen*·to de se·goo·ree·*da* pa·ra be·*bes*
  a babysitting service
  un club para niños
  oon kloob pa·ra *nee*·nyos
  a children's menu
  un menú infantil
  oon me·*noo* een·fan·*teel*
  (disposable) diapers/nappies
  pañales (de usar y tirar)
  pa·*nya*·les de oo·*sar* ee tee·*rar*
  an (English-speaking) babysitter
  una niñera (que habla inglesa)
  oo·na nee·*nye*·ra (ke a·bla een·*gle*·sa)
  formula (milk)
  leche en polvo
  le·che en *pol*·vo
  a highchair
  una silla para bebé
  oo·na *see*·ya pa·ra be·be
  a potty
  una bacinica
  oo·na ba·see·*nee*·ka
  a stroller
  una carreola
  oona ka·re·*o*·la

Also available from Lonely Planet:
Mexican Spanish Phrasebook

...nformation on the Spanish
...e the Language chapter (p251).
...f food and drink terms, see the
...Drink chapter (p47).

... – irrigation canal, often stone-lined, in Baja
...ja missions
...e – century plant
...be – sun-dried mud brick used for building
...bergue de juventud – youth hostel
...alto – stop; also means 'high'
Apdo – abbreviation of *Apartado* (Box); in addresses, stands for 'Post Office Box'
arroyo – brook, stream; often refers to a dry riverbed
asentamientos irregulares – shantytowns of Tijuana, Mexicali and other border towns
avenida – avenue

bahía – bay
bajacaliforniano – resident of Baja California
ballena – whale; also a colloquial term for a liter-size bottle of Pacífico beer
banda – style of music dominated by brass instruments, often without drums
barrio – neighborhood of a town or city, often a poor neighborhood
béisbol – baseball
billete – banknote
biznaga – barrel cactus
boleto – ticket
borrego – bighorn sheep, a rarely seen species in the sierras of Baja California that is frequently represented in the pre-Columbian rock art of the peninsula
burro – donkey

cabaña – cabin
caballero – gentleman
cabina – phone booth
caguama – any species of sea turtle, but most commonly the Pacific green turtle; also a colloquial term for a liter-size bottle of Tecate beer
cajero automático – automatic teller machine (ATM)
calle – street
callejón – alley
calzada – grand boulevard or avenue
cama matrimonial – double or queen bed
cambio – see *casa de cambio*
camino – road, path, way
campanario – bell tower

cardón – either of two species of *Pachycereus* cactus, a common genus in Baja
carga negra – hazardous cargo
carretera – highway
casa de cambio – currency exchange house
casa de huéspedes – guesthouse, a relatively inexpensive but uncommon form of accommodations in Baja
cascabel – rattlesnake
casita – cottage
central camionera – bus terminal
cerro – hill
charreada – rodeo, frequently held during fiestas and other special occasions; particularly popular in northern Mexico
charro – Mexican cowboy or horseman; mariachi bands often dress in gaudy charro clothing
chilango – native or resident of Mexico City; depending on context, the term can be very pejorative
chingar – literally 'to fuck'; it has a wide range of colloquial usages in Mexican Spanish equivalent to those in English
cholismo – rebellious youth movement, akin to punk, that has had some influence on the visual arts in Baja California
chubasco – in the Cape Region of southern Baja, a violent storm approaching hurricane force, associated with summer low-pressure areas in the tropical Pacific
cirio – a 'boojum' tree, a slow-growing species resembling an inverted carrot, common only within a limited range of the Sierra La Asamblea in north-central Baja
colonia – neighborhood in Tijuana or other large city; literally, 'colony'
comida corrida – set lunch
conquistador – early Spanish explorer-conqueror
cordillera – mountain range
correos – post office
corrida de toros – bullfight
corrido – folk ballad of the US-Mexico border region; corridos often have strong but subtle political content
Cotuco – Comité de Turismo y Convenciones (Committee on Tourism & Conventions)
coyote – smuggler who charges up to US$2000 to spirit illegal immigrants across the US-Mexican border
Cruz Roja – Red Cross
cuota – toll; a *vía cuota* is a toll road
curandero – folk healer

damas – ladies; seen on toilet doors
datilillo – yucca
desierto – desert

ejidatario – a member of an *ejido*

ejido – cooperative enterprise, usually of peasant agriculturalists, created under the land reform program of President Lázaro Cárdenas (1934-40); ejidos also participate in economic activities such as mining, ranching and tourism

encomienda – system of forced labor and tribute, which the Spanish crown instituted in mainland New Spain and other densely populated parts of its empire

fianza – bond posted against the return of a motor vehicle to the USA

fideicomiso – 30-year bank trust that has fostered the construction and acquisition of real estate by non-Mexicans in Baja California

Fonatur – Mexican federal government tourist agency

fraccionamiento – synonym for 'colonia' (see above)

frontera – border

fronterizo – an inhabitant of the US-Mexico border region

frontón – venue for jai alai (see below)

glorieta – city traffic circle; most numerous in Mexicali and Tijuana

gringo – term describing any light-skinned person, but most often a resident of the USA; often but not always pejorative

güero – 'blond,' a term often used to describe any fair-skinned person in Mexico

hacienda – local treasury department

hielo – ice

hipódromo – horseracing track

hombres – men; seen on toilet doors

huarache – woven leather sandal, often with tire tread as the sole

huerivo – aspen tree

INAH – Instituto Nacional de Antropología y Historia (National Institute of Anthropology & History), which administers museums and archeological monuments such as the cave paintings in the Desierto Central

iglesia – church

indígena – indigenous person

IVA – *impuesto de valor agregado,* or value-added tax

jai alai – game of Basque origin resembling squash

Judiciales – Mexican state and federal police

Ladatel – *Larga Distancia Automática,* or automatic long-distance phones

larga distancia – long-distance; usually refers to telephones

La Frontera – the area where Dominican priests built their missions in colonial times (from 1774); it extends from immediately south of present-day San Diego (m California) as far as El Rosario, at about the 30th

librería – bookstore

licorería – liquor store; also called *vinos y licores*

linea – line; *La linea* is the colloquial term for the M US border

llantera – tire-repair shop, common even in Baja's m out-of-the-way places

lleno – full, as with a car's fuel tank

lonchería – casual eatery, often a counter in markets, serving breakfast and lunch only

machismo – an exaggerated masculinity intended to impress other men more than women; usually innocuous if unpleasant

Magonistas – followers of the exiled Mexican intellectual Ricardo Flores Magón, who attempted to establish a regional power base in the towns of northern Baja California during the Mexican Revolution

maguey – any of several species of a common Mexico fiber plant (*Agave* spp), also used for producing alcoholic drinks like tequila, mescal and pulque

malecón – waterfront promenade

maquiladora – industrial plant in Tijuana, Mexicali or another border town that takes advantage of cheap Mexican labor to assemble US components for reexportation to the north

mariachi – small ensemble of street musicians playing traditional ballads on guitars and trumpets

matador – bullfighter

mercado – market; often a building near the center of a town, with shops and open-air stalls in the surrounding streets

mestizo – person of mixed Indian and European heritage

moneda nacional – national money, meaning the Mexican peso as distinguished from the US dollar (both use the symbol '$'); often abbreviated as 'm/n'

mono – human figure, as represented in the pre-Columbian rock art of the Desierto Central

mordida – bribe; literally, 'the bite'

municipio – administrative subdivision of Mexican states, roughly akin to a US county; Baja California (Norte) consists of five municipios, Baja California Sur of four

mujeres – women; seen on toilet doors

NAFTA – North American Free Trade Agreement, a pact between the USA, Canada and Mexico that reduces or eliminates customs duties and other trade barriers

nao – in colonial times, a Spanish galleon on the Acapulco-Manila trade route; such galleons frequently took shelter in Baja ports on their return voyages

neophyte – a new convert (in this case, of the Indians by the missionaries)

nopal – any cactus of the genus Opuntia that produces

ₜtuna), which was common in the diet of pre-
Baja and is still widely consumed today
water- or animal-driven mill
– north; El Norte is the colloquial term for the USA

ₙda – offering to a saint in exchange for a wish or
ₙes granted
ₐ – wave
tro lado – literally 'other side;' *el otro lado* refers col-
oquially to the USA

palafito – walled palapa
palapa – palm-leaf shelter
PAN – Partido de Acción Nacional, a free-market-oriented
populist party that is strong in Baja California (Norte); its
acronym, more than coincidentally, reproduces the Spanish
word for 'bread'
panga – fiberglass skiff used for fishing or whale-watching
panguero – one who owns or pilots a skiff; in practice,
the word is synonymous with 'fisherman'
parque nacional – national park
pastillas para purificar agua – water purification
tablets
peatonal – pedestrian walk
peligro – danger
Pemex – Petróleos Mexicanos, the Mexican government
oil monopoly
piñata – papier-mâché animal full of candy, broken open
by children at celebrations like Christmas and birthdays
pitahaya dulce – organ pipe cactus, a key element of
the traditional diet of Baja's native peoples
plaza de toros – bullring
pollero – synonymous with 'coyote'; a smuggler of undocumented immigrants (pollos, or 'chickens') into the USA
posada – at Christmas, a parade of costumed children
reenacting the journey of Mary and Joseph to Bethlehem
presidio – during colonial times, a military outpost
PRI – Partido Revolucionario Institucional, the official
party of government in Mexico from 1929 until 2000
propina – tip, at a restaurant or elsewhere
pueblo – town

ranchería – subsistence unit of hunter-gatherers in the
contact period with Europeans, or, later, units associated
with missions; implies a group of people rather than a place

rancho – tiny rural settlement, ranging from about 20
to 50 people

Secture – Secretaría de Turismo del Estado (State Tour-
ism Office)
SEDUE – Secretaría de Desarrollo Urbano y Ecología, a
Mexican government agency that regulates foreign hunt-
ing activity in Baja California and elsewhere in Mexico
Semarnap – Secretaría de Medio Ambiente, Recursos
Naturales y Pesca, the Mexican government's primary
conservation agency
Servicio Postal Mexicano – the Mexican national
postal service
Servicios Migratorios – Immigration office
SIDA – AIDS (Acquired Immune Deficiency Syndrome)
s/n (sin número) – street address without a specific
number

todo terreno – mountain bike
tombolo – sandspit beach
tope – speed bump
torote – elephant tree
tortillería – tortilla factory or shop
tortuga carey – hawksbill turtle
tortuga laúd – leatherback turtle
tranquilo – tranquil; mellow
trapiche – sugar mill
turista – tourist; also a colloquial name for diarrhea
contracted by tourists

ultramarino – small grocery store
Unesco – United Nations Educational, Scientific and
Cultural Organization

vado – ford, as of a river; can also refer to a dip in a road
vaquero – Mexican cowboy

zócalo – central plaza; term more common in mainland
Mexico than in Baja California
zona de tolerancia – in border cities like Tijuana and
Mexicali, an area in which prostitution and related activities are concentrated
zona hotelera – hotel zone

Behind the Scenes

THIS BOOK

The 6th edition of *Baja & Los Cabos* was researched and written by Danny Palmerlee, except for the Food & Drink chapter, written by Jim Peyton, and the Health chapter, adapted from text by Dr David Goldberg. Keith Jones wrote the 'Gray Whales of Baja' boxed text.

The last edition of this guide was written by Andrea Schulte-Peevers, David Peevers, Michele Matter and Sarah Long. Wayne Bernhardson wrote the third and fourth editions, and Scott Wayne wrote the first and second editions.

THANKS from the Authors

First, the hugest of hugs to Rebecca 'turn-left-at-the-cactus' Santana, who made the drive to Cabo a blast. Thanks to Don 'Pops' Santana, for sporting us ten nights' lodging (you rock, Don). To Michael Kieley in Tijuana, the cousin I never knew I had, thank you profusely for everything. Also in Tijuana, thanks to Jaime Chaidez for introducing me to the Tijuana music scene, and to Alfonzo López Camacho of Librería El Día. Thanks also to Max Mejía of Arte de Vivir. In San Diego, all my love to Aunt Candy and Uncle John for putting me up once again on my journey south – I love you guys. In La Paz, Joe Chamsi educated me on the city's great restaurants. To Lorena Hankins in La Candelaria, thanks for the wonderful afternoon and all your help. In San Ignacio, thanks to Sergio

Aguilar of INAH and to Eloy Gutiérrez for on my car. Blanca Acosta of Ensenada got the Fiesta de los Viñedos en Flor, even th didn't buy my ticket. Thanks! To Pete and Sw. thanks for helping me research the bars of E. nada, buey! And at home, many, many thanks my commissioning editor Suki Gear, whose guic ance and humor carried me through.

CREDITS

Baja & Los Cabos 6 was commissioned and developed in Lonely Planet's Oakland office by Suki Gear. Kathleen Munnelly and Erin Corrigan were the project managers, under direction of Regional Publishing Managers Maria Donohoe and David Zingarelli. Emily K Wolman edited the book and Tullan Spitz proofread. Bart Wright created all the maps. The book was laid out by Hayley Tsang, with assistance from Candice Jacobus. Candice designed the cover and the color pages. The index was compiled by Ken DellaPenta.

THANKS from Lonely Planet

Many thanks to the travelers who used the last edition and wrote to us with helpful hints, useful advice and interesting anecdotes:

A Francesca Ancona, James W Apgar, Kiersten Aschauer, Monica Auger, Eduardo Ayacardi **B** Stefan Bachschmid, Roger Baker, Martin Beebee,

THE LONELY PLANET STORY

The story begins with a classic travel adventure: Tony and Maureen Wheeler's 1972 journey across Europe and Asia to Australia. There was no useful information about the overland trail then, so Tony and Maureen published the first Lonely Planet guidebook to meet a growing need.

From a kitchen table, Lonely Planet has grown to become the largest independent travel publisher in the world, with offices in Melbourne (Australia), Oakland (USA), London (UK) and Paris (France).

Today Lonely Planet guidebooks cover the globe. There is an ever-growing list of books and information in a variety of media. Some things haven't changed. The main aim is still to make it possible for adventurous travelers to get out there – to explore and better understand the world.

At Lonely Planet we believe travelers can make a positive contribution to the countries they visit – if they respect their host communities and spend their money wisely. Since 1986 a percentage of the income from each book has been donated to aid projects and human rights campaigns, and, more recently, to wildlife conservation.

nyo Bianc, Luke Biggs, Scott Bish-
ers, Simon Briggs, Helen Burton,
C Mercedes Cisneros, IKU Collins,
David Croome, Gareth Cross D Jules
Davidson, Rosita De Decker, Morgan
Denny, Martin Dillig, Patrick Diveu, Mar-
haela Dohnalkova, Guy Dowman, Klaus
E David Eidell, Rob Erickson F Flavio Fer-
Annelies Florquin, Frank Fox, Astrid Frey G
Gerharter, Meghan Gibbons, Judy Gibson,
leen Gibson, Jeffrey Glazer, Stefan Goeddertz,
ter Gohler, M Guenza H Juliette Hayes, Maria
ealy, Jennifer Hess, Andresch Hiepel, Sebastian
Hoeft, Alison Hunter I Anneka Imkamp, Jim Isaacs
J Sue Jones K P Kalberer, Adam Kent, Michael
Kerr, Michael Kleinheinz L Rachele Lamontagne,
Andrew J Lampkin, Christopher Landreau, Lee
Lau, Lorna Lee, Sune Lolk, Harvey Lozano, Larry
Lunsford M Glenn MacCrimmon, Devin Mack,
Liene Maeckelburgh, Terry Marcer, Alessandro
Marcolin, Sheri Marcus, Michael McCann, Chris &
Jeff McFarland, Melissa McKay, George Merchant,
Jonathan Miles, Vicki Moellgaard, Dennis Moger-
man, Patrick Monney, Michael Monterey, Bea Mor-
row, Mark Mosbacher, Jack Munsee, Jean Munsee
N Barb Neelley, James Nelson, Joanna Nesbit,
Nancy Nixon, Steve Novosel O Ketra Oberlander,
Marie Olsen, Dennis Oman, Jack & Nancy Osthe-
imer, Pat Owsley P Jorgos-Rita Palimetakis, Lynda
Pedley, Wendy Postier, Harald Praschinger, Harald
Praschinger R Sri Redy, Keith Reher, Sage Rich,
Robin Ricker, Katja Rieger, Jack Romanski, Elad
Rubin, Mauro Ruffino, Paul Ruiz, Bruce Rumoge
S Scott Savage, Theodore H Schmidkonz, Thomas
Schmidt, Peter Seglow, Andy & Bea Sidler, Heidi
Smith, Laura Sobel, Peter Steiner, Bart Stephens,
Greg Sterne, Patrick Stoddard, Kevin Sweeney T
Candace Taylor-Webe, Mark Terry, R Tokgoz, Tom
Tyler V Steven Verdekel, Federica Vettor, Christian
Voigt, Paola Vozza W Jeff Walter, Sally Walton, Reik
Wetzig, Chandra White, Myra Winfield, Sean Witt,
Nancy Wright Z Hans R Zeller, Roberta Zibetti

Index

000 Map pages
000 Location of color photographs

LEGEND

ROUTES

Tollway	Walking Path
Freeway	Unsealed Road
Primary Road	Pedestrian Street
Secondary Road	Stepped Street
Tertiary Road	Tunnel
Lane	One Way Street
Walking Tour	Walking Tour Detour

TRANSPORT

Ferry	Rail
Metro	Rail (Underground)
Monorail	Tram

HYDROGRAPHY

River, Creek	Lake (Salt)
Intermittent River	Mudflats
Canal	Reef
Glacier	Swamp
Lake (Dry)	Water

BOUNDARIES

International	Ancient Wall
State, Provincial	Cliff
Regional, Suburb	Marine Park

POPULATION

○ CAPITAL (NATIONAL)	◉ CAPITAL (STATE)
● Large City	○ Medium City
● Small City	○ Town, Village

AREA FEATURES

Area of Interest	Land
Beach, Desert	Mall
Building	Market
Cemetery, Christian	Park
Cemetery, Other	Sports
Forest	Urban

SYMBOLS

SIGHTS/ACTIVITIES
- Beach
- Buddhist
- Castle, Fortress
- Christian
- Confician
- Diving, Snorkeling
- Hindu
- Islamic
- Jain
- Jewish
- Monument
- Museum, Gallery
- Picnic Area
- Point of Interest
- Ruin
- Shinto
- Sikh
- Skiing
- Taoist
- Winery, Vineyard
- Zoo, Bird Sanctuary

INFORMATION
- Bank, ATM
- Embassy/Consulate
- Hospital, Medical
- Information
- Internet Facilities
- Parking Area
- Petrol Station
- Police Station
- Post Office, GPO
- Telephone
- Toilets

SLEEPING
- Sleeping
- Camping

EATING
- Eating

DRINKING
- Drinking
- Café

ENTERTAINMENT
- Entertainment

SHOPPING
- Shopping

TRANSPORT
- Airport, Airfield
- Border Crossing
- Bus Station
- Cycling, Bicycle Path
- General Transport
- Taxi Rank
- Trail Head

GEOGRAPHIC
- Hazard
- Lighthouse
- Lookout
- Mountain, Volcano
- National Park
- Oasis
- Pass, Canyon
- River Flow
- Shelter, Hut
- Spot Height
- Waterfall

NOTE: Not all symbols displayed above appear in this guide.

LONELY PLANET OFFICES

Australia
Head Office
Locked Bag 1, Footscray, Victoria 3011
☎ 03 8379 8000, fax 03 8379 8111
talk2us@lonelyplanet.com.au

USA
150 Linden St, Oakland, CA 94607
☎ 510 893 8555, toll free 800 275 8555
fax 510 893 8572, info@lonelyplanet.com

UK
72–82 Rosebery Ave,
Clerkenwell, London EC1R 4RW
☎ 020 7841 9000, fax 020 7841 9001
go@lonelyplanet.co.uk

Published by Lonely Planet Publications Pty Ltd
ABN 36 005 607 983